5 Edition

The PRACTICE of RESEARCH in CRIMINOLOGY and CRIMINAL JUSTICE

*In loving memory of two pioneer women who homesteaded on the prairie in
South Dakota and instilled in me the importance of education and lifelong learning:*

To my great-aunt, Martha Geiken Lund, 1912–2002

and

To my grandmother, Anna Geiken Bachman, 1907–1989

—R. B.

To Elizabeth and Julia

—R. K. S.

The PRACTICE of RESEARCH in CRIMINOLOGY and CRIMINAL JUSTICE

RONET BACHMAN
University of Delaware

RUSSELL K. SCHUTT
University of Massachusetts Boston

Los Angeles | London | New Delhi
Singapore | Washington DC

Los Angeles | London | New Delhi
Singapore | Washington DC

FOR INFORMATION:

SAGE Publications, Inc.
2455 Teller Road
Thousand Oaks, California 91320
E-mail: order@sagepub.com

SAGE Publications Ltd.
1 Oliver's Yard
55 City Road
London EC1Y 1SP
United Kingdom

SAGE Publications India Pvt. Ltd.
B 1/I 1 Mohan Cooperative Industrial Area
Mathura Road, New Delhi 110 044
India

SAGE Publications Asia-Pacific Pte. Ltd.
3 Church Street
#10-04 Samsung Hub
Singapore 049483

Printed in the United States of America

A catalog record of this book is available from the Library of Congress.

978-1-4522-5819-5

Acquisitions Editor: Jerry Westby
Assistant Editor: Rachael Leblond
Publishing Associate: MaryAnn Vail
Production Editor: Eric Garner
Copy Editor: Lana Todorovic-Arndt
Typesetter: C&M Digitals (P) Ltd.
Proofreader: Jennifer Gritt
Indexer: Rick Hurd
Cover Designer: Michael Dubowe
Marketing Manager: Terra Schultz
Permissions Editor: Jennifer Barron

This book is printed on acid-free paper.

14 15 16 17 10 9 8 7 6 5 4 3 2

Brief Contents

On Student Study Site: www.sagepub.com/bachmanprccj5e

Appendix C: How to Use a Statistical Package: IBM SPSS Statistics

Appendix D: How to Use a Data Spreadsheet: Excel

Detailed Contents

On Student Study Site: www.sagepub.com/bachmanprccj5e

Preface

One of the most important aspects of teaching a research methods course is conveying to students the vital role that research plays in our discipline. After years of teaching courses in research methods, we have found that the best avenue of achieving this goal has been to link the teaching of key topics to contemporary research in the discipline. By combining discussions of research techniques with practical research examples from the field, students learn not only how to conduct research but also why it is important to do so. In the fifth edition of *The Practice of Research in Criminology and Criminal Justice*, we have drawn on comments by students in the classroom, insightful reviews by those who teach research methods, and our own continuing learning experience as scholars and teachers; we think the resulting innovations will add a great deal to your learning experience.

The purpose of this book is to introduce you to the scientific methods of research in criminology and criminal justice and show how they are actually used. Each chapter combines instructions in research methods with investigations of key research questions in our field: How do we measure offending and victimization? What are the causes of violent crime? What is the best police response to intimate partner violence? How do gang members perceive their world? Are boot camps effective in reducing recidivism? What is the impact of having a criminal record on finding a job? Do community police officers perceive their roles as different from regular patrol officers? These are just a sample of the many research examples used to demonstrate particular research methods.

You will learn not only the skills necessary for conducting research, but also the skills necessary to evaluate research done by others. You will learn to ask many questions as you consider whether research-based conclusions are appropriate and valid. What did the researchers set out to investigate? How were people or places selected for the study? What were the phenomena being studied, and how were they defined and measured? How was information analyzed? Throughout this book, you will learn what questions to ask when critiquing a research study and how to evaluate the answers.

Another goal of this book is to train you to actually do research. Substantive research examples will help you see how methods are used in practice. Exercises at the end of each chapter give you a way to try different methods alone or in a group. But research methods cannot be learned by rote and applied mechanically. It is our hope that you will realize that all research methods come with their own strengths and limitations. In fact, the underlying theme of our book is that employing a combination of methods together to answer the same research question is often preferable. You will come to appreciate why the results of particular research studies must always be interpreted within the context of prior research and through the lens of social and criminological theory.

Organization of the Book

The way this book is organized reflects our beliefs in making research methods interesting, teaching students how to critique research, and viewing specific research techniques as parts of an integrated research strategy. Our concern with ethical issues in all types of research is underscored by the fact that we have an entire chapter devoted exclusively to research ethics in addition to sections on ethics in every methodology chapter. The first two chapters introduce the why and how of research in general. Chapter 1 shows how research has helped us understand the magnitude of and the factors related to youth violence. Chapter 2 illustrates the basic stages of research with a series of experiments on the police response to intimate partner violence. Chapter 3 highlights issues of research ethics by taking you inside Philip Zimbardo's prison experiment and Stanley Milgram's research on obedience to authority. It also introduces you to different research philosophies. Chapters 4 and 5 discuss how to evaluate the way researchers design their measures and draw their samples. Chapter 6 explores issues related to making causal connections and a summary of the strengths and limitations of various research designs in making causal conclusions.

Chapters 7 through 9 present the three most important methods of data collection: experiments, surveys, and qualitative methods (including participant observation, intensive interviews, and focus groups). Chapter 10 examines methodologies that rely on existing content and includes a discussion of secondary data analysis, historical and comparative research, content analysis, and crime mapping, along with a discussion of triangulating methods. Chapter 11 covers evaluation research and policy analysis and highlights the different alternatives to evaluation along with a discussion of the most appropriate methods to use for each evaluation question (e.g., process versus impact). In this chapter, you will see how various methods have been used to investigate the effects of several programs and policies, including problem-oriented policing, boot camps, and mandatory sentencing laws. There are several examples within each of these methods chapters that use a mixed-methods approach to answer the same research question. However, because researchers are increasingly combining methods, we have added a new chapter, Chapter 12, which provides an overview of the philosophy and motivation for combining methods, the various techniques for doing so, and some exciting research examples to demonstrate the fruitfulness of such multiple methods projects.

In Chapter 13, we will work through an analysis of survey data on self-reported delinquency to see how these statistics are used to answer actual research questions. We finish up in Chapter 14 with an overview of the process of and techniques for reporting research results along with some ethical problems in writing.

The substantive studies in each of these chapters show how each methodology has been used to improve our understanding of criminal justice–related issues, including the factors related to violence, how question wording affects estimates of victimization in surveys, how gang members perceive their world, how community police officers describe their role in comparison to regular patrol officers, the perceptions of jurors who have participated in a death penalty case, the effects of inmates' classification on institutional misconduct in prison, and the effects of war on violence in a cross-national comparison, to name just a few of the examples provided.

Distinctive Features of the Fifth Edition

The most distinctive feature of this text compared to others in the field continues to be the integration into each chapter of in-depth substantive research examples from the real world. Examples from the literature are not simply dropped here and there to keep students' attention. Rather, each chapter presents a particular research method in the context of a substantive research story. When explaining a research method or design decision, we use narratives from researchers in the field that delineate the decision-making process. This serves several purposes; it illustrates the process of research in the real world, it underscores why particular methods were selected over others, and it highlights the important role research plays in policy decisions in our field. As such, this book's success is due in no small measure to the availability of so many excellent research examples in our discipline. New examples of research have been added in all data collection chapters. The following points are additional strengths of this text along with a few of the new innovations in this edition:

A new chapter on mixed methods research. We have added a new chapter on mixed methods (Chapter 12) that provides an overview of the philosophy and motivation for combining methods, the various techniques for doing so, and some exciting research examples to demonstrate the fruitfulness of such multiple methods projects.

New focus of qualitative data analysis using NVivo. Using a case study of interviews with drug-involved offenders, we highlight how the qualitative data software program NVivo helps researchers organize and analyze qualitative data (Chapter 9). We believe focusing on one software program instead of highlighting several will better illustrate the process of qualitative data analysis.

Recent developments in research methods. Research methods continue to change in response to the spread of cell phones and the use of the Internet, the growth of interdisciplinary scholarship, and concerns with community impact. Some researchers have begun to explore the Internet with qualitative techniques. We have expanded our coverage of these issues in various chapters including the chapters on sampling, surveys, and qualitative methods.

Updated examples of criminological research as they occur in real-world settings. We include interesting studies taken from the literature on a variety of topics including the effects of incarceration on employment, the efficacy of arrest for intimate partner assault, the perceptions of citizens regarding police misconduct, and an investigation into the lives of gang members, to name just a few. These real-world research examples illustrate the exigencies and complexities that shape the application of research methods.

Increased focus on international research. We have expanded our use of research conducted in countries around the globe, as well as continuing our focus on issues involving diversity in race, ethnicity, gender, and culture within the United Sates and in other countries.

New "research in the news" highlights. We have added new boxes in each chapter that highlight the research that has made headlines in the news to illustrate the impact of our research not just for researchers and practitioners in criminal justice, but on society as a whole.

Aids to effective study. The many effective study aids included in the previous editions have been updated, as needed. Lists of main points and key terms provide quick summaries at the end of each chapter. In addition, key terms are highlighted in boldface type when first introduced and defined in text. Definitions for these also can be found in the glossary/index at the end of the book.

It is a privilege to share with you the results of excellent research related to criminal justice and criminology. If this book communicates the excitement of research and the importance of evaluating carefully the methods we use in research, then we have succeeded in representing what social scientists interested in issues related to criminal justice and criminology do. We think it conveys the latest developments in research methodology and thereby demonstrates that researchers are committed to evaluating and improving their own methods of investigation.

We hope you enjoy learning how to investigate research questions related to criminal justice and criminology and perhaps do some research of your own along the way. We guarantee that the knowledge you develop about research methods will serve you well throughout your education, in your career, and in your community.

Ancillaries

Companion Student Study Site

This Web-based Student Study Site, available at **www.sagepub.com/bachmanprccj5e**, provides a variety of additional resources to enhance students' understanding of the book content and take their learning one step further. The site includes Web quizzes, eFlashcards, a "Learning From SAGE Journal Articles" feature, Web exercises, podcasts, videos, real crime data including a subset of the National Crime Victimization Survey data and the General Social Survey, and appendices on how to use a statistical package and how to use a qualitative analysis package.

Instructor Teaching Site

A password-protected instructor teaching site is available at **www.sagepub.com/bachmanprccj5e**. It offers a variety of resources to supplement the book material including lecture notes, PowerPoint slides, test questions with answers, and student project ideas. The site also contains SAGE journal articles, podcasts, videos, Web resources, and articles on teaching criminal justice research methods.

▣ A Note About Using IBM SPSS Statistics*

To carry out the SPSS exercises at the end of each chapter, you must have SPSS installed on your computer. The Student Study Site includes several subsets of data, including data from the National Crime Victimization Survey and the Uniform Crime Reports. Appendix C will get you up and running with SPSS for Windows as will Appendix D with Excel. You then may spend as much time as you like exploring the data sets provided, or you may even use your own data. You also may carry out analyses of the General Social Survey at the University of California, Berkeley, Web site (sda.berkeley.edu:7502/ archive.htm).

---

*IBM SPSS Statistics was formerly called PASW® Statistics.

Acknowledgments

We must first acknowledge our gratitude to Jerry Westby, whose hard work and guidance on this project are unrivaled. He has been more than an editor; he is an ideas man, a tenacious fact finder, a motivator, a therapist, and most important, a friend. We are also indebted to Megan Krattli for her supervision of the project and meticulous attention to detail in shuttling the manuscript through the appropriate channels, and to Lana Arndt for her meticulous attention to detail when editing the edition.

Gratitude also goes to the reviewers of this fifth edition, including Patrick R. Gartin, Missouri State University; Joy Hadwiger, Troy University; George E. Higgins, University of Louisville; E. Britt Patterson, Shippensburg University; Jennie K. Singer, California State University, Sacramento; Mary West-Smith, University of Northern Colorado; Reviewers of previous editions included; Hank J. Brightman, Saint Peter's College; Brian Colwell, Stanford University; Frank Cormier, University of Manitoba; Amy Craddock, Indiana State University; Cathy Coghlan, Texas Christian University; Michael J. DeValve, Fayetteville State University; Gennifer Furst, The College of New Jersey; Phyllis B. Gerstenfeld, California State University—Stanislaus; Lori Guevara, Fayetteville State University; Stephen Haas, Marshall University; Susan B. Haire, University of Georgia; Stephanie Halter, Plymouth State University; Timothy C. Hart, University of Nevada, Las Vegas; Pati K. Hendrickson, Tarleton State University; Susan M. Hilal, Metropolitan State University; Lucy Hochstein, Radford University; Kristy Holtfreter, Florida State University; Stanley S. Jacobs, Villanova University; Kristen Kuehnle, Salem State College; Satenik Margaryan, Montclair University; James R. Maupin, New Mexico State University; Eric Metchick, Salem State College; Wilson R. Palacios, University of South Florida; Ira Sommers, California State University—Los Angeles; Isaac Van Patten, Radford University; William Wells, Southern Illinois University—Carbondale; Mark Winton, University of Central Florida; and Lisa Anne Zilney, Montclair State University. Andre Rosay also provided an extensive and invaluable review of the first edition of this text. We also thank Lindsay R. Reed and Hanna S. Scott for their diligence and hard work in writing the instructor's manual, Ann Dupuis and Sharlene Hesse-Biber for the appendix on HyperRESEARCH software, Margarita Porteyeva for the appendix on Excel, and Peggy Plass, Kathryn Stoeckert, and Heather Albertson for additional interactive exercises.

We continue to be indebted to the many students we have had an opportunity to teach and mentor, at both the undergraduate and the graduate level. In many respects, this book could not have been written without these ongoing reciprocal teaching and learning experiences. You inspire us to become better teachers!

Ronet is indebted to her terrific colleagues in the Department of Sociology and Criminal Justice who are unwavering sources of support and inspiration. To a first-rate office staff who not only keep all the trains running on time in our department but also are wonderful friends: Christine Grott, Linda Keen, and Nancy Quillen. Ronet is also indebted to an amazing circle of friends who endured graduate school together and continue to hold retreats one weekend of the year (22 years and counting!) for guidance, support, therapy, and laughter: Dianne Carmody, Gerry King, Peggy Plass, and Barbara Wauchope. You are the most amazing women in the world, and I am so blessed to have you in my life. To Alex Alvarez and Michelle Meloy, my other kindred spirits for their support and guidance; to my mother, Jan, who remains my hero; and to my father, Ron, for his steadfast critical eye in all matters of life.

And most important, we both wish to thank our spouses, Raymond Paternoster and Elizabeth Schutt, for their love and support (and editorship!), and our children, John Bachman-Paternoster and Julia Schutt, for all the remarkable joy they have brought to our lives.

Science, Society, and Criminological Research

As this text was being sent to the printer, a 20-year-old man named Adam Lanza walked into an elementary school in Newtown, CT, armed with several semiautomatic weapons and killed 20 children and 6 adults. This was not the first school shooting, nor even the first in 2012. On February 27, 2012, 17-year-old T. J. Lane walked up to a cafeteria table at Chardon High School in Ohio and started shooting, killing three of his high school classmates and wounding three others. On March 11, 2009, 17-year-old Tim Kretschmer entered a high school in Winnenden, Germany, and opened fire killing nine students and three teachers. After fleeing, he killed four others before killing himself after a shootout with police. On April 16, 2007, Cho Seung-Hui killed 32 students, faculty, and staff and left over 30 others injured on the campus of Virginia Tech in Blacksburg, Virginia. Cho was armed with two semiautomatic handguns that he had legally purchased and a vest filled with ammunition. As police were closing in on the scene, he killed himself. The shooting rampage was the deadliest in all of U.S. history. Less than a year later, on February 14, 2008, Steven Kazmierczak, who was described as "an outstanding student," entered a large oceanography class that was in session at Northern Illinois University and opened fire using a shotgun and three handguns, which he had smuggled into the room using a guitar case. A total of 24 people were shot, six of whom died, including Kazmierczak, who shot himself before police arrived. The deadliest school shooting to take place in a high school occurred on April 20, 1999, when Eric Harris and Dylan Klebold killed 12 students and a teacher before killing themselves at Columbine High School in suburban Colorado.

None of these mass murder offenders were typical terrorists, and each of these incidents, as did the other school shootings in the past 20 years, caused a media frenzy. Headlines such as "The School Violence Crisis" and "School Crime Epidemic" were plastered across national newspapers and weekly news journals. From a statistical standpoint, these headlines seemed a little late, particularly because the juvenile arrest rate for murder had been declining. In addition, the thousands of other shootings that occurred in less privileged communities during the same period rarely made the national news, yet rates of murder in impoverished areas of the country are much higher than in privileged areas. You may say, "Well, these incidents received attention because they involved mass killing." We say, "What about murders in the same area involving single victims that still received little media attention?" For example, a 22-year-old gang member named Omar Sevilla was shot to death as he walked to a drug and alcohol treatment center. That same day, only a few blocks away from Sevilla's murder, a German tourist named Horst Fietze was killed during a robbery. While Sevilla's murder went largely unnoticed in the press, the murder of Fietze received national media attention (Alvarez and Bachman 2008).

Unfortunately, the media play a large role in how we perceive both problems and solutions. In fact, 95% of Americans say that mass media sources such as television and newspapers are their main source of information on crime and violence (Surrette 1998). What are your perceptions of violence committed by youth, and how did you acquire them? What do you believe are the causes of youth violence? Many factors have been blamed for youth violence in American society, including the easy availability of guns, the lack of guns in classrooms for protection, the use of weapons in movies and television, the moral decay of our nation, poor parenting, unaware teachers, school and class size, racial prejudice, teenage alienation, the Internet and the World Wide Web, anti-Semitism, and rap and rock music, and the list goes on.

You probably have your own ideas about the factors related to violence in general and youth violence in particular. However, these beliefs may not always be supported by empirical research. In fact, the factors often touted by politicians and the media to be related to violence are not always supported by empirical evidence. In the rest of this chapter, you will learn how the methods of social science research go beyond stories in the popular media to help us answer questions like "What are the causes of youth violence?" By the chapter's end, you should understand how scientific methods used in criminal justice and criminology can help us understand and answer research questions in this discipline.

▣ Reasoning About the Social World

The story of just one murderous youth raises many questions. Take a few minutes to read each of the following questions about one of the Columbine shooters and jot down your answers. Don't ruminate about the questions or worry about your responses. This is not a test; there are no wrong answers.

- How would you describe Eric Harris?
- Why do you think Eric Harris wanted to kill other students?
- Was Eric Harris typical of other murderers under 18 years of age?
- In general, why do people become murderers?
- How have you learned about youth violence?

Now let us consider the possible answers to some of these questions. The information about Eric Harris is somewhat inconsistent (Duggan, Shear, and Fisher 1999). He was the 18-year-old son of middle-class professionals. He had an older brother who attended the University of Colorado. Harris apparently thought of himself as a white supremacist, but he also loved music by antiracist rock bands. On his Web page, he quoted from KMFDM, a German rock band whose song "Waste" includes these lyrics: "What I don't say I don't do. What I don't do I don't like. What I don't like I waste." Online, Harris referred to himself as "Darkness."

Do you have enough information now to understand why he went on a shooting rampage in his school?

A year before the shootings at Columbine High School, Harris was arrested on a felony count of breaking into a car. A juvenile court put him on probation, required him to perform community service and take criminal justice classes, and sent him to a school counseling program. He was described by one of his probation officers as a "very bright young man who is likely to succeed in life."

Now can you construct an adequate description of Eric Harris? Can you explain the reason for his murderous rampage? Or do you feel you need to know more about Eric Harris, about his friends and the family he grew up in? How about his experiences in school and with the criminal justice system? We have attempted to investigate just one person's experiences, and already our investigation is spawning more questions than answers.

Questions and Answers

When research questions concern not just one person but many people or general social processes, the possible alternative answers multiply. For example, consider the question of why incidents of school violence occur. Responses to a survey of mothers with children between the ages of 12 and 15 found that the majority of mothers considered the most important factors that contributed to school violence to be parents who did not teach children morals (87%), parents who supported aggressive behavior (78%), and gang or peer pressure (70%) (Kandakai et al. 1999). Compare these answers with the opinion you recorded earlier. Was your idea about the causes of youth violence one of the more popular ones held by this sample of mothers?

We cannot avoid asking questions about the actions and attitudes of others. We all try to make sense of the social world, which is a very complex place, and to make sense of our position in it, in which we have quite a personal stake. In fact, the more that you begin to "think like a social scientist," the more questions will come to mind.

But why does each question have so many possible answers? Surely our perspective plays a role. One person may see a homicide offender as a victim of circumstance, and another person may see the same individual as inherently evil. Answers to questions we ask in the criminological sciences also vary because individual life experiences and circumstances vary. The study of mothers' perceptions conducted by Kandakai et al. (1999), summarized in Exhibit 1.1, gives some idea of how opinions about the causes and cures for school violence vary. Even though previous research has found that the general public believes school violence is worse in urban schools than in suburban and rural schools, only 14% of the mothers who had children in urban schools believed their child's school was more violent than other schools. However, a higher percentage of urban mothers (37%) than suburban mothers (17%) reported that their child had been involved in one or more fights at school. Somewhat surprisingly, even though these mothers perceived parental support for violence as a major contributor to school violence, 4 in 10 of them believed it was acceptable for their child to fight in certain situations.

Everyday Errors in Reasoning

People give different answers to research questions for yet another reason: It is simply too easy to make errors in logic, particularly when we are analyzing the social world in which we ourselves are conscious participants. We can call some of these everyday errors because they occur so frequently in the nonscientific, unreflective discourse about the social world that we hear on a daily basis.

For evidence of everyday errors, just listen to your conversations or the conversations of others for one day. At some point in the day, it is inevitable that you or someone you are talking with will say something like "Well, I knew a person

| Exhibit 1.1 | Mothers' Perceptions of the Factors Related to School Violence |

	Percentage Who Said Factor Contributed a Great Deal
Parents who do not teach their kids right from wrong	87
Parent support for aggressive behavior	78
Gang or peer pressure	70
Lack of family involvement	67
Sale of alcohol or cigarettes to children	61
Poor parent-teacher communication	60
Seeing violence in the community	53
Violent messages in rap music	47
Seeing violence in the media	44
Lack of a dress code	30

who did X, and Y happened." From this one piece of information, you therefore draw a conclusion about the likelihood of Y. Four general errors in everyday reasoning can be made: overgeneralization, selective or inaccurate observation, illogical reasoning, and resistance to change.

Overgeneralization

Overgeneralization, an error in reasoning, occurs when we conclude that what we have observed or what we know to be true for some cases is true for all cases. We are always drawing conclusions about people and social processes from our own interactions with them, but sometimes we forget that our experiences are limited. The social (and natural) world is, after all, a complex place. We have the ability (and inclination) to interact with just a small fraction of the individuals who inhabit the social world, especially in a limited span of time.

> **Overgeneralization** An error in reasoning that occurs when we conclude that what we have observed or know to be true for a subset of cases holds true for the entire set.

Selective or Inaccurate Observation

Selective observation is choosing to look only at things that are in accordance with our preferences or beliefs. When we are inclined to criticize individuals or institutions, it is all too easy to notice their every failing. For example, if we are convinced in advance that all kids who are violent are unlikely to be rehabilitated and will go on to commit violent offenses in adulthood, we will probably find many confirming instances. But what about other youths who have become productive and stable citizens after engaging in violence as adolescents? Or the child who was physically or sexually abused and joined a gang to satisfy the need for a family surrogate? If we acknowledge only the instances that confirm our predispositions, we are victims of our own selective observation. Exhibit 1.2 depicts the difference between selective observation and overgeneralization.

> **Selective observation** Observations chosen because they are in accord with preferences or beliefs of the observer.

Exhibit 1.2 The Difference Between Overgeneralization and Selective Observation

Recent research on cognitive functioning (how the brain works) helps explain why our feelings so readily shape our perceptions (Seidman 1997). Emotional responses to external stimuli travel a shorter circuit in the brain than do reasoned responses (see Exhibit 1.3). The result, according to some cognitive scientists, is "What something reminds us of can be far more important than what it is" (Goleman 1995:294–95). Our emotions can influence us even before we begin to reason about what we have observed.

Our observations also can simply be inaccurate. If a woman says she is *hungry* and we think she said she is hunted, we have made an **inaccurate observation**. If we think five people are standing on a street corner when seven actually are, we have made an inaccurate observation. Such errors occur often in casual conversation and in everyday observation of the world around us. In fact, our perceptions do not provide a direct window onto the world around us, for what we think we have sensed is not necessarily what we have seen (or heard, smelled, felt, or tasted). Even when our senses are functioning fully, our minds have to interpret what we have sensed (Humphrey 1992). For example, when looking at the optical illusion in Exhibit 1.4, your visual system deceives you so that the monster in the background seems larger, even though they are exactly the same size.

> **Inaccurate observation** Observations based on faulty perceptions of empirical reality.

Illogical Reasoning

When we prematurely jump to conclusions or argue on the basis of invalid assumptions, we are using **illogical reasoning**. For example, it is not reasonable to propose that depictions of violence in media such as television and movies cause violence if evidence indicates that the majority of those who watch such programs do not become violent. However, it is also illogical to

> **Illogical reasoning** Prematurely jumping to conclusions and arguing on the basis of invalid assumptions.

Exhibit 1.3 Anatomy of an Emotional Hijacking

Fight or Flight Response:
*Heart rate and blood pressure
increase. Large muscles prepare
for quick action.*

Source: From *Emotional Intelligence* by Daniel Goleman, Copyright © 1995 by Daniel Goleman. Used by permission of Bantam Books, a division of Random House, Inc.

assume that media depictions of gratuitous violence have no effect on individuals. Of course, logic that seems impeccable to one person can seem twisted to another; the problem usually is reasoning from different assumptions rather than failing to "think straight."

Resistance to Change

Resistance to change, the reluctance to change our ideas in light of new information, may occur for several reasons:

Ego-based commitments. We all learn to greet with some skepticism the claims by leaders of companies, schools, agencies, and so on that people in their organization are happy, that revenues are growing, that services are being delivered in the best possible way, and so forth. We know how tempting it is to make statements about the social world that conform to our own needs rather than to the observable facts. It also can be difficult to admit that we were wrong once we have staked out a position on an issue.

> **Resistance to change** Reluctance to change ideas in light of new information, due to ego-based commitments, excessive devotion to tradition, or uncritical agreement with authorities.

Excessive devotion to tradition. Some degree of devotion to tradition is necessary for the predictable functioning of society. Social life can be richer and more meaningful if it is allowed to flow along the paths charted by those who have preceded us. But too much devotion to tradition can stifle adaptation to changing circumstances. When we distort our observations or alter our reasoning so that we can maintain beliefs that "were good enough for my grandfather, so they're good enough for me," we hinder our ability to accept new findings and develop new knowledge. The consequences can be deadly, as residents of Hamburg, Germany, might have realized in 1892 (Freedman 1991). Until the last part of the 19th century, people believed that cholera, a potentially lethal disease, was due to minute, inanimate, airborne poison particles (miasmas). In 1850, English researcher John Snow demonstrated that cholera was, in fact, spread by contaminated water. When a cholera epidemic hit Hamburg in 1892, the authorities did what tradition deemed appropriate: digging up and carting away animal carcasses to prevent the generation of more miasmas. Despite their efforts, thousands died. New York City adopted a new approach based on Snow's discovery, which included boiling drinking water and disinfecting sewage. As a result, the death rate in New York City dropped to a tenth of what it had been in a previous epidemic.

Uncritical agreement with authority. If we do not have the courage to evaluate critically the ideas of those in positions of authority, we will have little basis for complaint if they exercise their authority over us in ways we do not like. And if we do not allow new discoveries to call our beliefs into question, our understanding of the social world will remain limited. As we will see in Chapter 3, an extreme example of this problem is obedience to authority figures that can harm and kill others, including acts of genocide.

Now take just a minute to reexamine the beliefs about youth violence that you recorded earlier. Did you grasp at a simple explanation even though reality was far more complex? Were your beliefs influenced by your own ego and feelings about your similarities to or differences from individuals prone to violence? Are your beliefs perhaps based on depictions of violence in the media or fiction? Did you weigh carefully the opinions of authority figures, including politicians, teachers, and even your parents, or just accept or reject those opinions out of hand? Could knowledge of research methods help improve your own understanding of the factors related to violent behavior? By now, we hope that you will see some of the challenges faced by social scientists studying issues related to crime and the criminal justice system.

You do not have to be a scientist or use sophisticated research techniques to recognize and avoid these four errors in reasoning. If you recognize these errors for what they are and make a conscious effort to avoid them, you can improve your own reasoning. In the process, you will also be heeding the admonishments of your parents (or minister, teacher, or other adviser) to refrain from stereotyping people, to avoid jumping to conclusions, and to look at the big picture. These are the same errors that the methods of social science are designed to help criminologists avoid.

Exhibit 1.4	An Optical Illusion

Which monster is larger?

  THE SOCIAL SCIENCE APPROACH

The **social science** approach to answering questions about the social world is designed to greatly reduce these potential sources of error in everyday reasoning. **Science** relies on logical and systematic methods to answer questions, and it does so in a way that allows others to inspect and evaluate its methods. In the realm of social research, these methods are not so unusual. After all, they involve asking questions, observing social groups, and counting people, which we

Social science The use of scientific methods to investigate individuals, societies, and social processes, including questions related to criminology and criminal justice; the knowledge produced by these investigations.

Science A set of logical, systematic, documented methods for investigating nature and natural processes; the knowledge produced by these investigations.

often do in our everyday lives. However, social scientists develop, refine, apply, and report their understanding of the social world more systematically, or specifically, than Joanna Q. Public:

- Social science research methods can reduce the likelihood of overgeneralization by using systematic procedures for selecting individuals or groups to study that are representative of the individuals or groups that we wish to generalize.

- Social science methods can reduce the risk of selective or inaccurate observation by requiring that we measure and sample phenomena systematically.

- To avoid illogical reasoning, social researchers use explicit criteria for identifying causes and for determining if these criteria are met in a particular instance.

- Because they require that we base our beliefs on evidence that can be examined and critiqued by others, scientific methods lessen the tendency to develop answers about the social world from ego-based commitments, excessive devotion to tradition, and/or unquestioning respect for authority.

Science Versus Pseudoscience

Epistemology A branch of philosophy that studies how knowledge is gained or acquired.

Transparent An important feature of the scientific method that requires procedures, methods, and data analyses of any study to be presented clearly for the purposes of replication.

Peer review A process in which a journal editor sends a submitted article to two or three experts who judge whether the paper should be accepted, revised and resubmitted, or rejected; the experts also provide comments to explain their decision and guide any revisions.

Pseudoscience Dubious but fascinating claims that are touted as "scientifically proven" and bolstered by fervent, public testimonials of believers who have experienced firsthand or have claimed to have witnessed the phenomenon; however, such evidence is not based on the principles of the scientific method.

Phrenology A now defunct field of study, once considered a science in the 19th century, that held that bumps and fissures of the skull determined the character and personality of a person.

In philosophical terms, the scientific method represents an **epistemology**, that is, a way of knowing that relies on objective, empirical investigation. Its techniques must be **transparent** so that the methods, procedures, and data analyses of any study can be replicated. This transparency allows other researchers to see if the same results can be reproduced. If findings can be replicated, we have greater confidence that the finding is real and not based on bias. Transparency also relies on **peer review**, the process by which other independent researchers evaluate the scientific merit of the study (you will learn more about this in Chapter 14).

In contrast, if we relied on findings based on intuition, gut reactions, or our own experience, we would be open to the errors we just covered above. If we based findings on these, it would not be science, but instead, it would fall under the classification of **pseudoscience**. Pseudoscientific beliefs are not based on the scientific method but rather on claims that may be touted as "scientifically proven," only bolstered by testimonials of believers who have experienced firsthand or who have claimed to have witnessed the phenomenon (Nester and Schutt 2012).

Of course, today's pseudoscience could be yesterday's science. In criminological research, **phrenology** is a good example. In the 19th century, phrenology was the belief that bumps and fissures of the skull determined the character and personality of a person. Doctors doing entry examinations at American prisons would examine a new inmate's head for bumps or cavities to develop a criminal profile. Advances in cognitive psychology neurology have largely discredited phrenology and placed it within the domain of pseudoscience. It didn't take a genius to question phrenology, but just a group of researchers adhering to the scientific method. When inmate's heads were compared to with individual heads in the general population, they were essentially the same!

Motives for Criminological Research

Like you, social scientists read stories about incidents of violence committed by youth, observe this violence occasionally in their lives, and try to make sense of what they see. For most, that is the end of it. But for some social scientists, the problem of youth violence has become a major research focus. The motivations for selecting this particular research focus, as with any social science topic, can be any one or some combination of the following:

Policy motivations. Many social service agencies and elected officials seek better assessments and descriptions of youth violence so they can identify needs and allocate responsibility among agencies that could meet these needs. For example, federal agencies such as the U.S. Department of Justice and the Centers for Disease Control and Prevention want to identify the magnitude of youth violence, and many state and local officials use social research to guide development of their social service budgets. Programs designed to rehabilitate young offenders often use research to learn more about the needs of their clientele. These policy guidance and program management needs have resulted in numerous research projects.

Academic motivations. Young offenders have been a logical focus for researchers interested in a number of questions ranging from how an individual's connection to parents and peers influences his or her behavior to how the social conditions under which an individual lives, such as poverty, affect his or her behavior. For example, social scientists have long been concerned with the impact that social disorganization has on individual behavior. Early in this century, researchers at the University of Chicago were interested in the effects that residential mobility and immigration had on levels of crime and delinquency in urban neighborhoods. Today researchers are exploring similar questions concerning the impact of disintegrating economic bases in central cities and their relationship to crime and violence. Other researchers have focused on individual-level explanations such as neurological damage. Those who study social policy also have sought to determine whether correctional programs such as boot camps and other forms of shock incarceration serve to decrease the probability of juveniles reoffending in the future.

Personal motivations. Many who conduct research on youth violence feel that by doing so they can help prevent it and/or ameliorate the consequences of this violence when it occurs. Some social scientists first volunteered with at-risk youth in such organizations as Big Brothers Big Sisters and only later began to develop a research agenda based on their experiences.

Social Criminological Research in Practice

Of course, youth violence is not a new phenomenon in the United States. It has always been a popular topic of social science research. However, the sharp increase in this violence in the United States that began in the late 1980s was unprecedented. Predictably, whenever a phenomenon is perceived as an epidemic, numerous explanations emerge to explain it. Unfortunately, most of these explanations are based on the media and popular culture, not on empirical research. Unlike the anecdotal information floating around in the mass media, social scientists interested in this phenomenon have amassed a substantial body of findings that have refined knowledge about the factors related to the problem and shaped social policy (Tonry and Moore 1998). These studies fall into the four categories of purposes for social scientific research:

Descriptive research. Defining and describing social phenomena of interest is a part of almost any research investigation, but **descriptive research** is the primary focus of many studies of youth crime and violence. Some of the central questions used in these studies were "How many people are victims of youth violence?" "How many youth are offenders?" "What are the most common crimes committed by youthful offenders?" and "How many youth are arrested and incarcerated each year for crime?" Measurement (see Chapter 4) and sampling (see Chapter 5) are central concerns in descriptive research.

> **Descriptive research** Research in which phenomena are defined and described.

> **Exploratory research** Research in which social phenomena are investigated without a priory expectations, in order to develop explanations of them.

Exploratory research. **Exploratory research** seeks to find out how people get along in the setting under question, what meanings they give to their actions, and what issues concern them. The goal is to answer the question "What is going on here?" and to investigate social phenomena without expectations. This purpose is associated with the use of methods that capture large amounts of relatively unstructured information. For example, researchers investigating the emergence of youth gangs in the 1980s were encountering a phenomenon with which they had no direct experience. Thus, an early goal was to find out what it was like to be a gang member and how gang members made sense of their situation. Exploratory research like this frequently involves qualitative methods (see Chapter 9).

Explanatory research. Many people consider explanation to be the premier goal of any science. **Explanatory research** seeks to identify causes and effects of social phenomena, to predict how one phenomenon will change or vary in response to variation in some other phenomenon. Researchers adopted explanation as a goal when they began to ask such questions as "Why do people become offenders?" and "Does the unemployment rate influence the frequency of youth crime?" Methods with which to identify causes and effects are the focus of Chapter 6.

> **Explanatory research** Research that seeks to identify causes and/or effects of social phenomena.

Evaluation research. **Evaluation research** seeks to determine the effects of a social program or other types of intervention. It is a type of explanatory research because it deals with cause and effect. However, evaluation research differs from other forms of explanatory research because evaluation research considers the implementation and effects of social policies and programs. These issues may not be relevant in other types of explanatory research. The increase of youth violence in the 1990s spawned many new government programs and, with them, evaluation research to assess the impact of these programs. Some of these studies are reviewed in Chapter 7, which covers experimental design, and in Chapter 11, which covers evaluation research.

We will now summarize one study in each of these four areas to give you a feel for the projects motivated by those different concerns.

> **Evaluation research** Research about social programs or interventions.

Description: How Prevalent Is Youth Violence?

Police reports. One of the most enduring sources of information on lethal violence in the United States is the Federal Bureau of Investigation's (FBI) Supplementary Homicide Reports (SHR). Homicide victimization rates indicate that for those under the age of 24, vulnerability to murder increased dramatically during the mid-1980s through about 1994 when rates began a steady decline. With some annual fluctuations from year to year, rates of homicide victimization for this age group leveled off after 2000 through 2008 (the most recent data available) (Cooper and Smith 2011). What accounted for this unprecedented rise in youth violence during the late 1980s and early 1990s? To answer this question, explanatory research is necessary. After their in-depth descriptive analysis of youth violence during this time, Cook and Laub (1998) contend that the increasing homicide rates began with the introduction of crack cocaine and the conflict that surrounded its marketing. However, the primary factor, they believe, was the increased easy availability of firepower: "All of the increase in homicide rates was with guns, and it appears to be changing access [to] and use of guns, rather than a change in the character of the youths, that best accounts for their increased involvement in lethal violence" (p. 60).

Data measuring the prevalence of nonlethal forms of violence such as robbery and assaults are a bit more complicated. How do we know how many young people assault victims each year? People who report their victimizations to police represent one avenue for these calculations. The FBI compiles these numbers in its Uniform Crime Reporting system, which is slowly being replaced by the National Incident-Based Reporting System (NIBRS). Both of these data sources rely on state, county, and city law enforcement agencies across the United States to voluntarily participate in the reporting program. Can you imagine why relying on these data sources may be problematic for estimating prevalence rates of violent victimizations? If victimizations are never reported to police, they are not counted. This is especially problematic for victimizations between intimate partners and other offenses like rape in which only a fraction of incidents are ever reported to police.

Surveys. Instead, most social scientists believe the best way to determine the magnitude of violent victimization is through random sample surveys. While we will discuss survey methodology in greater detail in Chapter 8, this basically means randomly selecting individuals in the population of interest and asking them about their victimization experiences. The only ongoing survey to do this on an annual basis is the National Crime Victimization Survey (NCVS), which is sponsored by the U.S. Department of Justice's Bureau of Justice Statistics. Among other questions, the NCVS asks questions like "Has anyone attacked or threatened you with a weapon, for instance, a gun or knife; by something thrown, such as a rock or bottle, include any grabbing, punching, or choking." Estimates indicate that youth aged 12 to 24 all have the highest rates of violent victimization, which have been declining steadily since the highs witnessed in the early 1990s, despite the recent increases observed in homicide rates for this age group in some locations.

Another large research survey that estimates the magnitude of youth violence (along with other risk-taking behavior such as taking drugs and smoking) is called the Youth Risk Behavior Survey (YRBS), which has been conducted every 2 years in the United States since 1990. Respondents to this survey are a national sample of approximately 16,000 high school students in Grades 9 through 12. To measure the extent of youth violence, students are asked the following questions: "During the past 30 days, on how many days did you carry a weapon such as a gun, knife, or club?" "During the past 12 months, how many times were you in a physical fight?" "During the past 12 months, how many times were you in a physical fight in which you were injured and had to be seen by a doctor or nurse?" "During the past 30 days, how many times did you carry a weapon such as a gun, knife, or club on school property?" "During the past 12 months, how many times were you in a physical fight on school property?" and "During the past 12 months, how many times did someone threaten or injure you with a gun, knife, or club on school property?"

Of course, another way to measure violence would be to ask respondents about their offending behaviors. Some surveys do this, including the National Youth Survey (NYS) and the Rochester Youth Development Study (RYDS). The RYDS sample consists of 1,000 students who were in the seventh and eighth grades of the Rochester, New York, public schools during the spring semester of the 1988 school year. This project has interviewed the original respondents at 12 different times (we will discuss longitudinal research of this kind in Chapter 6) including the last interview that took place in 1997 when respondents were in their early 20s (Thornberry et al. 2008). As you can imagine, respondents are typically more reluctant to reveal offending behavior compared to their victimization experiences. However, these surveys have been a useful tool for examining the factors related to violent offending and other delinquency. We should also point out that although this discussion has been specific to violence, the measures we have discussed in this section, along with their strengths and weaknesses, apply to measuring all crime in general.

Exploration: How Do Schools Respond to Gun Violence?

Research that is exploratory in nature is generally concerned with uncovering detailed information about a given phenomenon, learning as much as possible about particular people and/or events. Asmussen and Creswell (1995) were interested in the responses to school shooting incidents. Because school shootings are relatively rare and there was virtually no empirical literature that addressed the topic, Asmussen and Creswell performed an in-depth qualitative case study of a shooting incident that occurred at a large public university. The incident occurred in a senior-level actuarial science class when a male graduate student arrived early for the class one Monday morning armed with a vintage Korean War semiautomatic military rifle loaded with a 30-round clip of .30-caliber ammunition. He carried another 30-round clip in his pocket. Twenty of the 34 students in the class were already there, and most of them were quietly reading the student newspaper. The instructor was en route to class. The gunman pointed the rifle at the students, swept it across the room, and pulled the trigger. The gun jammed. Trying to unlock the rifle, he hit the butt of it on the desk and quickly tried firing it again. Again it did not fire. By this time, most students had realized what was happening and dropped to the floor, overturned their desks, and tried to hide behind them. After about 20 seconds, one of the students shoved a desk into the gunman, and students ran past him out into the hall and out of the building. The gunman hastily left the room and went out of the building to his parked car, which he had left running. He was captured by police within the hour.

Asmussen and Creswell (1995) were surprised to find that instead of seeking safety after leaving the classroom, all the students had stood together just outside the building. Although a few were openly emotional and crying, many were kidding about the incident, as if it had posed no real danger. This denial response is noted by the mental health literature, which finds that feelings of fear and anger usually follow an initial response of denial and disbelief. The researchers found that many people in addition to the students who witnessed it were traumatized by the incident. In fact, three distinct groups of people sought counseling services during the weeks following the event. The first group had some direct involvement with the assailant, either by seeing him the day of the gun incident or because they had known him personally. The second group was the "silent connection," comprising individuals who were indirectly involved and yet emotionally traumatized. A large number in this group were parents. The third group included people who had previously experienced a trauma and whose fears were retriggered by this incident.

Because the assailant's future was in the hands of the criminal justice system, the importance of information from this system became critical to feelings of safety. Two combined debriefing sessions by mental health counselors, the campus police chief, and two county attorneys were held for all those interested.

Another phenomenon observed on the campus was an increase in the number of professors and staff who were concerned with disruptive students or students who exhibited aberrant behavior in class. To manage this, the Student Judiciary Office advised departments on various methods of dealing with students who exhibited abnormal behavior in class. In addition, plainclothes police officers were sent to sit outside classrooms and offices whenever faculty and staff indicated concerns.

To their surprise, Asmussen and Creswell (1995) found that the campus did not establish a special unit to manage future incidents. The only structural change made was the installation of emergency phones throughout the campus. In addition, no discussion was reported about formal linkages with community agencies that might assist in the event of a future tragedy. In the end, Asmussen and Creswell's exploratory research illustrates the complexity involved in responding to a campus shooting.

Explanation: What Factors Are Related to Youth Delinquency and Violence?

What are some of the factors related to youth violence? Using the South Carolina YRBS, MacDonald et al. (2005) examined the efficacy of General Strain Theory (GST) (Agnew 1992) and Gottfredson and Hirschi's General Theory of Crime (1990) in predicting youth violence. GST generally contends that strain, such as disjunction between expectations and aspirations (e.g., wanting a good job but not being able to get one), increases the likelihood that individuals will experience negative emotions, which in turn increases the likelihood of antisocial or violent behavior. These negative emotions include anger, anxiety, dissatisfaction, and so on. The general theory of crime claims that self-control, which is primarily formed by the relationship children have with their parents and/or guardians, is the motivating factor for all crime. Individuals with low self-control, the theory predicts, will be more likely to pursue immediate gratification, be impulsive, prefer simple tasks, engage in risky behavior, have volatile tempers, and so on.

To measure violent behavior, the YRBS asks respondents how many times in the past 30 days they carried a weapon and how many times they were in a physical fight. To measure life satisfaction, MacDonald et al. (2005) used six questions that asked respondents to report on general satisfaction or the degree to which they felt "terrible" or "delighted" about family life, friendships, school, self, residential location, and overall life. To measure self-control, the authors used the indicators of smoking and sexual behavior to represent risky behaviors that are not illegal since they "reflect impulsivity and short-run hedonism" (p. 1502). When predicting violent behavior, they also controlled for a number of other factors like employment, drug use, family structure, and religious participation, along with age, race, and gender.

Consistent with the general theory of crime, MacDonald et al. (2005) found that high school students who reported more impulsive behaviors, indicative of low self-control, also reported greater participation in violent behavior. In addition, results indicated that students who were more satisfied with life were significantly less likely to have engaged in violence compared to their less satisfied peers.

Evaluation: Do Violence Prevention Programs in Schools Work?

To reduce violence and create a safer atmosphere at schools across the country, literally thousands of schools have adopted some form of violence prevention training (Powell, Muir-McClain, and Halasyamani 1995). These programs generally provide cognitive-behavioral and social skills training on various topics using a variety of methods. Such programs are commonly referred to as conflict resolution and peer mediation training. Many of these prevention programs are designed to improve interpersonal problem-solving skills among children and adolescents by training children in cognitive processing, such as identifying the interpersonal problem and generating nonaggressive solutions. There is limited evidence, however, that such programs are actually effective in reducing violence.

Grossman et al. (1997) assessed the efficacy of one such program for children in elementary school called "Second Step: A Violence Prevention Curriculum." The program involved 30 lessons, each lasting about 35 minutes, taught once or twice a week. Each lesson consisted of a photograph accompanied by a social scenario that formed the basis for discussion, role-playing, and conceptual activities. Lessons were arranged in three units: (1) empathy training, in which students identified their own feelings and those of others; (2) impulse control, in which students were presented with a problem-solving strategy and behavioral skills for affecting solutions (e.g., apologizing or dealing with peer pressure); and (3) anger management, in which students were presented with a coping strategy and behavioral skills for tense situations.

Twelve elementary schools in King County, Washington, were paired according to three criteria: the school district, the proportion of students receiving free or reduced-cost lunch, and the proportion of minority enrollment. After pairing, schools in each pair were randomly assigned either to receive the Second Step program (experimental groups) or to receive no violence prevention curriculum (control groups). Random assignment was necessary so the researchers could be more confident that any differences observed in aggression and violent behavior between the two groups after the program could be attributed to the program alone and not to some other factor. Violent and aggressive behavior was measured in three ways: teacher ratings of each child's behavior, parent ratings, and direct observation of students by trained observers in the classroom, on the playground, and in the cafeteria. Measures of aggression were taken at three time periods: before the start of the curriculum (baseline), 2 weeks after the conclusion of the curriculum, and 6 months after the curriculum.

To determine the effectiveness of the Second Step program, researchers examined the change in aggression between scores measured at baseline and those from the second and third periods of data collection. Grossman et al. (1997) found encouraging results: Observed physically aggressive behavior decreased significantly more among children who engaged in the curriculum than among children in the control group who were not exposed to the Second Step program. Moreover, prosocial behavior increased significantly among children in the Second Step program compared to the control group. Grossman et al. concluded, "This violence prevention curriculum appears to lead to modest reductions in levels of aggressive behavior and increases in neutral/prosocial behavior in school among second and third graders" (p. 1608).

▣ Strengths and Limitations of Social Research

These case studies are only four of the dozens of studies investigating youth violence, but they illustrate some of the questions criminological research can address, several different methods social scientists studying these issues can use, and ways criminological research can inform public policy. Notice how each of the four studies was designed to reduce the errors common in everyday reasoning:

- The clear definition of the population of interest in each study and the selection of a broad, representative sample of that population in two studies increased the researchers' ability to draw conclusions without overgeneralizing findings to groups to which they did not apply.

- The use of surveys in which each respondent was asked the same set of questions reduced the risk of selective or inaccurate observation.

- The risk of illogical reasoning was reduced by carefully describing each stage of the research, clearly presenting the findings, and carefully testing the basis for cause-and-effect conclusions.

- Resistance to change was reduced by using an experimental design that randomly assigned classes to an experimental treatment (the Second Step program) and a control group to fairly evaluate the efficacy of the program.

Nevertheless, we would be less than honest if we implied that you enter the realm of beauty, truth, and light whenever you engage in research or whenever you base your opinions only on the best available social research. Research always has some limitations and some flaws (as does any human endeavor), and findings are always subject to differing interpretations. Social research permits you to see more, to observe with fewer distortions, and to describe more clearly to others what your opinions are based on, but it will not settle all arguments. Other people will always have differing opinions, and some of those others will be social scientists who have conducted their own studies and drawn different conclusions. Do other programs similar to Second Step reduce levels of aggression among students? Only a handful of studies have used randomized controlled designs to examine these programs, and the results of these studies have been mixed. Like the Grossman et al. (1997) study, some researchers have found a reduction in aggressive behavior by children exposed to such social skills training programs, whereas others have not. Until more scientific research is conducted to evaluate these programs, it is difficult to determine whether the money poured into such programs by school districts is well spent.

But even in areas of research that are fraught with controversy, where social scientists differ in their interpretations of the evidence, the quest for new and more sophisticated research has value. What is most important for improving understanding of the social world and issues in criminology is not the result of any particular study but the accumulation of evidence from different studies of related issues. By designing new studies that focus on the weak points or controversial conclusions of prior research, social scientists contribute to a body of findings that gradually expands our knowledge about the social world and resolves some of the disagreements about it.

Social researchers investigating issues in criminal justice and criminology will always disagree somewhat because of their differing research opportunities, methodological approaches, and policy preferences. There are many heated debates in the criminological literature. For example, one issue that has recently received increased attention is how the availability of guns is related to overall levels of violence. Some research has found that greater gun availability is associated with more robberies, home burglaries, assaults, and homicides with guns. However, others have argued that gun ownership for self-defense can reduce robbery and home burglary completion rates, thus theoretically decreasing the rewards for these crimes and increasing the perceived risks to offenders. According to yet another view, someone who is planning an attack and fears that potential robbery and/or burglary victims are armed may simply decide to acquire superior firepower and carry out the attack regardless (for review, see Reiss and Roth 1993). As you can see, much more research is required using a variety of methods to resolve this debate.

Whether you plan to conduct your own research projects, read others' research reports, or just think about and act in the social world, knowing about research methods has many benefits. This knowledge will give you greater confidence in your own opinions, improve your ability to evaluate others' opinions, and encourage you to refine your questions, answers, and methods of inquiry about the social world.

Of course, the methods of social science, as careful as they may be, cannot answer all questions of interest to criminologists. Should we do unto others what we would have them do unto us? That is a very important question that has been asked throughout history, but we must turn to religion or philosophy to answer questions about values. Social research on the consequences of forgiveness or the sources of interpersonal conflict may help us understand and implement our values, but even the best research cannot tell us which values should guide our lives.

🔲 Types of Research Methods

As you will see in this book, the data we utilize in criminological research are derived from many different sources, and the research methods we employ in criminology and criminal justice are very diverse.

An **experimental approach** is used in criminological research, particularly when the efficacy of a program or policy is being evaluated. As we will see in Chapter 6, true experiments must have three things: two groups (one receiving the treatment or intervention and the other receiving no treatment or another form thereof), random assignment to these two groups, and an assessment of change in the outcome variable after the treatment or policy has been received. Quasi-experimental designs, experiments that lack one of these three ingredients, also are used in our discipline. Chapter 11 focuses exclusively on research designs used in evaluation research.

Asking people questions on **surveys** or **questionnaires**, as we highlighted above, is another popular method used by criminological researchers and is probably the most versatile. Most concepts about individuals can be defined in such a way that measurement with one or more questions becomes an option. These surveys can be self-administered by respondents (e.g., through the mail) or can be read by an interviewer (e.g., through a telephone survey).

Although in principle survey questions can be a straightforward and efficient means to measure individual characteristics, facts about events, level of knowledge, and opinions of any sort, in practice survey questions can result in misleading or inappropriate answers. All questions proposed for a survey must be screened carefully for their adherence to basic guidelines and then tested and revised until the researcher feels some confidence that they will be clear to the intended respondents (Fowler 1995). Some variables may prove to be inappropriate for measurement with any type of question. We have to recognize that memories and perceptions of the events about which we might like to ask can be limited. Specific guidelines for writing questions and developing surveys are presented in Chapter 8.

In other cases, a researcher may want to make her presence known and directly participate in the activity being observed. Included in this type of research design is **participant observation**, which involves developing a sustained relationship with people while they go about their normal activities. In other instances, the subject matter of interest may not be amenable to a survey, or perhaps we want more detailed and in-depth information than questions with fixed formats can answer. In these cases, we turn to research techniques such as participant observation and **intensive interviewing**. These methods are preferred when we seek in-depth information on an individual's feelings, experiences, and perceptions. Chapter 9 shows how these methods and other field research techniques can uncover aspects of the social world that we are likely to miss in experiments and surveys.

Secondary data analysis (Riedel 2000), which is the reanalysis of already existing data, is another method used by researchers. These data usually come from one of two places: from official sources such as local or federal agencies (e.g., rates of crime reported to police, information on incarcerated offenders from state correctional authorities, adjudication data from the courts) or from surveys sponsored by government agencies or conducted by other researchers. Virtually all the data

Experimental approach An approach in which the researcher assigns individuals to two or more groups in a way that equates the characteristics of individuals in the groups (with a certain chance of error), except for variation in the groups' exposure to the independent variable.

Surveys Popular and versatile research instruments using a question format. Surveys can either be self-administered or read by an interviewer.

Questionnaire The instrument containing the questions on a self-administered survey.

Participant observation A type of field research in which a researcher develops a sustained and intensive relationship with people while they go about their normal activities.

Intensive interviewing Open-ended, relatively unstructured questioning in which the interviewer seeks in-depth information on the interviewee's feelings, experiences, and/or perceptions.

Secondary data analysis Analysis of data collected by someone other than the researcher or the researcher's assistant.

Historical events research Research in which social events of only one time period in the past are studied.

Content analysis A research method for systematically analyzing and making inferences from text.

Crime mapping Geographical mapping strategies used to visualise a number of things including location, distance, and patterns of crime and their correlates.

collected by government agencies and a great deal of survey data collected by independent researchers are made available to the public through the Inter-University Consortium for Political and Social Research (ICPSR), which is located at the University of Michigan. When documents from the past, such as correspondence, newspaper accounts, and trial transcripts, are analyzed, the research is generally termed **historical events research**. Another type of indirect measurement is called **content analysis**. In this type of study, a researcher studies representations of the research topic in such media forms as news articles, TV shows, and radio talk shows. An investigation of the drinking climate on campuses might examine the amount of space devoted to ads for alcoholic beverages in a sample of issues of the student newspaper. Campus publications also might be coded to indicate the number of times that statements discouraging substance abuse appear. Content analysis techniques also can be applied to legal opinions, historical documents, novels, songs, or other cultural productions. With the advent of computer technology, **crime mapping** also has become a popular method for examining the relationship between criminal behavior and other social indicators. Chapter 10 covers each of these methodologies and illustrates the importance of these unobtrusive research techniques in criminology and criminal justice. Increasingly, researchers are combining methods to more reliably answer a single research question. Although examples of mixed methods research are highlighted in several chapters, Chapter 12 provides an overview of the philosophy and motivation for combining methods, along with the various techniques for doing so.

▣ Quantitative and Qualitative Methods

In general, research methods can be divided into two somewhat different domains called quantitative research methods and qualitative research methods. Did you notice the difference between the types of data the case studies discussed at the beginning of the chapter used? The data collected in the YRBS were counts of the responses students gave on the survey. These data were numerical, so we say that this study used **quantitative methods**. MacDonald

Quantitative methods Methods such as surveys and experiments that record variation in social life in terms of categories that vary in amount. Data that are treated as quantitative are either numbers or attributes that can be ordered in terms of magnitude.

et al. (2005) looked at the extent to which impulsivity and life satisfaction affected students' participation in violence; they examined this relationship with statistical methods like correlations and regression coefficients. This, too, represents quantitative methods. In contrast, Asmussen and Creswell's (1995) exploratory study used in-depth interviews with people who had experienced the attempted school shooting. This methodology was designed to capture the social reality of the participants as they experienced it, in their own words rather than in predetermined categories. Because the researchers focused on the participants' words rather than counts and numbers, we say that this study used **qualitative methods**.

Qualitative methods Methods such as participant observation, intensive interviewing, and focus groups that are designed to capture social life as participants experience it, rather than in categories predetermined by the researcher. Data that are treated as qualitative are mostly written or spoken words or observations that do not have a direct numerical interpretation.

The distinction between quantitative and qualitative methods involves more than just the type of data collected. Quantitative methods are most often used when the motives for research are explanation, description, or evaluation. Exploration is the most common motive for using qualitative methods, although researchers also use these methods for descriptive and evaluative purposes. The goals of quantitative and qualitative researchers also may differ. Whereas quantitative researchers generally accept the goal of developing an understanding that correctly reflects what is actually happening in the real world, some qualitative researchers instead emphasize the goal of developing an "authentic" understanding of a social process or social setting (Gubrium and Holstein 1997). An authentic understanding is one that reflects *fairly* the various perspectives of participants in that setting.

As important as it is, we do not want to place too much emphasis on the distinction between qualitative and quantitative methods because social scientists often combine these methods in order to enrich their research. For example, "qualitative knowing" about social settings can be essential for understanding patterns in quantitative data (Campbell and Russo 1999:141). Qualitative data can be converted to quantitative data, for example, when we count the frequency of particular words or phrases in a text or measure the time elapsed between different behaviors that we have observed. Surveys that collect primarily quantitative data also may include questions asking for written responses, and these responses may be used in a qualitative, textual analysis. Researchers using quantitative methods may engage in some exploration in order to find unexpected patterns in their data. Qualitative researchers may test explicit explanations of social phenomena using textual or observational data.

As noted above, the use of multiple methods to study one research question is called triangulation. The term suggests that a researcher can get a clearer picture of the social reality being studied by viewing it from several different perspectives. Each will have some liabilities in a specific research application, and all can benefit from a combination of one or more other methods (Brewer and Hunter 1989; Sechrest and Sidani 1995).

As you will see in the chapters that follow, the distinction between quantitative and qualitative data is not always sharp. We'll examine such "mixed method" possibilities in each of the chapters that review specific methods of data collection.

> ***Triangulation*** The use of multiple methods to study one research question. Also used to mean the use of two or more different measures of the same variable.

Conclusion

We hope this first chapter has given you an idea of what to expect in the rest of this book. Our aim is to introduce you to social research methods by describing what social scientists have learned about issues in criminology and criminal justice as well as how they learned it. The substance of social science inevitably is more interesting than its methods, but the methods also become more interesting when they are not taught as isolated techniques. We have focused attention on research on youth violence and delinquency in this chapter; in subsequent chapters, we will introduce research examples from other areas.

Chapter 2 continues to build the foundation for our study of social research by reviewing the types of problems that criminologists study, the role of theory, the major steps in the research process, and other sources of information that may be used in social research. We stress the importance of considering scientific standards in social research and review generally accepted ethical guidelines. Throughout the chapter, we use several studies of domestic violence to illustrate the research process.

Key Terms

Content analysis 16	Experimental approach 15	Inaccurate observation 5
Crime mapping 16	Explanatory research 10	Intensive interviewing 15
Descriptive research 9	Exploratory research 10	Overgeneralization 4
Epistemology 8	Historical events research 16	Participant observation 15
Evaluation research 10	Illogical reasoning 5	Peer review 8

Highlights

- Criminological research cannot resolve value questions or provide answers that will convince everyone and remain settled for all time.

- All empirically based methods of investigation are based on either direct experience or others' statements.

- Four common errors in reasoning are overgeneralization, selective or inaccurate observation, illogical reasoning, and resistance to change. Illogical reasoning is due to the complexity of the social world, self-interestedness, and human subjectivity. Resistance to change may be due to unquestioning acceptance of tradition or of those in positions of authority or to self-interested resistance to admitting the need to change one's beliefs.

- Social science is the use of logical, systematic, documented methods to investigate individuals, societies, and social processes, as well as the knowledge produced by these investigations.

- Pseudoscience are claims based on beliefs and/or public testimonials, not on the scientific method.

- Criminological research can be motivated by policy guidance and program management needs, academic concerns, and charitable impulses.

- Criminological research can be descriptive, exploratory, explanatory, evaluative, or some combination of these.

- Quantitative methods record variation in social life in terms of categories that vary in amount. Qualitative methods are designed to capture social life as participants experience it, rather than in categories predetermined by the researcher.

- Triangulation is the use of multiple research methods to study a single research question.

Research in the News

Are Youth Desensitized to Violence?

Oakland, California, had several shootings in 2011 that resulted in very young victims. For example, 5-year-old Gabriel Martinez, Jr. was shot as he played near his father's business. After several years of declining violent crime, shootings in Oakland increased rapidly, with about five people shot or shot at a day. In an article in the *New York Times*, the experts interviewed gave their perceptions of the reasons for the increased violence. For example, Anthony Del Toro of California Youth Outreach said, "To secure a gun in Oakland is like looking for some candy." Another youth worker believed that kids were too desensitized to violence because "Young people see it all the time." The police department appeared to blame the budget cuts they have sustained that has resulted in officer layoffs. How could these beliefs translate into more scientifically based facts?

Source: Walter, Shoshana. 2012. "Shootings Soar in Oakland: Children Often Victims." *The New York Times,* January 8: A29A.

Exercises

1. What criminological topic or issue would you focus on if you could design a research project without any concern for costs? What are your motives for studying this topic? List at least four of your beliefs about this phenomenon. Try to identify the sources of each belief (e.g., television, newspaper, parental influence).

2. Develop four research questions related to your chosen topic or issue, one for each of the four types of research (descriptive, exploratory, explanatory, and evaluative). Be specific.

3. Read the abstracts of each article in a recent issue of a major criminological journal. Identify the type of research conducted for each study.

4. Find a report of social science research in an article in a daily newspaper. What are the motives for the research? How much information is provided about the research design? What were the major findings? What additional evidence would you like to see in the article to increase your findings in the research conclusions?

Developing a Research Proposal

Will you develop a research proposal in this course? If so, you should begin to consider your alternatives.

1. What topic would you focus on if you could design a social research project without any concern for costs? What are your motives for studying this topic?

2. Develop four questions that you might investigate about the topic you just selected. Each question should reflect a different research motive: description, exploration, explanation, or evaluation. Be specific.

3. Which question most interests you? Would you prefer to attempt to answer that question with quantitative or qualitative methods? Why?

STUDENT STUDY SITE

Log on to the Web-based student study site at **www.sagepub.com/bachmanprccj5e** for additional study tools including eFlashcards, Web quizzes, links to SAGE journal articles, podcasts, videos, data sets and codebooks, Web exercises, Web resources, and additional appendices.

Web Exercises

1. You have been asked to prepare a brief presentation on a criminological topic or issue of interest to you. Go to the Bureau of Justice Statistics (BJS) Web site at www.ojp.usdoj.gov/bjs/. Browse the BJS publications for a topic that interests you. Write a short outline for a 5- to 10-minute presentation regarding your topic, including how the data were collected, statistics, and other relevant information.

2. Go to the Federal Bureau of Investigation (FBI) Web site at www.fbi .gov. Explore the types of programs and initiatives sponsored by the FBI. Discuss at least three of these programs or initiatives in terms of their purposes and goals. For each program or initiative examined, do you believe the program or initiative is effective? What are the major weaknesses? What changes would you propose the FBI make to more effectively meet the goals of the program or initiative?

3. Go to the Web site of a major newspaper and find an article that talks about the causes of violence. What conclusions does the article draw and what research methods does the author discuss to back up his or her claims?

Ethics Exercises

Throughout the book, we will be discussing the ethical challenges that arise in research on crime and criminal justice. At the end of each chapter, we will ask you to consider some questions about ethical issues related to that chapter's focus. We introduce this critical topic formally in Chapter 3, but we will begin here with some questions for you to ponder.

1. You have now learned about Asmussen and Creswell's (1995) qualitative study of a school shooting incident. We think it provided important information for policymakers about the social dynamics in these tragedies. But what would you do if you were conducting a similar study in a high school and you learned that another student was planning to bring a gun to school to kill some other students? What if he was only thinking about it? Or just talking with his friends about how "neat" it would be? Can you suggest some guidelines for researchers?

2. Grossman et al. (1997) found that the Second Step program reduced aggressive behavior in schools and increased pro-social behavior. If you were David Grossman, would you announce your findings in a press conference and encourage schools to adopt this program? If you were a school principal who heard about this research, would you agree to let another researcher replicate (repeat) the Grossman et al. study in your school, with some classrooms assigned to receive the Second Step program randomly (on the basis of the toss of a coin) and others not allowed to receive the program for the duration of the study?

SPSS or Excel Exercises

The SPSS exercises at the end of each chapter use the data sets included on the companion Web site. In NCVS.ASSAULT.POR, a sample of assault incidents from the National Crime Victimization Survey for 1992–2005, variable V2089, identifies the metropolitan statistical area (MSA) status (urban, suburban, or rural) of each assault incident included in the data set.

1. Create a bar chart of V2089 using the graph procedure to show the percentage of assault incidents occurring in urban, suburban, and rural areas. Be sure to leave out the missing values. What do you conclude about the distribution of assaults by geographic location?

2. Write four research questions, one for each type of social research (descriptive, exploratory, explanatory, and evaluative), regarding the distribution of assault incidents by MSA status.

3. Discuss the possible reasons (policy, academic, or personal) for conducting research on the location of assault incidents.

4. Now find the variable that indicates the relationship between the victim and the offender. After reviewing the frequency distribution for this variable (remember to make sure the missing cases are coded missing), by whom are we most likely to be attacked?

CHAPTER 2

The Process and Problems of Criminological Research

When the bloodied and bruised face of pop star Rihanna was splashed across television screens in 2009, the reality of intimate partner assault was once again brought to the forefront of public consciousness. In June 2009, R&B singer Chris Brown pleaded guilty to assaulting her. Intimate partner violence (violence between spouses or intimates), sometimes referred to as domestic violence, is a major problem in our society, with police responding to between 2 million and 8 million complaints of assault by a spouse or lover yearly (Sherman 1992). Moreover, it is estimated from victimization surveys that many of these assaults are never reported to police (Bachman 2000; Tjaden and Thoennes 2000). Domestic violence is not just a frequent crime; it is also costly not only in terms of the injuries suffered by the parties involved but also in terms of shattered families. What to do about this major social problem, then, is an important policy question. For over 30 years, the criminal justice system has attempted to effectively respond to intimate partner violence and other domestic assaults in a way that best protects victims and punishes offenders.

In 1981, a historic experiment was funded by the Police Foundation and the Minneapolis Police Department to determine whether immediately arresting accused spouse abusers on the spot would deter future offending incidents. For misdemeanor cases, the experimental course of action involved the random assignment of police to respond by either arresting the suspect or the suspect receiving a simple warning. The experimental treatment, then, was whether the suspect was arrested, and the researchers wanted to know whether arrest was better than not arresting the suspect in reducing recidivism (subsequent assaults against the same victim). The study's results, which were widely publicized, indicated that arrest did have a deterrent effect. Partly as a result of these findings, the percentage of urban police departments that made arrest the preferred response to complaints of domestic violence rose from 10% in 1984 to 90% in 1988 (Sherman 1992). Six other cities later carried out studies like the Minneapolis experiment (collectively, this was called the Spouse Assault Replication Program [SARP]), but city to city, the results were mixed (Buzawa and Buzawa 1996; Hirschel, Hutchison, and Dean 1992; Pate and Hamilton 1992; Sherman 1992; Sherman and Berk 1984). In some cities (and for some people), arrest did seem to prevent future incidents of domestic assault; in other cities, it seemed only to make matters worse, contributing to additional assault; and in still other cities, arrest seemed to have no discernible effect. After these replications of the original Minneapolis experiment, people still wondered, "Just what is the effect of arrest in reducing domestic violence cases, and how should the police respond to such cases?" The answer simply was not clear. The Minneapolis Experiment, the studies modeled after it, and the related controversies provide many examples for a systematic overview of the social research process. In this chapter, we use this body of research to illustrate the three main research strategies: deductive, inductive, and descriptive research. In all three, theory and data are inextricably linked. The chapter ends with scientific and ethical guidelines that should be adhered to no matter what the research strategy is, and it shows how the Minneapolis experiment followed these guidelines. By the chapter's end, you should be ready to formulate a criminological research question, design a general strategy for answering this question, and critique previous studies that addressed this question. You can think of Chapter 1 as having introduced the *why* of criminological research; Chapter 2 introduces the *how*.

▣ Criminological Research Questions

Criminological research question A question about some aspect of crime or criminals, the answer to which is sought through collection and analysis of the firsthand, verifiable, empirical data.

How does a criminologist decide what to study and research? A **criminological research question** is a question about some aspect of crime or criminals that you seek to answer through the collection and analysis of firsthand, verifiable, empirical data. The types of questions that can be asked are virtually limitless. For example, "Are children who are violent more likely than nonviolent children to use violence as adults?" "Does the race of a victim who is killed influence whether someone is sentenced to death rather than life imprisonment?" "Why do some kinds of neighborhoods have more crime than others? Is it due to the kinds of people who live there or characteristics of the neighborhood itself?" "Does community policing reduce the crime rate?" "Has the U.S. government's war on drugs done anything to reduce the use of illegal drugs?" So many research questions are possible in criminology that it is more of a challenge to specify what does not qualify as a social research question than to specify what does.

But that does not mean it is easy to specify a research question. In fact, formulating a good research question can be surprisingly difficult. We can break the process into three stages: identifying one or more questions for study, refining the questions, and then evaluating the questions.

Identifying Criminological Research Questions

Formulating a research question is often an intensely personal process in addition to being a scientific or professional one. Curiosity about the social world may emerge from your "personal troubles," as Mills (1959) put it, or your personal experiences. Examples of these troubles or experiences could range from an awareness you may have that crime is not randomly distributed within a city but that there seem to be "good" or safe parts of town and "bad" or unsafe areas. Can you think of other possible research questions that flow from your own experiences in the world?

The experience of others is another fruitful source of research questions. Knowing a relative who was abused by a spouse, seeing a TV special about violence, or reading a gang member's autobiography can stimulate questions about general criminological processes. Can you draft a research question based on a relative's experiences, a TV show, or a book?

Other researchers may also pose interesting questions for you to study. Most research articles end with some suggestions for additional research that highlight unresolved issues. For example, Sherman et al. (1992) concluded an article on some of the replications of the Minneapolis experiment on police responses to spouse abuse by suggesting that "deterrence may be effective for a substantial segment of the offender population. . . . However, the underlying mechanisms remain obscure" (p. 706). A new study could focus on the mechanisms: Why or under what conditions does the arrest of offenders who are employed deter them from future criminal acts? Exactly what occurs when someone is arrested for domestic violence that may lead him or her not to be violent against a spouse in the future? Is it the brute fear of being arrested and having to go to jail? Is it the fear that one's employer may find out and fire him or her? Is it the fear that members of the community may learn about the arrest and the offender may lose his or her good standing in the neighborhood? Is it all these? Any issue of a journal in your field is likely to have comments that point toward unresolved issues.

The primary source of research questions for many criminologists is criminological theory. As you will soon learn, criminological theory provides an explanation as to why crime occurs or to why it occurs in some places and under some conditions but not others. Theory, then, is a very rich source of research ideas. Some researchers spend much of their careers conducting research intended to refine an answer to one central question. For example, you may find rational choice theory to be a useful approach to understanding diverse forms of social behavior, like crime, because you think people do seem to make decisions on the basis of personal cost-benefit calculations. So you may ask whether rational choice theory can explain why some people commit crimes and others do not or why some people decide to quit committing crimes while others continue their criminal ways.

Some research questions adopt a very pragmatic rationale concerning their research design. You may focus on a research question posed by someone else because doing so seems to be to your professional or financial advantage. For instance, some criminologists conduct research on specific questions posed by a funding source in what is termed a request for proposals (RFP). (Sometimes the acronym RFA is used, meaning request for applications.) Or you may learn that the public defenders in your city are curious as to whether they are more successful in getting their clients acquitted of a criminal charge than private lawyers.

Refining Criminological Research Questions

As you may have guessed, coming up with interesting criminological questions for research is less problematic than focusing on a problem of manageable size. We are often interested in much more than we can reasonably investigate with our limited time and resources (or the limited resources of a funding agency). Researchers may worry about staking a research project (and thereby a grant) on a particular problem, so they commit to addressing several research questions at once, and often in a jumbled fashion. It may also seem risky to focus on a research question that may lead to results discrepant with our own cherished assumptions about the social world. In addition, the prospective commitment of time and effort for some research questions may seem overwhelming, resulting in a certain degree of paralysis (not that the authors have any experience with this!).

The best way to avoid these problems is to develop the research question one bit at a time with a step-by-step strategy. Do not keep hoping that the perfect research question will just spring forth from your pen. Instead, develop a list of possible research questions as you go along. At the appropriate time, you can look through this list for the research questions that appear more than once. Narrow your list to the most interesting, most workable candidates. Repeat this process as long as it helps improve your research questions. Keep in mind that the research you are currently working on will likely generate additional research questions for you to answer.

Evaluating Criminological Research Questions

In the third stage of selecting a criminological research question, you evaluate the best candidate against the criteria for good social research questions: feasibility, given the time and resources available, social importance, and scientific relevance (King, Keohane, and Verba 1994).

The research question in the Minneapolis Domestic Violence Experiment, "Does the formal sanction of police arrest versus nonarrest inhibit domestic violence?" certainly meets the criteria of social importance and scientific relevance, but it would not be a feasible question for a student project because it would require you to try to get the cooperation of a police department. You might instead ask the question "Do people (students) think that arrest will inhibit domestic violence?" This is a question that you could study with an on-campus survey. Or perhaps you could work out an arrangement with a local battered women's shelter to study the question "What leads some women to call the police when they are the victims of domestic violence, and why do they sometimes not call?" A review of the literature, however, might convince you that this and other questions may not be scientifically relevant because they have been studied enough.

Feasibility

You must be able to conduct any study within the time frame and with the resources you have. If time is limited, questions that involve long-term change may not be feasible—for example, "If a state has recently changed its law so that it now permits capital punishment for those convicted of murder, does it eventually see a reduction in the homicide rate over time?" This is an interesting and important question but one that requires years of data collection and research. Another issue is what people or groups you can expect to gain access to. Although well-experienced researchers may be granted access to police or correctional department files to do their research, less seasoned and lesser-known researchers or students may not be granted such access. It is also often difficult for even the most experienced of researchers to be given full access to the deliberations of a criminal jury. For someone interested in white-collar crime, recording the interactions that take place in corporate boardrooms may also be taboo.

Then you must consider whether you will have any additional resources, such as other researchers to collaborate with or research funds. Remember that there are severe limits on what one person can accomplish. On the other hand, you might work in an organization that collects data on employees, customers, or clients that are relevant to your research interests. Or you may be able to piggyback your research onto a larger research project.

You also must be prepared to handle large amounts of quantitative data. A computer and the skills to use it will be essential. Also take into account the constraints you face due to your schedule and other professional or personal commitments and obligations.

The Minneapolis Domestic Violence Experiment shows how ambitious social research questions can be when a team of seasoned researchers secures the backing of influential groups. The project required hundreds of thousands of dollars, the collaboration of many social scientists and criminal justice personnel, and the volunteer efforts of 41 Minneapolis police officers. But don't worry; many worthwhile research questions can be investigated with much more limited resources. You will read in subsequent chapters about studies that addressed important research questions with much fewer resources than the Minneapolis social scientists commanded.

Social Importance

Criminological research is not a simple undertaking, so you must focus on a substantive area that you feel is important and that is either important to the discipline and/or important for public policy. You also need to feel personally motivated to carry out the study; there is little point in trying to answer a question that does not interest you.

In addition, you should consider whether the research question is important to other people. Will an answer to the research question make a difference for society? Again, the Minneapolis Domestic Violence Experiment is an exemplary case. If that study showed that a certain type of police response to domestic violence reduced the risk of subsequent victimization, a great deal of future violence could be prevented. But clearly, criminology and criminal justice are far from lacking important research questions.

Scientific Relevance

Every research question in criminology should be grounded in the existing empirical literature. By *grounded* we mean the research we do must be informed by what others before us have done on the topic. Whether you formulate a research question because you have been stimulated by an academic article or are motivated by questions regarding your own personal experiences, you must turn to existing criminological literature to find out what has already been learned about this question. Even if your research topic has already been investigated by someone else, it would not necessarily be a bad idea for you to do research on the issue. It would be unreasonable to think of any criminological research question as being settled for all time. You can be sure that some prior study is relevant to almost any research question you can think of, and you can also think of better ways to do research than have been done in the past.

For example, the Minneapolis experiment was built on a substantial body of contradictory theorizing about the impact of punishment on criminality (Sherman and Berk 1984). Deterrence theory predicted that because it was a more severe penalty, arrest would better deter individuals from repeat offenses than not arresting them. Labeling theory, on the other hand, predicted that arrest would make repeat offenses more likely because it would stigmatize offenders. The researchers found one prior experimental study of this issue, but it was conducted with juveniles. Studies among adults and nonexperimental research had not yielded consistent findings about the effects of arrest on recidivism in domestic violence cases. Clearly, the Minneapolis researchers had good reason to perform another study. Prior research and theory also helped them develop the most effective research design.

Social Research Foundations

How do we find prior research on questions of interest? You may already know some of the relevant material from prior coursework or your independent reading, but that won't be enough. When you are about to launch an investigation of a new research question, you must apply a very different standard than when you are studying for a test or just seeking to "learn about domestic violence." You need to find reports of previous investigations that sought to answer the same research question that you wish to answer, not just those that were about a similar topic. If there have been no prior studies of exactly the same research question, you should find reports from investigations of very similar research questions. Once you have located reports from prior research similar to the research that you wish to conduct, you may expand your search to include investigations about related topics or studies that used similar methods. You want to be able to explain what your proposed study adds to prior research as well as how it takes into account what has already been learned about your research question.

Although it's most important when you're starting out, reviewing the literature is also important at later stages of the research process. Throughout a research project, you will uncover new issues and encounter unexpected problems; at each of these times, you should search the literature to locate prior research on these issues and to learn how others responded to similar problems. Published research that you ignored when you were seeking to find other research on domestic violence might become very relevant when you have to decide which questions to ask people about their attitudes toward police and other authorities.

Finding Information

Conducting a thorough search of the research literature and then reviewing critically what you have found lays an essential foundation for any research project. Fortunately, much of this information can be identified online, without leaving your desktop, and an increasing number of published journal articles can be downloaded directly onto your own computer (depending on your particular access privileges). But just because there's a lot available online doesn't mean that you need to find it *all*. Keep in mind that your goal is to find reports of prior research investigations; this means that you should focus on scholarly journals that choose articles for publication after they have been peer reviewed by other social scientists—**refereed journals**. Newspaper and magazine articles just won't do, although you may find some that raise important issues or that summarize social science research investigations.

Refereed journals Journals that selected research papers for publication based on the peer reviews of other social scientists.

Every year, the Web offers more and more useful material, including indexes of the published research literature. You may find copies of particular rating scales, reports from research in progress, papers that have been presented at professional conferences, and online discussions of related topics. Web search engines will also find academic journal articles that you can access directly online, although usually for a fee. Most of the published research literature will be available to you online only if you go through the Web site of your college or university library. The library pays a fee to companies that provide online journals so that you can retrieve this information without paying anything extra yourself. Of course, no library can afford to pay for every journal, so if you can't find a particular issue of a particular journal that you need online, you will have to order the article that you need through interlibrary loan or, if the hard copy of the journal is available, walk over to your library to read it.

You will also need to check out what is available through your library before you can begin to search effectively for published research on your topics of interest.

Reviewing Research

Your literature review will suggest specific research questions for further investigation and research methods with which to study those questions. Sherman and Berk (1984) learned from their literature review that there had been little empirical research about the impact of arrest policies in domestic violence cases. What prior research had been conducted did not use very rigorous research designs. There was thus potential value in conducting new research using a rigorous design. Subsequent researchers questioned whether Sherman and Berk's results would be replicated in other cities and whether some of their methods could be improved. When the original results did not replicate, researchers designed more investigations to find out why. In this way, reviewing the literature identifies unanswered questions and contradictory evidence.

Effective review of the prior research is an essential step in building the foundation for new research. You must assess carefully the quality of each research study, consider the implications of each article for your own plans, and expand your thinking about your research question to take account of new perspectives and alternative arguments. It is through reviewing the literature and using it to extend and sharpen your own ideas and methods that you become a part of the social science community. Instead of being just one individual studying an issue, you are building on an ever-growing body of knowledge that is being constructed by the entire community of scholars.

Sometimes you'll find that someone else has already searched the literature on your research question and discussed what he or she found in a special review article or book chapter. For example, Rosemary Chalk and Joel H. Garner (2001) published an excellent review of the research on arrest and domestic violence in the journal *New Directions for Evaluation.* Most of the research articles that you find will include a short literature review on the specific focus of the research. These reviews can help a lot, but they are no substitute for searching the literature yourself, selecting the articles and other sources that are most pertinent to your research question, and then reviewing what you have found. No one but you can decide what is relevant for your research question and the research circumstances you will be facing—the setting you will study, the timing of your study, the new issues that you want to include in your study, and your specific methods. And you can't depend on any published research review for information on the most recent works. New research results about many questions appear continually in scholarly journals and books, in research reports from government agencies and other organizations, and on Web sites all over the world; you'll need to check for new research like this yourself.

Caveat emptor (buyer beware) is the watchword when you search the Web from Google or another search engine. Instead of looking on the Internet in general, published scholarly journal literature can be identified in databases such as *Criminal Justice Abstracts, Sociological Abstracts*, *SocINDEX*, and *PsycINFO.* Because these literature databases follow a more standard format and use a careful process to decide what literature to include, they are the sources on which you should focus. This section concentrates on the procedures you should use for reviewing the articles you find in a search of the scholarly literature. These procedures can also be applied to reviews of research monographs—books that provide more information from a research project than that which can be contained in a journal article.

Reviewing the literature is really a two-stage process. In the first stage, you must assess each article separately. This assessment should follow a standard format such as that represented by the "Questions to Ask About a Research Article" in Appendix A. However, you should keep in mind that you can't adequately understand a research study if you just treat it as a series of discrete steps, involving a marriage of convenience among separate techniques. Any research project is an integrated whole, so you must be concerned with how each component of the research design influenced the others—for example, how the measurement approach might have affected the causal validity of the researcher's conclusions and how the sampling strategy might have altered the quality of measures.

The second stage of the review process is to assess the implications of the entire set of articles (and other materials) for the relevant aspects of your research question and procedures and then to write an integrated review that highlights these implications. Although you can find literature reviews that consist simply of assessments of one published article after another—that never gets beyond the first stage in the review process—your understanding of the literature and the quality of your own work will be much improved if you make the effort to write an integrated review.

In the next two sections, we will show how you might answer many of the questions in Appendix A as we review a research article about domestic violence. We will then show how the review of a single article can be used within an integrated review of the body of prior research on this research question. Because at this early point in the text you won't be familiar with all the terminology used in the article review, you might want to read through the more elaborate article review in Appendix B later in the course.

A Single-Article Review: Formal and Informal Deterrents to Domestic Violence

Antony Pate and Edwin Hamilton at the national Police Foundation designed one of the studies funded by the U.S. Department of Justice to replicate the Minneapolis Domestic Violence Experiment. In this section, we will examine the article that resulted from that replication, which was published in the *American Sociological Review* (Pate and Hamilton 1992). The numbers in square brackets refer to the article review questions in Appendix B.

The Research Question. Like Sherman and Berk's (1984) original Minneapolis study, Pate and Hamilton's (1992) Metro-Dade spouse assault experiment sought to test the deterrent effect of arrest in domestic violence cases but with an additional focus on the role of informal social control [1]. The purpose of the study was explanatory, because the goal was to explain variation in the propensity to commit spouse abuse [2]. Deterrence theory provided the theoretical framework for the study, but this framework was broadened to include the proposition by Williams and Hawkins (1986) that informal sanctions such as stigma and the loss of valued relationships augment the effect of formal sanctions such as arrest [3]. Pate and Hamilton's (1992) literature review referred, appropriately, to the original Sherman and Berk (1984) research, to the other studies that attempted to replicate the original findings, and to research on informal social control [4].

There is no explicit discussion of ethical guidelines in the article, although reference is made to a more complete unpublished report [6]. Clearly, important ethical issues had to be considered, given the experimental intervention in the police response to serious assaults, but the adherence to standard criminal justice procedures suggests attention to the welfare of victims as well as to the rights of suspects. We will consider these issues in more detail later in this chapter.

The Research Design. Developed as a follow-up to the original Minneapolis experiment, the Metro-Dade experiment exemplifies the guidelines for scientific research. It was designed systematically, with careful attention to specification of terms and clarification of assumptions, and focused on the possibility of different outcomes rather than certainty about one preferred outcome. The major concepts in the study, formal and informal deterrence, were defined clearly [7] and then measured with straightforward indicators—arrest or nonarrest for formal deterrence and marital status and employment status for informal deterrence. However, the specific measurement procedures for marital and employment status were not discussed, and no attempt was made to determine whether they captured adequately the concept of informal social control [9, 10].

Three hypotheses were stated and also related to the larger theoretical framework and prior research [8]. The study design focused on the behavior of individuals [11] and collected data over time, including records indicating subsequent assault up to 6 months after the initial arrest [14]. The project's experimental design was used appropriately to test for the causal effect of arrest on recidivism [15, 17]. The research project involved all eligible cases, rather than a sample of cases, but there were a number of eligibility criteria that narrow down the ability to generalize these results to the entire population of domestic assault cases in the Metro-Dade area or elsewhere [11]. There is a brief discussion of the 92 eligible cases that were not given the treatment to which they were assigned, but it does not clarify the reasons for the misassignment [15].

The Research Findings and Conclusion. Pate and Hamilton's (1992) analysis of the Metro-Dade experiment was motivated by concern with the effect of social context, because the replications in other cities of the original Minneapolis Domestic Violence Experiment had not had consistent results [19]. Their analysis gave strong support to the expectation that informal social control processes are important: As they had hypothesized, arrest had a deterrent effect on suspects who were employed but not on those who were unemployed (Exhibit 2.1). However, marital status had no such effect [20]. The subsequent discussion of these findings gives no attention to the implications of the lack of support for the effect of marital status [21], but the study represents an important improvement over earlier research that had not examined informal sanctions [22]. The need for additional research is highlighted, and the importance of the findings for social policy are discussed: Pate and Hamilton suggest that their finding that arrest deters only those who have something to lose (e.g., a job) must be taken into account when policing policies are established [23].

Overall, the Pate and Hamilton (1992) study represents an important contribution to understanding how informal social control processes influence the effectiveness of formal sanctions such as arrest. Although the use of a population of actual spouse assault cases precluded the use of very sophisticated measures of informal social control, the experimental design of the study and the researchers' ability to interpret the results in the context of several other comparable experiments distinguish this research as exceptionally worthwhile. It is not hard to understand why these studies continue to stimulate further research and ongoing policy discussions.

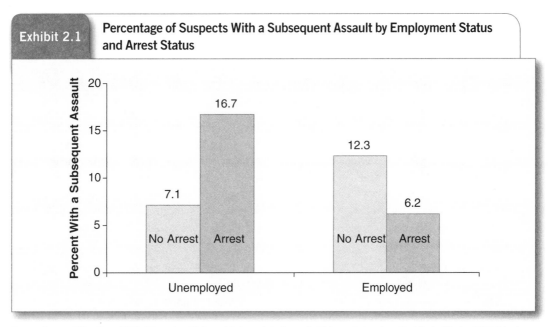

Exhibit 2.1 **Percentage of Suspects With a Subsequent Assault by Employment Status and Arrest Status**

Source: Pate and Hamilton, 1992. "Formal and Informal Deterrents to Domestic Violence." *American Sociological Review* 57(October), pp. 691–97. Fig. 1, p. 695.

An Integrated Literature Review: When Does Arrest Matter?

The goal of the second stage of the literature review process is to integrate the results of your separate article reviews and develop an overall assessment of the implications of prior research. The integrated literature review should accomplish three goals: (1) summarize prior research, (2) critique prior research, and (3) present pertinent conclusions (Hart 1998). We will discuss each of these goals in turn.

1. *Summarize prior research.* Your summary of prior research must focus on the particular research questions that you will address, but you may also need to provide some more general background. Carolyn Hoyle and Andrew Sanders (2000:14) begin their *British Journal of Criminology* research article about mandatory arrest policies in domestic violence cases with what they term a "provocative" question: What is the point of making it a crime for men to assault their female partners and ex-partners? They then review the different theories and supporting research that has justified different police policies: the "victim choice" position, the "pro-arrest" position, and the "victim empowerment" position. Finally, they review the research on the "controlling behaviors" of men that frames the specific research question on which they focus: How do victims view the value of criminal justice interventions in their own cases (Hoyle and Sanders 2000:15)?

   Ask yourself three questions about your summary of the literature:

   a. Have you been selective? If there have been more than a few prior investigations of your research question, you will need to narrow your focus to the most relevant and highest-quality studies. Don't cite a large number of prior articles "just because they are there."

   b. Is the research up-to-date? Be sure to include the most recent research, not just the "classic" studies.

   c. Have you used direct quotes sparingly? To focus your literature review, you need to express the key points from prior research in your own words. Use direct quotes only when they are essential for making an important point (Pyrczak 2005).

2. *Critique prior research.* Evaluate the strengths and weaknesses of the prior research. In addition to all the points that you develop as you answer the article review questions in Appendix B, you should also select articles for review that reflect work published in peer-reviewed journals and written by credible authors who have been funded by reputable sources. Consider the following questions as you decide how much weight to give each article:

   a. *How was the report reviewed prior to its publication or release?* Articles published in academic journals go through a rigorous review process, usually involving careful criticism and revision. Top "refereed" journals may accept only 10% of the submitted articles, so they can be very selective. Dissertations go through a lengthy process of criticism and revision by a few members of the dissertation writer's home institution. A report released directly by a research organization is likely to have had only a limited review, although some research organizations maintain a rigorous internal review process. Papers presented at professional meetings may have had little prior review. Needless to say, more confidence can be placed in research results that have been subject to a more rigorous review.

   b. *What is the author's reputation?* Reports by an author or a team of authors who have published other work on the research question should be given somewhat greater credibility at the outset.

   c. *Who funded and sponsored the research?* Major federal funding agencies and private foundations fund only research proposals that have been evaluated carefully and ranked highly by a panel of experts. They also often monitor closely the progress of the research. This does not guarantee that every such project report is good, but it goes a long way toward ensuring some worthwhile products. On the other hand, research that is funded by organizations that have a preference for a particular outcome should be given particularly close scrutiny (Locke, Silverman, and Spirduso 1998).

3. *Present pertinent conclusions.* Don't leave the reader guessing about the implications of the prior research for your own investigation. Present the conclusions you draw from the research you have reviewed. As you do so, follow several simple guidelines:

   a. Distinguish clearly your own opinion of prior research from the conclusions of the authors of the articles you have reviewed.

   b. Make it clear when your own approach is based on the theoretical framework that you use and not on the results of prior research.

   c. Acknowledge the potential limitations of any empirical research project. Don't emphasize problems in prior research that you can't avoid (Pyrczak 2005).

   d. Explain how the unanswered questions raised by prior research or the limitations of methods used in prior research make it important for you to conduct your own investigation (Fink 2005).

A good example of how to conclude an integrated literature review is provided by an article based on the replication in Milwaukee of the Minneapolis Domestic Violence Experiment. For this article, Paternoster et al. (1997) sought to determine whether police officers' use of fair procedures when arresting assault suspects would lessen the rate of subsequent domestic violence. For example, did suspects feel that their side of the story was heard? Did they feel that they were treated fairly? Paternoster et al. concluded that there was a major gap in the prior literature: "Even at the end of some seven experiments and millions of dollars, then, there is a great deal of ambiguity surrounding the question of how arrest impacts future spouse assault" (p. 164). Specifically, they noted that each of the seven experiments focused on the effect of arrest itself but ignored the possibility that "particular kinds of police procedure might inhibit the recurrence of spouse assault" (p. 165).

So Paternoster and his colleagues (1997) grounded their new analysis in additional literature on procedural justice and concluded that their new analysis would be "the first study to examine the effect of fairness judgments regarding a punitive criminal sanction (arrest) on serious criminal behavior (assaulting one's partner)" (p. 172).

The Role of Criminological Theory

We have already pointed out that criminological theory can be a rich source of research questions. What deserves more attention at this point is the larger role of **theory** in research. Criminological theories do many things:

> **Theory** A logically interrelated set of propositions about empirical reality. Examples of criminological theories include social learning, routine activities, labeling, general strain, and social disorganization theory.

- They help us explain or understand things like why some people commit crimes or more crimes than others; why some people quit and others continue; and what the expected effect of good families, harsh punishment, or other factors on crime might be.

- They help us make predictions about the criminological world: "What would be the expected effect on the homicide rate if we employed capital punishment rather than life imprisonment?" "What would be the effect on the rate of property crimes if unemployment were to substantially increase?"

- They help us organize and make sense of empirical findings in a discipline.

- They help guide future research.

- They help guide public policy: "What should we do to reduce the level of domestic violence?"

Social scientists, such as criminologists, who connect their work to theories in their discipline, can generate better ideas about what to look for in a study and develop conclusions with more implications for other research. Building and evaluating theory is therefore one of the most important objectives of a social science like criminology.

Theories usually contain what are called **theoretical constructs**. These theoretical constructs describe what is important to look at to understand, explain, predict, and "do something about" crime. For example, an important theoretical construct in differential association theory is the notion of "definitions favorable and unfavorable to the violation of law." Theories usually link one or more theoretical constructs to others in what are called *relationship statements*. Differential association theory, for

> **Theoretical constructs** Parts of a theory that describe what is important to look at to understand, explain, predict, and "do something about" the subject.

example, would link the theoretical construct of favorable or unfavorable definitions to the theoretical construct of involvement in crime to argue: "As one is exposed to more definitions favorable to the violation of law relative to definitions unfavorable to the violation of law, the more one is at risk for criminal behavior." This is a relationship statement that links two theoretical constructs; it states that as exposure to definitions favorable to the violation of law increases, the risk of crime also increases. This is essentially a hypothesis that the theory of differential association entertains; if the theory is true, then the expected relationship should be true. The purpose of much criminological research is to examine the truth value, or empirical validity, of such theoretical relationship statements or hypotheses. Some criminological theories reflect a substantial body of research and the thinking of many social scientists; others are formulated in the course of one investigation. A few have been widely accepted, at least for a time; others are the subject of vigorous controversy, with frequent changes and refinements in response to criticism and new research.

Most criminological research is guided by some theory, although the theory may be only partially developed in a particular study or may even be unrecognized by the researcher. When researchers are involved in conducting a research project or engrossed in writing a research report, they may easily lose sight of the larger picture. It is easy to focus on accumulating or clarifying particular findings rather than considering how the study's findings fit into a more general understanding of the social world. Furthermore, as we shall soon see, just as theory guides research, research findings also influence the development of theory.

We can use the studies of the police response to domestic assault to illustrate the value of theory for social research. Even in this very concrete and practical matter, we must draw on social theories to understand how people act and what should be done about those actions. Consider the three action options that police officers have when they confront a domestic assault suspect (Sherman and Berk 1984). Fellow officers might encourage separation to achieve short-term peace; police trainers might prefer mediation to resolve the underlying dispute; feminist groups may advocate arrest to protect the victim from further harm. None of these recommendations is really a theory, but each suggests a different perspective on crime and legal sanctions. You will encounter these different perspectives if you read much of the literature on domestic violence or even if you talk with your friends about it. In turn, these assumptions reflect different experiences with family conflict, police actions, and the legal system. What we believe about one crime and the appropriate response to it relates to a great many other ideas we have about the social world. Recognizing these relationships is a first step toward becoming a theoretically guided social researcher and a theoretically informed consumer of social research.

Remember that social theories do not provide the answers to research questions. Instead, social theories suggest the areas on which we should focus and the propositions that we should consider for a test. That is, theories suggest testable hypotheses about phenomena and research verifies whether those hypotheses are true. In fact, one of the most important requirements of theory is that it be testable, or what philosophers of science call **falsifiable**; theoretical statements must be capable of being proven wrong. If a body of thought cannot be empirically tested, it is more likely philosophy than theory. For example, Sherman and Berk's (1984) domestic violence research was actually a test of predictions derived from two alternative theories of the impact of punishment on crime, deterrence theory and labeling theory.

> **Falsifiable** When a theory can be tested and falsified or otherwise not supported by empirical evidence.

Deterrence theory presumes that human beings are at least marginally rational beings who are responsive to the expected costs and benefits of their actions. Committing a crime nets certain benefits for offenders; therefore, if we want to inhibit crime, there must be a compensating cost that outweighs the potential benefits associated with the offense. One cost is the criminal sanction (arrest, conviction, punishment). Deterrence theory expects punishment to inhibit crime in two ways. General deterrence occurs when people see that crime results in undesirable punishments for others, that "crime doesn't pay." Those who are punished serve as examples for those who have not yet committed an offense but might be thinking of what awaits them should they engage in similarly punishable acts. Specific deterrence occurs when persons who are punished decide not to commit another offense so they can avoid further punishment (Lempert and Sanders 1986). Deterrence theory leads to the prediction that arresting spouse abusers will reduce the likelihood of their reoffending when compared with a less serious sanction (not being arrested but being warned or counseled).

Labeling theory distinguishes between primary deviance, the acts of individuals that lead to public sanctions, and secondary deviance, the deviance that occurs in response to public sanction (Hagan 1994). Arrest or some other public sanction for misdeeds labels the offender as deviant in the eyes of others. Once the offender is labeled, others will treat the offender as a deviant, and he or she is then more likely to act in a way that is consistent with the deviant label. Ironically, the act of punishment stimulates more of the very behavior that it was intended to eliminate (Tannenbaum 1938). This theory suggests that persons arrested for intimate partner violence are more likely to reoffend than those who are caught but not punished because the formal sanction of arrest is more stigmatizing than being warned or counseled. This prediction about the effect of formal legal sanctions is the reverse of the deterrence theory prediction.

Theorizing about the logic behind formal legal punishment also can help us draw connections to more general theories about social processes. Deterrence theory reflects the assumptions of rational choice theory, which assumes behavior is shaped by practical calculations: People break the law if the benefits of doing so exceed the costs. If crime is a rational choice for some people, then increasing the certainty or severity of punishment for crime should shift the cost-benefit balance away from criminal behavior. Labeling theory is rooted in symbolic interactionism, which focuses on the symbolic meanings that people give to behavior (Hagan 1994). Instead of assuming that some forms of behavior are deviant in and of themselves (Scull 1988), symbolic interactionists would view deviance as a consequence of the application of rules and sanctions to an offender (Becker 1963). Exhibit 2.2 summarizes how these general theories relate to the question of whether to arrest spouse abusers.

Exhibit 2.2	Two Social Theories and Their Predictions About the Effect of Arrest for Intimate Partner Assault		
	Rational Choice Theory	*Symbolic Interactionism*
Theoretical assumption	People's behavior is shaped by calculations of the costs and benefits of their actions.	People give symbolic meanings to objects, behaviors, and other people.
Criminological component	Deterrence theory: People break the law if the benefits of doing so outweigh the costs.	Labeling theory: People label offenders as deviant, promoting further deviance.
Prediction (effect of arrest for domestic assault)	Abusing spouse, having seen the costs of abuse (namely, arrest), decides not to abuse again.	Abusing spo use, having been labeled as "an abuser," abuses more often.

Does either deterrence theory or labeling theory make sense to you as an explanation for the impact of punishment? Do these theories seem consistent with your observations of social life? Over a decade after Sherman and Berk's (1984) study, Paternoster et al. (1997) decided to study punishment of domestic violence from a different perspective. They turned to a social psychological theory called procedural justice theory, which explains law-abiding behavior as resulting from a sense of duty or morality (Tyler 1990). People obey the law from a sense of obligation that flows from seeing legal authorities as moral and legitimate. From this perspective, individuals who are arrested seem less likely to reoffend if they are treated fairly, irrespective of the outcome of their case, because fair treatment will enhance their view of legal authorities as moral and legitimate. Procedural justice theory expands our view of the punishment process by focusing attention on how police act and how authorities treat subjects, rather than just on the legal decisions they make. Are you now less certain about the likely effect of arrest for intimate partner violence? Will arrest decrease recidivism because abusers do not wish to suffer from legal sanctions again? Will it increase recidivism because abusers feel stigmatized by being arrested and thus are more likely to act like criminals? Or will arrest reduce abuse only if the abusers feel they have been treated fairly by the legal authorities? By posing such questions, social theory makes us much more sensitive to the possibilities and so helps us design better research. Before, during, and after a research investigation, we need to keep thinking theoretically.

Social Research Strategies

All social research, including criminological research, is the effort to connect theory and empirical data. As Exhibit 2.3 shows, theory and data have a two-way, mutually reinforcing relationship. Research that begins with a theory implying that certain data should be found involves **deductive reasoning**, which moves from general ideas (theory) to specific reality (data). In contrast, **inductive reasoning** moves from the specific to the general.

Both deductive reasoning and inductive reasoning are essential to criminologists. We cannot test an idea fairly unless we use deductive reasoning, stating our expectations in advance and then designing a way to test the validity of our claims. A theory that has not survived these kinds of tests can be regarded only as very tentative. Yet theories, no matter how cherished, cannot always make useful predictions for every social situation or research problem that we seek to investigate. We may find unexpected patterns in the data we collect, called

> **Deductive reasoning** The type of reasoning that moves from the general to the specific.

> **Inductive reasoning** The type of reasoning that moves from the specific to the general.

Exhibit 2.3   The Links Between Theory and Data

Ideas: What we think
Theory

Inductive reasoning

Deductive reasoning

Data
Reality: What we observe

Serendipitous findings (anomalous findings)
Unexpected patterns in data, which stimulate new ideas or theoretical approaches.

Research circle A diagram of the elements of the research process, including theories, hypotheses, data collection, and data analysis.

Deductive research The type of research in which a specific expectation is deduced from a general premise and is then tested.

Hyphothesis A tentative statement about empirical reality involving the relationship between two or more variables.

Example of a hypothesis: The higher the level of residential mobility in a community, the higher its rate of crime.

Variable Characteristics or properties that can vary (take on different values or attributes).

Constant A number that has a fixed value in a given situation; a characteristic or value that does not change.

serendipitous findings or anomalous findings. In either situation, we should reason inductively, making whatever theoretical sense we can of our unanticipated findings. Then, if the new findings seem sufficiently important, we can return to deductive reasoning and plan a new study to formally test our new ideas.

Explanatory Research

This process of conducting research, moving from theory to data and back again or from data to theory and back again, can be characterized as a research circle, as depicted in Exhibit 2.4. Note that it mirrors the relationship between theory and data shown in Exhibit 2.3 and that it comprises three main research strategies: deductive research, inductive research, and descriptive research.

Deductive Research

As Exhibit 2.4 shows, deductive research proceeds from theorizing to data collection and then back to theorizing. In essence, a specific expectation is deduced from a general premise and then tested.

Notice that a theory leads first to a hypothesis, which is a specific implication deduced from the more general theory. Researchers actually test a hypothesis, not the complete theory itself, because theories usually contain many hypotheses. As we stated earlier, a hypothesis proposes a relationship between two or more theoretical constructs or variables. A variable is a characteristic or property that can vary. A constant is a characteristic or property that cannot vary. For example, if we were to conduct some research in a male adult penitentiary, the theoretical construct "type of crime committed" would be a variable because persons will have been incarcerated for different offenses (one person is in for armed robbery, another for rape, etc.). However, the

Exhibit 2.4   The Research Circle

theoretical construct "gender" would be a constant because every inmate in the penitentiary would be male; gender does not vary—it is constant. Would age be a variable or a constant in this group? Would "criminal status" (offender or nonoffender) be a variable or a constant?

Variables are of critical importance in research because in a hypothesis, variation in one variable is proposed to predict, influence, or cause variation in the other variable. The proposed influence is the **independent variable**; its effect or consequence is the **dependent variable.** After the researchers formulate one or more hypotheses and develop research procedures, they collect data with which to test the hypothesis.

Hypotheses can be worded in several different ways, and identifying the independent and dependent variables is sometimes difficult. When in doubt, try to rephrase the hypothesis as an if-then statement: "If the independent variable increases (or decreases), then the dependent variable increases (or decreases)." Exhibit 2.5 presents several hypotheses with their independent and dependent variables and their if-then equivalents.

Exhibit 2.5 demonstrates another feature of hypotheses: **direction of association**. When researchers hypothesize that one variable increases as the other variable increases, the direction of the association is positive (Hypotheses 1 and 4 in the exhibit); when one variable decreases as the other variable decreases, the direction of association is also positive (Hypothesis 3). In a **positive relationship**, then, the independent and dependent variables move in the same direction (as one increases, the other increases, or as one decreases, the other decreases). But when one variable increases as the other decreases, or vice versa, the direction of association is negative, or inverse (Hypothesis 2). In a **negative relationship**, then, the independent and dependent variables move in opposite directions (as one increases, the other decreases, or as one decreases, the other increases). Hypothesis 5 is a special case, in which the

Independent variable A variable that is hypothesized to cause, or lead to, variation in another variable.

Example of an independent variable: Residential mobility (residents moving in and out of the community).

Dependent variable A variable that is hypothesized to change or vary depending on the variation in another variable.

Example of a dependent variable: The rate of crime in a community per 1,000 residents.

Direction of association A pattern in a cross-tabulation; the values of variables tend to change consistently in relation to change on the other variable. Direction of association can be either positive or negative.

Positive relationship The independent and dependent variables move in the same direction; as one increases the other decreases.

Negative relationship The independent and dependent variables move in opposite directions; as one increases the other decreases.

Exhibit 2.5	Examples of Hypotheses

Original Hypothesis	Independent Variable	Dependent Variable	If-Then Hypothesis
1. The greater the social disorganization in a community, the higher the rate of crime.	Social disorganization	Crime rate	If social disorganization is higher, then the crime rate is higher.
2. As one's self-control gets stronger, the fewer delinquent acts one commits.	Self-control	Self-reported delinquency	If self-control is higher, then the number of delinquent acts is lower.
3. As the unemployment rate in a community decreases, the community rate of property crime decreases.	Unemployment rate	Rate of property crime	If the unemployment rate is lower, then the rate of property crime is lower.
4. As the discrepancy between one's aspirations and expectations increases, one's level of strain increases.	Discrepancy between one's aspirations and expectations	Strain	If the discrepancy between one's aspirations and expectations is high, then the level of strain is high.
5. Crime is lower in those communities where the police patrol on foot.	Presence of foot patrols	Crime	If a community has police foot patrols, then the level of crime is lower.

independent variable is categorical. The independent variable cannot be said to increase or decrease. In this case, the concept of direction of association does not apply, and the hypothesis simply states that one category of the independent variable is associated with higher values on the dependent variable.

The motives for deductive research include both explanation and evaluation (as described in Chapter 1). Sherman and Berk's (1984) original study was evaluative because they sought to explain what sort of response by the authorities might keep an offender from repeating the offense. The researchers deduced from deterrence theory the expectation that arrest would deter domestic violence. They then collected data to test this expectation.

In both explanatory and evaluative research, the statement of expectations for the findings and the design of the research to test these expectations strengthen the confidence we can place in the test. The deductive researcher shows her hand or states her expectations in advance and then designs a fair test of those expectations. Then "the chips fall where they may"; in other words, the researcher accepts the resulting data as a more or less objective picture of reality.

Inductive Research

In contrast to deductive research, **inductive research** begins at the bottom of the research circle and then works upward (see Exhibit 2.4). The inductive researcher begins with specific data, which are then used to develop (induce) a general explanation (a theory) to account for the data. The patterns in the data are then summarized in one or more **empirical generalizations** (findings) that can be compared to the hypothesis. If these are those stated in the hypothesis, then the theory from which the hypothesis was deduced is supported. If the empirical generalizations are inconsistent with the hypothesis, then the theory is not supported (Wallace 1971).

> **Inductive research** The type of research in which specific data are used to develop (induce) a general explanation.
>
> **Empirical generalizations** Statements that describe patterns found in data.

The motive for inductive research is exploration. In Chapter 1, you read about an exploratory study of individuals' responses to an incident involving a school shooting (Asmussen and Creswell 1995). In strictly inductive research, the researcher already knows what he has found when he starts theorizing, or attempting to explain what accounts for these findings. The result can be new insights and provocative questions. But the adequacy of an explanation formulated after the fact is necessarily less certain than that of an explanation presented prior to the collection of data. Every phenomenon can always be explained in some way. Inductive explanations are thus more trustworthy if they are tested subsequently with deductive research.

Domestic Violence and the Research Circle

The Sherman and Berk (1984) study of domestic violence is a classic example of how the research circle works. In an attempt to determine ways to prevent the recurrence of spouse abuse, the researchers repeatedly linked theory and data, developing both hypotheses and empirical generalizations.

Phase 1: Deductive Research

The first phase of Sherman and Berk's (1984) study was designed to test a hypothesis. According to deterrence theory, punishment will reduce recidivism, or repeated offending. From this theory, Sherman and Berk deduced a specific hypothesis that arrest for spouse abuse would reduce the risk of repeat offenses. In this hypothesis, arrest is the independent variable, and variation in the risk of repeat offenses is the dependent variable (it is hypothesized to depend on arrest).

Sherman and Berk (1984) tested their hypothesis by setting up an experiment in which the police responded to complaints of spouse abuse in one of three ways, one of which was to arrest the offender. When the researchers examined their data (police records for the persons in their experiment), they found that of those arrested for assaulting their spouse, only 13% repeated the offense, compared to a 26% recidivism rate for those who were separated from their spouse by the police without any arrest. This pattern in the data, or empirical generalization, was consistent with the hypothesis that the researchers deduced from deterrence theory. The theory thus received support from the experiment (see Exhibit 2.6).

In designing their study, Sherman and Berk (1984) anticipated an important question: How valid is the connection between theory and data? The three dimensions of validity—measurement validity, generalizability, and causal validity—had to be taken into consideration.

Determining whether spouses were assaulted after the initial police intervention was the key

Exhibit 2.6 The Research Circle: Minneapolis Domestic Violence Experiment

Theory
Deterrence theory

Hypothesis
More arrests, less recidivism

Data
Measures for 330 domestic assault cases

Empirical Generalizations

Action	Recidivism
Arrest	13%
Separation	26%

measurement concern. Official records of subsequent assaults by the suspect would provide one measure. But most spousal assaults are not reported to the police, so research assistants also sought out the victims for interviews every 2 weeks during a 6-month follow-up period. Although fewer than half the victims completed all the follow-up interviews, the availability of the self-report measure allowed the researchers to shed some light on the validity of the official data. In general, the two measures yielded comparable results, although some discrepancies troubled critics.

The generalizability of the study's results was the researchers' greatest concern. Minneapolis is no more a typical U.S. city than any other, and we cannot assume that police policies that are effective in Minneapolis will be equally effective in cities with very different political histories, criminal justice agencies, and population characteristics. Sherman and Berk (1984) warned readers, "External validity will have to wait for replications" (p. 269)—that is, for repetitions of the study using the same research methods to answer the same research question.

Finally, Sherman and Berk's (1984) claims about the causal validity of their results rested primarily on the experimental design they used. The 330 domestic assault cases in the study were handled by the police in one of three ways: an arrest, an order that the offending spouse leave the house for 8 hours, or some type of verbal advice by the police officers. The officers were not allowed to choose which treatment to apply (except in extreme cases, such as when severe injury had occurred or when the spouse had demanded that an arrest be made). Instead, the treatments were carried out by police in random order, according to the color of the next report form on a pad that had been prepared by the researchers.

By insisting on the random assignment of cases to treatments, the researchers tried to ensure that police officers would not arrest just the toughest spouses or the spouses who seemed most obnoxious or the spouses they encountered late in the day. In other words, the random assignment procedure made it unlikely that arrested spouse abusers would differ, on average, from the other spouse abusers except for the fact that they were arrested (although, because of chance factors, the possibility of other differences cannot be completely ruled out). The researchers' conclusion that arrest caused a lower incidence of repeat offenses therefore seems valid.

Phase 2: Deductive Research

There still were doubts concerning the generalizability of their results, so Sherman and Berk, along with new collaborators, began to journey around the research circle again, with funding from the National Institute of Justice for **replications** (repetitions) of the experiment in six more cities. These replications used the same basic research approach but with some improvements. The random assignment process was tightened up in most of the cities so that police officers would be less likely to replace the assigned treatment with a treatment of their own choice. In addition, data were collected about repeat violence against other victims as well as against the original complainant. Some replications also examined different aspects of the arrest process, to see whether professional counseling helped and whether the length of time spent in jail after arrest mattered at all.

> **Replications** Repetitions of a study using the same research methods to answer the same research question.

By the time results were reported from five of the cities in the new study, a problem was apparent. In three cities—Omaha, Nebraska; Charlotte, North Carolina; and Milwaukee, Wisconsin—researchers were finding long-term increases in domestic violence incidents among arrestees. But in Colorado Springs, Colorado, and Dade County, Florida, the predicted deterrent effects seemed to be occurring (Sherman et al. 1992).

Researchers had now traversed the research circle twice in an attempt to answer the original research question, first in Minneapolis and then in six other cities. But rather than leading to more confidence in deterrence theory, the research results were calling it into question. Deterrence theory now seemed inadequate to explain empirical reality, at least as the researchers had measured this reality. So the researchers began to reanalyze the follow-up data from several cities to try to explain the discrepant results, thereby starting around the research circle once again (Berk et al. 1992; Pate and Hamilton 1992; Sherman et al. 1992).

Phase 3: Inductive Research

At this point, the researchers' approach became more inductive, and they began trying to make sense of the differing patterns in the data collected in the different cities. Inductive reasoning often enters into deductive research when we find unexpected patterns in the data we have collected for testing a hypothesis. We may call these patterns serendipitous findings or anomalous findings. Whether we begin by doing inductive research or add an inductive element later, the result of the inductive process can be new insights and provocative questions. But the adequacy of an explanation formulated after the fact is necessarily less certain than an explanation presented prior to the collection of data. Every phenomenon can always be explained in *some* way. Inductive explanations are thus more trustworthy if they are tested subsequently with deductive research.

Could systematic differences in the samples or in the implementation of arrest policies explain the differing outcomes? Or was the problem an inadequacy in the theoretical basis of the research? Was deterrence theory really the best way to explain the patterns in the data being collected? Sherman et al. (1992) now turned to control theory (Toby 1957), yet another broad explanation for social behavior. It predicts that having a stake in conformity (resulting from inclusion in social networks at work or in the community) decreases a person's likelihood of committing crimes. The implication is that people who are employed and married are more likely to be deterred by the threat of arrest than those without such stakes in conformity. This is because an arrest for domestic violence could jeopardize one's job and one's marriage, thus making arrest more costly for the employed and married. This is indeed what a reexamination of the data revealed: Individuals who were married and employed were deterred from repeat offenses by arrest, but individuals who were unmarried and unemployed were actually more likely to commit repeat offenses if they were arrested. This was an important theoretical insight, for it suggested that one powerful way that formal sanctions work is that they can potentially trigger informal sanctions or costs (e.g., loss of respect from friends and family).

Now the researchers had traversed the research circle almost three times, a process perhaps better described as a spiral (see Exhibit 2.7). The first two times the researchers had traversed the research circle in a deductive, hypothesis-testing way: They started with theory and then deduced and tested hypotheses. The third time they traversed the research circle in a more inductive, exploratory way: They started with empirical generalizations from the data they

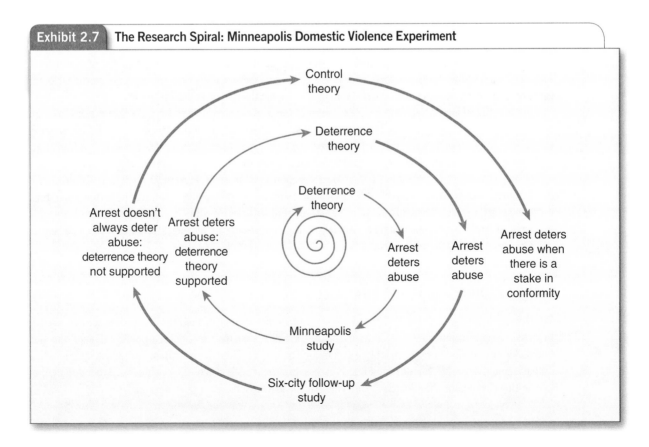

Exhibit 2.7 The Research Spiral: Minneapolis Domestic Violence Experiment

had already obtained and then turned to a new theory to account for the unexpected patterns in the data. At this point, they believed that deterrence theory makes correct predictions given certain conditions and that another theory, control theory, may specify what these conditions are.

After two and one-half cycles through the research circle, the picture became more complex but also conceptually richer. The researchers came closer to understanding how to inhibit domestic violence. But they cautioned us that their initial question, the research problem, was still not completely answered. Employment status and marital status alone do not measure the strength of social attachments; they also are related to how much people earn and the social standing of victims in court. So perhaps social ties are not really what makes arrest an effective deterrent to domestic violence. The real deterrent may be cost-benefit calculations ("If I have a higher income, jail is more costly to me") or perceptions about the actions of authorities ("If I am a married woman, judges will treat my complaint more seriously"). More research was still needed (Berk et al. 1992).

Phase 4: Deductive Research

In 1997, Paternoster et al. reexamined data from one of the replication sites in Milwaukee to test hypotheses derived from yet another theory, procedural justice theory. As explained earlier in this chapter, procedural justice theory predicts that people will comply with the law out of a sense of duty and obligation if they are treated fairly by legal authorities. In the Milwaukee sample, arrest had a criminogenic effect: Those who were arrested were subsequently more likely to abuse their spouses than those who were simply warned. Paternoster et al. thought that this effect might have been due to the way subjects were treated when they were arrested rather than simply to the fact that they were arrested. One of their hypotheses spells out the reasoning:

> Among those persons arrested for spouse assault, those who perceive themselves as being treated in a procedurally unfair manner will be more likely to commit acts of spouse assault in the future than those arrested persons who perceive themselves as being treated in a procedurally fair manner, net of other determinants of violence. (p. 173)

To carry out this study, Paternoster et al. (1997) reexamined data collected earlier in Milwaukee, where the findings had seemed anomalous. However, this reanalysis of the data qualifies as deductive research, because the hypotheses were derived from theory and then tested with the data, rather than being induced by the data.

The procedural justice hypotheses were supported: Persons who were arrested in the Milwaukee experiment became more likely to reoffend only if they perceived that they had been treated unfairly by the police. Otherwise, their rate of rearrest was similar to that for the persons who were not arrested. Thus, another element was added to our understanding of the effects of the police response to domestic violence.

Clearly our understanding of effective responses to domestic violence will never truly be complete, but research to date has greatly improved our knowledge of this social problem. The future should yield an even better understanding, even though at times it may be hard to make sense of conflicting findings from different studies. Science is an ongoing enterprise in which findings cumulate and eventually yield greater insight or even radical revisions in our understanding. Needless to say, researchers do not need to worry about running out of work to do.

Adding Exploration to the Mix

While researchers were grappling with the results of the randomized experiments, other researchers were engaged in inductive research by interviewing victims and offenders in depth and then developing an explanation for what was found. Because qualitative research is often exploratory and, hence, inductive, researchers often ask questions like "What is going on here?" "How do people interpret these experiences?" or "Why do people do what they do?" Rather than testing a hypothesis, the researchers are trying to make sense of some social phenomenon.

A Qualitative Exploration of the Response to Domestic Violence

Bennett, Goodman, and Dutton (1999) used this approach to investigate one of the problems that emerge when police arrest domestic batterers: The victims often decide not to press charges. Bennett et al. did not set out to test hypotheses with qualitative interviews (there was another, hypothesis-testing component in their research) but sought, inductively, to "add the voice of the victim to the discussion" and present "themes that emerged from [the] interviews" (p. 762).

Research assistants interviewed 49 victims of domestic violence in one court; Lauren Bennett also worked in the same court as a victim advocate. The researchers were able to cull from their qualitative data four reasons why victims became reluctant to press charges: Some were confused by the court procedures, others were frustrated by the delay, some were paralyzed by fear of retribution, and others did not want to send the batterer to jail.

Explanations developed inductively from qualitative research can feel authentic because we have heard what people have to say "in their own words" and we have tried to see the social world "as they see it." One victim interviewed by Bennett et al. (1999) felt that she "was doing time instead of the defendant"; another expressed her fear by saying that she would like "to keep him out of jail if that's what it takes to keep my kids safe" (pp. 768–69). Explanations derived from qualitative research will be richer and more finely textured than those resulting from quantitative research, but they are likely to be based on fewer cases from a limited area. We cannot assume that the people studied in this setting are like others or that other researchers would develop explanations similar to ours to make sense of what was observed or heard. Because we do not initially set up a test of a hypothesis according to some specific rules, another researcher cannot come along and conduct just the same test. However, by examining the results of both qualitative and quantitative research, we get a more detailed and nuanced picture of reality compared to using one set of methods alone.

🔲 Social Research Goals

A scientist seeks to develop an accurate understanding of empirical reality, the reality we encounter firsthand, by conducting research that leads to valid knowledge about the world. But when is knowledge valid? In general, we have reached the goal of validity when our statements or conclusions about empirical reality are correct. If you look out your window and observe that it is raining, this is probably a valid observation, if your eyes and ears are to be trusted. However, if you pick up the newspaper and read that the majority of Americans favor the death penalty, this conclusion is of questionable validity because it is probably based on an interpretation of a social survey. As you will see in Chapter 8, attitudes toward the death penalty vary substantially depending on the wording of the questions asked.

To some of you, the goal of validity may sound a bit far-fetched. After all, how can we really be sure our understandings of empirical phenomena are correct when we can perceive the world only through the filter of our own senses? You need not worry. Such skepticism will help you remember the tenuousness of all knowledge and will keep you properly skeptical about new discoveries.

This book is about validity more than anything else, about how to conduct research that leads to valid interpretations of the social world. We will refer to validity repeatedly, and we ask you to register it in your brain now as the central goal of all the research conducted in our field. The goal of research conducted by social scientists investigating issues related to criminology and criminal justice is not to come up with conclusions that people will like or conclusions that suit their personal preferences. The goal is to determine the most valid answers through empirical research methods.

We must be concerned with three aspects of validity: **measurement validity**, **generalizability**, and **causal validity** (also known as **internal validity**). Each of these three aspects of validity is essential: Conclusions based on invalid measures, invalid generalizations, or invalid causal inferences will themselves be invalid. We will also be concerned

Measurement validity The type of validity that is achieved when a measure measures what it is presumed to measure.

Generalizability The type of validity that is achieved when a conclusion holds true for the population, group, or groups that we say it does, given the conditions that we specify.

Causal validity (internal validity) The type of validity that is achieved when a conclusion that one phenomenon leads to or results in another phenomenon—or doesn't lead to or result in another—is correct.

Authenticity When the understanding of a social process or social setting is one that reflects fairly the various perspectives of participants in that setting.

with the goal of authenticity, a concern with reflecting fairly the perspectives of participants in a setting that we study.

Imagine that we survey a sample of 250 high school seniors and ask them two questions: "Do you have friends who have taken illegal drugs in the past 6 months?" (the measure of peer behavior) and "Have you taken illegal drugs in the past 6 months?" (individual use measure). We then compare the frequency of illegal drug use between students who have friends who have used illegal drugs and those whose friends have not used illegal drugs. We find that students who have friends who have used illegal drugs in the last 6 months are more likely to have used drugs themselves, and we conclude that drug use is, in part, due to the influence of peers.

But did our questions indeed tell us the frequency with which the students and their peers took illegal drugs? If they did, we achieved measurement validity. Do our results hold true of the larger adolescent population to which our conclusion referred? If so, our conclusion would satisfy the criterion for generalizability. Did the likelihood of students taking drugs actually increase if they had friends who also took drugs? If so, our conclusion is causally valid.

Measurement Validity

Measurement validity is our first concern in establishing the validity of research results, because without having measured what we think we measured, we really don't know what we're talking about. Measurement validity is the focus of Chapter 4.

Problems with measurement validity can occur for many reasons. In the study by MacDonald et al. (2005) highlighted in Chapter 1, were they really measuring impulsivity and self-control by using smoking and sexual behavior? The bottom line is that we cannot just *assume* that measures are valid.

Generalizability

The generalizability of a study is the extent to which it can be used to inform us about persons, places, or events that were not studied. MacDonald and his colleagues (2005) relied on responses from 5,545 students in the South Carolina Youth Risk Behavior Survey. They then generalized from what they found with those individuals to the entire U.S. high school population. Were they correct to do so? Were their generalizations valid? Chapter 5 on sampling will give you the tools you need to answer questions like these.

You also learned in this chapter that research on the police response to domestic violence led to different results in different cities. The researchers discovered that Sherman and Berk's (1984) findings in Minneapolis simply did not hold up in several other cities: The initial results could not be generalized. As you know, this led to additional research to figure out what accounted for the different patterns in different cities.

If every person or community we study were like every other one, generalizations based on observations of a small number would be valid. But that's not the case. We are on solid ground if we question the generalizability of statements about research based on the results of a restricted sample of the population or in just one community or other social context.

Generalizability has two aspects. Sample generalizability refers to the ability to generalize from a sample, or subset, of a larger population to that population itself. This is the most common meaning of generalizability. Cross-population generalizability refers to the ability to generalize from findings about one group, population, or setting to other groups, populations, or settings. Cross-population generalizability can also be referred to as **external validity**. (Some social scientists equate the term *external validity* to *generalizability*, but in this book we restrict its use to the more limited notion of cross-population generalizability.)

Sample generalizability is a key concern in survey research. Political pollsters may study a sample of likely voters, for example, and then generalize their findings to the entire population of likely voters. No one would be interested in the results of political polls if they represented only the relatively tiny sample that actually was surveyed rather than the entire population.

> *Sample generalizability* Exists when a conclusion based on a sample, or subset, of a larger population holds true for that population.
>
> *Cross-population generalizability (external validity)* Exists when findings about one group, population, or setting hold true for other groups, populations, or settings.

Cross-population generalizability occurs to the extent that the results of a study hold true for multiple populations; these populations may not all have been sampled, or they may be represented as subgroups within the sample studied. You have already learned that persons in Minneapolis who were arrested for domestic violence did not respond in the same way as persons arrested for the same crime in several other cities. As such, the conclusions from Sherman and Berk's (1984) initial research in Minneapolis were not "externally valid."

Generalizability is a key concern in research design. We rarely have the resources to study the entire population that is of interest to us, so we have to select cases to study that will allow our findings to be generalized to the population of interest. Nonetheless, because we can never be sure that our findings will hold under all conditions, we should be cautious in generalizing to populations or periods that we did not actually sample.

Causal Validity

Causal validity, also known as internal validity, refers to the truthfulness of an assertion that A causes B. It is the focus of Chapter 6.

Most research seeks to determine what causes what, so social scientists frequently must be concerned with causal validity. Sherman and Berk (1984) were concerned with the effect of arrest on the likelihood of recidivism by people accused of domestic violence. To test their causal hypothesis, they designed their experiment so that some accused persons were arrested and others were not. Of course, it may seem heavy-handed for social scientists to influence police actions for the purpose of a research project, but this step reflects just how difficult it can be to establish causally valid understandings about the social world. It was only because police officials did not know whether arrest caused spouse abusers to reduce their level of abuse that they were willing to allow an experiment to test the effect of different policies.

Chapters 6 and 7 will give you much more understanding of how some features of a research design can help us evaluate causal propositions. However, you will also learn that the solutions are neither easy nor perfect: We always have to consider critically the validity of causal statements that we hear or read.

Authenticity

The goal of authenticity is stressed by researchers who focus attention on the subjective dimension of the social world. An authentic understanding of a social process or social setting is one that reflects fairly the various perspectives of participants in that setting (Gubrium and Holstein 1997). Authenticity is one of several different standards proposed by some as uniquely suited to qualitative research; it reflects a belief that those who study the social world should focus first and foremost on how participants view that social world, not on developing a unique social scientists' interpretation of that world. Rather than expecting social scientists to be able to provide a valid mirror of reality, this perspective emphasizes the need for recognizing that what is understood by participants as reality is only a social construction of reality (Kvale 2002).

Conclusion

Criminological researchers can find many questions to study, but not all questions are equally worthy. The ones that warrant the expense and effort of social research are feasible, socially important, and scientifically relevant.

The simplicity of the research circle presented in this chapter belies the complexity of the social research process. In the following chapters, we will focus on particular aspects of that process. Chapter 4 examines the interrelated processes of conceptualization and measurement, arguably the most important part of research. Measurement validity is the foundation for the other two aspects of validity. Chapter 5 reviews the meaning of generalizability and the sampling strategies that help us achieve this goal. Chapter 6 introduces causal validity, the third aspect of validity, and illustrates different methods for achieving it, with particular emphasis on experimental designs. The following four chapters then introduce different approaches to data collection, including surveys, qualitative research methods, secondary data analysis, and evaluation research, that help us, in different ways, achieve validity.

As you encounter these specifics, do not lose sight of the basic guidelines that researchers need to follow to overcome the most common impediments to social research. Owning a large social science tool kit is no guarantee of making the right decisions about which tools to use and how to use them in the investigation of particular research problems. More important, our answers to research questions will never be complete or entirely certain. Thus, when we complete a research project, we should point out how the research could be extended and evaluate the confidence we have in our conclusions. Recall how the gradual elaboration of knowledge about the deterrence of domestic violence required sensitivity to research difficulties, careful weighing of the evidence, and identification of unanswered questions by several research teams.

Ethical issues also should be considered when evaluating research proposals and completed research studies. As Chapter 3 will show, ethical issues in social research are no less complex than the other issues that researchers confront. And it is inexcusable to jump into research on people without any attention to ethical considerations.

You are now forewarned about, and thus hopefully forearmed against, the difficulties that any scientists, but criminologists in particular, face in their work. We hope that you will return often to this chapter as you read the subsequent chapters, when you criticize the research literature, and when you design your own research projects. To be conscientious, thoughtful, and responsible is the mandate of every social scientist. If you formulate a feasible research problem, ask the right questions in advance, try to adhere to the research guidelines, and steer clear of the most common difficulties, you will be well along the road to fulfilling this mandate.

Key Terms

Anomalous findings
  (serendipitous findings)   34
Authenticity   42
Causal validity
  (internal validity)   41
Constant   34
Criminological
  research question   22
Cross-population generalizability (external
  validity)   42
Deductive reasoning   33
Deductive research   34

Dependent variable   35
Direction of association   35
Empirical generalizations   37
External validity (cross-population
  generalizability)   43
Falsifiable   32
Generalizability   41
Hypothesis   34
Independent variable   35
Inductive reasoning   33
Inductive research   36
Internal validity (causal validity)   41

Measurement validity   41
Negative relationship   35
Positive relationship   35
Refereed journals   26
Replications   38
Research circle   34
Sample generalizability   42
Serendipitous findings
  (anomalous findings)   34
Theoretical constructs   31
Theory   31
Variable   34

Highlights

- Research questions should be feasible (within the time frame and with the resources available), socially important, and scientifically relevant.

- Building criminological theory is a major objective of criminological research. Investigate relevant theories before starting criminological projects, and draw out the theoretical implications of research findings.

- The type of reasoning in most criminological research can be described as primarily deductive or inductive. Research based on deductive reasoning proceeds from general ideas, deduces specific expectations from these ideas, and then tests the ideas with empirical data. Research based on inductive reasoning begins with specific data and then develops general ideas or theories to explain patterns in the data.

- It may be possible to explain unanticipated research findings after the fact, but such explanations have less credibility than those that have been tested with data collected for the purpose of the study.

- The scientific process can be represented as circular, with connections from theory to hypotheses to data to empirical generalizations.

- Research investigations may begin at different points along the research circle and traverse different portions of it. Deductive research begins at the point of theory; inductive research begins with data but ends with theory. Descriptive research begins with data and ends with empirical generalizations.

- Replications of a study are essential to establish its generalizability in other situations. An ongoing line of research stemming from a particular question should include a series of studies that, collectively, traverse the research circle multiple times.

- Criminologists, like all social scientists, should structure their research so that their own ideas can be proved wrong, should disclose their methods for others to critique, and should recognize the possibility of error.

- Valid knowledge is the central concern of scientific research. The three components of validity are measurement validity, generalizability (both from the sample to the population from which it was selected and from the sample to other populations), and causal (internal) validity. The goal of authenticity is to reflect fairly the perspectives of participants in a setting that we study.

Research in the News

Investigating Child Abuse Doesn't Reduce It

Congress intended the 1974 Child Abuse Prevention and Treatment Act to increase documentation of child abuse, with hopes of reducing its prevalence. However, a review of records of 595 high-risk children nationwide ages 4 to 8 found that those children whose families were investigated were not doing any better than children whose families were not investigated. In addition, mothers in investigated families had more depressive symptoms than mothers in uninvestigated families. The services families were offered after being investigated failed to reduce the risk of future child abuse.

Source: Bakalar, Nicholas. 2010. "Child Abuse Investigations Didn't Reduce Risk, A Study Finds." *The New York Times.* October 12:D3.

Exercises

1. State a problem for research related to a criminological topic or issue of interest to you. Write down as many questions as you can about this topic.

   a. Considering your interest, your opportunities, and the work of others, which of your research questions does not seem feasible or interesting?

   b. Pick out one question that seems feasible and that your other coursework suggests has been the focus of prior research or theorizing. Write this research question in one sentence. Elaborate on your question in a single paragraph. List at least three reasons for why it is a good research question to investigate.

2. Search the scholarly literature on your topic of interest. Copy at least 10 citations to recent articles reporting research relevant to your research question.

   a. Look up at least three of these articles. Write a brief description of each article, and evaluate its relevance to your research question. What additions or changes to your thoughts about the research question are suggested by these sources?

   b. Would you characterize the findings of these articles as largely consistent or inconsistent? How would you explain discrepant findings?

   c. How well did the authors summarize their work in their abstracts for the articles you consulted? What important points would you have missed if you had relied on only the abstracts?

3. Using one of the research articles you consulted for Exercise 2, identify and look up one of the cited articles or Web sites. Compare the cited source to what was said about it in the original article or on the original site. Was the discussion in the cited source accurate?

4. Using the same research article you focused on for Exercise 3, identify the stages of the research project corresponding to the points on the research circle. Did the research cover all four stages? Identify the theories and hypotheses underlying the study. What data were collected or utilized for the study? What were the findings (empirical generalizations)?

Developing a Research Proposal

Now it is time to start writing the proposal. These next exercises are very critical first steps.

1. State a problem for research. If you have not already identified a problem for study or if you need to evaluate whether your research problem is doable, a few suggestions should help get the ball rolling and keep it on course:

   a. Jot down questions that have puzzled you in some area having to do with people and social relations, perhaps questions that have come to mind while reading textbooks or research articles or even while hearing news stories. Don't hesitate to jot down many questions, and don't bore yourself; try to identify questions that really interest you.

   b. Now take stock of your interests, your opportunities, and the work of others. Which of your research questions no longer seem feasible or interesting? What additional research questions come to mind? Pick out a question that is of interest and seems feasible and that your other coursework suggests has been the focus of some prior research or theorizing.

   c. Write out your research question in one sentence, and elaborate on it in one paragraph. List at least three reasons for why it is a good research question for you to investigate. Then present your proposal to your classmates and instructor for discussion and feedback.

2. Search the literature (and the Web) on the research question you identified. Refer to Appendix A for guidance on conducting the search. Copy down at least 10 citations to articles (with abstracts from *Criminal Justice Abstracts, Sociological Abstracts,* or *PsycINFO*) and five Web sites reporting research that seems highly relevant to your research question; then look up at least five of these articles and three of the sites. Inspect the article bibliographies and the links in the Web site and identify at least one more relevant article and Web site from each source. Write a brief description of each article and Web site you consulted and evaluate its relevance to your research question. What additions or changes to your thoughts about the research question are suggested by the sources?

3. Propose at least two hypotheses that pertain to your research question. Justify these hypotheses in terms of the literature you have read.

4. Which standards for the protection of human subjects might pose the most difficulty for researchers on your proposed topic? Explain your answers and suggest appropriate protection procedures for human subjects.

STUDENT STUDY SITE

Log on to the Web-based student study site at **www.sagepub.com/bachmanprccj5e** for additional study tools including eFlashcards, Web quizzes, links to SAGE journal articles, podcasts, videos, data sets and codebooks, Web exercises, Web resources, and additional appendices.

Web Exercises

1. You have been assigned to write a paper on domestic violence and the law. To start, you would like to find out what the American Bar Association's stance is on the issue. Go to the American Bar Association Commission on Domestic Violence's Web site at www .abanet.org/domviol/.

2. What is the American Bar Association's definition of domestic violence? How does it suggest one can identify a person as a victim of domestic violence? What does it identify as "basic warning signs"? Write your answers in a one- to two-page report.

3. Go to the Bureau of Justice Statistics (BJS) Web site at www.ojp .usdoj.gov/bjs/. Go to "Publications." Browse the list of publications for topics related to domestic violence. List the titles of all publications focusing on violence between intimate partners. Choose the most recent publication. How does the BJS define *intimate partners*? What are some of the characteristics of intimate partner violence? What trends are identified in the report?

Ethics Exercises

1. Review the ethical guidelines adopted by the American Sociological Association (1999:63). Indicate whether you think each guideline was followed in the Sherman and Berk (1984) research on the policy response to domestic violence. If you find it hard to give a simple "yes" or "no" answer for each guideline, indicate the issues that make this evaluation difficult.

2. Concern with how research results are used is one of the hallmarks of ethical researchers, but deciding what form that concern should take is often difficult. You learned in this chapter about the controversy that occurred after Sherman and Berk (1984) encouraged police departments to adopt a pro-arrest policy in domestic abuse cases, based on findings from their Minneapolis study. Do you agree with the researchers' decision to suggest policy changes to police departments based on their study, in an effort to minimize domestic abuse? Several replication studies failed to confirm the Minneapolis findings. Does this influence your evaluation of what the researchers should have done after the Minneapolis study was completed? What about Larry Sherman's argument that failure to publicize the Omaha study finding of the effectiveness of arrest warrants resulted in some cases of abuse that could have been prevented? In one paragraph, propose a policy that researchers should follow about how much publicity is warranted and at what point in the research it should occur.

SPSS or Excel Exercises

Browse the variables in YOUTH.POR, a survey of high school youth regarding attitudes toward delinquency and delinquent behavior.

1. From these variables (excluding sex of respondent), write two hypotheses about levels of delinquency (DELINQ1) among high school youth.

2. Create a bar chart for at least one of the variables you hypothesize to be associated with levels of delinquency.

3. Develop a hypothesis concerning the relationship between gender and delinquency. Now compare the distribution of delinquency across gender groups. Select all males (SEX = 1) and obtain the mean level of delinquency for males.

Then select all females (SEX = 2) and generate the mean level of delinquency for females. What do you conclude about mean levels of delinquency for males and females?

4. What other factors do you think may be responsible for the relationship between gender and delinquency? Some researchers believe that females are supervised more strictly by their parents compared to males. Find a variable in the data set that measures the degree of parental supervision for the respondent. After examining the differences in the distribution of this variable for males and females, do you think this may be a possible explanation?

CHAPTER 3

Research Ethics and Philosophies

L et's begin with a thought experiment (or a trip down memory lane, depending on your earlier exposure to this example). One day as you are drinking coffee and reading the newspaper during your summer in California, you notice a small ad recruiting college students for a study at Stanford University. Feeling a bit bored with your part-time waiting job and missing the campus environment you got used to in your previous year as a freshman, you go to the campus and complete an application.

Male college students needed for psychological study of prison life. $80 per day for 1–2 weeks beginning Aug. 14. For further information & applications, come to Room 248, Jordan Hall, Stanford U. (Zimbardo et al. 1973:38)

After you arrive at the university, you are given an information form with more details about the research (Zimbardo 1971).

Prison Life Study: General Information

Purpose: A simulated prison will be established somewhere in the vicinity of Palo Alto, Stanford, to study a number of problems of psychological and sociological relevance.

Paid volunteers will be randomly assigned to play the roles of either prisoners and guards [*sic*] for the duration of the study. This time period will vary somewhat from about 5 days to 2 weeks for any one volunteer—depending upon several factors, such as the "sentence" for the prisoner or the work effectiveness of the guards.

Payment will be $80 a day for performing various activities and work associated with the operation of our prison.

Each volunteer must enter a contractual arrangement with the principal investigator (Dr. P. G. Zimbardo) agreeing to participate for the full duration of the study. It is obviously essential that no prisoner can leave once jailed, except through established procedures. In addition, guards must report for their 8-hour work shifts promptly and regularly since surveillance by the guards will be around-the-clock—three work shifts will be rotated or guards will be assigned a regular shift—day, evening, or early morning. Failure to fulfill this contract will result in a partial loss of salary accumulated—according to a prearranged schedule to be agreed upon. Food and accommodations for the prisoners will be provided which will meet minimal standard nutrition, health and sanitation requirements.

A warden and several prison staff will be housed in adjacent cell blocks, meals and bedding also provided for them.

Medical and psychiatric facilities will be accessible should any of the participants desire or require such services.

All participants will agree to having their behavior observed and to be interviewed and perhaps also taking psychological tests. Films of parts of the study will be taken, participants agreeing to allow them to be shown, assuming their content has information of scientific value.

[The information form then summarizes two of the "problems to be studied" and provides a few more details.]

Thanks for your interest in this study. We hope it will be possible for you to participate and to share your experiences with us.

Philip G. Zimbardo, Ph.D.

Professor of Social Psychology Stanford University

Intrigued, you decide to continue. First you are asked to complete a long questionnaire about your family background, physical and mental health history, and prior criminal involvement; answer a researcher's questions in person; and sign a consent form. A few days later, you are informed that you and 20 other young men have been selected to participate in the experiment. You then return to the university to complete a battery of "psychological tests" and are told you will be picked up for the study the next day (Haney, Banks, and Zimbardo 1973:73).

The next morning, you hear a siren just before a squad car stops in front of your house. A police officer charges you with assault and battery, warns you of your constitutional rights, searches and handcuffs you, and drives you off to the police station. After fingerprinting and a short stay in a detention cell, you are blindfolded and driven to the "Stanford County Prison." Upon arrival, you are stripped naked, skin-searched, deloused, and issued a uniform (a loosely fitting smock with an ID number printed on it), bedding, soap, and a towel. You don't recognize anyone, but you notice that the other "prisoners" and the "guards" are college-age, apparently middle-class white men (and one Asian) like you (Haney et al. 1973; Zimbardo et al. 1973).

The prison warden welcomes you:

As you probably know, I'm your warden. All of you have shown that you are unable to function outside in the real world for one reason or another—that somehow you lack the responsibility of good citizens of this great country. We of this prison, your correctional staff, are going to help you learn what your responsibilities as citizens of this country are. . . . If you follow all of these rules and keep your hands clean, repent for your misdeeds and show a proper attitude of penitence, you and I will get along just fine. (Zimbardo et al. 1973:38)

Among other behavioral restrictions, the rules stipulate that prisoners must remain silent during rest periods, during meals, and after lights out; that they must address each other only by their assigned ID numbers; that they must address guards as "Mr. Correctional Officer"; and that they may be punished for any infractions (Zimbardo et al. 1973).

You can tell that you are in the basement of a building. You are led down a corridor to a small cell (6' x 9') with three cots, where you are locked behind a steel-barred black door with two other prisoners (Exhibit 3.1). There is a small solitary confinement room (2' x 2' x 7') across the hall for those who misbehave. There is little privacy, since you realize that the uniformed guards, behind their silver sunglasses, can always observe the prisoners. After you go to sleep, you are awakened by a whistle summoning you and the others for a roll call.

The next morning, you and the other eight prisoners must stand in line outside your cells and recite the rules until you remember all 17 of them. Prisoners must chant, "It's a wonderful day, Mr. Correctional Officer." Two prisoners who get out of line are put in the solitary confinement unit. After a bit, the prisoners in Cell 1 decide to resist: They barricade their cell door and call on the prisoners in other cells to join in their resistance. As punishment, the guards pull the beds out from the other cells and spray some inmates with a fire extinguisher.

The guards succeed in enforcing control and become more authoritarian, while the prisoners become increasingly docile. Punishments are meted out for infractions of rules and sometimes for seemingly no reason at all; punishments include doing push-ups, being stripped naked, having legs chained, and being repeatedly wakened during the night. Would you join in the resistance? How would you react to this deprivation of your liberty by these authoritarian guards?

Exhibit 3.1　Prisoner in His Cell

Source: From *The Lucifer Effect* by Philip G. Zimbardo, copyright © 2007 by Philip G. Zimbardo, Inc. Used by permission of Rider; Random House Inc., & Random House Ltd.

By the 5th day of the actual Stanford Prison Experiment, five student prisoners had to be released due to evident extreme stress (Zimbardo 2007). On the 6th day, Philip Zimbardo terminated the experiment. A prisoner subsequently reported,

The way we were made to degrade ourselves really brought us down and that's why we all sat docile towards the end of the experiment. (Haney et al. 1973:88)

One guard later recounted his experience:

I was surprised at myself . . . I made them call each other names and clean the toilets out with their bare hands. I practically considered the prisoners cattle, and I kept thinking: "I have to watch out for them in case they try something." (Zimbardo et al. 1973:174)

Exhibit 3.2 gives some idea of the difference in how the prisoners and guards behaved. What is most striking about this result is that all the guards and prisoners had been screened before the study began to ensure that they were physically and mentally healthy. The roles of guard and prisoner had been assigned randomly, by the toss of a coin, so the two groups were very similar when the study began. It seemed to be the "situation" that led to the deterioration of the mental state of the prisoners and the different behavior of the guards. Being a guard or a prisoner, with rules and physical arrangements reinforcing distinctive roles, changed their behavior.

Exhibit 3.2	Chart of Guard and Prisoner Behavior

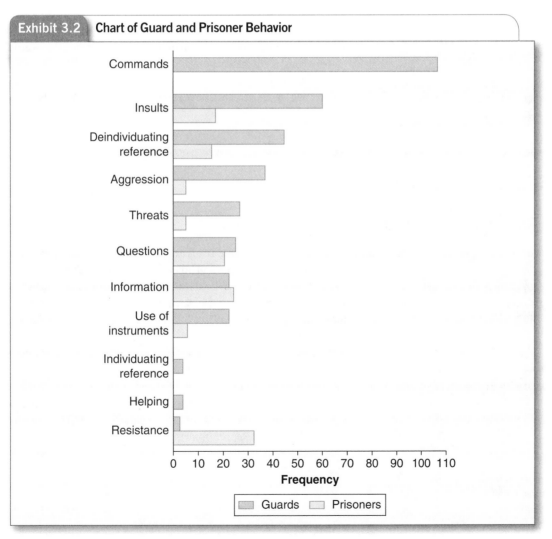

Are you surprised by the outcome of the experiment? By the guard's report of his unexpected, abusive behavior? By the prisoners' ultimate submissiveness and the considerable psychic distress some felt? (We leave it to you to assess how you would have responded if you had been an actual research participant.)

Of course, our purpose in introducing this small "experiment" is not to focus attention on the prediction of behavior in prisons; instead, we want to introduce the topic of research ethics by encouraging you to think about research from the standpoint of the people who are the subjects of research. We will refer to **Philip Zimbardo's Stanford Prison Experiment** throughout this chapter, since it is fair to say that this research ultimately had a profound influence on the way that social scientists think about research ethics as well as on the way that criminologists understand behavior in prisons. We will also refer to **Stanley Milgram's** (1963) **experiments on obedience to authority**, since that research also pertains to criminal justice issues and has stimulated much debate about research ethics.

Every criminal justice researcher needs to consider how to practice his or her discipline ethically. Whenever we interact with other people as social scientists, we must give paramount importance to the rational concerns and emotional needs that shape their responses to our actions. It is here that ethical research practice begins, with the recognition that our research procedures involve people who deserve as much respect for their well-being as we do for ours.

Philip Zimbardo's Stanford Prison Experiment A 2-week experiment that simulated the prison life of both prisoners and guards that was ended in just 6 days because of what the simulation was doing to college students who participated.

Stanley Milgram's experiments on obedience to authority Experiments by Stanley Milgram that sought to identify the conditions under which ordinary citizens would be obedient to authority figures' instructions to inflict pain on others.

🖾 Historical Background

Formal procedures for the protection of participants in research grew out of some widely publicized abuses. A defining event occurred in 1946, when the **Nuremberg War Crime Trials** exposed horrific medical experiments conducted by Nazi doctors and others in the name of "science." In the 1970s, Americans were shocked to learn that researchers funded by the U.S. Public Health Service had followed 399 low-income African American men with syphilis in the 1930s, collecting data to study the "natural" course of the illness (Exhibit 3.3). Many participants were not informed of their illness and were denied treatment until 1972, even though a cure (penicillin) was developed in the 1950s.

Egregious violations of human rights similar to these resulted, in the United States, in the creation of a National Commission for the Protection of Human Subjects of Biomedical and Behavioral Research. The commission's 1979 **Belmont Report** (from the Department of Health, Education, and Welfare) established three basic ethical principles for the protection of human subjects (Exhibit 3.4):

Nuremberg War Crime Trials U.S. court trials that exposed horrific medical experiments conducted by Nazi doctors and others in the name of "science."

Belmont Report A 1979 National Commission for the Protection of Human Subjects of Biomedical and Behavioral Research report that established three basic ethical principles for the protection of human subjects, including respect for persons, beneficence, and justice.

Respect for persons Treating persons as autonomous agents and protecting those with diminished autonomy.

Beneficence Minimizing possible harms and maximizing benefits.

Justice (in research) Distributing benefits and risks of research fairly.

- **Respect for persons**: treating persons as autonomous agents and protecting those with diminished autonomy;

- **Beneficence**: minimizing possible harms and maximizing benefits; and

- Justice: distributing benefits and risks of research fairly.

Exhibit 3.3	Tuskegee Syphilis Experiment

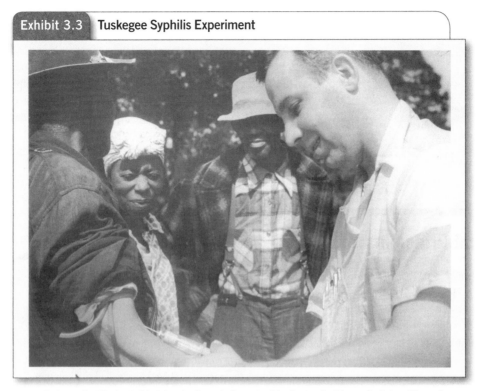

Source: Tuskegee Syphilis Study Administrative Records. Records of the Centers for Disease Control and Prevention. National Archives—Southeast Region (Atlanta).

The Department of Health and Human Services and the Food and Drug Administration then translated these principles into specific regulations that were adopted in 1991 as the **Federal Policy for the Protection of Human Subjects**. This policy has shaped the course of social science research ever since, and you will have to take it into account as you design your own research investigations. Professional associations such as the Academy of Criminal Justice Sciences, university review boards, and ethics committees in other organizations also set standards for the treatment of human subjects by their members, employees, and students, although these standards are all designed to comply with the federal policy. This section introduces these regulations.

Federal regulations require that every institution that seeks federal funding for biomedical or behavioral research on human subjects have an **institutional review board** (IRB) that reviews research proposals. IRBs at universities and other agencies apply ethical standards that are set by federal regulations but can be expanded or specified by the IRB itself (Sieber 1992). To promote adequate review of ethical issues, the regulations require that IRBs include members with diverse backgrounds. The **Office for Protection From Research Risks in the National Institutes of Health** monitors IRBs, with the exception of research involving drugs (which is the responsibility of the federal Food and Drug Administration).

Exhibit 3.4	Belmont Report Principles

Respect for Persons

Beneficence   **Justice**

Federal Policy for the Protection of Human Subjects
Federal regulations established in 1991 that are based on the principles of the Belmont Report.

> **Institutional review board (IRB)** Committee in all research organizations including universities that reviews research proposals to ensure the protection of human subjects.
>
> **Office for Protection From Research Risks in the National Institutes of Health** The organization within the federal government that monitors all IRBs, ensuring federal standards are followed.

The Academy of Criminal Justice Sciences (ACJS) and the American Society of Criminology (ASC), like most professional social science organizations, have adopted ethical guidelines for practicing criminologists that are more specific than the federal regulations. The ACJS Code of Ethics also establishes procedures for investigating and resolving complaints concerning the ethical conduct of the organization's members. The **Code of Ethics of the ACJS** (2000) is available on the ACJS Web site (www.acjs.org). The ASC follows the American Sociological Association's (ASA 1999) code of ethics, which is summarized on the ASA Web site (www.asanet.org/page .ww?section=Ethics&name=Ethics).

▣ Ethical Principles

Achieving Valid Results

Commitment to achieving valid results is the necessary starting point for ethical research practice. Simply put, we have no business asking people to answer questions, submit to observations, or participate in experimental procedures if we are simply seeking to verify our preexisting prejudices or convince others to take action on behalf of our personal inter-

> **Academy of Criminal Justice Sciences (ACJS), Code of Ethics** The Code of Ethics of ACJS sets forth 1) General Principles and 2) Ethical Standards that underlie members of the Academy's professional responsibilities and conduct, along with the 3) Policies and Procedures for enforcing those principles and standards. Membership in the Academy of Criminal Justice Sciences commits individual members to adhere to the ACJS Code of Ethics in determining ethical behavior in the context of their everyday professional activities.

ests. It is the pursuit of objective knowledge about human behavior—the goal of validity—that motivates and justifies our investigations and gives us some claim to the right to influence others to participate in our research. Knowledge is the foundation of human progress as well as the basis for our expectation that we, as social scientists, can help people achieve a brighter future. If we approach our research projects objectively, setting aside our personal predilections in the service of learning a bit more about human behavior, we can honestly represent our actions as potentially contributing to the advancement of knowledge.

The details in Zimbardo's articles and his recent book (2007) on the prison experiment make a compelling case for his commitment to achieving valid results—to learning how and why a prison-like situation influences behavior. In Zimbardo's (2009) own words,

Social-psychological studies were showing that human nature was more pliable than previously imagined and more responsive to situational pressures than we cared to acknowledge. . . . Missing from the body of social-science research at the time was the direct confrontation . . . of good people pitted against the forces inherent in bad situations. . . . I decided that what was needed was to create a situation in a controlled experimental setting in which we could array on one side a host of variables, such as . . . coercive rules, power differentials, anonymity. . . . On the other side, we lined up a collection of the "best and brightest" of young college men . . . I wanted to know who wins—good people or an evil situation—when they were brought into direct confrontation.

Zimbardo (Haney et al. 1973) devised his experiment so the situation would seem realistic to the participants and still allow careful measurement of important variables and observation of behavior at all times. Questionnaires and rating scales, interviews with participants as the research proceeded and after it was over, ongoing video and audio recording, and logs maintained by the guards all ensured that very little would escape the researcher's gaze.

Zimbardo's (Haney et al. 1973) attention to validity is also apparent in his design of the physical conditions and organizational procedures for the experiment. The "prison" was constructed in a basement without any windows so that participants would not have a sense of where they were. Their isolation was reinforced by the practice of placing paper bags over their heads when they went with a guard to use the bathroom, which was in a corridor apart from the prison area. Meals were bland, and conditions were generally demeaning. This was a very different "situation" for the participants; it was no college dorm experience.

However, not all social scientists agree that Zimbardo's approach achieved valid results. British psychologists Stephen Reicher and S. Alexander Haslam (2006) argue that guard behavior was not so consistent and that it was determined by the instructions Zimbardo gave the guards at the start of the experiment, rather than by becoming a guard in itself. For example, in another experiment, when guards were trained to respect prisoners, their behavior was less extreme (Lovibond, Mithiran, and Adams 1979).

In response to such criticism, Zimbardo (2007) has pointed to several replications of his basic experiment that support his conclusions—as well as to the evidence of patterns of abuse in the real world of prisons, including the behavior of guards who tormented prisoners at Abu Ghraib.

Do you agree with Zimbardo's assumption that the effects of being a prisoner or guard could fruitfully be studied in a mock prison, with "pretend" prisoners? Do you find merit in the criticisms? Will your evaluation of the ethics of Zimbardo's experiment be influenced by your answers to these questions? Should our ethical judgments differ when we are confident a study's results provide valid information about important social processes?

We can't answer these questions for you, but before you dismiss them as inappropriate when we are dealing with ethical standards for the treatment of human subjects, bear in mind that both Zimbardo and his critics buttress their ethical arguments with assertions about the validity (or invalidity) of the experimental results. It is hard to justify *any* risk for human subjects, or *any* expenditure of time and resources, if our findings tell us nothing about the reality of crime and punishment.

Honesty and Openness

The scientific concern with validity requires in turn that scientists be open in disclosing their methods and honest in presenting their findings. In contrast, research distorted by political or personal pressures to find particular outcomes or to achieve the most marketable results is unlikely to be carried out in an honest and open fashion. To assess the validity of a researcher's conclusions and the ethics of his or her procedures, you need to know exactly how the research was conducted. This means that articles or other reports must include a detailed methodology section, perhaps supplemented by appendices containing the research instruments or Web sites or an address where more information can be obtained.

Philip Zimbardo's research reports seemed to present an honest and open account of his methods. His initial article (Haney et al. 1973) included a detailed description of study procedures, including the physical aspects of the prison, the instructions to participants, the uniforms used, the induction procedure, and the specific data collection methods and measures. Many more details, including forms and pictures, are available on Zimbardo's Web site (www.prisonexperiment.org) and in his recent book (Zimbardo 2007).

The act of publication itself is a vital element in maintaining openness and honesty. Others can review and question study procedures and so generate an open dialogue with the researcher. Although Zimbardo disagreed sharply with his critics about many aspects of his experiment, their mutual commitment to public discourse in widely available publications resulted in a more comprehensive presentation of study procedures and a more thoughtful discourse about research ethics (Savin 1973; Zimbardo 1973). Almost 40 years later, this commentary continues to inform debates about research ethics (Reicher and Haslam 2006; Zimbardo 2007).

Openness about research procedures and results goes hand in hand with honesty in research design. Openness is also essential if researchers are to learn from the work of others. In spite of this need for openness, some researchers may hesitate to disclose their procedures or results to prevent others from building on their ideas and taking some of the credit. You might have heard of the long legal battle between a U.S. researcher, Dr. Robert Gallo, and a French researcher, Dr. Luc Montagnier, about how credit for discovering the AIDS virus should be allocated. Although a public dispute such as this one is unusual—even more unusual its resolution through an agreement announced by then-President Ronald Reagan and then-Prime Minister Jacques Chirac (Altman 1987)—concerns with priority of discovery are common. Scientists are like other people in their desire to be first. Enforcing standards of honesty and encouraging openness about research are the best solutions to these problems (as exemplified by the chronology of discovery that Gallo and Montagnier jointly developed as part of the agreement).

Protecting Research Participants

The ACJS code's standards concerning the treatment of human subjects include federal regulations and ethical guidelines emphasized by most professional social science organizations:

- Research should expose participants to no more than minimal risk of personal harm. (#16)

- Researchers should fully disclose the purposes of their research. (#13)

- Participation in research should be voluntary, and therefore subjects must give their informed consent to participate in the research. (#16)

- Confidentiality must be maintained for individual research participants unless it is voluntarily and explicitly waived. (#14, #18, #19)

Philip Zimbardo (2007) himself decided that his Stanford Prison Experiment was unethical because it violated the first two of these principles: Participants "did suffer considerable anguish . . . and [the experiment] resulted in such extreme stress and emotional turmoil that five of the sample of initially healthy young prisoners had to be released early" (pp. 233–34) and because the researchers did not disclose in advance the nature of the arrest or booking procedures at police headquarters; nor did they disclose to parents how bad the situation had become when they came to a visiting night. Nonetheless, Zimbardo (Zimbardo et al. 1973; Zimbardo 2007) argued that there was no long-lasting Zimbardo harm to participants and some long-term social benefits from this research. In particular, debriefing participants—discussing their experiences and revealing the logic behind the experiment—and follow-up interviews enabled the participants to recover from the experience without lasting harm. Also, the experience led several participants in the experiment, including Zimbardo, to dedicate their careers to investigating and improving prison conditions. As a result, publicity about the experiment has also helped focus attention on problems in prison management.

Do you agree with Zimbardo's conclusion that his experiment was not ethical? Do you think it should have been prevented from happening in the first place? Are you relieved to learn that current standards in the United States for the protection of human subjects in research would not allow his experiment to be conducted?

In contrast to Zimbardo, Stanley Milgram (1963) believed that his experiments on obedience to authority were ethical, so debate about this has been long-lasting. His experiments on obedience to authority raise most of the relevant issues we want to highlight here.

Milgram had recruited community members to participate in his experiment at Yale University. Milgram's research was stimulated by the success of Germany's Nazi regime of the 1930s and 1940s in enlisting the participation of ordinary citizens in unconscionable acts of terror and genocide. Milgram set out to identify through laboratory experiments the conditions under which ordinary citizens will be obedient to authority figures' instructions to inflict pain on others. He operationalized this obedience by asking subjects to deliver electric shocks (fake, of course) to students supposedly learning a memory task. Subjects ("teachers") were told to administer a shock to the learner each time he gave a wrong response and to move one level higher on the shock generator each additional time an incorrect response was given. They were told to increase the shocks over time and many did so, even after the supposed "students," behind a partition, began to cry out in (simulated) pain (Exhibit 3.5). The participants became very tense and some resisted as the shocks increased to the (supposedly) lethal range, but many still complied with the authority in that situation and increased the shocks. Like Zimbardo, Milgram debriefed participants afterward and followed up later to check on their well-being. It seemed that none had suffered long-term harm.

As we discuss how the ACJS Code of Ethics standards apply to Milgram's experiments, you will begin to realize that there is no simple answer to the question "What *is* (or *isn't*) ethical research practice?" The issues are just too complicated and the relevant principles too subject to different interpretations. But we do promise that by the time you finish this chapter, you will be aware of the major issues in research ethics and be able to make informed, defensible decisions about the ethical conduct of social science research.

Exhibit 3.5 Diagram of Milgram Experiment

Avoid Harming Research Participants

Although this standard may seem straightforward, it can be difficult to interpret in specific cases and harder yet to define in a way that is agreeable to all social scientists. Does it mean that subjects should not at all be harmed psychologically or physically? That they should feel no anxiety or distress whatsoever during the study or even after their involvement ends? Should the possibility of any harm, no matter how remote, deter research?

Before we address these questions with respect to Milgram's experiments, a verbatim transcript of one session will give you an idea of what participants experienced (Milgram 1965):

150 volts delivered.	You want me to keep going?
165 volts delivered.	That guy is hollering in there. There's a lot of them here. He's liable to have a heart condition. You want me to go on?
180 volts delivered.	He can't stand it! I'm not going to kill that man in there! You hear him hollering? He's hollering. He can't stand it. . . . I mean who is going to take responsibility if anything happens to that gentleman?
	[The experimenter accepts responsibility.] All right.
195 volts delivered.	You see he's hollering. Hear that. Gee, I don't know. *[The experimenter says: "The experiment requires that you go on."]* I know it does, sir, but I mean—Hugh—he don't know what he's in for. He's up to 195 volts.
	210 volts delivered.
	225 volts delivered.
	240 volts delivered. (p. 67)

This experimental manipulation generated "extraordinary tension" (Milgram 1963):

Subjects were observed to sweat, tremble, stutter, bite their lips, groan and dig their fingernails into their flesh. . . . Full-blown, uncontrollable seizures were observed for 3 subjects. [O]ne . . . seizure [was] so violently convulsive that it was necessary to call a halt to the experiment [for that individual]. (p. 375)

An observer (behind a one-way mirror) reported (Milgram 1963), "I observed a mature and initially poised businessman enter the laboratory smiling and confident. Within 20 minutes he was reduced to a twitching, stuttering wreck, who was rapidly approaching a point of nervous collapse" (p. 377).

Psychologist Diana Baumrind (1964) disagreed sharply with Milgram's approach, concluding that the emotional disturbance subjects experienced was "potentially harmful because it could easily affect an alteration in the subject's self-image or ability to trust adult authorities in the future" (p. 422). Stanley Milgram (1964) quickly countered,

> As the experiment progressed there was no indication of injurious effects in the subjects; and as the subjects themselves strongly endorsed the experiment, the judgment I made was to continue the experiment. (p. 849)

When Milgram (1964) surveyed the subjects in a follow-up, 83.7% endorsed the statement that they were "very glad" or "glad" "to have been in the experiment," 15.1% were "neither sorry nor glad," and just 1.3% were "sorry" or "very sorry" to have participated (p. 849). Interviews by a psychiatrist a year later found no evidence "of any traumatic reactions" (p. 197). Subsequently, Milgram (1974) argued that "the central moral justification for allowing my experiment is that it was judged acceptable by those who took part in it" (p. 21).

Milgram (1964) also attempted to minimize harm to subjects with postexperimental procedures "to assure that the subject would leave the laboratory in a state of well being" (p. 374). A friendly reconciliation was arranged between the subject and the victim, and an effort was made to reduce any tensions that arose as a result of the experiment.

In some cases, the "dehoaxing" (or "debriefing") discussion was extensive, and all subjects were promised (and later received) a comprehensive report (Milgram 1964:849).

In a later article, Baumrind (1985) dismissed the value of the self-reported "lack of harm" of subjects who had been willing to participate in the experiment—and noted that 16% did *not* endorse the statement that they were "glad" they had participated in the experiment (p. 168). Baumrind (1985) also argued that research indicates most students who have participated in a deception experiment report a decreased trust in authorities as a result—a tangible harm in itself.

Many social scientists, ethicists, and others concluded that Milgram's procedures had not harmed the subjects and so were justified for the knowledge they produced, but others sided with Baumrind's criticisms (Miller 1986). What is your opinion at this point? Does Milgram's debriefing process relieve your concerns? Are you as persuaded by the subjects' own endorsement of the procedures as was Milgram?

Would you ban such experiments because of the potential for harm to subjects? Does the fact that Zimbardo's and Milgram's experiments seemed to yield significant insights into the effect of a social situation on human behavior—insights that could be used to improve prisons or perhaps lessen the likelihood of another holocaust—make any difference (Reynolds 1979)? Do you believe that this benefit outweighs the foreseeable risks?

Obtain Informed Consent

The requirement of informed consent is also more difficult to define than it first appears. To be informed, consent must be given by the persons who are competent to consent, have consented voluntarily, are fully informed about the research, and have comprehended what they have been told (Reynolds 1979). Yet well-intentioned researchers may not foresee all the potential problems and so may not point them out in advance to potential participants (Baumrind 1985). Milgram (1974) reported that he and his colleagues were surprised by the subjects' willingness to carry out such severe shocks. In Zimbardo's prison simulation study, all the participants signed consent forms, but they were not "fully informed" in advance about potential risks. The researchers themselves did not realize that the study participants would experience so much stress so quickly, that some prisoners would have to be released for severe negative reactions within the first few days, or that even those who were not severely stressed would soon be begging to be released from the mock prison. But on the other hand, are you concerned that real harm "could result from *not doing* research on destructive obedience" and other troubling human behavior (Miller 1986:138)?

Obtaining informed consent creates additional challenges for researchers. The researcher's actions and body language should help convey his verbal assurance that consent is voluntary. The language of the consent form must be clear and understandable to the research participants yet sufficiently long and detailed to explain what will actually happen in the research. Examples A (Exhibit 3.6) and B (Exhibit 3.7) illustrate two different approaches to these trade-offs.

Consent form A was approved by the University of Delaware IRB for in-depth interviews with former inmates about their experiences after release from prison.

Consent form B is the one used by Philip Zimbardo. It is brief and to the point, leaving out many of the details that current standards for the protection of human subjects require. Zimbardo's consent form also released the researchers from any liability for problems arising out of the research (such a statement is no longer allowed).

As in Milgram's (1963) study, experimental researchers whose research design requires some type of subject deception try to minimize disclosure of experimental details by withholding some information before the experiment begins but then **debriefing** subjects at the end. In the debriefing, the researcher explains to the subjects what happened in the experiment and why and responds to their questions. A carefully designed debriefing procedure can help the research participants learn from the experimental research and grapple constructively with feelings elicited by the realization that they were deceived (Sieber 1992). However, even though

> **Debriefing** A researcher's informing subjects after an experiment about the experiment's purposes and methods and evaluating subjects' personal reactions to the experiment.

Exhibit 3.6	Consent Form A

INFORMED CONSENT

ROADS DIVERGE: LONG-TERM PATTERNS OF RELAPSE, RECIDIVISM AND DESISTANCE FOR A RE-ENTRY COHORT (National Institute of Justice, 2008-IJ-CX-0017)

PURPOSE: You are one of approximately 300 people being asked to participate in a research project conducted by the Center for Drug and Alcohol Studies at the University of Delaware. You were part of the original study of offenders in Delaware leaving prison in the 1990s, and we want to find out how things in your life have changed since that time. The overall purpose of this research is to help us understand what factors lead to changes in criminal activity and drug use over time.

PROCEDURES: If you agree to take part in this study, you will be asked to complete a survey, which will last approximately 60 to 90 minutes. We will ask you to provide us with some contact information so that we can locate you again if we are able to do another follow up study in the future. You will be asked about your employment, family history, criminal involvement, health history, drug use, and how these have changed over time. We will use this information, as well as information that you have previously provided or which is publicly available. We will <u>not</u> ask you for the names of anyone, or the specific dates or specific places of any of your activities. The interviews will be tape-recorded, but you will not be identified by name on the tape. The tapes will be stored in a locked cabinet until they can be transcribed to an electronic word processor. After the tapes have been transcribed and checked for accuracy they will be destroyed. Anonymous transcribed data will be kept indefinitely – no audio data will be kept.

RISKS: There are some risks to participating in this study. You may experience distress or discomfort when asked questions about your drug use, criminal history, and other experiences. Should this occur, you may choose not to answer such questions. If emotional distress occurs, our staff will make referrals to services you may need, including counseling, and drug abuse treatment and support services.

The risk that confidentiality could be broken is a concern, but it is very unlikely to occur. You will not be identified on the audiotape of the interview. We request that you not mention names of other people or places, but if this happens, those names will be deleted from the audiotape prior to transcription. All study materials are kept in locked file cabinets. Only three members of [the] research team will have access to study materials.

(Continued)

Exhibit 3.6 (Continued)

BENEFITS: You will have the opportunity to participate in an important research project, which may lead to the better understanding of what factors both help and prevent an individual's recovery from drug use and criminal activity.

COMPENSATION: You will receive $100 to compensate you for your time and travel costs for this interview.

CONFIDENTIALITY: Your records will be kept confidential. They will be kept under lock and key and will not be shared with anyone without your written permission. Your name will not appear on any data file or research report.

A Privacy Certificate has been approved by the U.S. Department of Justice. The data will be protected from being revealed to nonresearch interests by court subpoena in any federal, state, or local civil, criminal, administrative, legislative or other proceedings.

You should understand that a Privacy Certificate does not prevent you or a member of your family from voluntarily releasing information about yourself or your involvement in this research. If you give anyone written consent to receive research information, then we may not use the Certificate to withhold that information.

The Privacy Certificate does not prevent research staff from voluntary disclosures to authorities if we learn that you intend to harm yourself or someone else. These incidents would be reported as required by state and federal law. However, we will not ask you questions about these areas.

Because this research is paid for by the National Institute of Justice, staff of this research office may review copies of your records, but they also are required to keep that information confidential.

RIGHT TO QUIT THE STUDY: Participation in this research project is voluntary and you have the right to leave the study at any time. The researchers and their assistants have the right to remove you from this study if needed.

You may ask and will receive answers to any questions concerning this study. If you have any questions about this study, you may contact Ronet Bachman or Daniel O'Connell at (302) 831-6107. If you have any questions about your rights as a research participant you may contact the Chairperson of the University of Delaware's Human Subjects Review Board at (302) 831-2136.

CONSENT TO BE INTERVIEWED

I have read and understand this form (or it has been read to me), and I agree to participate in the in-depth interview portion of this research project.

_____

PARTICIPANT SIGNATURE   DATE

_____

SIGNATURE OF WITNESS/INTERVIEWER   DATE

CONSENT TO BE CONTACTED IN FUTURE

I have read and understand this form (or it has been read to me), and I agree to be recontacted in the future as part of this research project.

_____

PARTICIPANT SIGNATURE   DATE

_____

SIGNATURE OF WITNESS/INTERVIEWER   DATE

Ronet Bachman, Ph.D.
Principal Investigator
University of Delaware
Telephone: (302) 831-6107

Exhibit 3.7 Consent Form B

CONSENT

Prison Life Study
Dr. Zimbardo
August 1971

_____

(date) (name of volunteer)

I, _____, the undersigned, hereby consent to participate as a volunteer in a prison life study research project to be conducted by the Stanford University Psychology Department.

The nature of the research project has been fully explained to me, including, without limitation, the fact that paid volunteers will be randomly assigned to the roles of either "prisoners" or "guards" for the duration of the study. I understand that participation in the research project will involve a loss of privacy, that I will be expected to participate for the full duration of the study, that I will only be released from participation for reasons of health deemed adequate by the medical advisers to the research project or for other reasons deemed appropriate by Dr. Philip Zimbardo, Principal Investigator of the project, and that I will be expected to follow directions from staff members of the project or from other participants in the research project.

I am submitting myself for participation in this research project with full knowledge and understanding of the nature of the research project and of what will be expected of me. I specifically release the Principal Investigator and the staff members of the research project, Stanford University, its agents and employees, and the Federal Government, its agents and employees, from any liability to me arising in any way out of my participation in the project.

_____

(signature of volunteer)

Witness: _____

If volunteer is a minor:

_____

(signature of person authorized to consent for volunteer)

Witness: _____

_____

(relationship to volunteer)

---

debriefing can be viewed as a substitute, in some cases, for securing fully informed consent prior to the experiment, debriefed subjects who disclose the nature of the experiment to other participants can contaminate subsequent results (Adair, Dushenko, and Lindsay 1985). Unfortunately, if the debriefing process is delayed, the ability to lessen any harm resulting from the deception is also reduced.

If you were to serve on your university's IRB, would you allow this research to be conducted? Can students who are asked to participate in research by their professor be considered able to give informed consent? Do you consider informed consent to be meaningful if the true purpose or nature of an experimental manipulation is not revealed?

The process and even possibility of obtaining informed consent must take into account the capacity of prospective participants to give informed consent. Children cannot legally give consent to participate in research; instead, they must in most circumstances be given the opportunity to give or withhold their _assent_ to participate in research, usually by a verbal response to an explanation of the research. In addition, a child's legal guardian must give written informed consent to have the child participate in research (Sieber 1992). There are also special protections for other populations that are likely to be vulnerable to coercion—prisoners, pregnant women, mentally disabled persons, and educationally or economically disadvantaged persons. Would you allow research on prisoners, whose ability to give informed consent can be questioned? What special protections do you think would be appropriate?

Avoid Deception in Research, Except in Limited Circumstances

Deception occurs when subjects are misled about research procedures to determine how they would react to the treatment if they were not research subjects. Deception is a critical component of many social psychology experiments, in part because of the difficulty of simulating real-world stresses and dilemmas in a laboratory setting. The goal is to get subjects "to accept as true what is false or to give a false impression" (Korn 1997:4). In Milgram's (1963) experiment, for example, deception seemed necessary because the subjects could not be permitted to administer real electric shocks to the "student," yet it would not have made sense to order the subjects to do something that they didn't find to be so troubling. Milgram (1992) insisted that the deception was absolutely essential. The results of many other social psychological experiments would be worthless if subjects understood what was really happening to them while the experiment was in progress. The real question: Is this sufficient justification to allow the use of deception?

Gary Marshall and Philip Zimbardo (1979) sought to determine the physiological basis of emotion by injecting student volunteers with adrenaline so that their heart rate and sweating would increase and then by placing them in a room with a student "stooge" who acted silly. But the students were told that they were being injected with a vitamin supplement to test its effect on visual acuity (Korn 1997). Piliavin and Piliavin (1972) staged fake seizures on subway trains to study helpfulness (Korn 1997). Would you vote to allow such deceptive practices in research if you were a member of your university's IRB? What about less dramatic instances of deception in laboratory experiments with students like yourself? Do you react differently to the debriefing by Milgram compared to that by Zimbardo?

What scientific or educational or applied "value" would make deception justifiable, even if there is some potential for harm? Who determines whether a nondeceptive intervention is "equally effective" (Miller 1986:103)? Diana Baumrind (1985) suggested that personal "introspection" would have been sufficient to test Milgram's hypothesis and has argued subsequently that intentional deception in research violates the ethical principles of self-determination, protection of others, and maintenance of trust between people and so can never be justified. How much risk, discomfort, or unpleasantness might be seen as affecting willingness to participate? When should a postexperimental "attempt to correct any misconception" due to deception be deemed sufficient?

Can you see why an IRB, representing a range of perspectives, is an important tool for making reasonable, ethical research decisions when confronted with such ambiguity? Exhibit 3.8 shows a portion of the complex flowchart developed by the U.S. Department of Health and Human Services to help researchers decide what type of review will be needed for their research plans. Any research involving deception requires formal human subjects' review.

Maintain Privacy and Confidentiality

Maintaining privacy and confidentiality is another key ethical standard for protecting research participants, and the researcher's commitment to that standard should be included in the informed consent agreement (Sieber 1992). Procedures to protect each subject's privacy such as locking records and creating special identifying codes must be created to minimize the risk of access by unauthorized persons. However, statements about confidentiality should be realistic: Laws allow research records to be subpoenaed and may require reporting child abuse; a researcher may feel compelled to release information if a health- or life-threatening situation arises and participants need to be alerted. Also, the standard of confidentiality does not apply to observation in public places and information available in public records.

Privacy Certificate NIJ document that protects researchers from being legally required to disclose confidential information.

Certificate of Confidentiality NIH document that protects researchers from being legally required to disclose confidential information.

There are two exceptions to some of these constraints: The National Institute of Justice can issue a **Privacy Certificate**, and the National Institutes of Health can issue a **Certificate of Confidentiality**. Both of these documents protect researchers from being legally required to disclose confidential information. Researchers who are focusing on high-risk populations or behaviors, such as crime, substance abuse, sexual activity, or genetic information, can request such a certificate. Suspicions of child abuse or neglect must still be reported, and in some states researchers may still be required to report such crimes as elder abuse (Arwood and Panicker 2007).

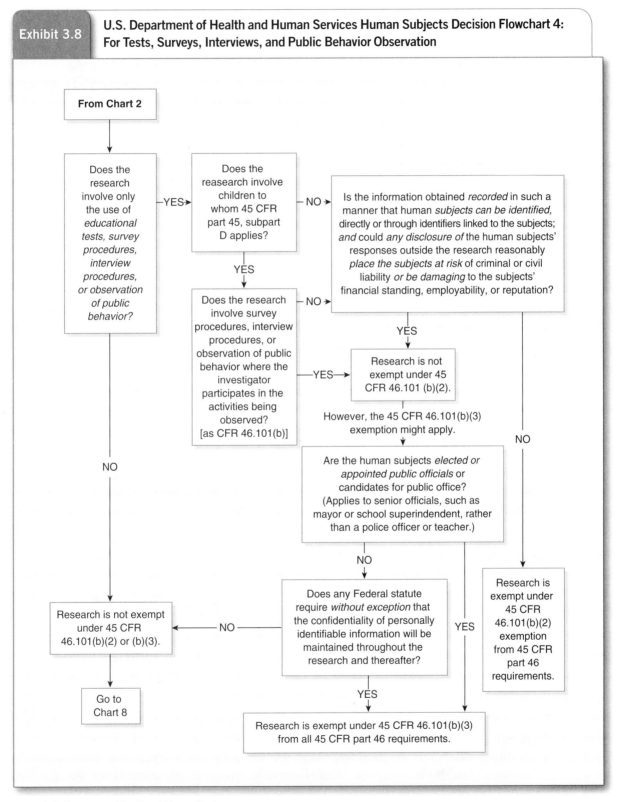

Exhibit 3.8 U.S. Department of Health and Human Services Human Subjects Decision Flowchart 4: For Tests, Surveys, Interviews, and Public Behavior Observation

From Chart 2

Does the research involve only the use of *educational tests, survey procedures, interview procedures, or observation of public behavior?*

—YES→

Does the reasearch involve children to whom 45 CFR part 45, subpart D applies?

— NO →

Is the information obtained *recorded* in such a manner that human *subjects can be identified,* directly or through identifiers linked to the subjects; *and* could *any disclosure of* the human subjects' responses outside the research reasonably *place the subjects at risk* of criminal or civil liability *or be damaging* to the subjects' financial standing, employability, or reputation?

YES

Does the research involve survey procedures, interview procedures, or observation of public behavior where the investigator participates in the activities being observed? [as CFR 46.101(b)]

— NO →

→YES→

Research is not exempt under 45 CFR 46.101 (b)(2).

However, the 45 CFR 46.101(b)(3) exemption might apply.

YES

NO

Are the human subjects *elected or appointed public officials* or candidates for public office? (Applies to senior officials, such as mayor or school superindendent, rather than a police officer or teacher.)

NO

NO

Research is not exempt under 45 CFR 46.101(b)(2) or (b)(3).

←— NO —

Does any Federal statute require *without exception* that the confidentiality of personally identifiable information will be maintained throughout the research and thereafter?

YES

Research is exempt under 45 CFR 46.101(b)(2) exemption from 45 CFR part 46 requirements.

Go to Chart 8

YES

Research is exempt under 45 CFR 46.101(b)(3) from all 45 CFR part 46 requirements.

Source: U.S. Department of Health and Human Services.

The Health Insurance Portability and Accountability Act (HIPAA) passed by Congress in 1996 created much more stringent regulations for the protection of health care data. As implemented by the U.S. Department of Health and Human Services in 2000 (and revised in 2002), the HIPAA Final Privacy Rule applies to oral, written, and electronic information that "relates to the past, present or future physical or mental health or condition of an individual." The HIPAA rule requires that researchers have valid authorization for any use or disclosure of "protected health information" (PHI) from a health care provider. Waivers of authorization can be granted in special circumstances (Cava, Cushman, and Goodman 2007).

The Uses of Research

Scientists must also consider the uses to which their research is put. Although many scientists believe that personal values should be left outside the laboratory, some feel that it is proper—even necessary—for scientists to concern themselves with the way their research is used.

Philip Zimbardo made it clear that he was concerned about the phenomenon of situational influence on behavior precisely because of its implications for people's welfare. As you have already learned, his first article (Haney et al. 1973) highlighted abuses in the treatment of prisoners. In his more comprehensive book, Zimbardo (2007) also used his findings to shed light on the atrocities committed at Abu Ghraib. He also urged reforms in prison policy.

It is also impossible to ignore the very practical implications of Milgram's investigations, which Milgram (1974) took pains to emphasize. His research highlighted the extent of obedience to authority and identified multiple factors that could be manipulated to lessen blind obedience (such as encouraging dissent by just one group member, removing the subject from direct contact with the authority figure, and increasing the contact between the subject and the victim).

The evaluation research by Lawrence Sherman and Richard Berk (1984) on the police response to domestic violence provides an interesting cautionary tale about the uses of science. As you recall from Chapter 2, the results of this field experiment indicated that those who were arrested were less likely to subsequently commit violent acts against their partners. Sherman (1993) explicitly cautioned police departments not to adopt mandatory arrest policies based solely on the results of the Minneapolis experiment, but the results were publicized in the mass media and encouraged many jurisdictions to change their policies (Binder and Meeker 1993; Lempert 1989). Although we now know that the original finding of a deterrent effect of arrest did not hold up in other cities where the experiment was repeated, Sherman (1992) later suggested that implementing mandatory arrest policies might have prevented some subsequent cases of spouse abuse. JoAnn Miller's (2003) analysis of victims' experiences and perceptions concerning their safety after the mandatory arrest experiment in Dade County, Florida, found that victims reported less violence if their abuser had been arrested (and/or assigned to a police-based counseling program called "Safe Streets") (Exhibit 3.9). Should this Dade County finding be publicized in the popular press so it could be used to improve police policies? What about the results of the other replication studies? The answers to such questions are never easy.

Social scientists who conduct research on behalf of specific organizations may face additional difficulties when the organization, instead of the researcher, controls the final report and the publicity it receives. If organizational leaders decide that particular research results are unwelcome, the researcher's desire to have findings used appropriately and reported fully can conflict with contractual obligations. Researchers can often anticipate such dilemmas in advance and resolve them when the contract for research is negotiated—or simply decline a particular research opportunity altogether. But often, such problems come up only after a report has been drafted, or the problems are ignored by a researcher who needs to have a job or needs to maintain particular personal relationships. These possibilities cannot be avoided entirely, but because of them, it is always important to acknowledge the source of research funding in reports and to consider carefully the sources of funding for research reports written by others.

The potential of withholding a beneficial treatment from some subjects also is a cause for ethical concern. The Sherman and Berk (1984) experiment required the random assignment of subjects to treatment conditions and thus had

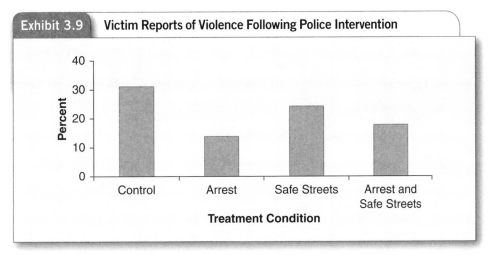

Exhibit 3.9 Victim Reports of Violence Following Police Intervention

Source: Adapted from Miller 2003:704.

the potential of causing harm to the victims of domestic violence whose batterers were not arrested. The justification for the study design, however, is quite persuasive: The researchers didn't know prior to the experiment which response to a domestic violence complaint would be most likely to deter future incidents (Sherman 1992). The experiment provided clear evidence about the value of arrest, so it can be argued that the benefits outweighed the risks.

Social Research Philosophies

What influences the choice of a research strategy? The motive for conducting research is critical: An explanatory or evaluative motive generally leads a researcher to use quantitative methods, whereas an exploratory motive often results in the use of qualitative methods. Of course, a descriptive motive means choosing a descriptive research strategy.

Positivism and Postpositivism

A researcher's philosophical perspective on reality and on the appropriate role of the researcher also will shape her methodological preferences. Researchers with a positivist philosophy believe that there is an objective reality that exists apart from the perceptions of those who observe it; the goal of science is to better understand this reality.

> Whatever nature "really" is, we assume that it presents itself in precisely the same way to the same human observer standing at different points in time and space. . . . We assume that it also presents itself in precisely the same way across different human observers standing at the same point in time and space. (Wallace 1983:461)

This philosophy is traditionally associated with science (Weber 1949), with the expectation that there are universal laws of human behavior, and with the belief that scientists must be objective and unbiased to see reality clearly.

Postpositivism is a philosophy of reality that is closely related to **positivism**. Postpositivists believe that there is an external, objective reality but are very sensitive to the complexity of this reality and the limitations of the scientists who study it—and, for social scientists, the biases they bring to the study of social beings like themselves (Guba and Lincoln 1994). As a result, they do not think scientists can ever be sure that their methods allow them to perceive objective reality; the goal of science can only be to achieve **intersubjective agreement** among scientists about the nature of reality (Wallace 1983). For example, postpositivists may worry that researchers' predispositions may bias them in favor of deterrence theory. Therefore, they will remain somewhat skeptical of results that support predictions based on deterrence until a number of researchers feel that they have found supportive evidence. The postpositivist retains much more confidence in the ability of the community of social researchers to develop an unbiased account of reality than in the ability of any individual social scientist to do so (Campbell and Russo 1999).

> **Positivism** The belief, shared by most scientists, that there is a reality that exists quite apart from our own perception of it, although our knowledge of this reality may never be complete.
>
> **Postpositivism** The belief that there is an empirical reality but that our understanding of it is limited by its complexity and by the biases and other limitations of researchers.
>
> **Intersubjective agreement** Agreement between scientists about the nature of reality; often upheld as a more reasonable goal for science than certainty about an objective reality.

Positivist Research Guidelines

To achieve an accurate, or valid, understanding of the social world, a researcher operating within the positivist or postpositivist tradition must adhere to some basic guidelines about how to conduct research:

1. *Test ideas against empirical reality without becoming too personally invested in a particular outcome.* This guideline requires a commitment to "testing," as opposed to just reacting to events as they happen or looking for what we want to see (Kincaid 1996).

2. *Plan and carry out investigations systematically.* Social researchers have little hope of conducting a careful test of their ideas if they do not think through in advance how they should go about the test and then proceed accordingly.

3. *Document all procedures and disclose them publicly.* Social researchers should disclose the methods on which their conclusions are based so that others can evaluate for themselves the likely soundness of these conclusions. Such disclosure is a key feature of science. It is the community of researchers, reacting to each other's work, that provides the best guarantee against purely self-interested conclusions (Kincaid 1996).

4. *Clarify assumptions.* No investigation is complete unto itself; whatever the researcher's method, the research rests on some background assumptions. For example, research to determine whether arrest has a deterrent effect assumes that potential law violators think rationally and that they calculate potential costs and benefits prior to committing crimes. By definition, research assumptions are not tested, so we do not know for sure whether they are correct. By taking the time to think about and disclose their assumptions, researchers provide important information for those who seek to evaluate the validity of research conclusions.

5. *Specify the meaning of all terms.* Words often have multiple or unclear meanings. "Recidivism," "self-control," "poverty," "overcrowded," and so on can mean different things to different people. In scientific research, all terms must be defined explicitly and used consistently.

6. *Maintain a skeptical stance toward current knowledge.* The results of any particular investigation must be examined critically, although confidence about interpretations of the social or natural world increases after repeated investigations yield similar results. A general skepticism about current knowledge stimulates researchers to improve the validity of current research results and expand the frontier of knowledge.

7. *Replicate research and build social theory.* No one study is definitive by itself. We cannot fully understand a single study's results apart from the larger body of knowledge to which it is related, and we cannot place much

confidence in these results until the study has been replicated. Theories organize the knowledge accumulated by numerous investigations into a coherent whole and serve as a guide to future inquiries.

8. *Search for regularities or patterns.* Positivist and postpositivist scientists assume that the natural world has some underlying order of relationships so that unique events and individuals can be understood at least in part in terms of general principles (Grinnell 1992).

Real investigations by social scientists do not always include much attention to theory, specific definitions of all terms, and so forth. But it behooves any social researcher to study these guidelines and to consider the consequences of not following any with which he or she does not agree.

A Positivist Research Goal: Advancing Knowledge

The goal of the traditional positivist scientific approach is to advance scientific knowledge. This goal is achieved when research results are published in academic journals or presented at academic conferences.

The positivist approach regards value considerations to be beyond the scope of science: "An empirical science cannot tell anyone what he should do—but rather what he can do—and under certain circumstances—what he wishes to do" (Weber 1949:54). The idea is that developing valid knowledge about how society is organized, or how we live our lives, does not tell us how society should be organized or how we should live our lives. The determination of empirical facts should be a separate process from the evaluation of these facts as satisfactory or unsatisfactory (Weber 1949).

The idea is not to ignore value considerations, because they are viewed as a legitimate basis for selecting a research problem to investigate. In addition, many scientists also consider it acceptable to encourage government officials or private organizations to act on the basis of a study's findings, after the research is over. During a research project, however, value considerations are to be held in abeyance.

Interpretivism and Constructivism

Qualitative research is often guided by a different, interpretivist philosophy. Interpretive social scientists believe that social reality is socially constructed and that the goal of social scientists is to understand what meanings people give to reality, not to determine how reality works apart from these interpretations. This philosophy rejects the positivist belief that there is a concrete, objective reality that scientific methods help us understand (Lynch and Bogen 1997); instead, interpretivists believe that scientists construct an image of reality based on their own preferences and prejudices and their interactions with others. Max Weber termed the goal of interpretivist research *verstehen*, or "understanding."

> **Interpretivism (interpretivist philosophy)** The belief that reality is socially constructed and that the goal of social scientists is to understand what meanings people give to that reality.
>
> **Verstehen** German term for "understanding."

Here is the basic argument: All the empirical data we collect come to us through our own senses and must be interpreted with our own minds. This suggests that we can never be sure that we have understood reality properly—or that we ever can—or that our own understandings can really be judged more valid than someone else's. Concerns like this have begun to appear in many areas of social science and have begun to shape some research methods. From this standpoint, the goal of validity becomes misleading: "Truth is a matter of the best-informed and most sophisticated construction on which there is consensus at a given time" (Schwandt 1994:128).

Searching for universally applicable social laws can distract from learning what people know and how they understand their lives. The interpretive social researcher examines meanings that have been socially constructed. . . . There is not one reality out there to be measured; objects and events are understood by different people differently, and those perceptions are the reality—or realities—that social science should focus on. (Rubin and Rubin 1995:35)

Constructivist paradigm Methodology based on rejection of belief in an external reality; it emphasizes the importance of exploring the way in which different stakeholders in a social setting construct their beliefs.

Hermeneutic circle Represents the dialectical process in which the researcher obtains information from multiple stakeholders in a setting, refines his or her understanding of the setting, and then tests that understanding with successive respondents.

The **constructivist paradigm** extends interpretivist philosophy by emphasizing the importance of exploring how different stakeholders in a social setting construct their beliefs (Guba and Lincoln 1989). It gives particular attention to the different goals of researchers and other participants in a research setting and seeks to develop a consensus among participants about how to understand the focus of inquiry. The constructivist research report will highlight different views of the social program or other issue and explain how a consensus can be reached among participants.

Constructivist inquiry uses an interactive research process, in which a researcher begins an evaluation in some social setting by identifying the different interest groups in that setting. The researcher goes on to learn what each group thinks and then gradually tries to develop a shared perspective on the problem being evaluated (Guba and Lincoln 1989).

These steps are diagrammed as a circular process in Exhibit 3.10. In this process, called a **hermeneutic circle**,

the constructions of a variety of individuals—deliberately chosen so as to uncover widely variable viewpoints—are elicited, challenged, and exposed to new information and new, more sophisticated ways of interpretation, until some level of consensus is reached (although there may be more than one focus for consensus). (Guba and Lincoln 1989:180–81)

The researcher conducts an open-ended interview with the first respondent (R1) to learn about her thoughts and feelings on the subject of inquiry, her "construction" (C1). The researcher then asks this respondent to nominate a second

Exhibit 3.10 The Hermeneutic Circle

KEY: R = Respondent
C = Construction

Source: Adapted from Guba and Lincoln 1989:152.

respondent (R2), who feels very differently. The second respondent is then interviewed in the same way but also asked to comment on the themes raised by the previous respondent. The process continues until all major perspectives are represented, and it may be repeated with the same set of respondents.

The final product is a **case report**.

A case report is very unlike the technical reports we are accustomed to seeing in positivist inquiries. It is not a depiction of a "true" or "real" state of affairs. . . . It does not culminate in judgments, conclusions, or recommendations except insofar as these are concurred on by relevant respondents.

> **Case report** A report that helps the reader realize (in the sense of making real) not only the states of affairs that are believed by constructors [research respondents] to exist but also of the underlying motives, feelings, and rationales leading to those beliefs.

The case report helps the reader come to a realization (in the sense of making real) not only of the states of affairs that are believed by constructors [research respondents] to exist but also of the underlying motives, feelings, and rationales leading to those beliefs. The case report is characterized by a thick description that not only clarifies the all-important context, but that makes it possible for the reader vicariously to experience it. (Guba and Lincoln 1989:180–81)

Interpretivist/Constructivist Research Guidelines

Researchers guided by an interpretivist philosophy reject some of the guidelines to which positivist researchers seek to adhere. In fact, there are a wide variety of specific approaches that can be termed "interpretivist," and each has some guidelines that it highlights. For those working within the constructivist perspective, Guba and Lincoln (1989:42) suggest four key steps for researchers, each of which may be repeated many times in a given study:

1. Identify stakeholders and solicit their "claims, concerns, and issues."
2. Introduce the claims, concerns, and issues of each stakeholder group to the other stakeholder groups and ask for their reactions.
3. Focus further information collection on claims, concerns, and issues about which there is disagreement among stakeholder groups.
4. Negotiate with stakeholder groups about the information collected and attempt to reach consensus on the issues about which there is disagreement.

An Interpretivist Research Goal: Creating Change

Some social researchers with an interpretivist or constructivist orientation often reject explicitly the traditional positivist distinction between facts and values (Sjoberg and Nett 1968). Bellah et al. (1985) have instead proposed a model of "social science as public philosophy." In this model, social scientists focus explicit attention on achieving a more just society:

> Social science makes assumptions about the nature of persons, the nature of society, and the relation between persons and society. It also, whether it admits it or not, makes assumptions about good persons and a good society and considers how far these conceptions are embodied in our actual society.

> Social science as public philosophy, by breaking through the iron curtain between the social sciences and the humanities, becomes a form of social self-understanding or self-interpretation. . . . By probing the past as well as the present, by looking at "values" as much as at "facts," such a social science is able to make connections that are not obvious and to ask difficult questions. (p. 301)

Whyte (1991) proposed a more activist approach to research called **participatory action research**. As the name implies, this approach encourages social researchers to get "out of the academic rut" and bring values into the research

Participatory action research A type of research in which the researcher involves some organizational members as active participants throughout the process of studying an organization; the goal is making changes in the organization.

process (p. 285). In participatory action research, the researcher involves as active participants some members of the setting studied. Both the organizational members and the researcher are assumed to want to develop valid conclusions, to bring unique insights, and to desire change, but Whyte (1991) believed these objectives were more likely to be obtained if the researcher collaborated actively with the persons he studied.

An Integrated Philosophy

It is tempting to think of positivism and postpositivism as representing an opposing research philosophy to interpretivism and constructivism. Then it seems that we should choose the one philosophy that seems closest to our own preferences and condemn the other as "unscientific," "uncaring," or perhaps just "unrealistic." But there are good reasons to prefer a research philosophy that integrates some of the differences between these philosophies (Smith 1991).

Society is a product of human action that in turn shapes how people act and think. The "sociology of knowledge" studies this process by which people make themselves as they construct society (Berger and Luckmann 1966). Individuals internalize the social order through the process of socialization, so their own beliefs and actions are not entirely of their own making but instead reflect the social order of which they are a part. This means that we should be very careful to consider how our research approaches and interpretations are shaped by our own social background, just as we are cautioned to do by interpretivist researchers.

When we peer below the surface of standardized research procedures, we also discover the importance of taking into account people's feelings and the meanings that they attach to these feelings. For example, Lavin and Maynard (2001) investigated how different survey research centers handle laughter by respondents during telephone surveys. The dilemma for the centers is this: When respondents laugh during an interview, it usually is an attempt to increase rapport with the interviewer, so turning down the "invitation" to laugh can make the interviewer seem unsympathetic. However, accepting this "invitation" to laugh injects an uncontrolled source of bias into what is supposed to be a standardized interview.

> As interviewers manage laughter in the interview, they artfully maneuver through the dilemma of adhering to standardization protocols while maintaining rapport with respondents that retains participation and continues to elicit answers. (p. 473)

As a result, what appear to be standardized interviews in fact vary in ways that are not apparent in the answers recorded by the interviewer. Recognition of this interpretive process can improve survey research conducted in the positivist tradition. Researchers cannot ignore the subjective aspects of human experience or expunge it entirely from the data collection process. This helps explain why the debate continues between positivist and interpretivist philosophies and why research can often be improved by drawing on insights from both. In the words of Stephen P. Turner (1980), "The distinctive empirical concerns of 'interpretive' and 'statistical' sociologies, usually thought of as antithetical or mutually irrelevant, can be made to mesh" (p. 99).

And what about the important positivist distinction between facts and values in social research? Here, too, there is evidence that neither the "value-free" presumption of positivists nor the constructivist critique of this position is entirely correct. For example, Savelsberg, King, and Cleveland (2002) examined influences on the focus and findings of published criminal justice scholarship. They found that criminal justice research was more likely to be oriented to topics and theories suggested by the state when it was funded by government agencies. This reflects a political influence on scholarship. However, government funding did not have any bearing on the researchers' conclusions about the criminal justice processes they examined. This suggests that scientific procedures can insulate the research process itself from political pressure.

Which philosophy makes the most sense to you? Do you agree with positivists and postpositivists that scientific methods can help us understand the social world as it is, not just as we would like to think it is? Does the interpretivist focus on meanings sound like a good idea? Whatever your answers to these questions, you would probably agree that developing a valid understanding of the social world is not an easy task for social scientists.

As we noted in Chapter 1, many scholars are beginning to advance mixed methods approaches to research that rely on both philosophies. We highlight mixed methods approaches throughout this book, and Chapter 12 focuses exclusively on the relative strengths of single method approaches versus a mixed methods approach. We argue that there is value to both positivist and interpretivist philosophies and that there are good reasons to prefer an integrated philosophy. Researchers influenced by a positivist philosophy should be careful to consider how their own social background shapes their research approaches and interpretations, just as interpretivist researchers caution us to do. Researchers influenced more by an interpretivist philosophy should be careful to ensure that they use rigorous procedures to check the trustworthiness of their interpretations of data (Riessman 2008). If we are not willing to ask hard questions about our research and the evidence we collect, we are not ready to investigate the social world.

Conclusion

The extent to which ethical issues are a problem for researchers and their subjects varies dramatically with the type of research design. Survey research, in particular, creates few ethical problems. In fact, researchers from Michigan's Institute for Social Research Survey Center interviewed a representative national sample of adults and found that 68% of those who had participated in a survey were somewhat or very interested in participating in another; the more times respondents had been interviewed, the more willing they were to participate again. Presumably, they would have felt differently if they had been treated unethically (Reynolds 1979). On the other hand, some experimental studies in the social sciences that have put people in uncomfortable or embarrassing situations have generated vociferous complaints and years of debate about ethics (Reynolds 1979; Sjoberg 1967).

The evaluation of ethical issues in a research project should be based on a realistic assessment of the overall potential for harm and benefit to research subjects rather than an apparent inconsistency between any particular aspect of a research plan and a specific ethical guideline. For example, full disclosure of "what is really going on" in an experimental study is unnecessary if subjects are unlikely to be harmed. Nevertheless, researchers should make every effort to foresee all possible risks and to weigh the possible benefits of the research against these risks. They should consult with individuals with different perspectives to develop a realistic risk-benefit assessment, and they should try to maximize the benefits to, as well as minimize the risks for, subjects of the research (Sieber 1992).

Ultimately, these decisions about ethical procedures are not just up to you, as a researcher, to make. Your university's IRB sets the human subjects' protection standards for your institution and will require that researchers—even, in most cases, students—submit their research proposal to the IRB for review. So we leave you with the instruction to review the human subjects guidelines of the ACJS or other professional association in your field, consult your university's procedures for the conduct of research with human subjects, and then proceed accordingly.

Key Terms

Academy of Criminal Justice Sciences (ACJS), Code of Ethics   54
Belmont Report   52
Beneficence   52
Case report   69
Certificate of Confidentiality   62
Constructivist paradigm   68
Debriefing   59
Federal Policy for the Protection of Human Subjects   53
Hermeneutic circle   68
Institutional review board (IRB)   53

Highlights

- Philip Zimbardo's prison simulation study and Stanley Milgram's obedience experiments led to intensive debate about the extent to which deception could be tolerated in social science research and how harm to subjects should be evaluated.

- Egregious violations of human rights by researchers, including scientists in Nazi Germany and researchers in the Tuskegee syphilis study, led to the adoption of federal ethical standards for research on human subjects.

- The 1979 Belmont Report developed by a national commission established three basic ethical standards for the protection of human subjects: respect for persons, beneficence, and justice.

- The Department of Health and Human Services adopted in 1991 a Federal Policy for the Protection of Human Subjects. This policy requires that every institution seeking federal funding for biomedical or behavioral research on human subjects have an institutional review board to exercise oversight.

- The ACJS standards for the protection of human subjects require avoiding harm, obtaining informed consent, avoiding deception except in limited circumstances, and maintaining privacy and confidentiality.

- Scientific research should maintain high standards for validity and be conducted and reported in an honest and open fashion.

- Effective debriefing of subjects after an experiment can help reduce the risk of harm due to the use of deception in the experiment.

- Positivism is the belief that there is a reality that exists quite apart from one's own perception of it that is amenable to observation.

- Intersubjective agreement is an agreement by different observers on what is happening in the natural or social world.

- Postpositivism is the belief that there is an empirical reality but that our understanding of it is limited by its complexity and by the biases and other limitations of researchers.

- Interpretivism is the belief that reality is socially constructed and the goal of social science should be to understand what meanings people give to that reality.

- The constructivist paradigm emphasizes the importance of exploring and representing the ways in which different stakeholders in a social setting construct their beliefs. Constructivists interact with research subjects to gradually develop a shared perspective on the issue being studied.

Research in the News

Syphilis Experiments in Guatemala

Between 1946 and 1948, the United States experimented with over 1,000 residents of Guatemala to determine the efficacy of drugs like penicillin to treat and prevent syphilis, gonorrhea, and chancres. Unfortunately, the study not only treated infected individuals, but to increase their sample size, the researchers actually infected some individuals. In 2010, these victims sued the U.S. government for the experiment but a U.S. District judge dismissed the lawsuit. The United States has apologized for the experiment, and President Obama has asked the Presidential Commission for the Study of Bioethical Issues to look into details of the research and to assure him that current rules protect people from unethical treatment.

Source: Castillo, Mariana. 2012. "Guatemalans to file appear over STD Experiments." CNN, Friday, June 15. Retrieved June 17, 2012 (http://www.cnn.com/2012/06/15/us/guatemala-std-experiments/index.html).

Exercises

1. Should criminologists be permitted to conduct replications of Zimbardo's prison simulation? Of Milgram's obedience experiments? Can you justify such research as permissible within the current ACJS ethical standards? If not, do you believe that these standards should be altered so as to permit this type of research?

2. How do you evaluate the current ACJS ethical code? Is it too strict, too lenient, or just about right? Are the enforcement provisions adequate? What provisions could be strengthened?

3. Why does unethical research occur? Is it inherent in science? Does it reflect "human nature"? What makes ethical research more or less likely?

4. Does debriefing solve the problem of subject deception? How much must researchers reveal after the experiment is over as well as before it begins?

5. What policy would you recommend that researchers such as Sherman and Berk (1984) follow in reporting the results of their research? Should social scientists try to correct misinformation in the popular press about their research, or should they just focus on what is published in academic journals? Should researchers speak to audiences like police conventions in order to influence policies related to their research results?

6. Investigate the standards and operations of your university's IRB. Interview one IRB member and one researcher whose research has been reviewed by the IRB (after receiving the appropriate permissions!). How well do typical IRB meetings work to identify the ethical issues in proposed research? Do researchers feel that their proposals are treated fairly? Why or why not?

7. Now go to the book's study site at www.sagepub.com/bachman prccj5e and choose the Learning From Journal Articles option. Read one article based on research involving human subjects. What ethical issues did the research pose, and how were they resolved? Does it seem that subjects were appropriately protected?

8. Continue the debate between positivism and interpretivism with an in-class discussion. Be sure to review the guidelines for these research philosophies and the associated goals. You might also consider whether an integrated philosophy is preferable.

9. Outline your own research philosophy. You can base your outline primarily on your reactions to the points you have read in this chapter, but try also to think seriously about which perspective seems more reasonable to you.

Developing a Research Proposal

Now it's time to consider the potential ethical issues in your proposed study and the research philosophy that will guide your research. The following exercises involve very critical "Decisions in Research."

1. List the elements in your research plans that an IRB might consider to be relevant to the protection of human subjects. Rate each element from 1 to 5, where 1 indicates no more than a minor ethical issue and 5 indicates a major ethical problem that probably cannot be resolved.

2. Write one page for the application to the IRB that explains how you will ensure that your research adheres to each relevant ASA standard.

3. Draft a consent form to be administered to your subjects when they enroll in your research. Use underlining and marginal notes to indicate where each standard for informed consent statements is met.

STUDENT STUDY SITE

Log on to the Web-based student study site at **www.sagepub.com/bachmanprccj5e** for additional study tools including eFlashcards, Web quizzes, links to SAGE journal articles, podcasts, videos, data sets and codebooks, Web exercises, Web resources, and additional appendices.

Web Exercises

1. The Collaborative Institutional Training Initiative (CITI) offers an extensive online training course in the basics of human subjects protections issues. Go to the public access CITI site at www.citiprogram.org/rcrpage.asp?affiliation=100 and complete the course in social and behavioral research. Write a short summary of what you have learned.

2. Philip Zimbardo provides extensive documentation about the Stanford Prison Experiment at www.prisonexperiment.org. Read several documents that you find on this Web site and write a short report about them.

3. Read the entire ACJS Code of Ethics at www.acjs.org. Discuss the meaning of each research standard.

4. There are many interesting Web sites that discuss philosophy of science issues. Read the summaries of positivism and interpretivism at www.misq.org/misq/downloads/download/editorial/25/. What do these summaries add to your understanding of these philosophical alternatives?

SPSS or Excel Exercises

1. Access HOMICIDE.POR. Obtain a pie chart for *MURCON*, which is a variable that gives the disposition of a homicide case according to three values: (1) no conviction, (2) a murder conviction, or (3) some other felony conviction. What do you conclude about this sample of homicide cases after analyzing the pie chart for this variable?

2. Using these same data, ask for a bar chart to be made for the variable giving the number of prior arrests the homicide defendant had (*PRIARR*). What do you conclude about the criminal history for this sample of homicide defendants?

3. Access YOUTH.POR. Ask for a frequency distribution for the variable *V63*, which provides information on how often respondents' parents know where they are when they are away from home using the following response options: 1 = never, 2 = sometimes, 3 = usually, 4 = always. You can also ask for a bar chart to be included in the output. What do you conclude about parents' knowledge of the whereabouts of their children from this sample of adolescents?

CHAPTER 4

Conceptualization and Measurement

A June 2009 editorial by the *New York Times* noted that binge drinking by young adults not attending college had significantly declined over a 27-year period, while binge drinking by the same-age cohorts who were attending college had not. This evidence, drawn from the National Survey on Drug Use and Health, appeared to indicate that it was something about attending college that increased the likelihood of binge drinking behavior. Many programs have been initiated to attempt to curtail binge drinking on college campuses. College students spend about $5.5 billion a year on alcohol, which is more than they spend on other beverages and books combined! Alcohol is also related to death; an average of 1,700 college student deaths a year are alcohol related (Brody 2008). But what do these concepts really mean? Some of these concepts—*alcohol, colleges, campuses,* and *programs*—are widely understood and commonly used. However, do we all have the same idea in mind when we hear these terms? For example, are junior colleges classified within the term *college?* Does the concept of *on campus* extend to fraternity houses that are not physically on college property?

Whether your goal is to examine the factors related to criminal offending, to deliver useful services, or to design effective social policies, at some point, you will probably need to read the research literature on substance abuse. Every time you begin to review or design relevant research, you will have to answer two questions: "What is meant by 'substance abuse' in this research?" (which concerns conceptualization) and "How was substance abuse measured?" (which concerns measurement). Both questions must be answered to evaluate the validity of substance abuse research. You cannot make sense of the results of a study until you know how the concepts were defined and measured. Nor are you ready to begin a research project until you have defined your concepts and constructed valid measures of them. Measurement validity is essential to successful research; in fact, without valid measures, it is fruitless to attempt to achieve the other two aspects of validity: causal validity (see Chapter 6) and generalizability (see Chapter 5).

In this chapter, we first address the issue of conceptualization, using substance abuse and related concepts as examples. We also provide examples of the conceptualization process for other terms like *community policing* and *street gangs*. We then focus on measurement, reviewing first how measures of substance abuse have been constructed, using such operations as available data, questions, observations, and less direct and obtrusive measures. Then we explain how to assess the validity and reliability of these measures. The final topic is the level of measurement reflected in different measures. By chapter's end, you should have a good understanding of measurement, the first of the three legs on which a research project's validity rests.

🔲 Concepts

Concepts such as *substance-free housing* require an explicit definition before they are used in research because we cannot be certain that all readers will share the same definition. It is even more important to define concepts that are somewhat abstract or unfamiliar. When we refer to concepts such as *poverty,* or *social control,* or *strain,* we cannot be certain that others know exactly what we mean.

> **Concept** A mental image that summarizes a set of similar observations, feelings, or ideas.

Clarifying the meaning of such **concepts** does not just benefit those unfamiliar with them; even experts often disagree about their meaning. We need not avoid using these concepts; we just have to specify clearly what we mean when we use them, and we must expect others to do the same.

Conceptualization in Practice

If we are to do an adequate job of **conceptualization**, we must do more than just think up some definition, any definition, for our concepts. We may need to distinguish subconcepts, or dimensions, of the concept. We also should ask how the concept's definition fits within the theoretical framework guiding the research and what assumptions underlie this framework.

Defining Youth Gangs

Do you have a clear image in mind when you hear the term *youth gangs*? Although this is a very ordinary term, social scientists' attempts to define precisely the concept, *youth gang*, have not yet succeeded: "Neither gang researchers nor law enforcement agencies can agree on a common definition . . . and a concerted national effort . . . failed to reach a consensus" (Howell 2003:75). Exhibit 4.1 lists a few of the many alternative definitions of youth gangs.

What is the basis of this conceptual difficulty? Howell (2003:27–28) suggests that defining the term *youth gangs* has been difficult for four reasons:

> ***Conceptualization*** The process of specifying what we mean by a term. In deductive research, conceptualization helps translate portions of an abstract theory into testable hypotheses involving specific variables. In inductive research, conceptualization is an important part of the process used to make sense of related observations.

1. Youth gangs are not particularly cohesive.

2. Individual gangs change their focus over time.

3. Many have a "hodgepodge of features," with diverse members and unclear rules.

4. There are many incorrect but popular "myths" about youth gangs.

In addition, youth gangs are only one type of social group, and it is important to define youth gangs in a way that distinguishes them from these other types of groups, for example, childhood play groups, youth subculture groups, delinquent groups, and adult criminal organizations. You can think of *social group* as a broader concept that has multiple dimensions, one of which may be a youth gang. In the same way, you can think of *substance abuse* as a concept with three dimensions: alcohol abuse, drug abuse, and polysubstance abuse. Whenever you define a concept, you need to consider whether the concept is unidimensional or multidimensional. If it is multidimensional, your job of

---

Exhibit 4.1   Alternative Definitions of Youth Gangs

- The term *gang* tends to designate collectivities that are marginal members of mainstream society, loosely organized, and without a clear, social purpose. (Ball and Curry 1995:227)

- The gang is an interstitial group (between childhood and maturity) originally formed spontaneously, and then integrated through conflict. (Thrasher 1927:18)

- [A gang is] any denotable adolescent group of youngsters who a) are generally perceived as a distinct aggregation by others in the neighborhood, b) recognize themselves as a denotable group (almost invariably with a group name), and c) have been involved in a sufficient number of delinquent incidents to call forth a consistently negative response from neighborhood residents and/or law enforcement agencies. (Klein 1971:13)

- A youth gang is a self-formed association of peers united by mutual interests with identifiable leadership and internal organization who act collectively or as individuals to achieve specific purposes, including the conduct of illegal activity and control of a particular territory, facility, or enterprise. (Miller 1992:21)

- [A gang is] an age-graded peer group that exhibits some permanence, engages in criminal activity, and has some symbolic representation of membership. (Decker and Van Winkle 1996:31)

- [A gang is] a self-identified group of kids who act corporately, at least sometimes, and violently, at least sometimes. (Kennedy, Piehl, and Braga 1996:158)

- A Criminal Street Gang is any ongoing organization, association, or group of three or more persons, whether formal or informal, having as one of its primary activities the commission of criminal acts. (Street Terrorism Enforcement and Prevention Act, 1988, California Penal Code sec. 186.22[f])

Source: Based on Howell 2003:76.

conceptualization is not complete until you have specified the related subconcepts that belong under the umbrella of the larger concept. And finally, the concept you define must capture an idea that is distinctly separate from related ideas.

Defining Substance Abuse

What observations or images should we associate with the concept *substance abuse*? Someone leaning against a building with a liquor bottle, barely able to speak coherently? College students drinking heavily at a party and passing out? Someone in an Alcoholics Anonymous group drinking one beer? A 12-year-old boy drinking a small glass of wine in an alley? A 12-year-old boy drinking a small glass of wine at the dinner table in France? Do all these images share something in common that we should define as substance abuse for the purposes of a particular research study? Do some of them? Should we take into account cultural differences? Social situations? Physical tolerance for alcohol? Individual standards?

Many researchers now use the definition of substance abuse contained in the *Diagnostic and Statistical Manual of Mental Disorders (DSM-IV)* of the American Psychiatric Association (1994), as noted by Mueser et al. (1990): "repeated use of a substance to the extent that it interferes with adequate social, vocational, or self-care functioning" (p. 33). In contrast, substance dependence is defined as "development of tolerance to a substance such that the person requires larger dosages to achieve the same psychoactive effect, and the experience of withdrawal symptoms and craving after a period of abstinence from the substance." Note that these definitions rely on behavioral and biological criteria rather than social expectations or cultural norms.

We cannot judge the *DSM-IV* definition of substance abuse as correct or incorrect. Each researcher has the right to conceptualize as he or she sees fit. However, we can say that the *DSM-IV* definition of substance abuse is useful, even good, in part because it has been very widely adopted. If we conceptualize substance abuse in the same way that the *DSM-IV* does, many others will share our definition and understand what we are talking about. This definition of substance abuse has two other attractive features: It is stated in clear and precise language that should minimize differences in interpretation and maximize understanding, and it can clearly be distinguished from the more specific concept of substance dependence.

One caution is in order. The definition of any one concept rests on a shared understanding of the terms used in the definition. So if our audience does not already have a shared understanding of terms such as *adequate social functioning*, *self-care functioning*, and *repeated use*, we must also define these terms before we are finished with the process of defining substance abuse.

Defining Community Policing

Most of us believe that the police are supposed to prevent crime, not just respond to it after it occurs. However, early research demonstrated that there was little difference in rates of crime between jurisdictions where there was a strong police presence in the form of visible patrols and those jurisdictions where there were virtually no patrols (Bayley 1994). In the 1980s, police began to acknowledge the limitations of basic patrols and seek more effective prevention strategies. David Bayley (1994) describes three insights that helped shape the new crime-prevention strategies that emerged: (1) that police could not prevent crime without community help, (2) that police must do more than react to crime, and (3) that simply patrolling an area is too passive. Most people label the crime-prevention efforts that emerged from these insights as "community policing." Unfortunately, there is still a large amount of variation and disagreement among practitioners and researchers alike on what exactly community policing really is. As Bayley describes,

I have heard police describe community policing as being foot patrol, aggressive enforcement of minor ordinances, electronic surveillance of shopping malls, enhanced traffic enforcement, and any police action that instills public confidence. . . . One police chief thought that any contact between the police and the public was community policing. (P. 104)

After examining the evolution of police practices from the common practice of basic patrolling to the new community approaches, Bayley (1994) observed that four elements were common: consultation, adaptation, mobilization, and problem solving. He conceptualized each of these elements as follows:

Consultation: Establishing new mechanisms for discussing police priorities and strategies with their communities.

Adaptation: Because crime and order needs vary from place to place, adaptation involves reshaping command structures so that local police commanders can use resources more flexibly.

Mobilization: Rather than relying on just their own efforts to prevent crime, mobilization involves police developing programs that enlist the active assistance of the public (e.g., Neighborhood Watch groups).

Problem Solving: Instead of simply responding to crimes after they have occurred, problem solving involves police studying conditions that lead to calls for their services, drawing up plans to correct these conditions, and taking the lead in evaluating and implementing remedial actions.

As you can see, community policing involves several different dimensions. There is wide variability in the extent to which police departments have adopted these different dimensions, and the future of community policing, at least in the United States, is unclear. However, in other industrialized countries, including Japan and Singapore, community policing has become entrenched (Bayley 1994).

Defining Poverty

Decisions about how to define a concept reflect the theoretical framework that guides the researchers. For example, the concept *poverty* has always been somewhat controversial, because different notions of what poverty is shape estimates of how prevalent it is and what can be done about it.

Most of the statistics that you see in the newspaper about the poverty rate reflect a conception of poverty that was formalized by Mollie Orshansky of the Social Security Administration in 1965 and subsequently adopted by the federal government and many researchers (Putnam 1977). She defined poverty as an absolute standard, based on the amount of money required to purchase an emergency diet that is estimated to be nutritionally adequate for about 2 months. The idea is that people are truly poor if they can barely purchase the food they need and other essential goods. This poverty standard is adjusted for household size and composition (number of children and adults), and the minimal amount needed for food is multiplied by 3 because a 1955 survey indicated that poor families spend about one third of their incomes on food (Orshansky 1977).

Some social scientists disagree with the absolute standard and have instead urged adoption of a relative poverty standard or income inequality (Blau and Blau 1982). The idea behind this relative conception is that poverty should be defined in terms of what is normal in a given society at a particular time.

Some social scientists prefer yet another conception of poverty. With the subjective approach, poverty is defined as what people think would be the minimal income they need to make ends meet. Of course, many have argued that this approach is influenced too much by the different standards that people use to estimate what they need (Ruggles 1990).

Which do you think is a more reasonable approach to defining poverty: an absolute standard, a relative standard, or a subjective standard? Our understanding of the concept of poverty is sharpened when we consider the theoretical ramifications of these alternative definitions.

Defining Strain

Some concepts have multiple dimensions, bringing together several related concepts under a larger conceptual umbrella. One such concept is strain, defined first by Merton (1938) and later by Cloward and Ohlin (1960). In its simplest form, strain theory contends that delinquency and other forms of criminality and/or deviance are the result of frustrated needs or wants; this frustration is generally believed to result from a breakdown in the relationship between socially induced aspirations or goals and socially approved ways of achieving these goals. According to strain theory, delinquency is a response to actual or anticipated failure to achieve socially induced needs or goals (e.g., status, wealth, power, social acceptance). To determine the relationship between perceived strain and delinquency in a sample of 13- through 19-year-olds from the National Youth Survey, Elliott, Huizinga, and Ageton (1985) conceptualized strain as goal expectation discrepancies in both home and school contexts. For example, strain would be increased at the individual level if being a good student was important to someone but he or she did not perceive that teachers thought of him or her as a good student.

Relying on Merton's (1938) earlier conceptualization, Messner and Rosenfeld (1994) utilized the macro-level analogue of strain called *anomie*. Anomie, in its most general formulation, is defined as a weakening in the normative regulation of behavior. Anomie theory posits that diminished normative regulation results from an overemphasis on cultural goals (e.g., wealth, prestige) relative to the legitimate means to achieve them (e.g., availability of a college education, high-status jobs) or from the differential distribution of opportunities to achieve highly valued goals (some groups in society may not have the same opportunities to achieve these goals as others). According to Messner and Rosenfeld, there are four cultural values within American society that contribute to anomie and therefore to crime in general: achievement, individualism, universalism, and materialism. To fully define anomie, Messner and Rosenfeld thus had to define these concepts. For example, to describe what they meant by the value of materialism, they state,

> In American culture, success is signified in a profoundly significant way: by the accumulation of monetary rewards. Money is awarded special priority in American culture. The point to emphasize here is not that Americans are uniquely materialistic, for a strong interest in material well-being can be found in most societies. Rather, the distinctive feature of American culture is the preeminent role of money as the "metric" of success. Monetary success is inherently open-ended. It is always possible in principle to have more money. Hence, the American Dream offers no final stopping point. It requires never-ending achievement. The pressure to accumulate money is therefore relentless, which entices people to pursue their monetary goals by any means necessary. (p. 71)

Concepts and Variables

After defining the concepts in a theory, we can identify variables corresponding to the concepts and develop procedures to measure them. Recall that a variable is a characteristic or property that can vary (e.g., religion, alcohol use, victimization). This is an important step. Consider the concept of social control, which Donald Black (1984) defines as all of the processes by which people define and respond to deviant behavior. What variables do you think represent this conceptualization of social control? Proportion of persons arrested in a community? Average length of sentences for crimes? Types of bystander reactions to public intoxication? Some combination of these?

Although we must proceed carefully to specify what we mean by a concept like social control, some concepts are represented well by the specific variables in the study and need not be defined so carefully. We may define binge drinking as heavy episodic drinking and measure it, as a variable, by asking people how many drinks they consumed in succession during some period (see Wechsler et al. 1994). That is pretty straightforward.

Be aware that not every concept in a study is represented by a variable. For example, if the term *tolerance of drinking* is defined as the absence of rules against drinking in a fraternity, it brings to mind a phenomenon that varies across different fraternities at different colleges. But if we study social life at only those fraternities that prohibit drinking, tolerance of drinking would not be a variable: In this hypothetical study, all the fraternities in the sample have the same level of tolerance, and thus tolerance of drinking is a constant and not a variable. Of course, the concept of tolerance of drinking would still be important for understanding social life in the "dry" fraternities.

⊡ Measurement Operations

After we have defined our concepts in the abstract—that is, after conceptualizing—and after we have identified the specific variables we want to measure, we must develop our measurement procedures. The goal is to devise **operations** that actually measure the concepts we intend to measure—in other words, to achieve measurement validity.

Exhibit 4.2 represents the **operationalization** process in three studies. The first researcher defines her concept (binge drinking) and chooses one variable (frequency of heavy episodic drinking) to represent it. This variable is then measured with responses to a single question, or indicator: "How often within the past 2 weeks did you consume 5 or more drinks containing alcohol in a row?" The second researcher defines her concept,

> **Operation** The procedure for actually measuring the concepts we intend to measure, identifying the value of a variable for each case.
>
> **Operationalization** The process of specifying the operations that will indicate the value of a variable for each case.
>
> **Indicator** The question or other operation used to indicate the value of cases on a variable.

poverty, as having two aspects or dimensions, subjective poverty and absolute poverty. Subjective poverty is measured with responses to a survey question: "Would you say you are poor?" Absolute poverty is measured by comparing family income to the poverty threshold. The third researcher decides that her concept, social class, can be indicated with three measured variables: income, education, and occupational prestige. The values of these three variables for each case studied are then combined into a single **indicator**.

Good conceptualization and operationalization can prevent confusion later in the research process. For example, a researcher may find that substance abusers who join a self-help group are less likely to drink again than those who receive hospital-based substance abuse treatment. But what is it about these treatment alternatives that is associated with successful abstinence? Level of peer support? Beliefs about the causes of alcoholism? Financial investment in the treatment? If the researcher had considered such aspects of the concept of substance abuse treatment before collecting her data, she might have been able to measure different elements of treatment and then identify which, if any, were associated with differences in abstinence rates. Because she did not measure these variables, she will not contribute as much as she might have to our understanding of substance abuse treatment.

Social researchers have many options for operationalizing their concepts. Measures can be based on activities as diverse as asking people questions, reading judicial opinions, observing social interactions, coding words in books,

---

Exhibit 4.2	Concepts, Variables, and Indicators	
Concepts	*Variables*	*Indicators*
Binge drinking	Frequency of heavy episodic drinking	"How often within the past 2 weeks did you consume 5 or more drinks containing alcohol in a row?"
Poverty	Subjective poverty	"Would you say you are poor?"
	Absolute poverty	Family income below Soc ial Security Administration poverty threshold
Social class	Income	Income + education + prestige
	Education	
	Occupational prestige	

checking census data, enumerating the contents of trash receptacles, or drawing urine and blood samples. We focus here on the operations of using published data, asking questions, observing behavior, and using unobtrusive means of measuring people's behavior and attitudes.

Using Available Data

Government reports are rich and readily accessible sources of criminal justice data, as are data sets available from nonprofit advocacy groups, university researchers, and some private businesses. For example, law-enforcement and health statistics provide several community-level indicators of substance abuse (Gruenewald et al. 1997). Statistics on arrests for the sale and possession of drugs, drunk driving arrests, and liquor law violations (such as sales to minors) can usually be obtained on an annual basis, and often quarterly, from local police departments or state crime information centers.

Still, indicators like these cannot be compared across communities or over time without reviewing carefully how they were constructed in each community. The level of alcohol in the blood that is legally required to establish intoxication can vary among communities, creating the appearance of different rates of substance abuse even though drinking and driving practices may be identical. Enforcement practices can vary among police jurisdictions and over time (Gruenewald et al. 1997). We also cannot assume that available data are accurate, even when they appear to measure the concept in which we are interested in a way that is consistent across communities. "Official" counts of homeless persons have been notoriously unreliable because of the difficulty of locating homeless persons on the streets, and government agencies have, at times, resorted to "guesstimates" by service providers (Rossi 1989). Even available data for such seemingly straightforward measures as cause of death can contain a surprising amount of error. For example, between 30% and 40% of death certificates incorrectly identify the cause of death (Altman 1998).

Government statistics that are generated through a central agency like the U.S. Bureau of the Census are often of high quality, but caution is warranted when using official data collected by local levels of government. For example, the Uniform Crime Reports (UCR) program administered by the Federal Bureau of Investigation (FBI) imposes standard classification criteria, with explicit guidelines and regular training at the local level, but data are still inconsistent for many crimes. Consider only a few of the many sources of inconsistency between jurisdictions: variation in the classification of forcible rape cases due to differences in what is considered to be "carnal knowledge of a female"; different decisions about what is considered "more than necessary force" in the definition of "strong-arm" robberies; and whether offenses in which threats were made but no physical injury occurred are classified as aggravated or simple assaults (Mosher, Miethe, and Phillips 2002:66). A new National Incident-Based Reporting System (NIBRS) corrects some of the problems with the UCR, but it requires much more training and documentation and has not yet been widely used (Mosher et al.). Moreover, as we learned in Chapter 1, both of these systems rely on victims to report their experiences to police in order to be counted.

In some cases, problems with an available indicator can be lessened by selecting a more precise indicator. For example, the number of single-vehicle nighttime crashes, whether fatal or not, is a more specific indicator of the frequency of drinking and driving than just the number of single-vehicle fatal accidents (Gruenewald et al. 1997). Focusing on a different level of aggregation may also improve data quality, because procedures for data collection may differ among cities, counties, states, and so on (Gruenewald et al. 1997:40–41). It is only after such factors as legal standards, enforcement practices, and measurement procedures have been taken into account that comparisons among communities become credible.

Constructing Questions

Asking people questions is the most common and probably the most versatile operation for measuring social variables. Most concepts about individuals can be defined in such a way that measurement with one or more questions becomes an option. In this section, we introduce some options for writing single questions; in Chapter 8, we explain why single questions can be inadequate measures of some concepts, and then we examine approaches that rely on multiple questions to measure a concept.

Measuring variables with single questions is very popular. Public opinion polls based on answers to single questions are reported frequently in newspaper articles and TV newscasts: "Do you favor or oppose U.S. policy in . . . ?" "If you had to vote today, for which candidate would you vote?" Criminal justice surveys also rely on single questions to measure many variables: "Overall, how satisfied are you with the police in your community?" "How would you rate your current level of safety?"

Single questions can be designed with or without explicit response choices. The question that follows is a **closed-ended (fixed-choice) question** because respondents are offered explicit responses to choose from. It has been selected from the Core Alcohol and Drug Survey distributed by the Core Institute (1994) at Southern Illinois University for the Fund for the Improvement of Postsecondary Education (FIPSE) Core Analysis Grantee Group (Presley, Meilman, and Lyerla 1994).

Compared to other campuses with which you are familiar, this campus's use of alcohol is . . . (*Mark one*)

_____ Greater than [that of] other campuses

_____ Less than [that of] other campuses

_____ About the same as [that of] other campuses

> **Closed-ended (fixed-choice) questions** Survey questions providing preformulated response choices for the respondent to circle or check.

Response choices should be mutually exclusive and exhaustive so that every respondent can find one and only one choice that applies to him or her (unless the question is of the "check all that apply" format). To make response choices exhaustive, researchers may need to offer at least one option with room for ambiguity. For example, a questionnaire asking college students to indicate their school status should not use *freshman, sophomore, junior, senior*, and *graduate student* as the only response choices. Most campuses also have students in a "special" category, so you might add *other (please specify)* to the five fixed responses to this question. If respondents do not find a response option that corresponds to their answer to the question, they may skip the question entirely or choose a response option that does not indicate what they are really thinking.

Most surveys of a large number of people contain primarily fixed-choice questions, which are easy to process with computers and analyze with statistics. With fixed-choice questions, respondents are also more likely to answer the question that the researcher really wants them to answer. Including response choices reduces ambiguity and makes it easier for respondents to answer. However, fixed-response choices can obscure what people really think if the choices do not match the range of possible responses to the question; many studies show that some respondents will choose response choices that do not apply to them simply to give some sort of answer (Peterson 2000). We will discuss question wording and response options in greater detail in Chapter 8.

Open-ended questions—namely, questions that have not previously been used in surveys, questions that are asked of new groups, and questions without explicit response choices, to which respondents write in their answers—are preferable when the range of responses cannot adequately be anticipated. Open-ended questions can also lessen confusion about the meaning of responses involving complex concepts. The next question is an open-ended version of the earlier fixed-choice question:

How would you say alcohol use on this campus compares to that on other campuses?

> **Open-ended questions** Survey questions to which the respondent replies in his or her own words, either by writing or by talking.

Making Observations

Observations can be used to measure characteristics of individuals, events, and places. The observations may be the primary form of measurement in a study, or they may supplement measures obtained through questioning.

Systemic social observation (SSO) A careful method of observing phenomena.

Reiss (1971) developed a careful method of observing phenomena that he termed **systematic social observation (SSO)**. In his study of police interaction with the public, Reiss's SSO method involved riding in police squad cars, observing police-citizen interactions, and recording features of these characteristics on a form.

Robert J. Sampson and Stephen W. Raudenbush (1999) and St. Jean (2007) used direct observation (and other techniques) in their studies of neighborhood disorder and crime, in addition to SSO. Teams drove in "a sport utility vehicle at a rate of 5 miles per hour down every street" in a sample of Chicago neighborhoods. On both sides of the vehicle, video cameras recorded activities while a trained observer completed a log for each block. Sampson and Raudenbush's research (1999) resulted in 23,816 observer logs containing information about building conditions and land use, while the videotapes were coded to measure features of streets, buildings, businesses, and social interaction on 15,141 blocks. Direct observation is often the method of choice for measuring behavior in natural settings, as long as it is possible to make the requisite observations.

Collecting Unobtrusive Measures

Unobtrusive measures allow us to collect data about individuals or groups without their direct knowledge or participation. In their classic book (now revised), Webb et al. ([1966] 2000) identified four types of unobtrusive measures:

Unobtrusive measures Measures that allow researchers to collect data about individuals or groups without their direct knowledge or participation.

physical trace evidence, archives (available data), simple observation, and contrived observation (using hidden recording hardware or manipulation to elicit a response). Let us consider the first two types in more detail: physical trace evidence and archives.

The physical traces of past behavior are one type of unobtrusive measure that is most useful when the behavior of interest cannot be directly observed (perhaps because it is hidden or occurred in the past) and has not been recorded in a source of available data. To measure the prevalence of drinking in college dorms or fraternity houses, we might count the number of empty bottles of alcoholic beverages in the surrounding Dumpsters. However, you can probably see that care must be taken to develop trace measures that are useful for comparative purposes. For instance, comparison of the number of empty bottles in Dumpsters outside different dorms can be misleading; at the very least, you would need to take into account the number of residents in the dorms, the time since the last trash collection, and the accessibility of each Dumpster to passersby.

Unobtrusive measures can also be created from such diverse forms of media as newspaper archives or magazine articles, TV or radio talk shows, legal opinions, historical documents, personal letters, or e-mail messages. An investigation of the drinking climate on campuses might include a count of the amount of space devoted to ads for alcoholic beverages in a sample of issues of the student newspaper. Campus publications also might be coded to indicate the number of times that statements discouraging substance abuse appear. With this tool, you could measure the frequency of articles reporting substance abuse-related crimes, the degree of approval of drinking expressed in TV shows or songs, or the relationship between region of the country and amount of space devoted in the print media to alcohol consumption.

Combining Measurement Operations

Using available data, asking questions, making observations, and using unobtrusive indicators are interrelated measurement tools, each of which may include or be supplemented by the others. From people's answers to survey questions, the U.S. Bureau of the Census develops widely consulted reports containing available data on people, firms, and geographic units in the United States. Data from employee surveys may be supplemented by information available in company records. Interviewers may record observations about those whom they question. Researchers may use insights gleaned from questioning participants to make sense of the social interaction they have observed. Unobtrusive indicators can be used to evaluate the honesty of survey responses.

Questioning can be a particularly poor approach for measuring behaviors that are very socially desirable, such as voting or attending church, or that are socially stigmatized or illegal, such as abusing alcohol or drugs. **Triangulation,** the use of two or more different measures of the same variable, can strengthen measurement considerably (Brewer and Hunter 1989). When we achieve similar results with different measures of the same variable, particularly when they are based on such different methods as survey questions and field-based observations, we can be more confident in the validity of each measure. If results diverge with different measures, it may indicate that one or more of these measures are influenced by more measurement error than we can tolerate. Divergence between measures could also indicate that they actually operationalize different concepts. An interesting example of this interpretation of divergent results comes from research on crime. Official crime statistics only indicate those crimes that are reported to and recorded by the police; when surveys are used to measure crimes with self-reports of victims, many "personal annoyances" are included as if they were crimes (Levine 1976). We will talk more about triangulation in Chapter 10.

> **Triangulation** The use of multiple methods to study one research question. Also used to mean the use of two or more different measures of the same variable.

▣ Did We Measure What We Wanted to Measure?

Do the operations developed to measure our concepts actually do so? Are they valid? If we have weighed our measurement options, carefully constructed our questions and observational procedures, and carefully selected indicators from the available data, we should be on the right track. We cannot have much confidence in a measure until we have empirically evaluated its validity. Additionally, we must also evaluate its reliability (consistency).

Measurement Validity

We can consider **measurement validity** the first concern in establishing the validity of research results, because without having measured what we think we measured, we really do not know what we are talking about.

As an example of measurement validity, consider the following question: "How prevalent is youth violence and delinquency in the United States; how many juveniles are involved in delinquency?" Data on the extent of juvenile delinquency come from two primary sources: official statistics and unofficial statistics. Official statistics are based on the aggregate records of juvenile offenders and offenses processed by agencies of the criminal justice system: police, courts, and corrections. One primary source of official statistics on juvenile delinquency is the UCR, produced by the FBI. Unofficial statistics are data produced by people or agencies outside the criminal justice system such as victimization surveys and self-report studies. The validity of official statistics for measuring the extent of juvenile delinquency is a heated debate among criminologists. Although some researchers believe official reports are a valid measure of serious delinquency, others contend that UCR data say more about the behavior of the police than about delinquency. These criminologists think the police are predisposed against certain groups of people or certain types of crimes.

Unquestionably, official reports underestimate the actual amount of delinquency because a great deal of delinquent behavior never comes to the attention of police (Mosher et al. 2002). Sometimes delinquent acts are committed and not observed, or they are observed and not reported. There is also evidence that the UCRs often reflect the political climate and police policies as much as they do criminal activity. Take the United States' "War on Drugs," which heated up in the 1980s. During this time, arrest rates for drug offenses soared, giving the illusion that drug use was increasing at an epidemic pace. However, self-report surveys that asked citizens directly about their drug use behavior during this

> **Measurement validity** The type of validity that is achieved when a measure measures what it is presumed to measure.

time period found that use of most illicit drugs was actually declining (Regoli and Hewitt 1994). In your opinion, then, which measure of drug use, the UCR or self-report surveys, was more valid? Before you answer this question, let us continue with the delinquency example.

Despite the limitations of official statistics for measuring delinquency, these data were relied on by criminologists and used as a valid measure of the prevalence of delinquency for many decades. As such, delinquency and other violent offenses were thought to primarily involve minority populations and/or disadvantaged youth. In 1947, however, Wallerstein and Wyle surveyed a sample of 700 juveniles and found that 91% admitted to having committed at least one offense that was punishable by 1 or more years in prison, and 99% admitted to at least one offense for which they could have been arrested had they been caught. Short and Nye (1957–1958) reported the results from the first large-scale self-report study involving juveniles from a variety of locations. In their research, Short and Nye concluded that delinquency was widespread throughout the adolescent population and that youth from high-income families were just as likely to engage in delinquency as youth from low-income families. Contemporary studies using self-report data from the National Youth Survey indicate that the actual amount of delinquency is much greater than that reported by the UCR and that unlike these official data, where nonwhites are overrepresented, self-report data indicate that white juveniles report nearly the identical number of delinquencies as nonwhites, but fewer of them are arrested (Elliott and Ageton 1980). This is just one example of measurement validity and should convince you that we must be very careful in designing our measures and in subsequently evaluating how well they have performed.

The extent to which measures indicate what they are intended to measure can be assessed with one or more of four basic approaches: face validation, content validation, criterion validation, and construct validation. Whatever the approach to validation, no one measure will be valid for all times and places. For example, the validity of self-report measures of substance abuse varies with such factors as whether the respondents are sober or intoxicated at the time of the interview, whether the measure refers to recent or lifetime abuse, and whether the respondents see their responses as affecting their chances at receiving housing, treatment, or some other desired outcome (Babor, Stephens, and Marlatt 1987). In addition, persons with severe mental illness are, in general, less likely to respond accurately (Corse, Hirschinger, and Zanis 1995). These types of possibilities should always be considered when evaluating measurement validity.

Face Validity

Researchers apply the term **face validity** to the confidence gained from careful inspection of a concept to see if it is appropriate "on its face," simply whether it appears to measure what it intends. For example, if college students' alcohol consumptions is what we are trying to measure, asking for student's favorite color seems unlikely on its face to tell us much about their drinking patterns. A measure with greater face validity would be a count of how many drinks they have consumed in the past week.

> **Face validity** The type of validity that exists when an inspection of the items used to measure a concept suggests that they are appropriate "on their face."

Although every measure should be inspected in this way, face validation, on its own, is not the gold standard of measurement validity. The question "How much beer or wine did you have to drink last week?" may look valid on its face as a measure of frequency of drinking, but people who drink heavily tend to underreport the amount they drink. So the question would be an invalid measure in a study that includes heavy drinkers.

Content Validity

> **Content validity** The type of validity that establishes a measure covers the full range of the concept's meaning.

Content validity establishes that the measure covers the full range of the concept's meaning. To determine that range of meaning, the researcher may solicit the opinions of experts and review literature that identifies the different aspects of the concept.

An example of a measure that covers a wide range of meaning is the Michigan Alcoholism Screening Test (MAST). The MAST includes 24 questions representing the following subscales: recognition of alcohol problems by self and others; legal, social, and work problems; help seeking; marital and family difficulties; and liver pathology (Skinner and Sheu 1982). Many experts familiar with the direct consequences of substance abuse agree that these dimensions capture the full range of possibilities. Thus, the MAST is believed to be valid from the standpoint of content validity.

Criterion Validity

Consider the following scenario: when people drink an alcoholic beverage, the alcohol is absorbed into their blood and then gradually metabolized (broken down into other chemicals) in their liver (National Institute on Alcohol Abuse and Alcoholism [NIAAA] 1997). The alcohol that remains in their blood at any point, unmetabolized, impairs both thinking and behavior (NIAAA 1994). As more alcohol is ingested, cognitive and behavioral consequences multiply. These biological processes can be identified with direct measures of alcohol concentration in the blood, urine, or breath. Questions about alcohol consumption, on the other hand, can be viewed as attempts to measure indirectly what biochemical tests measure directly.

Criterion validity is established when the scores obtained on one measure can be accurately compared to those obtained with a more direct or already validated measure of the same phenomenon (the criterion). A measure of blood-alcohol concentration or a urine test could serve as the criterion for validating a self-report measure of drinking, as long as the questions we ask about drinking refer to the same period. Observations of substance use by friends or relatives could also, in some circumstances, serve as a criterion for validating self-report substance use measures.

Criterion validation studies of substance abuse measures have yielded inconsistent results. Self-reports of drug use agreed with urinalysis results for about 85% of the drug users who volunteered for a health study in several cities (Weatherby et al. 1994). On the other hand, the posttreatment drinking behavior self-reported by 100 male alcoholics was substantially less than the drinking behavior observed by the alcoholics' friends or relatives (Watson et al. 1984). Such inconsistent findings can occur because of differences in the adequacy of measures across settings and populations. This underscores our point that you cannot assume that a measure that was validated in one study is also valid in another setting or with a different population.

An attempt at criterion validation is well worth the effort because it greatly increases confidence that the measure is actually measuring the concept of interest—the criterion validity basically offers evidence. However, often no other variable might reasonably be considered a criterion for individual feelings or beliefs or other subjective states. Even with variables for which a reasonable criterion exists, the researcher may not be able to gain access to the criterion, as would be the case with a tax return or employer document as a criterion for self-reported income.

> ***Criterion validity*** The type of validity that is established by comparing the scores obtained on the measure being validated to those obtained with a more direct or already validated measure of the same phenomenon (the criterion).

Construct Validity

Measurement validity also can be established by showing that a measure is related to a variety of other measures as specified in a theory. This validation approach, known as **construct validity**, is commonly used in social research when no clear criterion exists for validation purposes. For example, in one study of the validity of the Addiction Severity Index (ASI), McLellan and his colleagues (1985) compared subject scores on the ASI to a number of indicators that they felt from prior research should be related to substance abuse: medical problems, employment problems, legal problems, family problems, and psychiatric problems. They could not use a criterion validation approach because they did not have a more direct measure of abuse, such as laboratory test scores or observer reports. However, their extensive research on the subject had given them confidence that these sorts of other problems

> ***Construct validity*** The type of validity that is established by showing that a measure is related to other measures as specified in a theory.

were all related to substance abuse, and thus their measures seemed to be valid from the standpoint of construct validity. Indeed, the researchers found that individuals with higher ASI ratings tended to have more problems in each of these areas, giving us more confidence in the ASI's validity as a measure.

A somewhat different approach to construct validation is termed **discriminant validity**. In this approach, scores on the measure to be validated are compared to scores on another measure of the same variable and to scores on variables that measure different but related concepts. Discriminant validity is achieved if the measure to be validated is related most strongly to its comparison measure and less to the measures of other concepts. McLellan et al. (1985) found that the ASI passed this test, too: The ASI's measures of alcohol and drug problems were related more strongly to other measures of alcohol and drug problems than they were to measures of legal problems, family problems, medical problems, and the like.

> ***Discriminant validity*** An approach to construct validation; scores on the measure to be validated are compared to scores on another measure of the same variable and to scores on variables that measure different but related concepts. Discriminant validity is achieved if the measure to be validated is related most strongly to its comparison measure and less so to the measures of other concepts.

The distinction between criterion and construct validation is not always clear. Opinions can differ about whether a particular indicator is indeed a criterion for the concept that is to be measured. For example, if you need to validate a question-based measure of sales ability for applicants to a sales position, few would object to using actual sales performance as a criterion. But what if you want to validate a question-based measure of the amount of social support that people receive from their friends? Should you just ask people about the social support they have received? Could friends' reports of the amount of support they provided serve as a criterion? Are verbal accounts of the amount of support provided adequate? What about observations of social support that people receive? Even if you could observe people in the act of counseling or otherwise supporting their friends, can an observer be sure that the interaction is indeed supportive? There isn't really a criterion here, just related concepts that could be used in a construct validation strategy. Even biochemical measures of substance abuse are questionable as criteria for validating self-reported substance use. Urine test results can be altered by ingesting certain substances, and blood tests vary in their sensitivity to the presence of drugs over a particular period of time.

What construct and criterion validation have in common is the comparison of scores on one measure to scores on other measures that are predicted to be related. It is not so important that researchers agree that a particular comparison measure is a criterion rather than a related construct. But it is very important to think critically about the quality of the comparison measure and whether it actually represents a different measure of the same phenomenon. For example, it is only a weak indication of measurement validity to find that scores on a new self-report measure of alcohol use are associated with scores on a previously used self-report measure of alcohol use.

Reliability

> ***Reliability*** A measure is reliable when it yields consistent scores or observations of a given phenomenon on different occasions. Reliability is a prerequisite for measurement validity.

Reliability means that a measurement procedure yields consistent scores as long as the phenomenon being measured is not changing. For example, if we gave students a survey with the same questions asking them about their alcohol consumption, the measure would be reliable if the same students gave approximately the same answers 6 months later (assuming their drinking patterns had not changed much). If a measure is reliable, it is affected less by random error, or chance variation, than if it is unreliable. Reliability is a prerequisite for measurement validity; we cannot really measure a phenomenon if the measure we are using gives inconsistent results.

There are four possible methods for measuring the reliability of a measure: test-retest reliability, interitem reliability, alternate-forms reliability, and interobserver reliability.

Test-Retest Reliability

When researchers measure a phenomenon that does not change between two points separated by an interval of time, the degree to which the two measurements yield comparable, if not identical, values is the **test-retest reliability** of the measure. If you take a test of your math ability and then retake the test 2 months later, the test is performing reliably if you receive a similar score both times, presuming that nothing happened during the 2 months to change your math ability. Of course, if events between the test and the retest have changed the variable being measured, then the difference between the test and retest scores should reflect that change.

> **Test-retest reliability** A measurement showing that measures of a phenomenon at two points in time are highly correlated, if the phenomenon has not changed, or have changed only as much as the phenomenon itself.

One example of how test-retest reliability may be assessed is a study by Sobell et al. (1988) of alcohol abusers' past drinking behavior (using the Lifetime Drinking History questionnaire) and life changes (using the Recent Life Changes questionnaire). All 69 subjects in the study were patients in an addiction treatment program. They had not been drinking prior to the interview (determined by a breath test). The two questionnaires were administered by different interviewers about 2 or 3 weeks apart, both times asking the subjects to recall events 8 years prior to the interviews. Reliability was high: 92% of the subjects reported the same life events both times, and at least 81% of the subjects were classified consistently at both interviews as having had an alcohol problem or not. When asked about their inconsistent answers, subjects reported that in the earlier interview they had simply dated an event incorrectly, misunderstood the question, evaluated the importance of an event differently, or forgotten an event. Answers to past drinking questions were less reliable when they were very specific, apparently because the questions exceeded subjects' capacities to remember accurately.

Interitem Reliability (Internal Consistency)

When researchers use multiple items to measure a single concept, they are concerned with **interitem reliability** (or internal consistency). For example, if we are to have confidence that a set of questions (such as those in Exhibit 4.3) reliably measures attitudes toward violence, the answers to the questions should be highly associated with one another. The stronger the association among the individual items, and the more items that are included, the higher the reliability of the index.

> **Interitem reliability** An approach that calculates reliability based on the correlation among multiple items used to measure a single concept.

Exhibit 4.3	Questions Used in the Violent Defensive Values Index

Would you approve of a man punching a stranger who had hit the man's child after the child accidentally damaged the stranger's car?

_____ No (0)

_____ I don't know or not sure (1)

_____ Yes (2)

Would you approve of a man punching a stranger who was beating up a woman and the man saw it?

_____ No (0)

_____ I don't know or not sure (1)

_____ Yes (2)

Would you approve of a man punching a stranger who had broken into the man's house?

_____ No (0)

_____ I don't know or not sure (1)

_____ Yes (2)

Source: Cao, Adams, and Jensen 1997.

Alternate-forms reliability A procedure for testing the reliability of responses to survey questions in which subjects' answers are compared after the subjects have been asked slightly different versions of the questions or when randomly selected halves of the sample have been administered slightly different versions of the questions.

Split-halves reliability Reliability achieved when responses to the same questions by two randomly selected halves of a sample are about the same.

Intraobserver reliability (intrarater reliability) Consistency of ratings by an observer of an unchanging phenomenon at two or more points in time.

Interobserver reliability When similar measurements are obtained by different observers rating the same persons, events, or places.

Alternate-Forms Reliability

Researchers are testing **alternate-forms reliability** when they compare subjects' answers to slightly different versions of survey questions (Litwin 1995). A researcher may reverse the order of the response choices in an index or modify the question wording in minor ways and then readminister that index to subjects. If the two sets of responses are not too different, alternate-forms reliability is established.

A related test of reliability is the **split-halves reliability** approach. A survey sample is divided in two by flipping a coin or using some other random assignment method. These two halves of the sample are then administered the two forms of the questions. If the responses of the two halves of the sample are about the same, the measurer's reliability is established.

Intraobserver and Interobserver Reliability

When ratings by an observer, rather than ratings by the subjects themselves, are being assessed at two or more points in time, test-retest reliability is termed **intraobserver reliability** or **intrarater reliability**. Let's say a researcher observes a grade school cafeteria for signs of bullying behavior on multiple days. If her observations captured the same degree of bullying on every Friday, it can be said that her observations were reliable. When researchers use more than one observer to rate the same persons, events, or places, **interobserver reliability** is their goal. If observers are using the same instrument to rate the same thing, their ratings should be very similar. In this case, the researcher interested in cafeteria bullying would use more than one observer. If the measurement of bullying is similar across the observers, we can have much more confidence that the ratings reflect the actual degree of bullying behavior.

Ways to Improve Reliability and Validity

We must always assess the reliability of a measure if we hope to be able to establish its validity. Remember that a reliable measure is not necessarily a valid measure, as Exhibit 4.4 illustrates. This discrepancy is a common flaw of self-report measures of substance abuse. The multiple questions in self-report indexes of substance abuse are answered by most respondents in a consistent way, so the indexes are reliable. However, a number of respondents will not admit to drinking, even though they drink a lot. Their answers to the questions are consistent, but they are consistently misleading. So the indexes based on self-report are reliable but invalid. Such indexes are not useful and should be improved or discarded. Unfortunately, many measures are judged to be worthwhile on the basis only of a reliability test.

The reliability and validity of measures in any study must be tested after the fact to assess the quality of the information obtained. But then if it turns out that a measure cannot be considered reliable and valid, little can be done to save the study. Hence it is supremely important to select in the first place measures that are likely to be reliable and valid. In studies that use interviewers or observers, careful training is often essential to achieving a consistent approach. In most cases, however, the best strategy is to use measures that have been used before and whose reliability and validity have been established in other contexts. Know that the selection of "tried and true" measures still does not absolve researchers from the responsibility of testing the reliability and validity of the measure in their own studies.

| Exhibit 4.4 | The Difference Between Reliability and Validity: Drinking Behavior |

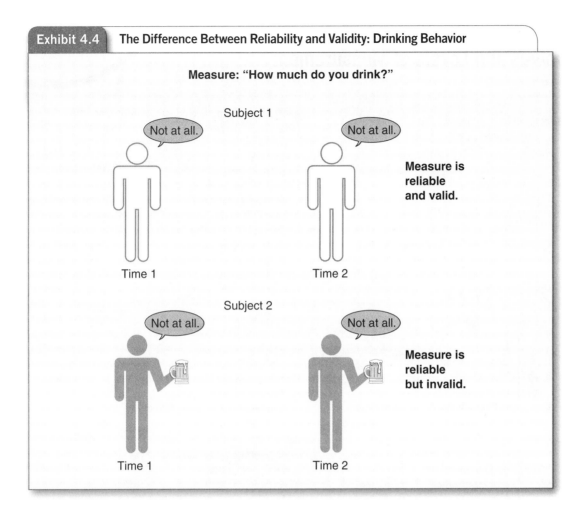

The process of evaluating the reliability and validity of measures about individuals is termed **psychometrics**. Measures of individuals that range from tests you take in school to personality assessments you complete on the job are advertised as "psychometrically valid" after multiple studies have demonstrated their reliability and validity. The process of evaluating the reliability and validity of measures about organizations, neighborhoods, or other collective units is termed **ecometrics**, a term coined by Raudenbush and Sampson (1999). For example, Raudenbush and Sampson's ecometric evaluation of their observational measures of Chicago neighborhoods included a test of the consistency of ratings by multiple observers of the same neighborhoods.

Psychometrics The process of evaluating the reliability and validity of measures about individuals.

Ecometrics The process of evaluating the reliability and validity of measures about organizations, neighborhoods, or other collective units.

It may be possible to improve the reliability and validity of measures in a study that already has been conducted if multiple measures were used. For example, in a study of housing for homeless mentally ill persons, residents' substance abuse was assessed with several different sets of direct questions as well as with reports from subjects' case managers and others (Goldfinger et al. 1996). It was discovered that the observational reports were often inconsistent with self-reports and that different self-report measures were not always in agreement and were thus unreliable. A more reliable measure of substance abuse was initial reports of lifetime substance abuse problems. This measure was extremely accurate in identifying all those who subsequently abused substances during the project.

🔲 Variables and Levels of Measurement

Level of measurement The complexity of the mathematical means that can be used to express the relationship between a variable's values. The nominal level of measurement, which is qualitative, has no mathematical interpretation; the quantitative levels of measurement (ordinal, interval, and ratio) are progressively more complex mathematically.

Whether we collect information through observations, questions, available data, or using unobtrusive measures, the data that result from our particular procedures may vary in mathematical precision. We express this level of precision as the variable's **level of measurement**. A variable's level of measurement also has important implications for the types of statistics that can be used with the variable, as you will learn in Chapter 13. There are four levels of measurement: nominal, ordinal, interval, and ratio. Exhibit 4.5 depicts the differences among these four levels.

Exhibit 4.5   Levels of Measurement

Nominal Level of Measurement

The **nominal level of measurement** (also called the categorical or qualitative level) identifies variables whose values have no mathematical interpretation; they only vary in kind or quality but not in amount. In fact, it is conventional to refer to the values of nominal variables as attributes instead of values. Gender is one example. The variable "gender" has two attributes (or categories or qualities): male and female. We might indicate male with the value 1 and female with the value 2, but these numbers do not tell us anything about the difference between male and female except that they are different. Female is not one unit more of "gender" than male, nor is it twice as much "gender."

> **Nominal level of measurement** Variables whose values have no mathematical interpretation; they vary in kind or quality but not in amount.

Ethnicity, occupation, religious affiliation, and region of the country are also measured at the nominal level. A person may be Spanish or Portuguese, but one ethnic group does not represent more ethnicity than another, just a different ethnicity. A person may be a doctor (arbitrarily valued as 5) or a truck driver (arbitrarily labeled 7), but one does not represent three units more occupation than the other. The values assigned to nominal variables should be thought of as codes, not numbers.

Although the attributes of categorical variables do not have a mathematical meaning, they must be assigned to cases with great care. The attributes we use to measure, or categorize, cases must be mutually exclusive and exhaustive:

- A variable's attributes or values are **mutually exclusive attributes** if every case can have only one attribute.

- A variable's attributes or values are **exhaustive attributes** when every case can be classified into one of the categories.

When a variable's attributes are mutually exclusive and exhaustive, every case corresponds to one, and only one, attribute. Imagine the challenge of coming up with an exhaustive set of attributes when a variable with a large number of attributes is being studied.

> **Mutually exclusive attributes** A variable's attributes or values are mutually exclusive if every case can have only one attribute.
>
> **Exhaustive attributes** A variable's attributes or values in which every case can be classified as having one attribute.

Ordinal Level of Measurement

The first of the three quantitative levels is the **ordinal level of measurement**. At this level, the numbers assigned to cases specify only the order of the cases, permitting greater-than and less-than distinctions; absolute mathematical distinctions cannot be made between categories. The Core Alcohol and Drug Survey (Core Institute 1994) measures substance abuse with a series of questions that permit ordinal distinctions (see Exhibit 4.6). Although these categories may seem at first to be mathematically distinct, you can really only determine the extent to which a respondent who checks one category consumes more or less than another respondent.

> **Ordinal level of measurement** A measurement of a variable in which the numbers indicating a variable's values specify only the order of the cases, permitting "greater than" and "less than" distinctions.

The properties of variables measured at the ordinal level are illustrated in Exhibit 4.5 by the contrast between the level of conflict in two groups. The first group, symbolized by two people shaking hands, has a low level of conflict. The second group, symbolized by two persons using fists against each other, has a higher level of conflict. The third group, symbolized by two people pointing guns at each other, has an even higher level of conflict. To measure conflict, we would put the groups "in order" by assigning the number 1 to the low-conflict group, the number 2 to the group using fists, and the number 3 to the high-conflict group using guns. The numbers thus indicate only the relative position or

| Exhibit 4.6 | Example of Ordinal Measures: Core Alcohol and Drug Survey |

Within the last year, about how often have you used . . . (mark one for each line)	Did Not Use	Once a Year	6 Times a Year	Once a Month	Twice a Month	Once a Week	3 Times a Week	5 Times a Week	Every Day
a. Tobacco (smoke, chew, snuff)									
b. Alcohol (beer, wine, liquor)									
c. Marijuana (pot, hash, hash oil)									
d. Cocaine (crack, rock, freebase)									
e. Amphetamines (diet pills, speed)									
f. Sedatives (downers, ludes)									
g. Hallucinogens (LSD, PCP)									
h. Opiates (heroin, smack, horse)									
i. Inhalants (glue, solvents, gas)									
j. Designer drugs (ecstasy, MDMA)									
k. Steroids									
l. Other illegal drugs									

Source: From Core Institute. 1994. "Core Alcohol and Drug Survey: Long Form." Carbondale. IL: FIPSE Core Analysis Grantee Group, Core Institute, Student Health Programs, Southern Illinois University.

order of the cases. Although low level of conflict is represented by the number 1, it is not mathematically two fewer units of conflict than the high level of conflict, which is represented by the number 3. These numbers really have no mathematical qualities; they are just used to represent relative rank in the measurement of conflict.

As with nominal variables, the different values of a variable measured at the ordinal level must be mutually exclusive and exhaustive. They must cover the range of observed values and allow each case to be assigned no more than one value.

Interval Level of Measurement

Interval level of measurement A measurement of a variable in which the numbers indicating a variable's values represent fixed measurement units, but have no absolute, or fixed, zero point.

The numbers indicating the values of a variable at the **interval level of measurement** represent fixed measurement units (e.g., the change between each value/unit is equal and incremental) but have no absolute, or fixed, zero point. This level of measurement is represented in Exhibit 4.5 by the difference between two Fahrenheit temperatures. Although 60 degrees is 30 degrees hotter than 30 degrees, 60 in this case is not twice as hot as 30. Why not? Because heat does not begin at 0 degrees on the Fahrenheit scale.

An interval-level measure is created by a scale that has fixed measurement units but no absolute, or fixed, zero point. The numbers can therefore be added and subtracted, but ratios are not meaningful. Again, the values must be mutually exclusive and exhaustive.

Social scientists often treat indexes that were created by combining responses to a series of variables measured at the ordinal level as interval-level measures. An index of this sort could be created with responses to the Core Institute's (1994) questions about friends' disapproval of substance use (see Exhibit 4.7). The survey has 13 questions on the topic, each of which has the same three response choices. If Do Not Disapprove is valued at 1, Disapprove is valued at 2, and Strongly Disapprove is valued at 3, the summed index of disapproval would range from 12 to 36. The average could then be treated as a fixed unit of measurement. So a score of 20 could be treated as if it were 4 more units than a score of 16.

Ratio Level of Measurement

The numbers indicating the values of a variable at the **ratio level of measurement** represent fixed measuring units and an absolute zero point (zero means absolutely no amount of whatever the variable measures or represents). On a ratio scale, 10 is two points higher than 8 and is also two times greater than 5. Ratio numbers can be added and subtracted, and because

> ***Ratio level of measurement*** A measurement of a variable in which the numbers indicating a variable's values represent fixed measuring units and an absolute zero point.

Exhibit 4.7	Ordinal-Level Variables Can Be Added to Create an Index With Interval-Level Properties: Core Alcohol and Drug Survey

How do you think your close friends feel (or would feel) about you . . . (mark one for each line)	Do Not Disapprove	Disapprove	Strongly Disapprove
a. Trying marijuana once or twice			
b. Smoking marijuana occasionally			
c. Smoking marijuana regularly			
d. Trying cocaine once or twice			
e. Taking cocaine regularly			
f. Trying LSD once or twice			
g. Taking LSD regularly			
h. Trying amphetamines once or twice			
i. Taking amphetamines regularly			
j. Taking one or two drinks of an alcoholic beverage (beer, wine, liquor) nearly every day			
k. Taking four or five drinks nearly every day			
l. Having five or more drinks in one sitting			
m. Taking steroids for bodybuilding or improved athletic performance			

Source: From Core Institute. 1994. "Core Alcohol and Drug Survey: Long Form." Carbondale. IL: FIPSE Core Analysis Grantee Group, Core Institute, Student Health Programs, Southern Illinois University.

the numbers begin at an absolute zero point, they can be multiplied and divided (so ratios can be formed between the numbers). For example, people's ages can be represented by values ranging from 0 years (or some fraction of a year) to 120 or more. A person who is 30 years old is 15 years older than someone who is 15 years old (30 – 15 = 15) and is twice as old as that person (30 ÷ 15 = 2). Of course, the numbers also are mutually exclusive and exhaustive, so every case can be assigned one and only one value.

Exhibit 4.5 displays an example of a variable measured at the ratio level. The number of people in the first group is 5, and the number in the second group is 7. The ratio of the two groups' sizes is then 1.4, a number that mirrors the relationship between the sizes of the groups. Note that there does not actually have to be any group with a size of 0; what is important is that the numbering scheme begins at an absolute zero, in this case, the absence of any people. The number of days a convicted felon was sentenced to prison would represent a ratio level of measurement because sentence length begins with an absolute 0 point. The number of days an addict stays clear after treatment, too, has a ratio level of measurement.

The Case of Dichotomies

Dichotomies, variables having only two values, are a special case from the standpoint of levels of measurement. Although variables with only two categories are generally thought of as nominally measured, we can also think of a dichotomy as indicating the presence or absence of an attribute. Suppose, for example, we were interested in differences between individuals who had never used illegal drugs in the last year and those who had used at least one illegal drug in the last year. We could create a variable that indicated this dichotomous distinction by coding those individuals who said they did not use any of the substances listed as 0 and all others as 1. Viewed in this way, there is an inherent order to the two values: In one group the attribute of consuming illegal substances is absent (those coded 0), and in another, it is present (those coded 1).

> **Dichotomy** A variable having only two values.

Comparison of Levels of Measurement

Exhibit 4.8 summarizes the types of comparisons that can be made with different levels of measurement, as well as the mathematical operations that are legitimate. All four levels of measurement allow researchers to assign different values to different cases. All three quantitative measures allow researchers to rank cases in order.

An important thing to remember is that researchers *choose* levels of measurement in the process of operationalizing the variables; the level of measurement is not inherent in the variable itself. Many variables can be measured at different levels, with different procedures. For example, the Core Alcohol and Drug Survey (Core Institute 1994) identifies binge drinking by asking students, "Think back over the last two weeks. How many times have you had five or more drinks at a sitting?" You might be ready to classify this as a ratio-level measure, but you must first examine

Exhibit 4.8	**Properties of Measurement Levels**					

Relevant Level of Measurement Examples of Comparison Statements	Appropriate Math Operations	Nominal	Ordinal	Interval	Ratio
A is equal to (not equal to) B	= (·)	√	√	√	√
A is greater than (less than) B	> (<)		√	√	√
A is three more than (less than) B	+ (−)			√	√
A is twice (half) as large as B					√

the fixed response options given to respondents. This is a closed-ended question, and students are asked to indicate their answer by checking None, Once, Twice, 3 to 5 times, 6 to 9 times, or 10 or more times. Use of these categories makes the level of measurement ordinal. The distance between any two cases cannot be clearly determined. A student with a response in the "6 to 9 times" category could have binged just one more time than a student who responded 3 to 5 times, or he or she could have binged four more times. With these response categories, you cannot mathematically distinguish the number of times a student binged, only the relative amount of binging behavior.

The more information available, the more ways you have to compare cases. You also have more possibilities for statistical analysis with quantitative than with qualitative variables. Thus, it often is a good idea to try to measure variables at the highest level of measurement possible, if doing so does not distort the meaning of the concept that is to be measured. For example, measure age in years, if possible, rather than in categories. You can always recategorize the responses into categories that compare teenagers to young adults, but it is impossible to obtain the actual age in years when the question is asked using an ordinal response format.

Be aware, however, that other considerations may preclude measurement at a high level. For example, many people are very reluctant to report their exact incomes, even in anonymous questionnaires. So asking respondents to report their income in categories (such as under $10,000, $10,000–$19,999, $20,000–$29,999, etc.) will result in more responses, and thus more valid data, than asking respondents for their income in dollars.

🔲 Conclusion

Remember always that measurement validity is a necessity for social research. Gathering data without careful conceptualization or conscientious efforts to operationalize key concepts often is a wasted effort.

The difficulties of achieving valid measurement vary with the concept being operationalized and the circumstances of the particular study. The examples in this chapter of difficulties in achieving valid measures of substance abuse should sensitize you to the need for caution, particularly when the concepts you wish to measure are socially stigmatized and/or illegal.

Planning ahead is the key to achieving valid measurement in your own research; careful evaluation is the key to sound decisions about the validity of measures in others' research. Statistical tests can help determine whether a given measure is valid after data have been collected, but if it appears after the fact that a measure is invalid, little can be done to correct the situation. If you cannot tell how key concepts were operationalized when you read a research report, do not trust the findings. And if a researcher does not indicate the results of tests used to establish the reliability and validity of key measures, remain skeptical.

Key Terms

Alternate-forms reliability   90
Closed-ended (fixed choice) question   83
Concept   76
Conceptualization   76
Construct validity   87
Content validity   86
Criterion validity   87
Dichotomy   96

Discriminant validity   88
Ecometrics   91
Exhaustive attributes   93
Face validity   86
Indicator   81
Interitem reliability   89
Interobserver reliability   90
Interval level of measurement   94

Intraobserver reliability (intrarater reliability)   90
Level of measurement   92
Measurement validity   85
Mutually exclusive attributes   93
Nominal level of measurement   93
Open-ended questions   83
Operation   81

Highlights

- Conceptualization plays a critical role in research. In deductive research, conceptualization guides the operationalization of specific variables; in inductive research, it guides efforts to make sense of related observations.

- Concepts are operationalized in research by one or more indicators, or measures, which may derive from observation, self-report, available records or statistics, books and other written documents, clinical indicators, discarded materials, or some combination.

- The validity of measures should always be tested. There are four basic approaches: face validation, content validation, criterion validation, and construct validation. Criterion validation provides the strongest evidence of measurement validity, but there often is no criterion to use in validating social science measures.

- Measurement reliability is a prerequisite for measurement validity, although reliable measures are not necessarily valid. Reliability can be assessed through test-retest procedures, in terms of interitem consistency, through a comparison of responses to alternate forms of the test, or in terms of consistency among observers.

- Level of measurement indicates the type of information obtained about a variable and the type of statistics that can be used to describe its variation. The four levels of measurement can be ordered by complexity of the mathematical operations they permit: nominal (least complex), ordinal, interval, ratio (most complex). The measurement level of a variable is determined by how the variable is operationalized. Dichotomies are a special case of measurement.

Research in the News

Curbing Binge Drinking Takes Group Effort

Noting that binge drinking is a behavior engaged in by over 4 in 10 college students (44%), the journalist next operationalized binge drinking as "consuming five or more drinks for men and four or more for women in a row, usually within two hours." Citing the Harvard School of Public Health College Alcohol Study, this article contends that reducing binge drinking requires a change in environmental and community factors including promotions in bars around campuses that encourage drinking to excess. This includes such promotions as selling alcohol in large containers like fishbowls, special women's nights, 25-cent beers, and so on. Strong drunk-driving policies and alcohol control policies like keg registration served to decreases binge drinking on some college campuses.

Source: Brody, Jane. 2008. "Curbing Binge Drinking Takes Group Effort." *The New York Times,* September 8, 2008: F7.

Exercises

1. Are important concepts in criminological research always defined clearly? Are they defined consistently? Search the literature for six articles that focus on "violent crime," "domestic violence," or some other concept suggested by your instructor. Is the concept defined clearly in each article? How similar are the definitions? Write what you have found in a short report.

2. What are some of the research questions you could attempt to answer with available statistical data? Visit your library and ask for an introduction to the government documents collection. Inspect the volumes from the Federal Bureau of Investigation's (FBI) Uniform Crime Report (UCR) or the *Sourcebook of Criminal Justice Statistics,* both of which report statistics on crimes

committed by offender characteristics. List 10 questions you could explore with such data.

3. Develop a plan for evaluating the validity of a measure. Your instructor will give you a copy of a questionnaire actually used in a study. Choose one question and define the concept that you believe it is intended to measure. Then develop a construct validation strategy involving other measures in the questionnaire that you think should be related to the question of interest—that is, if it measures what you think it measures.

4. Go the Bureau of Justice Statistics Web site or to your local library (in the government documents section) and select a recent publication on the death penalty. Now go through each table and define the levels of measurement for each variable described in the table.

Developing a Research Proposal

At this point you can begin the processes of conceptualization and operationalization. You will need to assume that your primary research method will be conducting a survey.

1. List at least 10 variables that will be measured in your research. No more than 2 of these should be sociodemographic indicators like race or age. The inclusion of each variable should be justified in terms of theory or prior research that suggests it would be an appropriate independent or dependent variable or will have some relation to either of these.

2. Write a conceptual definition for each variable. Whenever possible, this definition should come from the existing literature, either a book you have read for a course or the research literature that you have been searching. Ask two class members for feedback on your definitions.

3. Develop measurement operations for each variable. Several measures should be single questions and indexes that were used in prior research (search the Web and the journal literature in *Sociological Abstracts* or *PsycINFO*). Make up a few questions and one index yourself. Ask classmates to answer these questions and give you feedback on their clarity.

4. Propose tests of reliability and validity for four of the measures.

Web Exercises

1. Use the Web to find information regarding alcohol consumption and crime. Write a short report on your findings. How is "alcohol consumption" conceptualized and measured in the various sources you find?

2. How would you define *rape*? Write a brief definition. Based on this conceptualization, what circumstances constitute rape? Describe a method of measurement that would be valid for a study of rape (as you define it). Now go to the Rape Victim Advocates' Web site at www.rapevictimadvocates.org. Go to "Myths & Facts." Discuss some facts about rape that you were previously unaware of or some myths you believed. Rewrite your definition of rape based on your new knowledge. What additional circumstances constitute rape based on your new conceptualization?

3. How would you define a "hate crime." Now go to the Bureau of Justice Statistics (BJS) (bjs.ojp.usdoj.gov) website and find a publication that presents statistics on victimizations perceived to be motivated by hate. How does BJS define a hate crime. How do they actually measure the extent to which a victimization is motivated by hate? How does this compare to your definition of a hate crime?

4. Compare two different measures of substance abuse. A site maintained by the National Institute on Drug Abuse (www.drugabuse.gov/publications/media-guide/science-drug-abuse-addiction) provides many of the most popular measures. Pick two of them. What concept of substance abuse is reflected in each measure? Is either measure multidimensional? What do you think the relative advantages of each measure might be? What evidence is provided about their reliability and validity? What other test of validity would you suggest?

Ethics Exercises

1. In order to measure disorder in Chicago neighborhoods, Sampson and Raudenbush (1999) recorded the street scene with video cameras in a van with darkened windows. Do you judge this measurement procedure as ethical? Refer to each of the guidelines in Chapter 3. How could the guidelines about "anonymity/confidentiality" and "informed consent" be interpreted to permit this type of observational procedure?

2. Both some homeland security practices and inadvertent releases of Web searching records have raised new concerns about the use of unobtrusive measures of behavior and attitudes. If all identifying information is removed, do you think criminologists should be able to study who is stopped by police for traffic violations? What types of books are checked out in libraries in different communities? The extent of use of pornography in different cities by analyzing store purchases? How much alcohol different types of people use by linking credit card records to store purchases?

SPSS or Excel Exercises

HOMICIDE.POR contains a sample of homicide defendants from a sample of 33 U.S. counties.

1. Obtain a frequency distribution for the variables INTIMATE, NUMVICT, and PRITIME. At what levels (nominal or categorical, ordinal, interval, ratio) are each of these variables measured?

2. What conclusions do you make about the victim-offender relationship, number of victims, and length of sentence received based on these frequency distributions?

3. Access the data set STATE.POR. The units of analysis for these data are states. Take a look at the variables within the data set. Which variables would you describe as quantitative and which would you describe as qualitative?

Sampling

I n May 2012, Governor Andrew Cuomo proposed to decriminalize the possession of small amounts of marijuana in public view. Motivation for the measure was driven largely by the high number of arrests annually in New York City alone for the possession of small amounts of marijuana. The *New York Times* reported that in 2012 over 50,000 people, primarily African-American or Hispanic young men, were arrested for this crime typically after they had been stopped and frisked out on the street. These arrests cost the city over $75 million annually (Kaplan 2012). After Governor Cuomo's announcement, local news reports were full of stories asking people on the street how they felt about the new proposal. As you can imagine, opinions varied from fully supportive to believing that legalizing marijuana would lead to the downfall of civilization entirely. These "person-on-the-street" interviews tell us virtually nothing, however, about the attitudes of all New York residents about the proposed law. To find how the majority of New Yorkers feel about it, we would need to make sure that we asked a "random sample" of residents that was not biased in any way, and therefore, generalizable to all New York residents. How would we do this?

In this chapter, we first review the rationale for using sampling in social research and consider two alternatives to sampling. We then turn to the topic of specific sampling methods and when they are most appropriate, using a variety of examples from the criminological research literature. We also briefly introduce the concept of a sampling distribution and explain how it helps in estimating our degree of confidence in statistical generalizations. By the chapter's end, you should know which questions you need to ask to evaluate the generalizability of a study as well as what choices you need to make to design a sampling strategy. You will also realize that it is as important to select the right kind of sample to study as it is to take valid and reliable measurements of the phenomena of interest.

Sample Planning

You have encountered the problem of generalizability in each of the studies you have read about in this book. For example, MacDonald et al. (2005) generalized their sample-based explanation of adolescent aggression and violence to the population of high school students in the United States; Powell, Muir-McClain, and Halasyamani (1995) generalized their evaluation findings of violence prevention programs from an elementary school in King County, Washington, to all public elementary schools, and Sherman and Berk (1984) and others (Berk et al. 1992; Dunford, Huizinga, and Elliott 1990; Garner, Fagan, and Maxwell 1995; Hirschel, Hutchison, and Dean 1992; Pate and Hamilton 1992; Sherman et al. 1992) tried to determine the generalizability of findings from the original study of domestic violence in Minneapolis. As sampling is very common in social research, whether we are designing a sampling strategy or evaluating the generalizability of someone else's findings, we have to understand how and why researchers decide to sample.

Define Sample Components and the Population

Let's say that we are designing a survey about adult homeless persons in one city. We don't have the time or resources to study the entire adult **population** of the city, even though it consists of the set of individuals or other entities to which we wish to be able to generalize our findings. Even the city of Boston, which conducts an annual census of homeless persons, does not have the resources to actually survey the homeless persons it counts. So instead, we resolve to study a **sample**, a subset of this population. The individual members of this sample are called *elements*, or *elementary units*.

Population The entire set of elements (e.g., individuals, cities, states, countries, prisons, schools) in which we are interested.

Sample A subset of elements from the larger population.

Sampling frame A list of the elements of a population from which a sample actually is selected.

Enumeration units Units that contain one or more elements and that are listed in a sampling frame.

In many studies, we sample directly from the elements in the population of interest. We may survey a sample of the entire population of students in a school, based on a list obtained from the registrar's office. This list, from which the elements of the population are selected, is termed the **sampling frame**. The students who are selected and interviewed from that list are the elements.

In some studies, the entities that can be reached easily are not the same as the elements from which we want information, but they include those elements. For example, we may have a list of households but not a list of the entire population of a town, even though the adults are the elements that we actually want to sample. In this situation, we could draw a sample of households so that we can identify the adult individuals in these households. The households are termed **enumeration units**, and the adults in the households are the elements (Levy and Lemeshow 1999).

Sometimes, the individuals or other entities from which we collect information are not actually the elements in our study. For example, a researcher might sample schools for a survey about educational practices and then interview a sample of teachers in each sampled school to obtain the information about educational practices. Both the schools and the teachers are termed **sampling units**, because we sample from both (Levy and Lemeshow 1999). The schools are selected in the first stage of the sample, so they are the *primary sampling units* (in this case, they are also the elements in the study). The teachers are *secondary sampling units* (but they are not elements, because they are used to provide information about the entire school) (for another example, see Exhibit 5.1).

> ***Sampling units*** The units actually selected in each stage of sampling.

It is important to know exactly what population a sample can represent when you select or evaluate sample components. In a survey of "adult Americans," the general population may reasonably be construed as all residents of the United States who are at least 21 years old. But always be alert to ways in which the population may have been narrowed by the sample selection procedures. For example, perhaps only English-speaking residents of the United States were surveyed. The population for a study is the aggregation of elements that we actually focus on and sample from, not some larger aggregation that we really wish we could have studied.

Some populations, such as the homeless, are not identified by a simple criterion such as a geographic boundary or an organizational membership. Let's say we were interested in victimizations experienced by the homeless population.

Exhibit 5.1 **Sample Components in a Two-Stage Study**

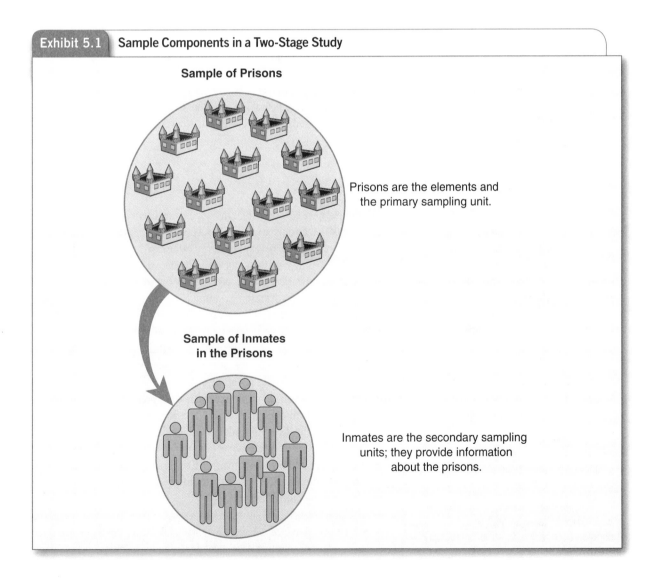

Sample of Prisons

Prisons are the elements and the primary sampling unit.

Sample of Inmates in the Prisons

Inmates are the secondary sampling units; they provide information about the prisons.

In this case, a clear definition of the homeless population is difficult but quite necessary. In research, anyone should be able to determine what population was actually studied. However, early studies of homeless persons "did not propose definitions, did not use screening questions to be sure that the people they interviewed were indeed homeless, and did not make major efforts to cover the universe of homeless people" (Burt 1996:15). For example, some studies relied on homeless persons in only one shelter. The result was "a collection of studies that could not be compared" (Burt 1996:15). Several studies of homeless persons in urban areas addressed the problem by employing a more explicit definition of the population: People are homeless if they have no home or permanent place to stay of their own (renting or owning) and no regular arrangement to stay at someone else's place (Burt 1996).

Even this more explicit definition still leaves some questions unanswered: What is a regular arrangement? How permanent does a permanent place have to be? In a study of homeless persons in Chicago, Sosin, Colson, and Grossman (1988) answered these questions in their definition of the population of interest:

> We define the homeless as those currently residing for at least one day but for less than fourteen with a friend or relative, not paying rent, and not sure that the length of stay will surpass fourteen days; those currently residing in a shelter, whether overnight or transitional; those currently without normal, acceptable shelter arrangements and thus sleeping on the street, in doorways, in abandoned buildings, in cars, in subway or bus stations, in alleys, and so forth; [and] those residing in a treatment center for the indigent who have lived at the facility for less than 90 days and who claim that they have no place to go, when released. (p. 22)

This definition accurately reflects these researchers' concept of homelessness and allows researchers in other locations or at other times to develop procedures for studying a comparable population. The more complete and explicit the definition of the population from which a sample is selected, the more precise our generalizations from a sample to that population can be.

Evaluate Generalizability

After we clearly define the population we will sample, we need to determine the scope of the generalizations we will seek to make from our sample. Let us say we were interested in the extent to which high school youth are fearful of being attacked or harmed at school or going to and from their schools. It would be easy to go down to the local high school and hand out a survey asking students to report their levels of fear in these situations. But what if our local high school were located in a remote and rural area of Alaska? Would this sample reflect levels of fear perceived by suburban youth in California or urban youth in New York City? Obviously not. Often, regardless of the sample utilized, researchers will go on to talk about "this percentage of high school students are fearful" or "freshman students are more fearful than seniors," as if their study results represent all high school students. Many social researchers and criminologists (and most everyone else, for that matter) are eager to draw conclusions about all individuals they are interested in, not just their samples. Generalizations make their work (and opinions) sound more important. If every high school student were like every other one, generalizations based on observations of one high school student would be valid. But of course, that is not the case.

As we noted in Chapter 2, generalizability has two aspects. **Sample generalizability** refers to the ability to generalize from a sample, or subset, of a larger population to that population itself. This is the most common meaning of generalizability. **Cross-population generalizability** refers to the ability to generalize from findings about one group, population, or setting to other groups, populations, or settings (see Exhibit 5.2). In this book, we use the term **external validity** to refer only to cross-population generalizability, not to sample generalizability.

Sample generalizability is a key concern in survey research, whether you are interested in measuring the extent of violent victimization, perceived levels of fear, or any other issue. A good example of the importance of sample generalizability comes from legitimate pollsters such as Gallup and Roper.

> **Sample generalizability** Exists when a conclusion based on a sample, or subset, of a larger population holds true for that population.
>
> **Cross-population generalizability (external validity)** Exists when findings about one group, population, or setting hold true for other groups, populations, or settings.

| Exhibit 5.2 | Sample and Cross-Population Generalizability |

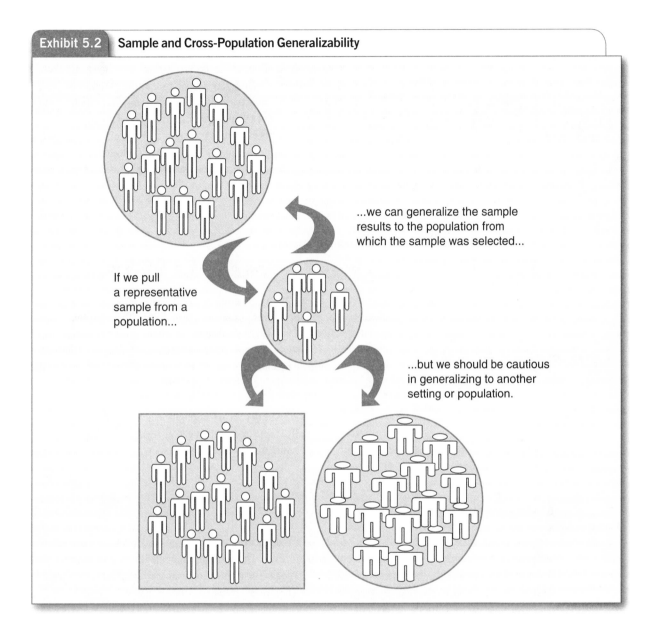

...we can generalize the sample results to the population from which the sample was selected...

If we pull a representative sample from a population...

...but we should be cautious in generalizing to another setting or population.

Say we were interested in the likely winner of the next presidential election. To determine this, these pollsters might study a sample of likely voters, for example, and then generalize their findings to the entire population of likely voters. No one would be interested in the results of political polls if they represented only the tiny sample that actually was surveyed rather than the entire population.

Cross-population generalizability occurs to the extent that the results of a study hold true for multiple populations; these populations may not all have been sampled, or they may be represented as subgroups within the sample studies. For example, our cross-population generalizability would be called into question if we said all high school students perceived low levels of fear while going to and from school and we only had our rural Alaskan sample.

Generalizability is a key concern in research design. We rarely have the resources to study the entire population that is of interest to us, so we have to select cases to study that will allow our findings to be generalized to the population of interest. We can never be sure that our propositions will hold under all conditions, so we should be cautious in generalizing to populations that we did not actually sample.

Sampling error Any difference between the characteristics of a sample and the characteristics of the population from which it was drawn. The larger the sampling error, the less representative the sample is of the population.

This chapter primarily focuses on the problem of sample generalizability: Can findings from a sample be generalized to the population from which the sample was drawn? This is the most basic question to ask about a sample, and social research methods provide many tools to address it.

Sample generalizability depends on sample quality, which is determined by the amount of **sampling error**. Sampling error can generally be defined as the difference between the characteristics of a sample and the characteristics of the population from which it was selected. The larger the sampling error, the less representative the sample, and thus the less generalizable the findings. To assess sample quality when you are planning or evaluating a study, ask yourself these questions:

- From what population were the cases selected?

- What method was used to select cases from this population?

- Do the cases that were studied represent, in the aggregate, the population from which they were selected?

In reality, researchers often project their theories onto groups or populations much larger than, or simply different from, those they have actually studied. The **target population** is a set of elements larger than or different from the population that was sampled and to which the researcher would like to generalize any study findings. When we generalize findings to target populations, we must be somewhat speculative. We must carefully consider the claim that the findings can be applied to other groups, geographic areas, cultures, or times.

Target population A set of elements larger than or different from the population sampled and to which the researcher would like to generalize study findings.

Because the validity of cross-population generalizations cannot be tested empirically, except by conducting more research in other settings, we do not focus much attention on this problem here. We will return to the problem of cross-population generalizability in Chapter 7, which addresses experimental research.

Assess Population Diversity

Sampling is unnecessary if all the units in the population are identical. Physicists do not need to select a representative sample of atomic particles to learn about basic physical processes. They can study a single atomic particle, because it is identical to every other particle of its type. Similarly, biologists do not need to sample a particular type of plant to determine whether a given chemical has toxic effects on it. The idea is "If you've seen one, you've seen 'em all."

What about people? Certainly all people are not identical; nor are animals in many respects. Nonetheless, if we are studying physical or psychological processes that are the same among all people, sampling is not needed to achieve generalizable findings. Psychologists and social psychologists often conduct experiments on college students to learn about processes that they think are identical for all individuals. They believe that most people will have the same reactions as the college students if they experience the same experimental conditions. Field researchers who observe group processes in a small community sometimes make the same assumption.

There is a potential problem with this assumption, however. There is no way to know if the processes being studied are identical for all people. In fact, experiments can give different results depending on the type of people studied or the conditions for the experiment. Milgram's (1965) classic experiments on obedience to authority, among the most replicated experiments in the history of social psychological research, illustrate this point very well. The Milgram experiments tested the willingness of male volunteers in New Haven, Connecticut, to comply with instructions from an authority figure to give electric shocks to someone else, even when these shocks seemed to harm the person receiving them. In most cases, the volunteers complied. Milgram concluded that people are very obedient to authority.

Were these results generalizable to all men, to men in the United States, or to men in New Haven? We have confidence in these findings because similar results were obtained in many replications of the Milgram experiments when the experimental conditions and subjects were similar to those studied by Milgram. Other studies, however, showed that some groups were less likely to react so obediently. Given certain conditions, such as another subject in the room who refused to administer the shocks, subjects were likely to resist authority.

So what do the experimental results tell us about how people will react to an authoritarian movement in the real world, when conditions are not so carefully controlled? In the real social world, people may be less likely to react obediently. Other individuals may argue against obedience to a particular leader's commands or people may see, on TV, the consequences of their actions. But alternatively, people may be even more obedient to authority than the experimental subjects, as they get swept up in mobs or are captivated by ideological fervor. Milgram's research gives us insight into human behavior, but there is no guarantee that what he found with particular groups in particular conditions can be generalized to the larger population (or to any particular population) in different settings.

Accurately generalizing the results of experiments and of participant observation is risky, because such research often studies a small number of people who do not represent a particular population. Researchers may put aside concerns about generalizability when they observe the social dynamics of specific clubs or college dorms or when they conduct a controlled experiment that tests the effect of, say, a violent movie on feelings for others. Nonetheless, we should still be cautious about generalizing the results of such studies.

The important point is that social scientists rarely can skirt the problem of demonstrating the generalizability of their findings. If a small sample has been studied in an experiment or a field research project, the study should be replicated in different settings or, preferably, with a **representative sample** of the population for which the generalizations are sought (see Exhibit 5.3).

The social world and the people in it are just too diverse to be considered identical units. Social psychological experiments and small field studies have produced good social science, but they need to be replicated in other settings, with other subjects, to claim any generalizability. Even when we believe that we have uncovered basic social processes in a laboratory experiment or field observation, we must seek confirmation in other samples and other research.

> **Representative sample** A sample that looks like the population from which it was selected in all respects that are potentially relevant to the study. The distribution of characteristics among the elements of a representative sample is the same as the distribution of those characteristics among the total population. In an unrepresentative sample, some characteristics are overrepresented or underrepresented and sampling error emerges.

Consider a Census

In some circumstances, researchers can bypass the issue of generalizability by conducting a **census** studying the entire population of interest rather than drawing a sample. The federal government tries to do this every 10 years with the U.S. Census. A census can also include studies of all the

> **Census** Research in which information is obtained through the responses that all available members of an entire population give to questions.

employees (or students) in small organizations (or universities), studies comparing all 50 states, and studies of the entire population of a particular type of organization in a particular area. However, in all these instances, except for the U.S. Census, the population studied is relatively small.

Social scientists do not often attempt to collect data from all the members of some large population simply because doing so is very expensive and time consuming. Some social scientists do conduct research with data from the U.S. Census, but this data is collected by the government For the 2000 census, the Bureau of the Census used half a million temporary workers just to follow up on the 34% of households that did not return their census form in the mail.

Even if the population of interest for a survey is a small town of 20,000 or students in a university of 10,000, researchers will have to sample. The costs of surveying just thousands of individuals far exceed the budgets for most research projects. In fact, even the U.S. Bureau of the Census cannot afford to have everyone answer all the questions that should be covered in the census. So it draws a sample. Every household must complete a short version of the census (it had seven questions in 2000), and a sample consisting of one in six households must complete a long form (with 53 additional questions) (Rosenbaum 2000).

| Exhibit 5.3 | Representative and Unrepresentative Samples |

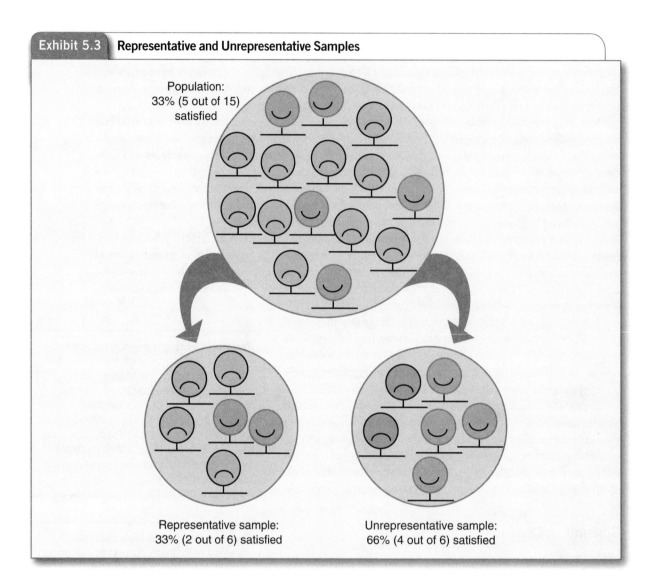

Population:
33% (5 out of 15)
satisfied

Representative sample:
33% (2 out of 6) satisfied

Unrepresentative sample:
66% (4 out of 6) satisfied

Another costly fact is that it is hard to get people to complete a survey. Even the U.S. Bureau of the Census (1999) must make multiple efforts to increase the rate of response in spite of the federal law requiring all citizens to complete their census questionnaire. After spending $167 million on publicity (Forero 2000), the bureau still planned up to six attempts to contact each household that did not respond by mail (U.S. Bureau of the Census 2000).

Sampling Methods

As you can probably guess, the most important feature to know about a sample is whether it is truly representative of the population from which it was selected. Sampling methods that allow us to know in advance how likely it is that any element of a population will be selected for the sample are **probability sampling methods**. Sampling methods that do not reveal the likelihood of selection in advance are **nonprobability sampling methods**.

Probability sampling methods rely on a random selection procedure. In principle, this is the same as flipping a coin to decide which person wins and which one loses. Heads and tails are equally likely to turn up in a coin toss, so both persons have an equal chance to win. That chance, or the **probability of selection**, is 1 out of 2, or .5.

Flipping a coin is a fair way to select one of two people, because the selection process harbors no systematic bias. You might win or lose the coin toss, but you know that the outcome was due simply to chance, not to bias (unless your opponent tossed a two-headed coin!). For the same reason, rolling a six-sided die is a fair way to choose one of six possible outcomes (the odds of selection are 1 out of 6, or .17). Dealing out a hand after shuffling a deck of cards is a fair way to allocate sets of cards in a poker game (the odds of each person getting a particular outcome, such as a full house or a flush, are the same). Similarly, state lotteries use a random process to select winning numbers. Thus, the odds of winning a lottery, the probability of selection, are known even though they are very small (perhaps 1 out of 1 million) compared to the odds of winning a coin toss. As you can see, the fundamental strategy in probability sampling is the **random selection** of elements into the sample. When a sample is randomly selected from the population, every element has a known and independent chance of being selected into the sample.

There is a natural tendency to confuse the concept of probability, in which cases are selected only on the basis of chance, with a haphazard method of sampling. On first impression, leaving things up to chance seems to imply the absence of control over the sampling method. But to ensure that nothing but chance influences the selection of cases, the researcher must actually proceed very methodically and leaving nothing to chance except the selection of the cases themselves. The researcher must carefully follow controlled procedures if a purely random process is to occur. In fact, when reading about sampling methods, do not assume that a random sample was obtained just because the researcher used a random selection method at some point in the sampling process. Look for these two particular problems: selecting elements from an incomplete list of the total population and failing to obtain an adequate response rate (say, only 45% of the people who were asked to participate actually agreed).

If the sampling frame, or list from which the elements of the population are selected is incomplete, a sample selected randomly from the list will not be random. How can it be when the sampling frame fails to include every element in the population? Even for a simple population like a university's student body, the registrar's list is likely to be at least a bit out of date at any given time. For example, some students will have dropped out, but their status will not yet be officially recorded. Although you may judge the amount of error introduced in this particular situation to be negligible, the problems are greatly compounded for a larger population. The sampling frame for a city, state, or nation is always likely to be incomplete because of constant migration into and out of the area. Even unavoidable omissions from the sampling frame can bias a sample against particular groups within the population.

A very inclusive sampling frame may still yield systematic bias if many sample members cannot be contacted or refuse to participate. **Nonresponse** is a major hazard in survey research because individuals who do not respond to a survey are likely to differ systematically from those who take the time to participate. You should not assume that findings from a randomly selected sample will be generalizable to the population from which the sample was selected if the rate of nonresponse is considerable (certainly not if it is much above 30%).

Probability sampling methods Sampling methods that rely on a random, or chance, selection method so that the probability of selection of population elements is known.

Nonprobability sampling methods Sampling methods in which the probability of selection of population elements is unknown.

Probability of selection The likelihood that an element will be selected from the population for inclusion in the sample. In a census of all the elements of a population, the probability that any particular element will be selected is 1.0 because everyone will be selected. If half the elements in the population will be sampled on the basis of chance (say, by tossing a coin), the probability of selection for each element is one half, or .5. When the size of the desired sample as a proportion of the population decreases, so does the probability of selection.

Random selection The fundamental element of probability samples; the essential characteristic of random selection is that every element of the population has a known and independent chance of being selected into the sample.

Nonresponse People or other entities who do not participate in a study although they are selected for the sample.

Probability Sampling Methods

Probability sampling methods require that the probability of selection is known and is not zero (so there is some chance of selecting each element). These methods randomly select elements and therefore have no systematic bias. Nothing but chance determines which elements are included in the sample. This feature of probability samples, sometimes referred to as random samples, makes them much more desirable than nonprobability samples when the goal is to generalize your findings to a larger population.

Even though a random sample has no systematic bias, it certainly will have some sampling error due to chance. The probability of selecting a head is .5 in a single toss of a coin and in 20, 30, or however many tosses of a coin you like. Be aware, however, that it is perfectly possible to toss a coin twice and get a head both times. The random sample of the two sides of the coin is selected in an unbiased fashion, but it still is unrepresentative. Imagine randomly selecting a sample of 10 people from a population comprising 50 men and 50 women. Just by chance, it is possible that your sample of 10 people will include seven women and only three men. Fortunately, we can determine mathematically the likely degree of sampling error in an estimate based on a random sample (as you will see later in this chapter), assuming that the sample's randomness has not been destroyed by a high rate of nonresponse or by poor control over the selection process.

In general, both the size of the sample and the homogeneity (sameness) of the population affect the degree of error due to chance; the proportion of the population that the sample represents does not. To elaborate:

The larger the sample, the more confidence we can have in the sample's representativeness of the population from which it was drawn. If we randomly pick five people to represent the entire population of our city, our sample is unlikely to be very representative of the entire population in terms of age, gender, race, attitudes, and so on. But if we randomly pick 100 people, the odds of having a representative sample are much better; with a random sample of 1,000, the odds become very good indeed.

The more homogeneous the population, the more confidence we can have in the representativeness of a sample of any particular size. Let us say we plan to draw samples of 50 from each of two communities to estimate mean family income. One community is very diverse, with family incomes ranging from $12,000 to $85,000. In the more homogeneous community, family incomes are concentrated in a narrower range, from $41,000 to $64,000. The estimated average family income based on the sample from the homogeneous community is more likely to be representative than is the estimate based on the sample from the more heterogeneous community. With less variation, fewer cases are needed to represent the larger population.

The fraction of the total population that a sample contains does not affect the sample's representativeness, unless that fraction is large. We can regard any sampling fraction under 2% with about the same degree of confidence (Sudman 1976). In fact, sample representativeness is not likely to increase much until the sampling fraction is quite a bit higher. Other things being equal, a sample of 1,000 from a population of 1 million (with a sampling fraction of 0.001, or 0.1%) is much better than a sample of 100 from a population of 10,000 (although the sampling fraction is 0.01, or 1%, which is 10 times higher). The size of a sample is what makes representativeness more likely, not the proportion of the whole that the sample represents.

Polls that predict presidential election outcomes illustrate both the value of random sampling and the problems that it cannot overcome. In most presidential elections, pollsters have accurately predicted the outcomes of the actual vote by using random sampling and, these days, phone interviewing to learn which candidate voters intend to choose. Exhibit 5.4 shows how close these sample-based predictions have been in the last 12 contests. The big exception was the 1980 election, when a third-party candidate had an unpredicted effect. Otherwise, the small discrepancies between the votes predicted through random sampling and the actual votes can be attributed to random error. In 2008, the final Gallup prediction of 55% for Obama was within 2 percentage points of his winning total of 53%. Because they do not disproportionately select particular groups within the population, random samples that are successfully implemented avoid systematic bias. The four most common methods for drawing random samples are simple random sampling, systematic random sampling, strati-fied random sampling, and cluster sampling.

Simple Random Sampling

Simple random sampling requires a procedure that generates numbers or identifies cases strictly on the basis of chance. As you know, flipping a coin and rolling a die can be used to identify cases strictly on the basis of chance, but these procedures are not very efficient tools for drawing a sample. A **random number table**, which can be obtained on many Web sites, simplifies the process considerably. The researcher numbers all the elements in the sampling frame and then uses a systematic procedure for picking corresponding numbers from the random number table. (Exercise 2 at the end of the chapter explains the process step by step.) Alternatively, a researcher may use a lottery procedure. Each case number is written on a small card, and then the cards are mixed up and the sample is selected from the cards.

When a large sample must be generated, these procedures are very cumbersome. Fortunately, a computer program can easily generate a random sample of any size. The researcher must first number all the elements to be sampled (the sampling frame) and then run the computer program to generate a random selection of the numbers within the desired range. The elements represented by these numbers are the sample.

Organizations that conduct phone surveys often draw random samples with another automated procedure called *random digit dialing* (RDD). A machine dials random numbers within the phone prefixes corresponding to the area in which the survey is to be conducted. RDD is particularly useful when a sampling frame is not available. The researcher simply replaces any inappropriate numbers (e.g., those no longer in service or for businesses) with the next randomly generated phone number.

As the percentage of the population that has only cell phones has increased (25% in 2011), it has become essential to explicitly sample cell phone number as well as landlines. Those who use cell phones only tend to be younger, more male, more single, and more likely to be black or Hispanic. As a result, failing to include cell phone numbers in a phone survey can introduce bias. In the National Intimate Partner and Sexual Violence Survey (NIPSVS) conducted by the Centers for Disease Control and Prevention (CDC), both landline and cell phone data bases of adult U.S. residents were selected through an RDD random sampling method (Black et al. 2011).

The probability of selection in a true simple random sample is equal for each element. If a sample of 500 is selected from a population of 17,000 (i.e., a sampling frame of 17,000), then the probability of selection for each element is 500 out of 17,000, or .03. Every element has an equal and independent chance of being selected, just like the odds in a toss of a coin (1 in 2) or a roll of a die (1 in 6). Thus, simple random sampling is an equal probability of selection method (EPSEM).

Exhibit 5.4	Election Outcomes: Predicted and Actual	
Winner (Year)	*Polls (%)*	*Result (%)*
Kennedy (1960)	51	50
Johnson (1964)	64	61
Nixon (1968)[b]	43	43
Nixon (1972)	62	62
Carter (1976)	48	50
Reagan (1980)[b]	47	51
Reagan (1984)	59	59
Bush (1988)	56	54
Clinton (1992)[b]	49	43
Clinton (1996)[b]	52	50
Bush, G. W. (2000)[b]	48	50
Bush, G. W. (2004)[b]	49	51
Obama (2008)[b]	55	53

Source: Gallup Poll Accuracy Record, 12-13-00, http://www.gallup.com/poll/111742/Obamas-Road-White-House-Gallup-Review.aspx for the 2008 presidential election. Copyright © 2008 Gallup, Inc. All rights reserved.

a. Final Gallup Poll prior to the election.

b. There was also a third-party candidate.

Simple random sampling A method of sampling in which every sample element is selected only on the basis of chance, through a random process.

Random number table A table containing lists of numbers that are ordered solely on the basis of chance; it is used for drawing a random sample.

Random digit dialing (RDD) The random dialing by a machine of numbers within designated phone prefixes, which creates a random sample for phone surveys.

> **Replacement sampling** A method of sampling in which sample elements are returned to the sampling frame after being selected, so they may be sampled again. Random samples may be selected with or without replacement.

Simple random sampling can be done either with or without replacement sampling. In **replacement sampling**, each element is returned to the sampling frame from which it is selected so that it may be sampled again. In sampling without replacement, each element selected for the sample is then excluded from the sampling frame. In practice it makes no difference whether sampled elements are replaced after selection, as long as the population is large and the sample is to contain only a small fraction of the population.

In the CDC's NIPSVS study mentioned above, noninstitutionalized (e.g., not in nursing homes, prison, and so on) English and/or Spanish-speaking residents aged 18 and older were randomly selected through an RDD sampling method in 2010. A total of 9,970 women and 8,079 men were selected. Approximately, 45% of the interviews were conducted by landline and 55% by cell phone. The final sample represented the U.S. population very well. For example, the proportion of the sample by gender, race/ethnicity, and age in the NIPSVS sample was very close to the sample proportions for the U.S. population as a whole.

How does this sample strike you? Let us assess sample quality using the questions posed earlier in the chapter:

- *From what population were the cases selected?* There is a clearly defined population: the adult residents of the continental United States (who live in households with phones).

- *What method was used to select cases from this population?* The case selection method is a random selection procedure, and there are no systematic biases in the sampling.

- *Do the cases that were studied represent, in the aggregate, the population from which they were selected?* The findings are very likely to represent the population sampled, because there were no biases in the sampling and a very large number of cases were selected. However, it must be remembered that an average of 30% of those selected for interviews could not be contacted or chose not to respond. This rate of nonresponse may have created a small bias in the sample for several characteristics.

We also must consider the issue of cross-population generalizability. Do findings from this sample have implications for any larger group beyond the population from which the sample was selected? Because a representative sample of the entire U.S. adult population was drawn, this question has to do with cross-national generalizations. Tjaden and Thoennes (2000) wisely do not make such generalizations because national cultures, norms, and social policies will undoubtedly be related to different rates of victimization.

Systematic Random Sampling

> **Systematic random sampling** A method of sampling in which sample elements are selected from a list or from sequential files, with every *n*th element being selected after the first element is selected randomly within the first interval.

Systematic random sampling is a variant of simple random sampling and is a little less time consuming. When you systematically select a random sample, the first element is selected randomly from a list or from sequential files, and then every *n*th element is systematically selected thereafter. This is a convenient method for drawing a random sample when the population elements are arranged sequentially. It is particularly efficient when the elements are not actually printed (i.e., there is no sampling frame) but instead are represented by folders in filing cabinets.

Systematic random sampling requires three steps:

1. The total number of cases in the population is divided by the number of cases required for the sample. This division yields the **sampling interval**, the number of cases from one sampled case to another. If 50 cases are to be selected out of 1,000, the sampling interval is 20 (1,000/50 = 20); every 20th case is selected.

2. A number between 1 and 20 (the sampling interval) is selected randomly. This number identifies the first case to be sampled, counting from the first case on the list or in the files.

> **Sampling interval** The number of cases from one sampled case to another in a systematic random sample.

3. After the first case is selected, every *n*th case is selected for the sample, where *n* is the sampling interval. If the sampling interval is not a whole number, the size of the sampling interval is systematically varied to yield the proper number of cases for the sample. For example, if the sampling interval is 30.5, the sampling interval alternates between 30 and 31.

In almost all sampling situations, systematic random sampling yields what is essentially a simple random sample. The exception is a situation in which the sequence of elements is affected by **periodicity**; that is, the sequence varies in some regular, periodic pattern. The list or folder device from which the elements are selected must be truly random in order to avoid sampling bias. For example, we could not have a list of convicted felons sorted by offense type, age, or some other characteristic of the population. If the list is sorted in any meaningful way, this will introduce bias to the sampling process, and the resulting sample is not likely to be representative of the population.

> **Periodicity** A sequence of elements (in a list to be sampled) that varies in some regular, periodic pattern.

Stratified Random Sampling

Although all probability sampling methods use random sampling, some add steps to the sampling process to make sampling more efficient or easier. Samples are easier to collect when they require less time, money, or prior information.

Stratified random sampling uses information known about the total population prior to sampling to make the sampling process more efficient. First, all elements in the population (i.e., in the sampling frame) are differentiated on the basis of their value on some relevant characteristic. This sorting step forms the sampling strata. Next, elements are sampled randomly from within these strata. For example, race may be the basis for distinguishing individuals in some population of interest. Within each racial category selected for the strata, individuals are then sampled randomly.

> **Stratified random sampling** A method of sampling in which sample elements are selected separately from population strata that are identified in advance by the researcher.

Why is this method more efficient than drawing a simple random sample? Well, imagine that you plan to draw a sample of 500 from an ethnically diverse neighborhood. The neighborhood population is 15% African American, 10% Hispanic, 5% Asian, and 70% Caucasian. If you drew a simple random sample, you might end up with disproportionate numbers of each group. But if you created sampling strata based on race and ethnicity, you could randomly select cases from each stratum: 75 African Americans (15% of the sample), 50 Hispanics (10%), 25 Asians (5%), and 350 Caucasians (70%). By using **propor-tionate stratified sampling**, you would eliminate any possibility of error in the sample's distribution of ethnicity. Each stratum would be represented exactly in proportion to its size in the population from which the sample was drawn (see Exhibit 5.5).

> **Proportionate stratified sampling** Sampling methods in which elements are selected from strata in exact proportion to their representation in the population.

In **disproportionate stratified sampling**, the proportion of each stratum that is included in the sample is intentionally varied from what it is in the population. In the case of the sample stratified by ethnicity, you might select equal numbers of cases from each racial or ethnic group: 125 African Americans (25% of the sample), 125 Hispanics (25%), 125 Asians (25%), and 125 Caucasians (25%). In this type of sample, the probability of selection of every case is known but unequal between strata. You know what the proportions are in the population, so you can easily adjust your combined

> **Disproportionate stratified sampling** Sampling in which elements are selected from strata in different proportions from those that appear in the population.

Exhibit 5.5 **Stratified Random Sampling**

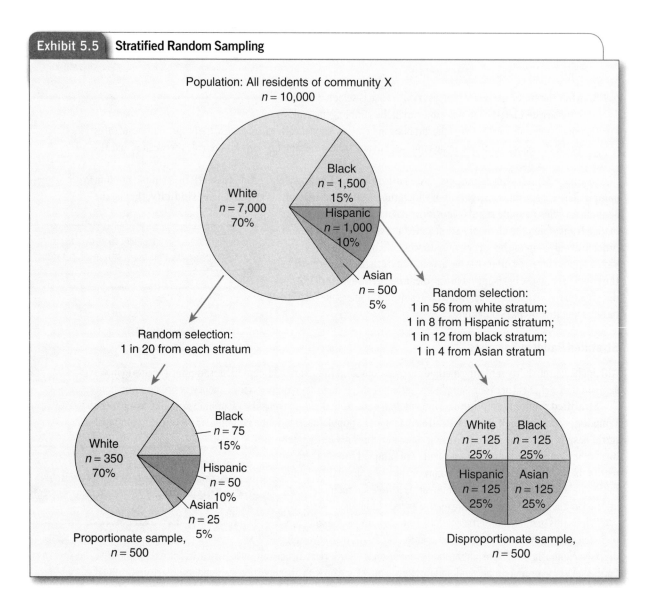

sample accordingly. For instance, if you want to combine the ethnic groups and estimate the average income of the total population, you would have to weight each case in the sample. The weight is a number you multiply by the value of each case based on the stratum it is in. For example, you would multiply the incomes of all African Americans in the sample by 0.6 (75/125), the incomes of all Hispanics by 0.4 (50/125), and so on. Weighting in this way reduces the influence of the oversampled strata and increases the influence of the undersampled strata to just what they would have been if pure probability sampling had been used.

Why would anyone select a sample that is so unrepresentative in the first place? The most common reason is to ensure that cases from smaller strata are included in the sample in sufficient numbers. Only then can separate statistical estimates and comparisons be made between strata (e.g., between African Americans and Caucasians). Remember that one determinant of sample quality is sample size. The same is true for subgroups within samples. If a key concern in a research project is to describe and compare the incomes of people from different racial and ethnic groups, then it is important that the researchers base the mean income of each group on enough cases to be a valid representation. If few members of a particular minority group are in the population, they need to be oversampled. Such disproportionate sampling may also result in a more efficient sampling design if the costs of data collection differ markedly between strata or if the variability (heterogeneity) of the strata differs.

Multistage Cluster Sampling

Although stratified sampling requires more information than usual prior to sampling (about the size of strata in the population), **multistage cluster sampling** requires less prior information. Specifically, cluster sampling can be useful when a sampling frame is not available, as often is the case for large populations spread across a wide geographic area or among many different organizations. In fact, if we wanted to obtain a sample from the entire U.S. population, there would be no list available. Yes, there

> **Multistage cluster sampling** Sampling in which elements are selected in two or more stages, with the first stage being the random selection of naturally occurring clusters and the last stage being the random selection of multilevel elements within clusters.

are lists in telephone books of residents in various places who have telephones, lists of those who have registered to vote, lists of those who hold driver's licenses, and so on. However, all these lists are incomplete; some people do not list their phone number or do not have a telephone, some people are not registered to vote, and so on. Using incomplete lists such as these would introduce selection bias into our sample.

In such cases, the sampling procedures become a little more complex, and we usually end up working toward the sample we want through a series of steps. First researchers extract a random sample of groups or clusters of elements that are available and then randomly sample the individual elements of interest from within these selected clusters. So what is a cluster? A **cluster** is a naturally occurring, mixed aggregate of elements of the population, with each element appearing in one and only one cluster. Schools could serve as clusters for sampling students, blocks could serve as clusters for sampling city residents, counties could serve as clusters for sampling the general population, and businesses could serve as clusters for sampling employees.

> **Cluster** A naturally occurring, mixed aggregate of elements of the population.

Drawing a cluster sample is at least a two-stage procedure. First, the researcher draws a random sample of clusters. A list of clusters should be much easier to obtain than a list of all the individuals in each cluster in the population. Next, the researcher draws a random sample of elements within each selected cluster. Because only a fraction of the total clusters are involved, obtaining the sampling frame at this stage should be much easier.

In a cluster sample of city residents, for example, blocks could be the first-stage clusters. A research assistant could walk around each selected block and record the addresses of all occupied dwelling units. Or in a cluster sample of students, a researcher could contact the schools selected in the first stage and make arrangements with the registrars to obtain lists of students at each school. Cluster samples often involve multiple stages (see Exhibit 5.6).

Exhibit 5.6 **Multistage Cluster Sampling**

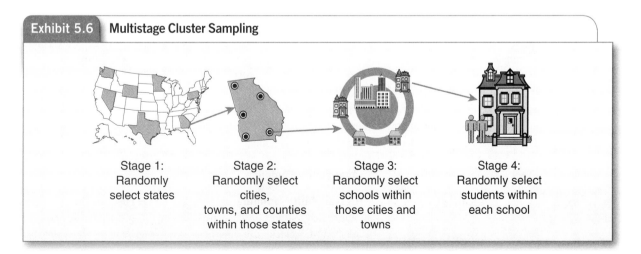

| Stage 1: Randomly select states | Stage 2: Randomly select cities, towns, and counties within those states | Stage 3: Randomly select schools within those cities and towns | Stage 4: Randomly select students within each school |

How many clusters and how many individuals within clusters should be selected? As a general rule, cases in the sample will be closer to the true population value if the researcher maximizes the number of clusters selected and minimizes the number of individuals within each cluster. Unfortunately, this strategy also maximizes the cost of the sample. The more clusters selected, the higher the travel costs. It also is important to take into account the homogeneity of the individuals within clusters; the more homogeneous the clusters, the fewer cases needed per cluster. This should make intuitive sense, as it is more likely that any selected element will represent other elements if they are alike. Although cluster sampling is a very popular method among survey researchers, it has one drawback: Sampling error is greater in a cluster sample than in a simple random sample. And as a general rule, this error increases as the number of clusters decreases.

Many federal government funded surveys use multistage cluster samples or even combinations of cluster and stratified probability sampling methods. For example, the U.S. Justice Department's National Crime Victimization Survey (NCVS) is an excellent example of a multistage cluster sample. In the NCVS, the first stage of clusters selected is referred to as primary sampling units (PSUs) and represents a sample of rural counties and large metropolitan areas. From these PSUs, the second stage of sampling involves the selection of geographic districts within each of the PSUs that have been listed by the U.S. Bureau of the Census population census. Finally, a probability sample of residential dwelling units is selected from these geographic districts. These dwelling units, or addresses, represent the final stage of the multistage sampling. Anyone who resides at a selected address who is 12 years of age or older and is a U.S. citizen is eligible for the NCVS sample. Approximately 50,500 housing units or other living quarters are designated for the NCVS each year and are selected in this manner.

How would we evaluate the NCVS sample, using the sample evaluation questions?

- *From what population were the cases selected?* The population was clearly defined for each cluster.

- *What method was used to select cases from this population?* The random selection method was carefully described.

- *Do the cases that were studied represent, in the aggregate, the population from which they were selected?* The unbiased selection procedures make us reasonably confident in the representativeness of the sample.

Nonprobability Sampling Methods

Unlike probability samples, when collecting a sample using nonprobability sampling techniques, elements within the population do not have a known probability of being selected into the sample. Thus, because the chance of any element being selected is unknown, we cannot be certain the selected sample actually represents our population. Why, you may be asking yourself right now, would we want to use such a sample if we cannot generalize our results to a larger population? These methods are useful for several purposes, including those situations in which we do not have a population list, when we are exploring a research question that does not concern a large population, or when we are doing a preliminary or exploratory study. Suppose, for example, that we were interested in the crime of shoplifting and wanted to investigate the rationalization used by shoplifters. It would be hard to define a population in this case because we do not have a list of shoplifters from which to randomly select. There may be lists of convicted shoplifters, but of course, they only represent those shoplifters who were actually caught.

There are four nonprobability sampling methods frequently used in criminological research: availability sampling, quota sampling, purposive sampling, and snowball sampling.

Availability Sampling

Availability sampling Sampling in which elements are selected on the basis of convenience.

In **availability sampling**, elements are selected because they are available or easy to find. Consequently, this sampling method is also known as haphazard, accidental, or convenience sampling. News reporters often use person-on-the-street interviews, a type of availability sample, to inject a personal perspective into a news story and show what ordinary people may think of a given topic. That is what reporters were doing on the streets of New York after Governor Cuomo proposed the new marijuana legislation mentioned at the beginning of the chapter. Availability samples are also used by university professors and researchers all the time. Have you ever been asked to complete a questionnaire before leaving one of your classes? If so, you may have been selected for inclusion in an availability sample.

Even though they are not generalizable, availability samples are often appropriate in research—for example, when a field researcher is exploring a new setting and trying to get some sense of prevailing attitudes or when a survey researcher conducts a preliminary test of a questionnaire. There are a variety of ways to select elements for an availability sample: standing on street corners and talking to anyone walking by, asking questions of employees who come to pick up their paychecks at a personnel office, or distributing questionnaires to an available and captive audience such as a class or a group at a meeting. Availability samples are also frequently used in fieldwork studies interested in obtaining detailed information about a particular group. For example, when Bourgois, Lettiere, and Quesada (1997) wanted to understand homeless heroin addicts, they immersed themselves in a community of addicts living in a public park in San Francisco. These addicts thus became the availability sample.

Another classic example of an availability sample used in research is found in John Irwin's *The Felon* (1970), a study of the postprison careers of a group of California criminal felons. To conduct his study, Irwin did not take a simple or systematic random sample of all felons released from the California Department of Corrections and Rehabilitation. Instead, because he resided and worked in the San Francisco area, Irwin studied offenders released on parole from penal institutions in San Francisco and Oakland parole districts who volunteered for his study.

When such samples are used, it is necessary to explicitly describe the sampling procedures used in the methodology section of research reports to acknowledge the nonrepresentativeness of the sample. For example, in a study investigating the prevalence problem behavior in a sample of students pursuing policing careers, Gray (2011) stated, "a convenience/purposive sample was used to survey students attending a medium-sized public, Midwestern university . . . to determine if differences existed between students majoring in criminal justice (CJ) and students with other majors in terms of deviance and delinquency, drinking and drug use, and an array of other behaviors" (p. 544). Those of you studying for a policing career will be interested to know that over ¼ of the CJ majors had engaged in serious forms of problematic behavior such as marijuana use. Students who engage in these forms of illegal activities, Gray points out, "should expect to have some level of difficulty with police application and hiring processes" (p. 549). But we digress.

How does this sample compare to the NIPSVS sample? There is no clearly definable population from which the respondents were drawn, and no systematic technique was used to select the respondents. Consequently, there is not much likelihood that the sample is representative of any target population; the problem is that we can never be sure.

Availability sampling often masquerades as a more rigorous form of research. Popular magazines and Internet sites periodically survey their readers by asking them to fill out questionnaires. Follow-up articles then appear in the magazine or on the site, displaying the results under such titles as "What You Think About the Death Penalty for Teenagers." If the magazine's circulation is large, a large sample can be achieved in this way. The problem is that usually only a tiny fraction of readers fill out the questionnaire, and these respondents are probably unlike other readers who did not have the interest or time to participate. So the survey is based on an availability sample. Polls conducted on specific Web sites (not Web surveys which we will discuss later) are also typically availability samples. Have you ever quickly answered the question of the day on CNN? These samples are not only availability samples, but electronic surveys also remain very susceptible to electronic ballot stuffing; few sites restrict access, so you can answer the posted questions as many times as you want. Because of their nonscientific basis, many Internet sites that conduct such polls, including ABC.com, now add this disclaimer to the online poll's question of the day: "Not a scientific poll; for entertainment only."

Quota Sampling

Quota sampling is intended to overcome availability sampling's biggest downfall: the likelihood that the sample will just consist of who or what

> **Quota sampling** A nonprobability sampling method in which elements are selected to ensure that the sample represents certain characteristics in proportion to their prevalence in the population.

is available, without any concern for its similarity to the population of interest. The distinguishing feature of a quota sample is that quotas are set to ensure that the sample represents certain characteristics in proportion to their prevalence in the population.

Quota samples are similar to stratified probability samples, but they are generally less rigorous and precise in their selection procedures. Quota sampling simply involves designating the population into proportions of some group that you want to be represented in your sample. Similar to stratified samples, in some cases, these proportions may actually represent the true proportions observed in the population. At other times, these quotas may represent predetermined proportions of subsets of people you deliberately want to oversample.

Suppose we are interested in investigating the crime of personal larceny with contact, which generally involves pocket picking and purse snatching. Because elderly citizens are disproportionately victimized by this crime, we would want to make sure we have enough elderly victims in our sample to make comparisons to their younger cohorts. For a study such as this, we may decide that we want 50% of the victims in our sample to consist of individuals 65 years of age or older and 50% to consist of those younger than 65 years of age. When these proportions are decided, they represent our *quotas*. Elements of the population are then collected until each quota is filled. In our example, we would select the sample until we have exactly 50% of the elements younger than 65 and 50% 65 years of age or older. Quota sampling may be more complex, in that we can add quotas to fill. For example, in addition to age, we may want to make sure that within each age group we have a certain proportion of African American men and women, a certain proportion of Hispanic men and women, and a certain proportion of Caucasian men and women.

The problem is that even when we know that a quota sample is representative of the particular characteristics for which quotas have been set, we have no way of knowing if the sample is representative in terms of any other characteristics. In Exhibit 5.7, for example, quotas have been set for gender only. Under the circumstances, it's no surprise that the sample is representative of the population only in terms of gender, not in terms of race. Interviewers are only human and guided by their own biases; they may avoid potential respondents with menacing dogs in the front yard, or they could seek out respondents who are physically attractive or who look like they would be easy to interview. Realistically, researchers can set quotas for only a small fraction of the characteristics relevant

---

Exhibit 5.7 **Quota Sampling**

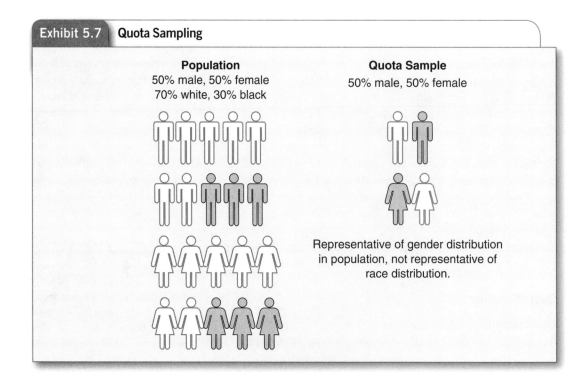

Population	Quota Sample
50% male, 50% female	50% male, 50% female
70% white, 30% black	

Representative of gender distribution in population, not representative of race distribution.

to a study, so a quota sample is really not much better than an availability sample (although following careful, consistent procedures for selecting cases within the quota limits always helps).

This last point leads to another limitation of quota sampling: You must know the characteristics of the entire population to set the right quotas. In most cases, researchers know what the population looks like in terms of no more than a few of the characteristics relevant to their concerns; and in some cases, they have no such information on the entire population. Exhibit 5.8 summarizes the differences between quota sampling and stratified random sampling. The key difference, of course, is quota sampling's lack of random selection. Thus, even though quota sampling techniques range from the simple to the rigorous, all quota samples are still considered nonprobability samples because they do not rely on random selection.

Purposive or Judgment Sampling

In **purposive sampling**, each sample element is selected for a purpose, usually because of the unique position of the sample elements. It is sometimes referred to as *judgment sampling*, because the researcher uses his or her own judgment about whom to select into the sample, rather than drawing sample elements randomly. Purposive sampling may involve studying the entire population of some limited group (members of a street gang) or a subset of a population (juvenile parolees). Or a purposive sample may be a key informant survey, which targets individuals who are particularly knowledgeable about the issues under investigation.

> **Purposive sampling** A nonprobability sampling method in which elements are selected for a purpose, usually because of their unique position. Sometimes referred to as *judgment sampling*.

Rubin and Rubin (1995) suggest three guidelines for selecting informants when designing any purposive sampling strategy. Informants should be

- knowledgeable about the cultural arena or situation or experience being studied;

- willing to talk; and

- representative of the range of points of view.

Exhibit 5.8 | **Unrepresentative Quota Sample Versus a Representative Stratified Sample**

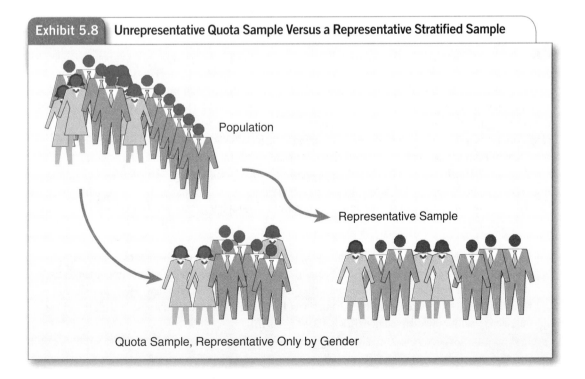

Population

Representative Sample

Quota Sample, Representative Only by Gender

In addition, Rubin and Rubin (1995) suggest continuing to select interviewees until you can pass two tests:

- *Completeness.* "What you hear provides an overall sense of the meaning of a concept, theme, or process" (p. 72).

- *Saturation.* "You gain confidence that you are learning little that is new from subsequent interview[s]" (p. 73).

Adhering to these guidelines will help ensure that a purposive sample adequately represents the setting or issues being studied.

Of course, purposive sampling does not produce a sample that represents some larger population, but it can be exactly what is needed in a case study of an organization, a community, or some other clearly defined and relatively limited group. For example, in their book *Crimes of the Middle Class*, Weisburd et al. (1991) examined a sample of white-collar criminal offenders convicted in seven federal judicial districts. These judicial districts were not randomly selected from an exhaustive list of all federal districts but were instead deliberately selected by the researchers because the seven districts were judged by them to provide a suitable amount of geographical diversity. They were also selected because they were believed to have a substantial proportion of white-collar crime cases. The cost of such nonprobability sampling, you should realize by now, is generalizability; we do not know if findings by Weisburd et al. hold true for white-collar crime in other areas of the country.

Snowball Sampling

For **snowball sampling**, you identify one member of the population and speak to him or her, then ask that person to identify others in the population and speak to them, then ask them to identify others, and so on. The sample size increases with time as a snowball would rolling down a slope. This technique is useful for hard-to-reach or hard-to-identify interconnected populations where at least some members of the population know each other, such as drug dealers, prostitutes, practicing criminals, gang leaders, and informal organizational leaders.

> **Snowball sampling** A method of sampling in which sample elements are selected as they are identified by successive informants or interviewees.

In their study of juvenile gangs in St. Louis, Missouri, Decker and Van Winkle (1996) utilized the technique of snowball sampling. Specifically, the snowball began with an earlier fieldwork project involving active residential burglars (Wright and Decker 1994). The young members from this sample, along with contacts a field ethnographer had with several active street criminals, started the referral process. The initial interviewees then nominated other gang members as potential interview subjects.

One problem with this technique is that the initial contacts may shape the entire sample and foreclose access to some members of the population of interest. Because Decker and Van Winkle (1996) wanted to interview members from several gangs, they had to restart the snowball sampling procedure many times to gain access to a large number of gangs. One problem, of course, was validating whether individuals claiming to be gang members, so-called wannabes, actually were legitimate members. Over 500 contacts were made before the final sample of 99 was complete.

St. Jean (2007) also used snowball sampling for recruiting offenders in a Chicago neighborhood for interviews. After several years of participant observation (see Chapter 9) within a Chicago community, St. Jean wanted to understand the logic offenders used for setting up street drug dealing and staging robberies. He explained his sampling technique as follows:

> I was introduced to the offenders mainly through referrals from relatives, customers, friends, and acquaintances who, after several months (sometimes years), trusted me as someone whose only motive was to understand life in their neighbourhood. For instance, the first three drug dealers I interviewed were introduced by their close relatives. Toward the end of each interview, I asked for leads to other subjects, with the first three interviews resulting in eleven additional leads. (St. Jean 2007:26)

More systematic versions of snowball sampling can also reduce the potential for bias. The most sophisticated version, *respondent-driven sampling*, gives financial incentives, also called gratuities, to respondents to recruit peers (Heckathorn 1997). Limitations on the number of incentives that any one respondent can receive increase the sample's diversity. Targeted incentives can steer the sample to include specific subgroups. When the sampling is repeated through several waves, with new respondents bringing in more peers, the composition of the sample converges on a more representative mix of characteristics. Exhibit 5.9 shows how the sample spreads out through successive recruitment waves to an increasingly diverse pool (Heckathorn 1997). As with all nonprobability sampling techniques, however, researchers using even the most systematic versions of snowball sampling cannot be confident that their sample is representative of the population of interest.

| Exhibit 5.9 | Respondent-Driven Sampling—A Version of Snowball Sampling |

Successive waves of sampling gradually produce a more representative sample than is typical of snowball sampling.

Instructions to respondents:
"We'll pay you $5 each for up to three names, but only one of those names can be somebody from your own town. The others have to be from somewhere else."

Lessons About Sample Quality

Some lessons are implicit in our evaluations of the samples in this chapter:

- We cannot evaluate the quality of a sample if we do not know what population it is supposed to represent. If the population is unspecified because the researchers were never clear about just what population they were trying to sample, then we can safely conclude that the sample itself is no good.

- We cannot evaluate the quality of a sample if we do not know exactly how cases in the sample were selected from the population. If the method was specified, we then need to know whether cases were selected in a systematic fashion or on the basis of chance. In any case, we know that a haphazard method of sampling (as in person-on-the-street interviews) undermines generalizability.

- Sample quality is determined by the sample actually obtained, not just by the sampling method itself. That is, findings are only as generalizable as the sample from which they are drawn. If many of the people (or other elements) selected for our sample do not respond or participate in the study, even though they have been selected for the sample, generalizability is compromised.

- We need to be aware that even researchers who obtain very good samples may talk about the implications of their findings for some group that is larger than or just different from the population they actually sampled. For example, findings from a representative sample of students in one university often are discussed as if they tell us about university students in general. And maybe they do; the problem is we just don't know.

▣ Sampling Distributions

A well-designed probability sample is one that is likely to be representative of the population from which it was selected. But as you have seen, random samples still are subject to sampling error due only to chance. To deal with that problem, social researchers take into account the properties of a sampling distribution, a hypothetical distribution of a statistic across an infinite number of random samples that could be drawn from a population. Any single random sample can be thought of as just one of an infinite number of random samples that, in theory, could have been selected from the population. If we had the finances of Bill Gates and the patience of Job, were able to draw an infinite number of samples, and calculated the same type of statistic (e.g., percentage of those in favor of three-strikes laws) for each of these samples, we would then have a **sampling distribution**. Understanding sampling distributions is the foundation for understanding how researchers can estimate sampling error.

> **Sampling distribution** A distribution of the value of a statistic from many samples.

What does a sampling distribution look like? Because a sampling distribution is based on some statistic calculated for different samples, we need to choose a statistic. Let's focus on the arithmetic average, or mean. We will explain the calculation of the mean in Chapter 12, but you may already be familiar with it: It is simply the arithmetic average of a variable distribution and is obtained by adding up the values of all the cases and then dividing this sum by the total number of cases. Let us say you draw a random sample of 500 families and find that their average (mean) family income is $36,239. This $36,239 would be the sample statistic for this one sample. But imagine that you then drew another random sample, and another, and another, and so on, and calculated the mean from each of these samples. Then imagine marking these means on graph paper. The resulting graph would be a sampling distribution of the mean.

Exhibit 5.10 demonstrates what happens when we do something very similar to what we just described. We did not take an infinite number of samples from a large population but used the General Social Survey (GSS) sample as if it were a population. We first drew 50 different random samples, each consisting of 30 cases, from the GSS. (The standard notation for the number of cases in each sample is $n = 30$.) Then we calculated for each random sample the approximate mean family income (approximate because the GSS does not record actual income in dollars). We then graphed the means of the 50 samples. Each column in Exhibit 5.10 shows how many samples had a particular family income. The mean for the population (the total sample) is $38,249, and you can see that the sampling distribution clusters around this value. Also notice, however, that although many of our selected sample means are close to the population mean, some are quite far from it. If you had calculated the mean from only one sample, it could have fallen

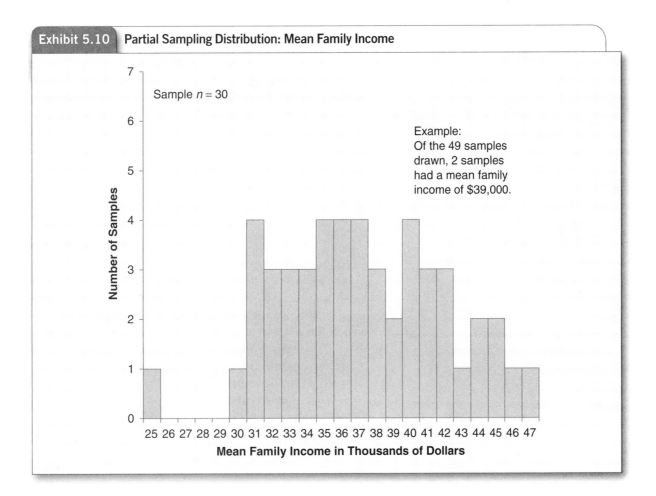

Exhibit 5.10 Partial Sampling Distribution: Mean Family Income

Sample *n* = 30

Example:
Of the 49 samples drawn, 2 samples had a mean family income of $39,000.

Number of Samples (y-axis: 0 to 7)

Mean Family Income in Thousands of Dollars (x-axis: 25 to 47)

anywhere in this distribution, from the low of $25,000 to the high of $47,000. From probability theory, however, we know that the one mean we actually obtain from our sample is unlikely to be far from the true population mean if, in fact, we have drawn a true random sample.

Estimating Sampling Error

In reality, we do not actually observe sampling distributions in real research; it would take too much time and money. Instead, researchers just draw the best sample they can. (Now you understand why it is important to have a sample that is representative of the population.) A sampling distribution usually remains hypothetical or a theoretical distribution. We can use the properties of sampling distributions, however, to calculate the amount of sampling error that was likely with the random sample used in a study. The tools for calculating sampling error are called **inferential statistics**.

Sampling distributions for many statistics, including the mean, have a normal shape. A graph of a **normal distribution** looks like a bell, with one hump in the middle, centered around the population mean, and the number of cases tapering off on both sides of the mean. Note that a normal distribution is symmetrical: If you fold it in half at its center (at the population mean), the two halves will match perfectly. This shape is produced by

Inferential statistics Mathematical tools for estimating how likely it is that a statistical result based on data from a random sample is representative of the population from which the sample was selected.

Normal distribution A symmetric distribution shaped like a bell and centered around the population mean, with the number of cases tapering off in a predictable pattern on both sides of the mean.

Systematic sampling error Overrepresentation or underrepresentation of some population characteristics in a sample due to the method used to select the sample. A sample affected by systematic sampling error is a biased sample.

Random sampling error Differences between the population and the sample that are due only to chance factors (random error), not to systematic sampling error. Random sampling error may or may not result in an unrepresentative sample. The magnitude of sampling error due to chance factors can be estimated statistically.

Sample statistic An estimated statistic (e.g., proportion, mean) from the one sample we actually selected from a population.

Population Parameter A statistic computed for the entire population.

random sampling error. The value of the statistic varies from sample to sample because of chance, so higher and lower values are equally likely. A good example of a normally shaped distribution is the grades that will be received in the class for which you are reading this text. The majority of students in the class will receive Cs, fewer will receive Bs and Ds, and fewer still will receive As and Fs. Unlike random sampling error, **systematic sampling error** occurs because of some bias inherent in the sampling process that creates an overrepresentation or underrepresentation of some population characteristics within our sample.

The partial sampling distribution in Exhibit 5.10 does not have a completely normal shape because it involves only a small number of samples (50), each of which has only 30 cases. Exhibit 5.11 shows what the sampling distribution of family incomes would look like if it formed a perfectly normal distribution if, rather than 50 random samples, we had selected thousands of random samples.

As stated earlier, in research, our goal is to generalize what we observe in our sample to the population of interest. In statistical terminology, a sample statistic is an estimate of the population parameter we want to estimate. The properties of a sampling distribution facilitate this process of statistical inference. In the sampling distribution, the most frequent value of the **sample statistic** (such as the mean) computed from sample data is identical to the **population parameter**, the statistic computed for the entire population. In other words, we can have a lot of confidence that the value at the peak of the bell curve represents the norm for the entire population.

In a normal distribution, a predictable proportion of cases also fall within certain ranges under the curve. Inferential statistics take advantage of this feature and allow us to estimate how likely it is that, given a particular sample, the true population value will be within some range around the statistic. For example, a statistician might conclude from a sample of 30 families that we

---

Exhibit 5.11 | **Normal Sampling Distribution: Mean Family Income**

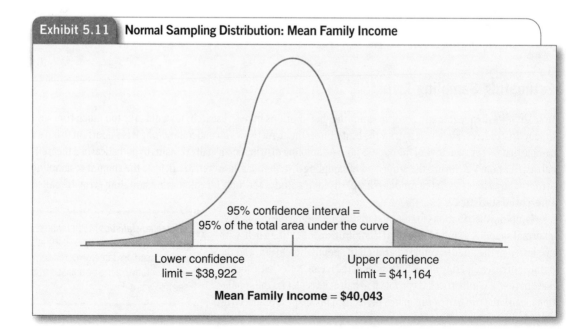

95% confidence interval =
95% of the total area under the curve

Lower confidence
limit = $38,922

Upper confidence
limit = $41,164

Mean Family Income = $40,043

can be 95% confident that the true mean family income in the total population is between $23,012 and $38,120. The interval from $23,012 to $38,120 would then be called the **confidence interval** for the mean. The upper ($38,120) and lower ($23,012) bounds of this interval are the **confidence limits**. Exhibit 5.11 marks such confidence limits, indicating the range that encompasses 95% of the area under the normal curve; in theory, then, 95% of all sample statistics would fall within this range.

Although all normal distributions have these same basic features, they differ in the extent to which they cluster around the mean. A sampling distribution is more compact when it is based on larger samples. Stated another way, we can be more confident in estimates based on large random samples because we know that a larger sample creates a more compact sampling distribution. This should make intuitive sense. If you want to estimate the average family income of residents in New York City and you only select a sample of 30 families, the mean you estimate from this sample of 30 is less likely to reflect New York City residents' annual family income than a sample of, say, 3,000. This should make intuitive sense.

Let us illustrate the importance of sample size for you. Compare the two sampling distributions of mean family income in Exhibit 5.12. Both depict the results for 50 samples. However, in one study each sample comprised 100 families, and in the other study each sample comprised only five families. Clearly, the larger samples ($n = 100$) result in a sampling distribution that is much more tightly clustered around the true mean of the population compared to the smaller samples ($n = 5$). The 95% confidence interval for mean family income for the entire GSS sample of 1,368 cases was $29,421 to $31,711, an interval only about $2,300 wide. But the 95% confidence interval for the mean family income in one GSS subsample of 100 cases was much wider, with limits of $25,733 and $35,399. And for a subsample of only five cases, the 95% confidence interval was very broad: $14,104 to $47,028. This wide interval reflects the fact that we are less confident in this sample estimate. Because the confidence we have in statistics obtained from such small samples is so low, they give us very little useful information about the population.

In most social science disciplines, including ours, researchers typically rely on 95% or 99% confidence intervals. In fact, every time you read the results of an opinion poll in the newspaper or hear about one on a news broadcast, you are really being given a confidence interval. For example, when a newspaper reports that 30% of high school seniors have used marijuana in the past 6 months, the reporter will also usually add the phrase "plus or minus 4 percentage points." This is a confidence interval. These conventional confidence limits reflect the conservatism inherent in classical statistical inference. As researchers, we cannot make an inferential statement (e.g., the population does or believes such and such) unless we are very confident (at least 95% confident) that it is correct.

Even though we have not explained how to calculate confidence intervals, all this discussion about theoretical sampling distributions and inferential statistics may have left you a little confused. We hope we have achieved our goal, however, and that you now have a sense of how researchers make inferences from a random sample to a population.

Now that you understand that more confidence can be placed in statistics obtained from large samples, you may wonder why researchers do not obtain large random samples all the time. The primary answer to this question is "Bucks!" Researchers often cannot afford to sample a large number of cases from their population of interest. They therefore try to determine during the design phase of their study how large a sample they must have to achieve their research purpose. This is usually done through a method called statistical power analysis (Kraemer and Thiemann 1987), which is a mathematical way to determine the sample size needed to find relationships between a given set of variables. Researchers also obtain some general guidance about sample sizes from the current practices of social scientists. For professional studies of the national population in which only a simple description is desired, professional social science studies typically use a sample size of 1,000 to 3,000 individuals. Studies of local or regional populations often sample only a few hundred people, in part because these studies lack sufficient funding to draw larger samples. The sampling error in these smaller studies, of course, is considerably larger than in a typical national study (Sudman 1976).

> **Confidence interval** The range defined by the confidence limits for a sample statistic.
>
> **Confidence limits** The upper and lower bounds around an estimate of a population parameter based on a sample statistic. The confidence limits show how much confidence can be placed in the estimate.

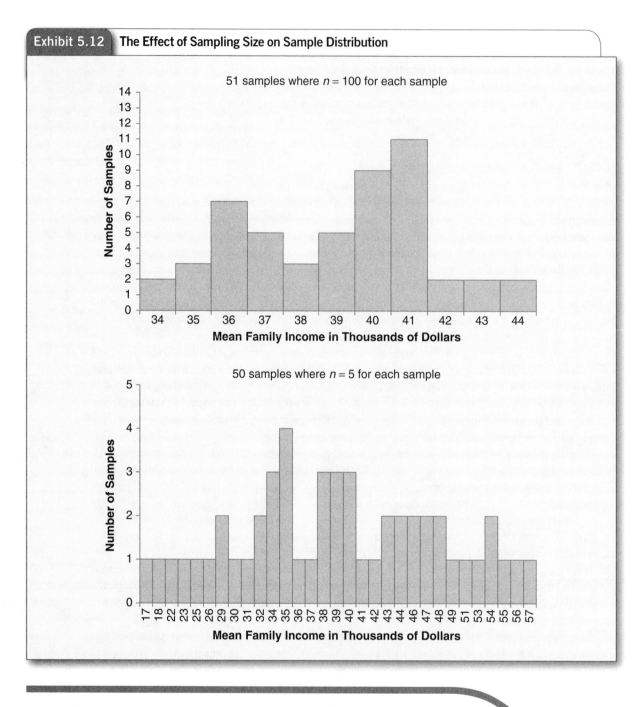

Exhibit 5.12 The Effect of Sampling Size on Sample Distribution

Units of Analysis and Errors in Causal Reasoning

In criminological research, we obtain samples from many different units, including individuals, groups, cities, prisons, countries, and so on. When we make generalizations from a sample to the population, it is very important to keep in mind the units under study, which are referred to as the **units of analysis**. These units of analysis are the level of social life on which the research question is focused, such as individuals, groups, or nations.

Individual and Group Units of Analysis

In most social science research, including criminological studies, the units of analysis are individuals. The researcher may collect survey data from individuals, analyze the data, and then report on how many individuals felt socially isolated and whether recidivism by individuals related to their feelings of social isolation. Data are collected from individuals, and the focus of analysis is on the individual.

> **Units of analysis** The level of social life on which a research question is focused, such as individuals.

In other instances, however, the units of analysis may instead be groups, such as families, schools, prisons, towns, states, or countries. For example, a researcher may collect data from town and police records on the number of accidents in which drivers were intoxicated and the presence or absence of a server liability law, which makes those who serve liquor liable for accidents caused by those they served. The researcher can then analyze the relationship between server liability laws and the frequency of accidents due to drunk driving (perhaps also taking into account town population). Because the data describe the towns, towns are the units of analysis.

In some studies, groups are the units of analysis, but data are collected from individuals. For example, Sampson, Raudenbush, and Earls (1997) studied influences on violent crime in Chicago neighborhoods. Collective efficacy was one variable they hypothesized as an influence on the neighborhood crime rate. This variable was a characteristic of the neighborhood residents who were likely to help other residents and were trusted by other residents, so they measured this variable in a survey of individuals. The responses of individual residents about their perceptions of their neighbors' helpfulness and trustworthiness were averaged to create a collective efficacy score for each neighborhood. It was this neighborhood measure of collective efficacy that was used to explain variation in the rate of violent crime between neighborhoods. The data were collected from individuals and were about individuals, but they were combined or aggregated to describe neighborhoods. The units of analysis were thus groups (neighborhoods).

In a study such as the one by Sampson et al. (1997), we can distinguish the concept of units of analysis from the units of observation. Data were collected from individuals, the units of observation, and then the data were aggregated and analyzed at the group level. In some studies, the units of observation and the units of analysis are the same while in others they are not. The important point is to know when this is true. A conclusion that crime increases with joblessness could imply that individuals who lose their jobs are more likely to commit a crime, that a community with a high unemployment rate is likely to have a high crime rate, or both. Whether we are drawing conclusions from data or interpreting others' conclusions, we have to be clear about which relationship is referenced.

> **Units of observation** The cases about which measures actually are obtained in a sample.

To interpret statistics appropriately, we also have to know the units of analysis. Measures of association tend to be stronger for group-level than for individual-level data because measurement errors at the individual level tend to cancel out at the group level (Bridges and Weis 1989).

The Ecological Fallacy and Reductionism

Researchers should make sure that their conclusions reflect the units of analysis in their study. For example, a conclusion that crime increases as unemployment increases could imply that individuals who lose their jobs are more likely to commit a crime, that a community with a high unemployment rate is also likely to have a high crime rate, or both. Conclusions about processes at the individual level should be based on individual-level data; conclusions about group-level processes should be based on data collected about groups. In most cases, violation of this rule creates one more reason to suspect the validity of the causal conclusions.

A researcher who draws conclusions about individual-level processes from group-level data is constructing an ecological fallacy (see Exhibit 5.13). The conclusions may or may not be correct, but we must recognize that group-level data do not describe individual-level processes. For example, a researcher

> **Ecological fallacy** An error in reasoning in which incorrect conclusions about individual level processes are drawn from group-level data.

Exhibit 5.13 **Errors in Causal Conclusions**

may examine prison employee records and find that the higher the percentage of correctional workers without college education in prisons, the higher the rate of inmate complaints of brutality by officers in prisons. But the researcher would commit an ecological fallacy if she then concluded that individual correctional officers without a college education were more likely to engage in acts of brutality against inmates. This conclusion is about an individual-level causal process (the relationship between the education and criminal propensities of individuals), even though the data describe groups (prisons). It could actually be that college-educated officers are the ones more likely to commit acts of brutality. If more officers in prison are not college educated, perhaps the college-educated officers feel they would not be suspected.

Bear in mind that conclusions about individual processes based on group-level data are not necessarily wrong. The data simply do not provide information about processes at the individual level. Suppose we find that communities with higher average incomes have lower crime rates. The only thing special about these communities may be that they have more individuals with higher incomes, who tend to commit fewer crimes. Even though we collected data at the group level and analyzed them at the group level, they reflect a causal process at the individual level (Sampson and Lauritsen 1994).

When data about individuals are used to make inferences about group-level processes, a problem occurs that can be thought of as the mirror image of the ecological fallacy: the **reductionist fallacy**, or **reductionism** (see Exhibit 5.13). For example, William Wilson (1987) notes that we can be misled into concluding from individual-level data that race has a causal effect on violence. However, community-level data reveal that almost 40% of poor African Americans lived in extremely poor areas in 1980, compared to only 7% of poor Caucasians. The concentration of African Americans in poverty areas, not the race or other characteristics of the individuals in these areas, may be the cause of higher rates of violence. Explaining violence in this case requires community-level data.

> *Reductionist fallacy (reductionism)* An error in reasoning that occurs when incorrect conclusions about group-level processes are based on individual-level data.

The fact that errors in causal reasoning can be made should not deter you from conducting research with aggregate data; nor should it make you unduly critical of researchers who make inferences about individuals on the basis of aggregate data. When considered broadly, many research questions point to relationships that could be manifested in many ways and on many levels. The study of urban violence by Sampson et al. (1987) is a case in point. Their analysis involved only aggregate data about cities, and they explained their research approach as, in part, a response to the failure of other researchers to examine this problem at the structural, aggregate level. Moreover, Sampson et al. argued that the rates of joblessness and family disruption in communities influence community social processes, not just the behavior of the specific individuals who are unemployed or who grew up without two parents. Yet Sampson et al. suggest that the experience of joblessness and poverty is what tends to reduce the propensity of individual men to marry and that the experience of growing up in a home without two parents in turn increases the propensity of individual juveniles to commit crimes. These conclusions about the behavior of individuals seem consistent with the patterns Sampson et al. found in their aggregate, city-level data, so it seems unlikely that they are committing an ecological fallacy.

The solution is to know what the units of analysis and units of observation were in a study and to take these into account when weighing the credibility of the researcher's conclusions. The goal is not to reject conclusions that refer to a level of analysis different from what was actually studied. Instead, the goal is to consider the likelihood that an ecological fallacy or a reductionist fallacy has been made when estimating the causal validity of the conclusions.

🔲 Conclusion

Sampling is the fundamental starting point in criminological research. Probability sampling methods allow a researcher to use the laws of chance, or probability, to draw samples from populations and maintain a standard of representativeness that can be estimated with a high degree of confidence. A sample of just 1,000 or 1,500 individuals can easily be used to reliably estimate the characteristics of the population of a nation comprising millions of individuals.

But researchers do not come by representative samples easily. Well-designed samples require careful planning, some advance knowledge about the population to be sampled, and adherence to systematic selection procedures so that the selection procedures are not biased. And even after the sample data are collected, the researcher's ability to generalize from the sample findings to the population is not completely certain. The best the researcher can do is to perform additional calculations that state the degree of confidence that can be placed in the sample statistic.

The alternatives to random, or probability-based, sampling methods are almost always much less desirable, even though they typically are less expensive. Without a method of selecting cases likely to represent the population in which the researcher is interested, research findings will have to be carefully qualified. Unrepresentative samples may help researchers understand which aspects of a social phenomenon are important, but questions about the generalizability of this understanding are left still unanswered.

Social scientists often seek to generalize their conclusions from the population that they studied to some larger target population. The validity of generalizations of this type is necessarily uncertain, for having a representative sample of a particular population does not at all ensure that what we find will hold true in other populations. Nonetheless, the accumulation of findings from studies based on local or otherwise unrepresentative populations can provide important information about broader populations.

Key Terms

Availability sampling   116
Census   107
Cluster   115
Confidence interval   125
Confidence limits   125
Cross-population generalizability (external validity)   104
Disproportionate stratified sampling   113
Ecological fallacy   127
Enumeration units   102
External validity (cross-population generalizability)   104
Inferential statistics   123

Multistage cluster sampling   115
Nonprobability sampling methods   108
Nonresponse   109
Normal distribution   123
Periodicity   113
Population   102
Population parameter   124
Probability of selection   109
Probability sampling methods   108
Proportionate stratified sampling   113
Purposive sampling   119
Quota sampling   117
Random digit dialing (RDD)   111

Random number table   111
Random sampling error   124
Random selection   109
Reductionist fallacy (reductionism)   128
Replacement sampling   112
Representative sample   107
Sample   102
Sample generalizability   104
Sample statistic   124
Sampling distribution   122
Sampling error   106
Sampling frame   102
Sampling interval   112

Highlights

- Sampling theory focuses on the generalizability of descriptive findings to the population from which the sample was drawn. It also considers whether statements can be generalized from one population to another.

- Sampling is usually necessary except in two conditions: (1) when the elements that would be sampled are identical, which is almost never the case, and (2) when you have the option of conducting a complete census of a population.

- Nonresponse undermines sample quality: It is the obtained sample, not the desired sample, that determines sample quality.

- Probability sampling methods rely on a random selection procedure to ensure there is no systematic bias in the selection of elements. In a probability sample, the odds of selecting elements are independent, equal, and known, and the method of selection is carefully controlled.

- A sampling frame (a list of elements in the population) is required in most probability sampling methods. The adequacy of the sampling frame is an important determinant of sample quality.

- Simple random sampling and systematic random sampling are equivalent probability sampling methods in most situations. However, systematic random sampling is inappropriate for sampling from lists of elements that have a regular, periodic structure.

- Stratified random sampling uses prior information about a population to make sampling more efficient. Stratified sampling may be either proportionate or disproportionate. Disproportionate stratified sampling is useful when a research question focuses on a stratum or on strata that make up a small proportion of the population.

- Cluster sampling is less efficient than simple random sampling but is useful when a sampling frame is unavailable. It is also useful for large populations spread out across a wide area or among many organizations.

- Nonprobability sampling methods can be useful when random sampling is not possible, when a research question does not concern a larger population, and when a preliminary exploratory study is appropriate. However, the representativeness of nonprobability samples cannot be determined.

- The likely degree of error in an estimate of a population characteristic based on a probability sample decreases as the size of the sample increases. Sampling error also decreases if the population from which the sample was selected is homogeneous. Sampling error is not affected by the proportion of the population that is sampled, except when that proportion is large. The degree of sampling error affecting a sample statistic can be estimated from the characteristics of the sample and knowledge of the properties of sampling distributions. Through these inferential statistics, we can estimate the degree of confidence we have in our findings.

- Invalid generalizations about causal relationships may occur when relationships between variables measured at the group level are assumed to apply at the individual level (the ecological fallacy) and when relationships between variables measured at the level of individuals are assumed to apply at the group level (the reductionist fallacy). Nonetheless, many research questions point to relationships at multiple levels and may profitably be answered by studying different units of analysis.

Research in the News

Department Engaged in Excessive Force

The U.S. Justice Department has concluded after an extensive investigation that the Seattle Police Department has used weapons either excessively or unnecessarily more than half the time during arrests. The investigation used many research methods including reviewing thousands of pages of documents (e.g., video footage, internal reports, investigative files), conducting hundreds of interviews, and examining a random sample of force reports between 2009 and 2011. The report noted that "This trend [excessive force] is pronounced in encounters with persons with mental illnesses or those under the influence of alcohol or drugs."

Source: Barnett, Jim. 2011. "Justice Department Finds Seattle Police Department Engaged in Excessive Force." CNN, December 16. Retrieved June 1, 2011 (http://www.cnn.com/2011/12/16/justice/washington-seattle-police/index.html).

Exercises

1. Assess two different polls offering opinions about the same heated topic related to crime—compare CNN.com with Slate.com, for example. What information does the article provide on the sample that was selected? What additional information do you need to determine whether the sample was a representative one? What do the responses tell you about the people who participated in the polls on these Web sites?

2. Select a random sample using a table of random numbers, which can be found on many Web sites (stattrek.com/statistics/random-number-generator.aspx). Compute a statistic based on your sample, and compare it to the corresponding figure for the entire population:

   a. First, select the crime statistics of your choice at the city or state level from the most recent Federal Bureau of Investigation's (FBI) Uniform Crime Report (UCR).

   b. Next, create your sampling frame, a numbered list of all elements in the population. If you are using a complete listing of all elements, such as state-level crime statistics, the sampling frame is the same as the list. Just number the elements (states). If your population is composed of cities, your sampling frame will be those cities that meet certain criteria (e.g., all cities with a population of 250,000 or greater); you may need to refer to another source, such as the U.S. Bureau of the Census, to determine which cities meet your criteria. Identify these cities, and then number them sequentially, starting with 1.

   c. Decide on a method of picking numbers out of the random number table that you obtained on the Internet, such as taking every number in each row, row by row, or by moving down or diagonally across the columns. Use only the first (or last) digit in each number if you need to select one to nine cases; select the first (or last) two digits if you want fewer than 100 cases.

   d. Pick a starting location in the random number table. It is important to pick a starting point in an unbiased way, perhaps by closing your eyes and then pointing to some part of the page.

   e. Record the numbers you encounter as you move from the starting location in the direction you decided in advance, until you have recorded as many random numbers as the number of cases you need in the sample. If you are selecting states, 10 might be a good number. Ignore numbers that are too large (or small) for the range of numbers used to identify the elements in the population. Discard duplicate numbers.

   f. Calculate the mean value (mathematical average) in your sample for the crime statistic you selected. Calculate the mean by adding up the values of all the elements in the sample and dividing by the number of elements in the sample.

   g. Go back to the sampling frame and calculate this same average for all the elements in the list. How close is the sample average to the population average?

3. Select three scholarly journal articles that describe criminological research using a sample drawn from some population (you can find articles on the Student Study Site). Identify the type of sample used in each study, and note any strong or weak points in how the sample was actually drawn. Did the researchers have a problem due to nonresponse? Considering the sample, how confident are you in the validity of generalizations about the population based on the sample? Do you need any additional information to evaluate the sample? Do you think a different sampling strategy would have been preferable? What larger population were the findings generalized to? Do you think these generalizations were warranted? Why or why not?

4. Draw a snowball sample of people who have some characteristic of interest that is not common (i.e., have been skydiving). Ask friends and relatives to locate a first contact, and then call or visit this person and ask for names of others. Stop when you have identified a sample of 10. Review the problems you encountered, and consider how you would proceed if you had to draw a larger sample.

5. All adult U.S. citizens are required to participate in the decennial census, but some do not. Some social scientists have argued for putting more resources into a large representative sample so that more resources are available to secure higher rates of response from hard-to-include groups. Do you think that the U.S. Census should shift to a probability-based sampling design? Why or why not?

6. What are the advantages and disadvantages of probability-based sampling designs compared with nonprobability-based designs? Could any of the research described in this chapter with a nonprobability-based design have been conducted instead with a probability-based design? What are the difficulties that might have been encountered in an attempt to use random selection? How would you discuss the degree of confidence you can place in the results obtained from research using a nonprobability-based sampling design?

7. Identify one article at the Student Study Site, www.sagepub.com/bachmanprccj5e, that used a survey research design. Describe the sampling procedure. What type was it? Why did the author(s) use this particular type of sample?

Developing a Research Proposal

Consider the possibilities for sampling.

1. Propose a sampling design that would be appropriate if you were to survey students on your campus only. Define the population, identify the sampling frame(s), and specify the elements and any other units at different stages. Indicate the exact procedure for selecting people to be included in the sample.

2. Propose a different sampling design for conducting your survey in a larger population, such as your city, your state, or the entire nation.

STUDENT STUDY SITE

Log on to the Web-based student study site at **www.sagepub.com/bachmanprccj5e** for additional study tools including eFlashcards, Web quizzes, links to SAGE journal articles, podcasts, videos, data sets and codebooks, Web exercises, Web resources, and additional appendices.

Web Exercises

1. What can you learn about sampling on the Web? Conduct a search on "sampling" and "population" and select a few of these sites. List a few new points that you learn about sampling and how the inclusion of cell phone users will steer future research findings.

2. Go to the INFOMINE Scholarly Internet Resource Collections Web site at infomine.ucr.edu. Search for five resources of information on crime or victimization. Briefly describe your sources and list the Web sites where they can be found. How do these sources of information differ in their approaches to collecting information? Do they report the sampling information? What statistics do they present? Do they report the sampling method used in the studies from which they obtained these statistics? What sampling methods were used? Evaluate the sampling methods in terms of representativeness and generalizability. How would you improve on the sampling methods to increase the representativeness and generalizability of the data? If no sampling methods are mentioned, propose one that would have been appropriate to obtain the statistics.

3. Check out some of the data sets collected by the Bureau of Justice Statistics at www.ojp.usdoj.gov/bjs/. Select a data set and describe the sampling procedures used to collect the data.

Ethics Exercises

1. How much pressure is too much pressure to participate in a probability-based sample survey? Is it OK for the U.S. government to mandate legally that all citizens participate in the decennial census? Should companies be able to require employees to participate in survey research about work-related issues? Should students be required to participate in surveys about teacher performance? Should parents be required to consent to the participation of their high school-age students in a survey about substance abuse and health issues? Is it OK to give monetary incentives for participation in a survey of homeless shelter clients? Can monetary incentives be coercive? Explain your decisions.

2. Federal regulations require special safeguards for research on persons with impaired cognitive capacity. Special safeguards are also required for research on prisoners and on children. Do you think special safeguards are necessary? Why or why not? Do you think it is possible for individuals in any of these groups to give "voluntary consent" to research participation? What procedures might help make consent to research truly voluntary in these situations? How could these procedures influence sampling plans and results?

3. As discussed in this chapter, the Centers of Disease Control and Prevention sampled adults using random digit dialing in order

to determine the prevalence of intimate partner violence and sexual assault. Do you believe that the researchers had any ethical obligation to take any action whatsoever when they learned that a respondent was currently being victimized? Are any of the ethical guidelines presented in Chapter 2 relevant to this situation?

Teachers and medical personnel are required by law to report cases they believe represent incidents of child abuse. Should researchers have the same obligation? How would this affect large-scale surveys using random digit dialing in which you want to preserve the anonymity of respondents?

SPSS or Excel Exercises

Using the data set NCVS.ASSAULT.POR, which contains a random sample of assault victimizations from the National Crime Victimization Survey from 1992 to 2005. The variable V2089 reports the location (urban, suburban, rural) of each assault incident.

1. Create a frequency distribution for this variable, and record the valid percentage for each category.

2. Select a random sample of approximately 5% of all cases. Create a second frequency distribution for the robbery location and record the valid percentage for each category.

3. Select a random sample containing approximately 1% of all cases. Create a third frequency distribution and record the valid percentage for each category.

4. Compare the three frequency distributions. How does sample size influence the results? Does the sample size affect the reliability or validity of where robbery is most likely to occur?

5. For those assault victims who were injured and lost time from work, describe the number of days of work lost (V4487). It is important to recode "don't know" and "residue" responses as missing for this analysis—you should include the values of 997 (don't know) and 998 (residue) as missing along with the values of 999, which is already specified as missing. Produce both a frequency distribution and a histogram for this variable. How would you describe the impact of assault victimizations on lost work productivity in America?

CHAPTER 6

Causation and Research Design

I dentifying causes, figuring out why things happen, is the goal of most social science research. Unfortunately, valid explanations of the causes of social phenomena do not come easily. According to the National Crime Victimization Survey (NCVS), violent crime victimization rates have been declining since the 1990s. However, decreases in violence rates have not been uniform across race or ethnicity, age, or geographic location. And in some cities, rates of violence have begun to increase significantly. For example, increases in homicide rates have been observed in various cities including Chicago, Illinois, Philadelphia, Pennsylvania, and Camden, New Jersey. For example, at the time of this writing in June 2012, there had already been 173 homicides in Philadelphia, which compared to only 143 for the same time period by June 2011 (Davey 2012).

There have been many explanations for these differential increases in violence across cities. Is the recent rise in violence observed in some cities due to the release of hard-core convicts who were imprisoned during the crime wave of the 1980s and early 1990s (Liptak 2004)? Simply a "crime-drop party is over" phenomenon, as criminologist James Alan Fox has suggested (cited in Lichtblau 2000:A2)? And why has the violent crime rate continued its downward trend in some cities like New York (Dewan 2004a)? Is it because of Compstat, the city's computer program that identifies to police where crimes are clustering (Dewan 2004b; Kaplan 2002)? Or in New York City, should credit be given to the "Safe Streets, Safe Cities" program, which increased the ranks of police officers (Rashbaum 2002)? What about better emergency room care causing a decline in the lethality of gunshot wounds (Harris et al. 2002)? To determine which of these factors may be causally related to increases or decreases in violence, we must design our research strategies carefully.

In this chapter, we first discuss the meaning of causation from two different perspectives—nomothetic and idiographic—and then review the criteria for achieving causally valid explanations. During this review, we give special attention to several key distinctions in research design that are related to our ability to come to causal conclusions: the use of an experimental or nonexperimental design and reliance on a cross-sectional or longitudinal design. By the end of the chapter, you should have a good grasp of the different meanings of causation and be able to ask the right questions to determine whether causal inferences are likely to be valid. You also may have a better answer about the causes of crime and violence.

🔲 Causal Explanation

A cause is an explanation for some characteristic, attitude, or behavior of groups, individuals, or other entities (such as families, organizations, or cities) or for events. Most social scientists seek causal explanations that reflect tests of the types of hypotheses with which you are familiar (see Chapter 2): In these tests, the independent variable is the presumed cause, and the dependent variable is the potential effect. For example, does problem-oriented policing (independent variable) reduce violent crime (dependent variable)? Does experiencing abuse as a child (independent variable) increase the likelihood that you will be a violent adult (dependent variable)? This type of causal explanation is termed *nomothetic*.

A different type of cause is the focus of some qualitative research (see Chapter 9) and our everyday conversations about causes. In this type of causal explanation, termed *idiographic*, individual events or the behavior of individuals are explained with a series of related, prior events. For example, you might explain a particular crime as resulting from several incidents in the life of the perpetrator that resulted in a tendency toward violence, coupled with stress resulting from a failed marriage and a chance meeting.

Nomothetic Causal Explanation

A **nomothetic causal explanation** is one involving the belief that variation in an independent variable will be followed by variation in the dependent variable, when all other things are equal (*ceteris paribus*), or when all other potentially influential conditions and factors are taken into consideration. For instance, researchers might claim that the likelihood of committing violent crimes is higher for individuals who were abused as

> *Nomothetic causal explanation* A type of causal explanation involving the belief that variation in an independent variable will be followed by variation in the dependent variable, when all other things are equal.

Causal effect (nomothetic perspective) When variation in one phenomenon, an independent variable, leads to or results, on average, in variation in another phenomenon, the dependent variable.

Example of a nomothetic causal effect: Individuals arrested for domestic assault tend to commit fewer subsequent assaults than do similar individuals who are accused in the same circumstances but not arrested.

Ceteris parabius Latin term meaning "all other things being equal."

Counterfactual The outcome that would have occurred if the subjects who were exposed to the treatment actually were not exposed but otherwise had had identical experiences to those they underwent during the experiment.

children than it would be if these same individuals had not been abused as children. Or, researchers might claim that the likelihood of committing violent crimes is higher for individuals exposed to media violence than it would be if these same individuals had not been exposed to media violence. The situation as it would have been in the absence of variation in the independent variable is termed the **counterfactual** (see Exhibit 6.1).

Of course, the fundamental difficulty with this perspective is that we never really know what would have happened at the same time to the same people (or groups, cities, and so on) if the independent variable had not varied, because it did. We cannot rerun real-life scenarios (King, Keohane, and Verba 1994). We could observe the aggressiveness of people's behavior before and after they were exposed to media violence. But this comparison involves an earlier time period, when, by definition, the people and their circumstances were not exactly the same.

Fortunately, we can design research to create conditions that are comparable indeed so that we can confidently assert our conclusions *ceteris paribus*. We can examine the impact on the dependent variable of

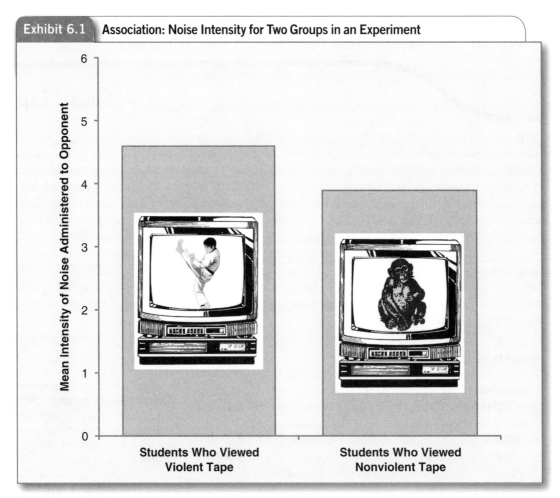

Exhibit 6.1 **Association: Noise Intensity for Two Groups in an Experiment**

Source: Adapted from Bushman 2012.

variation in the independent variable alone, even though we will not be able to compare the same people at the same time in exactly the same circumstances except for the variation in the independent variable. And by knowing the ideal standard of comparability, we can improve our research designs and strengthen our causal conclusions even when we cannot come so close to living up to the meaning of *ceteris paribus*.

Quantitative researchers seek to test nomothetic causal explanations with either experimental or nonexperimental research designs. However, the way in which experimental and nonexperimental designs attempt to identify causes differs quite a bit. It is very hard to meet some of the criteria for achieving valid nomothetic causal explanations using a nonexperimental design. Most of the rest of this chapter is devoted to a review of these causal criteria and a discussion of how experimental and nonexperimental designs can help establish them.

Idiographic Causal Explanation

The other meaning of the term *cause* is one that we have in mind very often in everyday speech. This is idiographic causal explanation: the concrete, individual sequence of events, thoughts, or actions that resulted in a particular outcome for a particular individual or that led to a particular event (Hage and Meeker 1988). An idiographic explanation also may be termed an *individualist* or a *historicist explanation*.

A causal explanation that is idiographic includes statements of initial conditions and then relates a series of events at different times that led to the outcome, or causal effect. This narrative, or story, is the critical element in an idiographic explanation, which may therefore be classified as narrative reasoning (Richardson 1995). Idiographic explanations focus on particular social actors, in particular social places, at particular social times (Abbott 1992). Idiographic explanations are also typically very concerned with context, with understanding the particular outcome as part of a larger set of interrelated circumstances. Idiographic explanations thus can be termed holistic.

Idiographic explanation is deterministic, focusing on what caused a particular event to occur or what caused a particular case to change. As in nomothetic explanations, idiographic causal explanations can involve counterfactuals, by trying to identify what would have happened if a different circumstance had occurred. But unlike nomothetic explanations, in idiographic explanations the notion of a probabilistic relationship, an average effect, does not really apply. A deterministic cause has an effect in every case under consideration.

Anderson's (1990) field research in a poor urban community produced a narrative account of how drug addiction can result in a downward slide into residential instability and crime:

> *Idiographic causal explanation* An explanation that identifies the concrete, individual sequence of events, thoughts, or actions that resulted in a particular outcome for a particular individual or that led to a particular event; may be termed an individualist or historicist explanation.
>
> *Causal effect (idiographic perspective)* When a series of concrete events, thoughts, or actions result in a particular event or individual outcome.
>
> *Example of an idiographic causal effect:* An individual is neglected by his parents. He comes to distrust others, has trouble maintaining friendships, has trouble in school, and eventually gets addicted to heroin. To support his habit, he starts selling drugs and is ultimately arrested and convicted for drug trafficking.

> *Context* A focus of causal explanation; a particular outcome is understood as part of a larger set of interrelated circumstances.

> When addicts deplete their resources, they may go to those closest to them, drawing them into their schemes. . . . The family may put up with the person for a while. They provide money if they can. . . . They come to realize that the person is on drugs. . . . Slowly the reality sets in more and more completely, and the family becomes drained of both financial and emotional resources. . . . Close relatives lose faith and begin to see the person as untrustworthy and weak. Eventually the addict begins to "mess up" in a variety of ways, taking furniture from the house [and] anything of value. . . . Relatives and friends begin to see the person . . . as "out there" in the streets. . . . One deviant act leads to another. (pp. 86–87)

An idiographic explanation like Anderson's (1990) pays close attention to time order and causal mechanisms. Nonetheless, it is difficult to make a convincing case that one particular causal narrative should be chosen over an alternative narrative (Abbott 1992). Does low self-esteem result in vulnerability to the appeals of drug dealers, or does a chance drug encounter precipitate a slide in self-esteem? The prudent causal analyst remains open to alternative explanations.

▣ Research Designs and Criteria for Causal Explanations

In the movie *The Basketball Diaries,* Jim Carroll, played by Leonardo DiCaprio, is a high school basketball player growing up in Manhattan in the 1960s. His life rotates around basketball and writing in his journal. At 16, he tries heroin for the first time and goes from a high school basketball star to a serious heroin addict. The film chronicles his downward spiral into addiction, homelessness, violent crime, and eventually prostitution. One scene in the movie shows a dream sequence in which DiCaprio guns down his teacher and some of his classmates. On December 1, 1997, Michael Carneal, a 14-year-old going to Heath High School in West Paducah, Kentucky, opened fire on a group of praying students, killing three girls and wounding five others. In 1999, the parents of three victims filed a lawsuit against the distributors of *The Basketball Diaries* and other media outlets claiming that the media violence depicted in the movie inspired Carneal to go on a shooting rampage and should therefore be held responsible. How would you evaluate this claim? What evidence do we need to develop a valid conclusion about a hypothesized causal effect? Imagine a friend saying, after reading about the incident, "See, media violence causes people to commit crimes." Of course, after reading Chapter 1 you would not be so quick to jump to such a conclusion. "Don't overgeneralize," you would remind yourself. When your friend insists, "But I recall that type of thing happening before," you might even suspect selective observation. As a blossoming criminological researcher, you now know that if we want to have confidence in the validity of our causal statements, we must meet a higher standard.

How research is designed influences our ability to draw causal conclusions. In this section, we will introduce the features that need to be considered in a research design in order to evaluate how well it can support nomothetic causal conclusions.

Five criteria must be considered when deciding whether a causal connection exists. When a research design leaves one or more of the criteria unmet, we may have some important doubts about causal assertions the researcher may have made. The first three of the criteria are generally considered the necessary and most important basis for identifying a nomothetic causal effect: empirical association, appropriate time order, and nonspuriousness. The other two criteria, identifying a causal mechanism and specifying the context in which the effect occurs, can also considerably strengthen causal explanations although many do not consider them as requirements for establishing a causal relationship.

Conditions necessary for determining causality:

1. Empirical association

2. Appropriate time order

3. Nonspuriousness

Conditions important in specifying causal relationships:

1. Mechanism

2. Context

◫ Case Study: Media Violence and Violent Behavior

We will use Brad Bushman's (see Bushman and Huesmann for review, 2012) experiments on media violence and aggression to illustrate the five criteria for establishing causal relationships. Bushman's study focused in part on this specific research question: Do individuals who view a violent videotape act more aggressively than individuals who view a nonviolent videotape?

Undergraduate psychology students were recruited to watch a 15-minute videotape in a screening room, one student at a time. Half of the students watched a movie excerpt that was violent, and half watched a nonviolent movie excerpt. After viewing the videotape, the students were told that they were to compete with another student, in a different room, on a reaction-time task. When the students saw a light cue, they were to react by trying to click a computer mouse faster than their opponent. On a computer screen, the students set a level of radio static that their opponents would hear when the opponents reacted more slowly. The students themselves heard this same type of noise when they reacted more slowly than their opponents, at the intensity level supposedly set by their opponents.

Each student in the study participated in 25 trials, or competitions, with the unseen opponent. Their aggressiveness was operationalized as the intensity of noise that they set for their opponents over the course of the 25 trials. The louder the noise level they set, the more aggressively they were considered to be behaving toward their opponents. The question that we will focus on first is whether students who watched the violent video behaved more aggressively than those who watched the nonviolent video.

Association

The results of Bushman's (2012) experiment are represented in Exhibit 6.1. The average intensity of noise administered to the opponent was indeed higher for students who watched the violent videotape than for those who watched the nonviolent videotape. But is Bushman justified in concluding from these results that viewing a violent videotape increased aggressive behavior in his subjects? Would this conclusion have any greater claim to causal validity than the statement that your friend made in response to *The Basketball Diaries* incident? Perhaps it would.

If for no other reason, we can have greater confidence in Bushman's (2012) conclusion because he did not observe just one student who watched a violent video and then acted aggressively, as was true in the *Basketball Diaries* incident. Instead, Bushman observed a number of students, some of whom watched a violent video and some of whom did not. So his conclusion is based on finding an **association** between the independent variable (viewing of a violent videotape) and the dependent variable (likelihood of aggressive behavior).

> **Association** A criterion for establishing a causal relationship between two variables: variation in one variable is related to variation in another variable as condition to determine causality.

Time Order

Association is a necessary criterion for establishing a causal effect, but it is not sufficient on its own. We must also ensure that the variation in the independent variable came *before* variation in the dependent variable— the cause must come before the presumed effect. This is the criterion of **time order**. Bushman's experiment satisfied this criterion because he controlled the variation in the independent variable: All the students saw the movie excerpts (which varied in violent content) before their level of aggressiveness was measured. As you can imagine, we cannot be so sure about time order when we use a survey or some other observation done at one point in time. Suppose you find in a survey that

> **Time order** A criterion for establishing a causal relation between two variables; the variation in the independent variable must come before variation in the dependent variable.

most people who have committed violent crimes have also watched the movie *The Basketball Diaries* and that most people who have not committed violent crimes have not watched the movie. You believe you have found an association between watching the movie and committing violent crimes. But imagine you learn that the movie was released after the crimes were committed. Thus, those people in your survey who said they had seen the movie had actually committed their crimes before the movie characters committed their crimes. Watching the movie, then, could not possibly have led to the crimes. Perhaps the criminals watched the movie because committing violent crimes made them interested in violent movies. This discussion points to the importance of the criterion of time order. To conclude that causation was involved, we must see that cases were exposed to variation in the independent variable *before* variation in the dependent variable.

Nonspuriousness

Even when research establishes that two variables are associated and that variation in the independent variable precedes variation in the dependent variable, we cannot be sure we have identified a causal relationship between the two variables. Have you heard the old adage "Correlation does not prove causation"? It is meant to remind us that an association between two variables might be caused by something else. If we measure children's shoe sizes and their academic knowledge, for example, we will find a positive association. However, the association results from the fact that older children have larger feet as well as more academic knowledge. As it turns out, shoe size does not cause knowledge or vice versa. We would say that the association between shoe size and knowledge is *spurious*.

Nonspuriousness A relationship that exists between two variables that is not due to variation in a third variable.

Spurious relationship A relationship between two variables that is due to variation in a third variable.

Extraneous variable A variable that influences both the independent and dependent variables so as to create a spurious association between them that disappears when the extraneous variable is controlled.

Before we conclude that variation in an independent variable causes variation in a dependent variable, we must have reason to believe that the relationship is nonspurious. **Nonspuriousness** is a relationship between two variables that is not due to variation in a third variable. When this third variable, an **extraneous variable**, causes the variation, it is said to have created a **spurious relationship** between the independent and dependent variables. We must design our research so that we can see what happens to the dependent variable when only the independent variable varies. If we cannot do this, there are other statistical methods we must use to control the effects of other variables we also believe are related to our dependent variable. (You will be relieved to know that a discussion of these statistical techniques is way beyond the scope of this text!)

In reality, then, the fact that someone went on a shooting spree after seeing the movie *The Basketball Diaries* might be related to the fact that he was already feeling enraged against society. This led him to seek out a violent movie for entertainment purposes (see Exhibit 6.2). Thus, seeing the violent movie itself in no way led him to commit the crime. We must be sure that all three conditions of association, time order, and nonspuriousness are met before we make such claims.

Does Bushman's (2012) claim of a causal effect rest on any stronger ground? To evaluate nonspuriousness, you need to know about one more feature of his experiment. He assigned students to watch either the violent video or the nonviolent video randomly—that is, by the toss of a coin. Because he used random assignment, the characteristics and attitudes that students already possessed when they were recruited for the experiment could not influence which video they watched. As a result, the students' characteristics and attitudes could not explain why one group reacted differently from the other after watching the videos. In fact, because Bushman used 296 students in his experiment, it is highly unlikely that the violent video group and the nonviolent video group differed in any relevant way at the outset, even on the basis of chance. This experimental research design meets the criterion of nonspuriousness. Bushman's conclusion that viewing video violence causes aggressive behavior thus rests on firm ground indeed.

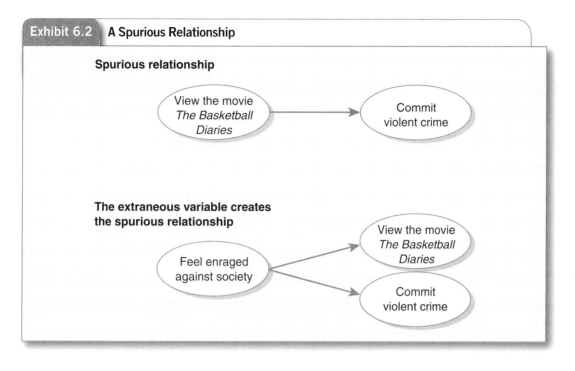

Exhibit 6.2 A Spurious Relationship

Causal (internal) validity is achieved by meeting the criteria of association, time order, and nonspuriousness. Others, however, believe that two additional criteria should also be considered: mechanism and context.

Mechanism

Confidence in a conclusion that two variables have a causal connection will be strengthened if a **mechanism**, some discernable means of creating a connection, can be identified (Cook and Campbell 1979; Marini and Singer

> **Mechanism** A discernible process that creates a causal connection between two variables.

1988). Many social scientists (and scientists in other fields) argue that a causal explanation is not adequate until a causal mechanism is identified. What process or mechanism actually is responsible for the relationship between the independent and dependent variables?

Bushman (2012) did not empirically identify a causal mechanism in his experiment, but he did suggest a possible causal mechanism for the effect of watching violent videos. Before we can explain this causal mechanism, we have to tell you about one more aspect of his research. He was not interested simply in whether viewing violent films resulted in aggressive behavior. Actually, his primary hypothesis was that individuals who were predisposed to aggression before the study began would be more influenced by a violent film than individuals who were not aggressive at the outset. And that is what happened: Individuals who were predisposed to aggression became more aggressive after watching Bushman's violent video, but individuals who were not predisposed to aggression did not become more aggressive.

After the experiment, Bushman (2012) proposed a causal mechanism to explain why aggressive individuals became even more aggressive after watching the film:

> High trait aggressive individuals [people predisposed to aggression] are more susceptible to the effects of violent media than are low trait aggressive individuals because they possess a relatively large network of aggressive associations that can be activated by violent cues. Habitual exposure to television violence might be partially responsible. (p. 959)

Note that this explanation relies more on speculation than on the actual empirical evidence from this particular experiment. Nonetheless, by proposing a reasonable causal mechanism that connects the variation in the independent and dependent variables, Bushman (2012) strengthens the argument for the causal validity of his conclusions.

It is often possible to go beyond speculation by designing research to test one or more possible causal mechanisms. Perhaps other researchers will design a new study to measure directly the size of individuals' networks of aggressive associations that Bushman (2012) contends are part of the mechanism by which video violence influences aggressive behavior.

Context

In the social world, it is virtually impossible to claim that one and only one independent variable is responsible for causing or affecting a dependent variable. Stated another way, no cause can be separated from the larger context in which it occurs. A cause is really only one of a set of interrelated factors required for the effect (Hage and Meeker 1988; Papineau 1978). When relationships among variables differ across geographic units like counties or across other social settings, researchers say there is a **contextual effect**. Identification of the context in which a causal relationship occurs can help us understand that relationship.

> ***Contextual effect*** Relationships between variables that vary between geographic units or other contexts.

Some researchers argue that we do not fully understand the causal effect of media violence on behavioral aggression unless we have identified these other related factors. As we have just seen, Bushman (2012) proposed at the outset of his research at least one other condition: Media violence would increase aggression only among individuals who were already predisposed to aggression.

Identification of the context in which a causal effect occurs is not a criterion for a valid causal conclusion. Some contextual factors may not turn out to be causes of the effect being investigated. The question for researchers is "How many contexts should we investigate?" In a classic study of children's aggressive behavior in response to media violence, Bandura, Ross, and Ross (1963) examined several contextual factors. They found that effects varied with the children's gender and with the gender of the opponent toward whom they acted aggressively but not with whether they saw a real (acted) or filmed violent incident. For example, children reacted more aggressively after observing men committing violent acts than after observing women committing these same acts. But Bandura et al. did not address the role of violence within the children's families or the role of participation in sports or many other factors that could be involved in children's responses to media violence. Bandura et al. strengthened their conclusions by focusing on a few likely contextual factors.

Specifying the context for a causal effect helps us understand that effect, but it is a process that can never really be complete. We can always ask what else might be important: In which country was the study conducted? What are the ages of the study participants? We need to carefully review the results of prior research and the implications of relevant theory to determine what contextual factors are likely to be important in a causal relationship. Our confidence in causal conclusions will be stronger when we know these factors are taken into account.

▣ Research Designs and Causality

How research is designed influences our ability to draw causal conclusions. Obviously, if you conclude that playing violent video games causes violent behavior after watching your 8-year-old nephew playing a violent video game and then hitting his 4-year-old brother, you would be on shaky empirical ground. In this section, we will introduce features that need to be considered in a research design in order to evaluate how well it can support nomothetic causal conclusions.

True Experiments

In a **true experiment**, the time order is determined by the researcher. The experimental design provides the most powerful design for testing causal hypotheses about the effect of a treatment or some other variable whose values can be manipulated by the researchers. It is so powerful for testing causal hypotheses because it allows us to establish the three criteria for causality with a great deal of confidence. The Bushman (1995) study we examined in the last section was a true experiment.

True experiments must have at least three things:

1. Two comparison groups, one receiving the experimental condition (e.g., treatment or intervention) termed the **experimental group** and the other receiving no treatment or intervention or another form thereof, termed the **control group** or **comparison group**.

2. **Random assignment** to the two (or more) comparison groups.

3. Assessment of change in the dependent variable for both groups after the experimental condition has been received.

The combination of these features permits us to have much greater confidence in the validity of causal conclusions than is possible in other research designs. Confidence in the validity of an experiment's findings is further enhanced by identification of the causal mechanism and control over the context of an experiment. We will discuss experimental designs in more detail in Chapter 7. For now, we want to highlight how true experimental designs lend themselves to meeting the criteria necessary for causality.

> **True experiment** Experiment in which subjects are assigned randomly to an experimental group that receives a treatment or other manipulation of the independent variable and a comparison group that does not receive the treatment or receives some other manipulation. Outcomes are measured in a posttest.
>
> **Experimental group** In an experiment, the group of subjects that receives the treatment or experimental manipulation.
>
> **Control or comparison group** The group of subjects who are either exposed to a different treatment than the experimental group or who receive no treatment at all.
>
> **Random assignment** A procedure by which each experimental subject is placed in a group randomly compared to random sampling.

Causality and True Experimental Designs

A prerequisite for meeting each of the three criteria to identify causal relations is maintaining control over the conditions subjects are exposed to after they are assigned to the experimental and comparison groups. If these conditions begin to differ, the variation between the experimental and comparison groups will not be what was intended. Even a subsequent difference in the distribution of cases on the dependent variable will not provide clear evidence of the effect of the independent variable. Such unintended variation is often not much of a problem in laboratory experiments where the researcher has almost complete control over the conditions and can ensure that these conditions are nearly identical for both groups. But control over conditions can become a very big concern for experiments that are conducted in the field in real-world settings, such as Sherman and Berk's (1984) study of the deterrent effects of arrest on intimate partner assaults.

Let us examine how well true experiments meet the criteria necessary for establishing causality in greater detail:

Association between the hypothesized independent and dependent variables. As you have seen, experiments can provide unambiguous evidence of association by randomly assigning subjects to experimental and comparison groups.

Time order of effects of one variable on the others. Unquestionably, the independent variable (treatment of condition) preceded the posttest measures in the experiments described so far. For example, arrest for partner abuse preceded recidivism in the Sherman and Berk (1984) study, and exposure to media violence preceded aggression in the Bushman (1995) experiment. In experiments with a pretest, time order can be established by comparing posttest to pretest scores. In experiments with random assignment of subjects to the experimental and comparison groups, time order can be established by comparison of posttest scores only.

Nonspurious relationships between variables. Nonspuriousness is difficult to establish; some would say it is impossible to establish in nonexperimental designs. The random assignment of subjects to experimental and comparison groups makes true experiments powerful designs for testing causal hypotheses. Random assignment controls a host of possible extraneous influences that can create misleading, spurious relationships in both experimental and nonexperimental data. If we determine that a design has used randomization successfully, we can be much more confident in the causal conclusions.

Mechanism that creates the causal effect. The features of a true experiment do not, in themselves, allow identification of causal mechanisms; as a result there can be some ambiguity about how the independent variable influenced the dependent variable and the causal conclusions.

Context in which change occurs. Control over conditions is more feasible in many experimental designs than it is in nonexperimental designs, but it is often difficult to control conditions in field experiments. In the next chapter, you will learn how the lack of control over experimental conditions can threaten internal validity.

Field Experiments: Determining the Effect of Incarceration on Employment

Experiments don't always have to be conducted in a laboratory. In fact, many experiments are conducted out in the real world. Whenever a method utilizes the conditions of an experimental method in a real-world setting, they are termed **field experiments**. All of the studies examining the effects of arrest on future intimate partner assaults discussed in Chapter 2 were field experiments. One recent innovative field experiment was conducted by Pager (2007) to determine the effects of incarceration on the likelihood of obtaining employment. This is an extremely important research question because the prison population in the United States has vastly increased over the past 30 years. Today, an unprecedented 2 million individuals are in some sort of correctional facility and nearly 5 million are under some sort of criminal justice supervision, bringing the total correctional population to over 7 million people. Of course, the majority of inmates are eventually returned to the community. In fact, over 650,000 inmates reenter society every year in the United States (Bureau of Justice Statistics 2009b). In addition to the laws barring ex-offenders in some states from obtaining employment in certain sectors, reentering offenders also face other obstacles in finding a job. How could we determine the effects of a formal record on the likelihood of getting a job? Well, we could examine employer attitudes about hiring ex-offenders through a survey, but as you now know, this would not help us isolate a causal relationship between having a record and getting a job. We could interview offenders reentering the community to find out their own experiences, but this too would tell us only about a few individuals' experiences. The best way to determine the effects of a criminal record on employment chances would be to conduct a field experiment.

Field experiment An experimental study conducted in a real-world setting.

Pager (2007) was interested in the negative consequences that being incarcerated had on future employment opportunities. She designed a field experiment in which pairs of applicants, one who had a criminal record and one who did not, applied for real jobs. Her study used two male teams of applicants, one team composed of two African Americans and one team composed of two whites. These individuals were actually college students in Milwaukee, Wisconsin, whom Pager refers to as "testers." The testers were matched on the basis of age, physical appearance, and general style of self-presentation, and all were assigned fictitious résumés that reflected equivalent levels of education (all had a high school education) and equivalent levels of steady work experience. However, one tester within each team was randomly assigned to have a criminal record and the other was not. The criminal record consisted of a felony drug conviction and 18 months of served prison time. This assignment rotated each week of the study (e.g., one individual played the job applicant with a record one week, and the other did so the next week) to control for unobserved differences between team members. Same-race testers (one with a criminal record and one without) applied for the same job, 1 day apart. The black team applied for a total of 200 jobs, and the white team applied for a total of 150 jobs.

The primary outcome of the study was the proportion of applications that elicited either callbacks from employers or on-the-spot job offers. The testers went through intensive training to become familiar with their assumed profiles and to respond similarly to potential interview questions. As such, the only difference between the two testers on each race team was that one had a criminal record and the other didn't. Because there was random assignment to these two conditions and the other characteristics of the testers were essentially the same, the differences observed in the percentage of callbacks between team members can be assumed to be related to the criminal record only and not to other factors.

The results of Pager's (2007) field experiment were stark. Testers with a criminal record were one-half to one-third less likely to receive a callback from employers, and the effect was even more pronounced for black applicants. Pager concludes, "Mere contact with the criminal justice system in the absence of any transformative or selective effects severely limits subsequent job prospects. The mark of a criminal record indeed represents a powerful barrier to employment" (p. 145). With such a powerful randomly assigned field experiment, the internal (causal) validity of these findings is strong. The implications of these findings in light of the hundreds of thousands of offenders who attempt to reenter society from prison each year are troubling indeed.

Nonexperimental Designs

Nonexperimental research designs can be either cross-sectional or longitudinal. In a **cross-sectional research design**, all data are collected at one point in time. Identifying the time order of effects—what happened first and so on—is critical for developing a causal analysis but can be an insurmountable problem with a cross-sectional design. In **longitudinal research designs**, data are collected at two or more points in time, and so identification of the time order of effects can be quite straightforward. You can think of an experiment as a type of longitudinal design because subjects are observed at two or more points in time.

> **Cross-sectional research design** A study in which data are collected at only one point in time.
>
> **Longitudinal research design** A study in which data are collected that can be ordered in time; also defined as research in which data are collected at two or more points in time.

Cross-Sectional Designs

Much of the research you have encountered so far in this text has been cross-sectional. Although each survey or interview takes some time to carry out, if it measures the actions, attitudes, and characteristics of respondents at only one time, it is considered cross-sectional. The name comes from the idea that a snapshot from a cross section of the population is obtained at one point in time.

As you learned in Chapter 4, Sampson and Raudenbush (1999) used a very ambitious cross-sectional design to study the effect of visible public social and physical disorder on the crime rate in Chicago neighborhoods. Their theoretical framework focused on the concept of informal social control: the ability of residents to regulate social activity in their neighborhoods through their collective efforts according to desired principles. They believed that informal social control would vary between neighborhoods, and they hypothesized that it was the strength of informal social control that would explain variation in crime rates rather than just the visible sign of disorder. They contrasted this prediction with the "broken windows" theory: the belief that signs of disorder themselves cause crime. Their findings supported their hypothesis: Both visible disorder and crime were consequences of low levels of informal social control (measured with an index of "collective efficacy"). One did not cause the other (see Exhibit 6.3).

In spite of these compelling findings (see Exhibit 6.4), Sampson and Raudenbush's (1999) cross-sectional design could not establish directly that the variation in the crime rate occurred after variation in informal social control. Maybe it was a high crime rate that led residents to stop trying to exert much control over deviant activities in the neighborhood, perhaps because of fear of crime. It is difficult to discount such a possibility when only cross-sectional data are available.

There are four special circumstances in which we can be more confident in drawing conclusions about time order on the basis of cross-sectional data. Because in these special circumstances the data can be ordered in time, they might even be thought of as longitudinal designs (Campbell 1992).

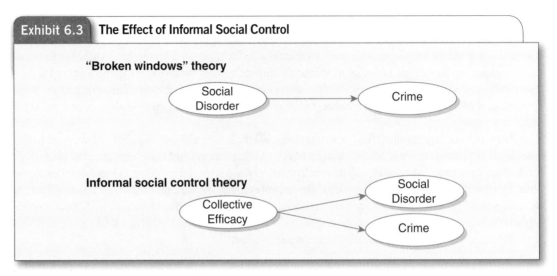

Exhibit 6.3 — The Effect of Informal Social Control

Source: Based on Sampson and Raudenbush 1999:635.

Exhibit 6.4 — Effect of Social Disorder and Collective Efficacy on Personal Violent Crimes

Source: Based on Sampson and Raudenbush 1999

The independent variable is fixed at some point prior to the variation in the dependent variable. So-called demographic variables that are determined at birth—such as sex, race, and age—are fixed in this way. So are variables like education and marital status, if we know when the value of cases on these variables was established and if we know that the value of cases on the dependent variable was set some time afterward. For example, say we hypothesize that educational opportunities in prison affect recidivism rates. Let us say we believe those inmates who are provided with greater educational and vocational opportunities in prison will be less likely to reoffend after release from prison. If we know that respondents completed their vocational or other educational training before leaving prison, we would satisfy the time order requirement even if we were to measure education at the same time we measure recidivism after release. However, if some respondents possibly went back to school after prison release, the time order requirement would not be satisfied.

We believe that respondents can give us reliable reports of what happened to them or what they thought at some earlier point in time. The reliability of recall is based on many factors including how far back in time respondents are queried and also the events they are asked to recall.

Our measures are based on records that contain information on cases in earlier periods. Government, agency, and organizational records are an excellent source of time-ordered data after the fact. However, sloppy record keeping and changes in data-collection policies can lead to inconsistencies, which must be taken into account. Another weakness of such archival data is that they usually contain measures of only a fraction of the variables that we think are important. This caution applies to the arrest records obtained by Lo and colleagues (2008) that we just described. For example, their research did not obtain arrest records from states other than Ohio, and as such, they may have missed important incidents that could have affected their results.

We know that the value of the dependent variable was similar for all cases prior to the treatment. For example, we may hypothesize that an anger management program (independent variable) improves the conflict resolution abilities (dependent variable) of individuals arrested for intimate partner assault. If we know that none of the arrested individuals could employ verbal techniques for resolving conflict prior to the training program, we can be confident that any subsequent variation in their ability to do so did not precede exposure to the training program. This is one way that traditional experiments establish time order: Two or more equivalent groups are formed prior to exposing one of them to some treatment.

Case Study Using Life Calendars: Do Offenders Specialize in Different Crimes?

Lo, Kim, and Cheng (2008) provide an interesting example of the use of such retrospective data. The researchers wanted to examine the characteristics of offenders that would lead them to repeat certain crimes. Specifically, they wanted to know if the type of crime committed early in someone's life was a reliable predictor of offenses committed later. Stated differently, do offenders specialize in different types of crime? Lo et al. obtained official arrest records from the age of 18 to the time of the study (typically around age 25) for a sample of young offenders who were incarcerated in county jails in Ohio. They then asked the inmates to reconstruct their drug and alcohol use among other things monthly for the same time period using a **life calendar** instrument based on the **Arrestee Drug Abuse Monitoring (ADAM)** interview schedule. This life calendar instrument helps respondents recall events in their past by displaying each month of a given year along with key dates noted within the calendar, such as birthdays, arrests, holidays, anniversaries, and so on. Respondents are given a calendar that displays these key dates, typically called **anchors**, and then are asked to recall the variables of interest (i.e., drug use, victimizations) that also occurred during the specified time frame. The use of a life calendar has been shown to improve the ability of respondents to recall events in the past compared to basic questions without a calendar (Belli, Stafford, and Alwin 2009).

> *Life calendar* An instrument that helps respondents recall events in their past by displaying each month of a given year along with key dates noted within the calendar, such as birthdays, arrests, holidays, anniversaries, etc.
>
> *Arrestee Drug Abuse Monitoring (ADAM)* Uses standardized drug testing methodologies and predictive models to measure the consequences of drug abuse within and across the United States boundaries.
>
> *Anchors* Key dates of important events like birthdays that help trigger recall for respondents.

Results of the research by Lo et al. (2008) were somewhat mixed regarding offender specialization. Most offenders engaged in a variety of offenses prior to their current arrest. However, compared to drug and property offenders, violent offenders were more likely to specialize as they were the most likely to have had violent arrest records prior to their current offenses.

It is important to note that retrospective data like these are often inadequate for measuring variation in past psychological states or behaviors, because what we recall about our feeling or actions in the past is likely to be influenced by what we feel in the present. For example, retrospective reports by both adult alcoholics and their parents appear to greatly overestimate the frequency of childhood problems (Vaillant 1995). People cannot report reliably the frequency and timing of many past events, from hospitalization to hours worked. However, retrospective data tend to be reliable when they concern major, persistent experiences in the past, such as what type of school someone went to or how a person's family was structured (Campbell 1992).

Longitudinal Designs

In longitudinal research, data are collected at two or more points in time and, as such, can be ordered in time. By measuring the value of cases on an independent variable and a dependent variable at different times, the researcher can determine whether variation in the independent variable precedes variation in the dependent variable.

In some longitudinal designs, the same sample (or panel) is followed over time; in other designs, sample members are rotated or completely replaced. The population from which the sample is selected may be defined broadly, as when a longitudinal survey of the general population is conducted. Or the population may be defined narrowly, as when members of a specific age group are sampled at multiple points in time. The frequency of follow-up measurement can vary, ranging from a before-and-after design with just one follow-up to studies in which various indicators are measured every month for many years.

Collecting data at two or more points in time can prove difficult for a number of reasons—lack of long-term funding, not being able to locate the original participants, and so on. But think of the many research questions that really should involve a much longer follow-up period: Does community-oriented policing decrease rates of violent crime? What is the impact of job training in prison on recidivism rates? How effective are batterer-treatment programs for individuals convicted of intimate partner assault? Do parenting programs for young mothers and fathers reduce the likelihood of their children becoming delinquent? It is safe to say that we will never have enough longitudinal data to answer many important research questions. Nonetheless, the value of longitudinal data is so great that every effort should be made to develop longitudinal research designs when they are appropriate for the research question asked. The following discussion of the three major types of longitudinal designs will give you a sense of the possibilities (see Exhibit 6.5).

Repeated Cross-Sectional Designs

Studies that use a **repeated cross-sectional design**, also known as **trend studies**, have become fixtures of the political arena around election time. Particularly in presidential election years, we accustom ourselves to reading weekly or even daily reports on the percentage of the population that supports each candidate. Similar polls are conducted to track sentiment on many other social issues. For example, the "Research in the News" box in the last chapter described the change in attitudes toward gun control from 1990 to 2010.

> **Repeated cross-sectional design (trend study)**
> A type of longitudinal study in which data are collected at two or more points in time from different samples of the same population.

Repeated cross-sectional surveys are conducted as follows:

1. A sample is drawn from a population at Time 1, and data are collected from the sample.

2. As time passes, some people leave the population, and others enter it.

3. At Time 2, a different sample is drawn from this population.

These features make the repeated cross-sectional design appropriate when the goal is to determine whether a population has changed over time. Has racial tolerance increased among Americans in the past 20 years? Are prisons more

Exhibit 6.5 Three Types of Longitudinal Design

likely to have drug-treatment programs available today than they were in the 1950s? These questions concern changes in the population as a whole, not changes in individuals within the population. We want to know whether racial tolerance increased in society, not whether this change was due to migration that brought more racially tolerant people into the country or to individual U.S. citizens becoming more tolerant. We are asking whether state prisons overall are more likely to have drug-treatment programs available today than they were a decade or two ago, not whether any such increase was due to an increase in prisoner needs or to individual prisons changing their program availability. When we do need to know whether individuals in the population changed, we must turn to a panel design.

Fixed-Sample Panel Designs

Panel designs allow us to identify changes in individuals, groups, or whatever we are studying. This is the process for conducting **fixed-sample panel designs**, also known as **panel studies**:

> ***Fixed-sample panel design (panel study)*** A type of longitudinal study in which data are collected from the same individuals—the panel—at two or more points in time. In another type of panel design, panel members who leave are replaced with new members.

1. A sample (called a panel) is drawn from a population at Time 1, and data are collected from the sample.

2. As time passes, some panel members become unavailable for follow-up, and the population changes.

3. At Time 2, data are collected from the same people as at Time 1 (the panel), except for those people who cannot be located.

Because a panel design follows the same individuals, it is better than a repeated cross-sectional design for testing causal hypotheses.

▣ Case Study: Offending Over the Life Course

Sampson and Laub (1990) used a fixed-sample panel design to investigate the effect of childhood deviance on adult crime. They studied a sample of white males in Boston when the subjects were between 10 and 17 years old and then followed up when the subjects were in their adult years. Data were collected from multiple sources, including the subjects themselves and criminal justice records. Sampson and Laub found that children who had been committed to a correctional school for persistent delinquency were much more likely than other children in the study to commit crimes as adults: 61% were arrested between the ages of 25 and 32, compared to 14% of those who had not been in correctional schools as juveniles. In this study, juvenile delinquency unquestionably occurred before adult criminality. If the researchers had used a cross-sectional design to study the past of adults, the juvenile delinquency measure might have been biased by memory lapses, by self-serving recollections about behavior as juveniles, or by loss of agency records.

If you now wonder why not every longitudinal study is designed as a panel study, you have understood the advantages of panel designs. However, remember that this design does not in itself establish causality. Variation in both the independent variable and the dependent variables may be due to some other variable, even to earlier variation in what is considered the dependent variable. In the example in Exhibit 6.6, there is a hypothesized association between delinquency in the 11th grade and grades obtained in the 12th grade (the dependent variable). The time order is clear. However, both variables are consequences of grades obtained in the 7th grade. The apparent effect of 11th-grade delinquency on 12th-grade grades is spurious because of variation in the dependent variable (grades) at an earlier time.

Panel designs are also a challenge to implement successfully, and often are not even attempted, because of two major difficulties:

Expense and attrition. It can be difficult, and very expensive, to keep track of individuals over a long period, and inevitably the proportion of panel members who can be located for follow-up will decline over time. Panel studies often lose more than one quarter of their members through attrition (Miller 1991), and those who are lost are often not necessarily like those who remain in the panel. As a result, a high rate of subject attrition may mean that the follow-up sample will no longer be representative of the population from which it was drawn and may no longer provide a sound

Exhibit 6.6 Causality in Panel Studies

Although delinquency in the 11th grade and grades in the 12th grade are clearly associated and the time order is clear, causality cannot be assumed. In reality, grades in the 7th grade also play a role.

basis for estimating change. Subjects who were lost to follow-up may have been those who changed the most, or the least, over time. For example, between 5% and 66% of subjects are lost in substance abuse prevention studies, and the dropouts typically begin such studies with higher rates of tobacco and marijuana use (Snow, Tebes, and Arthur 1992).

It does help to compare the baseline characteristics of those who are interviewed at follow-up with characteristics of those lost to follow-up. If these two groups of panel members were not very different at baseline, it is less likely that changes had anything to do with characteristics of the missing panel members. Even better, subject attrition can be reduced substantially if sufficient staff can be used to keep track of panel members. In their panel study, Sampson and Laub (1990) lost only 12 of the juveniles in the original sample (8 if you do not count those who died).

Subject fatigue. Panel members may grow weary of repeated interviews and drop out of the study, or they may become so used to answering the standard questions in the survey that they start giving stock answers rather than actually thinking about their current feelings or actions (Campbell 1992). This is called the problem of subject fatigue. Fortunately, subjects do not often seem to become fatigued in this way, particularly if the researchers have maintained positive relations with the subjects.

> *Subject fatigue* Problems caused by panel members growing weary of repeated interviews and dropping out of a study or becoming so used to answering the standard questions in the survey that they start giving stock or thoughtless answers.

Because panel studies are so useful, social researchers have developed increasingly effective techniques for keeping track of individuals and overcoming subject fatigue. But when resources do not permit use of these techniques to maintain an adequate panel, repeated cross-sectional designs usually can be employed at a cost that is not a great deal higher than that of a one-time-only cross-sectional study. The payoff in explanatory power should be well worth the cost.

Event-Based Designs

In an event-based design, often called a cohort study, the follow-up samples (at one or more times) are selected from the same cohort: people who all have experienced a similar event or a common starting point. Examples include the following:

- *Birth cohorts*: those who share a common period of birth (those born in the 1940s, 1950s, 1960s, etc.)

- *Seniority cohorts*: those who have worked at the same place for about 5 years, about 10 years, and so on

- *School cohorts*: freshmen, sophomores, juniors, and seniors

> *Event-based design (cohort study)* A type of longitudinal study in which data are collected at two or more points in time from individuals in a cohort.
>
> *Cohort* Individuals or groups with a common starting point. Examples of a cohort include college class of 1997, people who graduated from high school in the 1980s, General Motors employees who started work between 1990 and the year 2000, and people who were born in the late 1940s or the 1950s (the baby boom generation).

An event-based design can be a type of repeated cross-sectional design or a type of panel design. In an event-based repeated cross-sectional design, separate samples are drawn from the same cohort at two or more different times. In an event-based panel design, the same individuals from the same cohort are studied at two or more different times.

Causality in Nonexperimental Designs

How well do the research designs just described satisfy the criteria necessary to determine causality? Although it is relatively easy to establish that an empirical association exists between an independent and a dependent variable in these designs, the other criteria are much more difficult to assess.

Let us first illustrate the importance of time order and nonspuriousness using research that has examined the factors related to the gender and crime relationship. Based on both victimization data and official police reports, data indicate that males commit the majority of all crimes. Why is this? Gottfredson and Hirschi's (1990) General Theory of Crime (GTC) contends that the reason males engage in more criminality is that they have lower levels of self-control than females. The researchers also contend that socialization of children by parents is the primary factor in the development of self-control. However, based on a critique of the GTC by Miller and Burack (1993) and the power-control theory (Hagan, Gillis, and Simpson 1985), Blackwell and Piquero (2005) hypothesized that the power relationships that exist between parents in a household (e.g., patriarchy) would also affect the socialization experiences of boys and girls and ultimately their levels of self-control. To summarize briefly, Blackwell and Piquero examined the factors related to self-control acquisition in childhood using a sample of adults. Using this same sample of adults, they then examined the extent to which low-self control predicted the propensity for criminal offending. In a nutshell, they sought to explain the origins of self-control as well as the effects of self-control on criminal offending and how all this may be different for males and females from patriarchal families and for males and females from more egalitarian families. Using a random sample of 350 adults from Oklahoma City, Oklahoma, they found that there were indeed differences in the way power relationships between parents affected the acquisition of self-control for males and females. They also found, however, that there were essentially no differences in the ability of self-control to predict criminal aspirations; males and females with low self-control were more likely to self-report that they would engage in criminal behavior than their higher-self-control counterparts.

Do these findings establish that low self-control leads to crime through poor socialization of children by parents? Well, there are many assumptions being made here that we hope you can see right away. First, this study relied on the recollections of adults about their childhood socialization. It also assumed that levels of low self-control were subsequent to parental socialization and preceded individuals' aspirations to offend (time order). This may very well be the case. It may be that those adults who were more likely to offend had inadequate socialization, which created low self-control. However, it may be that offending behavior during their adolescence led to weak attachments to family and high attachments to other delinquent peers like themselves, which also decreased levels of self-control. In this case, the delinquent offending and peer associations would be a third variable responsible for both the low self-control and the criminal aspirations in adulthood (spurious relationship). The problem, of course, is that with cross-sectional data like these, the correct time order cannot be established and it is difficult to control for the effects of all important factors. Blackwell and Piquero (2005) stated this limitation well when they concluded, "Future research should attempt to examine the changing nature of parental socialization and self-control across gender in longitudinal studies" (p. 15).

To reduce the risk of spuriousness, Blackwell and Piquero (2005) used the technique of statistical control. Exhibit 6.7 represents the important concept of statistical control with a hypothetical study of the relationship between attending a boot camp in prison (a highly regimented, discipline-focused rehabilitation program) and the likelihood of committing crimes after prison (the recidivism rate). In Exhibit 6.7, the data for all prisoners show that prisoners who attended boot camp were less likely to return to committing crimes after they left prison. However, as the more detailed data show, more female prisoners attended boot camp than male prisoners, so gender may have played a significant role in recidivism. The researchers, however, reduced the risk of spuriousness by using two statistical control methods: They examined the association between attending boot camp and postprison criminality for men and for women. After doing this, researchers determined that boot camp did not reduce recidivism. It just appeared to do so, because women were more likely to attend boot camp and less likely to commit crimes after prison, regardless of whether they attended boot camp.

Similarly, Sampson and Raudenbush (1999) designed their study, in part, to determine whether the apparent effect of visible disorder on crime—the "broken windows" thesis—was spurious due to the effect of informal social control (see Exhibit 6.3). Exhibit 6.8 shows how statistical control was used to test this possibility. The data for all neighborhoods show

Statistical control A technique used in nonexperimental research to reduce the risk of spuriousness. One variable is held constant so the relationship between two or more other variables can be assessed without the influence of variation in the control variable.

Example of statistical control: Blackwell and Piquero (2005) found that self-control predicted criminal aspirations for individuals at all levels of income (a control variable). So an individual's level of income could not have caused the association between self control and criminal aspirations.

Exhibit 6.7 The Use of Statistical Control to Reduce Spuriousness

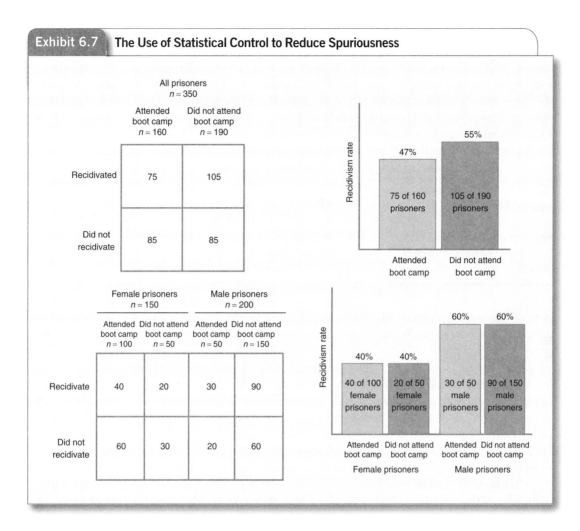

Exhibit 6.8 The Use of Statistical Control to Reduce Spuriousness

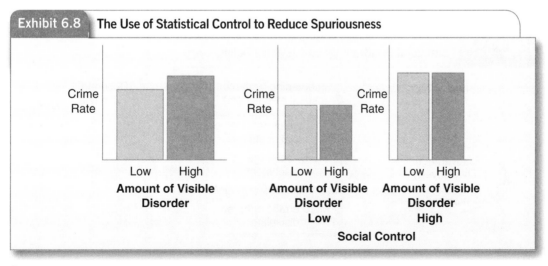

Source: Based on Sampson and Raudenbush 1999.

that neighborhoods with much visible disorder had higher crime rates than those with less visible disorder. However, when we examine the relationship between visible disorder and neighborhood crime rates separately for neighborhoods with high and low levels of informal social control—that is, when we statistically control for social control level—we see that the crime rate no longer varies with visible disorder. Therefore, we must conclude that the apparent effect of "broken windows" was spurious due to level of informal social control. Neighborhoods with low levels of social control were more likely to have high levels of visible social and physical disorder, and they were also more likely to have a high crime rate, but the visible disorder itself did not alter the crime rate.

Our confidence in causal conclusions based on nonexperimental research also increases with identification of a causal mechanism. These mechanisms are called **intervening variables** in nonexperimental research and help us understand how variation in the independent variable results in variation in the dependent variable. For example, in a study that reanalyzed data from Glueck and Glueck's (1950) path-breaking study of juvenile delinquency, Sampson and Laub (1993) found that children who grew up with such structural disadvantages as family poverty and geographic mobility were more likely to become juvenile delinquents. Why did this occur? Their analysis indicated that these structural disadvantages led to lower levels of informal social control in the family (less parent-child attachment, less maternal supervision, and more erratic or harsh discipline). Lower levels of informal social control resulted in a higher probability of delinquency (see Exhibit 6.9). Informal social control intervened in the relationship between structural context and delinquency.

> **Intervening variables** Variables that are influenced by an independent variable and in turn influence variation in a dependent variable, thus helping to explain the relationship between the independent and dependent variables.

Of course, identification of one (or two or three) intervening variables does not end the possibilities for clarifying the causal mechanisms. You might ask why structural disadvantage tends to result in lower levels of family social control or how family social control influences delinquency. You could then conduct research to identify the mechanisms that link, for example, family social control and juvenile delinquency. (Perhaps the children feel they are not cared for, so they become less concerned with conforming to social expectations.) This process could go on and on. The point is that identification of a mechanism through which the independent variable influences the dependent variable increases our confidence in the conclusion that a causal connection does indeed exist.

When you think about the role of variables in causal relationships, do not confuse variables that cause spurious relationships with variables that intervene in causal relationships, even though both are third variables that do not

Exhibit 6.9 Intervening Variables in Nonexperimental Research: Structural Disadvantage and Juvenile Delinquency

Independent Variable

Intervening Variable (causal mechanism)

Dependent Variable

Structural disadvantage Family poverty Geographic mobility

Informal social control: Low parent-child attachment Low maternal supervision More erratic or harsh discipline

Juvenile delinquency

Source: Based on Sampson and Laub 1993.

appear in the initial hypothesis. Intervening variables help explain the relationship between the independent variable (juvenile delinquency) and the dependent variable (adult criminality).

Nonexperimental research can be a very effective tool for exploring the context in which causal effects occur. Administering surveys in many different settings and to different types of individuals is usually much easier than administering various experiments. The difficulty of establishing nonspuriousness does not rule out using nonexperimental data to evaluate causal hypotheses. In fact, when enough nonexperimental data are collected to allow tests of multiple implications of the same causal hypothesis, the results can be very convincing (Freedman 1991).

In any case, nonexperimental tests of causal hypotheses will continue to be popular because the practical and ethical problems in randomly assigning people to different conditions preclude the test of many important hypotheses with an experimental design. Just remember to carefully consider possible sources of spuriousness and other problems when evaluating causal claims based on individual nonexperimental studies.

▣ Conclusion

In this chapter, you have learned about two alternative meanings of causation (nomothetic and idiographic). You have studied the five criteria used to evaluate the extent to which particular research designs may achieve causally valid findings. You have learned how our ability to meet these criteria is shaped by research design features including the use of true experimental designs, the use of cross-sectional or longitudinal designs, and the use of statistical control to deal with the problem of spuriousness. You have also seen why the distinction between experimental and nonexperimental designs has so many consequences for how, and how well, we are able to meet nomothetic criteria for causation.

It is important to remember that the results of any particular study are part of an always-changing body of empirical knowledge about social reality. Thus, our understandings of causal relationships are always partial. Researchers always wonder whether they have omitted some relevant variables from their controls, whether their experimental results would differ if the experiment were conducted in another setting, or whether they have overlooked a critical historical event. But by using consistent definitions of terms and maintaining clear standards for establishing the validity of research results and by expecting the same of others who do research, social researchers can contribute to a growing body of knowledge that can reliably guide social policy and social understanding.

When you read the results of a social scientific study, you should now be able to evaluate critically the validity of the study's findings. If you plan to engage in social research, you should now be able to plan an approach that will lead to valid findings. And with a good understanding of three dimensions of validity (measurement validity, generalizability, and causal [internal] validity) under your belt, you are ready to focus on the major methods of data collection used by social scientists.

Key Terms

Anchors   147
Arrestee Drug Abuse Monitoring
   (ADAM)   147
Association   139
Causal effect (idiographic perspective)   137

Causal effect (nomothetic
   perspective)   136
Ceteris paribus   135
Cohort   151
Cohort study (event-based design)   151

Context   137
Contextual effect   142
Control or comparison group   143
Counterfactual   136
Cross-sectional research design   145

Highlights

- Causation can be defined in either nomothetic or idiographic terms. Nomothetic causal explanations deal with effects on average. Idiographic causal explanations deal with the sequence of events that led to a particular outcome.

- The concept of nomothetic causal explanation relies on a comparison. The value of cases on the dependent variable is measured after they have been exposed to variation in an independent variable. This measurement is compared to what the value of cases on the dependent variable would have been if they had not been exposed to the variation in the independent variable (the counterfactual). The validity of nomothetic causal conclusions rests on how closely the comparison group comes to the ideal counterfactual.

- From a nomothetic perspective, three criteria are generally viewed as necessary for identifying a causal relationship: association between the variables, proper time order, and nonspuriousness of the association. In addition, the basis for concluding that a causal relationship exists is strengthened by identification of a causal mechanism and the context for the relationship.

- Association between two variables is in itself insufficient evidence of a causal relationship. This point is commonly made with the expression "Correlation does not prove causation."

- Experiments use random assignment to make comparison groups as similar as possible at the outset of an experiment in order to reduce the risk of spurious effects due to extraneous variables.

- Nonexperimental designs use statistical controls to reduce the risk of spuriousness. A variable is controlled when it is held constant so that the association between the independent and dependent variables can be assessed without being influenced by the control variable.

- Ethical and practical constraints often prevent the use of experimental designs.

- Idiographic causal explanations can be difficult to identify, because the starting and ending points of particular events and the determination of which events act as causes in particular sequences may be ambiguous.

- Longitudinal designs are usually preferable to cross-sectional designs for establishing the time order of effects. Longitudinal designs vary in terms of whether the same people are measured at different times, how the population of interests is defined, and how frequently follow-up measurements are taken. Fixed-sample panel designs provide the strongest test for the time order of effects, but they can be difficult to carry out successfully because of their expense as well as subject attrition and fatigue.

Research in the News

Gun Control's Prospects After Tucson

In 1990, 78% of the public told Gallup poll that they felt the laws covering the sale of firearms should be made stricter. In 2010, just 44% said this. This is related to political party: 70% of Republicans, but only 30% of Democrats, say it's more important to protect the rights of gun owners than to control gun ownership. It appears that the shooting incident in Arizona and the mass shooting at Virginia Teach have no lasting impact on public attitudes about the issues.

Source: The Washington Post. January 16, 2011. "Topic A: Gun Control's Prospects After Tucson." Retrieved June 10, 2012 (http://www.washingtonpost.com/wp-dyn/content/article/2011/01/14/AR2011011406881.html).

Exercises

1. Review articles in several newspapers, copying down all causal assertions. These might range from assertions that community policing was related to decreasing rates of violence, to assertions that the stock market declined because of uncertainty in the Middle East, and finally to explanations about why a murder was committed. Inspect the articles carefully, noting all evidence used to support the causal assertions. Are the explanations nomothetic, idiographic, or a combination of both? Which criteria for establishing causality in a nomothetic framework are met? How satisfactory are the idiographic explanations? What other potentially important influences on the reported outcome have been overlooked?

2. Select several research articles in professional journals that assert, or imply, that they have identified a causal relationship between two or more variables. Are all the criteria for establishing the existence of a causal relationship met? Find a study in which subjects were assigned randomly to experimental and comparison groups to reduce the risk of spurious influences on the supposedly causal relationship. How convinced are you by the study? Find a survey study that makes causal assertions based on the relationships, or correlations, among variables. What variables have been statistically controlled? List other variables that might be influencing the relationship but that have not been controlled. How convinced are you by the study?

3. Search *Criminal Justice Abstracts* or another index to the social literature for several articles on studies using any type of longitudinal design. You will be searching for article titles that use words like *longitudinal*, *panel*, *trend*, or *over time*. How successful were the researchers in carrying out the design? What steps did the researchers who used a panel design take to minimize panel attrition? How convinced are you by those using repeated cross-sectional designs that they have identified a process of change in individuals? Did any researchers use retrospective questions? How did they defend the validity of these measures?

4. Go to the Student Study Site, www.sagepub.com/bachmanprccj5e, and choose two research articles that include some attention to causality (as indicated by a check in that column of the article matrix). Describe the approach taken in each article to establishing causality. How do the approaches differ from each other? Which approach seems stronger to you?

5. Researchers often try to figure out how people have changed over time by conducting a cross-sectional survey of people of different ages. The idea is that if people who are in their 60s tend to be happier than people who are in their 20s, it is because people tend to "become happier" as they age. But maybe people who are in their 60s now were just as happy when they were in their 20s, and people in their 20s now will be just as unhappy when they are in their 60s. (That's called a "cohort effect.") Why can't we be sure unless we conduct a panel study (survey the same people at different ages)? What, in your experience, are the major differences between the generations today in social attitudes and behaviors? Which would you attribute to changes as people age, and which to differences between cohorts in what they have experienced (such as common orientations among baby boomers)? Explain your reasoning.

Developing a Research Proposal

How will you try to establish the causal effects you hypothesize?

1. Identify at least one hypothesis involving what you expect is a causal relationship.

2. Identify key variables that should be controlled in your survey design in order to increase your ability to avoid arriving at a spurious conclusion about the hypothesized causal effect.

Draw on relevant research literature and social theory to identify these variables.

3. Add a longitudinal component to your research design. Explain why you decided to use this particular longitudinal design.

4. Review the criteria for establishing a nomothetic causal effect and discuss your ability to satisfy each one.

STUDENT STUDY SITE

Log on to the Web-based student study site at **www.sagepub.com/bachmanprccj5e** for additional study tools including eFlashcards, Web quizzes, links to SAGE journal articles, podcasts, videos, data sets and codebooks, Web exercises, Web resources, and additional appendices.

Web Exercises

1. Go to the Disaster Center Web site at www.disastercenter.com/crime/. Review the crime rate nationally and, by picking out links to state reports, compare the recent crime rates in two states. Report on the prevalence of the crimes you have examined. Propose a causal explanation for variation in crime between states, over time, or both. What research design would you propose to test this explanation? Explain.

2. Go to Crime Stoppers USA's (CSUSA) Web site at www.crimestopusa.com. Check out "About Us" and "What is Crime Stoppers?" How is CSUSA "fighting crime"? What does CSUSA's approach assume about the cause of crime? Do you think CSUSA's approach to fighting crime is based on valid conclusions about causality? Explain.

3. What are the latest trends in crime? Write a short statement after inspecting the Federal Bureau of Investigation Uniform Crime Reports at www.fbi.gov (go to the "statistics" section under "Reports & Publications"). You will need to use Adobe Acrobat Reader to access some of these reports (those in PDF). Follow the instructions on the site if you are not familiar with this program.

Ethics Exercises

1. Bushman (1995) tested the impact of watching a violent video on students' level of aggressiveness. He found that watching the violent video increased aggressiveness. Do you consider it ethical to expose subjects to an intervention that might increase their aggressiveness? Are there any situations in which you would not approve of such research? Any types of subjects you would exclude from such research? Any limits you would draw on the type of intervention that could be tested? Would you impose any requirements for debriefing?

2. Lo, Kim, and Cheng (2008) surveyed inmates in county jails. Federal regulations require special safeguards for research on prisoners. Do you think special safeguards are necessary? Why or why not? What type of research would you allow with prisoners: experiments, surveys, observational studies? Do you think it is possible for prisoners to give "voluntary consent" to research participation? What procedures might help make prisoners' consent to research truly voluntary?

3. You learned in this chapter that Sampson and Raudenbush (1999) had observers drive down neighborhood streets in Chicago and record the level of disorder they observed. What should have been the observers' response if they observed a crime in progress? What if they just suspected that a crime was going to occur? What if the crime was a drug dealer interacting with a driver at the curb? What if it was a prostitute soliciting a customer? What, if any, ethical obligation does a researcher studying a neighborhood have to residents in that neighborhood? Should research results be shared at a neighborhood forum?

4. Under what conditions do you think that randomized assignment of subjects to a specific treatment is ethical in criminal justice research? Was it ethical for Sherman and Berk (1984) and the researchers who conducted the replication studies to randomly assign individuals accused of domestic violence to an arrest or nonarrest treatment? What about in a laboratory study with students like yourself? Do you think it would be ethical to assign students randomly to different groups, with some receiving stressful stimuli, like loud noises?

SPSS or Excel Exercises

We can use the GSS2004mini data to learn how causal hypotheses can be evaluated with nonexperimental data.

1. Specify four hypotheses in which CAPPUN is the dependent variable and the independent variable is also measured with a question in the GSS2004. The independent variables should have no more than 10 valid values (check the variable list).

   a. Inspect the frequency distributions of each independent variable in your hypotheses. If it appears that any have little valid data or were coded with more than 10 categories, substitute another independent variable.

   b. Generate cross tabulations that show the association between CAPPUN and each of the independent variables.

Make sure that CAPPUN is the row variable and that you select "Column Percents."

c. Does support for capital punishment vary across the categories of any of the independent variables? By how much? Would you conclude that there is an association, as hypothesized, for any pairs of variables?

d. Might one of the associations you have just identified be spurious due to the effect of a third variable? What might such an extraneous variable be? Look through the variable list and find a variable that might play this role. If you cannot think of any possible extraneous variables, or if you did not find an association in support of any of your hypotheses, try this: Examine the association between CAPPUN and WRKSTAT2. In the next step, control for sex (gender).

2. The idea is that there is an association between work status and support for capital punishment that might be spurious due to the effect of sex (gender). Produce a three-way table that controls for gender. Is the association between employment status and support for capital punishment affected by gender? Do you conclude that the association between CAPPUN and WRKSTAT2 seems to be spurious due to the effect of sex?

3. Does the association between support for capital punishment and any of your independent variables vary with social context? Marian Borg (1998) concluded that it did. Test this by reviewing the association between attitude toward African Americans (RACPUSH2) and CAPPUN. Take awhile to study this complex three-variable table. Does the association between CAPPUN and RACPUSH2 vary with region? How would you interpret this finding?

4. Now, how about the influence of an astrological sign on support for capital punishment? Create a cross tabulation in which ZODIAC is the independent (column) variable and CAPPUN is the dependent (row) variable (with column percents). What do you make of the results?

CHAPTER 7

Experimental Designs

A t the end of 2010, state and federal correctional authorities supervised approximately 1,612,395 prisoners. The imprisonment rate was 500 sentenced prisoners per 100,000 U.S. residents, or about 1 in 200 (Guerino, Harrison, and Sabol 2011). The large prison population coupled with lawsuits has prompted most correctional institutions to begin to classify inmates into differing levels of security (e.g., minimum, maximum) based on objective criteria such as the severity of their offenses, previous records, and so forth. Obviously, the security level of an institution in which an inmate is classified will affect his or her incarceration experience.

For example, someone who is assigned to a maximum security prison instead of one with a lower level of security will also have differential access to things like mental health services, drug treatment programs, and vocational training (Brennan and Austin 1997). But is the classification of inmates also related to their behavior while incarcerated? Do those assigned to maximum security prisons engage in more misconduct compared to inmates assigned to less secure facilities? How could you answer this question? If you compared rates of misconduct across prison settings, you would not have the answer because the inmates may have been very different at their time of incarceration. As such, any differences you observe in misconduct could be attributable to these "before incarceration" differences, not to the type of facility in which they are housed.

In the last chapter, you learned that experimental research provides the most powerful design for testing nomothetic causal hypotheses. This chapter examines experimental methodology in more detail. You will learn to distinguish different types of experimental designs (which include true experiments and quasi-experiments), to evaluate the utility of particular designs for reaching causally valid conclusions, to identify problems of generalizability with experiments, and to consider ethical problems in experimentation. We will also return to the relationship between prison security level and inmate misconduct later in the chapter.

▣ True Experiments

Recall from the last chapter that **true experiments** must have at least three things:

1. Two comparison groups, one receiving the experimental condition (e.g., treatment or intervention) and the other receiving no treatment or intervention or another form thereof.

2. Random assignment to the two (or more) comparison groups.

3. Assessment of change in the dependent variable for both groups after the experimental condition has been received.

> **True experiment** Experiment in which subjects are assigned randomly to an experimental group that receives a treatment or other manipulation of the independent variable and a comparison group that does not receive the treatment or receives some other manipulation. Outcomes are measured in a posttest.

Experimental and Comparison Groups

True experiments must have at least one **experimental group** (subjects who receive some treatment) and at least one **control or comparison group** (subjects to whom the experimental group can be compared). The control group differs from the experimental group by one or more independent variables, whose effects are being tested. In other words, the difference between the two groups is that the experimental group receives the treatment or condition we are interested in, whereas the comparison group does not.

An experiment can have more than one experimental group if the goal is to test several versions of the **treatment** (the independent variable) or several combinations of different treatments. An experiment also may have more than one comparison group, as when outcome scores for the treatment group need to be compared to more than one comparison group.

> **Experimental group** In an experiment, the group of subjects that receives the treatment or experimental manipulation.

> **Control or comparison group** A comparison group that receives no treatment.

> **Treatment** The manipulation that exposes subjects in an experiment to a particular value of the independent variable.

Pretest and Posttest Measures

All true experiments have a **posttest**—that is, measurement of the outcome in both groups after the experimental group has received the treatment. In fact, we might say that any hypothesis-testing research involves a posttest. The dependent variable is measured after the independent variable has had its effect, if any. True experiments also may have **pretests** that measure the dependent variable prior to the experimental intervention. A pretest is exactly the same as the post-test, just administered before the treatment. Strictly speaking, however, an experiment does not require a pretest. When researchers use **random assignment**, the groups' initial scores on the dependent variable and on all other variables will most likely be similar; we can be confident in this because of the random assignment. Any difference in outcome between the experimental group and the comparison group is likely caused by only the intervention or experimental condition.

Posttest Measurement of an outcome (dependent) variable after an experimental intervention or after a presumed independent variable has changed for some other reason.

Pretest Measurement of an outcome (dependent) variable prior to an experimental intervention or change in a presumed independent variable for some other reason. The pretest is exactly the same "test" as the posttest, but it is administered at a different time.

Random assignment A procedure by which each experimental and control group subjects are placed in a group randomly.

Having pretest scores, however, has many advantages. They provide a direct measure of how much the experimental and comparison groups changed over time. They allow the researcher to verify that randomization was successful (that chance factors did not lead to an initial difference between the groups). In addition, by identifying subjects' initial scores on the dependent variable, a pretest provides a more complete picture of the conditions in which the intervention had (or did not have) an effect (Mohr 1992).

An experiment may have multiple posttests and perhaps even multiple pretests. Multiple posttests can identify just when the treatment has its effect and for how long. They are particularly important for treatments delivered over time (Rossi and Freeman 1989).

Random Assignment

Random assignment, sometimes referred to as randomization, is what makes the comparison group in a true experiment such a powerful tool for identifying the effects of the treatment. If subjects are randomly assigned to either the experimental group or the comparison group, then a researcher can assume that the only difference between the two groups is that the experimental group received the treatment or intervention and the comparison group did not. Thus, a randomly assigned comparison group can provide a good estimate of the counterfactual, the outcome that would have occurred if the subjects had not been exposed to the treatment but had otherwise equal experiences (Mohr 1992; Rossi and Freeman 1989). If the comparison group differed from the experimental group in any way besides not receiving the treatment (or receiving a different treatment), a researcher would not be able to determine the unique effects of the treatment.

Assigning subjects randomly to the experimental and comparison groups ensures that systematic bias does not affect the assignment of subjects to groups. But of course, random assignment cannot guarantee that the groups are perfectly identical at the start of the experiment. Similar to random selection in sampling, random assignment removes bias from the assignment process but only by relying on chance, which itself can result in some intergroup differences. Fortunately, researchers can use statistical methods to determine the odds of ending up with groups that differ on the basis of chance alone; these odds are low even for groups of moderate size.

Although similar in procedure, it is important to note here that random assignment of subjects to experimental and comparison groups is not the same as random sampling of individuals from a larger population (see Exhibit 7.1). In fact, random assignment (randomization) does not help ensure that the research subjects are representative of some larger population; that is the goal of random sampling. What random assignment does by creating two or more equivalent groups is useful for ensuring internal validity, not generalizability.

Random assignment does share with random sampling the use of a chance selection method. In random assignment, a random procedure is used to determine the group into which each subject is placed. In random sampling, a random procedure is used to determine which cases are selected for the sample. The random procedure of tossing a

| Exhibit 7.1 | Random Sampling Versus Random Assignment |

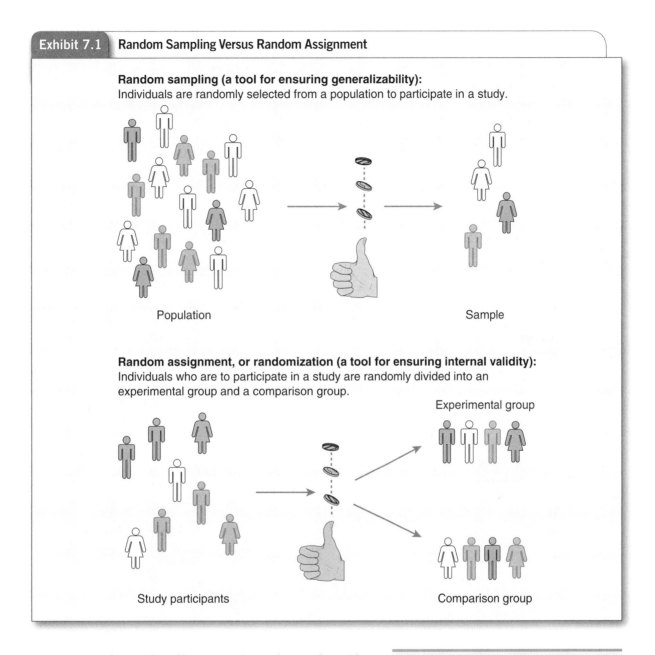

Random sampling (a tool for ensuring generalizability):
Individuals are randomly selected from a population to participate in a study.

Population   Sample

Random assignment, or randomization (a tool for ensuring internal validity):
Individuals who are to participate in a study are randomly divided into an
experimental group and a comparison group.

Experimental group

Study participants   Comparison group

coin, using a random number table, or generating random numbers with a
computer can be similar in both random assignment and random sampling.

Matching is another procedure sometimes used to equate experimental and comparison groups, but by itself, it is a poor substitute for randomization. Matching of individuals in a treatment group with those in a comparison group might involve pairing persons on the basis of similarity of gender, age, year in school, or some other characteristic. The basic problem is that, as a practical matter, individuals can be matched on only a few characteristics; unmatched differences between the experimental and comparison groups may still influence outcomes. However, matching combined with randomization can reduce the possibility of differences due

Matching A procedure for equating the characteristics of individuals in different comparison groups in an experiment. Matching can be done on either an individual or an aggregate basis. For individual matching, individuals who are similar in terms of key characteristics are paired prior to assignment, and then the two members of each pair are assigned to the two groups. For aggregate matching, groups are chosen for comparisons that are similar in terms of the distribution of key characteristics.

to chance. For example, if individuals are matched by gender and age, then the members of each matched pair are randomly assigned to the experimental and comparison groups, and the possibility of differences due to chance in the gender and age composition of the groups is eliminated (see Exhibit 7.2). Matching is also used in some quasi-experimental designs when randomization is not possible, as you will see later in this chapter.

We have already discussed two true experimental designs in this text: the Bushman experiment on media violence (for review, see Bushman and Huesmann 2012) and the Sherman and Berk (1984) experiment on the effects of arrest on intimate partner violence. Both are graphically displayed for you now in Exhibit 7.3. As you can see, in the Bushman experiment of media violence and aggression, the experimental design included a pretest. In this experiment, undergraduate college students were randomly assigned to experimental and control groups.

Recall from the last chapter that subjects in both groups were required to perform a learning task with a fake partner. In the task, subjects were to administer noises as a form of punishment to their partners when their partners gave an incorrect answer. The noise level was the operationalization of aggression for the experiment. The louder the noises administered, the higher the aggression score. Both experimental and control group subjects thus received a pretest score on their aggressiveness.

Subjects in both groups then watched a videotape; experimental group subjects watched a violent video, whereas control group subjects watched a nonviolent video. After viewing of the tapes, aggression levels were then similarly measured in the posttests. Using this design, Bushman was not only able to measure differences in aggression after the treatment (viewing the videotapes), but he was also able to determine whether aggression levels for the experimental and control subjects differentially changed from pretest to posttest. This illustrates the advantage of utilizing pretest measures in an experimental design.

The bottom panel of Exhibit 7.3 depicts the Sherman and Berk (1984) experiment. The subjects for the Sherman and Berk experiment were all reported offenders of misdemeanor intimate partner assault in Minneapolis, Minnesota, during the time of the experiment. The experimental treatment was arrest, and the control treatment was separation and no arrest. The key to this experimental design was that incidents were randomly assigned to the arrest

Exhibit 7.2   **Experimental Design Combining Matching and Random Assignment**

Experimental group

Comparison group

Study participants   Matched pairs

Exhibit 7.3 Experimental Design Used in the Bushman (1995) and Sherman and Berk (1984) Research

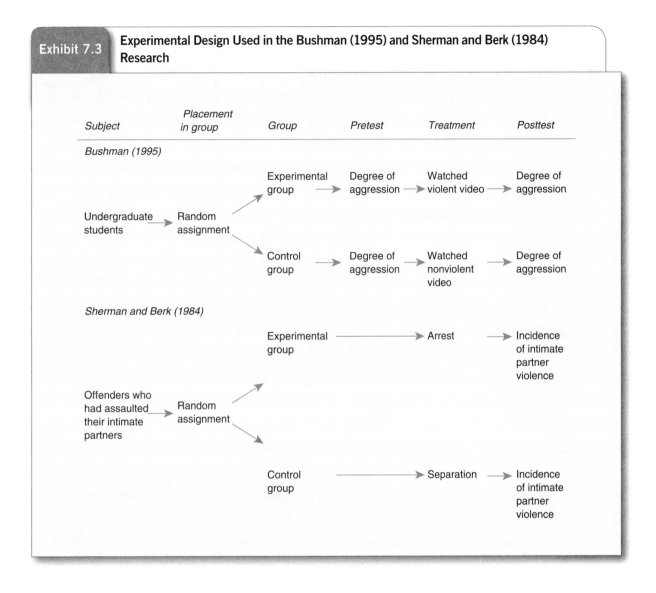

and nonarrest conditions. That is, when an officer arrived at the scene, he or she randomly assigned offenders to the treatment based on a randomly color-coded police record sheet. For example, if an officer arrived at the scene and the next sheet in his book was pink, he would make an arrest; if the sheet was white, he would not make an arrest. The posttest measurement was recidivism. If those offenders who were arrested were less likely than nonarrested offenders to have assaulted their partners 6 months after the incident, this decreased rate of assault could be attributed to the treatment of arrest. This, of course, is what happened.

Throughout the remainder of this chapter, you will learn more about each of these key features of experimental design. To help you understand the variability across different experimental designs, we will incorporate the use of simple diagrams. These diagrams also show at a glance just how well suited any experiment is to identifying causal relations, by indicating whether it has a comparison group, a pretest and a posttest, and random assignment. We will now turn to the question that we asked at the beginning of the chapter, "Does the type of security classification inmates are given affect their behavior?"

▣ Case Study: Prison Classification and Inmate Behavior

There is wide variability in the criteria used to classify prisoners across states. Regardless of how these classifications are made, once these labels are assigned, they have the effect that all labels have: They attach various expectations to prisoners. Bench and Allen (2003) state,

> An offender classified as maximum security instantly obtains an image of one who is hard to handle, disrespectful of authority, prone to fight with other inmates, and at a high risk for escape. In contrast, an offender classified as medium security is generally regarded as more manageable, less of an escape risk, and not requiring as much supervision as a maximum-security offender. (p. 369)

To examine whether prison classification actually affected inmate behavior, Bench and Allen (2003) obtained a random sample of 200 inmates admitted to the Utah State Prison who had been classified as maximum security following their initial assessment based on the following criteria: severity of current crime, expected length of incarceration, criminal violence history, escape history, prior institutional commitment, age, history of institutional adjustment, and substance abuse history.

From this group, inmates were randomly assigned to either an experimental group, in which inmates were reclassified to medium security status, or to a control group, in which inmates retained their maximum security status. The independent variable, then, was security classification. The dependent variable was the number of disciplinary infractions, or sanctions for violation of prison rules, received by each group. The severity of infractions were weighted to control for the severity of the violations (e.g., possession of unauthorized food was weighted lower than assaulting another inmate). The primary hypothesis was that the experimental group, those reclassified as medium security, would have a lower number of disciplinary infractions compared to the control group, the inmates who retained their maximum security classification. A diagram depicting the experiment is provided in Exhibit 7.4. Results indicated that, although inmates reclassified to medium security did not receive a lower number of infractions, both groups received about the same number of disciplinary infractions, regardless of security classification. Policy implications are obvious. Bench and Allen (2003) state,

> Maximum-security offenders who stand out on a number of dimensions such as length of sentence, severity of offense, prior incarcerations, and propensity for violence can be housed in medium-security environments with no increased risk of disciplinary involvement. . . . In addition, institutions that are considering expansion should give careful consideration to how much room actually is needed for costly maximum-security housing. (p. 378)

Exhibit 7.4 — **Experiment Examining the Effect of Prison Classification on Inmate Behavior (Bench and Allen 2003)**

To help you understand the procedures involved in true experimental designs, we will describe an experiment conducted by Colbert, Paternoster, and Bushway (2002), which investigated the effects of legal counsel at detainees' bail hearings.

▣ Case Study: The Effects of Counsel at Bail Hearings

While the Sixth Amendment guarantees a lawyer at trial for those whose freedom is as stake, this right does not extend to bail hearings. What this means is that many accused offenders, particularly those who cannot afford private counsel at a bail hearing, must wait for their trials in jail. The effects of this reality are important in light of burgeoning jail and prison populations. At a time when many jurisdictions are witnessing an increase in misdemeanor arrests because of zero-tolerance police practices, defendants awaiting trial in jail represent a huge cost to taxpayers. Moreover, incarcerated detainees often lose jobs, and families often lose an economic provider and/or a child caretaker. Would having legal representation at the bail stage make a difference in detention rates? Colbert et al. (2002) set out to answer this question using a randomized field experiment in Baltimore called the Lawyers at Bail Project. Only nonviolent defendants were eligible for the study. Of the approximately 300 nonviolent cases selected for the study, legal representation was randomly assigned by a staff of paralegals to an experimental group in which a lawyer was assigned to represent the detainee at his or her bail hearing or to a control group in which no legal counsel was provided. The authors noted, "The purpose of the random assignment of nonviolent cases was to ensure that the group of criminal suspects provided with attorneys were as comparable as possible to those not provided lawyers" (Colbert et al. 2002:1749). This study is diagrammed in Exhibit 7.5.

During the experiment, research staff composed primarily of graduate and law students attended each bail review hearing and recorded critical information about each case, such as the number and nature of the charges, whether the offense involved the use of violence, the offender's criminal history, the nature of the offender's ties to the community, and other demographic information. They also collected outcome measures including what the initial bail was, if this initial bail was modified by the bail review hearing officers, if the defendant was released on his or her own recognizance, if the suspect made bail, and the length of the hearing. The researchers also added a qualitative component to the study by interviewing suspects to obtain information about how they perceived the outcome and whether they believed they were treated fairly.

| Exhibit 7.5 | Experimental and Control Groups in the Colbert et al. (2002) Lawyers at Bail Hearings Experiment |

Source: Colbert et al. 2002.

Colbert and his colleagues (2002) found suspects provided with legal counsel were more than twice as likely to be released on their own recognizance. For those who were not released, the initial bail was set by a bail commissioner immediately after arrest and then reviewed at the bail review hearing. The bail officer then had three options: to leave the bail as it was set, to lower it, or to increase it. Here, too, defendants with lawyers also had an advantage: 59% of those with lawyers had their bail reduced while only 14% of those unrepresented did. Moreover, the average bail for those with lawyers was $2,441 while the mean bail amount for those without lawyers was $3,012. On average, the suspects with counsel had their bail reduced by nearly $1,000 while those without counsel had their bail reduced by an average of only $166. Clearly, having lawyers present at a bail hearing increased the likelihood that defendants would be released on their own recognizance and be more likely to have their bail set at a more affordable level. In sum, Colbert et al. (2002) estimate that providing counsel during the bail phase would save Baltimore City a huge amount of money!

The experiments we have discussed so far in this text are all true experiments. Now take a minute and think about how these studies meet the criteria necessary for determining causality that were discussed in Chapter 6. In the next section, we discuss quasi-experimental designs, that is, experiments in which at least one of the conditions of a true experiment is not met.

Quasi-Experiments

Often, testing a hypothesis with a true experimental design is not feasible. Such a test may be too costly, take too long to carry out, be inappropriate for the particular research problem, or presume ability to manipulate an intervention that already has occurred. To overcome these problems yet still benefit from the logic of the experimental method, researchers may use designs that retain several components of experimental design but differ in other important details.

Usually, the best alternative to an experimental design is a **quasi-experimental design**, maximizing internal validity. Although not defined consistently by all experts, in a quasi-experimental design the comparison group is predetermined to be comparable to the treatment group in critical ways, such as eligibility for the same services or attendance at the same school **cohort** (Rossi and Freeman 1989). However, because subjects are *not* randomly assigned to the comparison and experimental groups, these research designs are "quasi"-experimental. In other quasi-experimental designs, there may be just one group that is monitored before and after a treatment is delivered and no comparison group. In both cases, we cannot be as confident in their causal conclusions as we can with true experimental designs.

The following are the three major types of quasi-experimental designs (others can be found in Cook and Campbell 1979 or Mohr 1992):

- **Nonequivalent control group designs** have experimental and comparison groups designated before the treatment occurs and are not created by random assignment.

- **Before-and-after designs** have a pretest and posttest but no comparison group. In other words, the subjects exposed to the treatment served, at an earlier time, as their own controls.

Quasi-experimental design A research design in which there is a comparison group that is comparable to the experimental group in critical ways, but subjects are not randomly assigned to the comparison and experimental groups.

Cohort Individuals or groups with a common starting point. Examples of a cohort include college class of 1997, people who graduated from high school in the 1980s, General Motors employees who started work between 1990 and the year 2000, and people who were born in the late 1940s or the 1950s (the baby boom generation).

Nonequivalent control group designs A quasi-experimental design in which there are experimental and comparison groups that are designated before the treatment occurs but are not created by random assignment.

Before-and-after designs A quasi-experimental design may consist of before-and-after comparisons of the experimental group, but has no control group.

- Ex post facto control group designs, like nonequivalent control group designs, have experimental and comparison groups that are not created by random assignment. But unlike the groups in nonequivalent control group designs, the groups in ex post facto designs are designated after the treatment or intervention has occurred. For this reason, some researchers consider this design to be nonexperimental, not even quasi-experimental.

> **Ex post facto control group designs**
> Nonexperimental design in which comparison groups are selected after the treatment, program, or other variation in the independent variable has occurred.

Nonequivalent Control Group Designs

In this type of quasi-experimental design, a comparison group is selected to be as comparable as possible to the treatment group. Two selection methods can be used:

Individual matching. Individual cases in the treatment group are matched with similar individuals in the comparison group. A Mexican American male about 20 years old who is assigned to the treatment group may be matched with another Mexican American male about 20 years old who is assigned to the comparison group. The problem with this method is determining in advance which variables should be used for matching. It is also unlikely that a match can be found for all cases. However, in some situations matching can create a comparison group that is very similar to the experimental group. For example, some studies of the effect of Head Start, the government program that prepares disadvantaged toddlers for school, used participants' siblings as the comparison group. Therefore, they were similar to the experimental group.

Aggregate matching. Matching in the aggregate means finding a group with similar distributions on key variables such as the same average age, the same percentage of females, and so on. In this way, a comparison group is identified that matches the treatment group in the aggregate rather than trying to match individual cases. In most situations when random assignment is not possible, this method of matching makes sense. For this design to be considered even quasi-experimental, individuals cannot choose which group to join or where to seek services. In other words, the subjects cannot opt for or against the experimental treatment.

🔲 Case Study: The Effectiveness of Drug Courts

The study of the effectiveness of a drug court on recidivism by Listwan et al. (2003) illustrates a quasi-experimental nonequivalent control group design. Their quasi-experimental design is diagrammed in Exhibit 7.6. Reflecting the priority that policymakers place on controlling drug use and drug-related crime, drug courts have become extremely popular in the United States. They emerged as an alternative to correctional prison and jail-based responses to addicted offenders and generally rely on community-based treatment models. The assumption behind the drug court movement is that drug users and their drug-related crimes will increasingly clog the courts and fill our jails and prisons if their addictions are not remedied. Although drug court programs vary tremendously across jurisdictions, they generally integrate alcohol and drug treatment services with justice system case processing. In addition, they are designed to decrease case processing time, alleviate the demand of drug-related cases on the court, and decrease jail and prison commitments, all of which are supposed to decrease the cost of controlling drug offenders.

| Exhibit 7.6 | Quasi-Experimental Design of Drug Court Research |

Source: Adapted from Listwan et al. 2003.

Listwan and her colleagues (2003) examined whether participants in the Hamilton County Drug Court program in Cincinnati, Ohio, had lower rates of recidivism for both drug-related and other offenses. Exhibit 7.6 illustrates that there were two groups compared: those who participated in the drug court (experimental group) and those who were eligible but did not receive the drug court treatment services or the additional court supervision (control group). Importantly, the offenders were *not* randomly assigned to these groups. The researchers simply stated, "Members of the [the control group] . . . either refused drug treatment or were refused by the drug court team" (Listwan et al. 2003:396). Unfortunately, many evaluations of this nature do not have the ability to employ random assignment, thereby diluting the ability to determine the causal relationship between the treatment and the results. The researchers did examine the potential differences between the two groups and determined that they did not significantly differ in terms of age, race, education, or prior arrest for a drug-related offense, but the experimental group had a higher number of women and people with other prior records not related to drugs. Arrest and incarceration records for the participants were collected for up to 4 years after the program, but results were mixed. While participation in the program decreased the probability that offenders would be rearrested for drug-related offenses, it did not decrease the likelihood that they would be rearrested for other offenses.

Before-and-After Designs

The common feature of before-and-after designs is the absence of a comparison group. All cases are exposed to only the experimental treatment. The basis for comparison is provided by the pretreatment measures in the experimental group. These designs are useful for studies of interventions that are experienced by virtually every element in some population.

> **Fixed-sample panel design (panel study)** A type of longitudinal study in which data are collected from the same individuals—the panel—at two or more points in time. In another type of panel design, panel members who leave are replaced with new members.

The simplest type of before-and-after design is the **fixed-sample panel design (panel study)**. A panel design involves only one pretest and one posttest. It does not qualify as a quasi-experimental design because comparing subjects to themselves at only one earlier point in time does not provide an adequate comparison group. Many influences other than the experimental treatment may affect a subject following the pretest. Consequently, if there is a change in the dependent variable from pre- to postmeasures, we cannot be certain that the treatment itself is the sole cause of this change. Other before-and-after designs use repeated pretest and posttest measurements, such as the one we will see next to examine the effects of the Youth Criminal Justice Act in Canada.

回 Case Study: The Effects of the Youth Criminal Justice Act

Carrington and Schulenberg's (2008) study of the effect of the Youth Criminal Justice Act (YCJA) of 2002 in Canada on police discretion with apprehended young offenders illustrates a **time series design** often called a **repeated measures panel design**. This design typically includes many pretest and posttest observations that allow the researcher to study the process by which an intervention or a treatment has an impact over time. First, some background. One of the major objectives of the YCJA, which came into effect in 2003 in Canada, was to reduce the number of referrals to youth court. The YCJA generally requires police officers who are considering charging a minor with a crime to first consider extralegal judicial measures such as giving the youth an informal warning.

Time series design (repeated measures panel design) A quasi-experimental design consisting of many pretest and posttest observations of the same group.

To examine the effects of the YCJA, Carrington and Schulenberg (2008) examined the number of juveniles who were apprehended and charged from January 1, 1986, through December 31, 2006. The Canadian Uniform Crime Reporting Survey captures the number of minors who were charged, as well as the number who were "chargeable" but not charged. The researchers note, "A change in the charge ration, or proportion of chargeable youth who were charged, is an indication of a change in the use of police discretion with apprehended youth" (Carrington and Schulenberg 2008:355). To control for the actual crime rate of youth, the researchers also examined per capita ratios. Exhibit 7.7 displays the annual rates per 100,000 young persons who were (a) apprehended (i.e., chargeable),

| Exhibit 7.7 | **Results From a Repeated Measures Panel Design Used to Examine the Efficacy of the Youth Criminal Justice Act** |

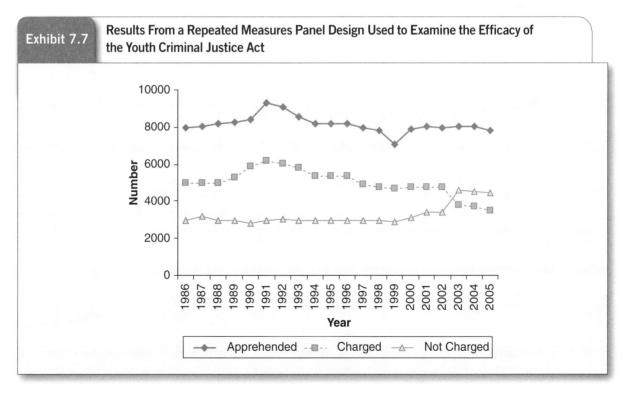

Source: From Canadian Centre for Justice Statistics and adapted from Carrington and Schulenberg 2008.

(b) charged, and (c) not charged. This clearly shows that the YCJA may have had the intended effect. Of course, the study design leaves open the possibility that something else in 2003 may have happened to effect this change in formal charges against juveniles. However, because there was no known event that could have had such a national impact, the conclusion that this effect is attributable to the YCJA is more plausible. As you can see, this time series design is particularly useful for studying the impact of new laws or social programs that affect everyone and can be readily assessed by ongoing measurement.

🔲 Case Study: Reduced Caseload and Intensive Supervision in Probation

Probation and parole professionals often contend that supervision outcomes would improve if caseloads were reduced, but research findings for this contention are inconsistent. For example, Jalbert and her colleagues (2010) studied the effect of reduced caseload size and intensive supervision on probation outcomes using a regression-discontinuity design. The probation office they examined identified the probationers most at risk of reoffending using a risk assessment tool that classifies probationers' risk of recidivism. Those with a high score on the measure are assigned to the highest level of supervision, called intensive supervision probation (ISP). This assessment tool score was used by Jalbert as the assignment variable. The researchers wanted to know if recidivism was actually different for those assigned to ISP compared to those assigned to a "high-normal" supervision caseload. Jalbert et al. describe their rational for using the regression-discontinuity design as follows, "The inference about treatment effectiveness is based on a comparison of the outcomes for offenders who are at the margins: those offenders who just failed to qualify for ISP and those offenders who just qualified for ISP" (2010:239). Results indicated that offenders supervised on both ISP and high normal caseloads had high rates of recidivism; over two-thirds were arrested for some new charge during or after supervision, although most of these offenses were minor public order offenses. At a 6-month follow-up, however, ISP reduced the likelihood of criminal recidivism compared to offenders assigned to the high-normal supervision. Importantly, the researchers also determined that ISP did *not* increase the likelihood of probationers receiving technical violations.

Ex Post Facto Control Group Designs

A design in which the treatment and comparison groups are designated after the treatment is administered is an ex post facto (after the fact) control group design. This design perhaps should be considered nonexperimental rather than quasi-experimental, because the comparison group may not be comparable to the treatment group. Carefully designed ex post facto studies, however, can result in comparisons between the treatment and control groups that give us almost as much confidence in the validity of their causal conclusions as we can have in the causal conclusions from a quasi-experimental design (Rossi and Freeman 1989).

🔲 Case Study: Does an Arrest Increase Delinquency?

Farrington's (1977) classic study of the deviance amplification process is an excellent example of an ex post facto control group design. Farrington was interested in testing the main hypothesis about deviance amplification from labeling theory. Becker (1963) describes deviance amplification thus: "One of the most crucial steps in the process of building a stable pattern of deviant behavior is likely to be the experience of being caught and publicly labeled as deviant" (p. 31). Accordingly, Farrington tested the hypothesis that individuals who were publicly labeled as deviant would increase their deviant behavior compared to those who were not so labeled. To measure the process of being publicly labeled, he used the criteria of whether individuals had been found guilty of a delinquent act in court.

To use a true experimental design to test this hypothesis, individuals who engaged in criminal behavior would have to be randomly assigned to either a group found guilty in court or a group not taken to court. It would then be possible to conclude that any subsequent differences between the groups resulted from the presence or absence of public labeling (being convicted) and did not reflect preexisting differences or the influence of any other factor. Because of ethical considerations, of course, such an experiment would be almost impossible to carry out.

Instead, Farrington (1977) used the Cambridge Study in Delinquent Development that interviewed adolescents from London at three different ages: 14, 16, and 18 years. (The Cambridge Study in Delinquent Development actually maintained intermittent contact with 400 London working-class youths from ages 8 to 18. In this study, only the interviews at ages 14, 16, and 18 were used.) At all three times, the youth were asked about their participation in delinquency. For example, the questionnaire given at age 18 included seven delinquent acts: breaking and entering, stealing from vehicles, stealing from slot machines, shoplifting, joyriding, damaging property, and buying stolen goods. The dependent variable, then, was the youth's self-reported delinquency score. The treatment or intervention was whether the youth was convicted of an offense by the Criminal Records Office. Pretest measures of self-reported delinquency were taken at age 14, and posttest scores were taken at age 18. Individuals convicted of an offense between the times of these interviews were considered the experimental publicly labeled group. Individuals who were not convicted were considered the control group (see Exhibit 7.8).

Farrington (1977) actually conducted many hypothesis tests with these data, trying to rule out the effects of other variables and to investigate the intervening processes or causal **mechanisms** linking public labeling and deviant acts. In conclusion, Farrington appropriately included a caveat about his methodology along with directions for future research:

> **Mechanism** A discernible process that creates a causal connection between two variables.

The results obtained with the quasi-experimental matching design, although less conclusive than would have been the case in a true experiment, were in agreement with the hypothesis that public labeling (measured by criminal convictions) increases deviant behavior (measured by self-reported delinquency scores). As a next step, it would be useful to establish the generality of this finding by investigating whether deviance amplification still occurred with different operational definitions of public labeling and deviant behavior, and with different samples of people in different places and at different times. (p. 123)

Exhibit 7.8	**Ex Post Facto Control Group Design: Farrington's (1977) Test of Deviance Amplification**				

Subject	Placement in group	Group	Pretest	Treatment	Posttest
		Experimental group	→ Delinquent acts at age 14	→ Convicted of offense	→ Delinquent acts at age 18
Adolescents from London	No random assignment				
		Control group	→ Delinquent acts at 14	→ Not Convicted of offense	→ Delinquent acts at age 18

▣ Validity in Experiments

Like any research design, experimental designs must be evaluated for their ability to yield valid conclusions. True experiments are particularly well suited to producing valid conclusions about causality (internal validity), but they are less likely to fare well in achieving generalizability. Quasi-experiments may provide more generalizable results than true experiments, but they are more prone to problems of internal invalidity (although some allow the researcher to rule out almost as many potential sources of internal invalidity as does a true experiment). Measurement validity is also a central concern, but an experimental design does not in itself offer any special tools or particular advantages or disadvantages in measurement. In this section you will learn more about the ways in which experiments help (or do not help) resolve potential problems of internal validity and generalizability.

Causal (Internal) Validity

> **Causal effect** The finding that change in one variable leads to change in another variable, *ceteris paribus* (other things being equal).

An experiment's ability to yield valid conclusions about **causal effects** is determined by the comparability of its experimental and comparison groups. First, of course, a comparison group must be created. Second, this comparison group must be so similar to the experimental group that it will show what the experimental group would be like if it did not receive the experimental treatment, if the independent variable was not varied. For example, the only difference between the two groups in Bushman's (1995) study was that one group watched a violent movie and the other group did not.

There are five basic sources of internal invalidity:

1. *Selection bias*: when characteristics of the experimental and comparison group subjects differ.

2. *Endogenous change*: when the subjects develop or change during the experiment as part of an ongoing process independent of the experimental treatment.

3. *External events or history effects*: when something occurs during the experiment, other than the treatment, that influences outcome scores.

4. *Contamination*: when either the experimental group or the comparison group is aware of the other group and is influenced in the posttest as a result (Mohr 1992).

5. *Treatment misidentification*: when variation in the independent variable (the treatment) is associated with variation in the observed outcome, but the change occurs through a process that the researcher has not identified.

Selection Bias

> **Selection bias** A source of internal (causal) invalidity that occurs when characteristics of experimental and comparison group subjects differ in any way that influences the outcome.

You may already realize that the composition of the experimental and comparison groups in a true experiment is unlikely to be affected by their difference. If it were affected, it would cause **selection bias**. Random assignment equates the groups' characteristics, though with some possibility for error due to chance. The likelihood of difference due to chance can be identified with appropriate statistics.

But in field experiments, what is planned as a random assignment process may deteriorate when it is delegated to frontline program staff. The staff may not always follow the process guidelines. This problem occurred in the Sherman and Berk (1984) domestic violence experiment in Minneapolis. Police officers sometimes violated the random assignment plan because they thought the circumstances warranted arresting a suspect who had been randomly assigned to receive only a warning. In several of the follow-up studies, the researchers maintained closer supervision over the assignment process so the randomization could be maintained.

Even when the random assignment plan works, the groups can differ over time because of **differential attrition**, or what can be thought of as deselection. That is, the groups become different because, for various reasons, subjects are more likely to drop out of groups. This is not a likely problem for a laboratory experiment that occurs in one session, but for laboratory experiments that occur over time, differential attrition may become a problem.

> **Differential attrition** A problem that occurs in experiments when comparison groups become different because subjects are more likely to drop out of one of the groups for various reasons.

Differential attrition is quite common in field experiments that evaluate the impact of social programs (Cook and Campbell 1979). Subjects who receive some advantageous program benefit are more likely to stay in the experiment (making themselves available for measurement in the posttest); subjects who do not receive program benefits are more likely to drop out. Another possibility is that individuals who may be more in need of a program, such as severe alcoholics in a detoxification study, are more likely to drop out (Rossi and Freeman 1989). The problem this creates is that the two groups are no longer equivalent, despite the fact that subjects were originally randomly assigned.

In **evaluation research** that monitors program impact over an extended period, the possibility of differential attrition can be high (evaluation research is discussed in detail in Chapter 11). When the treatment group is receiving some service or benefit that the control group is not, the individuals in the control group will be more likely to drop out of the study.

> **Evaluation research** Research about social programs or interventions.

When subjects are not randomly assigned to treatment and comparison groups, as in nonequivalent control group designs, there is a serious threat of selection bias. Even if the researcher selects a comparison group that matches the treatment group on important variables, there is no guarantee that the groups were similar initially in terms of the dependent variable or another characteristic that ultimately influences posttest scores. However, a pretest helps the researchers determine whether selection bias exists and control for it. Most variables that might influence outcome scores will also influence scores on the pretest. Statistically controlling for the pretest scores also serves to control for unmeasured variables that influence the pretest scores.

Endogenous Change

The type of problem considered an **endogenous change** occurs when natural developments in the subjects, independent of the experimental treatment, account for some or all of the observed changes between pretest and posttest. Endogenous change includes three specific threats to internal validity:

> **Endogenous change** A source of causal invalidity that occurs when natural developments or changes in the subjects (independent of the experimental treatment itself) account for some or all of the observed change from the pretest to the posttest.

Testing. Taking the pretest can in itself influence posttest scores. Subjects may learn something or be sensitized to an issue by the pretest and, as a result, respond differently when they are asked the same questions in the posttest.

Maturation. Changes in outcome scores during experiments that involve a lengthy treatment period may be due to maturation. Subjects may age, gain experience in school, or grow in knowledge, all as part of a natural maturational experience, and thus respond differently on the posttest than they did on the pretest.

Regression. People experience cyclical or episodic changes that result in different posttest scores, a phenomenon known as a **regression effect**. Subjects who are chosen for a study because they received very low scores on a test may show improvement in the posttest, on average, simply because some of the low scorers were having a bad day. On the other hand, individuals selected for an experiment because they are suffering from tooth decay will not show improvement in the posttest because a decaying tooth is not likely to improve in the natural course of things. It is hard, in many cases, to know whether a phenomenon is subject to naturally occurring fluctuations, so the possibility of regression effects should be considered whenever subjects are selected because of their extremely high or low values on the outcome variable (Mohr 1992).

> **Regression effect** A source of causal invalidity that occurs when subjects who are chosen for a study because of their extreme scores on the dependent variable become less extreme on the posttest due to natural cyclical or episodic change in the variable.

Testing, maturation, and regression effects are generally not a problem in true experiments. Both the experimental group and the comparison group take the pretest, so even if this experience itself leads to a change in posttest scores, the comparison between the experimental and comparison groups will not be affected. Of course, in experiments with no pretest, testing effects are not a problem. Similarly, both the experimental and comparison groups are equally subject to maturation and regression, since they are the same at the outset (unless chance factors led to a difference). These endogenous changes may affect outcome scores for both groups, but both groups should be equally affected. As a result, the estimates of treatment effects should not be biased.

Endogenous change is, however, a major problem with quasi-experimental designs, particularly before-and-after designs. In panel designs with a single pretest and a single posttest, any change may be due to testing, maturation, or regression. But a study that is completed within a short time would have little concern with maturation effects, and use of a diverse subject group will reassure those concerned about regression effects. Unfortunately, the possibility of endogenous change accounting for pretest-posttest change cannot be eliminated with before-and-after designs. Repeated measures panel studies and time series designs are more effective because they allow the researcher to trace the pattern of change or stability in the dependent variable up to and after the treatment. Ongoing effects of maturation and regression can thus be identified and taken into account.

External Events

External events, sometimes referred to as the **history effect** during the experiment—things that happen outside the experiment—can also change the subjects' outcome scores. An example of this is a newsworthy event that has to do with the focus of an experiment and the major disasters to which subjects are exposed. What if researchers were evaluating the effectiveness of a mandatory arrest policy in decreasing incidents of intimate partner assault, and assault of Rihanna by Chris Brown occurred during the experiment? This would clearly be a historical event that might compromise the results. The media were obsessed with this case, and as a result, intimate partner assault and homicide were given a tremendous amount of media attention. Because

> **External events (history effect)** A source of causal invalidity that occurs when something other than the treatment influences outcome scores; also called an effect of external events.

of this increased awareness, many victims of intimate partner violence reported their victimizations during this time; police agencies and women's shelters were flooded with calls. If a researcher had been using calls to police in a particular jurisdiction as an indicator of the incidence of intimate partner assault, this historical event would have seriously jeopardized the internal validity of his or her results. Why? Because the increase in calls to the police by other victims would have had more to do with the assault of Rihanna than with any recent change in arrest policies.

Causal conclusions can be invalid in true experiments because of the influence of external events, but not every experiment is affected by them. The specific features of an experiment must be considered carefully to evaluate the possibility of problems due to external events. For example, in an experiment in which subjects go to a particular location for the treatment and the control group subjects do not, something at the location unrelated to the treatment could influence the experimental subjects.

The more carefully controlled the conditions for experimental and comparison groups, the less likely external events will invalidate the causal conclusions of an experiment. External events seldom affect laboratory experiments. In addition, when using nonequivalent control group designs, a comparison group can minimize the effect of external events if the two groups are exposed to the same environment during the experiment. For example, the relatively constant level of seat-belt use in the comparison community in the Watson (1986) study suggests that a national series of TV announcements to encourage compliance is not what resulted in the changes in seat-belt use observed in the experimental community.

Before-and-after designs are much less prone to problems of external events and become quasi-experimental when the researchers make multiple before-and-after comparisons or when they apply multiple pretest and posttest measures to the same group in successive time intervals. If **multiple-group before-and-after designs** yield comparable results, the observed pretest-posttest change is less likely to be due to unique external events that would have affected only some of the comparisons.

> ***Multiple-group before-and-after designs*** A quasi-experimental design consisting of several before-and-after comparisons involving the same variables but different groups.

Contamination

Contamination occurs in an experiment when the comparison group is in some way affected by, or affects, the treatment group. This problem basically arises from failure to adequately control the conditions of the experiment. When comparison group members become aware that they are being denied some advantage, they may increase their efforts to compensate, creating a problem called **compensatory rivalry**, or the **John Henry effect** (Cook and Campbell 1979). (Saretsky, 1972, coined the term *John Henry effect* in honor of the steel driver who, when he learned that his output was to be compared to that of a steam drill, worked so hard that he outperformed the drill and died of overexertion.)

On the other hand, comparison group members may become demoralized if they feel that they have been left out of some valuable treatment and may perform worse than they would have outside the experiment. The treatment may seem, in comparison, to have a more beneficial effect than

> ***Contamination*** A source of causal invalidity that occurs when the experimental and/or the comparison group is aware of the other group and is influenced in the posttest as a result.
>
> ***Compensatory rivalry (John Henry effect)*** A type of contamination in experimental and quasi-experimental designs that occurs when control group members are aware that they are being denied some advantage and increase their efforts by way of compensation. This problem has also been referred to as the John Henry effect.

it actually did. Both compensatory rivalry and demoralization thus distort the impact of the experimental treatment. Similar problems could occur if members of the experimental group become aware of the control group and feel differently as a result.

Although the components of a true experiment guard against internal invalidity due to history and selection, the threat of contamination is always present. Careful inspection of the research design can determine whether contamination is likely to be a problem in a particular experiment. If the experiment is conducted in a laboratory, if members of the experimental group and the comparison group have no contact while the study is in progress, and if the treatment is relatively brief, contamination is not likely to be a problem. To the degree that these conditions are not met, the likelihood of contamination will increase. The threat of contamination is not necessarily any different in a quasi-experimental design than it is in a true experiment. Some nonequivalent control group designs minimize the threat of contamination by using a comparison group whose members will have no contact with the treatment group or awareness of the treatment.

Treatment Misidentification

Treatment misidentification occurs when the treatment itself does not cause the outcome but does cause some intervening process the researcher is not aware of and has not identified. This term can also refer to unknown concomitants or consequences for subjects in the control group that have to

> ***Treatment misidentification*** A problem that occurs in an experiment when the treatment itself is not what causes the outcome, but rather the outcome is caused by some intervening process that the researcher has not identified and is not aware of.

do with the experimental manipulation. In either case, the subjects experience something other than, or in addition to, what the researchers believe they will experience. Treatment misidentification has at least three sources:

1. *Expectancies of experimental staff.* Change among experimental subjects may be due to the positive **expectancies of the experimental staff** who are delivering the treatment rather than due to the treatment itself. This type of treatment misidentification can occur even in randomized experiments when well-trained staff convey their enthusiasm for an experimental program to the subjects in subtle ways. Such positive staff expectations create a **self-fulfilling prophecy**. Because social programs are delivered by human beings, such expectancy effects can be very difficult to control in field experiments. However, in some experiments on the effects of treatments such as medical drugs, **double-blind procedures** can be used. Staff will deliver the treatments without knowing which subjects are getting the treatment and which are receiving a placebo, something that looks like the treatment but has no effect. These procedures can be used in other experiments as well. In fact, the prison experiment discussed at the beginning of this chapter used a double-blind procedure to randomly assign inmates. In the experiment, only the executive director of the corrections department and the director of classification were aware of the research. Correctional staff, other individuals who worked with the inmates, and the inmates themselves were unaware of the study. In this way, any expectancies that the staff may have had were unlikely to affect inmate behavior.

> **Expectancies of the experimental staff (self-fulfilling prophecy)** A source of treatment misidentification in experiments and quasi-experiments that occurs when change among experimental subjects is due to the positive expectancies of the staff who are delivering the treatment, rather than to the treatment itself; also called a *self-fulfilling prophecy.*

> **Double-blind procedure** An experimental method in which neither subjects nor the staff delivering experimental treatments know which subjects are getting the treatment and which are receiving a placebo.

2. *Placebo effect.* Treatment misidentification may occur when subjects receive a treatment that they consider likely to be beneficial and then they improve because of that expectation rather than the treatment itself. In medical research the placebo is often a chemically inert substance that looks like the experimental drug but actually has no medical effect. Research indicates that the **placebo effect** produces positive health effects in two thirds of patients suffering   from relatively mild medical problems (Goleman 1993). Placebo effects can also occur in social science research. The only way to reduce this threat to internal validity is to treat the comparison group with something similar.

3. *Hawthorne effect.* Members of the treatment group may change in terms of the dependent variable because their participation in the study makes them feel special. This problem can occur when treatment group members compare their situation to that of the control group members, who are not receiving the treatment. In this case, this is a type of contamination effect. But experimental group members could feel special simply because they are in the experiment. The **Hawthorne effect** is named after a famous productivity experiment at the Hawthorne electric plant outside Chicago. Workers were moved to a special room for a study of the effects of lighting intensity and other work conditions on their productivity. After this move, the workers began to increase their output no matter what change was made in their working conditions, even when the conditions became worse. The researchers concluded that the workers felt they should work harder because they were part of a special experiment. By the time the study was over, the researchers were convinced that it was social interaction among workers, not physical arrangements, that largely determined their output. Most management historians believe that the human relations school of management began with this insight.

> **Placebo effect** A source of treatment misidentification that can occur when subjects receive a treatment that they consider likely to be beneficial, and improve because of that expectation rather than because of the treatment itself.

> **Hawthorne effect** A type of contamination in experimental and quasi-experimental designs that occurs when members of the treatment group change in terms of the dependent variable because their participation in the study makes them feel special.

In a **process analysis**, periodic measures are taken throughout the experiment to assess whether the treatment is being delivered as planned. To avoid treatment misidentification, field researchers are now using process analysis more often than in the past. Process analysis is also a necessary component of evaluation studies, when researchers need to be very confident that the effects they observe are caused by the policy or program change they are studying (Hunt 1985).

> ***Process analysis*** A research design in which periodic measures are taken to determine whether a treatment is being delivered as planned, usually in a field experiment.

Generalizability

The need for generalizable findings can be thought of as the Achilles' heel of the true experimental design. The design components that are essential for a true experiment and minimize the threats to causal (internal) validity make it more difficult to achieve **sample generalizability**, the ability to apply the findings to a clearly defined, larger population. In contrast, cross-population generalizability is no more or less achievable with experiments than with other research designs. As you learned in Chapter 1, the extent to which treatment effects can be generalized across subgroups and to other populations and settings is **external validity**.

> ***Sample generalilzability*** Exists when a conclusion based on a sample, or subset, of a larger population holds true for that population.
>
> ***Example of sample generalizability:*** Sherman et al. (1992) found that arrest reduced repeat offenses for a sample of offenders in Minneapolis. If this finding is assumed to be true for all misdemeanour assaults in that occurred in Minneapolis, researchers could say their sample results were generalizable to the population.
>
> ***External validity (cross-population generalizability)*** A type of validity that occurs when a treatment effect (or noneffect) occurs across subgroups within an experiment or other study or across different populations, times, or settings.
>
> ***Example of external validity:*** Sherman et al. (1992) found that arrest reduced repeat offenses for employed subjects but not for unemployed subjects. The effect of arrest thus varied with employment status, so a conclusion that arrest deters recidivism would not be externally valid.

Sample Generalizability

Subjects who can be recruited for a laboratory experiment, randomly assigned to a group, and kept under carefully controlled conditions for the study's duration are unlikely to be a representative sample of any large population of interest to social scientists. In fact, most are recruited from college populations. Can they be expected to react to the experimental treatment in the same way as members of the larger population? The more artificial the experimental arrangements, the greater the problem (Campbell and Stanley 1966). As you learned in Chapter 5, randomly selecting a sample from a population is the best way to ensure sample generalizability (this has nothing to do with randomly assigning the sample to the control or experimental group). A large percentage of laboratory experiments, including those performed by Bushman (1995), utilize availability samples such as college students. Field experiments conducted out in the real world, like many of those we have examined in this chapter, are more generalizable.

It is not only the characteristics of the subjects themselves that determine the generalizability of the experimental results. The generalizability of the treatment and of the setting for the experiment also must be considered (Cook and Campbell 1979). However, researchers can take steps both before and after an experiment to increase a study's generalizability. Field experiments are likely to yield findings that are more generalizable to broader populations than are laboratory experiments using subjects who must volunteer. Sherman and Berk's (1984) experimental study of arrest and domestic violence and the study of the effects of counsel at bail hearings by Colbert et al. (2002) were both conducted while elements of the criminal justice system engaged in their normal activities in real communities, greatly increasing our confidence in the studies' generalizability. However, in other experiments, neither random selection from the population nor selection of the entire population is possible. Potential subjects must make a conscious decision to participate. This undoubtedly increases the possibility that the resulting sample is an unrepresentative pool of volunteers. Even in the Sherman and Berk study, many police officers did not participate, so the attempt to include all domestic assault cases that met study criteria did not succeed. The results of the study may not have been generalizable even to the two precincts.

When random selection is not feasible, the researchers may be able to increase generalizability by selecting several sites for conducting the experiments that offer obvious contrasts in the key variables of the population. The follow-up studies to Sherman and Berk's (1984) work, for example, were conducted in cities that differed from Minneapolis, the original site, in social class and ethnic composition. As a result, although the findings are not statistically generalizable to a larger population, they do give some indication of the original study's general applicability (Cook and Campbell 1979).

▣ Factorial Survey Design

> **Factorial survey** A survey in which randomly selected subsets of respondents are asked different questions, or are asked to respond to different vignettes, in order to determine the causal effect of the variables represented by these differences.

Factorial surveys embed the features of true experiments into a survey design in order to maximize generalizability. In the most common type of factorial survey, respondents are asked for their likely responses to one or more vignettes about hypothetical situations. The content of these vignettes is varied randomly among survey respondents so as to create "treatment groups" that differ in terms of particular variables reflected in the vignettes.

▣ Case Study: How Citizens View Police Misconduct

To assess how citizens judge fair punishments for police misconduct, Seron, Pereira, and Kovath (2006) used a factorial survey of 1,100 residents in New York City (randomly selected using random digit dialing). Regulations for police officers generally dictate they avoid unnecessary use of force, abuse of authority, discourteous behavior, and offensive language in their dealings with citizens. The authors explained their rationale for using a factorial survey this way, "Even when a respondent does not have firsthand, "real-life," experience with a subject such as police misconduct, a factorial survey allows respondents to make judgments based on a "contrived but enriched set of choices" arrayed in vignettes..." (p. 931). The researchers designed their vignettes after analyzing a sample of closed and redacted cases of police misconduct in New York City. Several dimensions were varied in the vignettes including the civilian response to discourtesy or abuse by the police officer. An example of a vignette was provided:

A police officer stops a Jamaican, teenaged, male walking down the street, because of some odd behavior and asks, "What are you doing?" The teen politely asks the police officer why he is being questioned. The police officer says to the teen, "go back to your country, you filthy immigrant." The teen says, "Who the f*** do you think you guys are?" As a result of the interaction, the teen suffers mental trauma.

Respondents were asked to rate the level of misconduct perceived in each vignette on a scale from zero (0) "not misconduct" to ten (10) "serious misconduct." They were also asked to suggest the appropriate punishment for the officers using a nine-point scale from (1) "written warning to (9) "prison or jail time of 1 year or more." Findings indicate that citizens were most likely to score vignettes high on misconduct if they used "unnecessary use of force" and also if the civilian in the vignette sustained physical injuries.

External Validity

Researchers are often interested in determining whether the treatment effects identified in an experiment hold true for subgroups of subjects or across different populations. Of course, determining that a relationship between the treatment

Exhibit 7.9	Examples of Conditions Manipulated in a Factorial Survey Design to Examine Judgments of Police Misconduct

Dimension 5—Civilian Initial response

The civilian does exactly what the police officer says.

The civilian attempts to explain what is going on.

The civilian seems nervous.

The civilian flees from officer, dropping a gun.

The civilian repeatedly tells PO, "I didn't do anything wrong!"

The civilian repeatedly tells PO, "I know my rights!"

The civilian flees from officer.

Dimension 7—Abuse of Authority—Officer threatens to arrest civilian

Officer threatens to grab and kick civilian.

Officer threatens to beat civilian.

Officer searches civilian.

Officer refuses to provide a name or badge number.

Officer gives the civilian a false name and badge number.

Officer threatens "I'm going to send you back to NJ in a body bag!"

Officer searches, handcuffs, and arrests civilian without apparent cause.

Officer threatens to use his baton on civilian while he is in custody.

Officer says to civilian, "Don't say another word or you're going to jail!"

Source: Adapted from Seron, C., Pereira, J., & Kovath, J. 2006. "How citizens assess just punishment for police misconduct." *Criminology* 44(4): 925–60.

and the outcome variable holds true for certain subgroups does not establish that the same relationship also holds true for these subgroups in the larger population, but it does suggest that the relationship might be externally valid.

Imagine a field experiment in which subjects were randomly sampled from the population of interest but in which the treatment effect occurred only for some subgroups. Suppose, for example, that you conduct an experiment on the effects of alcohol on violent behavior and find that alcohol increases the probability for males to act violently, but not females. The finding about the overall effect of alcohol, then, would not apply to all groups within the population. In this instance, the external validity of the conclusions would be equivalent to their cross-population generalizability.

Ultimately, the external validity of experimental results will increase with the success of replications taking place at different times and places, using different forms of the treatment. As indicated by the replications of the Sherman and Berk (1984) study of arrest for domestic violence, the result may be a more detailed, nuanced understanding of the hypothesized effect.

Interaction of Testing and Treatment

A variation of the problem of external validity occurs when the experimental treatment is effective only when particular conditions created by the experiment occur. For example, if subjects have had a pretest it may sensitize them to a particular issue, so when they are exposed to the treatment, their reaction is different from what it would have been if they had not taken the pretest. In other words, testing and treatment interact to produce the outcome.

Suppose you were interested in the effects of a diversity training film on prejudicial attitudes. After answering questions in a pretest about their attitudes on various topics related to diversity (e.g., racial or sexual prejudice), the subjects generally became more sensitive to the issue of prejudice without seeing the training film. On the posttest, then, their attitudes may be different from pretest attitudes simply because they have become sensitized to the issue of diversity through pretesting. In this situation, the treatment may actually have an effect, but it would be difficult to determine how much of the effect was attributable to the sensitizing pretest and how much was due to seeing the film.

Researchers sometimes deliberately take advantage of the interaction of testing and treatment to increase external validity. One design for doing so, the **Solomon four-group design**, randomly assigns subjects to at least two experimental groups and at least two comparison groups. One experimental group and one comparison group will have a pretest, and the other two groups will not have a pretest (see Exhibit 7.10). If testing and treatment do interact, the difference in outcome scores between the experimental and comparison groups will differ between subjects who took the pretest and those who did not.

> ***Solomon four-group design*** An experimental design in which there are four groups. Two of the groups represent a classic experimental design in which there is an experimental and a control group that each receive a pretest. The final two groups represent an experimental and a control group but neither receives a pretest. This design helps to identify the interaction of testing and treatment.

Ethical Issues in Experimental Research

Exhibit 7.10	Solomon Four-Group Design Testing the Interaction of Pretesting and Treatment			
Experimental group	R	O$_1$	X	O$_2$
Comparison group	R	O$_1$		O$_2$
Experimental group	R		X	O$_2$
Comparison group	R			O$_2$

Note: R = random assignment; O = observation (pretest or posttest); X = experimental treatment.

> ***Distribution of benefits*** An ethical issue about how much researchers can influence the benefits subjects receive as part of the treatment being studied in a field experiment.

Social science experiments often raise difficult ethical issues. You have already read in Chapter 3 that Philip Zimbardo (2004) ended his Stanford Prison Experiment after only 6 days, rather than after the planned 2 weeks, because of the psychological harm that seemed to result from the unexpectedly sadistic behavior of some of the "guards." Although Zimbardo's follow-up research convinced him that there had been no lasting harm to subjects, concern about the potential for harm would preclude many such experiments today.

In spite of the ethical standard of informed consent by subjects, deception is an essential part of many experimental designs. As a result, contentious debate continues about the interpretation of this standard. Experimental evaluation of social programs also poses ethical dilemmas because they require researchers to withhold possibly beneficial treatment from some of the subjects just on the basis of chance (Boruch 1997). In this section, we will give special attention to the problems of deception and the **distribution of benefits** in experimental research.

Deception

Deception is used in social experiments to create more "realistic" treatments, often within the confines of a laboratory. You learned in Chapter 3 about Stanley Milgram's (1965) use of deception in his classic study of obedience to authority. Volunteers were recruited for what they were told was a study of the learning process, not a study of "obedience to authority." The experimenter told the volunteers that they were administering electric shocks to a "student" in the next room, when there were actually neither students nor shocks. Subjects seemed to believe the deception.

Whether or not you believe that you could be deceived in this way, you are not likely to be invited to participate in an experiment such as Milgram's. Current federal regulations preclude deception in research that might trigger such upsetting feelings. However, deception is still routine in many college laboratories. The question that must always be answered is "Is there sufficient justification to allow the use of deception?"

The American Sociological Association's Code of Ethics (1999), which is also used by the American Society of Criminology, does not discuss experimentation explicitly, but it does highlight the ethical dilemma posed by deceptive research:

> 12.05 Use of Deception in Research: (a) Sociologists do not use deceptive techniques (1) unless they have determined that their use will not be harmful to research participants; is justified by the study's prospective scientific, educational, or applied value; and that equally effective alternative procedures that do not use deception are not feasible, and (2) unless they have obtained the approval of institutional review boards or, in the absence of such boards, with another authoritative body with expertise on the ethics of research. (b) Sociologists never deceive research participants about significant aspects of the research that would affect their willingness to participate, such as physical risks, discomfort, or unpleasant emotional experiences. (c) When deception is an integral feature of the design and conduct of research, sociologists attempt to correct any misconception that research participants may have no longer than at the conclusion of the research.

This approach is to allow deception when it is unlikely to cause harm, is necessary for the research, and is followed by adequate explanation after the experiment is over.

Selective Distribution of Benefits

Field experiments conducted to evaluate social programs also can involve issues of informed consent (Hunt 1985). One ethical issue that is somewhat unique to field experiments is the distribution of benefits: How much are subjects harmed by the way treatments are distributed in the experiment? For example, Sherman and Berk's (1984) experiment, and its successors, required police to make arrests in domestic violence cases largely on the basis of a random process. When arrests were not made, did the subjects' abused spouses suffer? Price, Van Ryn, and Vinokur (1992) randomly assigned unemployed individuals who had volunteered for job-search help to an intensive program. Were the unemployed volunteers assigned to the comparison group at a big disadvantage?

Is it ethical to give some potentially advantageous or disadvantageous treatment to people on a random basis? Would randomly assigning all those who wanted the additional treatment to drug courts or not have been ethical? Random distribution of benefits is justified when the researchers do not know whether some treatment actually is beneficial—and, of course, it is the goal of the experiment to find out. Chance is as reasonable a basis for distributing the treatment as any other. Also, if insufficient resources are available to fully fund a benefit for every eligible person, distribution of the benefit on the basis of chance to equally needy persons is ethically defensible (Boruch 1997).

Individuals who were the subjects of domestic violence complaints in the Sherman and Berk (1984) study had no choice about being arrested or receiving a warning, nor were they aware that they were in a research study. Perhaps it seems unreasonable to let a random procedure determine how police resolve cases of domestic violence. And, indeed, it would be unreasonable if this procedure were a regular police practice. The Sherman and Berk experiment and its successors do pass ethical muster, however, when seen for what they were: a way of learning how to increase the effectiveness of police responses to this all-too-common crime. The initial Sherman and Berk findings encouraged police departments to make many more arrests for these crimes, and the follow-up studies resulted in a better understanding of when arrests are not likely to be effective. The implications of this research may be complex and difficult to implement, but the research provides a much stronger factual basis for policy development.

▣ Conclusion

True experiments play two critical roles in criminological research. First, they are the best research design for testing causal hypotheses. Even when conditions preclude the use of a true experimental design, many research designs can be improved by adding experimental components. Second, true experiments provide a comparison point for evaluating the ability of the other research designs to achieve causally valid results.

In spite of their obvious strengths, true experiments are used infrequently to study many research problems related to criminology and criminal justice. There are three basic reasons for this:

1. The experiments required to test many important hypotheses require more resources than most social scientists can access.

2. Most research problems of interest to social scientists simply are not amenable to experimental designs, for reasons ranging from ethical considerations to the limited possibilities for randomly assigning people to different conditions in the real world.

3. The requirements of experimental design usually preclude large-scale studies and so limit generalizability to a degree that is unacceptable to many social scientists.

And just because it is possible to test a hypothesis with an experiment, it may not always be desirable to do so. When a program is first developed and its elements are in flux, it is not a good idea to begin a large evaluation study that cannot possibly succeed unless the program design remains constant. Researchers should wait until the program design stabilizes somewhat. It also does not make sense for evaluation researchers to test the impact of programs that cannot actually be implemented or that are unlikely to be implemented in the real world due to financial or political problems (Rossi and Freeman 1989).

Even laboratory experiments are inadvisable when they do not test the real hypothesis of interest but instead test a limited version amenable to laboratory manipulation. The intersecting complexity of societies, social relationships, and social beings of people and the groups to which they belong is so great that it often defies reduction to the simplicity of a laboratory or restriction to the requirements of experimental design. Yet the virtues of experimental designs indicate they should always be considered when explanatory research is planned.

When a true experimental design is not feasible, researchers may instead use a quasi-experimental design, including nonequivalent control group designs, before-and-after designs, and ex post facto control group designs. These research designs are termed "quasi"-experimental because the units under study are not randomly assigned to the comparison and experimental groups. As a result, we cannot be as confident in the comparability of the groups in these designs. However, there are several steps that can be taken, such as matching certain individual or group characteristics across the two groups that allow us to have more confidence in the results of quasi-experimental research.

Key Terms

Before-and-after design   168
Causal effect   174
Cohort   168

Compensatory rivalry (John Henry
   effect)   177
Contamination   177

Control or comparison group   161
Differential attrition   175
Distribution of benefits   182

Highlights

- The independent variable in an experiment is represented by a treatment or another intervention. Experiments have a comparison group that represents what subjects are like on the dependent variable without the treatment. In true experiments, subjects are randomly assigned to comparison and experimental groups.

- Experimental research designs have three essential components: use of at least two groups of subjects for comparison, measurement of the change that occurs as a result of the experimental treatment, and use of random assignment. In addition, experiments may include identification of a causal mechanism and control over experimental conditions.

- Random assignment of subjects to experimental and comparison groups eliminates systematic bias in group assignment. The odds of a difference between the experimental and comparison groups on the basis of chance can be calculated.

- Both random assignment and random sampling rely on a chance selection procedure, but their purposes differ. Random assignment involves placing predesignated subjects into two or more groups on the basis of chance; random sampling involves selecting subjects out of a larger population on the basis of chance. Matching cases in the experimental and comparison groups is a poor substitute for randomization because it is not possible to identify in advance all important variables to use for the match. However, matching can improve the comparability of groups when it is used to supplement randomization.

- Causal conclusions derived from experiments can be invalid due to selection bias, endogenous change, the effects of external events, cross-group contamination, or treatment misidentification. In true experiments, randomization should eliminate selection bias and bias due to endogenous change. External events, cross-group contamination, and treatment misidentification can threaten the validity of causal conclusions in both true experiments and quasi-experiments.

- Process analysis can be used in experiments to identify how the treatment had (or did not have) its effect, a matter of particular concern in field experiments. Treatment misidentification is less likely when process analysis is used.

- The generalizability of experimental results declines if the study conditions are artificial and the experimental subjects are unique. Field experiments are likely to produce more generalizable results than experiments conducted in the laboratory.

- Causal conclusions can be considered externally valid if they apply to all the subgroups in a study. When causal conclusions do not apply to all the subgroups, they are not generalizable to corresponding subgroups in the population and are not externally valid. Causal conclusions can also be considered externally invalid when they occur only under the experimental conditions.

- Nonexperimental designs use statistical controls to reduce the risk of spuriousness. A variable is controlled when it is held constant so that the association between the independent and dependent variables can be assessed without being influenced by the control variable.

- Subject deception is common in laboratory experiments and poses unique ethical issues. Researchers must weigh the potential harm to subjects and debrief subjects who have been deceived. In field experiments, a common ethical problem is selective distribution of benefits. Random assignment may be the fairest way of allocating treatment when treatment openings are insufficient for all eligible individuals and when the efficacy of the treatment is unknown.

Research in the News

Sending the Police Before There's a Crime

In Santa Cruz, California, two women were arrested as they were peering in parked cars in a parking garage. Police were monitoring the parking garage because a computer program predicted that particular parking garage was likely to experience car burglaries that day. Sound far-fetched? The program is part of an experiment being conducted by the Santa Cruz Police Department in predictive policing, which is essentially deploying officers to places where crimes are likely to occur in the future. Unlike CompStat systems, which targets areas based on past crimes, this new program actually predicts new crimes. The article notes that empirical evidence on the effectiveness of the experiment are not yet available.

Source: Goode, Erica. 2011. "Sending the Police Before There's a Crime." *The New York Times,* August 16, A11.

Exercises

1. Read the original article reporting one of the experiments described in this chapter. Critique the article, using as your guide the article review questions presented in Appendix B. Focus on the extent to which experimental conditions were controlled and the causal mechanism was identified. Did inadequate control over conditions or inadequate identification of the causal mechanism make you feel uncertain about the causal conclusions?

2. Design a laboratory experiment to determine whether alcohol consumption leads to increased violent attitudes or actions. Describe how your design incorporates the three components of experiments. Evaluate how well your design meets the criteria for identifying causality. What are the ethical issues you face in this experiment?

3. Select a true experiment, from the *Journal of Experimental Criminology,* the *Journal of Experimental Social Psychology,* the *Journal of Personality and Social Psychology,* or sources suggested by your instructor. Diagram the experiment using Exhibits 7.3 and 7.4 in this chapter as models. Discuss the extent to which experimental conditions were controlled and the causal mechanism was identified. How confident can you be in the causal conclusions from the study, based on review of the threats to internal validity discussed in this chapter: selection bias, endogenous change, external events, contamination, and treatment misidentification?

4. Repeat Exercise 3 with a quasi-experiment.

5. Critique the ethics of one of the articles from Exercise 3 or 4. What specific rules do you think should guide researchers' decision about subject deception and the selective distribution of benefits?

6. Volunteer for an experiment! Contact the psychology department and ask about opportunities for participating in laboratory experiments. Discuss this experience with your classmates.

7. Take a few minutes to review "sources of internal invalidity" with the interactive exercises on the study site. It will be time well spent!

Developing a Research Proposal

1. Design a laboratory experiment to test one of your hypotheses or a related hypothesis. Describe the experimental design, commenting on each component of a true experiment. Specify clearly how the independent variable will be manipulated and how the dependent variable will be measured.

2. Assume that your experiment will be conducted on campus. Formulate recruitment and randomization procedures.

3. Discuss the extent to which each source of internal validity is a problem in the study. Propose procedures like process analysis to cope with these sources of invalidity.

4. How generalizable would you expect the study's findings to be? What can be done to increase generalizability?

5. Develop appropriate procedures for the protection of human subjects in your experiment, including a consent form. Give particular attention to any aspects of the study that are likely to raise ethical concerns.

Web Exercises

1. Go to SocioSite at www.sociosite.net. Choose "Subject Areas." Choose "Crime" or "Criminology." Find an example of research that has been done using experimental methods. Explain the experiment. Choose at least five of the key terms listed at the end of this chapter that are relevant to and incorporated in the research experiment you have located on the Web. Explain how each of the five key terms you have chosen plays a role in the research example you have found on the Web.

2. Go to the Stanford Prison Experiment Web site at www.prisonexp .org. Read the information provided about the Stanford Prison Experiment.

   a. Write a brief essay on the study, including the purpose of the study, the type of experiment, the participant selection process, the problems encountered during the study, and the results.

   b. Go to the discussion questions provided on the Web site. Answer the questions listed. What conclusions do you make about the Stanford Prison Experiment?

3. Go to Crime Stoppers USA's (CSUSA) Web site at www.crimesto pusa.com. Check out "About Us" and then "What is Crime Stoppers?" How is CSUSA "fighting crime"? What does CSUSA's approach assume about the cause of crime? Do you think CSUSA's approach to fighting crime is based on valid conclusions about causality? Explain.

4. What are the latest trends in crime? Write a short statement after inspecting the Federal Bureau of Investigation Uniform Crime Reports at www.fbi.gov (go to the "statistics" section under "Reports & Publications"). You will need to use Adobe Acrobat Reader to access some of these reports (those in PDF format). Do any of the publications discuss the "causes" of crime? If so, on what research do they base these statements?

Ethics Exercises

1. Under what conditions do you think that randomized assignment of subjects to a specific treatment is ethical in criminal justice research? Was it ethical for Sherman and Berk (1984) and the researchers who conducted the replication studies to randomly assign individuals accused of domestic violence to an arrest or a nonarrest treatment? What about in a laboratory study with students like yourself? Do you think it would be ethical to assign students randomly to be "prisoners" in a study like Zimbardo's (2007)?

2. Critique the ethics of one of the articles from Exercise 3 or 4 above. What specific rules do you think should guide researchers' decisions about subject deception and the selective distribution of benefits?

SPSS or Excel Exercises

1. How do homicide offender characteristics influence length of sentence? You can test various hypotheses by comparing means across categories for the characteristics of interest using HOMICIDE.POR.

   a. Obtain frequency distributions for whether or not the defendant knew the victim (KNOWN), race of the defendant (RACE), and sex of the defendant (SEX).

b. Pose at least three hypotheses about the relationship between homicide defendant characteristics and length of sentence.

c. Test these hypotheses by comparing the mean sentence length in days received by defendants (PRITIME) between categories of the independent variables listed in Part a. Which of your hypotheses appear to be supported? What do you theorize the cause of these findings to be?

2. Do prior convictions influence the number of days to which homicide defendants are sentenced?

a. Obtain a frequency distribution for the variable PRCONV (prior convictions). According to the data, do homicide defendants frequently have prior convictions? What do you hypothesize is the relationship between prior convictions and sentence length? Why?

b. Compare the mean sentence length in days received by defendants against their number of prior convictions. For example, do defendants who have no prior convictions receive a shorter sentence length compared to those with at least one prior conviction? Do the data support your hypothesis? Do any of the categories deviate from what you hypothesized? Explain.

c. Recode the PRCONV variable into a new dichotomous variable, measuring whether the homicide defendant had prior convictions or no prior convictions. If necessary, reword your hypothesis to reflect the dichotomous nature of the new variable.

d. Test your hypothesis by comparing the mean sentence length in days received by defendants with prior convictions and those with no prior convictions. What conclusions do you make about the relationship between prior convictions and sentence length of homicide defendants?

Survey Research

Despite over three decades of research, the magnitude of rape, stalking, and intimate-perpetrated violence (IPV) against men and women is still frequently disputed. For many reasons, including the historical stigma attached to these crimes, fear of retaliation from their perpetrators, and other safety concerns, estimating incidence rates of this violence has always been a difficult task. As we noted in Chapter 1, the most enduring source of statistical information about violent crime in the United States is the Uniform Crime Reporting (UCR) Program compiled by the Federal Bureau of Investigation (FBI), but this data source relies on victimizations reported to the police. This is problematic since we know that fewer than 50% of these offenses are ever reported to police. Due to this weakness in estimating rates of this violence, random sample surveys of the population are now being used as a social science tool of choice for uncovering incidents of violence within families. However, as can be expected, surveys employing diverse methodologies and different definitions of violence result in tremendously diverse estimates.

To increase our understanding of violent victimization, the National Institute of Justice and the Centers for Disease Control and Prevention cosponsored a national telephone survey called the National Violence Against Men and Women (NVAMW) Survey (Tjaden and Thoennes 2000). Respondents to the NVAMW Survey were asked about a number of health and safety issues, including physical assault they experienced as children by adult caretakers, physical assault they experienced as adults by any type of perpetrator, and forcible rape or stalking they experienced at any time in their life by any type of perpetrator. In this chapter, we will use this project along with the U.S. Justice Department's National Crime Victimization Survey (NCVS) to illustrate some key features of survey research. After an initial review of the reasons for using survey methods, we explain the major steps in questionnaire design and then consider the features of four types of surveys, highlighting the unique problems of each and suggesting possible solutions. Important ethical issues are discussed in the final section. By the chapter's end, you should be well on your way to becoming an informed consumer of survey reports and a knowledgeable developer of survey designs. In addition, you will become a more informed student of the methodological issues surrounding the measurement of violent victimization in the United States.

🔲 Survey Research in the Social Sciences

Survey research involves the collection of information from a sample of individuals through their responses to questions. In addition to social scientists, many newspaper editors, political pundits, and marketing gurus have turned to survey research because it is an efficient method for systematically collecting data from a broad spectrum of individuals and social settings. The results of surveys are broadcast daily on most network news programs. In fact, surveys have become such a vital part of our nation's social fabric that we cannot assess much of what we read in the newspaper or see on TV without having some understanding of this method of data collection (Converse 1984).

> **Survey research** Research in which information is obtained from a sample of individuals through their responses to questions about themselves or others comparison of designs.

Modern survey research methods were developed in the early and middle years of the 20th century (Lazarsfeld and Oberschall 1965; Oberschall 1972). Beginning in the 1920s, psychologists used surveys to test the abilities of students, employees, and army recruits. For their part, sociologists conducted a few ambitious attitude surveys of the general population, such as Emory S. Bogardus's study of race relations, which had a sample of 1,725 respondents (Converse 1984). Industrial psychologists began to rely on surveys to study employee morale and other attitudes. Psychologist Paul F. Lazarsfeld studied consumers' reactions to particular products before moving into sociology and becoming one of the discipline's leading survey proponents (Converse 1984).

Political demands also stimulated the growth of survey research. Professional polling became a regular fixture after the 1936 presidential election. Professional polling firms such as the one operated by George Gallup correctly predicted that President Franklin Delano Roosevelt would win reelection, whereas the poorly designed *Literary Digest* poll led to an infamous forecast that challenger Alfred M. Landon would win (see Chapter 5). The U.S. Bureau of the Census began to supplement its 10-year census with more frequent surveys of population samples to monitor respondents' income and other economic variables. And in 1973, the U.S. Department of Justice implemented the National Crime Victimization Survey to capture incidents of crime victimization not reported to police.

Since the early days of survey research, professional survey organizations have provided a base of support for social science researchers affiliated with universities. The development of electronic computers also aided the growth of survey research, allowing for great increases in the speed and accuracy of processing and reporting data. Surveys soon became the most popular research method in the social sciences.

Attractive Features of Survey Research

Regardless of its scope, survey research owes its continuing popularity to three features: versatility, efficiency, and generalizability.

Versatility

The first and foremost reason for the popularity of survey methods is their versatility. Researchers can ask respondents questions about almost any topic you can imagine. Although a survey is not the ideal method for testing all hypotheses or learning about every social process, a well-designed survey can enhance our understanding of just about any social issue. In fact, there is hardly any topic of interest to social scientists that has not been studied at some time with survey methods.

Efficiency

Surveys also are popular because data can be collected from many people at relatively low cost and, depending on the survey design, relatively quickly. For the NVAMW Survey, Tjaden and Thoennes (2000) contracted with Schulman, Ronca, and Bucuvalas, Inc. (SRBI) to conduct the telephone survey, primarily because SRBI had conducted nationally representative sample surveys before on sensitive subject matters such as victimization. Surveys were conducted from November 1995 to May 1996 with an average cost of $30 per respondent. Large, mailed surveys are less expensive, at $10 to $15 per potential respondent, but the cost can increase greatly when intensive follow-up efforts are made. Surveys of the general population using personal interviews are much more expensive, with costs ranging from $100 per potential respondent for studies in a limited geographical area to $300 or more when lengthy travel or repeat visits are needed to connect with respondents (Floyd J. Fowler, personal communication, January 7, 1998, Center for Survey Research, University of Massachusetts Boston; see also Dillman 1982; Groves and Kahn 1979). As you would expect, phone surveys are the quickest survey method, which accounts for their popularity in political polling.

Surveys are efficient research methods because many variables can be measured without substantially increasing the time or cost of data collection. Mailed questionnaires can include up to 10 pages of questions before respondents lose interest (and before more postage must be added). The maximum time limit for phone surveys seems to be about 45 minutes. In-person interviews can last much longer, taking more than an hour. For example, the 1991 General Social Survey included 196 questions, many with multiple parts, and was 75 pages long.

Of course, the efficiency of the surveys can be attained only in a place with a reliable communications infrastructure (Labaw 1980). A reliable postal service, required for mail surveys, has generally been available in the United States, and phone surveys can be effective in the United States because 95% of its households have phones (Czaja and Blair

1996). Also important to efficiency are the services of the many survey organizations that provide the trained staff and the proper equipment for conducting high-quality surveys.

Generalizability

Survey methods lend themselves to probability sampling from large populations. Thus, survey research is very appealing when sample generalizability is a central research goal. In fact, survey research is often the only means available for developing a representative picture of the attitudes and characteristics of a large population.

Surveys also are the research method of choice when cross-population generalizability is a primary concern. They allow a range of social contexts and subgroups to be sampled, and the consistency of relationships can be examined across the various subgroups.

The Omnibus Survey

Most surveys are directed at a specific research question. In contrast, an **omnibus survey** covers a range of topics of interest to different social scientists. It has multiple sponsors or is designed to generate data useful to a broad segment of the social science community rather than answer one particular research question.

> **Omnibus survey** A survey that covers a range of topics of interest to different social scientists.

One of the most successful omnibus surveys is the General Social Survey (GSS) of the National Opinion Research Center at the University of Chicago. After taking a teaching position at Dartmouth College, James A. Davis, who worked at the National Opinion Research Center for 10 years, was dismayed to discover how difficult it was for faculty in small schools to obtain worthwhile survey data. Starting in 1972, the National Science Foundation agreed to fund the GSS as an annual, publicly available national survey on topics of general interest to sociologists. In 1992, the GSS changed to a biennial schedule.

Today, the GSS is administered every 2 years as a 90-minute interview to a probability sample of almost 3,000 Americans. It includes more than 500 questions about background characteristics and opinions, with an emphasis on social stratification, race relations, family issues, law and social control, and morale. It explores political views, work experiences, social ties, news sources, and views on law, health, and religion. Questions and topic areas are chosen by a board of overseers drawn from the best survey researchers.

The core of the GSS is the set of questions asked in every survey. Other questions are repeated only in alternating surveys, and some questions are added in single or multiyear supplements paid for by special grants. Since 1988, most of the questions have been asked in each survey, but many of them have been asked of only a randomly selected subset of respondents. This **split-ballot design** allows the inclusion of more questions without increasing the survey's cost. The split-ballot design also allows for experiments on the effect of question wording; different phrasings of the same question are included in the split-ballot subsets.

> **Split-ballot design** Unique questions or other modifications in a survey administered to randomly selected subsets of the total survey sample, so that more questions can be included in the entire survey or so that responses to different question versions can be compared.

Although the NVAMW Survey is not exactly an omnibus survey, it was developed to obtain detailed information on a number of phenomena related to victimization. For example, because the Centers for Disease Control and Prevention was a cosponsor of the survey, many questions were added to obtain detailed information on a respondent's history of health and injuries in addition to injuries resulting from victimization.

The deficiency of the omnibus approach is the limited depth that can be achieved in any one substantive area. In some years, the GSS avoids this problem by going into greater depth in one particular area. But the best way to get survey data about one particular topic is still the survey developed around the topic alone. The surveys we are going to highlight in this chapter were all developed to measure one topic, victimization.

▣ Questionnaire Development and Assessment

The questionnaire or interview schedule, as it is often called in interview-based studies) is the central feature of the survey process. Without a well-designed questionnaire tailored to the study's purposes, survey researchers have little hope of achieving their research goals.

The correct design of a questionnaire varies with the specific survey method used and the other particulars of a survey project. There is no precise formula for a well-designed questionnaire. Nonetheless, some key principles should guide the design of any questionnaire, and some systematic procedures should be considered for refining it.

> **Questionnaire** The survey instrument containing the questions for a self-administered survey.
>
> **Interview schedule** The survey instrument containing the questions asked by the interviewer for an in-person interview or phone survey.

Maintain Focus

A survey (with the exception of an omnibus survey) should be guided by a well-defined inquiry and a definitively targeted population. Does the study seek to describe some phenomenon in detail, explain some behavior, or explore some type of social relationship? And is your aim to explain that behavior for everyone or as it pertains to a select group? Until the research objective is clearly formulated, survey design cannot begin. Throughout the process of questionnaire design, this objective should be the primary basis for making decisions about what to include and exclude, and what to emphasize or treat with less importance. Moreover, the questionnaire should be viewed as an integrated whole, in which each section and every question serves a clear purpose related to the study's objective and is a complement to other sections or questions.

Surveys often include too many irrelevant questions and fail to include questions that the researchers realize later are crucial. One way to ensure that all possibly relevant questions are asked is to use questions suggested by prior research, theory, or experience or by experts (including participants) who are knowledgeable about the setting under investigation. Of course, even the best researcher cannot anticipate every question that could be worthwhile, nor can one anticipate those that are worthless.

Build on Existing Instruments

When another researcher already has designed a set of questions to measure a key concept in your study, that existing set of questions can be called a survey instrument. If evidence from previous surveys indicates that these already formulated questions provide a good measure of the concept or behaviors you are interested in, then use them! Measurement tools have already been established for many concepts, especially those of interest to criminological research including delinquency, self-control, depression, and so on. In the case study that follows, you will see how researchers rarely have to reinvent the wheel.

Consider Translation

Should the survey be translated into one or more languages? In the 21st century, no survey plan in the United States or many other countries can be considered complete until this issue has been considered. In the U.S. in 2008, 15.3% of persons aged 18 years and older were foreign born (Pew Hispanic Center 2008) and more than half of these adults said that they did not speak English very well. In some areas of the U.S., these proportions can be much higher.

Many first generation immigrants are not fluent in English (Hakimzadeh and Cohn 2007). As a result, they can only be included in a survey if it is translated into their native language.

This does not simply mean picking up a bilingual dictionary and clicking "translate" in a Web browser, or even hiring a translator to translate the questions. You must ensure that the concepts you are measuring have equivalence in different cultures, which is often a time-consuming task, and typically involves teams of experts both in the language and in the culture for which the questionnaire is intended. Many government sponsored surveys are currently translated into Spanish, including the NVAMWS highlighted in this chapter.

Case Study: Measuring Violent Victimizations

To measure incidents of physical assault, Tjaden and Thoennes (2000) modified a survey instrument that had already been widely used in the literature: the Conflict Tactics Scale (CTS) (Straus 1979). To measure incidents of rape and sexual victimization, Tjaden and Thoennes utilized questions that had already been used by Kilpatrick et al. at the University of South Carolina in the National Women's Study (National Victim Center and the Crime Victims Research and Treatment Center 1992). As you can see in Exhibit 8.1, these questions were very specific in nature and covered all behaviors that are legally defined as rape or sexual assault in most states. In contrast, you will also see in Exhibit 8.1 that the screening questions used today by the NCVS to uncover incidents of rape and sexual assault still do not use these graphic behavior-specific questions, which have been proven to uncover more reports of victimization (Fisher 2009).

Respondents to the NVAMW Survey who answered yes to any of these screening questions were asked many specific questions about the nature of the victimization, including information about the offender, injuries sustained, and reports to police. Respondents to the NCVS who answered yes to their screening questions were further queried, "Do you mean forced or coerced sexual intercourse?" Only if respondents answered yes to this question were they counted as rape victims; the others were classified as other sexual assault victims. In the end, both surveys purport to measure incidents of rape in the United States, but which methodology is most appropriate? In the next section, we will provide you with some specific guidelines for writing questions and you will see that the answer to this question is not so clear-cut.

Writing Questions

Asking people questions is the most common operation for measuring social variables, and probably the most versatile. In principle, survey questions can be a straightforward and efficient means of measuring individual characteristics, facts about events, levels of knowledge, and opinions of any sort. In practice, survey questions, if misleading or unclear, can result in inappropriate and unintended answers. All questions proposed for a survey must adhere to basic guidelines and then tested and revised until the researcher feels confident they will be clear to the intended respondents (Fowler 1995). Structurally, questions on surveys generally fall into two categories: those with and those without explicit response choices. Recall from Chapter 4 that open-ended questions are those without explicit response choices. This type of question is usually used only for explorative purposes when there is little known about a particular topic and you want to uncover as much about it as possible without restricting responses. For example, if you are

Open-ended questions Survey questions to which the respondent replies in his or her own words, either by writing or by talking.

Exhibit 8.1 | **Rape Screening Questions Used by the NVAMW Survey and by the NCVS Survey**

National Violence Against Men and Women (NVAMW) Survey

[For females only] Regardless of how long ago it happened, has a man ever made you have sex by using force or threatening to harm you or someone close to you? Just so there is no mistake, by sex we mean putting a penis in your vagina.

[For males and females] Has anyone, male or female, ever made you have oral sex by using force or threat of harm? Just so there is no mistake, by oral sex we mean that a man or boy put his penis in your mouth or someone, male or female, penetrated your vagina or anus with their mouth or tongue.

[For males and females] Has anyone ever made you have anal sex by using force or threat of harm? Just so there is no mistake, by anal sex we mean that a man or boy put his penis in your anus.

[For males and females] Has anyone, male or female, ever put fingers or objects in your vagina or anus against your will by using force or threats?

[For males and females] Has anyone, male or female, ever attempted to make you have vaginal, oral, or anal sex against your will, but intercourse or penetration did not occur?

National Crime Victimization Survey (NCVS)

Incidents involving forced or unwanted sexual acts are often difficult to talk about. Have you been forced or coerced to engage in unwanted sexual activity by

    a. someone you didn't know before,

    b. a casual acquaintance, or

    c. someone you know well?

---

investigating the perceptions of residents regarding a new community policing program instituted in the neighborhood, open-ended questions such as the following one could be very informative:

> "In your opinion, what have been the benefits of the community policing program in your neighborhood?"

The information obtained from open-ended questions such as this could then be used as the basis for questions with fixed responses in future studies that evaluate the efficacy of community policing.

Open-ended questions are also excellent tools for obtaining respondents' interpretations in greater detail and can often illuminate flaws in other questions. A survey researcher can also try to understand what respondents mean by their responses after the fact by including additional open-ended questions in the survey. Adding such **interpretive questions** after key survey questions is always a good idea, but it is of utmost importance when the questions in a survey have not been pretested. An example from a study of people with motor-vehicle driving violations illustrates the importance of interpretive questions:

> **Interpretive questions** Questions included in a questionnaire or interview schedule to help explain answers to other important questions.

> When asked whether their emotionaol state affected their driving at all, respondents would reply that their emotions had very little effect on their driving habits. Then, when asked to describe the circumstances surrounding their last traffic violation, respondents typically replied, "I was mad at my girlfriend," or "I had a quarrel with my wife," or "We had a family quarrel," or "I was angry with my boss." (Labaw 1980:71)

Were these respondents lying in response to the first question? Probably not. More likely, they simply did not interpret their own behavior in terms of a general concept such as "emotional state." But their responses to the first question were likely to tell a different story without the further detail provided by answers to the second.

In summary, one strength of open-ended questions is the wealth of information they provide. This wealth of information, however, is exactly why many researchers do not use them. The verbatim text narratives obtained from open-ended questions take a great deal of time and energy to organize and summarize. In addition, many respondents may feel overwhelmed about writing a lengthy essay. If you want to ask a large number of open-ended questions, it is perhaps best to consider an in-person interview or a phone interview instead of a questionnaire (both of which are discussed later in this chapter).

> **Fixed-choice questions (closed-ended question)**
> A question format in which respondents are provided with explicit responses from which to select.

When respondents are offered explicit responses to choose from, this type of question is referred to as a **closed-ended question** or a **fixed-choice question**. For example, in the NVAMW Survey, respondents were asked:

Overall, would you say that personal safety in this country has improved since you were a child, gotten worse since you were a child, or stayed about the same?

- Improved

- Gotten worse

- Stayed about the same

Most surveys of a large number of people primarily contain fixed-choice questions, which are easy to process and analyze with the use of computers and statistical software. With fixed-choice questions, respondents are also more likely to answer the question that researchers want them to answer. By including the response choices, the survey reduces ambiguity. However, fixed-choice questions can also obscure what people really think unless the choices are carefully designed to match the range of all possible responses to the question.

Regardless of the format used for questions, there are several rules to follow and pitfalls to avoid that will maximize the validity of your survey instrument. We will highlight these in the next section.

Constructing Clear and Meaningful Questions

All hope for achieving measurement validity is lost unless survey questions are clear and convey the intended meaning to respondents. Just because you pose questions all the time and have no trouble understanding the responses you receive, clear and meaningful survey questions would not present a challenge. Consider just a few of the differences between everyday conversations and standardized surveys. Survey questions must be asked of many people, not just one person:

- The same survey questions must be used with each person, not tailored to the specifics of a given conversation.

- Survey questions must be understood in the same way by people who differ in many ways.

- You will not be able to rephrase a survey question if someone does not understand it because that would alter the question, and it would not be the same as the one posed to other participants.

- Survey respondents do not know you and so cannot be expected to share the nuances of expression that you and those close to you use to communicate.

These features make a survey very different from natural conversation and make question writing a challenging and important task for survey researchers.

Questions must be very clear and specific about what is being asked of respondents. Note the differences in specificity between the rape screening questions used by the NVAMW Survey and the NCVS displayed in Exhibit 8.1. It is logical that the multiple, behaviorally specific questions from the NVAMW Survey will be associated with greater disclosure by survey respondents compared to the one question about sexual intercourse posed by the NCVS. In fact, results of the two surveys indicate that the NVAMW Survey uncovers about four times as many rapes as does the NCVS (Bachman 2000).

Another powerful illustration of the effect of questions on responses comes from the redesign of the NCVS itself. The NCVS was implemented in 1972 to complement what was known about crime from police reporting data from the UCR. In the 1980s, the survey's sponsor, the Bureau of Justice Statistics (BJS), redesigned the screening instrument used by the NCVS to more accurately measure incidents of violent crime, particularly those perpetrated by known offenders such as intimates and other family members (Bachman and Taylor 1994). Among the most important changes to the questionnaire were (a) additional cues to help survey respondents recall incidents, (b) questions encouraging respondents to report victimizations that they themselves may not define as crimes, (c) more direct questions on rape and sexual assault, and (d) new questions to encourage disclosure of victimizations by nonstrangers.

Exhibit 8.2 displays the old screening questions of the NCVS along with the redesigned violent crime screen questions that were implemented into a small percentage of the total NCVS sample beginning in 1989; by 1992 the entire sample was asked these questions. As you can see, not only are there more questions in the redesigned instrument, but the questions also are much more behaviorally specific than those in the old questionnaire. In fact, note that the old questionnaire did not contain a specific question about rape. Prior to the redesign, only those respondents who said they were "attacked some other way" and who self-reported that attack as a rape were classified as rape victims.

Exhibit 8.2	Comparison of the Redesigned and Old Screener Questions Used by the National Crime Victimization Survey

Screener questions for violent crimes
New (beginning January 1992)*

1. Has anyone attacked or threatened you in any of these ways—
   a. With any weapon, for instance, a gun or knife—
   b. With anything like a baseball bat, frying pan, scissors, or stick—
   c. By something thrown, such as a rock or bottle—
   d. Include any grabbing, punching, or choking,
   e. Any rape, attempted rape, or other type of sexual assault—
   f. Any face to face threats—

OR

   g. Any attack or threat or use of force by anyone at all? Please mention it even if you were not certain it was a crime.

2. Incidents involving forced or unwanted sexual acts are often difficult to talk about. Have you been forced or coerced to engage in unwanted sexual activity by—
   a. Someone you didn't know before
   b. A casual acquaintance OR
   c. Someone you know well.

Old (1972–1992)

1. Did anyone take something directly from you by using force, such as by a stickup, mugging, or threat?
2. Did anyone TRY to rob you by using force or threatening to harm you?
3. Did anyone beat you up, attack you, or hit you with something, such as a rock or bottle?
4. Were you knifed, shot at, or attacked with some other weapon by anyone at all?

(Continued)

Exhibit 8.2 (Continued)

5. Did anyone THREATEN to beat you up or THREATEN you with a knife, gun, or some other weapon, NOT including telephone threats?

6. Did anyone TRY to attack you in some other way?

*During 1992 half of the sampled households responded to the old questionnaire, and half to the redesigned survey.

Screener questions for all types of crimes
New

1. Were you attacked or threatened OR did you have something stolen from you—
   a. At home including the porch or yard—
   b. At or near a friend's, relative's, or neighbor's home—
   c. At work or school—
   d. In a place such as a storage shed or laundry room, a shopping mail, restaurant, bank or airport—
   e. While riding in any vehicle—
   f. On the street or in a parking lot—
   g. At such places as a party, theater, gym, picnic area, bowling lanes, or while fishing or hunting.

OR

   h. Did anyone ATTEMPT to attack or attempt to steal anything belonging to you from any of these places?

2. People often don't think of incidents committed by someone they know. Did you have something stolen from you OR were you attacked or threatened by—
   a. Someone at work or school—
   b. A neighbor or friend—
   c. A relative or family member—
   d. Any other person you've met or known?

3. Did you call the police to report something that happened to YOU which you thought was a crime?

4. Did anything happen to you which you thought was a crime, but did NOT report to the police?

Old

1. Was anything stolen from you while you were away from home, for instance, at work, in a theater or restaurant, or while traveling?

2. Did you call the police to report something that happened to YOU that you thought was a crime?

3. Did anything happen to YOU that you thought was a crime, but did NOT report to the police?

In 1994, the BJS began publishing the results of the redesigned survey. Not surprisingly to survey methodologists, rates of violent crime such as rape, intimate-perpetrated assault, and other family violence increased dramatically. Exhibit 8.3 displays the rate changes for various types of violent crime against men and women. Do these dramatic increases from 1991 to 1992 actually reflect increases in victimizations? Obviously not. The increase is due primarily to the new screening questionnaire. The more specific questions increased the extent to which respondents disclosed their victimizations. As you might imagine, the BJS had to educate the media and public about this methodology before these rates were released, to avoid headlines such as "The Justice Department Finds Rates of Family Violence Skyrocketing."

In addition to writing clear and meaningful questions, there are several other rules to follow and pitfalls to avoid that we will highlight in the next section.

| Exhibit 8.3 | Comparison of Violent Crime Rates per 1,000 Males and Females by Victim-Offender Relationship Obtained by the Redesigned Screener and the Older Screener of the NCVS |

Relationship	Female Rate	Male Rate
Older Questionnaire		
Intimate	5.4	.5
Other relative	1.1	.7
Acquaintance/friend	7.6	13.0
Stranger	5.4	12.2
Redesigned Questionnaire		
Intimate	9.3	1.4
Other relative	2.8	1.2
Acquaintance/friend	12.9	17.2
Stranger	7.4	19.0

Source: R. Bachman and L. Saltzman. 1995. *Violence Against Women: Estimates From the Redesigned Survey* (NCJ-154348), Appendix Table. Washington, DC: Bureau of Justice Statistics, U.S. Department of Justice.

Avoid Confusing Phrasing and Vagueness

Good grammar is a basic requirement for clear questions. Clearly and simply phrased questions are most likely to have the same meaning for different respondents. So, be brief and to the point. The wordier and longer the question, the more likely you are to lose respondent's attention and focus.

Virtually all questions about behavior and feelings will be more reliable if they refer to specific times or events (Turner and Martin 1984). Without a **reference period**, or time frame around which a question is being asked, a researcher will not know how to interpret an answer. For example, the question "How often do you carry a method of self-protection such as pepper spray?" will produce answers that have no common reference period and can therefore not be reliably compared to answers from other respondents. A more specific way to ask the question is "In the last month, how many days did you carry a method of self-protection such as pepper spray?"

> **Reference period** A time frame in which a survey question asks respondents to place a particular behavior (e.g., in the last 6 months).

In general, research shows that the longer the reference period, the greater the underreporting of a given behavior (Cantor 1984, 1985; Kobelarcik et al. 1983). As a general rule, when respondents are being asked about mundane or day-to-day activities, reference periods should be no longer than "in the past month." However, when rare events are being measured, such as experiences with victimizations, "in the last 6 months," as utilized by the NCVS Survey, or "in the past 12 months," as used by the NVAMW, are both more appropriate. By using longer reference periods like this, we will more likely capture these rarer events.

Avoid Negatives and Double Negatives

Picture yourself answering the following question: "Do you disagree that juveniles should not be tried as adults if they commit murder?" It probably took a long time for you to figure out if you would actually agree or disagree with this statement, because it is written as a **double-negative question**. For example, if you think juveniles who commit

> **Double-negative question** A question or statement that contains two negatives, which can muddy the meaning.

murder should be tried as adults, you would actually agree with this statement. Even questions that are written with a single negative are usually difficult to answer. For example, suppose you were asked to respond to "I can't stop thinking about the terrorist attacks on 9/11" using a five-point response set of "very rarely" to "very often." A person who marks "very rarely" is actually saying, "I very rarely can't stop thinking about the terrorist attacks on 9/11." Confusing, isn't it? Even the most experienced survey researchers can unintentionally make this mistake.

Avoid Double-Barreled Questions

When a question is really asking more than one question, it is called a **double-barreled question**. For example, the statement "I believe we should stop spending so much money building prisons and put it into building more schools" is

> **Double-barreled question** A single survey question that actually asks two questions but allows only one answer.

really asking respondents two different questions. Some respondents may believe we should stop building so many prisons but may not want the revenue to go into building more schools. Double-barreled questions can also show up in the response categories. For example, the item below is really asking two questions:

Do you know anyone who has ever used cocaine?

_____ Yes _____ No _✓_ I have used cocaine

Avoid Making Either Disagreement or Agreement Disagreeable

People often tend to "agree" with a statement just to avoid seeming disagreeable. You can see the impact of this human tendency in a 1974 Michigan Survey Research Center survey that asked who was to blame for crime and lawlessness in the United States (Schuman and Presser 1981). When one question stated that individuals were more to blame than social conditions, 60% of the respondents agreed. But when the question was rephrased so respondents were asked, in a balanced fashion, whether individuals or social conditions were more to blame, only 46% chose individuals.

You can take several steps to reduce the likelihood of agreement bias. As a general rule, you should impartially present both sides of attitude scales in the question itself: "In general, do you believe that *individuals* or *social conditions* are more to blame for crime and lawlessness in the United States?" (Dillman 2000:61–62). The response choices themselves should be phrased to make each one seem as socially approved, or as "agreeable," as the others. You should also consider replacing the word "agree" with a range of response alternatives. For example, "To what extent do you support or oppose the new health care plan?" (response choices range from "strongly support" to "strongly oppose") is probably a better approach than the question "To what extent do you agree or disagree with the statement 'The new health care plan is worthy of support'?" (response choices range from "strongly agree" to "strongly disagree").

When an illegal or socially disapproved behavior or attitude is the focus, we have to be concerned that some respondents will be reluctant to agree that they have ever done or thought such a thing. In this situation, the goal is to write a question and response choices that make agreement seem more acceptable or at the very least, not stigmatizing. For example, Dillman (2000) suggests that we ask, "Have you ever taken anything from a store without paying for it?" rather than "Have you ever shoplifted something from a store?" (p. 75). Asking about a variety of behaviors or attitudes that range from socially acceptable to socially unacceptable will also soften the impact of agreeing with those that are socially unacceptable.

Additional Guidelines for Fixed-Response Questions

Creating questions that are clear and meaningful is only half of the formula to creating a good survey instrument. The choices you provide respondents in fixed-choice questions are also important. In this section, we provide you with several rules that will help ensure that the response choices you provide to your questions will also be clear, concise, and exhaustive.

Response Choices Should Be Mutually Exclusive

When you want respondents to make only one choice, the fixed-response categories must not overlap. For example, if you were interested in the ways foot patrol officers spent their time while working, you might ask the following question:

On average, how much time do you spend on the job each week taking care of traffic violations?

- Less than 1 hour
- 1–3 hours
- 3–6 hours
- 6–10 hours
- 10 hours or more

The choices provided for respondents in this question are not **mutually exclusive responses**, because they overlap. Which choice would an officer select if he or she spent an hour a week on traffic violations? Choices that are mutually exclusive would look like this:

> **Mutually exclusive responses** Response choices on a survey that do not overlap.

- Less than 1 hour
- 2–3 hours
- 4–6 hours
- 7–10 hours
- 11 hours or more

Make the Response Categories Exhaustive

In addition to mutual exclusivity, fixed-response categories must also allow all respondents to select an option. Consider the same research question about foot patrol officers. Suppose we asked a question such as this:

In what activity do you spend the most time in an average week on the job?

_____ Traffic violations

_____ Disturbance-related issues

_____ Felony arrests

_____ Misdemeanor arrests

Regardless of how exhaustive we think the response categories are, there must always be an option for respondents who require another choice. Response categories can easily be made **exhaustive** if respondents are provided with a choice labeled:

> **Exhaustive responses** A variable's attributes or values in which every case can be classified as having one attribute.

_____ Other, please specify: _____

Note, however, that "Other" should be used only after you have included all options that you believe to be relevant. Otherwise, a large percentage of respondents will select the "Other" category and you will have to spend time coding their responses.

Utilize Likert-Type Response Categories

> **Likert-type responses** Survey responses in which respondents indicate the extent to which they agree or disagree with statements.

Likert-type responses generally ask respondents to indicate the extent to which they agree or disagree with statements. Why the name? Well, this format is generally believed to have been developed by Rensis Likert in the 1930s. Likert-type response categories list choices for respondents to select their level of agreement with a statement and may look something like this:

"Three-strikes" laws that increase penalties for individuals convicted of three or more felonies will help decrease the crime rate.

1	2	3	4
Strongly Agree	Agree	Disagree	Strongly Disagree

Minimize Fence-Sitting and Floating

Two related problems in question writing stem from the respondent's desire to choose an acceptable or socially desirable answer and those who want to get through the survey as fast as possible. There is no uniformly correct solution to these problems, so you must carefully select an alternative.

Fence-sitters are people who see themselves as neutral in their attitudes toward a particular issue. If you are truly interested in those who do not have strong feelings on an issue, one alternative is to provide a neutral or undecided response option. The disadvantage to these options is that they may encourage some respondents to take the easy way out rather than really thinking about their feelings. They may also provide an out for respondents who do not want to reveal how they truly feel about an issue. On the other hand, not providing respondents who really have no opinion on an issue with an option such as "undecided" can be very frustrating and may encourage them to leave the item blank altogether. Whatever you decide, it is generally a good idea to provide respondents with instructions that ask them to

> **Fence-sitters** Survey respondents who see themselves as being neutral on an issue and choose a middle (neutral) response that is offered.

"select the choice in each item that most closely reflects your opinion." This should help make all respondents feel more comfortable about their answers, particularly those who only slightly feel one way or the other.

Floaters are respondents who choose a substantive answer even when they do not know anything about a particular question. For example, research has shown that a third of the public will provide an opinion on a proposed law they know nothing about if they are not provided with a "Don't know" response option (Schuman and Presser 1981). Of course, providing a "don't know" option has the same disadvantage as providing a neutral response option; its inclusion leads some people who have an option to take the easy way out.

> **Floaters** Survey respondents who provide an opinion on a topic in response to a closed-ended question that does not include a "don't know" option, but will choose "don't know" if it is available.

If you are really interested in informed opinions about an issue, it is best to provide detailed information about that issue when asking a question. For example, let us say we were interested in attitudes about the treatment of juvenile offenders by the criminal justice system. Suppose we asked respondents to provide their opinion on the following statement: "The Juvenile Justice Bill before Congress will help reduce crime committed by juveniles." Do you know what the Juvenile Justice Bill is? If we did not provide a "don't know" option, respondents who knew nothing about the Juvenile Justice Bill would be forced to select a response that would not be meaningful and may bias the results of the entire survey. Instead of a "don't know" option, another way to handle the problem is to provide details of the issue you are interested in. For example, you could tell respondents that one component of the bill encourages states to adjudicate all juvenile homicide offenders 13 years of age or older as adults and then ask respondents their opinion about this particular issue. If you are truly interested in the extent to which respondents have knowledge about a particular issue and you want to include a "don't know" response, it should be set apart from the other choices so that respondents do not mistake it as a neutral or undecided choice. Of course, as with all questions, there should be clear instructions about what the response options actually mean. For example, if you wanted to examine citizens' knowledge and opinion about the Independent Counsel statute, you could ask:

Instructions: For each statement, check the box that best indicates your agreement about the statement. If you do not have enough information about a statement to determine your level of agreement, leave the boxes blank and put an X on the box next to "Don't Know."

I think the Independent Counsel law should remain as it is.

- Strongly Agree
- Agree
- Disagree
- Strongly Disagree
- Don't Know

Utilize Filter Questions

The use of filter questions is important to ensure that questions are asked only of relevant respondents. For example, if you are interested in the utilization of police services by robbery victims, you would first need to establish victimization with a **filter question**. These filter questions create **skip patterns**. For example, respondents who answer "no" to one question are directed to skip ahead to another question, but respondents who answer yes go on to the **contingent question** or questions. That's why these questions are sometimes called contingency questions. Skip patterns should be indicated clearly with arrows or other direction in the questionnaire, as demonstrated in Exhibit 8.4.

> **Filter question** A survey question used to identify a subset of respondents who then are asked other questions.
>
> **Skip patterns** The unique combination of questions created in a survey by filter questions and contingent questions.
>
> **Contingent question** Questions that are asked of only a subset of survey respondents.

Combining Questions Into an Index

Measuring variables with single questions is very popular. Public opinion polls based on answers to single questions are reported frequently in newspaper articles and TV newscasts: "Do you favor or oppose U.S. policy in . . . ?" "If you had to vote today, for which candidate would you vote?" The primary problem with using a single question is that if respondents misunderstand the question or have some other problem with the phrasing, there is no way to tell. Single questions are prone to this **idiosyncratic variation**, which occurs when individuals' responses vary because of their reactions

> **Idiosyncratic variation** Variation in responses to questions that is caused by individuals' reactions to particular words or ideas in the question instead of by variation in the concept that the question is intended to measure.

to particular words or ideas in the question. Differences in respondents' backgrounds, knowledge, and beliefs almost guarantee that they will understand the same question differently. If some respondents do not know some of the words in a question, we may misinterpret their answers—if they answer at all. If a question is too complex, respondents may

---

Exhibit 8.4   Filter Questions and Skip Patterns

14. In the past 6 months, has anyone taken something from you by force or the threat of force?

    _____ Yes (If yes, please answer questions 15 through 16)

    _____ No (If no, please skip to question 17)

15. What was the approximate monetary value of the items taken?

    _____ Under $50

    _____ $51 to $99

    _____ $100 to $299

    _____ $300 to $500

    _____ Over $500

16. Was the incident reported to the police?

    _____ Yes

    _____ No

17. How fearful are you of walking alone at night in your neighborhood?

    _____ Extremely afraid

    _____ Afraid

    _____ Unafraid

    _____ Extremely unafraid

---

focus on different parts of the question. If prior experiences or culturally biased orientations lead different groups in the sample to interpret questions differently, answers will not have a consistent meaning because the question meant something different to each respondent.

If just one question is used to measure a variable, the researcher may not realize respondents had trouble with a particular word or phrase in the questions. Although writing carefully worded questions will help reduce idiosyncratic variation, when measuring concepts, the best option is to devise an index of multiple rather than single questions.

> **Index** A composite measure based on summing, averaging, or otherwise combining the responses to multiple questions that are intended to measure the same variable.
>
> **Scale** A composite measure of one concept created from a series of two or more questions.

When several questions are used to measure one concept, the responses may be combined by taking the sum or average of the responses. A composite measure based on this type of sum or average is called an **index** or a **scale.** The idea is that idiosyncratic variation in response to single questions will average out, so the main influence on the combined measure will be the concept focused on by the questions. In addition, the index can be considered a more complete measure of the concept than can any one of the component questions.

Creating an index, however, is not just a matter of writing a few questions that seem to focus on one concept. Questions that seem to you to measure a common concept might seem to respondents to concern several different issues. The only way to know that a given set of questions does effectively form an index is to administer the questions in a pretest to people similar to the sample you plan to study. If a common concept is being measured, people's responses to the different questions should display some

> **Reliability measures** Special statistics that help researchers decide whether responses are consistent.

consistency. Special statistics called **reliability measures** help researchers decide whether responses are consistent. Most respondent attitudes are complex and consist of many elements.

Be aware of response sets when constructing an index measuring attitudes. For example, some people tend to agree with almost everything asked of them, whereas others tend to disagree. Still others are prone to answer neutrally to everything if given the option. To decrease the likelihood of this happening, it is a good idea to make some statements both favorable and unfavorable to a particular attitude to vary the response choices and still reach an understanding of individuals' opinions. In this way, respondents are forced to be more careful in their responses to individual items. Exhibit 8.5 displays a hypothetical set of questions designed to solicit respondents' attitudes toward police in their community.

When scoring an index or scale made up of both favorable and unfavorable statements, you must remember to reverse code the unfavorable items. For example, marking "strongly agree" to the first item in Exhibit 8.5 should not be scored the same as a "strongly agree" response to the second item.

Due to the popularity of survey research, indexes already have been developed to measure many concepts, and some of these indexes have proved to be reliable in a range of studies. It usually is much better to use these indexes to measure concepts than to try to devise new questions to form a new index. As noted earlier in this chapter, the use of a preexisting measure both simplifies the work involved in designing a study and facilitates a comparison of findings to those obtained in previous studies.

One index available in the NCVS is designed to measure what is referred to in criminological literature as *routine activities*. To explain crime victimization, the Routine Activities Theory focuses on the circumstances in which crimes are committed rather than on the circumstances of the offender. According to Cohen and Felson (1979), each criminal act requires the convergence of three elements: likely and motivated offenders, suitable targets, and an absence of capable guardians to prevent the would-be offender from committing the crime. Thus, the routine patterns of work, play, and leisure time affect the convergence in time and place of the motivated offenders, the suitable targets, and the absence of guardians. To measure the extent to which respondents engage in routine activities away from the home, the NCVS asks three questions that are displayed in Exhibit 8.6. These questions measure different types of activities people routinely engage in away from the home and, when combined, create a better measure of an individual's activities away from the home than would a single question.

Exhibit 8.5 **Items in an "Attitude Toward Police" Index**

1. Police officers are generally fair to all people regardless of their race or ethnicity.

   _____ Strongly Agree _____ Agree _____ Disagree _____ Strongly Disagree

2. Police officers are given too much freedom to stop and frisk community residents.

   _____ Strongly Agree _____ Agree _____ Disagree _____ Strongly Disagree

3. If someone resisted arrest, even a little, most police officers would become assaultive if they thought they could get away with it.

   _____ Strongly Agree _____ Agree _____ Disagree _____ Strongly Disagree

4. Police officers put their lives on the line every day trying to make it safe for residents of this community.

   _____ Strongly Agree _____ Agree _____ Disagree _____ Strongly Disagree

5. The majority of police officers have lied under oath at least once.

   _____ Strongly Agree _____ Agree _____ Disagree _____ Strongly Disagree

6. The majority of police officers are honest and fair.

   _____ Strongly Agree _____ Agree _____ Disagree _____ Strongly Disagree

Exhibit 8.6	Example of an Index: NCVS Questions Used to Make Up an Index of Routine Activities Away From the Home

Before we get to the crime questions, I'd like to ask you about some of your usual activities. We have found that people with different lifestyles may be more or less likely to become victims of crime.

30. On average, during the past 6 months, that is since _____, 20 _____, how often have you gone shopping? For example, at drug, clothing, grocery, hardware, and convenience stores. (Read answer categories until respondent answers yes.)

   _____ Almost every day (or more frequently)

   _____ At least once a week

   _____ At least once a month

   _____ Less often

   _____ Never

   _____ Don't know

31. On average, during the past 6 months, how often have you spent the evening away from home for work, school, or entertainment? (Read answer categories until respondent answers yes.)

   _____ Almost every day (or more frequently)

   _____ At least once a week

   _____ At least once a month

   _____ Less often

   _____ Never

   _____ Don't know

32. On average, during the past 6 months, how often have you ridden public transportation? Do not include school buses. (Read answer categories until respondent answers yes.)

   _____ Almost every day (or more frequently)

   _____ At least once a week

   _____ At least once a month

   _____ Less often

   _____ Never

   _____ Don't know

Another example of an index is that used to measure student perceptions of tolerance for substance abuse on college campuses (Core Institute 1994). An excerpt from this is shown in Exhibit 8.7. Alone, no single question would be sufficient to capture the overall tolerance of substance abuse on campus. A person's total response to these questions is likely to provide a more accurate indication of tolerance for substance abuse than would a single, general question such as "Do students on this campus feel that drinking or using drugs is OK?"

The advantages of using indexes rather than single questions to measure important concepts are very clear. Surveys often include sets of multiple-item questions, and the following are four cautions to consider:

Our presupposition that each component question is indeed measuring the same concept may be mistaken. Although we may include multiple questions in a survey to measure one concept, we may find that answers to the questions are not related to one another, and so the index cannot be created. Alternatively, we may find that answers to just a few of the questions are not related to the answers given to most of the other questions. We may therefore decide to discard these particular questions before computing the average that comprises the index.

Exhibit 8.7 **Example of an Index: Excerpt From the Index of Student Tolerance of Substance Abuse**

37. During the past 30 days, to what extent have you engaged in any of the following behaviors?

(Mark one for each line)	0 Times	1 Time	2 Times	3–5 Times	6–9 Times	10 or More Times
a. Refused an offer of alcohol or other drugs						
b. Bragged about your alcohol or other drug use						
c. Heard someone else brag about his or her alcohol or other drug use						
d. Carried a weapon such as a gun, knife, and so on (do not count hunting situations or weapons used as part of your job)						
e. Experienced peer pressure to drink or use drugs						
f. Held a drink to have people stop bothering you about why you weren't drinking						
g. Thought a sexual partner was not attractive because he or she was						
h. Told a sexual partner that he or she was not attractive because he or she was drunk						

Source: Core Institute 1994. "Core Alcohol and Drug Survey: Long Form." Carbondale. IL: FIPSE Core Analysis Grantee Group, Core Institute, Student Health Programs, Southern Illinois University.

Combining responses to specific questions can obscure important differences in meaning among the questions. Schutt, Gunston, and O'Brien's (1992) research projects on the impact of AIDS prevention education in shelters for the homeless provide an example. In this research, Schutt et al. asked a series of questions to ascertain respondents' knowledge about HIV risk factors and about methods of preventing exposure to those risk factors. After combining the responses into an overall knowledge index, they were surprised to find that the knowledge index scores were no higher in a shelter with an AIDS education program than in a shelter without such a program. Further analysis, however, showed that respondents in the shelter with an AIDS education program were more knowledgeable than the other respondents about the specific ways to prevent AIDS, which were in fact the primary focus of the program. Combining the responses to these questions with the other responses about general knowledge of HIV risk factors obscured this important finding (Schutt et al. 1992).

The questions in an index may cluster together in subsets. All the questions may measure the intended concept, but we may conclude that the concept actually has several different aspects. A multidimensional index has then been obtained. This conclusion can in turn help us refine our understanding of the original concept. For example, over two decades of work have culminated in the development of a multidimensional index of stress at the state level. Research has found that this index, the State Stress Index (SSI), is related to a number of aggressive behaviors also measured at the state level such as state rates of homicide and rape (Linsky, Bachman, and Straus 1995). The SSI is based on the life-events theory of stress, which holds that the more events such as divorce or movement to a new community to which individuals must adapt, the greater risk they have of not being able to cope. The administration and scoring of life-event measures of stressors experienced by an individual are straightforward. Respondents are asked to indicate events on the list they experienced in the recent past. The number of life events is then added to provide a score that indicates the extent to which the respondent has experienced these stressful events. The SSI is a translation of the life-events approach from the original individual level to the macro or societal level. The basic strategy was to measure the rate at which these events occurred in each state to evaluate the stressfulness of living in each state. What developed was a multidimensional index composed of 15 indicators that statistically fell into three categories: economic stressors, family stressors, and community stressors. The specific variables used to make up the SSI are presented in Exhibit 8.8.

Sometimes particular questions are counted, or weighted, more than others in the calculation of the index. Some questions may be more central to the concept being measured than others and so may be given greater weight in the index score. It is difficult to justify this approach without extensive testing, but some well-established indexes do involve differential weighting. Another approach to creating an index score is by giving different weights to the responses to different questions before summing or averaging the responses. Such a weighted index is also termed a scale. The scaling procedure might be as simple as arbitrarily counting responses to one question as worth two or three times as much as responses to another question, but most often, the weight applied to each question is determined through empirical testing. For example, based on Mooney and Lee's (1995) research on abortion law reform, the scoring procedure for a scale of support for abortion might give a "1" to agreement that abortion should be allowed "when a pregnancy results from rape or incest" and a "4" to agreement with the statement that abortion should be allowed "whenever a woman decides she wants one." In other words, agreeing that abortion is allowable in any circumstances is much stronger support for abortion rights than agreeing that abortion should be allowed in the case of rape or incest.

Demographic Questions

Almost all questionnaires include a section on demographic information such as sex, age, race or ethnicity, income, and religion. For many research studies, these questions are important independent variables. For example, research

---

Exhibit 8.8 **Life-Events Indicators in the 1992 State Stress Index (SSI)**

Economic Stressors
Business failures per 1 million population, 1982
Unemployment claims per 100 thousand adults age 18 and over, 1982
Striking workers per 100 thousand adults age 18 and over, 1981
Bankruptcy cases per 100 thousand population, 1982
Mortgage foreclosures per 100 thousand population, 1982

Family Stressors
Divorces per 1 thousand population, 1982
Abortions per 100 thousand population, 1982
Illegitimate births per 100 thousand population age 14 and over, 1982
Infant deaths per 1 thousand live births, 1982
Fetal deaths per 1 thousand live births, 1982

Community Stressors
Disaster assistance per 100 thousand population, 1982
Percentage residing in state less than 5 years, 1980
New housing units per 1 thousand population, 1982
New welfare recipients per 100 thousand population, 1982
High school dropouts per 100 thousand population, 1982

Source: Linsky, Bachman, and Straus 1995.

has shown that all five of these factors are related to the probability of victimization. Many researchers, however, include demographic questions that are not necessary for purposes of their research. Try to avoid this, particularly for questions on income because it makes the questionnaire more intrusive than necessary. In fact, many respondents feel that questions about their income invade their privacy. If you believe income is an essential variable for your study, providing fixed responses that include a range of values to select from is less intrusive than asking respondents for specific annual incomes. This format was utilized by the NVAMW Survey, as shown in Exhibit 8.9.

Exhibit 8.9   Question on Income From the NVAMW Survey

Including income from all sources, such as work, child support, and AFDC [Aid to Families with Dependent Children], how much income did you personally receive in 1995 before taxes? Stop me when I get to the category that applies. Was it:

01	Less than $5,000
02	$5,001 to $10,000
03	$10,001 to $15,000
04	$15,001 to $20,000
05	$20,001 to $25,000
06	$25,001 to $35,000
07	$35,001 to $50,000
08	$50,001 to $80,000
09	$80,001 to $100,000
10	Over $100,001
11	(Volunteer) None
12	(Volunteer) Don't Know
13	(Volunteer) Refused

Source: Tjaden and Thoennes 2000.

Care should also be taken when writing questions about race and ethnicity. Many people are justifiably sensitive to these questions. Even the U.S. Bureau of the Census has been struggling with appropriate categories to offer respondents. In fact, the bureau still utilizes two questions, one of race and one for respondent ethnicity (Hispanic or non-Hispanic), which is obviously problematic. Most survey researchers now include questions such as the following:

Which of the following best describes your racial or ethnic background? Please check one.

- Asian

- Black or African American

- White or Caucasian

- Hispanic (may be of any race)

- Native American

- Of Mixed Race or Ethnicity

- Other (Please specify: _____)

Deciding which categories to include remains difficult. Some researchers still prefer to exclude the Mixed category, because they believe most respondents will identify primarily with one race.

Questions on marital status can also be tricky to compose. The traditional categories of Married, Single, Divorced, and Widowed, still used by unsavvy researchers, can be interpreted very differently by respondents. Why? Well, isn't someone who is currently divorced also single? And what about someone not officially divorced but separated? To avoid confusing respondents, the U.S. Bureau of the Census adopted the following response categories: Married, Separated, Widowed, Divorced, and Never Married.

Because demographic questions are usually perceived as private by respondents, some researchers place them in a section at the end of the questionnaire with an introduction reassuring respondents that the information will remain confidential. However, when the information being gathered in the rest of the questionnaire is even more sensitive, such as violence respondents may have experienced at the hands of a family member or an intimate partner, some researchers opt to keep demographic questions near the beginning of the questionnaire. For example, the NVAMW Survey asked demographic questions after the first section, which asked respondents about their general perceptions of fear and safety.

Don't Forget to Pretest!

Adhering to the preceding question-writing guidelines will go a long way toward producing a useful questionnaire. However, simply asking what appear to be clear questions does not ensure that people have a consistent understanding of what you are asking. You need some external feedback, and the more of it the better.

No questionnaire should be considered ready for use until it has been **pretested**. Try answering the questionnaire yourself, and then revise it. Try it out on some colleagues or other friends, and then revise it. Then select a small sample of individuals from the population you are studying or one very similar to it, and try out the questionnaire on them. Audiotape the test interviews for later review, or for a written questionnaire, include in the pretest version some space for individuals to add comments on each key question.

> **Pretested** When a questionnaire is taken by a small subsample of respondents to uncover any problems with the questions or response categories.

The NVAMW Survey was pretested in *four* different trials on a total of 107 respondents. Yes, four! The pretests were used to assess the effectiveness of the interview introduction, identify confusion and awkwardness in question wording and response categories, and evaluate the flow and length of the interview. Once the fourth pretest established that the instrument was workable, it was then fielded to replicate samples of 500, 1,000, or 2,000 completed interviews. This additional pretesting allowed Tjaden and Thoennes (2000) to determine whether they should retain, drop, or revise particular questions.

Another important form of feedback results from simply discussing the questionnaire content with others. Persons to consult should include other researchers, key figures in the locale or organization to be surveyed (such as elected representatives, company presidents, and community leaders), and some individuals from the population to be sampled. If you find you have to explain a particular question in detail, you probably need to rewrite it. Run your list of variables and specific questions by such figures whenever you have a chance. Reviewing the relevant literature to find results obtained with similar surveys and comparable questions is also an important step to take. Of course, you should have already conducted such a review before writing your questions!

Another increasingly popular form of feedback comes from guided discussions among potential respondents, called focus groups, to check for consistent understanding of terms and to identify the range of events or experiences about which people will be asked to report. By listening and observing the focus group discussions, researchers can validate their assumptions about what level of vocabulary is appropriate and what people are going to be reporting (Fowler 1995).

Professional survey researchers have also developed a technique for evaluating questions called the **cognitive interview** (Fowler 1995). Although the specifics vary, the basic approach is to ask people test questions, and then probe with follow-up questions to learn how they understood the questions and what their answers mean.

Review the distribution of responses to each question, listen to the audiotapes, or read all the comments, and then code what you heard or read to identify problems in question wording or delivery. Revise any questions that respondents do not seem to interpret as you had intended or that are not working well for other reasons.

> **Cognitive interview** A technique for evaluating questions in which researchers ask people test questions, then probe with follow-up questions to learn how they understood the questions and what their answers mean.

To create a good questionnaire takes several drafts. By the time you have gone through just a couple of drafts, you may not be scanning the instrument as clearly as you think. A very honest illustration of this is provided by Don Dillman, the director of the Social and Economic Sciences Research Center at Washington State University. His research team was about ready to mail a questionnaire with the following response categories:

What is your opinion?

1	2	3	4	5
Strongly Oppose	Oppose	Neither Oppose nor Favor	Favor	Strongly Oppose

This Likert-type response format slipped not only by Dillman but by his typist, a research assistant, and another person working on the project. He explains:

> By the time a would-be surveyor has reached the final draft, he or she is often scanning the questionnaire for errors but not absorbing the detail. . . . All of us were looking for other things, such as spacing, punctuation, and content. The uniform appearance of the response categories looked right to all of us. (Seltzer 1996:98)

A careful scrutiny of your questionnaire using the procedures outlined in this section will help you detect these and other problems.

🔲 Organization of the Questionnaire

Once the basic topics and specific variables for a questionnaire have been identified, they can be sorted into categories (which may become separate sections) listed in tentative order, and later adjusted to develop the questionnaire's polish and coherence. Throughout the question-writing process, the grouping of variables into sections and the ordering of questions within sections can be adjusted. These adjustments will in turn require changes in the specific questions, in an iterative process that leads to a polished, coherent questionnaire.

The first thing needed is a descriptive title for the questionnaire that indicates the overall topic. The title is essential because it sets the context for the entire survey. For example, both the NCVS and the NVAMW Survey are interested in measuring the magnitude of crime victimization in the United States. The NVAMW Survey, however, was presented as a survey interested in a number of personal safety–related issues, including tactics used in conflict resolution. The

NCVS is named a crime survey and is a survey interested in obtaining information only about crimes respondents have experienced. Unfortunately, some survey participants still may not view assaults they have experienced by intimates and other family members as criminal acts.

Even though many of the behaviors conveyed in the screening instruments (e.g., kicking and punching) are the same for both surveys, the context in which these questions are asked must inevitably play a role in the candor respondents are willing to provide. The contextual message of crime may take precedence over the questions and may discourage respondents from reporting incidents they do not perceive as crimes. Lynch (1996) illuminates the importance of context by citing a study undertaken by the BJS in 1975 when a fear-of-crime supplement was asked of a subsample of the NCVS prior to the screening interview. Reports of victimization in the subsample that received the fear-of-crime supplement increased significantly; this finding was attributed to a warm-up effect of the fear supplement, such that the additional questions about fear of crime stimulated recall of crime events.

In addition to the title, question order and the use of multiple questions to uncover attitudes about emotional charged attitudes are important because these factors also can influence responses. Consider the issue of capital punishment. For example, a 1986 Gallup poll revealed that 70% of those surveyed approved of the death penalty for murder. However, when respondents were given the alternative punishment of life imprisonment without the possibility of parole, the support declined to 55%. This suggests that public opinion questions that simply ask whether the person approves of capital punishment for convicted murderers are a misleading indicator of the strength of support for the death penalty. As Paternoster (1991) explains,

> What Americans may be expressing, however, is a desire for protection against dangerous criminals, not a desire for capital punishment. More sophisticated polling questions indicate that the public does not necessarily want to repay one life with another, but wants the murderer to be unable to offend again, and to ease the hardship and loss for those left behind. (p. 30)

A similar phenomenon has been observed with questions about abortion. When a sample of the general public was asked, "Do you think it should be possible for a pregnant woman to obtain a legal abortion if she is married and does not want any more children?" There were 58% of the respondents who said yes. However, when this abortion question was preceded by one asking whether the respondent would allow abortion of a damaged fetus, only 40% said yes to the more permissive question. Clearly, the first question altered the respondents' frame of reference, perhaps by making abortion as a simple way to avoid having more children seem frivolous compared to the problem of having a damaged fetus (Turner and Martin 1984). The point to take away from these cases is that question order is extremely important. As Schuman and Presser (1981) acknowledge,

> Both examples illustrate the potential impact of question order on the respondents' answers. This potential is greatest when two or more questions concern the same issue or closely related issues so that asking one question affects reactions to the next question. The impact of question order also tends to be greatest for general summary-type questions. (p. 23)

There is no real cure for this potential problem, although the split-ballot technique may help identify the problem when the question order is reversed on a subset of the questionnaires. What is most important is to be aware of the potential for problems due to question order and carefully evaluate the likelihood of their occurrence in any particular questionnaire. Those who survey results should mention, at least in a footnote, the order in which key questions were asked when more than one such question was used (Labaw 1980). Questionnaires should conform to several other organizational guidelines as well:

- Major topic divisions within the questionnaire should be organized in separate sections, and each section should be introduced with a brief statement. This helps respondents understand the organization of the questionnaire.

- Instructions should be used liberally to minimize respondent confusion. Instructions should explain how each type of question is to be answered (such as circling a number or writing a response) in a neutral way that is not likely to influence responses. This type of instruction is particularly important with groups of questions that have standard answers laid out in a matrix format. The same set of response choices appears next to each question, because many respondents do not realize that they should circle one response on each line. Instructions also should guide respondents through skip patterns.

- Instructions may also be used to clarify for respondents why some information is included in the questionnaire (such as the implicit instruction to skip a set-off box of lines that are "For coding purposes only").

- The questionnaire should look attractive, be easy to complete, and have substantial open space. Resist the temptation to cram as many questions as possible onto one page. Response choices should be printed in a font or format and location different from the questions.

- Response choices should be designated by numbers to facilitate coding and data entry after the questionnaire is completed.

There were several sections in the NVAMW Survey, including sections on fear of violence and accommodation behavior, previous relationships, current partner (spouse, boyfriend or girlfriend) characteristics, sexual victimization, physical victimization, stalking victimization, violence in current relationships, and threat victimization. Exhibit 8.10 presents the introduction and a portion of the section on stalking victimization given to female respondents. Even though this questionnaire was given over the phone by professional interviewers, notice the specific instructions provided throughout.

The **cover letter** for a mailed questionnaire and the introductory statement read by interviewers in telephone or in-person interviews are also critical to the survey's success. Similar to the context set by the title of the survey, the initial statement of the cover letter sets the tone for the entire questionnaire. For example, the first thing interviewers said to respondents of the NVAMW Survey was, "Hello, I'm _____ from SRBI, the national research organization. We are conducting a national survey

> ***Cover letter*** The letter sent with a mailed questionnaire. It explains the survey's purpose and auspices and encourages the respondent to participate.

on personal safety for the Center for Policy Research, under a grant from the federal government." Notice that even though the survey's primary purpose was to uncover incidents of victimization, it was presented to respondents as a survey interested in issues of personal safety. This was done to increase the probability of respondents disclosing incidents of victimization even if they did not perceive them as crimes. Also note that the introductory statement disclosed the researcher's affiliation and the project sponsor. In addition, the purposes of the survey should also be briefly described, and a contact number of those who wish to ask questions or register complaints should be included.

A carefully prepared cover letter or initial statement should increase the response rate and result in more honest and complete answers to the survey questions; a poorly prepared cover letter or initial statement can have the reverse effects. There is no opportunity to clarify misunderstandings.

The cover letter or introductory statement must have the following characteristics:

Credible. The letter should establish that the research is conducted by a researcher or organization the respondent is likely to accept as a credible, unbiased authority. Research conducted by government agencies, university personnel, and recognized research organizations (such as Gallup or RAND) is usually considered credible. On the other hand, a questionnaire from an animal rights group on the topic of animal rights will probably be viewed as biased.

Personalized. The cover letter should include a personalized salutation (not just "Dear Student"), refer to the respondent in the second person ("Your participation . . ."), and close with the researcher's signature.

Exhibit 8.10	Section of the NVAMW Survey on Stalking Victimizations Given to Female Respondents

SECTION H: STALKING VICTIMIZATION

H1. Now I'd like to ask you some questions about following or harassment you may have experienced on more than one occasion by strangers, friends, relatives, or even husbands and partners. Not including all bill collectors, telephone solicitors or other sales people, has anyone, male or female, ever. . . . MARK ALL THAT APPLY

    01   Followed you or spied on you?

    02   Sent you unsolicited letters or written correspondence?

    03   Made unsolicited phone calls to you?

    04   Stood outside your home, school, or workplace?

    05   Showed up at places you were even though he or she had no business being there?

    06   Left unwanted items for you to find?

    07   Tried to communicate with you in ways against your will?

    08   Vandalized your pregnancy or destroyed something you loved?

    09   (Volunteered) Don't Know   GO TO SECTION I

    10   (Volunteered) Refused   GO TO SECTION I

    11   (Volunteered) None   GO TO SECTION I

H2. If H1 = ANY OF 1–8 (RESPONDENT HAS BEEN STALKED) GO TO H3, ELSE GO TO SECTION I.

H3. Has anyone ever done any of these things to you on more than one occasion?

    1   Yes

    2   No   GO TO SECTION I

    3   (Volunteered) Don't Know   GO TO SECTION I

    4   (Volunteered) Refused   GO TO SECTION I

H4. How many different people have ever done this to you on more than one occasion?

    _____ Number of people [RANGE IS 1–97]

    98   (Volunteered) Don't Know   GO TO SECTION I

    99   (Volunteered) Refused   GO TO SECTION I

H5. Was this person or these persons. . . . MARK ALL THAT APPLY

    01   Your current spouse?

    02   An ex-spouse?

    03   A male live-in partner?

    04   A female live-in partner?

    05   A relative?

    06   Someone else you know?

    07   A stranger?

    08   (Volunteered) Don't Know

    09   (Volunteered) Refused

Source: Tjaden and Thoennes 2000.

Interesting. The statement should interest the respondent in the contents of the questionnaire. Never make the mistake of assuming that what interests you will also interest your respondents. Try to put yourself in their shoes before composing the statement, and then test your appeal with a variety of potential respondents.

Responsible. Reassure the respondent that the information you obtain will be treated confidentially, and include a phone number the respondent can use if he or she has questions or would like a summary of the final report. Point out that the respondent's participation is completely voluntary (Dillman 1978). For example, in the NVAMW Survey, respondents were told, "I will be asking you about your personal experiences and opinions. You don't have to answer any questions you don't want to. All your answers will be treated as strictly confidential. Your participation is completely voluntary, but very important to the study. You can confirm the authenticity of the survey by calling our 800 number and asking for the Women's Safety Survey Coordinator."

Survey Designs

The five basic survey designs are the mailed survey, group-administered survey, phone survey, in-person survey, and **electronic or Web-based survey**. Exhibit 8.11 summarizes the typical features of the five different survey designs. Each survey design varies in its arrangement and application:

Manner of administration. The five survey designs differ in the manner in which the questionnaire is administered. Mailed, group, and electronic surveys are completed by the respondents themselves. During phone and in-person interviews, however, the researcher or a staff person asks the questions and records the respondent's answers.

> **Electronic survey (Web-based survey)** A survey that is sent and answered by computer, either through e-mail or on the Web.

Questionnaire structure. Survey designs also differ in the extent to which the content and order of questions are structured in advance by the researcher. Most mailed, group, phone, and electronic surveys are highly structured, fixing in advance the content and order of questions and response choices. Some of these types of surveys, particularly mailed surveys, may include some open-ended questions (respondents write in their answers rather than checking off one of several response choices). In-person interviews are often highly structured, but they may include many questions without fixed response choices. Moreover, some interviews may proceed from an interview guide rather than a fixed set of questions. In these relatively unstructured interviews, the interviewer covers the same topics with

Exhibit 8.11 Typical Features of the Five Survey Designs

Design	Manner of Administration	Setting	Questionnaire Structure	Cost
Mailed survey	Self	Individual	Mostly structured	Low
Group survey	Self	Group	Mostly structured	Very low
Phone survey	Professional	Individual	Structured	Moderate
In-person interview	Professional	Individual	Structured or unstructured	High
Web survey	Self	Individual	Mostly structured	Very low

respondents but varies questions according to the respondent's answers to previous questions. Extra questions are added as needed to clarify or explore answers to the most important questions.

Setting. Most mail and electronic questionnaires and phone interviews are intended for completion by only one respondent. The same is usually true of in-person interviews, although sometimes researchers interview several family members at once. On the other hand, a variant of the standard survey is a questionnaire distributed simultaneously to a group of respondents, who complete the survey while the researcher (or assistant) waits. Students in classrooms are typically the group involved, although this type of group distribution also occurs in surveys administered to employees and members of voluntary groups.

Cost. As mentioned earlier, in-person interviews are the most expensive type of survey. Phone interviews are much less expensive, but surveying by mail is cheaper yet. Electronic surveys are now the least expensive method because there are no interviewer costs, no mailing costs, and, for many designs, almost no costs for data entry. Of course extra staff time and expertise is required to prepare an electronic questionnaire.

Because of their different features, the five designs vary in the types of errors to which they are most prone and the situations in which they are most appropriate. The rest of this section focuses on the unique advantages and disadvantages of each design.

Mailed, Self-Administered Surveys

A **mailed (self-administered) survey** is conducted by mailing a questionnaire to respondents, who then administer the survey themselves. The principal drawback in using this method of survey administration is the difficulty maximizing the response rate—we have to rely on people to voluntarily return the surveys! The final response rate is unlikely to be much above 80% and almost surely will be below 70% unless procedures to maximize the response rate are precisely followed. A response rate below 60% is a disaster, and even a 70% response rate is not much more than minimally acceptable. It is hard to justify the representativeness of the sample if more than a third of those surveyed fail to respond.

> **Mailed (self-administered) survey** A survey involving a mailed questionnaire to be completed by the respondent.

Some ways to maximize the response rate (Fowler 1988; Mangione 1995; Miller 1991) include the following:

- Make the questionnaire attractive, with plenty of white space.

- Use contingent questions and skip patterns infrequently. When they are necessary, guide respondents visually through the pattern.

- Make individual questions clear and understandable to all the respondents. No interviewers will be on hand to clarify the meaning of the questions or probe for additional details.

- Use no more than a few open-ended questions. Respondents are likely to be put off by the idea of having to write out answers.

- Include a personalized and professional cover letter. Using an altruistic appeal (informing respondents that their response will do some good) seems to produce a response rate 7% higher than indicating that respondents will receive something for their participation.

- Have a credible research sponsor. According to one investigation, a sponsor known to respondents may increase the rate of response by as much as 17%. The next most credible sponsors are the state headquarters of an organization and then other people in a similar field. Publishing firms, college professors or students, and private associations elicit the lowest response rates.

- Write an identifying number on the questionnaire so you can determine the nonrespondents.

- A small incentive can help. Even a coupon or ticket worth $2 can be enough to increase the response rate.

- Include a stamped, self-addressed return envelope with the questionnaire.

Most important, use follow-up mailings to encourage initial nonrespondents to return a completed questionnaire. Dillman (1978) recommends a standard procedure for follow-up mailings:

1. Send a reminder postcard, thanking respondents and reminding nonrespondents, to all sample members 2 weeks after the initial mailing.

2. Send a replacement questionnaire with a new cover letter only to nonrespondents about 3 or 4 weeks after the initial mailing.

3. Send another replacement questionnaire with a new cover letter 8 weeks after the initial mailing by certified mail if possible (it's pretty expensive). If enough time and resources are available for telephone contacts or in-person visits for interviews, they will also help.

If Dillman's (1978) procedures are followed, and if the guidelines for cover letters and questionnaire design are followed, the response rate is almost certain to approach 70%. One review of studies using Dillman's method to survey the general population indicates that the average response to a first mailing will be about 24%; the response rate will rise to 42% after the postcard follow-up, to 50% after the first replacement questionnaire, and to 72% after a second replacement questionnaire is sent by certified mail (Dillman et al. 1974).

Related to the threat of nonresponse in mailed surveys is the hazard of incomplete response. Some respondents may skip some questions or just stop answering questions at some point in the questionnaire. Fortunately, this problem does not often occur with well-designed questionnaires. Potential respondents who decide to participate in the survey will usually complete it. But there are many exceptions to this observation, since questions that are poorly written, too complex, or about sensitive personal issues simply turn off some respondents. Revising or eliminating such questions during the design phase should minimize the problem. Still, many researchers continue to rely on mailed surveys because they are relatively inexpensive and respondents are free to answer questions at their leisure, without the scrutiny of a survey administrator.

Group-Administered Surveys

A **group-administered survey** is completed by individual respondents assembled in a group. The response rate is not usually a concern in surveys that are distributed and collected in a group setting because most group members will participate. The difficulty with this method is that assembling a group is seldom feasible because it requires a captive audience.

> **Group-administered survey** A survey that is completed by individual respondents who are assembled in a group.

Individuals going about their daily activities are usually not amenable to group-administered surveys. With the exception of students, employees, members of the armed forces, and some institutionalized populations, most populations cannot be sampled in such a setting.

One issue of special concern with group-administered surveys is the possibility that respondents will feel coerced to participate and as a result will be less likely to answer questions honestly.

Also, because administering a survey to a group probably requires the approval of the group's supervisor, and if survey is conducted on the organization's premises, respondents may infer that the researcher is not at all independent of the sponsor. Even those who volunteer may still feel uncomfortable answering all questions, which may bias their responses. No complete solution to this problem exists, but it helps to make an introductory statement that emphasizes the researcher's independence, assures respondents that their surveys will be completely anonymous, and gives participants a chance to ask questions about the survey.

Surveys by Telephone

In a **phone survey**, interviewers question respondents over the phone and then record respondents' answers. Phone interviewing has become a very popular method of conducting surveys in the United States because almost all families have phones. But two matters may undermine the validity of a phone survey: not reaching the proper sampling units and not getting enough complete responses to make the results generalizable.

> **Phone survey** A survey in which interviewers question respondents over the phone and then record their answers.

Reaching Sampling Units

Today, drawing a random sample is easier than ever due to random digit dialing (RDD) (Lavrakas 1987). A machine calls random phone numbers within designated exchanges, regardless of whether the numbers are published. When the machine reaches an inappropriate household (such as a business in a survey directed to the general population), the phone number is simply replaced with another. Also, several recent surveys have used both landline and cell phone data bases to capture individuals whom no longer have landlines.

The NVAMW Survey collected a national probability sample of 8,000 English- and Spanish-speaking women and 8,000 English- and Spanish-speaking men 18 years of age and older residing in households throughout the United States through RDD. The generation of the NVAMW Survey sample is described below:

> The geographic frame for the sample was the fifty states and the District of Columbia. Within this geographic frame SRBI systematically selected household telephone bands and conducted a random digit dialing (RDD) sampling screen for gender and age eligible respondents. In households with more than one eligible respondent a designated respondent was randomly selected using the "most recent birthday method." If the interviewer encountered a language barrier, either with the person answering the phone or with the designated respondent, the interviewer thanked the person and terminated the call. If a case was designated as Spanish language, it was turned over to a Spanish-speaking interviewer. (Tjaden and Thoennes 1998)

However households are contacted, the interviewers must always ask a series of questions at the start of the survey to ensure that they are speaking to the appropriate member of the household. Exhibit 8.12 displays the beginning of the phone interview schedule utilized by the NVAMW Survey. This example shows how to distinguish appropriate and inappropriate households in a phone survey so the interviewer is guided to the correct respondent.

Maximizing Response to Phone Surveys

Three issues require special attention in phone surveys. First, because people often are not home, multiple callbacks will be necessary for many sample members. In addition, interviewers must be prepared for distractions if the respondent is interrupted by other household members. Sprinkling interesting questions throughout the questionnaire may help maintain respondent interest. In general, rapport between the interviewer and the respondent is likely to be lower with phone surveys than in-person interviews, as respondents may tire and refuse to answer all the questions (Miller 1991).

The number of callbacks needed to reach respondents by telephone has increased greatly in the past 20 years, with increasing numbers of single-person households, dual-earner families, and out-of-home activities. The growth of telemarketing has also created another problem for telephone survey researchers: Individuals are more accustomed to just "saying no" to calls from strangers or simply use their answering machines or caller ID mechanism to screen

| Exhibit 8.12 | Phone Interview Procedures for Respondent Designation in the NVAMW Survey |

CONTROL FORM

Respondent Number:

ID   1:1-6

Interview Date:

MO   1:7-8
DAY   1:9-10
YEAR   1:11-12

Telephone Number:

PHONE   1:13-22

Interviewer Gender: 1 Male   2 Female

IGENDER   1:23

Respondent Gender: 1 Male   2 Female

RGENDER   1:24

Zip Code:

ZIP   1:25-29

FIPS Code:

FIPS   1:30-34

(Continued)

Exhibit 8.12 (Continued)

State Code:

01	Alabama	27	Montana
02	Alaska	28	Nebraska
03	Arizona	29	Nevada
04	Arkansas	30	New Hampshire
05	California	31	New Jersey
06	Colorado	32	New Mexico
07	Connecticut	33	New York
08	Delaware	34	North Carolina
09	District of Columbia	35	North Dakota
10	Florida	36	Ohio
11	Georgia	37	Oklahoma
12	Hawaii	38	Oregon
13	Idaho	39	Pennsylvania
14	Illinois	40	Rhode Island
15	Indiana	41	South Carolina
16	Iowa	42	South Dakota
17	Kansas	43	Tennessee
18	Kentucky	44	Texas
19	Louisiana	45	Utah
20	Maine	46	Vermont
21	Maryland	47	Virginia
22	Massachusetts	48	Washington
23	Michigan	49	West Virginia
24	Minnesota	50	Wisconsin
25	Mississippi	51	Wyoming
26	Missouri		

STATE   1:35-36

Region Code:

01	New England	06	ESC
02	Mid-Atlantic	07	WSC
03	ENC	08	Mountain
04	WNC	09	Pacific
05	South Atlantic		

REGION   1:37-38

Survey Wave:

1	Cf/m	4	Ff/m
2	Df/m	5	Af
3	Ef/m	6	Bf

WAVE   1:39

CF2   How many persons, age 18 and older, live in this household?
       [RANGE IS 0-20, 21=Don't know; 22=Refused]

PERS18   1:40-41

CF3   How many of these adults are:

A   Women [RANGE IS 0-99]
B   Men [RANGE IS 0-99]in household
C   Refused [1=Don't know/refused; O = Other]

WOMEN18   1:42-43
MEN18   1:44-45
REF18   1:46-47

Source: Tjaden and Thoennes 2000.

unwanted calls. The response rate of most surveys, even those sponsored by the U.S. government have been decreasing over the past two decades. For example, the individual response rate for the National Crime Victimization Survey was 91% in 1996, but by 2007, it had fallen to 85% (Groves and Cork 2008).

Phone surveys also must cope with difficulties due to the impersonal nature of phone contact. Visual aids cannot be used, so the interviewer must be able to verbally convey all information about response choices and skip patterns. With phone surveys, instructions for the interviewer must clarify how to ask each question, and the response choices must be short.

Careful interviewer training is essential for phone surveys. Below is a brief description of how SRBI interviewers were trained before conducting the NVAMW Survey:

> Because of the complexity of the survey, only the most experienced SRBI interviewers worked on the survey. Before fielding the survey, interviewers received specialized training on the general principles of survey research and the requirements of the study at hand. Interviewers were also trained to recognize and respond appropriately to cues that the respondent may have been concerned about being overheard. Telephone numbers of local support services (e.g., domestic violence shelters, rape crisis hotlines, child protective services) were offered to respondents who disclosed current abuse or appeared in distress. (Tjaden and Thoennes 1998)

Procedures can be standardized more effectively, quality control maintained, and processing speed maximized when phone interviewers are assisted by computers. This **computer-assisted telephone interview** has become known as **CATI**, and most large surveys are now performed in this way. There are several advantages to using CATI, but perhaps the foremost advantage is that data collection and data entry can occur concurrently. Second, the CATI system has several machine edit features that help minimize data entry error. For example, by automatically assigning single-punch fields of appropriate width for each data item in the questionnaire, the CATI system eliminates the possibility of over-punching and the possibility of including blanks as legitimate values. Third, by programming the skip patterns into its data entry program, the CATI system ensures that the aggregated database is comprehensive and accurate.

> **Computer-assisted telephone interview (CATI)** A telephone interview in which a questionnaire is programmed into a computer, along with relevant skip patterns that must be followed. It essentially combines the tasks of interviewing, data entry, and some data cleaning.

One method that avoids the interviewer altogether is **computerized interactive voice response (IVR)** survey technology. In an IVR survey, respondents receive automated calls and answer questions by pressing numbers on their touch-tone phones or speaking numbers that are interpreted by computerized voice recognition software. These surveys can also record verbal responses to open-ended questions for later transcription. Although they present some difficulties when many answer choices must be used or skip patterns must be followed, IVR surveys have been used successfully with short questionnaires and when respondents are highly motivated to participate (Dillman 2000). When these conditions are not met, potential respondents may be put off by the impersonality of this computer-driven approach.

> **Computer interactive voice response (IVR)** Software that uses a touch-tone telephone to interact with people in order to acquire information from or enter data into a database.

In summary, phone surveying is the best method to use for relatively short surveys of the general population. Response rates in phone surveys tend to be very high, often above 80%, because few individuals will hang up on a polite caller or refuse to stop answering questions (at least within the first 30 minutes or so). The NVAMW Survey obtained a response rate of 72% in the female survey and 69% in the male survey by conducting interviews via telephone.

In-Person Interviews

What is unique to the **in-person interview**, compared to the other survey designs, is the face-to-face social interaction between interviewer and respondent. If financial resources are available for hiring interviewers to go out and personally conduct the surveys with respondents, in-person interviewing is often the best survey design.

In-person interview A survey in which an interviewer questions respondents and records their answers.

Although time-consuming and costly, in-person interviewing has several advantages. Response rates are higher for this survey design than with any other, when potential respondents are approached by a courteous interviewer. For example, respondents for the NCVS actually stay in the sample for 3 years. The first of these surveys is performed in person. This is one reason the NCVS obtains a very high response rate of approximately 95%. In addition, in-person interviews can be much longer than mailed or phone surveys; the questionnaire can be complex, with both open-ended and closed-ended questions and frequent branching patterns. The order in which questions are read and answered can be controlled by the interviewer and the physical and social circumstances of the interview can be monitored. Lastly, respondents' interpretations of questions can be probed and clarified.

Researchers must be alert to some special hazards due to the presence of an interviewer. Respondents should experience the interview process as a personalized interaction with an interviewer who is very interested in their experiences and opinions. At the same time, however, every respondent should have the same interview experience and be asked the same questions in the same way by the same type of person, who reacts similarly to the answers. Therein lies the researcher's challenge: to plan an interview process that will be personal, engaging, consistent, and nonreactive and to hire interviewers who can carry out the plan. Without a personalized approach, the rate of response will be lower, and answers will be less thoughtful and potentially less valid. Without a consistent approach, information obtained from different respondents will not be comparable because it is less reliable and less valid.

Balancing Rapport and Control

Adherence to some basic guidelines for interacting with respondents can help interviewers maintain an appropriate balance between personalization and standardization:

- Project a professional image in the interview, that of someone who is sympathetic to the respondent but nonetheless has a job to do.

- Establish rapport at the outset by explaining what the interview is about and how it will work and by reading the consent form. Ask the respondent if he or she has any questions or concerns, and respond to these honestly and fully. Emphasize that everything the respondent says is confidential.

- During the interview, ask questions at a close but not intimate distance. Stay focused on the respondent, and be certain your posture conveys interest. Maintain eye contact, respond with appropriate facial expressions, and speak in a conversational tone of voice.

- Be sure to maintain a consistent approach; deliver each question as written and in the same tone of voice. Listen empathically, but avoid self-expression or loaded reactions.

- Repeat questions if the respondent is confused. Use nondirective probes such as "Can you tell me more about that?" for open-ended questions.

Computer-assisted personal interviewing (CAPI) An interview in which the interviewer carries a laptop computer programmed to display the interview questions and processes the responses that the interviewer types in, as well as checking that these responses fall within the allowed ranges.

Computer-assisted self-interviewing (CASI) A system within which respondents interact with a computer-administered questionnaire by using a mouse and following audio instructions delivered via headphones.

As with phone interviewing, computers can be used to increase control of the in-person interview. In a **computer-assisted personal interviewing (CAPI)** project, interviewers carry a laptop computer programmed to display the interview questions and process the responses that the interviewer types in, as well as to check that these responses fall within the allowed ranges. Interviewers seem to like CAPI, and the data obtained are at least as good in quality as a noncomputerized interview (Shepherd et al. 1996). **Computer-assisted self-interviewing (CASI)** is also an alternative. With audio-CASI, respondents interact with a computer-administered questionnaire by using a mouse and following audio instructions delivered via headphones. Audio-CASI is considered the most reliable way to administer questionnaires that probe sensitive or potentially stigmatizing information such as offending or victimization information (Miller et al. 1998; Tourangeau and Smith 1996; Turner et al. 1998). Wolff et al. (2006) used this technology to obtain information about the physical and sexual victimization experiences of male and female state prison inmates. They explain, "The survey was administered using audio-CASI (computed assisted self interviewing) and was available in English and Spanish. There were 30 computer stations set up at each facility and members of the research team were available to answer any questions and assist with the technology as needed" (p. 1350).

The presence of an interviewer may make it more difficult for respondents to give honest answers to questions about sensitive personal matters. If you are not using a CASI, interviewers may hand respondents a separate, self-administered questionnaire containing the more sensitive questions. After answering these questions, the respondent can then seal the separate questionnaire in an envelope so that the interviewer does not know the answers.

Although in-person interview procedures are typically designed with the expectation that the interview will involve only the interviewer and the respondent, one or more other household members are often within earshot. This is particularly problematic if you are asking respondents about issues related to other family members, such as victimizations by family members. Although the NVAMW Survey only interviewed one member of each household, the NCVS interviews all members of a selected household. Thus, all family members are asked the same set of screening questions regarding their victimization experiences with both known and unknown offenders. Even though respondents are instructed to reschedule a telephone or personal interview for a more convenient time (e.g., when others are not present), this situation may nevertheless prevent some respondents from disclosing incidents of violence to interviewers, particularly those incidents perpetrated by intimate partners within the household.

Maximizing Response to Interviews

Even if the right balance is struck between maintaining control over interviews and achieving good rapport with respondents, in-person interviews can still have a problem. Due to the difficulty of catching all the members of a sample, response rates may suffer. Exhibit 8.13 displays the breakdown of nonrespondents to the 1990 General Social

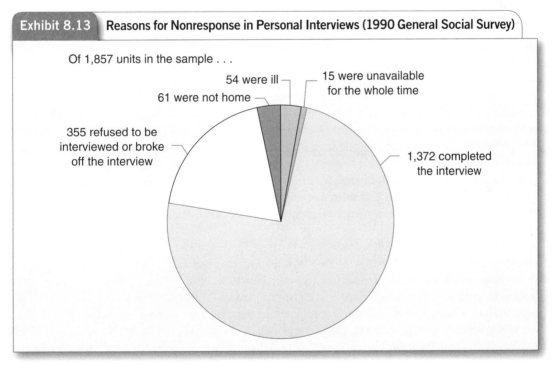

Exhibit 8.13 | **Reasons for Nonresponse in Personal Interviews (1990 General Social Survey)**

Of 1,857 units in the sample . . .

54 were ill
61 were not home
15 were unavailable for the whole time
355 refused to be interviewed or broke off the interview
1,372 completed the interview

Source: Data from Davis and Smith 1992:54.

Survey. From the total original sample of 2,165, only 86% (1,857) were determined to be valid selections of dwelling units with potentially eligible respondents. Among these potentially eligible respondents, the response rate was 74%. The GSS is a well-designed survey using carefully trained and supervised interviewers, so this response rate indicates the difficulty of securing respondents from a sample of the general population even when everything is done "by the book."

Several factors affect the response rate in interview studies. Contact rates tend to be lower in cities, in part because of difficulties in finding people at home and gaining access to high-rise apartments and in part because of interviewer reluctance to visit some areas at night, when people are more likely to be home (Fowler 1988). Households with young children or elderly adults tend to be easier to contact, whereas single-person households are more difficult to reach (Groves and Couper 1998).

Refusal rates vary with some respondent characteristics. People with less education participate somewhat less in surveys of political issues (perhaps because they are less aware of current political issues). Less education is also associated with higher rates of "don't know" responses (Groves 1989). High-income persons tend to participate less in surveys about income and economic behavior (perhaps because they are suspicious about why others want to know about their situation). Unusual strains and disillusionment in a society can also undermine the general credibility of research efforts and the ability of interviewers to achieve an acceptable response rate. These problems can be lessened with an advance letter introducing the survey project and by multiple contact attempts throughout the day and evening, but they cannot entirely be avoided (Fowler 1988; Groves and Couper 1998).

Web Surveys

Web-based surveys have become increasingly useful for two reasons: growth in the fraction of the population using the Internet and technological advances that make Web-based survey design relatively easy.

However, it is still not possible to obtain a true representative sample of the U.S. population on the Web, since not everyone is connected or has access to the Internet. Households without Internet access also tend to be older and poorer than those that are connected (Tourangeau 2004). However, many specific populations have very high rates of Internet use, making Internet-based surveys of groups such as professionals, middle-class communities, and of course, college students a viable alternative to other survey methods. Due to the Internet's global reach, Web surveys also make it possible to conduct large, international surveys.

There are several different approaches to conducting Web-based surveys, each with unique advantages and somewhat different effects on the coverage problem. Many Web-based surveys begin with an e-mail message to potential respondents that contains a direct "hotlink" to the survey Web site. If a defined population with known e-mail addresses is to be surveyed, a researcher can send e-mail invitations to a representative sample without difficulty. To ensure that the appropriate people respond to a Web-based survey, researchers may require that respondents enter a PIN (personal identification number) to gain access to the Web survey (Dillman 2000). However, lists of unique e-mail addresses for the members of defined populations generally do not exist outside of organizational settings. Many people have more than one e-mail address, and often, there is no apparent link between an e-mail address and the name or location of the person it is assigned to. As a result, there is no available method for drawing a random sample of e-mail addresses for people from any general population, even if the focus is only on those with Internet access (Dillman 2007).

Some Web surveys are instead linked to a Web site that is used by the intended population, and everyone who visits that site is invited to complete the survey. Although this approach can generate a very large number of respondents, the resulting sample will necessarily reflect the type of people who visit that Web site (middle-class, young North Americans) and thus be a biased representation of the larger population (Dillman 2000). Some control over the resulting sample can be maintained by requiring participants to meet certain inclusion criteria (Selm and Jankowski 2006).

When they are appropriate for a particular population, Web surveys have some unique advantages (Selm and Jankowski 2006). Questionnaires completed on the Web can elicit more honest reports of illicit behavior and of victimization as compared with phone interviews (Parks, Pardi, and Bradizza 2006). They are relatively easy to complete, as respondents simply click on response boxes and the survey can be programmed to move respondents easily through sets of questions, not presenting questions that do not apply to the respondent. Pictures, sounds, and animation can be used as a focus of particular questions, and graphic and typographic variation can be used to enhance visual survey appeal. Definitions of terms can "pop up" when respondents scroll over them (Dillman 2007). In these ways, a skilled Web programmer can generate a survey layout with many attractive features that make it more likely that respondents will give their answers—and have a clear understanding of the question (Smyth et al. 2004). Responses can quickly be checked to make sure they fall within the allowable range. Because answers are recorded directly in the researcher's database, data entry errors are almost eliminated, and results can be reported quickly. There are many free online services to aid you in developing a Web survey, like SurveyMonkey. However, many universities have also subscribed to more sophisticated survey engines such as Qualtrics.

Using a random sample of University of Delaware students, the Center for Drug and Alcohol Studies conducted a College Risk Behavior Survey, using Qualtrics. Exhibit 8.14 displays one screen of the survey, which was devoted to ascertaining the extent to which students engaged in all types of risky behavior including drinking and driving, using drugs, cheating, victimizations, stealing, fighting, gambling, and illegally downloading material. Notice that

Exhibit 8.14 | **A Page From the College Risk Behavior Survey**

the top of the screen told respondents how much of the survey they had left before they were finished. To enhance their response rate, the researchers offered students who completed the survey a $5 voucher that could be used at any university eating establishment.

Mixed-Mode Surveys

Survey researchers increasingly are combining different survey designs. **Mixed-mode surveys** allow the strengths of one survey design to compensate for the weaknesses of another and can maximize the likelihood of securing data from different types of respondents. For example, a survey may be sent electronically to sample members who have e-mail addresses and be mailed to those who do not. Alternatively, nonrespondents in a mailed survey may be interviewed in person or over the phone. As noted previously, an interviewer may use a self-administered questionnaire to present sensitive questions to a respondent.

> **Mixed-mode survey** Surveys that are conducted by more than one method, allowing the strengths of one survey design to compensate for the weaknesses of another and maximizing the likelihood of securing data from different types of respondents; for example, nonrespondents in a mailed survey may be interviewed in person or over the phone.

Mixing survey designs like this makes it possible that respondents will give different answers to different questions because of the mode in which they are asked, rather than because they actually have different opinions. However, use of what Dillman (2000:232–40) calls "unimode design" reduces this possibility substantially. A unimode design uses questions and response choices that are least likely to yield different answers according to the survey mode that is used. Unimode design principles include use of the same question structures, response choices, and skip instructions across modes, as well as using a small number of response choices for each question.

A Comparison of Survey Designs

Which survey design should be used when? Group-administered surveys are similar in most respects to mailed surveys, except they require the unusual circumstance of having access to the sample in a group setting. We therefore do not need to consider this survey design by itself; what applies to mailed survey designs applies to group-administered survey designs, with the exception of sampling issues. Thus, we can focus our comparison on the four survey designs that involve the use of a questionnaire with individuals sampled from a larger population: mailed surveys, phone surveys, in-person surveys, and electronic surveys. Exhibit 8.15 summarizes their strong and weak points.

The most important consideration in comparing the advantages and disadvantages of the four survey designs is the likely response rate they will generate. Because of the great weakness of mailed surveys in this respect, they must be considered the least preferred survey design from a sampling standpoint. However, researchers may still prefer a mailed survey when they have to reach a widely dispersed population and do not have enough financial resources to hire and train an interview staff or to contract with a survey organization that already has an interview staff available in many locations.

Contracting with an established survey research organization for a phone survey is often the best alternative to a mailed survey. The persistent follow-up attempts necessary to secure an adequate response rate are much easier over the phone than in person or via mail. But the process is not simple:

> Initial telephone contact with households was attempted during hours of the day and days of the week which had the greatest probability of respondent contact (between 5:30 P.M. and 10:00 P.M. on weekdays, between 9:00 A.M. and 10:00 P.M. on Saturdays, and between 10:00 A.M. and 10:00 P.M. on Sundays). Interviewers made five attempts to ringing unanswered telephones on different days and at different times over a period of at least three weeks in order to obtain the highest possible response rate. If the interview could not be conducted or completed at the time of the initial contact, the interviewer rescheduled the interview at a time convenient to the respondent. (From a description of the NVAMW Survey)

| Exhibit 8.15 | Advantages and Disadvantages of Four Survey Designs |

Characteristics of Design	Mail Survey	Phone Survey	In-Person Survey	Web Survey
Representative sample				
Opportunity for inclusion is known				
For completely listed populations	High	High	High	Medium
For incompletely listed populations	Medium	Medium	High	Low
Selection within sampling units is controlled (e.g., specific family members must respond)	Medium	High	High	Low
Respondents are likely to be located				
If samples are heterogeneous	Medium	Medium	High	Low
If samples are homogeneous and specialized	High	High	High	High
Questionnaire construction and question design				
Allowable length of questionnaire	Medium	Medium	High	Medium
Ability to include				
Complex questions	Medium	Low	High	High
Open questions	Low	High	High	Medium
Screening questions	Low	High	High	High
Tedious, boring questions	Low	High	High	Low
Ability to control question sequence	Low	High	High	High
Ability to ensure questionnaire completion	Medium	High	High	Low
Distortion of answers				
Odds of avoiding social desirability bias	High	Medium	Low	High
Odds of avoiding interviewer distortion	High	Medium	Low	High
Odds of avoiding contamination by others	Medium	High	Medium	Medium
Administrative goals				
Odds of meeting personnel requirements	High	High	Low	Medium
Odds of implementing quickly	Low	High	Low	High
Odds of keeping costs low	High	Medium	Low	High

In-person surveys are clearly preferable in terms of the possible length and complexity of the questionnaire itself, as well as the researcher's ability to monitor conditions while the questionnaire is being completed. Mailed surveys often are preferable for asking sensitive questions, although this problem can be lessened in an interview by giving respondents a separate sheet to fill out on their own. Although interviewers may themselves distort results, either by changing the wording of questions or failing to record answers properly, this problem can be lessened by careful training, monitoring, and tape-recording the answers.

A phone survey limits the length and complexity of the questionnaire but offers the possibility of very carefully monitoring interviewers (Dillman 1978; Fowler 1988). For the NVAMW Survey, SRBI ensures quality control over its interviewers in the following manner:

> Throughout the project, interviewers were silently monitored by a supervisor at least twice during each of their interviewing shifts to evaluate the manner in which interviewers were conducting the interview and the accuracy with which they were entering responses. (Tjaden and Thoennes 1998)

The advantages and disadvantages of electronic surveys must be weighed in light of the capabilities at the time that the survey is to be conducted. At this time, too many people lack Internet connections for general use of Internet surveying, and too many people who have computers lack adequate computer capacity for displaying complex Web pages.

These various points about the different survey designs lead to two general conclusions. First, in-person interviews are the strongest design and generally preferable when sufficient resources and a trained interview staff are available; telephone surveys have many of the advantages of in-person interviews at a much lower cost. Second, the "best" survey design for any particular study will be determined by the study's unique features and goals rather than by any absolute standard of what the best survey is.

Ethical Issues in Survey Research

Survey research usually poses fewer ethical dilemmas than do experimental or field research designs. Potential respondents to a survey can easily decline to participate, and a cover letter or an introductory statement that identifies the sponsors of and motivations for the survey gives them the information required to make this decision. The methods of data collection are quite obvious in a survey, so little is concealed from the respondents. The primary ethical issue in survey research involves protecting respondents.

Protection of Respondents

If the survey could possibly have any harmful effects for the respondents, these should be disclosed fully in the cover letter or introductory statement (recall the Informed Consent Form outlined in Chapter 3). The procedures used to reduce such effects should also be delineated, including how the researcher will keep interviews confidential and anonymous. In addition, surveys such as the NVAMW Survey and NCVS that attempt to measure sensitive subject matter such as rape and intimate-perpetrated assault should also have other protections in place. When asking about victimizations, particularly those that are perpetrated by known offenders and family members, the World Health Organization (WHO) has been at the forefront of establishing policies to protect respondents. As WHO notes, "The primary ethical concern related to researching VAW is the potential for inflicting harm to respondents through their participation in the study" (Ellsberg and Heise 2005:38). Because many perpetrators of intimate partner violence use control as form of abuse, a respondent may suffer physical harm if an abuser finds out that she disclosed information about their relationship to an interviewer. Guidelines to prevent this from happening include interviewing only one person in the household (Ellsberg and Heise 2005). In addition, a graduated informed consent process is also recommended. For example, when first contacting a potential respondent, the initial person who answered the telephone should be provided only general information about the survey topic (e.g., on health-related issues). Only after a respondent is selected from a household should they be told about the specific topics that would be covered (e.g., violent victimizations). Interviewers should also remind respondents that they can stop the interview at any time, and safety plans should be established between the interviewer and the respondents.

Minimizing respondents' distress by reliving victimization events and providing them with information on services and resources that can help their situation are also necessary. For example, the NVAWS provided telephone numbers for the National Domestic Violence Hotline and the Rape, Abuse, and Incest National Network at the end of interviews. The College Risk Behavior Survey discussed earlier in this chapter also gave respondents information about a number of avenues for help-seeking including the phone numbers to the University of Delaware Center for Counseling and Student Development, the Delaware Council on Gambling Problems, and the Delaware 24-hour Rape Crisis Hotline. As you can see in Exhibit 8.16, the last screen of the survey provided this information to respondents

Respondent protection is even more complicated when asking about victimizations against minor children, as the NCVS does (e.g., it interviews individuals aged 12 or older). Currently, researchers do not fall under the purview of "mandatory reporters" according to most state statutes, and the WHO claims there is no consensus internationally about how to handle cases of child abuse (Ellsberg and Heise 2005). This is true for cases of elder abuse that are reported by respondents as well. Regardless of statutes not explicitly listing researchers as mandatory reporters, however, interviewers should certainly be required to develop protocols to act in the best interests of a child or an elder when cases of these forms of abuse are revealed.

Confidentiality

Do any of the questions have the potential to embarrass respondents or otherwise subject them to adverse consequences such as legal sanctions? If the answer to this question is no, and it often is in surveys about general social issues, other ethical problems are unlikely. But if the questionnaire includes questions about attitudes or behaviors that are socially stigmatized or generally considered to be private or questions about actions that are illegal, the researcher must proceed carefully and ensure that respondents' rights are protected.

The first step to take with potentially troublesome questions is to consider omitting or modifying them. Researchers often include some questions in surveys just out of curiosity or out of a suspicion that the questions might prove to be important. If sensitive questions fall into this category, they probably should be omitted. There is no point in asking, "Have you ever been convicted of a felony?" if the answers are unlikely to be used in the analysis of survey results.

Many surveys do include some essential questions that might prove damaging to the subjects if their answers were disclosed, particularly surveys interested in delinquent or criminal offending behavior. To prevent any possibility of harm to subjects due to disclosure of such information, it is critical to preserve subject confidentiality. No one other than research personnel should have access to information that could be used to link respondents to their responses, and even that access should be limited to what is necessary for specific research purposes. Only numbers should be used to identify respondents on their questionnaires, and the researcher should keep the names that correspond to these numbers in a separate, safe, and private location, unavailable to others who might otherwise come across them. Follow-up mailings or contact attempts that require linking the ID numbers with names and addresses should be carried out by trustworthy assistants under close supervision.

Only if no identifying information about respondents is obtained can surveys provide true **anonymity** to respondents. In this way, no identifying information is ever recorded to link respondents with their responses. However, the main problem with anonymous surveys is that they preclude follow-up attempts to encourage participation by initial nonrespondents, and they prevent panel designs, which measure change through repeated surveys of the same individuals. In-person surveys rarely can be anonymous because an interviewer must in almost all cases know the name and address of the interviewee. However, phone surveys that are meant only to sample opinions at one point in time, as in political polls, can

> ***Anonymity*** Provided by research in which no identifying information is recorded that could be used to link respondents to their responses.

Exhibit 8.16 | **Information Provided to Respondents From the College Risk Behavior Survey**

UNIVERSITY OF DELAWARE
2009 College Survey

Your responses to the previous section have been recorded.

Thank you for your participation. Before finishing the survey, we would like to provide you with the following information. After reading the information, please use the button at the bottom of the page to complete the survey and receive information about the $5 voucher.

ADDITIONAL INFORMATION THAT MAY BE HELPFUL TO YOU

We want to thank you for your participation in this survey. The survey touched on a number of subjects that may have raised concerns in you, either about yourself or about someone else. We want to make sure that you know of places to go to get more information or to talk to someone. All of these services are confidential and available to you free of charge.

Under any circumstances if you have a **dire emergency** involving the safety of someone, **University Police** should be contacted.

If calling from on-campus, dial: 911
If calling from off-campus, dial: 302-831-2222

For health emergencies, the **Student Health Service** in Laurel Hall is open 24 hours a day when classes are in session except during holidays, breaks and summers.

If you or a student you know is feeling extremely depressed or anxious, please call the **Center for Counseling & Student Development** (CCSD) at 831-2141. For emergencies in the evenings, or on weekends: Contact the Student Health Service (302-831-2226). You can get more information about the Counseling Center at the University at http://www.udel.edu/Counseling/

The **Center for Counseling & Student Development** is also the place to go if you or a student you know is having trouble with alcohol or other drug abuse. They have a program for students called MOSAIC that is designed to help when a student has a substance abuse problem.

For Smoking concerns, please call the **Delaware Quitline** at: 1-866-409-1858. They are available 24 hours a day to help you with programs and materials to curtail tobacco use. More information on the Quitline is available at their webpage http://www.dhss.delaware.gov/dhss/dph/dpc/quitline.html/

For Gambling concerns, please call the **Delaware Council on Gambling Problems** at 1-888-850-8888. The Council offers confidential assistance. More information is available at http://www.dcgp.org/

For concerns about sexual assault, please call the **Delaware 24-hour Rape Crisis Hotline Contact Lifeline** at 1-800-262-9800.

If you want information on a variety of issues related to your health and well-being, please contact Wellspring, the University's Student Wellness Program. You can also access their website at http://www.udel.edu/wellspring/

Finally, if you would like more information about suicide and mental health in college students, one resource is the Ulifeline web site that is funded by the Jed Foundation: http://www.ulifeline.org/

Please use the button below to complete the survey and receive information about the $5 voucher:

Next Section

safely be completely anonymous. When no follow-up is desired, group-administered surveys also can be anonymous. To provide anonymity in a mail survey, the researcher should omit identifying codes from the questionnaire but could include a self-addressed, stamped postcard so the respondent can notify the researcher that the questionnaire has been returned, without being linked to the questionnaire itself (Mangione 1995).

Any survey can allow anonymous responses to a subset of particularly sensitive questions. A tear-off sheet containing these questions and a separate return envelope, without identifying information, can be included with a mailed survey. In an in-person interview, this special section can be left with the respondent to be completed later and returned by mail. Of course, a response obtained in this way cannot be linked with the response of the same subject to the same question in some later follow-up survey. But if it increases the response rate, this method can provide more valid results for the initial survey.

🔲 Conclusion

Survey research is an exceptionally efficient and productive method for investigating a wide array of social research questions. In addition to the potential benefits for social science, considerations of time and expense frequently make a survey the preferred data-collection method. One or more of the four survey designs reviewed in this chapter can be applied to almost any research question. It is no wonder that surveys have become the most popular research method in sociology and that they frequently influence discussion and planning about important social and political questions.

The relative ease of conducting at least some types of survey research leads many people to imagine that no particular training or systematic procedures are required. Nothing could be further from the truth. As a result of this widespread misconception, you will encounter a great many worthless survey results. You must be prepared to carefully examine the procedures used in any survey before accepting its finding as credible. And if you decide to conduct a survey, you must be prepared to invest the time and effort required to follow proper procedures.

Key Terms

Highlights

- Surveys are the most popular form of social research because of their versatility, efficiency, and generalizability. Many survey data sets, such as the General Social Survey (GSS), are available for social scientists to use in teaching and research.

- Surveys can fail to produce useful results due to problems in sampling, measurement, and overall survey design. Political polling can produce inconsistent results because of rapid changes in popular sentiment.

- A survey questionnaire or interview schedule should be designed as an integrated whole, with each question and section serving some clear purpose and complementing the others.

- Questions must be worded carefully to avoid confusing the respondents or encouraging a less-than-honest response. Inclusion of "don't know" choices and neutral responses may help, but the presence of such options also affects the distribution of answers. Open-ended questions can be used to determine the meaning that respondents attach to their answers. Answers to any survey questions may be affected by the questions that precede them in a questionnaire or an interview schedule.

- Every questionnaire and interview schedule should be pretested on a small sample that is like the sample to be surveyed.

- The cover letter for a mailed questionnaire and the introductory statement for an interview should be credible, personalized, interesting, and responsible.

- Response rates in mailed surveys are typically well below 70% unless multiple mailings are made to nonrespondents and the questionnaire and cover letter are attractive, interesting, and fully planned. Response rates for group-administered surveys are usually much higher.

- Phone interviews using random digit dialing allow fast turnaround and efficient sampling. Multiple callbacks may be required, but once the people are contacted, most can be interviewed by phone for 30 to 45 minutes.

- In-person interviews have several advantages over other types of surveys: They allow longer and more complex interview schedules, monitoring of the conditions when the questions are answered, probing for respondents' understanding of the questions, and high response rates.

- Web surveys may be e-mailed or posted on the Web. Interactive voice-response systems using the telephone are another option. At this time, use of the Internet is not sufficiently widespread to allow e-mail or Web surveys of the general population, but these approaches can be fast and efficient for populations with high rates of computer use.

- Mixed-mode surveys allow the strengths of one survey design to compensate for the weaknesses of another. However, questions and procedures must be designed carefully, using "unimode design" principles, to reduce the possibility that responses to the same question will vary as a result of the mode of delivery.

- Most survey research poses few ethical problems because respondents are able to decline to participate. This option should be stated clearly in the cover letter or introductory statement. Special care must be taken when questionnaires are administered in group settings (to captive audiences) and when sensitive personal questions are to be asked; subject confidentiality should always be preserved.

Research in the News

Drunken Driving Declines in U.S. but Drug Use Still Troubling

According to a random sample survey of over 9,000 people who entered road survey sites and provided breath-alcohol measurements to the National Highway Traffic Safety Administration, just over 2% had a blood alcohol content of .08 or higher, compared to 7.5% in 1973. Unfortunately, from blood and urine samples submitted by over 3,000 drivers, it was found that about 1 in 6 drivers on weekend nights is on drugs.

Source: CNN. 2012. "Drunken Driving Declines in U.S.: Drug Use 'Troubling' Agency Says." Retrieved June 10, 2012 (http://www.cnn.com/2009/CRIME/07/13/drunken.driving/index.html).

Exercises

1. Read the original article reporting one of the surveys described in this book (check the text of the chapters for ideas). Critique the article using the questions presented in Appendix B as your guide. Focus particular attention on sampling, measurement, and survey design.

2. Write 8 to 10 questions for a one-page questionnaire on fear of crime among students. Include some questions to measure characteristics (such as income or year in school) that might help explain the attitudes. Make all but one of your questions closed-ended.

3. By interviewing two students, conduct a preliminary pretest of the questionnaire you wrote for Exercise 2. Follow up the closed-ended questions with open-ended questions that ask the students what they meant by each response or what came to mind when they were asked each question. Take account of the answers when you revise your questions.

4. Make any necessary revisions to the questionnaire you wrote in Exercise 2. Write a cover letter that presumes the survey will be administered to students in a class at your school. Submit the questionnaire and cover letter to your instructor for comment and evaluation.

5. Test your understanding of survey research terminology by completing one set of interactive exercises from the study site on survey design. Be sure to review the text on the pages indicated in relation to any answers you get wrong!

Developing a Research Proposal

1. Write 10 questions for a one-page questionnaire that concerns your proposed research question. Your questions should operationalize at least three of the variables on which you have focused, including at least one independent and one dependent variable (you may have multiple questions to measure some variables). Make all but one of your questions closed-ended. If you completed the "research proposal" exercises in Chapter 3, you can select your questions from the ones you developed for those exercises.

2. Conduct a preliminary pretest of the questionnaire by conducting cognitive interviews with two students or other persons like those to whom the survey is directed. Follow up the closed-ended questions with open-ended probes that ask the students what they meant by each response or what came to mind when they were asked each question. Take account of the feedback you receive when you revise your questions.

3. Polish up the organization and layout of the questionnaire, following the guidelines in this chapter. Prepare a rationale for the order of questions in your questionnaire. Write a cover letter directed to the appropriate population that contains appropriate statements about research ethics (human subjects issues).

STUDENT STUDY SITE

Log on to the Web-based student study site at **www.sagepub.com/bachmanprccj5e** for additional study tools including eFlashcards, Web quizzes, links to SAGE journal articles, podcasts, videos, data sets and codebooks, Web exercises, Web resources, and additional appendices.

Web Exercises

1. Go to the Social Science Information Gateway (SOSIG) at www.mcli.dist.maricopa.edu/smc/ml/ssinfogateway.html. Search SOSIG for electronic journal articles that use surveys to collect information on crime, criminal behavior, or criminal victimization. Find at least five articles and briefly describe each.

2. Go to the Council of European Social Science Data Archives (CESSDA) at www.nsd.uib.no/cessda /index.html. Go to "Accessing Data," and then click on "CESSDA Catalogue." From here you can browse the catalogue by topic, keyword, or publisher. Browse the publications list or conduct a search at the site for at least three countries for studies that use surveys to collect information on crime, criminal behavior, or criminal victimization. What type of information did you find? If possible, do a cross-national comparison between the studies reviewed in Web Exercise 1 and the studies found in this exercise.

3. Who does survey research, and how do they do it? These questions can be answered through careful inspection of ongoing surveys and the organizations that administer them at www.ciser.cornell .edu/info/polls.shtml. Spend some time reading about the different survey research organizations, and write a brief summary of

the types of research they conduct, the projects in which they are involved, and the resources they offer on their Web sites. What are the distinctive features of different survey research organizations?

4. Go to the Research Triangle Institute site at www.rti.org. Click on "Survey Research and Services" and then on "Capabilities." Read about the institute's methods for computer-assisted interviewing and mixed-mode data collection. Next, click on "Methodologies" at the bottom of the screen, and then access "Questionnaire Design and Evaluation," to learn about innovative techniques including cognitive pretesting. What does this add to your treatment of these topics in this chapter?

5. Go to The Pew Research Center at www.pewsocialtrends.org. Browse a few of their recent surveys and review 10 questions. Critique them in terms of the principles for question writing that you have learned.

Ethics Exercises

1. In this chapter, we posed the questions "How can researchers ameliorate the negative consequences that responding to these surveys may have?" and "What responsibility do researchers have in providing respondents safety should they need it?" Write a short statement in response to each question.

2. Tjaden and Thoennes (2000) sampled adults with random digit dialing in order to study violent victimization from a nationally representative sample of adults. We already asked you about the ethical dilemmas of reporting victimizations in Chapter 8. But what about respondents who are minors and are under the age of 18? What about children under the age of 12? Teachers and medical personnel are required by law to report cases they believe to represent incidents of child abuse. Should researchers have the same obligation? How would this affect large-scale surveys using random digit dialing in which you want to preserve the anonymity of respondents?

3. Group-administered surveys are easier to conduct than other types of surveys, but they always raise an ethical dilemma. If a teacher allows a researcher to survey a class, or if an employer allows employees to complete a survey on company time, are the surveys really voluntary? Is it sufficient to read a statement to the group stating that their participation is entirely up to them? What general guidelines should be followed in such situations?

SPSS or Excel Exercises

Injuries are often sustained by victims of violent crime. Using NCVS.Assault.POR, which includes assault victimizations from the National Crime Victimization Survey from 1992 to 2005, you can explore what factors most often lead to injury for victims of assault.

1. Browse the variables in the data set. What factors do you think are related to whether or not a victim of assault is injured?

2. Choose at least three of these variables and state your hypotheses about the relationship between each of these variables and injury.

3. Generate cross-tabulations of your chosen variables and INJURY. (If you have had a statistics course, you may want to request the CHI-SQUARE statistic for each of the cross-tabulations.)

4. Describe the relationship you have found, noting the difference in the distribution of the dependent (row) variables between the categories of each independent (column) variable.

5. Now do the same for the issue of police reporting. What factors do you think are related to whether or not a victim of assault reports his or her victimization to police?

CHAPTER 9

Qualitative Methods and Analysis

Observing, Participating, and Listening

"I mean, you try to touch on me, I'm gonna check you. If you try to touch on me, you being disrespectful. I'm saying, you engaged in sexual harassment. Some girls just play that. Laughing at it. That's how you know if a girl is a freak or not. That she wants to be touched for real." This was one young women's description of her reaction to sexual harassment. The young woman was part of a study examining gendered violence that Jody Miller (2008) conducted using intensive interviewing techniques with 75 inner city high school–aged men and women. In this chapter, you will learn how qualitative methods were used to illuminate the relationships, both individually and collectively, that gang members have with other social institutions (Decker and Van Winkle 1996). You will also get an inside look at community policing in action (Miller 1999). Throughout the chapter, you will learn, from a variety of other examples, that some of our greatest insights into social processes can result from what appear to be very ordinary activities: observing, participating, listening, and talking.

But you will also learn that qualitative research is much more than just doing what comes naturally in social situations. Qualitative researchers must keenly observe respondents, sensitively plan their participation, systematically take notes, and strategically question respondents. They must also prepare to spend more time and invest more of their whole selves than often occurs with experiments or surveys. Moreover, if we are to have any confidence in the validity of a qualitative study's conclusions, each element of its design must be reviewed as carefully as the elements of an experiment or survey.

The chapter begins with an overview of the major features of qualitative research, as reflected in Venkatesh's (1997) study of Blackstone (the fictitious name given to the residential area). The next section discusses the various approaches to participant observation research, which is the most distinctive qualitative method, and reviews the stages of research using participant observation. We then review, in some detail, the issues involved in intensive interviewing, before briefly explaining focus groups, an increasingly popular qualitative method. The last two sections cover issues that are of concern in any type of qualitative research project: analyzing the data collected and making ethical decisions. By the chapter's end, you should appreciate the hard work required to translate "doing what comes naturally" into systematic research, be able to recognize strong and weak points in qualitative studies, and be ready to do some research yourself.

Fundamentals of Qualitative Methods

Qualitative methods can often be used to enrich experiments and surveys, and refer to three distinctive research designs: participant observation, intensive interviewing, and focus groups. Participant observation and intensive interviewing are often used in the same project; focus groups combine some elements of these two approaches into a unique data-collection strategy.

Although these three qualitative designs differ in many respects, they share several features that distinguish them from experimental and survey research designs (Denzin and Lincoln 1994; Maxwell 1996; Wolcott 1995).

Collection primarily of qualitative rather than quantitative data. Any research design may collect both qualitative and quantitative data, but qualitative methods emphasize observations about natural behavior and artifacts that capture social life as it is experienced by the participants rather than in categories predetermined by the researcher.

Exploratory research questions, with a commitment to inductive reasoning. Qualitative researchers typically begin their projects seeking not to test preformulated hypotheses but to discover what people think and how and why they act in certain social settings. Only after many observations do qualitative researchers try to develop general principles to account for their observations.

A focus on previously unstudied processes and unanticipated phenomena. Previously unstudied attitudes and actions cannot adequately be understood with a structured set of questions or within a highly controlled experiment. Therefore, qualitative methods have their greatest appeal when we need to explore new issues, investigate hard-to-study groups, or determine the meaning people give to their lives and actions.

An orientation to social context, to the interconnections between social phenomena rather than to their discrete features. The context of concern may be a program, an organization, a neighborhood, or a broader social context. For example, in Venkatesh's (1997) analysis of the social space occupied by a street gang, he observed,

> The result of their [Saint's street gang] corporatization was the emergence of a novel social space in Blackstone, that is, a new orientation to local geography in which the symbolic distinctions of local street gangs challenged the building-centered distinctions that had previously underwritten the power of the Councils. (p. 7)

A focus on human subjectivity, on the meanings that participants attach to events and people give to their lives. "Through life stories, people account for their lives. . . . The themes people create are the means by which they interpret and evaluate their life experiences and attempt to integrate these experiences to form a self-concept" (Kaufman 1986:24–25).

A focus on the events leading up to a particular event or outcome instead of general causal explanations. With its focus on particular actors and situations and the processes that connect them, qualitative research tends to identify causes of particular events embedded within an unfolding, interconnected action sequence (Maxwell 1996:20–21). The language of variables and hypotheses appears only rarely in the qualitative literature.

Reflexive research design. The design develops as the research progresses:

> Each component of the design may need to be reconsidered or modified in response to new developments or to changes in some other component. . . . The activities of collecting and analyzing data, developing and modifying theory, elaborating or refocusing the research questions, and identifying and eliminating validity threats are usually all going on more or less simultaneously, each influencing all of the others. (Maxwell 1996:2–3)

Qualitative methods Methods such as participant observation, intensive interviewing, and focus groups that are designed to capture social life as participants experience it, rather than in categories predetermined by the researcher. These methods typically involve explanatory research questions, inductive reasoning, an orientation to social context and human subjectivity, and the meanings attached by participants to events and to their lives.

Participant observation A type of field research in which a researcher develops a sustained and intensive relationship with people while they go about their normal activities

Intensive interviewing Open-ended, relatively unstructured questioning in which the interviewer seeks in-depth information on the interviewee's feelings, experiences, and/or perceptions.

Focus groups Unstructured group interviews in which the focus group leader actively encourages discussion among participants on the topics of interest.

Sensitivity to the subjective role of the researcher. Little pretense is made of achieving an objective perspective on social phenomena. Miller and Crabtree (1999a) capture the entire process of qualitative research in a simple diagram (see Exhibit 9.1). In this diagram, qualitative research begins with the qualitative researcher reflecting on the setting and her relation to it and interpretations of it. The researcher then describes the goals and means for the research. This description is followed by *sampling and collecting* data, describing the data, and *organizing* those data. Thus, the *gathering process* and the *analysis process* proceed together, with repeated description and analysis of data as they are collected. As the data are organized, *connections* are identified between different data segments, and efforts are made to corroborate the credibility of these connections. This *interpretive process* begins to emerge in a written account that represents what has been done and how the data have been interpreted. Each of these steps in the research process informs the others and is repeated throughout the research process.

Origins of Qualitative Research

Field research Research in which natural social processes are studied as they happen and left relatively undisturbed.

Anthropologists and sociologists laid the foundation for modern qualitative methods while doing **field research** in the early decades of the 20th century. Dissatisfied with studies of native peoples that relied on secondhand accounts and inspection of artifacts, anthropologists Franz Boas and

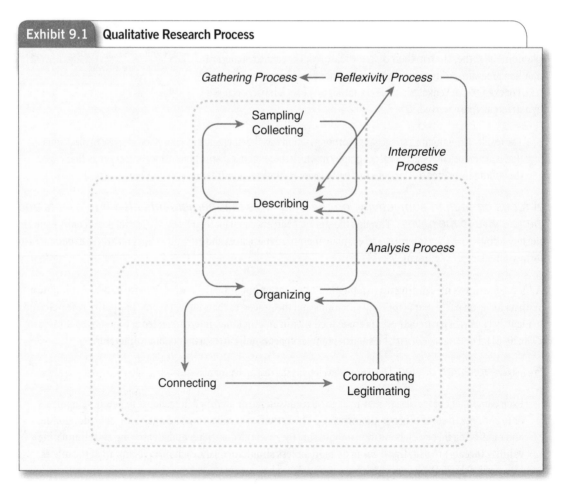

Exhibit 9.1   Qualitative Research Process

Source: Adapted from Miller and Crabtree 1999a:16.

Bronislaw Malinowski went to live in or near the communities they studied. Boas visited Native American villages in the American Northwest; Malinowski lived among New Guinea natives. Neither truly participated in the ongoing social life of those they studied, but both helped establish the value of intimate familiarity with the community of interest and thus laid the basis for modern anthropology (Emerson 1983).

Many of sociology's field research pioneers were former social workers and reformers. Some brought their missionary concern with the welfare of new immigrants to the Department of Sociology and Anthropology at the University of Chicago. Their successors continued to focus on sources of community cohesion and urban strain but came to view the city as a social science laboratory. They adopted the fieldwork methods of anthropology for studying the "natural areas" of the city and the social life of small towns (Vidich and Lyman 1994). By the 1930s, 1940s, and 1950s, qualitative researchers were emphasizing the value of direct participation in community life and sharing in subjects' perceptions and interpretations of events (Emerson 1983).

🔲 Case Study: Life in a Gang

The use of fieldwork techniques to study gangs has a long tradition in a variety of cities, including Thrasher's (1927) classic study of gangs in Chicago, and others, including Whyte (1943), Hagedorn (1988), Vigil (1988), Padilla (1992), Sanchez-Jankowski (1991), and Moore (1978, 1991), who spent over two decades studying the "home-boys" of Hispanic barrios all over the country. All these researchers employed a fieldwork approach to the study of gangs rather than the more structured approaches offered by quantitative methods.

You can get a better feel for qualitative methods by reading the following excerpts from Decker and Van Winkle's (1996) book about gangs, *Life in the Gang: Family, Friends, and Violence*, and by reasoning inductively from their observations. See if you can induce from these particulars some of the general features of field research. Ask yourself, "What were the research questions?" "How were the issues of generalizability, measurement, and causation approached?" "How did social factors influence the research?"

One of the first issues Decker and Van Winkle (1996) were challenged with was precisely defining a gang (recall Chapter 4). After all, the term *gang* could refer to many groups of youth, including high school Debate Society or the Young Republicans. After reviewing the literature, Decker and Van Winkle developed a working definition of a gang as an "age-graded peer group that exhibits some permanence, engages in criminal activity, and has some symbolic representation of membership" (p. 31). To operationalize who was a gang member, they relied on self-identification. "Are you claiming . . ." was a key screening question that was also verified, as often as possible, with other gang members.

Decker and Van Winkle (1996) were interested in several questions:

Our study revolved around a number of activities, both gang and nongang related, that our subjects were likely to engage in. First, we were interested in motivations to join gangs, the process of joining the gang, the symbols of gang membership, the strength of associational ties, the structure or hierarchy within the gang, motivations to stay (or leave) the gang….The second set of issues concerned the activities gang members engaged in. These included such things as turf protection, drug sales and use, and violence, as well as conventional activities. An accurate picture of gang members must portray both the nature of their gang involvement and the legal status of their activities. (pp. 54–55)

With these research questions in mind, Decker and Van Winkle (1996) explain why they chose a fieldwork approach: "A single premise guided our study; the best information about gangs and gang activity would come from gang members contacted directly in the field" (p. 27). As stated earlier, Decker and Van Winkle combined two methods of qualitative data collection. With the help of a field ethnographer who spent the majority of each day "on the streets," direct observation was conducted along with the intensive interviewing conducted by Decker and Van Winkle.

You may wonder what the difference is between the interviews conducted by qualitative researchers and those discussed in the last chapter. The difference is structure. For example, the interviews did not use closed-ended questions, but relied on open-ended questions using probes to clarify answers. As they state:

> Learning about gangs and gang members can be best accomplished by hearing the gang member's story directly from the individuals involved. . . . We went to great lengths to ensure that each person we interviewed felt they had received the opportunity to "tell their story in their own words." (p. 45)

As for their method, it was inductive. First they gathered data. Then, as data collection continued, they figured out how to interpret the data, how to make sense of the social situations they were studying. Their analytic categories ultimately came not from social theory but from the categories by which the gang members themselves described one another and their activities and how they made sense of their social world.

To summarize, Decker and Van Winkle's (1996) research began with exploratory questions and proceeded inductively throughout, developing general concepts to make sense of specific observations. Although the researchers were not gang members themselves, with observational data collected on the streets and transcripts from intensive interviews, Decker and Van Winkle were able to share many gang members' experiences and perspectives. They provided the field of criminology with in-depth descriptions and idiographic connections of sequences of events that could not have been obtained through other methodologies. They successfully used field research to explore human experiences in depth, carefully analyzing the social contexts in which the experiences occurred. As you will see, the goal of much qualitative research is to create a **thick description** of the setting being studied, a description that provides a sense of what it is like to experience that setting or group from the standpoint of the participants in that setting (Geertz 1973).

Thick description A rich description that conveys a sense of what it is like from the standpoint of the participants in that setting.

回 Participant Observation

Other researchers have utilized a more direct observational strategy for studying gangs. For example, to illuminate the nuances and complexities of the role of a street gang in community social life, Venkatesh (1997) conducted intensive participant observation in Blackstone, a midsize public housing development located in a poor ghetto of a large Midwestern city. As Venkatesh describes, "Having befriended these gang members, I moved into their world, accompanying them into Blackstone and other spaces where they were actively involved in illicit economic activities, member recruitment, and the general expansion of their street-based organization" (p. 4). Participant observation, called fieldwork in anthropology, is a method of studying natural social processes as they happen (in the field rather than in the laboratory), leaving them relatively undisturbed, and minimizing your presence as a researcher. It is the seminal field research method, a means for seeing the social world as the research subjects see it, in its totality, and for understanding subjects' interpretations of that world (Wolcott 1995). By observing people and interacting with them in the course of their normal activities, participant observers seek to avoid the artificiality of experimental designs and the unnatural structured questioning of survey research (Koegel 1987).

The term *participant observer* actually represents a continuum of roles (see Exhibit 9.2), ranging from being a complete observer who does not participate in group activities and is publicly defined as a researcher, to being a covert participant who acts just like other group members and does not disclose his or her research role. Many field

Exhibit 9.2   The Observational Continuum

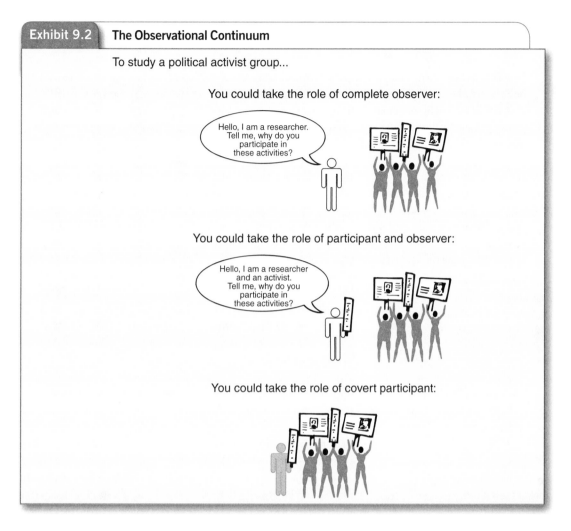

researchers develop a role between these extremes, publicly acknowledging being a researcher but nonetheless participating in group activities. In some settings, it also is possible to observe covertly without acknowledging being a researcher or participating.

Choosing a Role

The first concern of all participant observers is to decide what balance to strike between observing and participating and whether to reveal their role as researchers. These decisions must take into account the specifics of the social situation being studied, the researcher's own background and personality, the larger sociopolitical context, and ethical concerns. The balance of participating and observing that is most appropriate also changes during most projects, often many times. Ultimately, the researcher's ability to maintain either a covert or an overt role can be challenged many times throughout the research effort.

Complete Observation

In her study of community policing, Susan Miller (1999) adopted the role of a complete observer when she conducted research on community policing. Community policing, as most of you probably know, is an approach to policing that emphasizes building closer ties between police and members of the community. Miller was particularly interested in how gender affected the attitudes and behavior of community-police liaisons or neighborhood police officers (NPOs):

> I was curious as to whether the interpersonal dynamics I observed with Officer Terry [a female officer] would be like those when a male NPO was involved. I wanted to delve into the heads and hearts of the NPOs, to see for myself what worked in community policing and to see what they felt did not. I wanted to examine how such a paradigm shift in the theory and practice of policing would affect the officers who desire street action, and how they would assess their new "walk and talk" colleagues. (p. x)

In complete observation, researchers try to see things as they happen, without disrupting the participants. Along with intensive interviews with police officers, Miller (1999) also observed police officers on their daily shifts:

> Both neighborhood and patrol officers' shifts were observed, either on foot with neighborhood officers, or in squad cars with patrol officers. This component of the project also permitted gathering some observational information about citizens' reactions to police delivery of services. . . . Typically, we tried to work the same shifts as the neighborhood police officers, and we shadowed the NPO and each corresponding patrol officer during the same shift. Shadowing both permitted a cross-check of how neighborhood officers perceived the role of patrol officers and of how patrol officers saw their role in conjunction with, or opposition to, the neighborhood policing concept. (pp. 232–33)

Complete observation A role in participant observation in which the researcher does not participate in group activities and is publicly defined as a researcher.

As clearly depicted in this quote, the "shadowing" is visible. Of course, the researcher's presence as an observer alters the social situation being observed. It is not natural in most social situations to have an observer present, one who will record at some point her or his observations for research and publication purposes. The observer thus sees what individuals do when they are being observed, which is not necessarily what they would do without an observer. This is called a **reactive effect**, and the extent to which it can be a problem varies with the situation. In Miller's (1999) study, the extended amount of time she spent as an observer made her presence commonplace, thereby serving to decrease the problem of reactive effects. She states,

Reactive effect The changes in individual or group behavior that are due to being observed or otherwise studied.

> Since I had spent so many hours over eighteen months with the Jackson City Police Department [fictional name], I had grown to be a familiar face; this, I believe, decreased respondents' tendencies toward social desirability. Officers took my presence for granted in the briefing room, the hallways, the interview rooms, and in the field, including me in jokes and informal conversation in the coffee shop. (p. 235)

Generally, in social settings involving many people, an observer may not attract attention. On the other hand, when the social setting involves few people and observing is apparent rather than camouflaged, or when the observer differs in obvious respects from the participants, the complete observer is more likely to have an impact.

Participation and Observation

Most field researchers adopt a role that involves some active participation in the setting. Usually they inform at least some group members of their research interests, but then they participate in enough group activities to develop trust and rapport with members and to gain a direct sense of what group members experience. This is not an easy balancing act:

The key to participant observation as a fieldwork strategy is to take seriously the challenge it poses to participate more, and to play the role of the aloof observer less. Do not think of yourself as someone who needs to wear a white lab coat and carry a clipboard to learn about how humans go about their everyday lives. (Wolcott 1995:100)

In his classic study of corner gangs and other social organizations in the poor Boston community he called Cornerville, Whyte (1943) spent a large part of nearly 4 years trying to be accepted by the community and seen as a good fellow. He describes his efforts:

My aim was to gain an intimate view of Cornerville life. My first problem, therefore, was to establish myself as a participant in the society so that I would have a position from which to observe. I began by going to live in Cornerville, finding a room with an Italian family. . . . It was not enough simply to make the acquaintance of various groups of people. The sort of information that I sought required that I establish intimate social relations, and that presented special problems. Since illegal activities are prevalent in Cornerville, every newcomer is under suspicion. . . . I put in a great deal of time simply hanging around with them [the men] and participating in their various activities. This active participation gave me something in common with them so that we had other things to talk about besides the weather. (pp. v–vii)

Because of the great deal of time he spent with each gang and social organization he was studying, Whyte (1943) became accepted into each group and the community. Sudhir Alladi Venkatesh's (2000) book about gangs in Chicago, *American Project*, will almost certainly become a classic as well. In it, he describes the evolution of his research methodology from structured interviews to participant observation:

They read my survey instrument, informed me that I was "not going to learn shit by asking these questions," and said I would need to "hang out with them" if I really wanted to understand the experiences of African-American youth in the city. Over the next few months, I met with many of them informally to play racquetball, drink beer on the shores of Lake Michigan, attend their parties, and eat dinner with their families. . . . Over an eighteen-month period, I logged notes on the activities of their gang, called the Black Kings. But it was the gang's relationship with other people in the housing development that piqued my interest. Gang members were also schoolchildren, nephews, churchgoers, fathers, husbands, and so on. They were "gang members" at certain times and in certain contexts, such as narcotics trafficking and meetings in open park space, but most of the time their lives were characterized by involvement with work, family, school, and peers. (pp. xiv)

Disclosing your research to participants has two clear ethical advantages. Because group members know the researcher's real role in the group, they can choose to keep some information or attitudes hidden. By the same token, the researcher can decline to participate in unethical or dangerous activities without fear of exposing his or her identity.

Most field researchers who opt for disclosure get the feeling that, after they have become known and at least somewhat trusted figures in the group, their presence does not have a palpable effect on members' actions. The major influences on individual actions and attitudes are past experiences, personality, group structure, and so on, and these continue to exert their influence even when an outside observer is present. The participant observer can presumably be ethical about identity disclosure and still observe the natural social world. Of course, the argument is less persuasive when the behavior to be observed is illegal or stigmatized, giving participants reason to fear the consequences of disclosure to any outsider. In practice, it can be difficult to maintain a fully open research role even in a setting without these special characteristics.

Even when researchers maintain a public identity as researchers, the ethical dilemmas arising from participation in group activities do not go away. In fact, researchers may have to prove themselves to group members by joining in some of their questionable activities. For example, police officers gave Van Maanen (1982) a nonstandard and technically prohibited pistol to carry on police patrols. Pepinsky (1980) witnessed police harassment of a citizen but did not intervene when the citizen was arrested. Experienced participant observers try to lessen some of the problems of identity disclosure by evaluating both their effect on others in the setting and the effect of others on the observers. The observers must write about these effects throughout the time they are in the field and as they analyze their data. While in the field they must preserve some regular time when they can concentrate on their research and schedule occasional meetings with other researchers to review the fieldwork. Participant observers modify their role as circumstances seem to require, perhaps not always disclosing their research role at casual social gatherings or group outings but always informing new members of their role.

Covert Participation

> **Covert (complete) participation** A role in field research in which the researcher does not reveal his or her identity as a researcher to those who are observed. The covert participant has adopted the role of a "complete participant."

To lessen the potential for reactive effects and to gain entry to otherwise inaccessible settings, some field researchers have adopted the role of covert participant. By doing so, they keep their research secret and do their best to act like other participants in a social setting or group. **Covert participation** is also known as **complete participation**. Laud Humphreys (1970) served as a "watch queen" so that he could learn about men engaging in homosexual acts in a public restroom. Randall Alfred (1976) joined a group of Satanists to investigate group members and their interaction. Goffman (1961) worked as a state hospital assistant while studying the treatment of psychiatric patients.

Although the role of covert participant lessens some of the reactive effects encountered by the complete observer, covert participants confront other problems. The following are a few examples:

- *Covert participants cannot openly take notes or use any obvious recording devices.* They must write up notes based solely on memory and must do so at times when it is natural for them to be away from group members.

- *Covert participants cannot ask questions that will arouse suspicion.* Thus, they often have trouble clarifying the meaning of other participants' attitudes or actions.

- *The role of covert participation is difficult to play successfully.* Covert participants will not know how regular participants act in every situation in which the researchers find themselves. Regular participants enter the observed situation with social backgrounds and goals different from the researchers, whose spontaneous reactions to every event are unlikely to be consistent with those of the regular participants. Suspicion that researchers are not "one of us" may then have reactive effects, obviating the value of complete participation (Erikson 1967). In his study of the Satanists, for example, Alfred (1976) pretended to be a regular group participant until he completed his research, at which time he informed the group leader of his covert role. Rather than act surprised, the leader told Alfred that he had long considered Alfred to be strange, not like the others. We will never be certain how Alfred's observations were affected.

- *Covert participants must keep up the act at all times while in the setting under study.* Researchers may experience enormous psychological strain, particularly in situations where they are expected to choose sides in intragroup conflict or to participate in criminal or other acts. Of course, some covert observers may become so wrapped up in their role that they adopt not just the mannerisms but also the perspectives and goals of the regular participants; they "go native." At this point, they abandon research goals and cease to critically evaluate their observations.

Ethical issues have been at the forefront of debate over the strategy of covert participation. Erikson (1967) argues that covert participation is by its very nature unethical and should not be allowed except in public settings. Covert researchers cannot anticipate the unintended consequences (e.g. gang violence) of their actions for research subjects, Erikson points out. If others suspect the researcher's identity or if the researcher contributes to, or impedes, group action, these consequences can be adverse. In addition, other social research is harmed when covert research is disclosed, either during the research or upon its publication, because distrust of social scientists increases and future access to research opportunities may decrease.

But a total ban on covert participation would "kill many a project stone dead" (Punch 1994:90). For example, when studying the behavior of male-for-male escorts, Pruitt (2008) contends that "it is unlikely that many escorts would respond to an e-mail from a self-identified Sociologist" (p. 71). In fact, he demonstrated that escorts who received an e-mail from a sociologist asking them about their business responded 15% of the time while escorts who received the same e-mail message that he sent as a potential client received a response 60% of the time. These findings, Pruitt believes, support his contention that certain populations would be inaccessible without using deception.

Others agree. "The crux of the matter is that some deception, passive or active, enables you to get at data not obtainable by other means" (Punch 1994:91). Therefore, some field researchers argue that covert participation is legitimate in certain circumstances. If the researcher maintains the confidentiality of others, keeps their commitments to them, and does not directly lie to the participants, some degree of deception may be justified in exchange for the knowledge gained (Punch 1994). According to the American Sociological Association's (1997) ethical guidelines, which are followed by the American Society of Criminology (see Chapter 3), deceptive techniques can only be used if researchers

> have determined that their use will not be harmful to research participants; is justified by the study's prospective scientific, educational, or applied value; and that equally effective alternative procedures that do not use deception are not feasible . . . or, on rare occasions, sociologists may need to conceal their identity in order to undertake research that could not practicably be carried out were they to be known as researchers. Under such circumstances, sociologists undertake the research if it involves no more than minimal risk for the research participants and if they have obtained approval to proceed in this manner from an institutional review board.

Entering the Field

Entering the field or the setting under investigation is a critical stage in a participant observation project as the introduction can shape many subsequent experiences. Some background work is necessary before entering the field, at least enough to develop a clear understanding of what the research questions are likely to be and to review one's personal stance toward the people and problems likely to be encountered. With participant observation, researchers must also learn in advance about the participants' dress and their typical activities to avoid being caught completely unprepared.

Entering the field even required Whyte (1943) to learn a new language:

> Since the mother and father of the family spoke no English, I began studying Italian. Conversations with them and practice with the Linguaphone enabled me to learn enough to talk fairly fluently with the older generation. As I became largely concerned with the second-generation men, who conducted their activities in English, Italian was not essential to me; but the fact that I made the effort to learn the language was important, since it gave the impression that I had a sincere and sympathetic interest in Cornerville people. (p. v)

Developing trust with at least one member of the research setting is a necessity in qualitative research. Such a person can become a valuable informant throughout the project, and most participant observers make a point of developing trust with at least one informant in a group under study. Miller (1999) gained access to the police department she studied through a chief of police who was extremely open to research. She also had two friends on the police force at the time of her study:

> Both of my friends were well-liked on the force and had great credibility with their colleagues. They vouched for me to others, tracked down retired officers for me to interview, helped with scheduling, answered my questions, and provided clarification and other assistance as the need arose. . . . Whenever I encountered scheduling snafus or any reluctance by a police offer to schedule an interview or a walk-along, my friends on the force would make a call and easily arrange the time I needed with other officers. (p. 230)

In short, field researchers must be very sensitive to the impression they make and the ties they establish when entering the field. This state of research lays the groundwork for collecting data from people who have different perspectives and for developing relationships that the researcher can use to overcome the problems that inevitably arise in the field.

Developing and Maintaining Relationships

Researchers must be careful to manage their relationships in the research setting so they can continue to observe and interview diverse members of the social setting throughout the long period typical of participant observation (Maxwell 1996). Every action the researcher takes can develop or undermine this relationship. As Decker and Van Winkle (1996) describe,

> There are a number of groups and individuals with whom field relationships must be maintained. Doing so effectively often involves balancing the competing demands of confidentiality, trust, and danger that emerge in a field study of individuals actively engaged in offending. (p. 45)

Maintaining trust is the cornerstone to successful research engagement, as Decker and Van Winkle (1996) further elaborate:

> We were able to maintain good field relations with our subjects by strictly observing our own commitment to the confidentiality of their statements. Since we interviewed many individuals from the same gang, it was often the case that one member would want to know what an earlier participant had told us. We refused to honor such inquiries, reminding them that the same confidentiality that applied to their own answers also covered those of their fellow gang members. We received numerous requests from gang members to sit in on the interview of a fellow member. These requests were declined as well. The strict confidentiality we were committed to was respected by our subjects, and appeared to enhance our own credibility as "solid" in their eyes. (p. 46)

Experienced participant observers (Whyte 1943; Wolcott 1995) have developed some sound advice for others seeking to maintain relationships in the field:

- Develop a plausible (and honest) explanation for yourself and your study.

- Maintain the support of key individuals in groups or organizations under study.

- Don't be too aggressive in questioning others (e.g., don't violate implicit norms that preclude discussion of illegal activity with outsiders). Being a researcher requires that you not simultaneously try to be the guardian of law and order.

- Don't fake social similarity with your subjects. Taking a friendly interest in them should be an adequate basis for developing trust.

- Avoid giving and receiving monetary or other tangible gifts, but do not violate norms of reciprocity. Living with other people, taking others' time for conversations, and going out for a social evening all create expectations and incur social obligations. You cannot be an active participant without occasionally helping others. But you will lose your ability to function as a researcher if you are seen as someone who gives away money or other favors. Such small forms of assistance as an occasional ride to the store or advice on applying to college may strike the right balance.

- Be prepared for special difficulties and tensions if multiple groups are involved. It is hard to avoid taking sides or being used in situations of intergroup conflict.

Jody Miller (2000) describes her efforts to develop trust with the female gang members she interviewed for her book *One of the Guys*:

> First, my research approach proved useful for establishing rapport. The survey began with relatively innocuous questions (demographics, living arrangements, attitudes toward school) and slowly made the transition from these to more sensitive questions about gang involvement, delinquency, and victimization. In addition, completing the survey interview first allowed me to establish a relationship with each young woman, so that when we completed the in-depth interview, there was a preexisting level of familiarity between us. . . . In addition, I worked to develop trust in the young women I interviewed through my efforts to protect their confidentiality. (pp. 29–30)

Sampling People and Events

Decisions to study one setting or several settings and to pay attention to specific people and events will shape field researchers' ability to generalize about what they have found as well as the confidence that others can place in the results of their study. Limiting a particular study to a single setting allows a more intensive portrait of actors and activities in that setting but also makes generalization of the findings questionable.

It is easy to be reassured by information indicating that a typical case was selected for study or that the case selected was appropriate in some way for the research question. We also must keep in mind that many of the most insightful participant observation studies were conducted in only one setting and draw their credibility precisely from the researcher's thorough understanding of that setting. Nonetheless, studying more than one case or setting almost always strengthens the causal conclusions and makes the findings more generalizable (King, Keohane, and Verba 1994).

Most qualitative researchers utilize a purposive sampling technique (Chapter 5), often adding a snowball aspect by asking respondents to recommend others. Decker and Van Winkle (1996) utilized the technique of snowball sampling. To make their findings more generalizable, they interviewed members of several different gangs. Specifically, the snowball began with an earlier fieldwork project on active residential burglars (Wright and Decker 1994). The young members from this sample, along with contacts the field ethnographer had with several active street criminals, started the referral process. The initial interviewees then nominated other gang members as potential interview subjects. Because they wanted to interview members from several gangs, they had to restart the snowball sampling procedure many times to gain access to a large number of gangs. One problem, of course, was validating whether individuals claiming to be gang members, so-called "wannabes," actually were legitimate members. Over 500 contacts were made before the final sample of 99 was complete.

Theoretical sampling is a systematic approach to sampling in participant observational research (Glaser and Strauss 1967). Decker and Van Winkle (1996) used this technique to ensure that various subgroups such as race, sex, and type of gang were represented within their sample. When field researchers discover in an investigation that particular processes seem to be important, implying that certain comparisons should be made or that similar instances should be checked, the researchers then modify their settings and choose new individuals, as diagrammed in Exhibit 9.3 (Ragin 1994). Based on the existing literature and anecdotal knowledge, Decker and Van Winkle (1996) knew that not all gang members were young minority-group males. They describe their strategy to obtain a full range of gang members as follows:

> We aggressively pursued leads for female gangs and gang members as well as opportunities to locate older and nonblack gang members. These leads were more difficult to find and often caused us to miss chances to interview other gang members. Despite these "missed opportunities," our sample is strengthened in that it more accurately represents the diverse nature of gangs and gang members in St. Louis. (p. 43)

> *Theoretical sampling* A sampling method recommended for field researchers by Glaser and Strauss (1967). A theoretical sample is drawn in a sequential fashion, with settings or individuals selected for study as earlier observations or interviews indicate that these settings or individuals are influential.

Exhibit 9.3 **Theoretical Sampling**

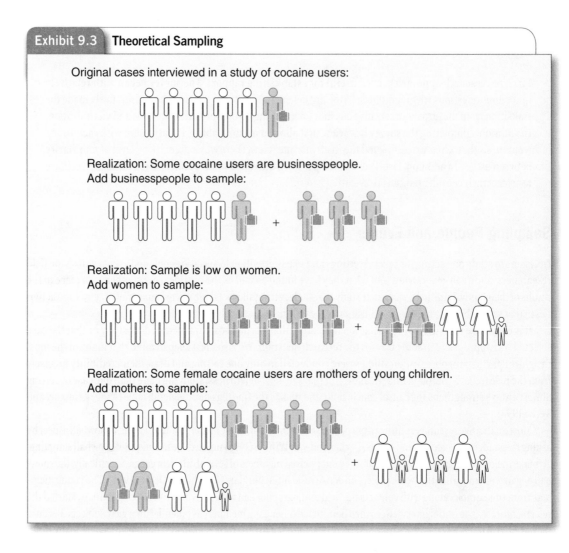

Original cases interviewed in a study of cocaine users:

Realization: Some cocaine users are businesspeople.
Add businesspeople to sample:

Realization: Sample is low on women.
Add women to sample:

Realization: Some female cocaine users are mothers of young children.
Add mothers to sample:

The resulting sample of gang members in Decker and Van Winkle's (1996) study represented 29 different gangs. Thus, Decker and Van Winkle's ability to draw from different gangs in developing conclusions gives us greater confidence in their studies' generalizability.

You already learned in Chapter 5 about nonprobability sampling methods, which can also be used to develop a more representative range of opinions and events in a field setting. Purposive sampling, which is a type of theoretical sampling, can be used to identify opinion leaders and representatives of different roles. With snowball sampling, field researchers learn from participants about who represents different subgroups in a setting. Quota sampling also may be employed to ensure the representation of particular categories of participants. Using some type of intentional sampling strategy within a particular setting can allow tests of some hypotheses that would otherwise have to wait until comparative data could be collected from several settings (King et al. 1994).

When field studies do not require ongoing, intensive involvement by researchers in the setting, the **experience sampling method (ESM)** can be used. The experiences, thoughts, and feelings of a number of people are randomly sampled as they go about their daily activities. Participants in an ESM study carry an electronic pager and fill out reports when they are beeped.

Experience sampling method (ESM) A technique for drawing a representative sample of everyday activities, thoughts, and experiences; participants carry a pager and are beeped at random times over several days or weeks; upon hearing the beep, participants complete a report designed by the researcher.

Taking Notes

Written **field notes** are the primary means of recording participant observation data (Emerson, Fretz, and Shaw 1995). It is almost always a mistake to try to take comprehensive notes while engaged in the field; the process of writing extensively is just too disruptive. The usual procedure (see Exhibit 9.4) is to jot down brief notes about the highlights of the observation period. These brief notes, called **jottings**, then serve as memory joggers when writing the actual field notes at a later time. With the aid of the brief notes and some practice, researchers usually remember a great deal of what happened, as long as the comprehensive field notes are written within the next 24 hours, that night or upon arising the next day. Many field researchers jot down partial notes while observing and then retreat to their computers to write up more complete notes on a daily basis. The computerized text can then be inspected and organized after it is printed out, or it can be marked up and organized for analysis using one of several computer programs designed especially for the task.

> **Field notes** Notes that describe what has been observed, heard, or otherwise experienced in a participant observation study; these notes usually are written after the observational session data analysis.
>
> **Jottings** Brief notes that are jotted down quickly during the observation period that will be expanded into more extensive field notes.

Usually, writing up notes takes as long as making the observations. Field notes must be as complete, detailed, and true to what was observed and heard as possible. Quotes should be clearly distinguished from the researcher's observations and phrased in the local vernacular; pauses and interruptions should be indicated. The surrounding context should receive as much attention as possible, and a map of the setting always should be included, with indications of where individuals were at different times.

Careful note taking yields a big payoff for the researcher. On page after page, field notes will suggest new concepts, causal connections, and theoretical propositions. Social processes and settings can be described in rich detail, with ample illustrations. Exhibit 9.5, for example, contains field notes recorded by Miller (1999) for her study of community police officers. The notes include observations of the setting, the questions Miller asked and the answers she received, and her analytic thoughts about one of the police officers. What can be learned from just this one page of field notes? You can vividly visualize the neighborhood patrolled on the evening described. Key concepts and phrases are identified in the notes, such as "the hole," which refers to the worst apartment houses in the city ("absent landlords, repairs unattended"), and "jackets," which are tiny bags used to sell crack. The notes depict the nature and tone of the interactions between the patrol officer and several residents, with the officer knowing most of the residents by name and asking about other family members.

Exhibit 9.4	The Note-Taking Process

Notes jotted down while in the field... are transformed within 24 hours... into comprehensive, well-organized field notes.

| Exhibit 9.5 | Field Notes From Susan Miller's (1999) Study of Community Policing |

(7–6–95, Officer P, NBH #4)

Once the sergeant arrived, we walked around in groups for high visibility in the 1900 block, "the hole" (worst apartment houses: absent landlords, repairs unattended, no background check for tenants). Planned to search some of the basements for drugs. Several officers commented that "Linc" was seen hanging around the hole more frequently than usual—could indicate increased drug activity. We drove towards the hole. When we got within a block, Officer P. slowed down and asked over radio if everybody was ready. In we went. We parked by the other police mini-station in case anyone wanted sodas later. P. noticed that the windows had been broken, with rocks around. A white woman (early 30s) from the apt across the street came over and said it happened Wed night, and she had already reported it to the other neighborhood officers. Unclear if break happened after incidents on Wed or even if they were related. P. felt they were related since they picked police windows to break. She was very friendly and cooperative, as were her kid (white 12 years old) and her boyfriend (black). We started to walk up to the building on the way 1900 block. Kids came up to us to say hi to P. Adults (mostly black) asked P. how he was doing and how things were since the mini-riot last night. Residents seemed to know him, and they answered his questions with ease, some volunteering more information than others. P. knew many by name and often asked about other family members. Easy rapport. At each building, P. would knock on the door of one of the ground floor apartments to ask for a basement key. Women always answered and were friendly and cooperative. Before P. got to the door with a key, one of the private security guards had already forced it open with a knife. The women, upon seeing this, complained to P. that everyone got in that way. (All women are African American unless otherwise noted.) One woman ran after P. asking him to get the landlord to fix the lock on the basement door. P. whipped out his cell phone and dialed right there in front of her (she was happy about that). In the basements, officers poked at the insulation where the walls met ceilings. Last week, they found a gun hidden there, and often find stashes of drugs. Our search found two different baggies full of "jackets," which is a way to sell crack (tiny bags) and a bag of pot. Corners of baggies used to sell crack in $20 quantities on the street. P. documented all of this to show the absent landlord. Back outside (around 8:10), several officers and squad cars surrounding a bunch of on-lookers as well as 3 young males (2 black, 1 white, in 20s) being frisked. They were spotted going from their car into an apartment where they don't live—a known apt where people went to do heroin. One of the bystanders (black, mid 20s) took P. aside to talk about getting some of his personal items back from jail (P. had visited him earlier in jail to get his version of the mini-riot). Search revealed a rock of cocaine.

Source: From Miller, S. L., *Gender and Community Policing: Walking the Talk.* Copyright © 1999, University Press of New England, Lebanon, NH. Reprinted with permission, page 36.

Complete field notes must provide more than only a record of what was observed or heard. Notes also should include descriptions of the methodology: where researchers were standing while observing, how they chose people for conversation or observation, and what numerical counts of people or events they made and why. Sprinkled throughout the notes also should be a record of the researchers' feelings and thoughts while observing: when they were disgusted by some statement or act, when they felt threatened or intimidated, why their attention shifted from one group to another. Notes like these provide a foundation for later review of the likelihood of bias or inattention to some salient features of the situation.

Managing the Personal Dimensions

Our overview of participant observation is not complete without considering its personal dimensions. Because field researchers become a part of the social situation they are studying, they cannot help but be affected on a personal, emotional level. At the same time, those being studied react to researchers not just as researchers but as personal acquaintances, often as friends, and sometimes as personal rivals. Managing and learning from this personal side of field research is an important part of any qualitative project.

The impact of personal issues varies with the depth of researchers' involvement in the setting. The more involved researchers are in multiple aspects of the ongoing social situation, the more important personal issues become and the greater the risk of "going native." Even when researchers acknowledge their role, "increased contact brings sympathy, and sympathy in its turn dulls the edge of criticism" (Fenno 1978:277). To study the social life of "corner boys," however, Whyte (1943) could not stay so disengaged. Recall that he moved into an apartment with a Cornerville family and lived for about 4 years in the community he was investigating:

> The researcher, like his informants, is a social animal. He has a role to play, and he has his own personality needs that must be met in some degree if he is to function successfully. Where the researcher operates out of a university, just going into the field for a few hours at a time, he can keep his personal social life separate from field activity. His problem of role is not quite so complicated. If, on the other hand, the researcher is living for an extended period in the community he is studying, his personal life is inextricably mixed with his research. (p. 279)

There is no formula for successfully managing the personal dimension of field research. It is much more art than science and flows more from the researcher's own personality and natural approach to other people than from formal training. Novice field researchers often neglect to consider how they will manage personal relationships when they plan and carry out their projects. Then suddenly, they find themselves doing something they do not believe they should, just to stay in the good graces of research subjects, or juggling the emotions resulting from conflict within the group. These issues are even more salient when researchers place themselves in potentially dangerous situations. As Decker and Van Winkle (1996) explain,

> In part, gang members were of interest to us because of their involvement in violence. Because of this, we took steps to insure our own safety. One of the guiding principles was to limit the number of people being separately interviewed at the same time and location. In addition, we steadfastly avoided interviewing members of rival gangs at the same time. Despite our best efforts, there were occasions when these precautions did not work. The field ethnographer witnessed several drive-by shootings while on the way to pick up interview subjects, and on one occasion, he saw three of our subjects shot while waiting to be picked up for an interview. . . . Not all exposure to risk of physical danger comes through such obvious means; however, during one interview, when asked whether he owned any guns, a gang member reached into his coat pocket and pulled out a .32 caliber pistol. We assured him that we would have taken his word for it. (p. 46)

If you plan a field research project, there are some general guidelines to follow:

- Take the time to consider how you want to relate to your potential subjects as people.

- Speculate about what personal problems might arise and how you will respond to them.

- Keep in touch with other researchers and personal friends outside the research setting.

- Maintain standards of conduct that make you comfortable as a person and that respect the integrity of your subjects. (Whyte 1943)

When you evaluate participant observers' reports, pay attention to how they defined their role in the setting and dealt with personal problems. Do not place too much confidence in such research unless the report provides this information.

Systematic Observation

> **Systematic observation** A strategy that increases the reliability of observational data by using explicit rules that standardize coding practices across observers.

Observations can be made in a more systematic, standardized design that allows systematic comparisons and more confident generalizations. A researcher using systematic observation develops a standard form on which to record variation within the observed setting in terms of variables of interest. Such variables might include the frequency of some behavior(s), the particular people observed, the weather or other environmental conditions, and the number and state of repair of physical structures. In some systematic observation studies, records will be obtained from a random sample of places or times.

Case Study: Studying Public Disorder and Crime

You first learned about Robert Sampson and Stephen Raudenbush's (1999) study of disorder and crime in urban neighborhoods in Chapter 4. In this section, we'll elaborate on their use of the method of systematic social observation of public spaces to learn about these neighborhoods. A systematic observational strategy increases the reliability of observational data by using explicit rules that standardize coding practices across observers (Reiss 1971).

Sampson and Raudenbush's (1999) study was a multiple methods investigation that combined observational research, survey research, and archival research. The observational component involved a stratified probability (random) sample of 196 Chicago census tracts. A specially equipped sport utility vehicle was driven down each street in these tracts at the rate of 5 miles per hour. Two video recorders taped the blocks on both sides of the street, while two observers peered out the vehicle's windows and recorded their observations in logs. The result was an observational record of 23,816 face blocks (the block on one side of the street is a face block). The observers recorded codes that indicated land use, traffic, physical conditions, and evidence of physical disorder (see Exhibit 9.6). Physical disorder was measured by counting such features as cigarettes or cigars in the street, garbage, empty beer bottles, graffiti, condoms, and syringes. Indicators of social

Exhibit 9.6 | **Neighborhood Disorder Indicators Used in Systematic Observation Log**

Variable	Category	Frequency
Physical Disorder		
Cigarettes, cigars on street or gutter	no	6815
	yes	16758
Garbage, litter on street or sidewalk	no	11680
	yes	11925
Empty beer bottles visible in street	no	17653
	yes	5870

Source: Raudenbush, Stephen W. and Robert J. Sampson. 1999. "Ecometrics: Toward a Science of Assessing Ecological Settings, With Application to the Systematic Social Observation of Neighborhoods." *Sociological Methodology* 29:1–41.

Variable	Category	Frequency
Tagging graffiti	no	12859
	yes	2252
Graffiti painted over	no	13390
	yes	1721
Gang graffiti	no	14138
	yes	973
Abandoned cars	no	22782
	yes	806
Condoms on sidewalk	no	23331
	yes	231
Needles or syringes on sidewalk	no	23392
	yes	173
Political message graffiti	no	15097
	yes	14
Social Disorder		
Adults loitering or congregating	no	14250
	yes	861
People drinking alcohol	no	15075
	yes	36
Peer group, gang indicators present	no	15091
	yes	20
People intoxicated	no	15093
Adults fighting or hostilely arguing	no	15099
	yes	12
Prostitutes on street	no	15100
	yes	11
People selling drugs	no	15099
	yes	12

Source: Raudenbush, Stephen W. and Robert J. Sampson. 1999. "Ecometrics: Toward a Science of Assessing Ecological Settings, With Application to the Systematic Social Observation of Neighborhoods." *Sociological Methodology* 29:1–41.

disorder included adults loitering, drinking alcohol in public, fighting, and selling drugs. To check for reliability, a different set of coders recoded the videos for 10 of the blocks. The repeat codes achieved 98% agreement with the original codes.

Sampson and Raudenbush (1999) also measured crime levels with data from police records, census tract socioeconomic characteristics with census data, and resident attitudes and behavior with a survey. As you learned in Chapter 6, the combination of data from these sources allowed a test of the relative impact on the crime rate of informal social control efforts by residents and of the appearance of social and physical disorder.

Peter St. Jean (2007) advanced the research of Sampson and Raudenbush by examining the variation in collective efficacy, community disorder, and crime within specific blocks in one high-crime police district in Chicago. After examining official data and combining them with interviews asking residents where crime typically took place in the neighbourhood, St. Jean found that "pockets of crime" emerged whereby most crimes occurred on particular blocks while other blocks remained relatively untouched. The goal of St. Jean's work was to determine why. He used multiple methods for this project including resident surveys, participant observation, in-depth interviews with residents and offenders, and systematic social observation. For the latter, video cameras were mounted on each side of a vehicle while it was slowly driven through neighborhood streets so that physical and social appearances could be captured. An example of the video St. Jean captured is available on the Student Study Site for this text. Using the tapes, neighborhoods were then coded for social disorder by using the conditions of the buildings, properties, and vacant lots and the prevalence of behaviors like loitering, public drinking, and panhandling. A snapshot from one of St. Jean's videos is displayed in Exhibit 9.7.

Innovatively, St. Jean (2007) not only coded the videos; he used the footage as a visual cue when interviewing offenders about their reasons for selecting particular locations and victims. He explains,

> For instance, drug dealers and robbers were able to use the [Systematic Social Observation] movie to explain in detail how and why certain locations are more attractive than others. It also allowed offenders to identify the specific features of neighbourhoods that they considered distasteful, and to explain associated meanings, especially as such meanings pertain to the crimes they commit . . . it refreshed the subjects' memories of relevant events that they often claimed they would have forgotten to mention [without the video]. (p. 27)

Exhibit 9.7 **One Building in St. Jean's (2007) Study**

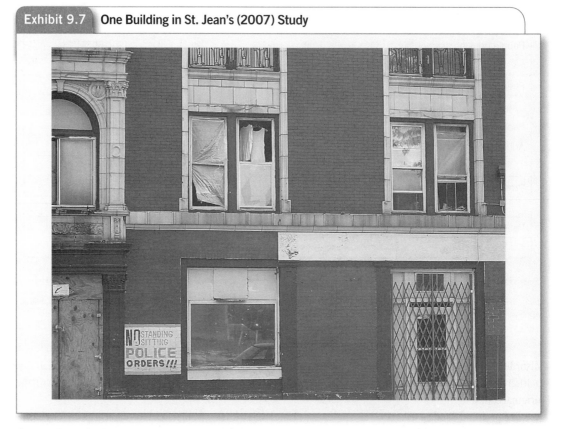

Source: © Peter K. B. St. Jean. Reprinted with permission.

Among other things, St. Jean discovered that even when offenders faced opposition from neighborhood reformers, they were not deterred from engaging in crime in an area when it offered "ecological advantages" such as retail establishments and bus stops.

These studies illustrate both the value of multiple methods and the technique of recording observations in a form from which quantitative data can be obtained. The systematic observations when combined with residents' own perceptions provide us with much greater confidence in the measurement of relative neighborhood disorder. When these are combined with rich narrative accounts from neighborhood residents and active offenders, both the measurement validity of the constructs and the overall validity of the findings are significantly enhanced.

⊡ Intensive Interviewing

Asking questions is part of almost all qualitative research designs (Wolcott 1995). Many qualitative researchers employ intensive interviewing exclusively. Unlike the more structured interviewing that may be used in survey research (discussed in Chapter 8), intensive interviewing relies on open-ended questions. Qualitative researchers do not presume to know the range of answers that respondents might give, and they seek to hear these answers in the respondents' own words. Rather than asking standard questions in a fixed order, intensive interviewers allow the specific content and order of questions to vary from one interviewee to another.

What distinguishes intensive interviewing from more structured forms of questioning is consistency and thoroughness. The goal is to develop a comprehensive picture of the interviewees' background, attitudes, and actions, in their own terms—to "listen to people as they describe how they understand the worlds in which they live and work" (Rubin and Rubin 1995:3). For example, even though Decker and Van Winkle (1996) had an interview guide, they encouraged elaboration on the part of their respondents and "went to great lengths to insure that each person we interviewed felt they had received the opportunity to tell their story in their own words" (p. 45).

Intensive interview studies do not directly reveal the social context in which action is taken and opinions are formed. Similar to participant observation studies, intensive interviewing engages researchers more actively with their subjects than does standard survey research. The researchers must listen to lengthy explanations, ask follow-up questions tailored to the preceding answers, and seek to learn about interrelated belief systems or personal approaches to things rather than measure a limited set of variables. As a result, intensive interviews are often much longer than standardized interviews, sometimes as long as 15 hours, conducted in several different sessions (Kaufman 1986).

The intensive interview becomes more like a conversation between partners than between a researcher and a respondent. Intensive interviewers actively try to probe understandings and engage interviewees in a dialogue about the intended meaning of their comments. The interview typically follows a preplanned outline of topics, which often are asked of selected group members or other participants in a reasonably consistent manner. Some projects may use relatively structured interviews, particularly when the focus is on developing knowledge about prior events or some narrowly defined topic. But more exploratory projects, particularly those aimed at learning the interviewees' interpretations of the world, may let each interview flow in a unique direction in response to the interviewee's experiences and interests (Kvale 1996; Rubin and Rubin 1995; Wolcott 1995). In either case, qualitative interviewers must nimbly adapt throughout the interview, paying attention to nonverbal cues, expressions with symbolic value, and the ebb and flow of the interviewee's feelings and interests. "You have to be free to follow your data where they lead" (Rubin and Rubin 1995:64).

Random selection is rarely used to select respondents for intensive interviews, but the selection method still must be carefully considered. If interviewees are selected in a haphazard manner, as by speaking just to those who happen to be available at the time that the researcher is on site, the interviews are likely to be of less value than when a more purposive selection strategy is used. Researchers should try to select interviewees who are knowledgeable about

Saturation point The point at which subject selection is ended in intensive interviewing, when new interviews seem to yield little additional information.

the subject of the interview, who are open to talking, and who represent the range of perspectives (Rubin and Rubin 1995). Selection of new interviewees should continue, if possible, at least until the saturation point is reached, the point when new interviews seem to yield little additional information (see Exhibit 9.8). As new issues are uncovered, additional interviewees may be selected to represent different opinions about these issues.

| Exhibit 9.8 | **The Saturation Point in Intensive Interviewing** |

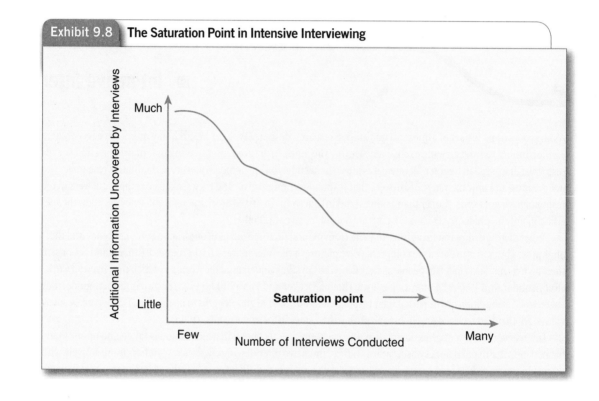

Case Study: Jurors' Stories of Death

A book by Fleury-Steiner (2003) that examines the thoughts and emotions of jurors in death penalty cases is an excellent illustration of the tremendous insights that can be uncovered through intensive interviewing. In *Jurors' Stories of Death*, Fleury-Steiner reports on his work with the Capital Jury Project (CJP), which was a national study of the experiences of citizens who served as jurors on death penalty cases. To encourage respondents to tell stories about their experiences, the CJP survey explicitly asked jurors to tell interviewers about important moments during the trial and deliberations, and their impressions of the defendant. Fleury-Steiner states, "The goal of these questions was to facilitate jurors to construct their responses in their own ways. . . . Given the leeway to answer as they saw fit, in many instances jurors' stories emerged when I least expected them to" (p. 44).

The inductive analytic process of generating theory and making conclusions based on intensive interview narratives is often a time-consuming process. Fleury-Steiner (2003) explains,

Through numerous rounds of retranscribing and revising, I was able to clarify my interpretations of jurors' stories. . . . Expanding beyond a literal interpretation of what was on the page, I began to notice consistencies in the way jurors made sense in their stories, including the taken for granted normative grammars of both speaker and listener. By privileging the "telling" of jurors' stories, I was able to make subsequent analytical interpretation. Indeed, the more I returned to the data, the more I began to connect the particularities of jurors' stories to broader sociohistorical, cultural, and institutional interpretations of identity, morality, and punishment. (p. 47)

Establishing and Maintaining a Partnership

Because intensive interviewing does not engage researchers as participants in subjects' daily affairs, the problems associated with entering the field are greatly reduced. However, the logistics of arranging long periods for personal interviews can still be fairly complicated. It is important to establish rapport with subjects by considering in advance how they will react to the interview arrangement and by developing an approach that does not violate their standards for social behavior. Interviewees should be treated with respect, as knowledgeable partners whose time is valued. (In other words, avoid coming late for appointments.) Once again, a commitment to confidentiality should be stated and honored (Rubin and Rubin 1995).

It is important to highlight, however, that the intensive interviewer's relationship with the interviewee is not an equal partnership, for the researcher seeks to gain certain types of information and strategizes throughout to maintain an appropriate relationship (Kvale 1996). In the first few minutes of the interview, the goal is to show interest in the interviewee and to clearly explain the purpose of the interview (Kvale 1996). During the interview, the interviewer should maintain an appropriate distance from the interviewee, one that does not violate cultural norms; the interviewer should maintain eye contact and not engage in distracting behavior. An appropriate pace is also important; pause to allow the interviewee to reflect, elaborate, and generally not feel rushed (Gordon 1992). When an interview covers emotional or otherwise stressful topics, at the end the interviewer should give the interviewee an opportunity to unwind (Rubin and Rubin 1995).

Asking Questions and Recording Answers

Intensive interviewers must plan their main questions around an outline of the interview topic. The questions should generally be short and to the point. More details can then be elicited through nondirective probes (such as "Can you tell me more about that?"), and follow-up questions can be tailored to answers to the main questions. Interviewers should strategize throughout an interview about how best to achieve their objectives while taking into account interviewees' answers.

Decker and Van Winkle's (1996) interview narrative illustrates this well:

Nearly half of the gang members identified leaders as persons who could provide material advantage, thus ascribing a functional character to leadership within the gang. Since half of our sample was in their early teens, someone with the ability to procure cars, drugs, guns, or alcohol could play a valuable role in the gang. Consequently, it was no surprise to find that over half of gang members identified leaders as persons who could "deliver." Because of the situational nature of leadership, persons moved in and out of this role. This was especially true in the case of being able to provide drugs in large quantities for street sales:

Q: Does someone have more juice in the gang?

A: Yeah, you always got someone that got more juice.

Q: What is the type of person who usually has more juice?

A: The one who got the connection with the drugs.

Q: Who has the most juice?

A: Dude named T-Loc.

Q: Why does he have more juice than everybody else?

A: 'Cause he travels a lot. Gets the good stuff.

Q: What's the good stuff?

A: Like guns, cocaine, weed.

Q: What gives him the juice? (pp. 97–98)

Do you see how the interviewer actively encouraged the subject to elaborate on answers? More important, intensive interviews can also uncover true meanings that questions utilizing fixed formats would surely miss. For example, during an interview with a female gang member, Decker and Van Winkle (1996) discovered that some gang members were actually confused about what marijuana (weed) actually was:

Q: What drugs are being sold?

A: Coke, crack, marijuana.

Q: Anything else?

A: Weed, that's all.

Q: Weed is marijuana?

A: No.

Q: What is marijuana then?

A: I don't know.

Q: What is weed?

A: Stuff you smoke.

Tape recorders commonly are used to record intensive interviews. Most researchers who have tape-recorded interviews feel that they do not inhibit most interviewees and, in fact, are routinely ignored. The occasional respondent who is very concerned with his or her public image may speak "for the tape recorder," but such individuals are unlikely to speak frankly in any research interview. In any case, constant note taking during an interview prevents adequate displays of interest and appreciation by the interviewer and hinders the degree of concentration that results in the best interviews.

Of course, there are exceptions to every rule. Fenno (1978) presents a compelling argument for avoiding the tape recorder when interviewing public figures who are concerned with their public image:

My belief is that the only chance to get a nonroutine, nonreflexive interview [from many of the members of Congress] is to converse casually, pursuing targets of opportunity without the presence of a recording instrument other than myself. If [worse] comes to worst, they can always deny what they have said in person; on tape they leave themselves no room for escape. I believe they are not unaware of the difference. (p. 280)

Combining Participant Observation and Intensive Interviewing

Many large research projects aimed at uncovering detailed information about a particular phenomenon often combine the qualitative research techniques of participant observation and intensive interviewing. As we have already seen, Decker and Van Winkle (1996) utilized this double strategy. Miller (1999) also combined participant observation with intensive interviewing in her study of community policing. The information obtained from both methodologies was vital to her conclusions. For example, the observational component of Miller's research shows how traditional patrol officers' perceptions and experiences differ from those of neighborhood patrol officers. Her observations also uncovered how rarely the paths of patrol officers crossed with their community policing counterparts. These limited interactions contributed, Miller believed, to patrol officers' misconceptions about community policing. Patrol officers believed that neighborhood police officers did not do real police work and spent too much time responding to residents and political needs, not to crime-fighting goals.

Through both methods, Miller (1999) also uncovered differences in what was observed in group settings compared to what was revealed in one-on-one interviews with the officers. On ride-alongs with patrol officers, Miller observed that it was customary to gather during the shift at a predetermined place for dinner or in an uncrowded parking lot. She observed that although these meetings involved both women and men, the discussions usually revolved around "guy stuff," such as joking about guns and pretending to pull out a gun. Miller describes,

> Their language was full of expletives, with some version of "f—k" being the most common. . . . Common topics of conversation were upcoming shooting competitions, physical training, qualifications, and similar physical activities. The men tended to tell us, the researchers, what kind of exercise regimens they followed, and which officers helped with running, training, and weight lifting at the police academy. These topics reinforced the tough, masculine, crime-fighting image of policing. Patrolwomen who were part of these "jawing" sessions engaged in the conversation with equal heartiness. (pp. 175–76)

If Miller (1999) had only performed this observation, she would not have discovered the more gendered nature of the patrol officers' perceptions and experiences that was uncovered in her intensive interviews:

> Even though the patrolwomen joined in the banter and told their share of crime-fighting war stories, it became clear during one-on-one conversations with them they dropped their aggressive facade when their actions were less visible to other patrol officers. The women were more than superficially involved in some of the local people's lives, particularly with the children. (p. 176)

Focus Groups

Focus groups are groups of individuals that are formed by a researcher and then led in group discussion of a topic. The researcher asks specific questions and guides the discussion to ensure that group members address these questions, but the resulting information is qualitative and relatively unstructured. Unlike most other survey designs, focus groups do not involve representative samples; instead, a few individuals are recruited for the group who have the time to participate and who share key characteristics with the target population. Focus groups have their roots in the interviewing techniques developed in the 1930s by sociologists and psychologists who were dissatisfied with traditional surveys. Traditionally, in a questionnaire survey, subjects are directed to consider certain issues and particular response options in a predetermined order. The spontaneous exchange and development of ideas that characterize social life outside the survey situation are lost, as are, some social scientists fear, the prospects for validity.

Focus groups were used by the military in World War II to investigate morale and then were popularized by the great American sociologist Robert K. Merton and two collaborators, Marjorie Fiske and Patricia Kendall, in *The Focused Interview* (1956). But marketing researchers were the first to adopt focus groups as a widespread methodology. Marketing researchers use focus groups to investigate likely popular reactions to possible advertising themes and techniques. Their success has prompted other social scientists to use focus groups to evaluate social programs and to assess social needs (Krueger 1988).

Most focus groups involve seven to 10 people, a number that facilitates discussion by all in attendance. Although participants usually do not know one another, they are chosen so that they are relatively homogeneous, which tends to reduce their inhibitions in discussion. Of course, the characteristics of individuals that determine their inclusion are based on the researcher's conception of the target population for the study. Focus group leaders must begin the discussion by creating the expectation that all will participate and that the researcher will not favor any particular perspective or participant.

Focus groups are interviewed to collect qualitative data using open-ended questions posed by the researcher (or group leader). Thus, a focused discussion mimics the natural process of forming and expressing opinions and may give some sense of validity. The researcher may also want to conduct a more traditional survey, asking a representative sample of the target population to answer closed-ended questions, to weigh the validity of data obtained from the focus group. No formal procedure exists for determining the generalizability of focus group answers, but the careful researcher should conduct at least several focus groups on the same topic and check for consistency in the findings as a partial test of generalizability.

The study of mothers' perceptions of violence in schools by Kandakai et al. (1999) provides a good example of the effective use of focus groups in research. Recall from Chapter 1 that this research involved survey methodology and examined the reasons mothers most often gave for school violence. Before Kandakai et al. designed their questionnaire, however, they conducted focus groups with mothers to identify in a more detailed manner their perceptions of the causes of school violence. Specifically, four focus groups of six to eight mothers of junior high school students from both urban and suburban areas were conducted to ascertain mothers' most salient beliefs regarding school violence. Responses that were given at least three times during a focus group were then added to the final questionnaire. For example, if during the course of a focus group, at least three mothers mentioned that the lack of supervision in schools was an important factor related to school violence, then this reason was included as a response choice in the questionnaire.

As with other field research techniques, focus group methods share an emphasis on discovering unanticipated findings and exploring hidden meanings. Although they do not provide a means for developing reliable, generalizable results (the traditional strong suits of survey research), focus groups can be an indispensable aid for developing hypotheses and survey questions, for investigating the meaning of survey results, and for quickly identifying the range of opinion about an issue.

Combining Focus Groups With Official Records: An Analysis of Police Searches

Racial profiling has generally been defined as the use of race as a key factor in deciding whether to make a traffic stop (Williams and Stahl 2008). As a response to lawsuits alleging racial profiling, many state and local law enforcement agencies have been mandated or have volunteered to collect traffic stop data to monitor the behavior of officers to determine the extent of such profiling. However, to actually determine if racial minorities like African Americans are stopped for speeding more than whites, researchers would first have to determine the percentage of African American drivers relative to white who were actually driving along a given highway, and then the percent of these motorists who were actually speeding to get a true base rate of speeding per population group. This would entail many hours of monitoring a given highway during various times of day. While some researchers have actually collected these data, Williams and Stahl decided to examine whether race was a determining factor in the search process, not in the original police stop. The questions they asked were, "Who is being searched, and what are the results of these searches?" Using data collected in 24 local Kentucky law enforcement agencies along with two state agencies, they concluded that of the motorists pulled over on the interstate for compliance and courtesy stops, African American and Hispanic motorists were significantly more likely to be searched compared to white motorists. To test the second question, they examined whether there were differences in positive search results (e.g., finding contraband) across race/ethnic groups. Not surprisingly, based on other research, there was no statistical difference in the likelihood that white, African American, or Hispanic motorists who were searched had illegal material. In fact, although not significantly different, whites who were searched were more likely to be carrying contraband than either African Americans or Hispanics.

To better contextualize these quantitative findings, Williams and Stahl (2008) also conducted focus groups with police officers to determine their perceptions about a number of issues including whether traffic stops and searches were effective in preventing some of the problems in their communities. A purposive sample of 24 officers participated in five focus groups. After comparing the perceptions, attitudes, and experiences across groups and individual officers, several themes emerged. The first was that drugs and drinking and driving were major community problems regarding traffic stops. The second was that if you wanted to target a particular problem, you had to target a particular group: African Americans were perceived to be associated with crack cocaine, driving under the influence was perceived to be associated with Hispanic motorists, and methamphetamine was perceived to be associated with whites. Moreover, officers were confident that traffic stops helped deter the drug trade and improve the quality of life of their local communities. Williams and Stahl concluded that the officers shared a perception that they were community problem solvers who profile the problems and not a particular group. However, these qualitative data combined with the quantitative analysis of search data led the researchers to conclude, "If police want to be efficient and effective in their efforts to stop drugs, it seems that they need to disregard the 'profile' as our analysis has found that it is an ineffective tool for turning up illegal substances" (p. 238). This triangulation of methods, or mixed methods approach, was extremely helpful in placing the quantitative data within the perceptions shared by police officers.

Analyzing Qualitative Data

"I don't think most girls would go out there and kill somebody. It just depends on how crazy you are and how much you hate that person. But I don't really think, I don't think they would do it as much as the boys would do. I wouldn't. I wouldn't go out there and kill somebody just 'cause they wearin' that color. I wouldn't do that. I might beat 'em up or get me, I might get beat up. But I would never go out to that certain extent to kill 'em" (Miller 2000:36). This statement, along with other narratives about the reality of violence in gang life for female gang members, led Jody Miller to conclude that female gang members were less likely to resort to serious violence compared to their male counterparts. Narratives such as these often represent the type of data that are analyzed in qualitative data analysis. The first difference, then, between qualitative and quantitative data analysis is that the data to be analyzed are text, rather than numbers, at least when the analysis first begins.

Exhibit 9.9 outlines the different techniques that are shared by most approaches to qualitative data analysis:

1. Documentation of the data and the process of data collection

2. Organization or categorization of the data into concepts

3. Connection of the data to show how one concept may influence another

4. Corroboration or legitimization, by evaluating alternative explanations, disconfirming evidence, and searching for negative cases

5. Representing the account (reporting the findings)

Exhibit 9.9 **Flow Model of Qualitative Data Analysis Components**

Source: Huberman and Miles 1994:10, Figure 1.3.

The analysis of qualitative research notes begins in the field, at the time of observation, interviewing, or both, as the researcher identifies problems and concepts that appear likely to help in understanding the situation. Simply reading the notes or transcripts is an important step in the analytic process. Researchers should make frequent notes in the margins to identify important statements and to propose ways of coding the data: "husband/wife conflict," perhaps, or "tension reduction strategy."

An interim stage may consist of listing the concepts reflected in the notes and diagramming the relationships among concepts (Maxwell 1996). In a large project, weekly team meetings are an important part of this process. Miller (1999) described this process in her study of neighborhood police officers. Miller's research team met both to go over their field notes and to resolve points of confusion, as well as to dialogue with other skilled researchers who helped identify emerging concepts:

> The fieldwork team met weekly to talk about situations that were unclear and to troubleshoot any problems. We also made use of peer-debriefing techniques. Here, multiple colleagues, who were familiar with qualitative data analysis but not involved in our research, participated in preliminary analysis of our findings. (p. 233)

This process continues throughout the project and should assist in refining concepts during the report-writing phase, long after data collection has ceased. As you can imagine, there is often a huge amount of data to analyze, from field observations to interview transcripts and so on. What to do with all this material? Many field research projects slow to a halt when a novice researcher becomes overwhelmed by the quantity of information that has been collected. A 1-hour interview can generate 20 to 25 pages of single-spaced text (Kvale 1996). Analysis is less daunting, however, if the researcher maintains a disciplined transcription schedule.

The process of qualitative data analysis is described by some as involving as much "art" as science, as a "dance," in the words of Miller and Crabtree (1999b). In this artful way, analyzing text involves both inductive and deductive processes. The researcher generates concepts and linkages between them based on reading the text and also checks the text to see whether those concepts and interpretations are reflected. Qualitative data analysis is reflexive process that begins as data are being collected rather than after data collection has ceased (Stake 1995). Next to her field notes or interview transcripts, the qualitative analyst jots down ideas about the meaning of the text and how it might relate to other issues.

This process of reading through the data and interpreting them continues throughout the project. The analyst adjusts the data-collection process itself when it begins to appear that additional concepts need to be investigated or new relationships explored. This process is termed **progressive focusing** (Parlett and Hamilton 1976).

> **Progressive focusing** The process by which a qualitative analyst interacts with the data and gradually refines his or her focus.

Let's examine each of the stages of qualitative analysis in more detail.

Documentation

The first formal analytical step is **documentation**. The various contacts, interviews, written documents, and whatever it is that preserves a record of what happened all need to be saved and listed. Documentation is critical to qualitative research for several reasons: It is essential for keeping track of what will be a rapidly growing volume of notes, tapes, and documents; it provides a way of developing an outline for the analytic process; and it encourages ongoing conceptualizing and strategizing about the text.

> **Documentation** A list and/or copy of all contacts, interviews, and written documents that preserves a record of the project.

An excellent example of a documentation guide is provided by Tammy Anderson (2009), who conducted a large study of drug use and victimization in nightclub events (e.g., raves, hip-hop, and electronic dance music events) in Philadelphia. When she and her team entered an event for direct observation, they followed a guideline form, which cued the researcher to obtain information about all pertinent data points (see Exhibit 9.10).

Conceptualization, Coding, and Categorizing

Identifying and refining important concepts is a key part of the iterative process of qualitative research. Sometimes, conceptualizing begins with a simple observation that is interpreted directly, "pulled apart," and then put back together more meaningfully. Stake (1995) provides an example:

> When Adam ran a pushbroom into the feet of the children nearby, I jumped to conclusions about his interactions with other children: aggressive, teasing, arresting. Of course, just a few minutes earlier I had seen him block the children climbing the steps in a similar moment of smiling bombast. So I was aggregating, and testing my unrealized hypotheses about what kind of kid he was, not postponing my interpreting. . . . My disposition was to keep my eyes on him. (p. 74)

The focus in this conceptualization "on the fly" is to provide a detailed description of what was observed and a sense of why that was important.

More often, analytic insights are tested against new observations; the initial statement of problems and concepts is refined; the researcher then collects more data and interacts with the data again; and the process continues. Elijah Anderson (2003) recounts how his conceptualization of social stratification at Jelly's bar developed over a long period of time:

> I could see the social pyramid, how certain guys would group themselves and say in effect, "I'm here and you're there." I made sense of these crowds [initially] as the "respectables," the "non-respectables," and the "near-respectables." . . . Inside, such non-respectables might sit on the crates, but if a respectable came along and wanted to sit there, the lower status person would have to move. (pp. 18–19)

But this initial conceptualization changed with experience, as Anderson (2003) realized that the participants themselves used other terms to differentiate social status: "winehead," "hoodlum," and "regular" (p. 28). What did

Exhibit 9.10	Example of a Direct Observation Form for Nightclub Observation

1. Site:
2. Period of observation:
3. Type of event:
4. Description of clubber demographics:
5. Description of conversations with clubbers and staff:
6. Description of response to ethnographer's presence, conversations:

Social organization of event	Physical layout (chill areas, dance floor, dj box, exits, bars)	Utilization of area by clubbers	Clubbers' interactions within areas	Entertainment personnel
Social organization of event II	Staffing patterns	Roles and behaviors	Interaction with clubbers by security, managers, bartenders	Entertainment personnel
Club's cultural ethos	Vibe	Music	Norms	Identity markers or props
Outside support agencies	Public safety	Law enforcement	Medical personnel	
Behaviors at event	Type	Frequency	Impact	
Clubbers' typologies	Dress and props	Status indicators	Clubbing motives	
Drug or alcohol consumption	Clubbers	Staff	Consequences	
Victimization	Observed	Rumored	Victim or offender	Consequences (e.g., clubber and staff reaction)
Personal reflections				

Source: Anderson, T. 2009.

they mean by these terms? "The 'regulars' basically valued 'decency.' They associated decency with conventionality but also with 'working for a living,' or having a 'visible means of support'" (p. 29). In this way, Anderson progressively refined his concept as he gained experience in the setting.

Miller (2000) provides another excellent illustration of this iterative process of conceptualization in her study of girls in gangs:

I paid close attention to and took seriously respondents' reactions to themes raised in interviews, particularly instances in which they "talked back" by labeling a topic irrelevant, pointing out what they saw as misinterpretations on my part, or offering corrections. In my research, the women talked back the most in response to my efforts to get them to articulate how gender inequality shaped their experiences in the gang. Despite stories they told to the contrary, many maintained a strong belief in their equality within the gang. Consequently, I developed an entire theoretical discussion around the contradictory operation of gender within the subject. As the research progressed, I also took emerging themes back to respondents in subsequent interviews to see if they felt I had gotten it right. (p. 30)

The process described in this quote illustrates the reflexive nature of qualitative data collection and analysis. In qualitative research, the collection of data and their analysis are not typically separate activities. This excerpt shows how the researcher first was alerted to a concept by observations in the field and then refined her understanding of this concept by investigating its meaning. By observing the concept's frequency of use, she came to realize its importance.

Examining Relationships and Displaying Data

Examining relationships is the centerpiece of the analytic process, because it allows the researcher to move from simple description of the people and settings to explanations of why things happened as they did with those people in that setting. The process of examining relationships can be captured in a **matrix** that shows how different concepts are connected, or perhaps what causes are linked with what effects.

> **Matrix** A form that systematically records particular features of multiple cases or instances and how they are related.

Exhibit 9.11 provides an excellent example of a causal model developed by Baskin and Sommers (1998) to explain the desistance process for the sample of violent female offenders they interviewed in the state of New York. They described the process for the women who made it out of their lives of crime as follows:

> Desistance is a process as complex and lengthy as the process of initial involvement. It was interesting to find that some of the key concepts in initiation of deviance—social bonding, differential association, deterrence, age—were equally important in the process of desistance. We see the aging offender take the threat of punishment seriously, reestablish links with conventional society and sever associations with subcultural street elements. We found, too, that the decision to give up crime was triggered by a shock of some sort that was followed by a period of crisis. They arrived at a point at which the deviant way of life seemed senseless. (p. 139)

Authenticating Conclusions

No set standards exist for evaluating the validity or "authenticity" of conclusions in a qualitative study, but the need to consider carefully the evidence and methods on which conclusions are based is just as great as with other types of research. Individual items of information can be assessed in terms of at least three criteria (Becker 1958):

- *How credible was the informant?* Were statements made by someone with whom the researcher had a relationship of trust or by someone the researcher had just met? Did the informant have reason to lie? If the statements do not seem to be trustworthy as indicators of actual events, can they at least be used to help understand the informant's perspective?

- *Were statements made in response to the researcher's questions, or were they spontaneous?* Spontaneous statements are more likely to indicate what would have been said had the researcher not been present.

- *How does the presence or absence of the researcher or the researcher's informant influence the actions and statements of other group members?* Reactivity to being observed can never be ruled out as a possible explanation for some directly observed social phenomenon. However, if the researcher carefully compares what the informant says goes on when the researcher is not present, what the researcher observes directly, and what other group members say about their normal practices, the extent of reactivity can be assessed to some extent.

> **Tacit knowledge** In field research, a credible sense of understanding of social processes that reflects the researcher's awareness of participants' actions as well as their words, and of what they fail to state, feel deeply, and take for granted.

A qualitative researcher's conclusions should also be assessed by their ability to provide a credible explanation for some aspect of social life. That explanation should capture group members' **tacit knowledge** of the social processes that were observed, not just their verbal statements about these

Exhibit 9.11	The Desistance Process for Violent Female Offenders

Stage 1: Problems Associated With Criminal Participation

Socially Disjunctive Experiences	*Delayed Deterrence*
Hitting rock bottom	Increased probability of punishment
Fear of death	Increased difficulty in "doing time"
Tiredness	Increased severity of sanctions
Illness	Increasing fear

Assessment

Reappraisal of life and goals
Psychic change

Decision

Decision to quit or initial attempts at desistance
Continuing possibility of criminal participation

Stage 2: Restructuring of Self

Public pronouncement of decision to end criminal participation
Claim to a new identity

Stage 3: Maintenance of the Decision to Stop

Ability to successfully renegotiate identity
Support of significant others
Integration into new social networks
Ties to conventional roles
Stabilization of new social identity

Source: From *Casualties of Community Disorder: Women's Careers in Violent Crime* by Deborah R. Baskin and Ira B. Sommers. Copyright © 1998. Reprinted by permission of Westview Press, a member of Perseus Books Group.

processes. Tacit knowledge, "the largely unarticulated, contextual understanding that is often manifested in nods, silences, humor, and naughty nuances " is reflected in participants' actions as well as their words and in what they fail to state but nonetheless feel deeply and even take for granted (Altheide and Johnson 1994:492–93). These features are evident in Whyte's (1955) analysis of Cornerville social patterns:

> The corner-gang structure arises out of the habitual association of the members over a long period of time. The nuclei of most gangs can be traced back to early boyhood. . . . Home plays a very small role in the group activities of the corner boy. . . . The life of the corner boy proceeds along regular and narrowly circumscribed channels. . . . Out of [social interaction within the group] arises a system of mutual obligations which is fundamental to group cohesion. . . . The code of the corner boy requires him to help his friends when he can and to refrain from doing anything to harm them. When life in the group runs smoothly, the obligations binding members to one another are not explicitly recognized. (pp. 255–57)

Comparing conclusions from a qualitative research project to those obtained by other researchers conducting similar projects can also increase confidence in their authenticity.

Reflexivity

Confidence in the conclusions from a field research study is also strengthened by an honest and informative account about how the researcher interacted with subjects in the field, what problems he or she encountered, and how these problems were or were not resolved. Such a "natural history" of the development of the evidence, sometimes termed **reflexivity**, enables others to evaluate the findings. Such an account is important primarily because of the evolving nature of field research.

> **Reflexivity** An accounting by a qualitative researcher that describes the natural history of the development of evidence; this enables others to more adequately evaluate the findings.

Qualitative data analysts, more often than quantitative researchers, display real sensitivity to how a social situation or process is interpreted from a particular background and set of values and not simply based on the situation itself (Altheide and Johnson 1994). Researchers are only human, after all, and must rely on their own senses to process information through their own minds. By reporting how and why they think they did what they did, they can help others determine whether, or how, the researchers' perspectives influenced their conclusions.

Anderson's (2003) memoir about the Jelly's bar research illustrates the type of "tracks" that an ethnographer makes as well as how he can describe those tracks. Anderson acknowledges that his tracks began as a child:

> While growing up in the segregated black community of South Bend, from an early age, I was curious about the goings on in the neighborhood, but particularly streets, and more particularly, the corner taverns that my uncles and my dad would go to hang out and drink in. . . . Hence, my selection of Jelly's as a field setting was a matter of my background, intuition, reason, and with a little bit of luck. (pp. 1–2)

🔲 Alternatives in Qualitative Data Analysis

The qualitative data analyst can choose from many interesting alternative approaches. Of course, the research question under investigation should shape the selection of an analytic approach, but the researcher's preferences and experiences will inevitably steer the research method selection. The alternative approaches we present here (ethnography, ethnomethodology, qualitative comparative analysis, narrative analysis, conversation analysis, case-oriented understanding, and grounded theory) give you a good sense of the different possibilities (Patton 2002).

Ethnography

Ethnography is the study of a culture or cultures that a group of people share (Van Maanen 1995). As a method, it usually is meant to refer to the process of participant observation by a single investigator who immerses himself or herself in the group for a long period of time (often 1 or more

> **Etnography** The study of a culture or cultures that some group of people shares, using participant observation over an extended period of time.

years). Ethnographic research can also be called "naturalistic," because it seeks to describe and understand the natural social world as it really is, in all its richness and detail. But there are no particular methodological techniques associated with ethnography, other than just "being there." The analytic process relies on the thoroughness and insight of the researcher to "tell it like it is" in the setting, as he or she experienced it.

Code of the Street, Anderson's (1999) study of Philadelphia's inner city, captures the flavor of this approach:

> My primary aim in this work is to render ethnographically the social and cultural dynamics of the interpersonal violence that is currently undermining the quality of life of too many urban neighborhoods. . . . How do the people of the setting perceive their situation? What assumptions do they bring to their decision making? (pp. 10–11)

The methods of investigation are described in the book's preface: participant observation, including direct observation and in-depth interviews; impressionistic materials drawn from various social settings around the city; and interviews with a wide variety of people. Like most traditional ethnographers, Anderson (1999) describes his concern with being "as objective as possible" and using his training as other ethnographers do "to look for and to recognize underlying assumptions, their own and those of their subjects, and to try to override the former and uncover the latter" (p. 11).

From analysis of the data obtained in these ways, a rich description emerges of life in the inner city. Although we often do not "hear" the residents speak, we feel the community's pain in Anderson's (1999) description of "the aftermath of death":

> When a young life is cut down, almost everyone goes into mourning. The first thing that happens is that a crowd gathers about the site of the shooting or the incident. The police then arrive, drawing more of a crowd. Since such a death often occurs close to the victim's house, his mother or his close relatives and friends may be on the scene of the killing. When they arrive, the women and girls often wail and moan, crying out their grief for all to hear, while the young men simply look on, in studied silence. . . . Soon the ambulance arrives. (p. 138)

Anderson (1999) uses these descriptions as a foundation on which he develops the key concepts in his analysis, such as "code of the street":

> The "code of the street" is not the goal or product of any individual's action but is the fabric of everyday life, a vivid and pressing milieu within which all local residents must shape their personal routines, income strategies, and orientations to schooling, as well as their mating, parenting, and neighbor relations. (p. 326)

Anderson's (2003) report on his Jelly's bar study illustrates how an ethnographic analysis deepened as he became more socially integrated into the Jelly's bar group. He thus became more successful at "blending the local knowledge one has learned with what we already know sociologically about such settings" (p. 39):

> I engaged the denizens of the corner and wrote detailed field notes about my experiences, and from time to time looked for patterns and relationships in my notes. In this way, an understanding of the setting came to me in time, especially as I participated more fully in the life of the corner and wrote my field notes about my experiences; as my notes accumulated, and as I reviewed them occasionally and supplemented them with conceptual memos to myself, their meanings became more clear, while even more questions emerged. (p. 15)

This rich ethnographic tradition is being abandoned by some qualitative data analysts, however. Many have become skeptical of the ability of social scientists to perceive the social world in a way that is not distorted by their own subjective biases or to receive impressions from the actors in that social world that are not altered by the fact of being studied (Van Maanen 2002). As a result, both specific techniques and alternative approaches to qualitative data analysis have proliferated. The next sections introduce several of these alternative approaches.

Ethnomethodology

Ethnomethodology focuses on the way that participants construct the social world in which they live, how they "create reality," rather than on describing the social world itself. In fact, ethnomethodologists do not necessarily believe that we can find an objective reality; it is the way that participants come to create and sustain a sense of "reality" that is of interest. In the words of Gubrium and Holstein (1997), in ethnomethodology, as compared to the naturalistic orientation of ethnography,

---

Ethnomethodology A qualitative research method focused on the way that participants in a social setting create and sustain a sense of reality.

The focus shifts from the scenic features of everyday life onto the ways through which the world comes to be experienced as real, concrete, factual, and "out there." An interest in members' methods of constituting their world supersedes the naturalistic project of describing members' worlds as they know them. (p. 41)

Unlike the ethnographic analyst, who seeks to describe the social world as the participants see it, the ethnomethodological analyst seeks to maintain some distance from that world. The ethnomethodologist views a "code" of conduct like that described by Anderson (2003) not as a description of a real normative force that constrains social action but as the way that people in the setting create a sense of order and social structure (Gubrium and Holstein 1997). The ethnomethodologist focuses on how reality is constructed, not on what it *is*.

Qualitative Comparative Analysis

In previous chapters, we discussed many studies that have attempted to explain violent crime. Another novel approach to the study of violence, specifically of homicide, was recently undertaken by Miethe, Regoeczi, and Drass (2004). In their book *Rethinking Homicide*, instead of focusing on the victim or the offender, they analyzed the homicide situation as the unit of analysis, exploring the structure and process underlying the lethal outcome. They state, "Homicide situations are defined by the nexus of offender, victim, and offense elements in time and space. It is the combination of these elements, not their operation in isolation, which provides the context for lethal violence" (p. xvii).

To analyze the homicide narratives from cases from four large cities in the United States, Miethe et al. (2004) used **qualitative comparative analysis (QCA).** They describe why QCA was the most appropriate methodology for their study:

> *Qualitative comparative analysis (QCA)* A systematic type of qualitative analysis that identifies the combination of factors that had to be present across multiple cases to produce a particular outcome.

As an analytical method for case comparisons, QCA considers cases holistically, as complex configurations of attributes measured by a set of variables. It also assumes that events or outcomes are produced by variables acting together in combination. Under this specification, the effect of any particular variable may be different from one case to another, depending upon the values of other attributes of a case. QCA places importance on the total context of elements to assess whether the same outcome can be produced by different combinations of variables. (p. 50)

It is beyond the scope of this book to detail the process of QCA here. Readers who want more information should seek other sources (Amenta and Poulsen 1994). QCA actually combines elements of quantitative and qualitative analysis and, as such, is a hybrid of sorts. For example, similar to a statistical analysis, QCA requires the specification of a model relating a set of independent variables to an outcome variable. But it examines the data holistically by developing typologies across a complex arrangement of cases and variables.

After their QCA analysis of over 400,000 homicides, Miethe et al. (2004) concluded that most homicides occur in situational contexts that have changed little over the past three decades. They found expressive homicides involving disputes and arguments to be more prevalent than instrumental homicides with males being the primary perpetrators of both, but particularly of instrumental homicides. Contrary to previous research that characterized confrontational homicides to involve public disputes among marginalized males, Miethe et al. also found that these "character contests" did most often involve males, but they also involved female offenders, occurred in both public and private settings, and were not restricted to minority group members. Like other research, they found that these conflicts often involved what many would call "trivial altercations" where alcohol was involved and where the victim often provoked the offender in some way (e.g., with an insult). This was particularly true for youth homicides wherein many contained elements of honor contests and issues of respect.

Narrative Analysis

> *Narrative analysis* A form of qualitative analysis in which the analyst focuses on how respondents impose order on the flow of experience in their lives and so make sense of events and actions in which they have participated.

Narrative "displays the goals and intentions of human actors; it makes individuals, cultures, societies, and historical epochs comprehensible as wholes" (Richardson 1995:200). **Narrative analysis** focuses on "the story itself" and seeks to preserve the integrity of personal biographies or a series of events that cannot adequately be understood in terms of their discrete elements (Riessman 2002:218). The coding for a narrative analysis is typically of the narratives as a whole, rather than of the different elements within them. The coding strategy revolves around reading the stories and classifying them into general patterns.

For example, Morrill et al. (2000) read through 254 conflict narratives written by the ninth graders they studied and found four different types of stories:

1. *Action tales*, in which the author represents himself or herself and others as acting within the parameters of taken-for-granted assumptions about what is expected for particular roles among peers.

2. *Expressive tales*, in which the author focuses on strong, negative emotional responses to someone who has wronged him or her.

3. *Moral tales*, in which the author recounts explicit norms that shaped his or her behavior in the story and influenced the behavior of others.

4. *Rational tales*, in which the author represents him- or herself as a rational decision maker navigating through the events of the story.

You can contrast that "action tale" with the following narrative, which Morrill et al. (2000) classifies as a "moral tale," in which the students explicitly tell about their moral reasoning, often referring to how normative commitments shape their decision making"

I . . . got into a fight because I wasn't allowed into the basketball game. I was being harassed by the captains that wouldn't pick me and also many of the players. The same type of things had happened almost every day where they called me bad words so I decided to teach the ring leader a lesson. I've never been in a fight before but I realized that sometimes you have to make a stand against the people that constantly hurt you, especially emotionally. I hit him in the face a couple of times and I got respect I finally deserved. (pp. 545–46)

How does such an analysis contribute to our understanding of youth violence? Morrill et al. (2000) first emphasize that their narratives "suggest that consciousness of conflict among youths—like that among adults—is not a singular entity, but comprises a rich and diverse range of perspectives" (p. 551). Theorizing inductively, Morrill et al. then attempt to explain why action tales were much more common than the more adult-oriented normative, rational, or emotionally expressive tales. Morrill et al.'s narrative analysis allowed an understanding of youth conflict to emerge from the youths' own stories while also informing our understanding of broader social theories and processes.

Conversation Analysis

Conversation analysis is a specific qualitative method for analyzing ordinary conversation. Unlike narrative analysis, it focuses on the sequence and details of conversational interaction, rather than on the "stories" that people are telling. Like ethnomethodology, from which it developed, conversation analysis focuses on how reality is constructed, rather than on what it *is*. Three premises guide conversation analysis (Gubrium and Holstein 2000):

> **Conversation analysis** Developed from ethnomethodology, this qualitative method focuses on the sequence and details of conversational interaction and focuses on how reality is constructed.

1. Interaction is sequentially organized, and talk can be analyzed in terms of the process of social interaction rather than in terms of motives or social status.

2. Talk, as a process of social interaction, is contextually oriented; it both is shaped by interaction and creates the social context of that interaction.

3. These processes are involved in all social interaction, so no interactive details are irrelevant to understanding it.

Consider these premises as you read the following dialogue between British researcher Ann Phoenix (2003) and a boy she called "Thomas" in her study of notions of masculinity, bullying, and academic performance among 11- to 14-year-old boys in 12 London schools.

Thomas: It's your attitude, but some people are bullied for no reason whatsoever just because other people are jealous of them. . . .

Q: How do they get bullied?

Thomas: There's a boy in our year called James, and he's really clever and he's basically got no friends, and that's really sad . . . He gets top marks in every test and everyone hates him. I mean, I like him. (p. 235)

Phoenix (2003) notes that here,

Thomas dealt with the dilemma that arose from attempting to present himself as both a boy and sympathetic to school achievement. He . . . distanced himself from . . . being one of those who bullies a boy just because they are jealous of his academic attainments . . . [and] constructed for himself the position of being kind and morally responsible. (p. 235)

Do you see how Thomas's presentation of himself reflected his interchange with the researcher, as she probed his orientation? Do you imagine that his talk would have been quite different if this conversation had been with other boys?

Case-Oriented Understanding

A **case-oriented understanding** attempts to understand a phenomenon from the standpoint of the participants. The case-oriented understanding method reflects an interpretive research philosophy that is not geared to identifying causes, but provides a different way to explain social phenomena. For example, Fischer and Wertz (2002) constructed such an explanation of the effect of being criminally victimized. They first recounted crime victims' stories and then identified common themes in these stories.

> **Case-oriented understanding** An understanding of social processes in a group, formal organization, community, or other collectivity that reflects accurately the standpoint of participants.

Their explanation began with a description of what they termed the process of "living routinely" before the crime: "He/she . . . feels that the defended against crime could never happen to him/her. I said, 'nah, you've got to be kidding.'"

In a second stage, "being disrupted," the victim copes with the discovered crime and fears worse outcomes: "You imagine the worst when it's happening. . . . I just kept thinking my baby's upstairs." In a later stage, "reintegrating," the victim begins to assimilate the violation by taking some protective action: "But I clean out my purse now since then and I leave very little of that kind of stuff in there."

Finally, when the victim is "going on," he or she reflects on the changes the crime produced: "I don't think it made me stronger. It made me smarter."

You can see how Fischer and Wertz (2002:288–90) constructed an explanation of the effect of crime on its victims through this analysis of the process of responding to the experience. This effort to "understand" what happened in these cases gives us a much better sense of why things happened as they did.

Grounded Theory

Theory development occurs continually in qualitative data analysis (Coffey and Atkinson 1996) but the goal of many qualitative researchers is to create **grounded theory**—that is, to build up inductively a systematic theory that is "grounded" in, or based on, the observations. The observations are summarized into conceptual categories, which are tested directly in the research setting with more observations. Over time, as the conceptual categories are refined and linked, a theory evolves (Glaser and Strauss 1967; Huberman and Miles 1994). Exhibit 9.12 illustrates this process.

As observation, interviewing, and reflection continue, researchers refine their definitions of problems and concepts and select indicators. They can then check the frequency and distribution of phenomena: How many people made a particular type of comment? How often did social interaction lead to arguments? Social system models may then be developed, which specify the relationships among different phenomena. These models are modified as researchers gain experience in the setting. For the final analysis, the researchers check their models carefully against their notes and make a concerted attempt to discover negative evidence that might suggest the model is incorrect.

Grounded theory Systematic theory developed inductively, based on observations that are summarized into conceptual categories, reevaluated in the research setting, and gradually refined and linked to other conceptual categories.

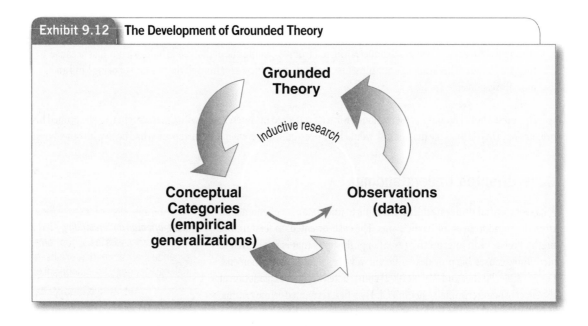

Exhibit 9.12   The Development of Grounded Theory

Computer-Assisted Qualitative Data Analysis

Computer-assisted qualitative data analysis Uses special computer software to assist qualitative analyses through creating, applying and refining categories; tracing linkages between concepts; and making comparisons between cases and events.

The analysis process can be enhanced in various ways by using a computer. Programs designed for qualitative data can speed up the analysis process, make it easier for researchers to experiment with different codes, test different hypotheses about relationships, and facilitate diagrams of emerging theories and preparation of research reports (Coffey and Atkinson 1996; Richards and Richards 1994). The steps involved in **computer-assisted qualitative data analysis** parallel those used traditionally to analyze such text as notes, documents, or interview transcripts: preparation, coding, analysis, and reporting. There are several of these programs available that analyze qualitative data including HyperRESEARCH, ATLAS.ti, and QSR NVivo. In this section, we will focus on QSR NVivo to illustrate the basic steps of qualitative data analysis.

This section is not meant to be a "primer" on learning NVivo. We simply want to show you the things that are possible when examining qualitative data with the aid of a computer program. Importantly, a computer software program like this does *not* think for you, but simply helps you work through narrative or pictorial data. Text preparation using this software program begins with typing or scanning text in a word processor or directly into NVivo's text editor. NVivo will create or import a rich text file, a WORD file, or even videos or other narrative material. The collective term for research material in NVivo is called "sources," and data that is imported directly into NVivo are called "internals." Data that cannot be imported but can still be used by creating summaries of their content are called "externals."

🔳 Case Study: Addicts' Narratives of Getting Clean

One of the textbook authors is currently involved in a research project examining the factors related to desistance for a sample of drug-involved offenders (Bachman et al. 2012). One phase of the project involved intensive interviews with over 300 individuals originally released from prison in the early 1990s. Interviews lasted between 1 ½ to 2 hours and were primarily open-ended and resembled conversations rather than formal questions and answers. The goal of the interviews was to uncover what Agnew (2006) refers to as "storylines" in understanding criminal offending. A storyline is a "temporally limited, interrelated set of events and conditions that increase the likelihood that individuals will engage in crime" (p. 121). As you can imagine, there were many hundreds of pages of transcripts! Exhibit 9.13 displays the basic NVivo program with the Internals in this screen shot listing the interview ID numbers from respondents.

The first step for our coding team was to categorize particular text segments within these interviews. This is the foundation of much qualitative analysis. You can assign a code to any segment of text. You can make up codes as you go through a document and also assign codes that you have already developed to text segments. You can also have the program "autocode" text by identifying a word or phrase that should always receive the same code. NVivo also lets you examine the coded text "in context," embedded in its place in the original document.

How did we begin? The coding process began with a list of initial categories developed from the existing literature on desistance including such key indicators as turning points, indicators of agency and readiness for change, the psychological indicators of discontent and fear. Before coding began, training sessions ensured that definitions of each category were understood along with the coding guidelines. Next, all researchers coded the same transcripts and discussed their coding strategies in group meetings. In these team meetings, the decision to add new categories was adjudicated and coding discrepancies were illuminated. The coding process continued with weekly "marathon" reliability meetings in which the same interview was coded by all four researchers. Not only did this increase inter-coder reliability, but these meetings also were forums for the discussion of emerging categories and opportunities to clarify coding strategies for ambiguous narratives.

Codes in our scheme ranged from purely descriptive (e.g., narrative describing first arrest or first incarceration) to more interpretive concepts such as reflections of whether respondents ever perceived themselves as addicts, when they wanted to get clean, etc. All themes that emerged from the interview transcripts were coded; this resulted in over 20 main categories (e.g., Discontent, Turning Points, Incarceration) with over 100 subcategories used in the coding scheme.

After all interviews were coded, NVivo allowed us to perform analyses by viewing all interview narratives that had been coded within a particular

Interviewer: So I know people say all the time "I just got tired." You used the word "crushed." What does that mean?

Respondent: I'll be honest with you, more than tire, I got scared. The last time I went back I said, "I can't do this anymore." I told myself over and over again "I can't do this anymore." I'm hurting myself, my loved ones, I was afraid that I'd be alone in life. And I didn't know whether I liked myself so I had to work hard to make myself better. . . . It scared the hell out of me. I finally realized I was my own worst enemy.

Exhibit 9.13   Screenshot of NVivo with Interview Narratives listed as "Internals"

---

domain. For example, some respondents that had gotten clean and stayed out of prison were motivated by fear; they often feared who they would become if they continued to use drugs or engage in crime. Indicators of this phenomenon included statements such as, "I was afraid of dying alone in prison without my family." Or "I knew that if I didn't get clean, I would never be able to get my family back and I would end up on the street alone." We coded all narratives reflecting these sentiments under the larger domain of "desistance" within a subdomain of "fear." One example of such a narrative was from a 54-year white male:

Another respondent, an African American woman, talked about almost dying from a heroin overdose:

> I overdosed and I was in a coma for 9 days. They told my mom that if I was gonna live, I was going to be a complete vegetable, there was a time to start making funeral arrangements. I had no brain waves or anything. It was a complete miracle. They had no explanation why I lived or why I woke up . . . when I woke up, I had to gain back all my muscle strength, I couldn't even walk . . . my mom had to take care of me. That's how I got clean. It scared the shit out of me.

The actual term for a code in NVivo is a "node," and you can have large domain "nodes" (e.g., drugs) with small subgroup nodes that fall within the larger domain. For example, we had a large domain node labelled "Drugs," and within this domain there were several subgroup nodes including "age at first use," "drug of choice," "relapse," and so on.

Once your data are coded, you can begin your analysis. In NVivo, you can examine all interview transcripts that were coded within particular nodes (coding categories). These analyses are called "Queries." For example, Exhibit 9.14 displays narratives that were coded under the node called "relapse." When a query is performed on a single node, it will display the source number (in this case, internals/1009 stands for interview number 1009) along with the text that was coded within that particular category (node). As can be seen, respondent 1009 talked about getting out of prison the first time and ending up with the same "people, places, and things" that led to his drug use, which eventually led to relapse.

NVivo will also allow you to examine a domain separately based on other variables. For example, we could examine how fear was expressed differently for males and females in the sample, or by race or age. When a multiple query like this is performed, called a "Matrix Coding Query," NVivo will first present a table displaying how many times each interview was coded within the grouping variable (usually a demographic indicator), and the category (nodes). Exhibit 9.15 displays one of these tables for a Matrix Coding Query grouped by Gender (1 = male, 2 = female) and by the nodes called "periods of abstinence" and "relapse." You can see that within the interviews, 78 of the male interviews had narratives coded for "periods of abstinence" along with 54 females, and so on. When you click directly on a cell within this table, the text narratives that were coded will appear so that narratives can be compared and contrasted.

As you can see, computer software programs like NVivo are an extremely useful way to organize and analyze qualitative data. In fact, when there is a great deal of data to be analyzed, a computer software program is not only a luxury, but a necessity!

Exhibit 9.14 | **Result of Query in NVivo for "Relapse"**

Exhibit 9.15	Results of a Matrix Query in NVivo for Gender and "Periods of Abstinence" and "Relapse"

Ethical Issues in Qualitative Research

Qualitative research can raise some complex ethical issues. No matter how hard the field researcher strives to study the social world naturally, leaving no traces, the very act of research itself imposes something unnatural on the situation. It is up to the researchers to identify and take responsibility for the consequences of their involvement. Six main ethical issues arise: voluntary participation, subject well-being, identity disclosure, confidentiality, appropriate boundaries, and researcher safety:

1. *Voluntary Participation:* Ensuring that subjects are participating in a study voluntarily is not often a problem with intensive interviewing and focus group research, but it is often a point of contention in participant observation studies. Few researchers or institutional review boards are willing to condone covert participation because it does not offer a way to ensure that participation by the subjects is voluntary. Even when the researcher's role is more open, interpreting the standard of voluntary participation still can be difficult. Practically, much field research would be impossible if the participant observer were required to request permission of everyone having some contact, no matter how minimal, with a group or setting being observed. And should the requirement of voluntary participation apply equally to every member of an organization being observed? What if the manager consents, the workers are ambivalent, and the union says no? Requiring everyone's consent would limit participant observation research only to settings without serious conflicts of interest.

The issue of voluntary participation is particularly important when interviewing or observing minors. At what age can individuals validly give their voluntary consent to participate in a project? It is customary for human subjects committees to want the consent of parents when their children are participating in research. This requirement poses a problem for research that may be investigating issues that parents or guardians may not want uncovered, such as abuse or neglect. In other instances, alerting parents or guardians about the nature of the study may compromise the confidentiality of the participants. For example, if Decker and Van Winkle (1996) had been forced to obtain parental approval for their gang member interviews, it would have violated the confidentiality they tried to provide to their respondents. To assure the human subjects committee that their participants understood their rights, Decker and Van Winkle obtained an advocate for each juvenile member of their sample. This advocate was responsible for making sure that the juveniles each understood their right to refuse or quit the interview at any time without penalty, and the confidential nature of the project. Only after these issues were carefully explained did the participant sign a consent form.

2. *Subject Well-Being:* Before beginning a project, every field researcher should carefully consider how to avoid harm to subjects. It is not possible to avoid every theoretical possibility of harm, nor is it possible to be sure that any project will not cause adverse consequences to any individual. Some of the Cornerville men read Whyte's (1943) book and felt discomfited by it (others found it enlightening). Some police accused Van Maanen (1982) of damaging their reputations with his studies. But such consequences could follow from any research, even from any public discourse. Direct harm to the reputations or feelings of particular individuals is what researchers must carefully avoid. They can do so in part by maintaining the confidentiality of research subjects. They must also avoid adversely affecting the course of events while engaged in a setting. Whyte (1943) found himself regretting having recommended that a particular politician be allowed to speak to a social club he was observing because the speech led to serious dissension in the club and strains between Whyte and some club members. These problems are rare in intensive interviewing and focus groups, but even there, researchers should try to identify negative feelings and help distressed subjects cope with their feelings through debriefing or referrals for professional help.

Jody Miller (2000) encountered a unique ethical dilemma while she was recruiting young women from a residential facility by paying them to refer other girls who were gang members to her research. These referral gratuities are common in snowball samples like this. Unfortunately, in this case, one young woman decided to cash in on the deal by initiating new young women into her gang. The ethical dilemma regarding "subject well-being" in this case was that the initiation ceremony for this particular gang involved recruits to the gang being "beaten into the gang." Miller decided to stop conducting research at this location and ultimately lost several interviews. She states,

> It was a difficult decision to make because I had struggled for so long to locate gang girls in Columbus [Missouri]. Ultimately, I believe it was the right thing to do. My presence had stirred up trouble for the agency, and I had an ethical obligation to back away, regardless of the cost to me. (p. 26)

3. *Identity Disclosure:* We already have considered the problems of identity disclosure, particularly in the case of covert participation. But how much disclosure about the study is necessary, and how hard should researchers try to make sure that their research purposes are understood? Less-educated subjects may not readily comprehend what a researcher is or be able to weigh the possible consequences of the research for themselves. Should researchers inform subjects if the study's interests and foci change while it is in progress? Current ethical standards require informed consent of research subjects; can this standard be met in any meaningful way if researchers do not fully disclose their identity? But isn't some degree of dissimulation a natural part of social life (Punch 1994)? Can a balance be struck between the disclosure of critical facts and a coherent research strategy?

4. *Confidentiality:* Field researchers normally use fictitious names for the characters in their reports, but doing so does not always guarantee confidentiality to their research subjects. Individuals in the setting

studied may be able to identify those whose actions are described and may thus become privy to some knowledge about their colleagues or neighbors that had formerly been kept from them. Researchers should thus make every effort to expunge possible identifying material from published information and to alter unimportant aspects of a description when necessary to prevent identity disclosure. In any case, no field research project should begin if some participants clearly will suffer serious harm by being identified in project publications.

Confidentiality is particularly important if the research is uncovering deviant or illegal behavior. In research such as Decker and Van Winkle's (1996), it was almost inevitable that their information about illegal activity would be revealed during the course of observing or interviewing. Because they had promised confidentiality to their interviewees, Decker and Van Winkle did not use specific information they gained about past crimes; they would only refer to this activity in an aggregate form to describe the activities of gang members in general. They state, "Had we violated this promise [of confidentiality], we would have placed the lives of several individuals (including the field-worker) in jeopardy." In addition, Decker and Van Winkle told their subjects that they did not want to know about information concerning future crimes, as this information would not be protected by their pledge of confidentiality.

5. *Appropriate Boundaries:* This is an ethical issue that cuts across several of the others, including identity disclosure, subject well-being, and voluntary participation. You probably are familiar with this issue in the context of guidelines for professional practice: Therapists are cautioned to maintain appropriate boundaries with patients; teachers must maintain appropriate boundaries with students. This is a special issue in qualitative research because it often involves lessening the boundary between the "researcher" and the research "subject." Qualitative researchers may seek to build rapport with those they plan to interview by expressing an interest in their concerns and conveying empathy for their situation. Is this just "faking friendship" for the purpose of the research? Jean Duncombe and Julie Jessop (2002) posed the dilemma clearly in a book chapter titled "'Doing Rapport' and the Ethics of 'Faking Friendship.'"

> With deeper rapport, interviewees become more likely to explore their more intimate experiences and emotions. Yet they also become more likely to discover and disclose experiences and feelings which, upon reflection, they would have preferred to keep private from others . . . or not to acknowledge even to themselves. (p. 112)

6. *Researcher Safety:* Research "in the field," whether researchers are studying gang life or anything else, should not begin until any potential risks to researcher safety have been evaluated. Qualitative methods may provide the only opportunity to learn about organized crime in Russian ports (Belousov et al. 2007), street crime in the Dominican Republic (Gill 2004), or the other studies examined in this chapter, but they should not be used if the risks to the researchers are unacceptably high. Safety needs to be considered at the time of designing the research, not as an afterthought on arriving in the research site. As Hannah Gill learned in the Dominican Republic, such advance planning can require more investigation than just reading the local newspapers: "Due to the community's marginality, most crimes, including murders, were never reported in newspapers, making it impossible to have known the insecurity of the field site ahead of time" (p. 2).

But being realistic about evaluating risk does not mean simply accepting misleading assumptions about unfamiliar situations or communities. For example, reports of a widespread breakdown in law and order in New Orleans were broadcast repeatedly after Hurricane Katrina, but researchers found that most nontraditional behavior in that period was actually "prosocial," rather than antisocial (Rodríguez, Trainor, and Quarantelli 2004):

> One group named itself the "Robin Hood Looters." The core of this group consisted of eleven friends who, after getting their own families out of the area, decided to remain at some high ground and, after the floodwaters rose, commandeered boats and started to rescue their neighbors. . . . For about two weeks they kept searching in the area. . . . They foraged for food and water from abandoned homes, and hence their group name.

Among the important norms that developed were that they were going to retrieve only survivors and not bodies and that group members would not carry weapons. The group also developed informal understandings with the police and the National Guard. (p. 91)

These ethical issues cannot be evaluated independently. The final decision to proceed must be made after weighing the relative benefits and risks to participants. Few qualitative research projects will be barred by consideration of these ethical issues, except for those involving covert participation. The more important concern for researchers is to identify the ethically troublesome aspects of their proposed research, resolve them before the project begins, and act on new ethical issues as they come up during the project. Combining methods is often the best strategy.

回 Conclusion

Qualitative research allows the careful investigator to obtain a richer and more intimate view of the social world than can be achieved with more structured methods. It is not hard to understand why so many qualitative studies have become classics in the literature. And the emphases in qualitative research on inductive reasoning and incremental understanding help stimulate and inform other research approaches. Exploratory research to chart the dimensions of previously unstudied social settings and intensive investigations of the subjective meanings that motivate individual action are particularly well served by the techniques of participant observation, intensive interviewing, and focus groups.

The very characteristics that make qualitative research techniques so appealing restrict their use to a limited set of research problems. It is not possible to draw representative samples for study using participant observation, and for this reason the generalizability of any particular field study's results cannot really be known. Only the accumulation of findings from numerous qualitative studies permits confident generalization, but here again the time and effort required to collect and analyze the data make it unlikely that many particular field research studies will be replicated.

Even if qualitative researchers made an effort to replicate key studies, their notion of developing and grounding explanations inductively in the observations made in a particular setting would hamper comparison of findings. Measurement reliability is thereby hindered, as are systematic tests for the validity of key indicators and formal tests for causal connections.

In the final analysis, qualitative research involves a mode of thinking and investigating different from that used in experimental and survey research. Qualitative research is inductive and idiographic; experiments and surveys tend to be conducted in a deductive, quantitative framework. Both approaches can help social scientists learn about the social world; the proficient researcher must be ready to use either. Qualitative data are often supplemented with many quantitative characteristics or activities. And as you have already seen, quantitative data are often enriched with written comments and observations, and focus groups have become a common tool of survey researchers seeking to develop their questionnaires. Thus, the distinction between qualitative and quantitative research techniques is not always clear-cut.

Key Terms

Case-oriented understanding 271
Conversation analysis 270
Complete observation 241

Computer-assisted qualitative data
analysis 272
Covert (complete) participation 244

Documentation 263
Ethnography 267
Ethnomethodology 268

Highlights

- Qualitative methods are most useful in exploring new issues, investigating hard-to-study groups, and determining the meaning people give to their lives and actions. In addition, most social research projects can be improved in some respects by taking advantage of qualitative techniques.

- Qualitative researchers tend to develop ideas inductively, try to understand the social context and sequential nature of attitudes and actions, and explore the subjective meanings that participants attach to events. They rely primarily on participant observation, intensive interviewing, and in recent years, focus groups.

- Participant observers may adopt one of several roles for a particular research project. Each role represents a different balance between observing and participating, which may or may not include public acknowledgment of the researcher's real identity. Many field researchers prefer a moderate role, participating as well as observing in a group but publicly acknowledging the researcher role. Such a role avoids the ethical issues posed by covert participation while still allowing the customary insights into the social world derived from directly participating in it. The role that the participant observer chooses should be based on an evaluation of the problems likely to arise from reactive effects, the ethical dilemmas of covert observation, and the consequences of identity disclosure in the particular setting.

- Field researchers must develop strategies for entering the field, developing and maintaining relations in the field, sampling, and recording and analyzing data. Sampling techniques commonly used in field research include theoretical sampling, purposive sampling, snowball sampling, quota sampling, and in special circumstances, random selection with the experience sampling method.

- Recording and analyzing notes is a crucial step in field research. Detailed notes should be recorded and analyzed daily to refine methods and to develop concepts, indicators, and models of the social system observed.

- Intensive interviews involve open-ended questions and follow-up probes, with specific question content and order varying from one interview to another. Intensive interviews can supplement participant observation data.

- Focus groups combine elements of participant observation and intensive interviewing. They can increase the validity of attitude measurement by revealing what people say when presenting their opinions in a group context.

- The four main ethical issues in field research concern voluntary participation, subject well-being, identity disclosure, and confidentiality.

Research in the News

Put to the Test

Concerned with high rates of adolescent substance abuse, hundreds of middle and high schools have begun randomly drug testing their students. The Supreme Court has ruled that the schools may conduct random drug tests among students who wish to participate in school-sponsored extracurricular activities such as sports, marching band, or a foreign language club. To examine community support and reactions to the random drug tests, many school districts perform focus group with parents and community members before and after the new programs begin.

Source: Roan, Shari. 2007. "Put to the Test." *The Los Angeles Times,* May 21:A15.

Exercises

1. Review the experiments and surveys described in previous chapters. Choose one and propose a field research design that would focus on the same research question but with participant observation techniques in a local setting. Propose the role that you would play in the setting, along the participant observation continuum, and explain why you would favor this role. Describe the stages of your field research study, including your plans for entering the field, developing and maintaining relationships, sampling, and recording and analyzing data. Then discuss what you would expect your study to add to the findings resulting from the study described in the book.

2. Explore a qualitative project using the software HyperRESEARCH (see Student Study Site) and your own data. Conduct a brief observational study in a public location on campus where students congregate. A cafeteria, a building lobby, or a lounge would be ideal. You can sit and observe, taking occasional notes unobtrusively, without violating any expectations of privacy. Observe for 30 minutes. Write up field notes, being sure to include a description of the setting and a commentary on your own behavior and your reactions to what you observed. Then load the demonstration copy of HyperRESEARCH, and make your own project.

3. Develop an interview guide that focuses on a research question addressed in one of the studies in this book. Using this guide, conduct an intensive interview with one person who is involved with the topic in some way. Take only brief notes during the interview, and then write as complete a record of the interviews as you can immediately afterward. Turn in an evaluation of your performance as an interviewer and note taker, together with your notes.

4. Read about focus groups in one of the references cited in this chapter and then devise a plan for using a focus group to explore and explain student perspectives about crime on campus. How would you recruit students for the group? What types of students would you try to include? How would you introduce the topic and the method to the group? What questions would you ask? What problems would you anticipate (e.g., discord between focus group members or digressions from the chosen topic)? How would you respond to these problems?

5. Read and summarize one of the qualitative studies discussed in this chapter or another classic study recommended by your instructor. Review and critique the study using the article review questions presented in Appendix B. What questions are answered by the study? What questions are raised for further investigation?

6. The April 1992 issue of the *Journal of Contemporary Ethnography* is devoted to a series of essays reevaluating Whyte's (1943) classic field study, *Street Corner Society*. A social scientist interviewed some of the people described in Whyte's book and concluded that the researcher had made methodological and ethical errors. Whyte and others offer able rejoinders and further commentary. Reading the entire issue of this journal will improve your appreciation of the issues that field researchers confront.

7. Find the Qualitative Research lesson in the interactive exercises on the Student Study Site (www.sagepub.com/bachmanprccj5e). Answer the questions in this lesson in order to review the types of ethical issues that can arise in the course of participant observation research.

Developing a Research Proposal

Add a qualitative component to your proposed study. You can choose to do this with a participant observation project or intensive interviewing. Pick the method that seems most likely to help answer the research question for the overall survey project.

1. For a participant observation component, propose an observational plan that would complement the overall survey project. Present in your proposal the following information about your plan: (a) Choose a site and justify its selection in terms of its likely value for the research, (b) choose a role along the participation-observation continuum and justify your choice, (c) describe access procedures and note any likely problems, (d) discuss how you will develop and maintain relations in the site, (e) review any sampling issues, and (f) present an overview of the way in which you will analyze the data you collect.

2. For an intensive interview component, propose a focus for the intensive interviews that you believe will add the most to findings from the survey project. Present in your proposal the following information about your plan: (a) Present and justify a method for selecting individuals to interview, (b) write out three introductory biographical questions and five "grand tour" questions for your interview schedule, (c) list at least six different probes you

may use, (d) present and justify at least two follow-up questions for one of your grand tour questions, and (e) explain what you expect this intensive interview component to add to your overall survey project.

3. Which qualitative data analysis alternative is most appropriate for the qualitative data you propose to collect for your project? Using this approach, develop a strategy for using the techniques to analyze your textual data.

STUDENT STUDY SITE

Log on to the Web-based student study site at **www.sagepub.com/bachmanprccj5e** for additional study tools including eFlashcards, Web quizzes, links to SAGE journal articles, podcasts, videos, data sets and codebooks, Web exercises, Web resources, and additional appendices.

Web Exercises

1. Check your library's online holdings to see if it subscribes to the online version of the *Annual Review of Sociology*. If it does, go to the *Annual Review of Sociology's* Web site by following the publication link at www.annualreviews.org/journal/soc. Search for articles that use field research as the primary method of gathering data on gangs or delinquency. Find at least three articles and report on the specific method of field research used in each.

2. Go to RTI International site at www.rti.org/ and conduct a search for "qualitative methods." Now choose three or four interesting research reports or articles to find out more about the topic. Explore the sites to find out what information they provide regarding field research, what kinds of projects are being done that

involve field research, and the purposes that specific field research methods are being used for.

3. Search the Web for information on focus groups (previous, upcoming, or ongoing) involving victims, offenders, fear of crime, crime prevention, or another criminological topic. List the Web sites you found, and write a paragraph about the purpose of each focus group and the sample involved. How might these focus groups be used to influence public policy?

4. *The Qualitative Report* is an online journal about qualitative research. Inspect the table of contents for a recent issue at www .nova.edu/ssss/QR/index.html. Read one of the articles and write a brief article review.

Ethics Exercises

1. Covert participation may be the only way for researchers to observe the inner workings of some criminal or other deviant groups, but this strategy is likely to result in the researcher witnessing, and perhaps being asked to participate in, illegal acts. Do you think that covert participation is ever ethical? If so, under what conditions? Can the standards of "no harm to subjects," "identity disclosure," and "voluntary" participation be maintained in covert research?

2. A *New York Times* reporter (Wines 2006) talked about the dilemma many reporters have: whether or not to provide monetary or other compensation like food or medical supplies to people they interview for a story. In journalism, paying for information is a "cardinal sin" because journalists are "indoctrinated with the notion that they are observers." They are trained to report on situations, but not to

influence a situation. This is what many scholars believe a researcher's role should be. Nevertheless, as we learned in this chapter, it is common in research to offer small gratuities for information and interviews. However, does paying for information unduly influence the truthfulness of the information being sought? Do you believe some people will say anything to earn money? What are your thoughts on paying for information? What if you were investigating the problems faced by families living below the poverty level and, during an interview, you noticed that the family refrigerator and cupboards were empty and the baby was crying from hunger? What is the ethical reaction? If you believe the most ethical response would be to provide food or money for food, is it fair that there is another family next door in the same condition that did not happen to be on your interview list? How should gratuities be handled? Write a paragraph on how gratuities should be handled.

3. Should any requirements be imposed on researchers who seek to study other cultures, to ensure that procedures are appropriate and interpretations are culturally sensitive? What practices would you suggest for cross-cultural researchers to ensure that ethical guidelines are followed? (Consider the wording of consent forms and the procedures for gaining voluntary cooperation.)

SPSS or Excel Exercises

The YOUTH.POR data set includes some questions on opinions regarding friends' attitudes toward delinquent acts and the extent to which getting caught for committing a crime would negatively affect the respondent's life.

1. Describe the opinions about friends' attitudes and personal misfortune based on the frequencies for these variables (V77; V79; V109; V119).

2. What explanation can you develop (inductively) for these attitudes? Do you believe that either friends' attitudes toward delinquent acts or getting caught for committing a crime would influence behavior? Explain.

3. Propose a participant observation, a focus group, or an intensive interview study to explore these attitudes further. Identify the sample for the study and describe how you would carry out your observations, focus groups, or interviews.

CHAPTER 10

Analyzing Content

Historical, Secondary, and Content Analysis and Crime Mapping

The research methods we have examined so far in this text have relied on researchers collecting the data or information themselves. Increasingly, however, those interested in criminological research questions are relying on data previously collected by other investigators (Riedel 2000). As we noted in Chapter 1, this is referred to as **secondary data analysis**. Secondary data analysis is simply the act of collecting or analyzing data that were originally collected by someone else at another time (Riedel 2000). Thus, if a researcher goes to a police department and personally compiles information from police reports to examine a research question, she is still engaging in secondary data analysis because the police records were originally collected prior to her own research.

Secondary data analysis Analysis of data collected by someone other than the researcher or the researcher's assistant.

Secondary data analysis has a long history. Since the latter part of the 17th century, people have been monitoring the state of their localities by examining rates of population, mortality, marriage, disease, climate, and crime. Adolphe Quételet, an ambitious Belgian mathematician, was one of the first to show that the annual number of murders reported in France from 1826 to 1831 was relatively constant and, further, that the proportion of murders committed with guns, swords, knives, stones, kicks and punches, and strangulation was also relatively constant. He concluded that although we may not know who will kill whom by what means, we do know, with a high degree of probability, that a certain number of murders of a certain type will happen every year in France (Menand 2001). This was one of the first attempts to apply the methods of science to social phenomena. You are also probably familiar with Émile Durkheim's ([1951] 1987) use of official statistics on suicide rates in different areas to examine the relationship between religion and suicide.

In this chapter, we will tell you about a number of data sets including surveys and official records that are publicly available for research purposes. Then we will examine several research methods that rely on secondary data, including historical events research, cross-cultural research, content analysis, and crime mapping. And finally, because using data originally gathered for other purposes poses unique concerns for a researcher, we will spend the latter part of the chapter highlighting these methodological issues.

Analyzing Secondary Data

In general, there are four major types of secondary data: surveys, official statistics, official records, and other historical documents. Although a data set can be obtained by an agreement between two or more researchers, many researchers obtain data through the Inter-University Consortium for Political and Social Research (ICPSR) (www.icpsr.umich.edu). Data stored at ICPSR primarily include surveys, official records, and official statistics. ICPSR stores data and information for nearly 5,000 sources and studies, including those conducted independently and those conducted by the U.S. government. Riedel (2000) has documented the majority of data sets that are available from ICPSR and that are appropriate for crime research, including the following:

Census enumerations: historical and contemporary population characteristics. The most well-known data sets within this category are the surveys conducted every decade by the Bureau of the Census. Linking information from this data set (e.g., neighborhood characteristics including such things as poverty and residential mobility) to crime data at the same level (e.g., census block, county) has provided researchers with a rich source of data to test theories of crime.

The National Archive of Criminal Justice Data (NACJD). The Bureau of Justice Statistics and National Institute of Justice cosponsored NACJD, which provides more than 600 criminal justice data collections to the public. A sample of these data sets includes the following:

- Capital Punishment in the United States
- Expenditure and Employment Data for the Criminal Justice System
- Gang Involvement in Rock Cocaine Trafficking in Los Angeles, 1984–1985
- Criminal Careers and Crime Control in Massachusetts

- Longitudinal Research Design, Phase I, 1940–1965
- Changing Patterns of Drug Use and Criminality Among Crack Cocaine Users in New York City: Criminal Histories and CJ Processing, 1983–1984, 1986
- The National Crime Victimization Survey, ongoing
- National Jail Census
- National Judicial Reporting Program
- National Survey of Jails
- Survey of Adults on Probation
- Survey of Inmates of Federal Correctional Facilities
- Survey of Inmates of Local Jails
- Survey of Inmates of State Correctional Facilities
- Federal Bureau of Investigation (FBI) Uniform Crime Reporting (UCR) Program data, including the Supplementary Homicide Reports (SHR)

Social indicators and behavior. There is a series of annual surveys under this heading including the General Social Survey, which has been conducted annually by the National Opinion Research Center since 1972. In addition, Monitoring the Future: A Continuing Study of the Lifestyles and Values of Youth is a survey of a nationally representative sample of high school seniors that asks them for many things including self-reports of drug and alcohol use and their attitudes toward a number of issues. The National Youth Survey Series (1976–1980 and 1983) is another survey available at ICPSR that examines factors related to delinquency.

▣ Case Study: Police Protection by Neighborhood

As you can see, the research possibilities are almost limitless with the wealth of data already made available to researchers interested in issues of criminology and criminal justice. Using Uniform Crime Reporting data on the number of police officers and civilians employed within specific jurisdictions, David Thacher (2011) recently examined whether the racial/ethnic distribution and its socioeconomic status influenced the degree to which a jurisdiction was "protected" by these resources. To answer his question, Thacher matched the UCR police data with U.S. Census data. He stated, "With these data on police strength and the composition of the population served by each agency, I am able to describe the distribution of policing by race and class in the same way that the educational literature has analyzed the distribution of educational resources" (Thacher 2011:283). To measure poverty, he created a measure called the Concentration Index (CI), which is actually a measure of income inequality.

Thacher (2011) found that when police strength was measured as the number of police employees per crime, it varied substantially between rich and poor areas (see Exhibit 10.1 for comparative results). For example, wealthier jurisdictions tended to have significantly more police employees per 100 index crimes compared to poorer areas. This finding runs counter to the contention that cities generally allocate police resources equitably. Thacher (2011) states, "police protection has become more concentrated in the most advantaged communities—those with the highest per-capita incomes and the largest share of white residents" (p. 286). What has changed, Thacher believes, is the crime rates. For example, when police protection per capita (number of individuals in jurisdiction) are examined, police

Exhibit 10.1	Police Protection by Race and Class Composition of Jurisdiction, 2000

	Average # of Police Employees Per		
	1,000 Residents	100 Index crimes	100 Violent Crimes
Richest jurisdictions comprising			
5% of U.S. Population	2.78	21.48	418.04
Poorest jurisdictions comprising			
5% of U.S. Population	2.69	11.967	120.01

Source: Adapted from Thacher, David. The Distribution of Police Protection. *Journal of Quantitative Criminology, 27*(3):275–298, Table 1. September 2011.

protection has not changed much since 1970 across jurisdictions. However, because crime became more concentrated in the poorest communities during that time, police resources per crime have become less egalitarian. What does this mean in the real world? "The result is a growing workload disparity between rich and poor jurisdictions. In rich jurisdictions, each police officer has responsibility for fewer and fewer crimes over time, while in poor jurisdictions this part of the police workload has either remained constant or grown" (Thacher 2011:289).

🔲 Historical Events Research

The central insight behind considering the causes and impacts of historical events is that we can improve our understanding of social processes when we make comparisons to other times and places. Although there are no rules for determining how far in the past the focus of research must be in order for it to be considered historical, in practice, research tends to be considered historical when it focuses on a period prior to the experience of most of those conducting research (Abbott 1994).

Historical research in the social sciences differs from traditional historical research because researchers seek to develop general theoretical explanations of historical events and processes instead of just detailed, "fact-centered" descriptions of them (Monkkonen 1994:8). Social scientists do not ignore the details of historical events; rather, they "unravel" unique events to identify general patterns (Abrams 1982:200). However, as in traditional history, the focus on the past presents special methodological challenges. Documents and other evidence may have been lost or damaged, and what evidence there is may represent a sample biased toward those who were more newsworthy figures or who were more prone to writing. The feelings of individuals involved in past events may be hard, if not impossible, to reconstruct. Nonetheless, in many situations the historical record may support very systematic research on what occurred in the past.

When research on past events does not follow processes for a long period of time, when it is basically cross-sectional, it is usually referred to as **historical events research**. Investigations of past events may be motivated by the belief that they had a critical impact on subsequent developments or because they provide opportunities for testing the implications of a general theory (Kohn 1987).

Historical events research Research in which social events of only one time period in the past are studied.

Event-structure analysis A systematic method of developing a causal diagram showing the structure of action underlying some chronology of events; the end result is an idiographic causal explanation.

One technique useful in historical events research is called **event-structure analysis**. Event-structure analysis is a qualitative approach that relies on a systematic coding of key events or national characteristics to identify the underlying structure of action in a chronology of events. The codes are then used to construct event sequences, make comparisons between cases, and develop an ideographic causal explanation for a key event. An event-structure analysis consists of the following steps:

1. Classifying historical information into discrete events

2. Ordering events into a temporal sequence

3. Identifying prior steps that are prerequisites for subsequent events

4. Representing connections between events in a diagram

5. Eliminating from the diagram connections that are not necessary to explain the focal event

Case Study: A Lynching in Mississippi

Larry Griffin (1993) used event-structure analysis to explain a lynching in the 1930s in Mississippi. According to published accounts and legal records, the lynching occurred after David Harris, an African American who sold moonshine from his home, was accused of killing a white tenant farmer. After the killing was reported, the local deputy was called and a citizen search party was formed. The deputy did not intervene as the search party trailed Harris and then captured and killed him. Meanwhile, Harris's friends killed another African American who had revealed Harris's hiding place. This series of events is outlined in Exhibit 10.2.

Which among the numerous events occurring between the time that the tenant farmer confronted Harris and the time that the mob killed Harris had a causal influence on the outcome? To identify these ideographic causal lings, Griffin identified plausible counterfactual possibilities—events that might have occurred but did not—and considered whether the outcome might have been changed if a counterfactual had occurred instead of a particular event. He concluded:

> If, contrary to what actually happened, the deputy had attempted to stop the mob, might the lynching have been averted? . . . Given what happened in comparable cases and the Bolivar County deputy's clear knowledge of the existence of the mob and of its early activities, his forceful intervention to prevent the lynching thus appears an objective possibility. (Griffin 1993:1112)

Case Study: The Martinsville Seven

Another exemplary model of more general historical events research is the book *The Martinsville Seven: Race, Rape, and Capital Punishment* by Eric Rise (1995). The book examines the trial of seven young black men who were accused of violently raping a white woman in Martinsville, Virginia in 1949. These men became known as the "Martinsville Seven." Within 2 days of the allegation, state and local police had arrested and obtained confessions from each of the suspects. In a rapid succession of brief trials held over the course of 11 days, six separate juries convicted the

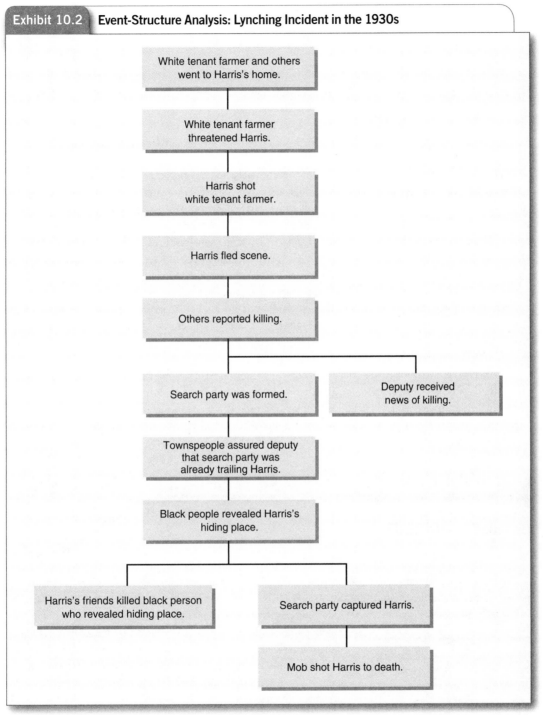

Exhibit 10.2 Event-Structure Analysis: Lynching Incident in the 1930s

White tenant farmer and others went to Harris's home.

White tenant farmer threatened Harris.

Harris shot white tenant farmer.

Harris fled scene.

Others reported killing.

Search party was formed.

Deputy received news of killing.

Townspeople assured deputy that search party was already trailing Harris.

Black people revealed Harris's hiding place.

Harris's friends killed black person who revealed hiding place.

Search party captured Harris.

Mob shot Harris to death.

Source: Adapted from Larry J. Griffin "Narrative, Event-Structure Analysis, and Causal Interpretation in Historical Sociology" *American Journal of Sociology*, Vol. 98, No. 5, March 1993. University Chicago Press. Pp. 1094–1133.

defendants of rape and sentenced each to death. During the first week of February 1951, each of the "Martinsville Seven" died in the electric chair of the Virginia State Penitentiary. At a time when African Americans were beginning to assert their civil rights vigorously, the executions provided a stark reminder of the harsh treatment reserved for African Americans who violated southern racial codes.

In his analysis of the case, Rise (1995) examined a wealth of historical documents:

1. Legal papers that the lawyers involved in the case made available

2. Official transcripts of the cases

3. Briefs and petitions to the Virginia State Supreme Court

4. Related case law from the Supreme Court

5. Annual reports from the Virginia Department of Corrections 1946–1951 and newspaper accounts

The large number of defendants, the rapid pace of the trials, and the specter of multiple executions attracted national media attention and brought sentencing disparity arguments to the foreground of contemporary race relations. Rise's (1995) analysis of historical documents and correspondence revealed extreme conflict between two organizations while they were both vying for top billing in representing the Martinsville Seven, The National Association for the Advancement of Colored People (NAACP) and the Civil Rights Congress (CRC). The inherent goal of the CRC was not so much to seek justice for the seven men but to "reveal the capitalist conspiracy of racial and economic oppression in America. The divergent manner in which each organization proposed to handle the cases highlighted fundamental disagreements over strategy, ingrained suspicions of motive, and fierce competition for membership" (p. 68). Because cooperation was never established through the appeals process, both organizations continued to pursue the cases in a manner consistent with their own ideological and institutional interests. The result, of course, was deadly. As Rise notes, "Never before had a state executed so many men for a single rape incident, nor had a lynching of that magnitude for men accused of rape ever been reported" (p. 3).

Rise's (1995) analysis revealed the critical effect that this historical event had on subsequent developments. The revelation that capital sentencing disparities existed between white and African American defendants during the appeals process of the Martinsville Seven was significant for modern jurisprudence. Specifically, the Martinsville case was the first time courtroom attorneys presented equal protection arguments that challenged the racial disparity of death sentences for rape. Subsequent to the Martinsville case, civil rights lawyers have not only used the equal protection strategy in the pursuit of equal justice for African Americans, but they also have used it as evidence for the abolition of the death penalty.

Comparative Methods

The limitations of examining data from a single location have encouraged many social scientists to turn to comparisons among many geographical entities. As noted in the 2001 American Academy of Criminal Justice Sciences' Presidential Address by Richard Bennett (2004), **comparative research** in criminal justice and criminology took on a new importance after September 11. Of course, the limitations of examining data from a single location had encouraged many social scientists to turn to comparisons among many geographical entities, and the increase in comparative research has burgeoned recently. Bennett described two types of comparative research:

> **Comparative research** Research comparing data from more than one time period and/or more than one nation.

1. Research that seeks to understand the structure, nature, or scope of a nation's or nations' criminal justice systems or rates of crime is descriptive comparative research.

2. Research that seeks to understand how national systems work and the factors related to their operations is analytic comparative research.

There is also variability in the scope of comparative research. Studies can analyze single nations, make a comparison across several nations, or conduct **transnational research**, which generally explores how cultures and nations deal with crime that transcends their borders. Investigating terrorism is one emerging form of transnational research. Bennett (2004) notes, "One of the outcomes of the terrorist attacks in 2001 was a shocking awareness that terrorism is international and inextricably tied to trans-national criminal activity. . . . We need to understand how criminal and terrorist organizations fund themselves and exploit our inability to link and analyze criminal activity that transcends national borders" (p. 8). Although comparative methods are often associated with cross-national comparisons, research examining smaller aggregates such as states

> **Descriptive comparative research** Research that seeks to understand the structure, nature, or scope of a nation's or nations' criminal justice systems or rates of crime.
>
> **Analytic comparative research** Research that seeks to understand how national systems work and the factors related to their operations.
>
> **Transnational research** Explores how cultures and nations deal with crime that transcends their borders.

and cities can also be subsumed under the comparative research umbrella. Comparative research methods allow for a broader vision about social relations than is possible with cross-sectional research limited to one location.

🖻 Case Study: Homicide Across Nations

One of the first large comparative research projects undertaken in criminology was the development of the Comparative Crime Data File (CCDF), which was created by Archer and Gartner (1984). Archer and Gartner articulated the need for comparative research in the field succinctly:

> The need for cross-national comparisons seems particularly acute for research on crime and violence since national differences on these phenomena are of a remarkable magnitude. In some societies, homicide is an hourly, highly visible, and therefore somewhat unexceptional cause of death. In other nations, homicides are so infrequent that, when they do occur, they receive national attention and lasting notoriety. (p. 4)

The CCDF continues to be updated but originally contained crime and violence data from 110 nations and 44 major international cities covering the period from approximately 1900 to 1970. In their work, Archer and Gartner (1984) examined many research questions using the CCDF. One of these questions is related to the idea that war might increase the level of postwar homicide within nations involved in wars. There are several theoretical models that speculate about the possible effects of wars on postwar violence within a nation. For example, the social solidarity model posits a wartime *decrease* in violence because of the increase in social solidarity among a nation's citizenry. At a more individual level, the violent veteran model predicts that postwar levels of violence within a nation will *increase* as a result of the violent acts of returning war veterans. At a societal level, the legitimization of violence model postu-lates that during a war, a society reverses its prohibitions against killing and instead honors acts of violence that would be regarded as murderous in peacetime. This social approval or legitimation of violence, this model predicts, may produce a lasting reduction of inhibitions against taking human life, even after the war, thereby increasing levels of violence within nations.

To examine the effects of war on postwar violence, Archer and Gartner (1984) compared national rates of homicide before and after many wars, both small and large, including the two world wars. Exhibit 10.3 displays the increase or decrease of homicide rates in combatant nations and a sample of control nations that were not involved in World War I and World War II. The researchers also controlled for a number of other factors related to war, including the number of combat deaths in war, whether nations were victorious or defeated, and whether the nation's postwar eco-nomics were improved or worsened, and for several types of homicide offenses committed by both men and women.

| Exhibit 10.3 | Homicide Rate Changes in Combatant and Control Nations After World War I and World War II |

Combatant Nations

Rates Decreased	Rates Remained Unchanged	Rates Increased
Australia (I)	England (I)	Belgium
Canada (I)	France (I)	Bulgaria
Hungary (I)	S. Africa (I)	Germany
Finland (II)	Canada (II)	Italy (I)
N. Ireland (II)		Japan (I)
U.S. (II)		Portugal (I)
		Scotland (I)
		U.S. (I)
		Australia (II)
		Denmark (II)
		England (II)
		France (II)
		Italy (II)
		Japan (II)
		Netherlands (II)
		New Zealand (II)
		Norway (II)
		Scotland (II)
		S. Africa (II)

Control Nations

Rates Decreased	Rates Remained Unchanged	Rates Increased
Norway (I)	Ceylon (I)	Finland (I)
Ceylon (II)	Chile (1)	Thailand (I)
Chile (II)	Netherlands (I)	Colombia (II)
El Salvador (II)		Sweden (I)
Ireland (II)		Turkey (II)
Switzerland (II)		
Thailand (II)		

Source: From *Violence and Crime in Cross-National Perspective* by Archer, D. & Gartner, R., copyright © 1984. Reprinted with permission of Yale University Press.

The researchers found that most combatant nations in their analysis experienced substantial postwar increases in their rates of homicide after both small and large wars. Archer and Gartner concluded,

> The one model that appears to be fully consistent with the evidence is the legitimation of violence model, which suggests that the presence of authorized or sanctioned killing during war has a residual effect on the level of homicide in peacetime society. (p. 96)

More recently, Savage, Bennett, and Danner (2008) examined the relationship between social welfare spending and homicide. Does welfare spending encourage dependency and weaken personal initiative, thereby increasing crime, or does it redress the imbalance of opportunities available in society and alleviate the resulting tensions that arise from such inequality, thereby decreasing crime? When looking at variation in welfare spending across localities in the United States, evidence tends to support the latter. Savage et al. (2008) used a data set called the Correlates of Crime (COC), which contains data for a sample of 52 diverse nations from every region of the globe for 1960 through 1984. It includes data from the International Criminal Police Organization (Interpol), the United Nations (UN), the World Bank (WB), the International Labour Organization (ILO), and other sources.

Social welfare spending was operationalized as the amount of governmental spending in U.S. dollar equivalents for social welfare programs per person, adjusted to 1980 dollars. The variable was computed by dividing the total amount of social welfare spending per country per year by the population and further dividing it by the consumer price index. Savage et al. (2008) also controlled other factors including the gross domestic product (GDP), the percent of the population residing in urban areas, female labor force participation, and unemployment, among others. In addition to rates of homicide, they used rates of theft as another dependent variable. Over the time period studied, they found that social welfare spending was negatively related to both theft and homicide; that is, as social welfare spending increased, rates of these crimes generally decreased.

🖳 Content Analysis

Do media accounts of crime, such as newspaper and television news coverage, accurately portray the true nature of crime? The methodologies discussed thus far may not be helpful for answering this question. **Content analysis**, or "the systematic, objective, quantitative analysis of message characteristics" (Neuendorf 2002:1) would be an appropriate tool. Using this method, we can learn a great deal about popular culture and many other issues through studying the characteristics of messages delivered through the mass media and other sources.

> **Content analysis** A research method for systematically analyzing and making inferences from text.

The goal of a content analysis is to develop inferences from text (Weber 1990). You can think of a content analysis as a "survey" of some documents or other records of prior communication. In fact, a content analysis is a survey designed with fixed-choice responses so that it produces quantitative data that can be analyzed statistically. This method was first applied to the study of newspaper and film content and then developed systematically for the analysis of Nazi propaganda broadcasts in World War II, but it can also be used to study historical documents, records of speeches, and other "voices from the past" (Neuendorf 2002:31–37).

Content analysis bears some similarities to qualitative data analysis, because it involves coding and categorizing text, discovering relationships among constructs identified in the text, and a statistical analysis of those findings. Content analysis also bears some similarities to secondary data analysis, because it involves taking data, texts, that already exist and subjecting them to a new form of "analysis," but unlike secondary analysis of previously collected quantitative data, content analysis also involves sampling and measurement of primary data. Unlike the secondary analyst of qualitative data, the content analyst, by definition, applies primarily quantitative techniques to the coding and analysis of her data. These distinctions become even fuzzier, however, when we recognize that content analysis techniques can be used with all forms of messages, including visual images, sounds, and interaction patterns, as well as written text (Neuendorf 2002).

Identifying a Population of Documents or Other Textual Sources

The population of documents that is selected for analysis should be appropriate to the research question of interest. The units that can be surveyed in a content analysis are numerous and can range from newspapers, books, films, nomination speeches, or TV shows to persons referred to in other communications, themes expressed in documents, or propositions made in different statements. Often, a comprehensive archive can provide the primary data for the analysis (Neuendorf 2002). For a fee, the LexisNexis service makes a large archive of newspapers available for analysis. Words or other features of these units are then coded in order to measure the variables involved in the research question. The content analysis proceeds through several stages (Weber 1985).

Identify a population of documents or other textual sources for study. This population should be selected so that it is appropriate to the research question of interest. Perhaps the population will be all newspapers published in the United States, college student newspapers, nomination speeches at political party conventions, or "state of the nation" speeches by national leaders.

Determine the units of analysis. These could be newspaper articles, whole newspapers, television episodes, speeches, or political conventions.

Select a sample of units from the population. The simplest strategy might be a simple random sample of documents. However, a stratified sample might be needed to ensure adequate representation of community newspapers in large and small cities, of weekday and Sunday papers, or of political speeches during election years and in off years (see Chapter 4).

Design coding procedures for the variables to be measured. This requires deciding what unit of text to code, such as words, sentences, paragraphs, or newspaper pages. Then the categories into which the units are to be coded must be defined. These categories may be broad, such as "supports democracy," or narrow, such as "supports universal suffrage."

Test and refine the coding procedures. Clear instructions and careful training of coders are essential.

Base statistical analyses on counting occurrences of particular items. These could be words, themes, or phrases. You will also need to test relations between different variables.

Developing reliable and valid coding procedures is not an easy task. The meaning of words and phrases is often ambiguous. Homographs (words such as *mine* that have different meanings in different contexts) create special problems, as do many phrases that have special meanings (such as *point of no return*) (Weber 1985). As a result, coding procedures cannot simply categorize and count words; text segments in which the words are embedded must also be inspected before codes are finalized. Because different coders may perceive different meanings in the same text segments, explicit coding rules are required to ensure coding consistency. Special dictionaries can be developed to keep track of how the categories of interest are defined in the study (Weber 1985).

After coding procedures are developed, their reliability should be assessed by comparing different coders' codes for the same variables. Computer program content analysis can be used to enhance reliability (Weber 1985). Whatever rules the computer is programmed to use to code text will be applied consistently. The criteria for judging quantitative content analyses of text reflect the same standards of validity applied to data collected with other quantitative methods. We must review the sampling approach, the reliability and validity of the measures, and the controls used to strengthen any causal conclusions.

The various steps in a content analysis are represented in the flowchart in Exhibit 10.4. Note that the steps are comparable to the procedures in quantitative survey research. Use this flowchart as a checklist when you design or critique a content analysis project.

回 Case Study: Media Representations of Crime

Researchers interested in the media and crime have used content analysis in a number of ways. For example, scholars analyzing crime depictions presented in the media often conclude that newspaper and television coverage of crime is frequently inaccurate and misleading; stories disproportionately report violent crimes, and reporters tend to focus attention on sensational matters such as the capture of criminal or high-status offenders.

One type of television program presents vignettes depicting actual crimes in which theories of crime are dramatized. These dramatizations feature actors, actual photographs or film footage, and interviews conducted with participants and the police. Viewers are urged to call the police or program representatives with information related to the crime, and police officers are on standby in the television studio would be available to take these calls and facilitate action. Two examples of these sorts of programs are *America's Most Wanted* (AMW) and *Unsolved Mysteries* (UM).

To analyze the images these programs revealed to viewers, Cavender and Bond-Maupin (2000) conducted a content analysis of AMW and UM programs that aired between January 25 and May 31, 1989. All programs that aired during this time period were videotaped, and a subsample of 16 episodes that contained 77 crime vignettes was randomly selected. The crime vignettes served as the study's units of analysis. The coding protocol used for data collection was focused on three aspects of the programs:

1. *Demographics.* Types of crime and general information on the crime, criminals, and victims

2. *Characterizations.* Specific depictions of crime, criminals, and victims, such as brutality, dangerousness, or a victim's vulnerability

3. *Worldview.* The relative safety of people and places, the terror and randomness of crime, and what the audience should do about crime

Exhibit 10.5 presents the percentage of program vignettes that depicted offense types for both AMW and UM. Cavender and Bond-Maupin (2000) concluded that the overwhelming majority of criminals on these shows were depicted as dangerous people who were beyond the help of social control or rehabilitation. In addition, both shows regularly featured criminals who were characterized with deviant psychological labels such as *crazed killer*, *psycho*, *maniac*, *schizophrenic*, *emotionally disturbed*, or *showing no emotion*. Other criminals were portrayed as Satanists, gang members, and drug dealers. On the other hand, victims were usually presented as upstanding citizens whom you would like to have as a neighbor. The camera most often took the victims' perspective as well, achieving what Cavender and Bond-Maupin called the "good/evil dichotomy," with the victim and the audience aligned against the criminal.

Cavender and Bond-Maupin (2000) were particularly interested in how the shows' cinematographic techniques were used to make the dramas entertaining. They found that in a majority of the violent crimes, graphic details of the incident were depicted, including the number and location of a victim's wounds. For example, one victim was stabbed 30 times through the heart, and another victim was shot 5 times and ultimately died of massive bleeding.

Exhibit 10.4 Flowchart for the Typical Process of Content Analysis Research

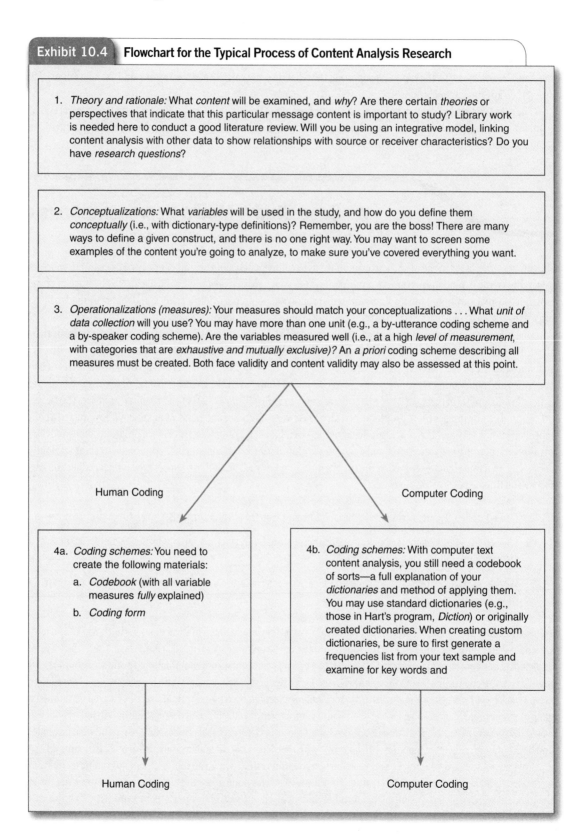

1. *Theory and rationale:* What *content* will be examined, and *why*? Are there certain *theories* or perspectives that indicate that this particular message content is important to study? Library work is needed here to conduct a good literature review. Will you be using an integrative model, linking content analysis with other data to show relationships with source or receiver characteristics? Do you have *research questions*?

2. *Conceptualizations:* What *variables* will be used in the study, and how do you define them *conceptually* (i.e., with dictionary-type definitions)? Remember, you are the boss! There are many ways to define a given construct, and there is no one right way. You may want to screen some examples of the content you're going to analyze, to make sure you've covered everything you want.

3. *Operationalizations (measures):* Your measures should match your conceptualizations . . . What *unit of data collection* will you use? You may have more than one unit (e.g., a by-utterance coding scheme and a by-speaker coding scheme). Are the variables measured well (i.e., at a high *level of measurement*, with categories that are *exhaustive and mutually exclusive)?* An *a priori* coding scheme describing all measures must be created. Both face validity and content validity may also be assessed at this point.

Human Coding

Computer Coding

4a. *Coding schemes:* You need to create the following materials:

    a. *Codebook* (with all variable measures *fully* explained)

    b. *Coding form*

4b. *Coding schemes:* With computer text content analysis, you still need a codebook of sorts—a full explanation of your *dictionaries* and method of applying them. You may use standard dictionaries (e.g., those in Hart's program, *Diction*) or originally created dictionaries. When creating custom dictionaries, be sure to first generate a frequencies list from your text sample and examine for key words and

Human Coding

Computer Coding

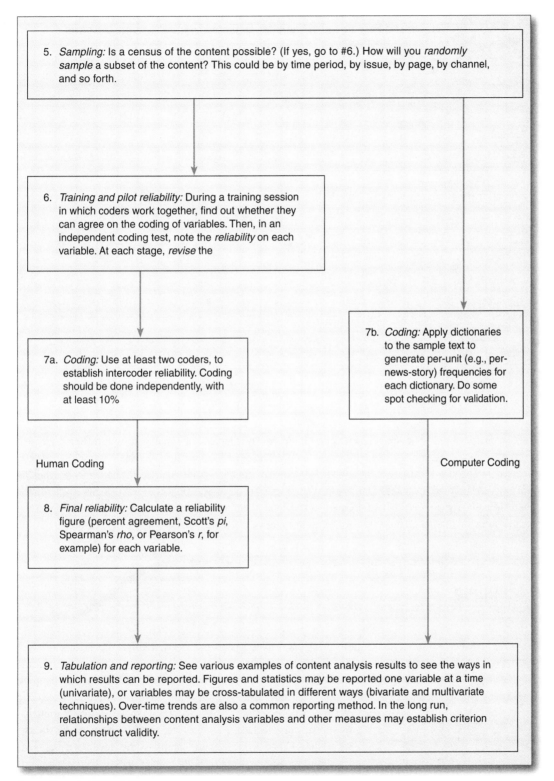

5. *Sampling:* Is a census of the content possible? (If yes, go to #6.) How will you *randomly sample* a subset of the content? This could be by time period, by issue, by page, by channel, and so forth.

6. *Training and pilot reliability:* During a training session in which coders work together, find out whether they can agree on the coding of variables. Then, in an independent coding test, note the *reliability* on each variable. At each stage, *revise* the

7b. *Coding:* Apply dictionaries to the sample text to generate per-unit (e.g., per-news-story) frequencies for each dictionary. Do some spot checking for validation.

7a. *Coding:* Use at least two coders, to establish intercoder reliability. Coding should be done independently, with at least 10%

Human Coding

Computer Coding

8. *Final reliability:* Calculate a reliability figure (percent agreement, Scott's *pi*, Spearman's *rho*, or Pearson's *r*, for example) for each variable.

9. *Tabulation and reporting:* See various examples of content analysis results to see the ways in which results can be reported. Figures and statistics may be reported one variable at a time (univariate), or variables may be cross-tabulated in different ways (bivariate and multivariate techniques). Over-time trends are also a common reporting method. In the long run, relationships between content analysis variables and other measures may establish criterion and construct validity.

Source: Neuendorf 2002:50–51.

Exhibit 10.5	Number and Percentage of Vignettes Depicted by the Programs *Unsolved Mysteries* and *America's Most Wanted*	
Murder	*52*	*40*
Theft or fraud extortion	13	10
Escape	12	9
Bank robbery or armed robbery	10	8
Illegal arms or terrorism	3	2
Unexplained death or missing	7	5
Rape	5	4
Kidnapping	5	4
Child molestation	5	4
Attempted murder	3	2
Drug dealing	3	2
Other	7	5

Source: Adapted from Cavender and Bond-Maupin 1993

To sensationalize these acts, in some vignettes, the film speed was reduced to slow motion to capture the muzzle flash as a criminal drew a gun and shot the victim. What Cavender and Bond-Maupin called "fear cues" were also frequently employed by the shows to capture the attention of viewers. For example, in one vignette, the host emerges from the night on a deserted road and makes reference to a common fear of driving on a lonely stretch of highway where one's cries for help would go unheeded. In sum, Cavender and Bond-Maupin concluded that the message sent to viewers by both programs was that danger lurks everywhere, awaiting the victim and, by implication, the viewer at home.

Crime Mapping

Many of us have adopted the image of crime mapping that involves a police precinct wall with pushpins stuck all over it identifying the location of crime incidents. Shows like the *Wire* have also presented the drama behind the use of crime mapping in generating crime counts within various police beats that are monitored very closely. But **crime mapping** for research purposes has a very long history and is generally used to identify the spatial distribution of crime along with the social indicators such as poverty and social disorganization that are similarly distributed across areas (e.g., neighborhood, census tracks). Rachel Boba (2009) defines crime mapping as "the process of using a geographic information system to conduct special analysis of crime problems and other police-related issues" (p. 7). She also describes the three main functions of crime mapping:

Crime mapping Geographical mapping strategies used to visualize a number of things including location, distance, and patterns of crime and their correlates.

1. It provides visual and statistical analyses of the spatial nature of crime and other events.

2. It allows the linkage of crime data to other data sources, such as census information on poverty or school information, which allows relationships between variables to be established.

3. It provides maps to visually communicate analysis results.

Although applied crime mapping like this has been used for over 100 years to assist the police in criminal apprehension and crime prevention, the type of crime mapping we will discuss here is related to mapping techniques used for traditional research purposes (e.g., testing theory about the causes of crime), not for investigative purposes. With the advent of computing technology, however, crime mapping has become an advanced form of statistical data analysis. The **geographic information system (GIS)** is the software tool that has made crime mapping increasingly available to researchers since the 1990s.

> **Geographic information system (GIS)** The software tool that has made crime mapping increasingly available to researchers since the 1990s.

📇 Case Study: Social Disorganization and the Chicago School

Crime mapping for general research purposes has a long history in criminological research and has generally been used to identify the spatial distribution of crime along with the social indicators such as poverty and social disorganization that are similarly distributed across areas (e.g., neighborhood, census tracts). Although not the first to use crime mapping, Shaw and McKay (1942) conducted a landmark analysis in criminology on juvenile delinquency in Chicago neighborhoods back in the 1930s. These researchers mapped thousands of incidents of juvenile delinquency and analyzed relationships between delinquency and various social conditions such as social disorganization. After analyzing rates of police arrests for delinquency, using police records to determine the names and addresses of those arrested in Chicago between 1927 and 1935, Shaw and McKay observed a striking pattern that persisted over the years.

Exhibit 10.6 displays one of the maps Shaw and McKay (1942) created that illuminates the spatial distribution of delinquency within concentric circles of Chicago that spread out to the suburbs from the city's center. As noted in Exhibit 10.5, there is a linear decrease in rates of delinquency as the distance from the Loop (city center) increases. When rates of other community characteristics were similarly mapped (e.g., infant mortality, tuberculosis cases, percentage of families who own their own homes, percentage of foreign-born residents, percentage of families on relief), the conclusions were obvious. Shaw and McKay concluded,

> It may be observed, in the first instance, that the variations in rates of officially recorded delinquents in communities of the city correspond very closely with variations in economic status. The communities with the highest rates of delinquents are occupied by these segments of the population whose position is most disadvantageous in relation to the distribution of economic, social, and cultural values. Of all the communities in the city, these have the fewest facilities for acquiring the economic goods indicative of status and success in our conventional culture. . . . In the low-income areas, where there is the greatest deprivation and frustration, where, in the history of the city, immigrant and migrant groups have brought together the widest variety of divergent cultural traditions and institutions, and where there exists the greatest disparity between the social values to which the people aspire and the availability of facilities for acquiring these values in conventional ways, the development of crime as an organized way of life is most marked. (pp. 318–19)

▣ Case Study: Gang Homicides in St. Louis

Contemporary researchers interested in issues related to crime and criminology have access to more sophisticated computer technology that allows for the creation of more enhanced crime maps. The purpose of crime maps, however, remains the same: to illuminate the relationship between some category of crime and corresponding characteristics such as poverty and disorganization across given locations. Rosenfeld, Bray, and Egley (1999) examined the mechanisms through which gangs facilitate violent offending in St. Louis, Missouri. The primary purpose of this research was to examine whether gang membership impels members to engage in violence or merely exposes them to violent persons and situations. Rosenfeld et al. compared gang-affiliated, gang-motivated, and nongang youth homicides occurring in St. Louis between 1985 and 1995. In one part of their analysis, they examined the spatial distribution of gang and nongang youth homicide in relation to attributes of the neighborhood context (e.g., economic deprivation) in which the incidents occurred.

Rosenfeld et al. (1999) did not rely on the police classification of homicides as gang-related; they coded homicide reports themselves. Operationally, a homicide was coded gang-motivated if it resulted from gang behavior or relationships, such as an initiation ritual, the "throwing" of gang signs, or a gang fight. A case was coded as gang-affiliated if the homicide involved a suspect or victim identified in the police report as a gang member but did not arise from gang activity. For example, an incident in which a gang member was killed during a robbery would be gang-affiliated but not gang-motivated. A youth homicide was coded as nongang-related if no indication of gang activity or affiliation was present in the case file and the suspect was between 10 and 24 years of age. To examine the spatial relationship among these three types of homicides and the relationship they had to neighborhood disadvantage (such as economic deprivation or social disorganization) and instability (such as residents moving in and out of the neighborhood), the researchers used the census block group as their unit of analysis. Exhibit 10.7 displays the map of block groups where gang-affiliated and gang-motivated homicides occurred, along with the extent of neighborhood disadvantage in each block for 1990–1995 (Rosenfeld et al. 1999). Exhibit 10.8 displays this same information for nongang youth homicides.

From these maps, you can see that both gang and nongang homicides were concentrated in disadvantaged areas. Other maps revealed a similar finding with regard to neighborhood instability; homicides were concentrated in neighborhoods with moderate levels of instability regardless of whether they were gang-affiliated, gang-motivated, or nongang-related. Rosenfeld and his colleagues (1999) conclude,

> Our results offer powerful evidence of the clustering of both gang and nongang youth homicides in areas characterized by high levels of social-economic disadvantage and racial isolation. Although the accumulated evidence for gang facilitation of violence is quite compelling, our results serve as a reminder that concentrated disadvantage and racial isolation remain the fundamental sources of lethal violence in urban areas. (p. 514)

These conclusions echo those made over a half-century earlier by Shaw and McKay (1942). As such, we are compelled to note Ernest W. Burgess's words in the introduction of Shaw and McKay's original work:

> We must realize that the brightest hope in reformation is in changing the neighborhood and in control of the gang in which the boy moves, lives, and has his being and to which he returns after this institutional treatment. . . . We must reaffirm our faith in prevention, which is so much easier, cheaper, and more effective than cure and which begins with the home, the play group, the local school, the church, and the neighborhood. (p. xiii)

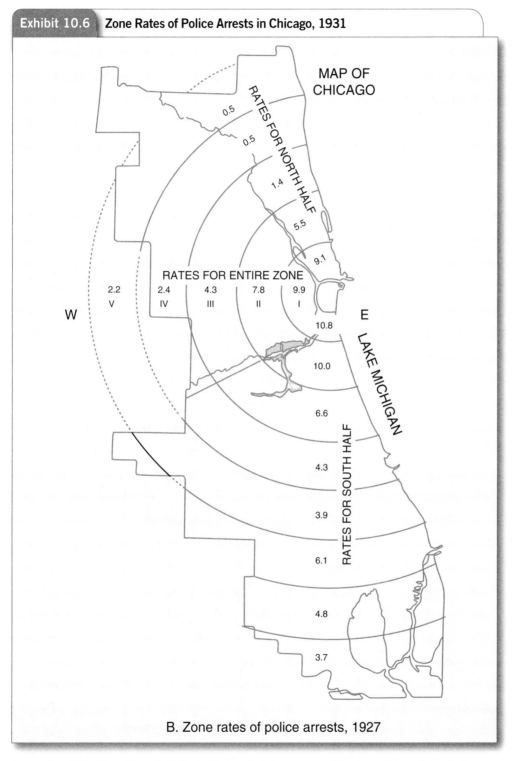

Exhibit 10.6 Zone Rates of Police Arrests in Chicago, 1931

MAP OF CHICAGO

RATES FOR NORTH HALF

0.5
0.5
1.4
5.5
9.1

RATES FOR ENTIRE ZONE

| 2.2 | 2.4 | 4.3 | 7.8 | 9.9 |
| V | IV | III | II | I |

W

E

10.8

LAKE MICHIGAN

10.0

6.6

RATES FOR SOUTH HALF

4.3

3.9

6.1

4.8

3.7

B. Zone rates of police arrests, 1927

Source: Shaw, Clifford R. and Henry D. McKay. 1942. *Juvenile Delinquency and Urban Areas.* Chicago: University of Chicago Press.

Exhibit 10.7	Neighborhoods in St. Louis Where Gang-Affiliated and Gang-Motivated Homicides Occurred

Gang-Affiliated and Gang-Motivated Homicides
  S   **Gang Affiliated**
  Ñ   **Gang Motivated**
St. Louis Block Groups
  Not Disadvantaged
  Disadvantaged
  Very Disadvantaged

2   0   2   4 **Miles**

N

Source: Rosenfeld et al. 1999. Facilitating Violence: A Comparison of Gang-Motivated, Gang-Affiliated, and Nongang Youth Homicides."
Journal of Quantitative Criminology 15(4):496–516.

Exhibit 10.8 Neighborhoods in St. Louis Where Nongang Homicides Occurred

Source: Rosenfeld et al. 1999. "Facilitating Violence: A Comparison of Gang-Motivated, Gang-Affiliated, and Nongang Youth Homicides." *Journal of Quantitative Criminology* 15(4):496–516.

🔲 Case Study: Using Google Earth to Track Sexual Offending Recidivism

While the GIS software that was utilized by Rosenfeld et al. (1999) has many research advantages for displaying the spatial distributions of crime, other researchers have begun to take advantage of other research mapping tools including Google Earth. One such endeavor was conducted by Duwe, Donnay, and Tewksbury (2008), who sought to determine the effects of Minnesota's residency restriction statute on the recidivism behavior of registered sex offenders. Many states have passed legislation that restricts where sex offenders are allowed to live. These policies are primarily intended to protect children from child molesters by deterring direct contact with schools, day care centers, parks, and so on. Most of these statutes are applied to all sex offenders, regardless of their offending history or perceived risk of reoffense. The impact of such laws on sexual recidivism, however, remains unclear. Duwe et al. (2008) attempted to fill this gap in our knowledge. They examined 224 sex offenders who had been reincarcerated for a new sex offense between 1990 and 2005 and asked several research questions including "Where did offenders initially establish contact with their victims, and where did they commit the offense?" and "What were the physical distances between an offender's residence and both the offense and first contact locations?" (Duwe et al. 2008:488). The researchers used Google Earth to calculate the distance between an offender's place of residence, the place where first contact with the victim occurred, and the location of offense.

Duwe and his colleagues (2008) investigated four criteria to classify a reoffense as preventable: (a) the means by which offenders established contact with their victims, (b) the distance between an offender's residence and where first contact was established (i.e., 1,000 feet, 2,500 feet, or 1 mile), (c) the type of location where contact was established (e.g., was it a place where children congregated?), and (d) whether the victim was under the age of 18. To be classified as preventable through housing restrictions, an offense had to meet certain criteria. For example, the offender would have had to establish direct contact with a juvenile victim within 1 mile of his residence at a place where children congregate (e.g., park, school). Results indicated that the majority of offenders, as in all cases of sexual violence, victimized someone they already knew. Only 35% of the sex offender recidivists established new direct contact with a victim, but these victims were more likely to be adults than children, and the contact usually occurred more than a mile away from the offender's residence. Of the few offenders who directly established new contact with a juvenile victim within close proximity of their residence, none did so near a school, a park, a playground, or other locations included in residential restriction laws.

The authors concluded that residency restriction laws were not that effective in preventing sexual recidivism among child molesters. Duwe et al. (2008) state,

> Why does residential proximity appear to matter so little with regard to sexual reoffending? Much of it has to do with the patterns of sexual offending in general. . . . Sex offenders are much more likely to victimize someone they know. For example, one of the most common victim-offender relationships in this study [for those who victimized children] was that of a male offender developing a romantic relationship with a woman who had children. . . . They used their relationships with these women to gain access to their victims. . . . It was also common for offenders to gain access to victims through babysitting for an acquaintance or co-worker. (p. 500)

Clearly, the power of mapping technologies has changed not only the way law enforcement officials are preventing crime but also the way in which researchers are examining the factors related to crime and crime control.

🔲 **Methodological Issues When Using Secondary Data**

Each of the methods we have discussed in this chapter presents unique methodological challenges. For example, in historical events research and comparative research, small numbers of cases, spotty historical records, variable cross-national record-keeping practices, and different cultural and linguistic contexts limit the confidence that can be placed in measures, samples, and causal conclusions. Just to identify many of the potential problems for a comparative historical research project requires detailed knowledge of the times and of the nations or other units investigated (Kohn 1987). This requirement often serves as a barrier to in-depth historical research and to comparisons between nations.

Analysis of secondary data presents several challenges, ranging from uncertainty about the methods of data collection to the lack of maximal fit between the concepts that the primary study measured and each of the concepts that are the focus of the current investigation. Responsible use of secondary data requires a good understanding of the primary data source. The researcher should be able to answer the following questions (most of which were adopted from Riedel 2000:55–69; and Stewart 1984:23–30):

1. What were the agency's goals in collecting the data? If the primary data were obtained in a research project, what were the project's purposes?

2. Who was responsible for data collection, and what were their qualifications? Are they available to answer questions about the data? Each step in the data collection process should be charted and the personnel involved identified.

3. What data were collected, and what were they intended to measure?

4. When was the information collected?

5. What methods were used for data collection? Copies of the forms used for data collection should be obtained, and the way in which these data are processed by the agency or agencies should be reviewed.

6. How is the information organized (by date, event, etc.)? Are there identifiers that are used to identify the different types of data available on the same case? In what form are the data available (computer tapes, disks, paper files)? Answers to these questions can have a major bearing on the work that will be needed to carry out the study.

7. How consistent are the data with data available from other sources?

8. What is known about the success of the data collection effort? How are missing data indicated? What kind of documentation is available?

Answering these questions helps ensure that the researcher is familiar with the data he or she will analyze and can help identify any problems with it.

Data quality is always a concern with secondary data, even when the data are collected by an official government agency. The need for concern is much greater in research across national boundaries, because different data-collection systems and definitions of key variables may have been used (Glover 1996). Census counts can be distorted by incorrect answers to census questions as well as by inadequate coverage of the entire population (see Chapter 5; Rives and Serow 1988:32–35). Social and political pressures may influence the success of a census in different ways in different countries. These influences on records are particularly acute for crime data. For example,

Archer and Gartner (1984) note, "It is possible, of course, that many other nations also try to use crime rate fluctuations for domestic political purposes—to use 'good' trends to justify the current administration or 'bad' trends to provide a mandate for the next" (p. 16).

Researchers who rely on secondary data inevitably make trade-offs between their ability to use a particular data set and the specific hypotheses they can test. If a concept that is critical to a hypothesis was not measured adequately in a secondary data source, the study might have to be abandoned until a more adequate source of data can be found. Alternatively, hypotheses or even the research question itself may be modified in order to match the analytic possibilities presented by the available data (Riedel 2000).

Measuring Across Contexts

One problem that historical and comparative research projects often confront is the lack of data from some historical periods or geographical units (Rueschemeyer, Stephens, and Stephens 1992; Walters, James, and McCammon 1997). The widely used U.S. Uniform Crime Reporting Program did not begin until 1930 (Rosen 1995). Missing data prevented Olzak, Shanahan, and McEneaney (1996) from including more than 55 out of a total of 212 standard metropolitan statistical areas (SMSAs) in their analysis of race riots. Sometimes alternative sources of documents or estimates for missing quantitative data can fill in gaps (Zaret 1996), but even when measures can be created for key concepts, multiple measures of the same concepts are likely to be out of the question; as a result, tests of reliability and validity may not be feasible. Whatever the situation, researchers must assess the problem honestly and openly (Bollen, Entwisle, and Alderson 1993).

Those measures that are available are not always adequate. What remains in the historical archives may be an unrepresentative selection of materials from the past. At various times, some documents could have been discarded, lost, or transferred elsewhere for a variety of reasons. "Original" documents may be transcriptions of spoken words or handwritten pages and could have been modified slightly in the process; they could also be outright distortions (Erikson 1966; Zaret 1996). When relevant data are obtained from previous publications, it is easy to overlook problems of data quality, but this simply makes it all the more important to evaluate the primary sources. Developing a systematic plan for identifying relevant documents and evaluating them is very important.

A somewhat more subtle measurement problem is that of establishing measurement equivalence. The meaning of concepts and the operational definition of variables may change over time and between nations or regions (Erikson 1966). The value of statistics for particular geographic units like counties may vary over time simply due to change in the boundaries of these units (Walters et al. 1997). As Archer and Gartner (1984) note,

> These comparative crime data were recorded across the moving history of changing societies. In some cases, this history spanned gradual changes in the political and social conditions of a nation. In other cases, it encompassed transformations so acute that it seems arguable whether the same nation existed before and after. (p. 15)

Such possibilities should be considered, and any available opportunity should be taken to test for their effects.

A different measurement concern can arise as a consequence of the simplifications made to facilitate comparative analysis. In many qualitative comparative analyses, the values of continuous variables are dichotomized. For example, nations may be coded as "democratic" or "authoritarian." This introduces an imprecise and arbitrary element into the analysis (Lieberson 1991). On the other hand, for some comparisons, qualitative distinctions such as "simple majority rule" or "unanimity required" may capture the important differences between cases better than quantitative distinctions. It is essential to inspect carefully the categorization rules for any such analysis and to consider what form of measurement is both feasible and appropriate for the research question being investigated (King, Keohane, and Verba 1994).

Sampling Across Time and Place

The simplest type of sample is the selection of one case for a historical study. Although a great deal can be learned from the intensive focus on one nation or another unit, the lack of a comparative element shapes the type of explanations that are developed. Explanations for change within one nation are likely to focus on factors that have changed within it, such as the decisions of a political leader, rather than factors like political systems that vary between nations (Rueschemeyer et al. 1992). However, comparisons between nations may reveal that differences in political systems are much more important than voluntary decisions by individual political leaders. It is only when the political system changes over time within one nation that its impact can be evaluated empirically (Rueschemeyer et al. 1992).

Qualitative comparative historical studies are likely to rely on availability samples or purposive samples of cases. In an availability sample, researchers study a case or multiple cases simply because they are familiar with or have access to them. When using a purposive sampling strategy, researchers select cases because they reflect theoretically important distinctions. Quantitative historical comparative researchers often select entire populations of cases for which the appropriate measures can be obtained.

When geographic units like nations are sampled for comparative purposes, it is assumed that the nations are independent of each other in terms of the variables examined. Each nation can then be treated as a separate case for identifying possible chains of causes and effects. However, in a very interdependent world, this assumption may be misplaced; nations may develop as they do because of how other nations are developing (and the same can be said of cities and other units). As a result, comparing the particular histories of different nations may overlook the influence of global culture, international organizations, or economic dependency. These common international influences may cause the same pattern of changes to emerge in different nations; looking within the history of these nations for the explanatory influences would lead to spurious conclusions. The possibility of such complex interrelations should always be considered when evaluating the plausibility of a causal argument based on a comparison between two apparently independent cases (Jervis 1996).

Identifying Causes

The restriction of historical research to one setting in the past limits possibilities for testing causal connections, because explanations applied to these events can seem arbitrary (Skocpol 1984). The researcher can reduce this problem by making some comparisons to other events in the past or present. However, the interdependence of sampled units (noted in the previous section) may mean that several cases available for comparison should be treated as just one larger case. There may also be too many possible combinations of causal factors to test and not enough cases to test them with.

The inductive approach taken by many qualitative comparative researchers can also make it seem that whatever the causal explanation developed, it has been tailored to fit the particulars of the historical record and so is unlikely to be confirmed by other cases (Rueschemeyer et al. 1992).

Some comparative researchers use a systematic method for identifying causes, developed by the English philosopher John Stuart Mill (1872), called the **method of agreement** (see Exhibit 10.9). The core of this approach is the comparison of nations (*cases*) in terms of similarities and differences on potential causal variables and the phenomenon to be explained. For example, suppose three nations that have all developed democratic political systems are compared in terms of four socioeconomic variables hypothesized by different theories to influence violent crime. If the nations differ in terms of three of the variables but are similar in terms of the fourth, this is evidence that the fourth variable influences violent crime.

> ***Method of agreement*** A method proposed by John Stuart Mill for establishing a causal relation, in which the values of cases that agree on an outcome variable also agree on the value of the variable hypothesized to have a causal effect, whereas they differ in terms of other variables.

Exhibit 10.9	John Stuart Mill's Method of Agreement		
Variable	Case 1	Case 2	Case 3
A	Different	Different	Different
B	Different	Same	Same
C	Different	Different	Different
D[a]	Same	Same	Same
Outcome	Same	Same	Same

Source: Adapted from Skocpol 1984:379.

a. D is considered the cause of the outcome.

The features of the cases selected for comparison have a large impact on the ability to identify influences using the method of agreement. Cases should be chosen for their difference in terms of key factors hypothesized to influence the outcome of interest and their similarity on other, possibly confounding factors (Skocpol 1984). For example, in order to understand how unemployment influences violent crime, you would need to select cases for comparison that differ in unemployment rates so that you could then see if they differ in rates of violence (King et al. 1994).

This **deterministic causal approach** (Ragin 1987) requires that there be no deviations from the combination of factors that are identified as determining the outcome for each nation. Yet there are likely to be exceptions to any explanatory rule that we establish (Lieberson 1991). A careful analyst will evaluate the extent to which exceptions should be allowed in particular analyses.

Deterministic causal approach An approach in which there is a relationship between an independent and a dependent variable; the independent variable has an effect on the dependent variable in every case under consideration.

With these cautions in mind, the combination of historical and comparative methods allows for rich descriptions of social and political processes in different nations or regions as well as for causal inferences that reflect a systematic, defensible weighing of the evidence. Data of increasingly good quality are available on a rapidly expanding number of nations, creating many opportunities for comparative research. We cannot expect one study comparing the histories of a few nations to control adequately for every plausible alternative causal influence, but repeated investigations can refine our understanding and lead to increasingly accurate causal conclusions (King et al. 1994).

Ethical Issues When Analyzing Available Data and Content

When analyzing historical documents or quantitative data collected by others, the potential for harm to human subjects that can be a concern when collecting primary data is greatly reduced. It is still, however, important to be honest and responsible in working out arrangements for data access and protection. Researchers who conclude that they are being denied access to public records of the federal government may be able to obtain the data by filing a Freedom of

Information Act (FOIA) request. The FOIA stipulates that all persons have a right to access all federal agency records unless the records are specifically exempted (Riedel 2000). Researchers who review historical or government documents must also try to avoid embarrassing or otherwise harming named individuals or their descendants by disclosing sensitive information.

Subject confidentiality is a key concern when original records are analyzed. Whenever possible, all information that could identify individuals should be removed from the records to be analyzed so that no link is possible to the identities of living subjects or the living descendants of subjects (Huston and Naylor 1996). When you use data that have already been archived, you need to find out what procedures were used to preserve subject confidentiality. The work required to ensure subject confidentiality probably will have been done for you by the data archivist. For example, ICPSR examines carefully all data deposited in the archive for the possibility of disclosure risk. All data that might be used to identify respondents are altered to ensure confidentiality, including removal of information such as birth dates or service dates, specific incomes, or place of residence that could be used to identify subjects indirectly (see www.icpsr.umich.edu/icpsrweb/ICPSR/access/restricted/). If all information that could be used in any way to identify respondents cannot be removed from a data set without diminishing data set quality (such as by preventing links to other essential data records), ICPSR restricts access to the data and requires that investigators agree to conditions of use that preserve subject confidentiality.

It is not up to you to decide whether there are any issues of concern regarding human subjects when you acquire a data set for secondary analysis from a responsible source. The institutional review board (IRB) for the protection of human subjects at your college or university or other institution has the responsibility to decide whether it needs to review and approve proposals for secondary data analysis. The federal regulations are not entirely clear on this point, so the acceptable procedures will vary between institutions based on what their IRBs have decided.

Ethical concerns are multiplied when surveys are conducted or other data are collected in other countries. If the outside researcher lacks much knowledge of local norms, values, and routine activities, the potential for inadvertently harming subjects is substantial. For this reason, cross-cultural researchers should spend time learning about each of the countries in which they plan to collect primary data and establish collaborations with researchers in those countries (Hantrais and Mangen 1996). Local advisory groups may also be formed in each country so that a broader range of opinion is solicited when key decisions must be made. Such collaboration can also be invaluable when designing instruments, collecting data, and interpreting results.

▣ Conclusion

Each of these methods can help researchers gain new insights into numerous processes related to criminal justice or criminological inquiry. Historical and comparative social science investigations use a variety of techniques that range from narrative histories having much in common with qualitative methods to analyses of secondary data that in many respects are like traditional survey research. They encourage intimate familiarity with the course of development of the nations studied and thereby stimulate inductive reasoning about the interrelations among different historical events. Systematic historical and comparative techniques can be used to test deductive hypotheses concerning international differences as well as historical events.

Most historical and comparative methods encourage causal reasoning. They require the researcher to consider systematically the causal mechanism, or historical sequences of events, by which earlier events influence later outcomes. They also encourage attention to causal context, with a particular focus on the ways in which different cultures and social structures may result in different effects on other variables. There is much to be gained by continuing to use and develop these methods.

Key Terms

Highlights

- Secondary data analysis is the act of collecting or analyzing data that were originally collected for another purpose.

- In general, there are four major types of secondary data: surveys, official statistics, official records, and other historical documents including written text or media representations (e.g., trial transcripts, newspaper articles, television shows).

- The central insight behind historical and comparative methods is that we can improve our understanding of social processes when we make comparisons to other times and places.

- When research on past events does not follow processes for some long period of time, when it is basically cross-sectional, then it is usually referred to as historical events research.

- Content analysis is a tool for systematic analysis of documents and other textual data. It requires careful testing and control of coding procedures to achieve reliable measures.

- Event-structure analysis is a type of historical events research that develops a causal diagram showing the structure of action underling some chronology of events.

- Crime mapping for research purposes is generally used to identify the spatial distribution of crime along with the social indicators such as poverty and social disorganization that are similarly distributed across areas (e.g., neighborhoods, census tracts).

- Secondary data for historical and comparative research are available from many sources. The Inter-University Consortium for Political and Social Research (ICPSR) provides the most comprehensive data archive.

Research in the News

Data on Rape in the European Union Difficult to Compare

Most data available for the Europe Union nations, of which there are 27, is relatively easy to compare. But information on rape and domestic violence is different. In fact, most individual EU member states that do collect such data often have generally relied on police reports, not on surveys. As such, countries have are working hard to improve conditions for rape victims and victims of intimate partner violence, tend to have increasing rates of victimization because more victims are willing to come forward. As such, comparing the true magnitude of victimization for these crimes across EU countries is virtually impossible.

Source: Loftus, Louise. 2011. "Data on Rape in E.U. Difficult to Compare." *The New York Times*, October, 24. Retrieved June 12, 2012 (http://www.nytimes.com/2011/10/25/world/europe/data-on-rape-in-eu-difficult-to-compare.html).

Exercises

1. Read the original article reporting one of the studies described in this chapter. Critique the article, using the article review questions presented in Appendix B as your guide. Focus particular attention on procedures for measurement, sampling, and establishing causal relations.

2. What historical events have had a major influence on social patterns in the nation? The possible answers are too numerous to list, ranging from any of the wars to major internal political conflicts, economic booms and busts, scientific discoveries, and legal changes. Pick one such event in your own nation for this exercise.

Find one historical book on this event and list the sources of evidence used. What additional evidence would you suggest for a social science investigation of the event?

3. Using your library's government documents collection or the U.S. Census site on the Web (www.census.gov), select one report by the U.S. Bureau of the Census about the population of the United States or some segment of it. Outline the report and list all the tables included in it. Summarize the report in two paragraphs. Suggest a historical or comparative study for which this report would be useful.

4. Review the survey data sets available through the Inter-University Consortium for Political and Social Research (ICPSR), using either its published directory or its Internet site (www.icpsr.umich.edu). Select two data sets that might be used to study a research question in which you are interested. Use the information ICPSR reports about them to answer Questions 1–5 in the section "Methodological Issues When Using Secondary Data" earlier in this chapter. Is the information adequate to answer these questions? What are the advantages and disadvantages of using one of these data sets to answer your research question compared to designing a new study?

5. Find a magazine or newspaper report on crime in the United States or in some city or state. Explain how one of the key demographic concepts could be used or was used to improve understanding of this issue.

6. Select a current crime or political topic that has been the focus of news articles. Propose a content analysis strategy for this topic, using newspaper articles or editorials as your units of analysis. Your strategy should include a definition of the population, selection of the units of analysis, a sampling plan, and coding procedures for key variables. Now find an article on this topic and use it to develop your coding procedures. Test and refine your coding procedures with another article on the same topic.

Developing a Research Proposal

Add a historical or comparative dimension to your proposed study.

1. Consider which of the four types of comparative-historical methods would be most suited to an investigation of your research question. Think of possibilities for qualitative and quantitative research on your topic with the method you prefer. Will you conduct a variable-oriented or case-oriented study? Write a brief statement justifying the approach you choose.

2. Review the possible sources of data for your comparative-historical project. Search the Web and relevant government, historical, and international organization sites or publications. Search the social science literature for similar studies and read about the data sources that they used.

3. Specify the hypotheses you will test or the causal sequences you will investigate. Describe what your cases will be (nations, regions, years, etc.). Explain how you will select cases. List the sources of your measures and describe the specific type of data you expect to obtain for each measure.

4. Review the list of potential problems in comparative-historical research and discuss those that you believe will be most troublesome in your proposed investigation. Explain your reasoning.

STUDENT STUDY SITE

Log on to the Web-based student study site at **www.sagepub.com/bachmanprccj5e** for additional study tools including eFlashcards, Web quizzes, links to SAGE journal articles, podcasts, videos, data sets and codebooks, Web exercises, Web resources, and additional appendices.

Web Exercises

1. The Bureau of Justice Statistics (BJS) home page can be found at www.ojp.usdoj.gov/bjs. The site contains an extensive list of reports published by the BJS along with links to the data used in the reports. You can access tables of data that display phenomena over time and across various geographical locations.

a. Using data and/or reports available from the National Crime Victimization Survey, conduct an analysis of the rates of violent victimization from 1993 until the most recent date available in the data report. What do you conclude about the trends of violent victimization?

b. Find a report available on the site that makes cross-national comparisons. Summarize the methods by which the data were collected. Now summarize the findings of the report.

2. The National Institute of Justice has a wealth of information on crime mapping located at www.ncjrs.gov. Search the site for information on "crime mapping," and you will find that the site contains a multitude of information, including the latest technological advances in crime mapping strategies for police departments as well as full-text articles discussing recent research that uses crime mapping techniques. Select a report available online and summarize its findings.

3. The World Bank offers numerous resources that are useful for comparative research. Visit the World Bank Web site at www.worldbank.org. You will find data listed by countries; select a random sample of countries along with social indicators of your choice. Now summarize the differences and similarities you have identified between the countries.

4. The U.S. Bureau of Labor Statistics (BLS) provides extensive economic indicator data on the Web for regions, states, and cities. Go to the BLS Web page, which offers statistics by location: stats.bls.gov/eag/. Click on a region and explore the types of data that

are available. Write out a description of the steps you would have to take to conduct a comparative analysis using the data available from the BLS Web site.

5. The U.S. Census Bureau's home page can be found at www.census.gov. This site contains extensive reporting of census data including population data, economic indicators, and other information acquired through the U.S. Census. This Web site allows you to collect information on numerous subjects and topics, which can be used to make comparisons between different states or cities. Find the "State and County QuickFacts" option and choose your own state. Now pick the county in which you live and copy down several statistics of interest. Repeat this process for other counties in your state. Use the data you have collected to compare your county with other counties in the state. Write a one-page report summarizing your findings.

6. Go to the International Association of Law Enforcement Intelligence Analysts (IALEIA) Web site at www.ialeia.org. On the site you can download papers and information regarding numerous topics, including crime mapping. Provide a review of at least one of these applications. You can also link to IALEIA's journal (Hank Brightman, Editor, Saint Peter's College, The Jesuit College of New Jersey) to read the latest publications in this area.

Ethics Exercises

1. Do you think researchers conducting research using cross-national data should be sensitive to the cultural ideals of the societies they are studying? Should advisory groups of local residents or researchers be constructed to advise cross-national research? What other protections should be taken?

2. Should any requirements be imposed on researchers who seek to study other cultures, in order to ensure that procedures are appropriate and interpretations are culturally sensitive? What practices would you suggest for cross-cultural researchers in order to ensure that ethical guidelines are followed? (Consider the wording of consent forms and the procedures for gaining voluntary cooperation.)

3. Oral historians can uncover disturbing facts about the past. What if a researcher were conducting an oral history project such as the Depression Writer's Project and learned from an interviewee about his previously undisclosed involvement in a predatory sex crime many years ago? Should the researcher report what he learned to a government attorney who might decide to bring criminal charges? What about informing the victim and/or her surviving relatives? Would it matter if the statute of limitations had expired so that the offender could not be prosecuted any longer? Would it matter if the researcher were subpoenaed to testify before a grand jury?

SPSS or Excel Exercises

1. Using the data set STATE2000, examine the rates of violence and murder across the four regions of the country (REGION). The best procedure to use for this is called MEANS. You can access this under ANALYZE, then COMPARE MEANS, then click on MEANS.

In the Mean dialog box, place the rate of violence you wish to compare first (VIOLENT or MURDER) in the dependent variables box and REGION in the independent variable box. Summarize your findings.

Now, using this same procedure, examine whether there are similar differences across regions for rates of poverty, which are often found to be associated with rates of violence. That is, geographical locations that have higher rates of poverty and overdeprivation also tend to have higher rates of violence. What do you conclude?

2. Because the General Social Survey (GSS) file is cross-sectional, we cannot use it to conduct historical research. However, we can develop some interesting historical questions by examining differences in the attitudes of Americans in different birth cohorts.

    a. Inspect the distributions of the same set of variables. Would you expect any of these attitudes and behaviors to have changed over the 20th century? State your expectations in the form of hypotheses.

    b. Request a cross-tabulation of these variables by birth COHORT.

    c. What appear to be the differences among the cohorts? Which differences do you think are due to historical change, and which do you think are due to the aging process? Which attitudes and behaviors would you expect to still differentiate the baby boom generation and the post-Vietnam generation in 20 years?

CHAPTER **11**

Evaluation and Policy Analysis

Every year, the U.S. Department of Justice (DOJ) spends an average of $3 billion in grants to help state and local law enforcement and communities prevent and ameliorate the consequences of crime. Not only does the money go for such stereotypical prevention programs as after-school recreation programs, but it also supports such efforts as community-oriented policing, drug raids, prisoner rehabilitation, boot camps, home confinement and electronic monitoring, job corps and vocational training for prison inmates, preschool education programs, and other programs too numerous to mention. Most of the Department of Justice money set aside for prevention, however, is allocated most heavily in police and prisons, with very little support for prevention programs in other institutions (Sherman et al. 1997).

Many of the studies we have already highlighted in this text were conducted to evaluate the effectiveness of some program or policy (e.g., violent prevention programs in schools, mandatory arrest policies, the effects of a lawyer at bail hearings, the effects of drug courts). In this chapter, we will illustrate other research focused on different types of evaluation. Although all the research we have discussed in this text is ultimately useful, evaluation research is inherently so because the results generally have an impact on policy choices in the immediate future. As such, evaluation research is often referred to as **applied research** because the findings can immediately be utilized and applied.

We will first provide you with a brief history of evaluation research. Then, after describing the different types of evaluation research, we will provide you with case studies that illustrate the various methodologies used to assess the impacts of programs and policies in criminology and criminal justice. We will conclude with a discussion of the differences between basic science and applied research and highlight the emerging demand for evidence-based policy.

> **Applied research** Research that has an impact on policy and can be immediately utilized and applied.

> **Evidence-based policy** A policy that has been evaluated with a methodologically rigorous design and has been proven to be effective.

🖫 A Brief History of Evaluation Research

Evaluation research is not a method of data collection, like survey research or experiments, nor is it a unique component of research designs, like sampling or measurement. Instead, evaluation research is social research that is conducted for a distinctive purpose: to investigate social programs (such as substance abuse treatment programs, welfare programs, criminal justice programs, or employment and training programs). For each project, an evaluation researcher must select a research design and method of data collection that are useful for answering the particular research questions posed and appropriate for the particular program investigated.

You can see why we placed this chapter after most of the others in the text: When you review or plan evaluation research, you have to think about the research process as a whole and how different parts of that process can best be combined.

Although scientific research methods had been used prior to the 1950s (in fact as early as the 1700s) to evaluate outcomes of particular social experiments and programs, it was not until the end of the 1950s that social research became immersed in the workings of government with the common goal of improving society. As Weiss (1993) observed, social science was expected to bring rationality to the untidy world of government:

> It would provide hard data for planning and give cause-and-effect theories for policy making, so that statesmen would know which variables to alter in order to effect the desired outcomes. . . . And once policies were in operation, it would provide objective evaluation of their effectiveness so that necessary modifications could be made to improve performance. (p. 4)

During the 1960s, the practice of evaluation research increased dramatically not only in the United States but also around the world. One of the main initiatives that spawned this growth of evaluation research in the United States was the so-called War on Poverty that was part of the Great Society legislation of the 1960s. When the federal government began to take a major role in alleviating poverty and the social problems associated with it, such as delinquency and crime, the public wanted accountability for the tax dollars spent on such programs. Were these programs actually having their intended effects? Did the benefits outweigh the costs? During this time, the methods of social science were utilized like never before to evaluate this proliferation of new programs.

In 1967, Edward Suchman put forth his seminal definition of evaluation research as the application of social research techniques to the study of large-scale human service programs. In fact, a version of this definition is still utilized by some scholars today. For example, Rossi and Freeman (1989) encompass his definition in their more recent version: "Evaluation research is the systematic application of social research procedures for assessing the conceptualization, design, implementation, and utility of social intervention programs" (p. 18). What exactly does *systematic* mean? Well, regardless of what treatment or program is being examined, evaluations are systematic because they employ social research approaches to gathering valid and reliable data. Note the plural *approaches* instead of the singular *approach*. Evaluation research covers the spectrum of research methods that we have discussed in this text.

By the mid-1970s, evaluators were called on not only to assess the overall effectiveness of programs but also to determine whether programs were being implemented as intended and to provide feedback to help solve programming problems as well. As an indication of the growth of evaluation research during this time, several professional organizations emerged to assist in the dissemination of ideas from the burgeoning number of social scientists engaged in this type of research in the United States, along with similar organizations in other countries (Patton 1997).

By the 1990s, the public wanted even more accountability. Unfortunately, clear answers were not readily available. Few social programs could provide hard data on results achieved and outcomes obtained. Of course, government bureaucrats had produced a wealth of data on other things, including exactly how funds in particular programs were spent, for whom this money was spent, and for how many. However, these data primarily measured whether government staff were following the rules and regulations, not whether the desired results were being achieved. Instead of being rewarded for making their programs produce the intended outcomes (e.g., more jobs, fewer delinquents), the bureaucracy of government had made it enough simply to do the required paperwork of program monitoring. The results of evaluations that were conducted rarely saw the light of day. This, in turn, was interpreted by many politicians and individual citizens alike as "nothing works."

Utility The utility standards are intended to ensure that an evaluation will serve the practical information needs of intended users.

Feasibility The feasibility standards are intended to ensure that an evaluation will be realistic, prudent, diplomatic, and frugal.

Propriety The propriety standards are intended to ensure that an evaluation will be conducted legally, ethically, and with due regard for the welfare of those involved in the evaluation, as well as those affected by its results.

Accuracy The accuracy standards are intended to ensure that an evaluation will reveal and convey technically adequate information about the features that determine worth or merit of the program being evaluated.

Professional evaluation researchers soon realized that it was not enough simply to perform rigorous experiments to determine program efficacy; they must also be responsible for making sure their results could be understood and utilized by the practitioners (e.g., government officials, corporations, and nonprofit agencies) to make decisions about scrapping or modifying existing programs. In addition, there was increased concern in the field regarding fiscal accountability, documenting the worth of social program expenditures in relation to their costs.

It was in this context that professional evaluators began discussing standards for the field of evaluation research. In 1981, a Joint Committee on Standards published the list of features all evaluations should have. These standards still exist today (Joint Committee 1994, as cited in Patton 1997:17): **utility, feasibility, propriety,** and **accuracy.**

To the surprise of many in the field, utility was at the top of the list. This conveyed the idea that an evaluation only met the standards if, in fact, it served the needs of intended users. Professionals in the field responded accordingly. For example, Patton (1997) developed the practice of and coined the term *utilization-focused evaluation* as a way to fulfill the utility standard. Utilization-focused evaluation offered both a philosophy of evaluation and a practical framework for designing and conducting evaluations. The primary premise of this method was that evaluations should be judged by their utility and actual use. Use concerned how real people in the real world applied evaluation findings and experienced the evaluation process. As such, the focus in utilization-focused evaluation was on intended use by intended users. Like the field as a whole, utilization-focused evaluation does not advocate any particular evaluation content, model, method, or theory. Rather, it stresses an interactive process between an evaluator and primary intended users to select the most appropriate content, model, and methods for their particular situation. To stress this process, Patton offers the following definition of program evaluation:

> Program evaluation is the systematic collection of information about the activities, characteristics, and outcomes of programs to make judgments about the program, improve program effectiveness, and/or inform decisions about future programming. Utilization-focused evaluation (as opposed to program evaluation in general) is evaluation done for and with specific, intended primary users for specific, intended uses. (p. 23)

Evaluation Basics

Exhibit 11.1 illustrates the process of evaluation research as a simple systems model. First, clients, customers, students, or some other persons or units—cases—enter the program as **inputs**. (You will notice that this model treats programs like machines, with people functioning as raw materials to be processed.) Students may begin a new D.A.R.E. (Drug Abuse Resistance Education) program, sex offenders may enter a new intense probation program, or crime victims may be sent to a victim advocate. Resources and staff required by a program are also program inputs.

Inputs Resources, raw materials, clients, and staff that go into a program.

Next, some service or treatment is provided to the cases. This may be attendance in a class, assistance with a health problem, residence in new housing, or receipt of special cash benefits. The process of service delivery (**program process**) may be simple or complicated, short or long, but it is designed to have some impact on the cases, as inputs are consumed and outputs are produced.

Program process The complete treatment or service delivered by the program.

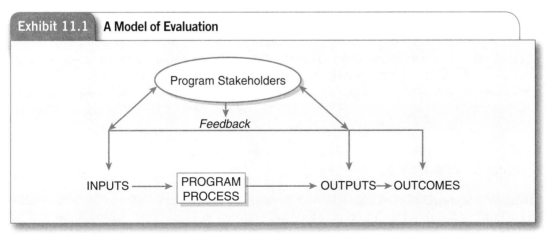

Exhibit 11.1 A Model of Evaluation

Source: Adapted from Lawrence and Kettner 1996.

The direct product of the program's service delivery process is its output. Program outputs may include clients served, case managers trained, food parcels delivered, or arrests made. The program outputs may be desirable in themselves, but they primarily serve to indicate that the program is operating.

> **Outputs** The services delivered or new products produced by the program process.

> **Outcomes** The impact of the program process on the cases processed.

> **Feedback** Information about service delivery system outputs, outcomes, or operations that is available to any program inputs.

Program outcomes indicate the impact of the program on the cases that have been processed. Outcomes can range from improved test scores or higher rates of job retention to fewer criminal offenses and lower rates of poverty. There are likely to be multiple outcomes of any social program, some intended and some unintended, some positive and others that are viewed as negative.

Variation in both outputs and outcomes in turn influences the inputs to the program through a feedback process. If not enough clients are being served, recruitment of new clients may increase. If too many negative side effects result from a trial medication, the trials may be limited or terminated. If a program does not appear to lead to improved outcomes, clients may go elsewhere.

Evaluation research enters into this picture as a more systematic approach to feedback that strengthens the feedback loop through credible analyses of program operations and outcomes. Evaluation research also broadens this loop to include connections to parties outside of the program itself. A funding agency or political authority may mandate the research, outside experts may be brought in to conduct the research, and the evaluation research findings may be released to the public, or at least funders, in a formal report.

The evaluation process as a whole, and the feedback process in particular, can only be understood in relation to the interests and perspectives of program stakeholders. Stakeholders are those individuals and groups who have some basis of concern with the program. They might be clients, staff, managers,

> **Stakeholders** Individuals and groups who have some basis of concern with the program.

funders, or the public. The board of a program or agency, the parents or spouses of clients, the foundations that award program grants, the auditors who monitor program spending, the members of Congress—each is a potential program stakeholder, and each has an interest in the outcome of any program evaluation. Some may fund the evaluation; some may provide research data; some may review, even approve, the research report (Martin and Kettner 1996). Who the program stakeholders are and what role they play in the program evaluation will have tremendous consequences for the research.

Can you see the difference between evaluation research and traditional social science research? Unlike explanatory social science research, evaluation research is not designed to test the implications of a social theory; the basic issue is often just "What is the program's impact?" Process evaluation often uses qualitative methods, but unlike traditional exploratory research, the goal is not to create a broad theoretical explanation for what is discovered; instead, the question is "How does the program do what it does?" Unlike social science research, the researchers cannot design evaluation studies simply in accord with the highest scientific standards and the most important research questions; instead, it is program stakeholders who set the agenda, but there is no sharp boundary between the two: In their attempt to explain how and why the program has an impact and whether the program is needed, evaluation researchers often bring social theories into their projects.

Evaluation Alternatives

Today, the field of evaluation research remains somewhat of a dichotomy. There are those who conduct evaluation research for the sake of knowledge alone, whereas others strive to make their products useful for some action. Regardless of the emphasis, however, all evaluation is empirical and data driven. Both program evaluation and evaluation research in general offer empirical answers to questions of policy and policy effectiveness. Objective and empirical assessments of policies and programs are the cornerstone of the evaluation field. Because there will never be an infinite amount of financial resources to fund all the programs we think will work, social scientists will always have work to do. As Patton (1997) so eloquently states, "As not everything can be done, there must be basis for deciding which things are worth doing. Enter evaluation" (p. 11).

Entire manuscripts have been devoted to delineating the various theories and methodologies utilized in evaluation research. Because this is a methods text, we are going to concentrate on the research methodologies most often utilized in criminology for evaluation purposes. Methods are always driven by research questions, however, so it is important to say something about the types of questions addressed by evaluation research. Patton (1997) distinguishes these three general question types:

Judgment-oriented evaluation. Evaluations aimed at determining the overall merit, worth, or value of something are **judgment-oriented evaluations**. Merit refers to the intrinsic value of a program. Questions addressed in this type of research include "How effective is the program in meeting the needs of those it is intended to help?" and "Does the program have the desired outcomes?"

> ***Judgment-oriented evaluation*** Evaluations aimed at determining the overall merit, worth, or value of something.

Improvement-oriented evaluation. Using evaluation results to improve a program turns out, in practice, to be fundamentally different from rendering judgment about overall effectiveness, merit, or worth. **Improvement-oriented evaluation** focuses on making things better, rather than just rendering summative judgment. Although the questions addressed in this research are similar to those addressed in a judgment-oriented study, they are somewhat different: "What are the program's strengths and weaknesses?" and "To what extent are participants progressing toward the desired outcomes (e.g., are there any barriers to overcome in the delivery of services)?"

> ***Improvement-oriented evaluation*** Evaluations that seek to improve a program rather than simply rendering a summative judgment about the program's merit or effectiveness.

Knowledge-oriented evaluation. Contrary to the instrumental use of results of both judgment- and improvement-oriented evaluations, **knowledge-oriented evaluation** is used to influence thinking about issues in a general way. This knowledge can be as specific as clarifying a program's model, testing a theory, or figuring out how to measure outcomes. Academic researchers often initiate this type of an evaluation simply because the knowledge gained may fill a gap or add significantly to a particular research literature. For example, when Sherman and Berk (1984) began their experiment that examined the effect of arrest on recidivism rates of men who had assaulted their partners, they were concerned not only with the specific effect of arrest but also with testing some basic tenets of deterrence theory such as "Are would-be offenders really deterred by the threat of formal sanctions like arrest and imprisonment?" and "Does the severity of the sanction effect the deterrent effect of formal sanctions?"

> ***Knowledge-oriented evaluation*** Used to influence thinking about issues in a general way.

As these questions illustrate, evaluation research may be undertaken for a variety of reasons: for management and administrative purposes, to test hypotheses derived from theory, to identify ways to improve the delivery of services, or to decide whether to continue, cut, or modify a particular program. The goal of evaluation research, however, is primarily the same as the goal for all social science research, to design and implement a study that is objective and grounded in the rules of scientific methodology. These methods span the gamut of the methods we have discussed in this text. They can range from the strictly quantitative experimental and quasi-experimental designs to the qualitative methodologies of observation and intensive interviewing.

Evaluation projects can focus on several questions related to the operation of social programs and the impact they have:

- Is the program needed? (evaluation of need)
- Can the program be evaluated? (evaluability assessment)

- How does the program operate? (process evaluation)

- What is the program's impact? (impact evaluation)

- How efficient is the program? (efficiency analysis)

The specific methods used in an evaluation research project depend, in part, on which of these questions is being addressed.

The Evaluation of Need, or Needs Assessment

Is a new program needed or an old one still required? Is there a need at all? A **needs assessment** attempts to answer these questions with systematic, credible evidence. The initial impetus for implementing programs to alleviate social problems and other societal ailments typically comes from a variety of sources, includ-

> **Needs assessment** A type of evaluation research that attempts to determine the needs of some population that might be met with a social program.

ing advocacy groups, moral leaders, community advocates, and political figures. Before a program is designed and implemented, however, it is essential to obtain reliable information on the nature and scope of the problem and the target population in need of the intervention. Evaluation researchers often contribute to these efforts by applying research tools to answer such questions as "What is the magnitude of this problem in this community?" "How many people in this community are in need of this program?" "What are the demographic characteristics of these people (e.g., age, gender, and race or ethnicity)?" and "Is the proposed program or intervention appropriate for this population?"

Rossi and Freeman (1989) provide several examples of the problems encountered in program implementation when these questions are not adequately answered. For example, during the early 1990s, when juvenile crime and delinquency were increasing, a suburban community in the Midwest implemented a program designed to prevent adolescent criminal behavior. However, after the program was started, it was discovered that there was virtually no juvenile crime in that particular community to begin with. The community planners had wrongly assumed that because juvenile delinquency was a social problem nationally, it was a problem in their community as well. Consequently, a lot of time, effort, and financial resources were wasted.

An empirical assessment by a social researcher of the community's needs in this area could have avoided this costly mistake. This research could have taken several forms, including doing an in-depth records search of local police agencies to determine the extent of crime and delinquency committed by juveniles in the area. A survey is another appropriate method used to determine the incidence of crime among juveniles in the community. For example, questionnaires could have been distributed in the schools to determine whether the rate of juvenile offending was serious enough in the community to warrant allocating the financial resources for the prevention programs.

Evaluability Assessment

> **Evaluability assessment** A type of evaluation research conducted to determine whether it is feasible to evaluate a program's effects within the available time and resources.

Evaluation research will be pointless if the program itself cannot be evaluated. Yes, some type of study is always possible, but a study specifically to identify the effects of a particular program may not be possible within the available time and resources. So researchers may conduct an **evaluability assessment** to learn this in advance, rather than expend time and effort on a fruitless project.

Why might a social program not be evaluable?

- Management only wants to have its superior performance confirmed and does not really care whether the program is having its intended effects. This is a very common problem.

- Staff are so alienated from the agency that they do not trust any attempt sponsored by management to check on their performance.

- Program personnel are just "helping people" or "putting in time" without any clear sense of what the program is trying to achieve.

- The program is not clearly distinct from other services delivered from the agency and so cannot be evaluated by itself. (Patton 2002:164)

An evaluability assessment can help solve the problems identified. Discussion with program managers and staff can result in changes in program operations. The evaluators may use the evaluability assessment to "sell" the evaluation to participants and sensitize them to the importance of clarifying their goals and objectives. Knowledge about the program gleaned through the evaluability assessment can be used to refine evaluation plans.

Because they are preliminary studies to "check things out," evaluability assessments often rely on qualitative methods. Program managers and key staff may be interviewed in depth, or program sponsors may be asked about the importance they attach to different goals. These assessments also may have an "action research" aspect, because the researcher presents the findings to program managers and encourages changes in program operations.

When evaluating the effectiveness of teen courts in Maryland, Stickle and colleagues (2008) used a 3-day workshop called the Program Development and Evaluation (PDE) with court personnel to facilitate an evaluability assessment. The purpose of this workshop was to standardize the goals, objectives, interventions, and operating standards for the participating courts. The goals and objectives agreed upon were then translated into outcome measures for the impact evaluation.

Process Evaluation (Program Monitoring)

What actually happens in a program? Once a program has been started, evaluators are often called on to document the extent to which implementation has taken place, whether the program is reaching the target individuals or groups, whether the program is actually operating as expected, and what resources are being expended (e.g., bucks spent!) in the conduct of the program. Rossi and Freeman (1989) define process evaluation or program monitoring as the

> **Process evaluation (program monitoring)**
> Evaluation research that investigates the process of service delivery.

systematic attempt by evaluation researchers to examine program coverage and delivery. Assessing program coverage consists of estimating the extent to which a program is reaching its intended target population; evaluating program delivery consists of measuring the degree of congruence between the plan for providing services and treatments and the ways they are actually provided. (p. 170)

Process evaluations are extremely important primarily because there is no way to reliably determine whether the intended outcomes have occurred without being certain the program is working according to plan. For example, imagine you are responsible for determining whether an anti-bullying curriculum given in a school has been successful in decreasing the amount of bullying behavior by the students. You conduct a survey of the students both before and after the curriculum was given and determine that rates of bullying have not significantly changed in the school since the curriculum was given. After you write your report, however, you find out that instead of being given in a 5-day series of 1-hour sessions as intended, the curriculum was actually crammed into a 2-hour format delivered on a Friday afternoon. A process evaluation would have revealed this implementation problem. If a program has not been implemented as intended, there is obviously no need to ask whether it had the intended outcomes.

A process evaluation can take many forms. Because most government and private organizations inherently monitor their activities through such things as application forms, receipts, and stock inventories, it should be relatively easy to obtain quantitative data for monitoring the delivery of services. This information can be summarized to describe things such as the clients served and the services provided. In addition to this quantitative information, a process evaluation will also likely benefit from qualitative methodologies such as unstructured interviews with people using the service or program. Interviews can also be conducted with staff to illuminate what they perceive to be obstacles to their delivery of services. As Posavac and Carey (1997) state, "Such qualitative information often provides points of view that neither evaluators nor service providers had considered" (p. 8).

Process evaluation is even more important when more complex programs are evaluated. Many social programs comprise multiple elements and are delivered over an extended period of time, often by different providers in different areas. Due to this complexity, it is quite possible that the program as delivered is not the same for all program recipients or consistent with the formal program design.

Case Study: Evaluating the D.A.R.E. Program

The evaluation of D.A.R.E. by Research Triangle Institute researchers Ringwalt et al. (1994) included a process evaluation with three objectives:

1. Assess the organizational structure and operation of representative D.A.R.E. programs nationwide.

2. Review and assess factors that contribute to the effective implementation of D.A.R.E. programs nationwide.

3. Assess how D.A.R.E. and other school-based drug prevention programs are tailored to meet the needs of specific populations. (p. 7)

The process evaluation (the researchers called it an "implementation assessment") was an ambitious research project in itself, with site visits, informal interviews, discussions, and surveys of D.A.R.E. program coordinators and advisors. These data indicated that D.A.R.E. was operating as designed and was running relatively smoothly. As shown in Exhibit 11.2, drug prevention coordinators in D.A.R.E. school districts rated the program components as much more satisfactory than did coordinators in school districts with other types of alcohol and drug prevention programs.

Process evaluation also can be used to identify the specific aspects of the service delivery process that have an impact. This, in turn, will help explain why the program has an effect and which conditions are required for these effects. Implementation problems identified in site visits included insufficient numbers of officers to carry out the program as planned and a lack of Spanish-language D.A.R.E. books in a largely Hispanic school. Classroom observations indicated engaging presentations and active student participation (Ringwalt et al. 1994).

When a Process Evaluation Finds a Problem

Process analysis of this sort can also help show how apparently unambiguous findings may be incorrect. The apparently disappointing results of the Transitional Aid Research Project (TARP) provide an instructive lesson of this sort. TARP was a social experiment designed to determine whether financial aid during the transition from prison to the community would help released prisoners find employment and avoid returning to crime. A total of 2,000 participants in Georgia and Texas were randomized to receive either a particular level of benefits over a particular period of time or no benefits at all (the control group). Initially, it seemed that the payments had no effect: The rate of subsequent arrests for both property and nonproperty crimes was not affected by TARP treatment condition.

Exhibit 11.2	Components of D.A.R.E. and Other Alcohol and Drug Prevention Programs Rated as Very Satisfactory (in Percentages)	

Component	D.A.R.E. Program (N = 222)	Other AOD Programs (N = 406)
Curriculum	67.5	34.2
Teaching	69.7	29.8
Administrative requirements	55.7	23.1
Receptivity of students	76.5	34.6
Effects on students	63.2	22.8

Source: Ringwalt et al. 1994:58.

But this wasn't the end of the story. Peter Rossi tested a more elaborate causal model of TARP effects that is summarized in Exhibit 11.3 (Chen 1990). Participants who received TARP payments had more income to begin with and so had more to lose if they were arrested; therefore, they were less likely to commit crimes. However, TARP payments also created a disincentive to work and therefore increased the time available in which to commit crimes. Thus, the positive direct effect of TARP (more to lose) was cancelled out by its negative indirect effect (more free time).

The term **formative evaluation** may be used instead of process evaluation when the evaluation findings are used to help shape and refine the program (Rossi and Freeman 1989). Formative evaluation procedures that are incorporated into the initial development of the service program can specify the treatment process and lead to changes in recruitment procedures, program delivery, or measurement tools (Patton 2002).

> **Formative evaluation** Process evaluation that is used to shape and refine program operations.

Process evaluation can employ a wide range of methods. Program coverage can be monitored through program records, participant surveys, community surveys, or utilizers versus dropouts and ineligibles. Service delivery can be monitored through service records completed by program staff, a management information system maintained by program administrators, or reports by program recipients (Rossi and Freeman 1989).

Qualitative methods are often a key component of process evaluation studies because they can be used to elucidate and understand internal program dynamics, even those that were not anticipated (Patton 2002; Posavac and Carey 1997). Qualitative researchers may develop detailed descriptions of how program participants engage with each other, how the program experience varies for different people, and how the program changes and evolves over time.

The Evaluation of Impact or Outcomes

If a process study shows that the implementation of the program has been delivered to the target population as planned, the next role for an evaluator is to assess the extent to which the program achieved its goals. "Did the program work?" "Did the program have the intended consequences?" This question should by now be familiar to you; stated more like a research question we are used to, "Did the treatment or program (independent variable) effect change in the dependent variable?" It all comes back to the issue of causality. This part of the research is variously called **impact analysis** or **impact evaluation**.

> **Impact evaluation (or impact analysis)** Analysis of the extent to which a treatment or other service has the intended effect.

Exhibit 11.3 Model of TARP Effects

Source: From Chen 1990:210.

The bulk of the published evaluation studies in our field are devoted to some type of impact assessment. Have new seat-belt laws increased rates of seat-belt usage? Have rape reform statutes increased the willingness of rape victims to report their victimizations to police? Are boot camps more likely to reduce recidivism among juveniles compared to more traditional juvenile detention settings? Have mandatory minimum sentencing guidelines decreased the probability that extralegal factors such as sex and race will affect an individual's sentence? The list could go on and on.

The D.A.R.E. program (independent variable), for instance, tries to reduce drug use (dependent variable). When the program is present, we expect less drug use. In a more elaborate study, we might have multiple values of the independent variable; for instance, we might look at "no program," "D.A.R.E. program," and "other drug or alcohol education" conditions and compare the results of each.

Case Study: How Does the Risk Skills Training Program (RSTP) Compare to D.A.R.E.?

Experimental designs Refers to a plan for assigning subjects to treatment conditions. A good experimental design serves three purposes: causation, which allows the experimenter to make causal inferences about the relationship between independent variables and a dependent variable; control, which allows the experimenter to rule out alternative explanations due to the confounding effects of extraneous variables (i.e., variables other than the independent variables); and variability, which reduces variability within treatment conditions, which makes it easier to detect differences in treatment outcomes.

D'Amico and Fromme's (2002) study of a new Risk Skills Training Program (RSTP) is a good example of a more elaborate study. They compared the impact of RSTP on children 14 to 19 years of age to that of an abbreviated version of D.A.R.E. and to a control group. The impacts they examined included positive and negative "alcohol expectancies" (the anticipated effects of drinking) as well as perceptions of peer risk taking and actual alcohol consumption. D'Amico and Fromme found that negative alcohol expectancies increased for the RSTP group in the posttest but not for the D.A.R.E. group or the control group, while weekly drinking and "positive expectancies" for drinking outcomes actually *increased* for the D.A.R.E. group and/or the control group by the 6-month follow-up but not for the RSTP group (see Exhibit 11.4).

As in other areas of research, a true **experimental design** (see Chapters 6 and 7) is the preferred method for maximizing internal

Exhibit 11.4 Impact of Risk Skills Training Program (RSTP), DARE-A.

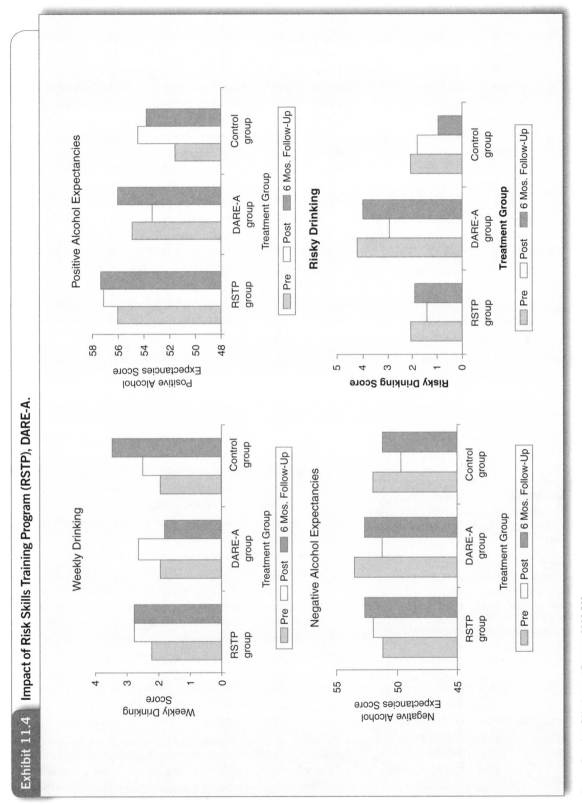

Source: Based on D'Amico and Fromme 2002:569.

validity—that is, for making sure your causal claims about program impact are justified. Cases are assigned randomly to one or more experimental treatment groups and to a control group so that there is no systematic difference between the groups at the outset. The goal is to achieve a fair, unbiased test of the program itself so that the judgment about the program's impact is not influenced by differences between the types of people who are in the different groups. It can be a difficult goal to achieve, because the usual practice in social programs is to let people decide for themselves whether they want to enter a program and also to establish eligibility criteria that ensure that people who enter the program are different from those who do not (Boruch 1997). In either case, a selection bias is introduced.

Of course, program impact may also be evaluated with quasi-experimental designs (see Chapter 7) or survey or field research methods, without a randomized experimental design. But if current participants who are already in a program are compared to nonparticipants, it is unlikely that the treatment group will be comparable to the control group. Participants will probably be a selected group, different at the outset from nonparticipants. As a result, causal conclusions about program impact will be on much shakier ground. For instance, when a study at New York's maximum-security prison for women found that "Income Education [i.e., classes] Is Found to Lower Risk of New Arrest," the conclusions were immediately suspect: The research design did not ensure that the women who enrolled in the prison classes were the same as those who had not enrolled in the classes, "leaving open the possibility that the results were due, at least in part, to self-selection, with the women most motivated to avoid reincarceration being the ones who took the college classes" (Lewin 2001:A18).

Impact analysis is an important undertaking that fully deserves the attention it has been given in government program funding requirements. However, you should realize that more rigorous evaluation designs are less likely to conclude that a program has the desired effect; as the standard of proof goes up, success is harder to demonstrate. We will provide other case studies of impact evaluations at the end of the chapter.

The Evaluation of Efficiency

Whatever the program's benefits, are they sufficient to offset the program's costs? Are the taxpayers getting their money's worth? What resources are required by the program? These efficiency questions can be the primary reason that funders require evaluation of the programs they fund. As a result, **efficiency analysis**, which compares program effects to costs, is often a necessary component of an evaluation research project.

> **Efficiency analysis** A type of evaluation research that compares program costs to program effects. It can be either a cost-benefit analysis or a cost-effectiveness analysis.
>
> **Cost-benefit analysis** A type of evaluation research that compares program costs to the economic value of program benefits.
>
> **Cost-effectiveness analysis** A type of evaluation research that compares program costs to actual program outcomes.

A **cost-benefit analysis** must identify the specific program costs and the procedures for estimating the economic value of specific program benefits. This type of analysis also requires that the analyst identify whose perspective will be used in order to determine what can be considered a benefit rather than a cost.

A **cost-effectiveness analysis** focuses attention directly on the program's outcomes rather than on the economic value of those outcomes. In a cost-effectiveness analysis, the specific costs of the program are compared to the program's outcomes, such as the number of jobs obtained, the extent of improvement in reading scores, or the degree of decline in crimes committed. For example, one result might be an estimate of how much it cost the program for each job obtained by a program participant.

Social science training often does not include much attention to cost-benefit analysis, so it can be helpful to review possible costs and benefits with an economist or a business school professor or student. Once potential costs and benefits have been identified, they must be measured. It is a need highlighted in recent government programs:

> The Governmental Accounting Standards Board's (GASB) mission is to establish and improve standards of accounting and financial reporting for state and local governments in the United States. . . . The new reporting will provide information that citizens and other users can utilize to gain an understanding of the financial position and cost of programs for a government and a descriptive management's discussion and analysis to assist in understanding a government's financial results. (Campbell 2002:1)

In addition to measuring services and their associated costs, a cost-benefit analysis must be able to make some type of estimation of how clients benefited from the program. Normally, this will involve a comparison of some indicators of client status before and after clients received program services or between clients who received program services and a comparable group who did not.

📖 Case Study: Cost-Benefit Analysis of Therapeutic Communities

A recent study of therapeutic communities provides a clear illustration. A therapeutic community is an alternative to the traditional correctional response to drug addiction, which is typically incarceration for those convicted of either the possession or trafficking of illegal substances. In therapeutic communities, abusers participate in an intensive, structured living experience with other addicts who are attempting to stay sober. Because the treatment involves residential support as well as other types of services, it can be quite costly. Are those costs worth it?

Sacks et al. (2002) conducted a cost-benefit analysis of a modified therapeutic community (TC). A total of 342 homeless mentally ill chemical abusers were randomly assigned to either a TC or a "treatment-as-usual" comparison group. Employment status, criminal activity, and utilization of health care services were each measured for the 3 months prior to entering treatment and the 3 months after treatment. Earnings from employment in each period were adjusted for costs incurred by criminal activity and utilization of health care services.

Was it worth it? The average cost of TC treatment for a client was $20,361. In comparison, the economic benefit (based on earnings) to the average TC client was $305,273, which declined to $273,698 after comparing post- to pre-program earnings, but was still $253,337 even after adjustment for costs. The resulting benefit-cost ratio was 13:1, although this ratio declined to only 5.2:1 after further adjustments (for cases with extreme values). Nonetheless, the TC program studied seems to have had a substantial benefit relative to its costs.

The goal of most policymakers, of course, is to offer services that will justify the investment of funds. In a business, these cost-benefit analyses are relatively straightforward. When delivering human services, however, the evaluation of efficiency is a bit trickier, because the benefits are usually hard to convert into a dollar figure. The procedures involved in these types of analyses are highly technical and, as such, are beyond the scope of this book. It is important, however, to understand the concept of efficiency analysis. Sherman (1997) succinctly describes the importance of this type of evaluation:

> Even though scientific evaluation results are a key part of rational policy analysis, those results cannot automatically select the best policy. This is due not just to the scientific limitations of generalizing results from one setting to the next. Another reason is that evaluations often omit key data on cost-benefit ratios; the fact that a program is "effective" may be irrelevant if the financial or social costs are too high. (p. 11)

📖 Design Decisions

Once we have decided on, or identified, the goal or focus for a program evaluation, there are still important decisions to be made about how to design the specific evaluation project. The most important decisions are the following:

- Black box or program theory: Do we care how the program gets results?
- Researcher or stakeholder orientation: Whose goals matter most?
- Quantitative or qualitative methods: Which methods provide the best answers?
- Simple or complex outcomes: How complicated should the findings be?

Black Box Evaluation or Program Theory

The "meat and potatoes" of most evaluation research involves determining whether a program has the intended effect. If the effect occurred, the program "worked"; if the effect didn't occur, then, some would say, the program should be abandoned or redesigned. In this approach, the process by which a program has an effect on outcomes is often treated as a **black box**; that is, the focus of the evaluation researcher is on whether cases seem to have changed as a result of their exposure to the program, between the time they entered the program as inputs and when they exited the program as outputs (Chen 1990). The assumption is that program evaluation requires only the test of a simple input/output model. There may be no attempt to open the black box of the program process.

> **Black box evaluation** This type of evaluation occurs when an evaluation of program outcomes ignores, and does not identify, the process by which the program produced the effect.

> **Program theory** A descriptive or prescriptive model of how a program operates and produces its effects.

> **Theory-driven evaluation** A program evaluation that is guided by a theory that specifies the process by which the program has an effect.

If an investigation of program process is conducted, a **program theory** may be developed. A program theory describes what has been learned about how the program has its effect. When a researcher has sufficient knowledge before the investigation begins, outlining a program theory can help guide the investigation of program process in the most productive directions. This is termed a *theory-driven evaluation*.

A program theory specifies how the program is expected to operate and identifies which program elements are operational (Chen 1990). In addition, a program theory specifies how a program is to produce its effects and so improves understanding of the relationship between the independent variable (the program) and the dependent variable (the outcome or outcomes). For example, Exhibit 11.5 illustrates the theory for an alcoholism treatment program. It shows that persons entering the program are expected to respond to the combination of motivational interviewing and peer support. A program theory can also decrease the risk of failure when the program is transported to other settings, because it will help identify the conditions required for the program to have its intended effect.

Program theory can be either descriptive or prescriptive (Chen 1990). Descriptive theory specifies what impacts are generated and how they occur. It suggests a causal mechanism, including intervening factors, and the necessary

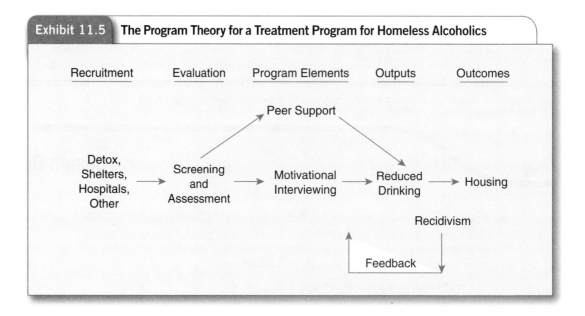

Exhibit 11.5 The Program Theory for a Treatment Program for Homeless Alcoholics

context for the effects. Descriptive theories are generally empirically based. On the other hand, prescriptive theory specifies what ought to be done by the program and is not actually tested. Prescriptive theory specifies how to design or implement the treatment, what outcomes should be expected, and how performance should be judged. Comparison of the descriptive and prescriptive theories of the program can help identify implementation difficulties and incorrect understandings that can be corrected (Patton 2002).

Researcher or Stakeholder Orientation?

Whose prescriptions specify how the program should operate, what outcomes it should try to achieve, or whom it should serve? Most social science research assumes that the researcher specifies the research questions, the applicable theory or theories, and the outcomes to be investigated. Social science research results are most often reported in a professional journal or at professional conferences where scientific standards determine how the research is received. In program evaluation, however, the research question is often set by the program sponsors or the government agency that is responsible for reviewing the program. In consulting projects for businesses, the client—a manager, perhaps, or a division president—decides what question researchers will study. It is to these authorities that research findings are reported. Most often this authority also specifies the outcomes to be investigated. The first evaluator of the evaluation research is the funding agency, then, not the professional social science community. Evaluation research is research for a client, and its results may directly affect the services, treatments, or even punishments (e.g., in the case of prison studies) that program users receive. In this case, the person who pays the piper gets to call the tune.

Should the evaluation researcher insist on designing the evaluation project and specifying its goals, or should she accept the suggestions and adopt the goals of the funding agency? What role should the preferences of program staff or clients play? What responsibility does the evaluation researcher have to politicians and taxpayers when evaluating government-funded programs? The different answers that various evaluation researchers have given to these questions are reflected in different approaches to evaluation (Chen 1990).

Stakeholder approaches encourage researchers to be responsive to program stakeholders (so this approach is also termed **responsive evaluation**). Issues for study are to be based on the views of people involved with the program, and reports are to be made to program participants (Shadish, Cook, and Leviton 1991). The program theory is developed by the researcher to clarify and develop the key stakeholders' theory of the program (Shadish et al. 1991). In one stakeholder approach, termed *utilization-focused evaluation*, the evaluator forms a task force of program stakeholders who help shape the evaluation project so that they are most likely to use its results (Patton 2002). In evaluation research termed *action research* or *participatory research*, program participants are engaged with the researchers as coresearchers and help design, conduct, and report the research. One research approach that has been termed *appreciative inquiry* eliminates the professional researcher altogether in favor of a structured dialogue about needed changes among program participants themselves (Patton 2002).

> *Stakeholder approaches (responsive evaluation)*
> An orientation to evaluation research that expects researchers to be responsive primarily to the people involved with the program.

In their book, *Fourth Generation Evaluation*, Guba and Lincoln (1989) argue for evaluations oriented toward stakeholders:

> The stakeholders and others who may be drawn into the evaluation are welcomed as equal partners in every aspect of design, implementation, interpretation, and resulting action of an evaluation—that is, they are accorded a full measure of political parity and control . . . determining what questions are to be asked and what information is to be collected on the basis of stakeholder inputs. (P. 11)

Because different stakeholders may differ on their reports about or assessment of the program, there is not likely to be one conclusion about program impact. The evaluators are primarily concerned with helping participants understand the views of other stakeholders and generate productive dialogue. Abma (2005) took this approach in a study of an injury prevention program at a dance school in the Netherlands:

> The evaluators acted as facilitators, paying deliberate attention to the development of trust and a respectful, open and comfortable climate. . . . Furthermore, the evaluation stimulated a public discourse about issues that were taboo, created a space for reflection fostered dynamics and motivated participants to think about ways to improve the quality of their teaching practice. (pp. 284–85)

Social science approaches An orientation to evaluation research that expects researchers to emphasize the importance of researcher expertise and maintenance of autonomy from program stakeholders.

Social science approaches emphasize the importance of researcher expertise and maintenance of some autonomy in order to develop the most trustworthy, unbiased program evaluation. It is assumed that "evaluators cannot passively accept the values and views of the other stakeholders" (Chen 1990:78). Evaluators who adopt this approach derive a program theory from information they obtain on how the program operates and extant social science theory and knowledge, not from the views of stakeholders. In one somewhat extreme form of this approach, *goal-free evaluation*, researchers do not even permit themselves to learn what goals the program stakeholders have for the program. Instead, the researcher assesses and then compares the needs of participants to a wide array of program outcomes (Scriven 1972). The goal-free evaluator wants to see the unanticipated outcomes and to remove any biases caused by knowing the program goals in advance.

Of course, there are disadvantages to both stakeholder and social science approaches to program evaluation. If stakeholders are ignored, researchers may find that participants are uncooperative, that their reports are unused, and that the next project remains unfunded. On the other hand, if social science procedures are neglected, standards of evidence will be compromised, conclusions about program effects will likely be invalid, and results are unlikely to be generalizable to other settings. These equally undesirable possibilities have led to several attempts to develop more integrated approaches to evaluation research.

Integrative approaches An orientation to evaluation research that expects researchers to respond to concerns of people involved with stakeholders as well as to the standards and goals of the social scientific community.

Integrative approaches attempt to cover issues of concern to both stakeholders and evaluators, as well as to include stakeholders in the group from which guidance is routinely sought (Chen and Rossi 1987). The emphasis given to either stakeholder or social concern is expected to vary with the specific project circumstances. Integrated approaches seek to balance the goal of carrying out a project that is responsive to stakeholder concerns with the goal of objective, scientifically trustworthy, and generalizable results. When the research is planned, evaluators are expected to communicate and negotiate regularly with key stakeholders and to take stakeholder concerns into account. Findings from preliminary inquiries are reported back to program decision makers so that they can make improvements in the program before it is formally evaluated. When the actual evaluation is conducted, the evaluation research team is expected to operate more autonomously, minimizing intrusions from program stakeholders.

Many evaluation researchers now recognize that they must take account of multiple values in their research and be sensitive to the perspectives of different stakeholders, in addition to maintaining a commitment to the goals of measurement validity, internal validity, and generalizability (Chen 1990). Ultimately, evaluation research takes place in a political context, in which program stakeholders may be competing or collaborating to increase program funding or to emphasize particular program goals. It is a political process that creates social programs, and it is a political process that determines whether these programs are evaluated and what is done with evaluation findings (Weiss 1993). Developing supportive relations with stakeholder groups will increase the odds that political processes will not undermine evaluation practice. You do not want to find out after you are all done that "people operating ineffective programs who depend on them for their jobs" are able to prevent an evaluation report from having any impact ("'Get Tough' Youth Programs Are Ineffective, Panel Says" 2004:25).

Simple or Complex Outcomes

Does the program have only one outcome? Unlikely. How many outcomes are anticipated? How many might be unintended? Which are direct consequences of program action, and which are indirect effects that occur as a result of the direct effects (Mohr 1992)? Do the longer-term outcomes follow directly from the immediate program outputs? Does the output (the increase in test scores at the end of the preparation course) result surely in the desired outcomes (increased rates of college admission)? Due to these and other possibilities, the selection of outcome measures is a critical step in evaluation research.

The decision to focus on one outcome rather than another, or on a single outcome or on several, can have enormous implications. When Sherman and Berk (1984) evaluated the impact of an immediate arrest policy in cases of domestic violence in Minneapolis, Minnesota, they focused on recidivism as the key outcome. Similarly, the reduction of recidivism was the single desired outcome of prison "boot camps" opened in the 1990s. Boot camps are military-style programs for prison inmates that provide tough, highly regimented activities and harsh punishment for disciplinary infractions, with the goal of scaring inmates "straight." They were very popular in the 1990s, and the researchers who evaluated their impact understandably focused on criminal recidivism.

But these single-purpose programs turned out not to be quite so simple to evaluate. The Minneapolis researchers found that there was no adequate single source for records of recidivism in domestic violence cases, so they had to hunt for evidence from court and police records, follow-up interviews with victims, and family member reports. More easily measured variables, such as partners' ratings of the accused's subsequent behavior, eventually received more attention. Boot camp researchers soon concluded that the experience did not reduce recidivism: "Many communities are wasting a great deal of money on those types of programs" (Robert L. Johnson quoted in "'Get Tough' Youth Programs Are Ineffective, Panel Says" 2004:25). However, some participants felt the study had missed something:

> [A staff member] saw things unfold that he had never witnessed among inmates and their caretakers. Those experiences profoundly affected the drill instructors and their charges, who still call to talk to the guards they once saw as torturers. Graduation ceremonies routinely reduced inmates, relatives, and sometimes even supervisors to tears. (Latour 2002:B7)

Former boot camp superintendent Michael Corsini compared a Massachusetts boot camp to other correctional facilities and concluded, "Here, it was a totally different experience" (Latour 2002:B7).

Some now argue that the failure of boot camps to reduce recidivism was due to the lack of post-prison support rather than a failure of the camps to promote positive change in inmates. Looking only at recidivism rates would ignore some important positive results.

So in spite of the additional difficulties introduced by measuring multiple outcomes, most evaluation researchers attempt to do so (Mohr 1992). The result usually is a much more realistic, and richer, understanding of program impact.

Of course, there is a potential downside to the collection of multiple outcomes. Policymakers may choose to publicize those outcomes that support their own policy preferences and ignore the rest. Often, evaluation researchers themselves have little ability to publicize a more complete story.

In a sense, all these choices (black box or program theory, researcher or stakeholder interests, etc.) hinge on (a) what your real goals are in doing the project and (b) how able you will be in a "research for hire" setting to achieve those goals. Not every agency really wants to know if its programs work, especially if the answer is no. Dealing with such issues and the choices they require is part of what makes evaluation research both scientifically and politically fascinating.

▣ Evaluation in Action

Case Study: Problem-Oriented Policing in Violent Crime Areas—A Randomized Controlled Experiment

Several studies have found that over half of all crimes in a city are committed at a few criminogenic places within communities. These places have been called "hot spots" by some criminologists (Sherman, Gartin, and Buerger 1989; Weisburd, Maher, and Sherman 1992). Even within the most crime-ridden neighborhoods, it has been found that crime clusters at a few discrete locations while other areas remain relatively crime-free. The clustering of violent crime at particular locations suggests that there are important features or dynamics at these locations that give rise to violent situations. As such, focused crime prevention efforts should be able to modify these criminogenic conditions and reduce violence.

Problem-oriented policing strategies are increasingly utilized by urban jurisdictions to reduce crime in these high-activity crime places. Problem-oriented policing challenges officers to identify and analyze the causes of problems behind a string of criminal incidents. Once the underlying conditions that give rise to crime problems are known, police officers can then develop and implement appropriate responses. Despite the increasing use of problem-oriented policing strategies, however, there has been very little evaluation research conducted to determine whether such strategies are actually effective in decreasing crime rates.

Braga et al. (1999) created a novel experiment designed to determine the effectiveness of problem-oriented policing to decrease the incidence of violent street crime in Jersey City, New Jersey. The methodology they employed for their study was a true randomized experimental design. Recall from Chapter 6 that this design allows researchers to assume that the only systematic difference between a control and an experimental group is the presence of the intervention, in this case the presence or absence of problem-oriented policing strategies.

To determine which places would receive the problem-oriented strategies and which places would not, Braga et al. (1999) used computerized mapping technologies to analyze all robbery and assault incidents and emergency citizen calls for services in Jersey City. These incidents were then matched to intersection areas (the intersection and its four adjoining street segments) and counted. Braga et al. then identified 56 discrete high-activity violent crime places. These 56 places were then matched into 28 pairs. Matching was done on a number of variables, including the primary offenses in each place (e.g., places with lower numbers of robberies and higher numbers of assaults were grouped together), types of problems at a place (e.g., robberies of commuters versus robberies of convenience stores), known dynamics of the place (e.g., the presence of active drug markets), and physical characteristics (e.g., presence of a park or school). A coin was flipped by the researchers to randomly determine which of the places within the pair would receive the problem-oriented policing treatment (experimental places). Remember that a key feature of true experimental designs is this **random assignment**. The places that were not selected from the flip in each pair did not receive the new policing strategies (control places). The design of this experimental evaluation is illustrated in Exhibit 11.6.

> **Random assignment** A procedure by which each experimental and control group subjects are placed in a group randomly.

In each of the experimental places, police officers from the violent crime unit (VCU) of the Jersey City police department established networks consistent with problem-oriented policing. For example, community members were used as information sources to discuss the nature of the problems the community faced, the possible effectiveness of proposed responses, and the assessment of implemented responses. In most places, the VCU officers believed that the violence that distinguished these places from other areas of the city was closely related to the disorder of the place. Although specific tactics varied from place to place, most attempts to control violence in these places were actually targeted at the social disorder

Exhibit 11.6 Randomized Experimental Design Used to Evaluate Problem-Oriented Policing Strategies

Source: Braga et al. 1999.

problems. For example, some tactics included cleaning up the environment of the place through aggressive order maintenance and making physical improvements such as securing vacant lots or removing trash from the street. Other tactics included aggressive interventions to control the social disorder of a place, such as repeat foot and radio car patrols, dispersing groups of loiterers, and stop-and-frisks of suspicious persons. In addition, in places where drug markets were located, VCU officers increased their investigations to disrupt both the selling and the consumption of illicit drugs. The independent variable or treatment, then, was the use of problem-oriented policing, which comprised a number of specific tactics implemented by police officers to control the physical and social disorder at experimental violent places. In contrast, control places did not receive these problem-solving efforts; they received traditional policing strategies such as arbitrary patrol interventions and routine follow-up investigations by detectives. No problem-oriented strategies were employed.

Braga et al. (1999) examined the efficacy of these problem-oriented policing strategies by using three separate dependent variables. The first two were traditional indicators of crime, incident report data and citizen emergency calls for service within each place. The third variable was a physical observation of each place during the pretest and posttest periods. This variable was used to indicate changes in both physical incivilities at places such as vacant lots, trash, graffiti, or broken windows and social incivilities such as drinking in public and loitering. These variables were measured for 6-month preintervention and postintervention periods. If the problem-oriented policing approach was effective, then Braga et al. should have seen a decrease in incidents and emergency calls for service in the experimental areas in the posttest compared to the control areas. They should also have seen decreased signs of physical and social incivilities in the experimental areas compared to the control areas.

Results indicated that the total number of criminal incidents and the total number of citizen calls for service were significantly reduced at the experimental places relative to the control places. This effect was true for most specific crime types examined as well. Examination of the observational data indicated that both physical disorder and social disorder were reduced in 91 of the experimental places compared to the control places. Thus, the problem-oriented policing strategies examined in this evaluation research appear to have had a great deal of success in controlling and preventing crime.

Recall from Chapter 7 that although randomized experiments do allow us to determine whether the independent variable had an effect on the dependent variable, they do not tell us why. That is, they do not provide us with information about the causal **mechanisms** that may be producing this effect. Braga et al. (1999), however, utilized several theories to speculate on how these problem-oriented strategies may have changed the dynamics of a place in ways that resulted in a decrease in crime. For example, based on rational choice theory, which asserts that offenders consider risks, effort, and reward when contemplating criminal acts, the

> **Mechanism** A discernible process that creates a causal connection between two variables.

researchers speculated that the increased presence and order maintenance activities at the experimental places may have served as a powerful deterrent by communicating to offenders that disorderly behavior would no longer be tolerated. Braga et al. correctly pointed out, however, that the study did not gather data to determine the specific causal mechanisms responsible for the reductions found in crime. To do this, other forms of research would be necessary, such as interviewing offenders to determine their perceptions regarding their decisions to offend or to desist from offending in particular places.

What is certain from this research is that problem-oriented policing strategies are more effective in reducing both incidents of violent crime and citizen calls for emergency service than traditional policing strategies. Braga and his colleagues (1999) concluded,

> Law enforcement agencies interested in controlling violence should consider implementing problem-oriented policing programs that focus on the places where violence clusters by developing tailored interventions addressing the underlying conditions and dynamics that give rise to violent situations. (P. 571)

Strengths of Randomized Experimental Design in Impact Evaluations

The research design used by Braga et al. (1999) meets all three criteria for a true experimental design. First, they used at least two comparison groups. In the Braga et al. research, some communities received the problem-oriented patrol strategies (experimental groups) while the other comparison communities received traditional police patrol (control groups). And finally, the assessment of change in the dependent variables used in their study was performed after the experimental condition (problem-oriented strategies) had been delivered.

Recall the three criteria necessary for establishing a causal relationship between independent and dependent variables (see Chapter 6):

1. Association between the independent and dependent variables

2. Correct time order (the independent variable precedes the dependent)

3. Nonspuriousness (rule out influence of other variables)

Data obtained from a true experimental design provide the best way to determine that all three of these criteria have been met.

Because the communities in the study by Braga et al. (1999) were randomly assigned to receive either problem-oriented or traditional patrol strategies, the relationship found between these strategies (independent variable) and the dependent variables (incidents of crime, etc.) is unambiguous. Braga et al. monitored their dependent variables both before and after the different policing strategies were implemented, so there is also no question that the strategies came before the change in the dependent variable. Finally, the random assignment of the communities to either the problem-oriented or traditional police conditions controlled for a host of possible extraneous influences that may have created spurious relationships.

The extent to which the findings of these studies can be generalized to the larger population, however, is another issue. Can findings by Braga et al. (1999) be generalized to the larger population in New Jersey (sample generalizability) or to other states and communities (external validity)? Issues of sample generalizability, you will recall, are related to selecting a random sample from the population in the first place (random selection), not random assignment. However, because the study by Braga et al. utilized several experimental and control communities, this increases the likelihood that their findings are generalizable to their respective populations. In addition, because the study was a field experiment (i.e., real world) and not in a laboratory, their findings are more likely to be generalizable to the larger population.

回 Quasi-Experimental Designs in Evaluation Research

We have already learned that many research questions or situations are not amenable to a true experimental design. The same is true in evaluation research. There are many reasons why it may be impossible to use randomized experiments to evaluate the impacts of programs and policies. The primary reason why randomization is not possible in evaluation research is that the program is usually outside the control of the evaluator. As Rossi and Freeman (1989) state, "For political, human subject or other considerations, program staff, sponsors, or other powerful stakeholders resist randomization" (p. 313). Obtaining the cooperation of the program staff and sponsors is often an obstacle in evaluation research. In fact, when there are several locations implementing similar programs, the sites included in an evaluation study may be selected based primarily on the cooperation of the staff and sponsors. For example, in their evaluation study of treatment alternatives to street crime (TASC), Anglin, Longshore, and Turner (1999) state, "The program's ability to negotiate successfully with local officials to ensure their cooperation with evaluation activities was also a condition of study inclusion" (p. 172).

In general, **quasi-experimental designs** are the most powerful alternatives to true randomized experimental designs. The more alike the experimental and control groups are to each other, particularly on characteristics thought to be related to the intervention or treatment, the more confident we can be in a study's findings. In this section, we will discuss two types of quasi-experimental designs that are often utilized in criminology and criminal justice to determine the impacts of programs. To illustrate the first type, a **nonequivalent control group design**, we will use research that has been done to evaluate whether boot camps are more likely to reduce recidivism after release compared to traditional incarceration. The second type of quasi-experimental design we will highlight is the **time series design**. To illustrate this design, we will use a study that evaluated the impact of mandatory sentences for gun crimes.

> ***Quasi-experimental design*** A research design in which there is a comparison group that is comparable to the experimental group in critical ways, but subjects are not randomly assigned to the comparison and experimental groups.
>
> ***Nonequivalent control group design*** A quasi-experimental design in which there are experimental and comparison groups that are designated before the treatment occurs but are not created by random assignment.
>
> ***Time series design*** A quasi-experimental design consisting of many pretest and posttest observations of the same group.

回 Case Study: Boot Camps

As noted above, the use of correctional boot camps, sometimes called shock incarceration programs, has skyrocketed in both state and federal prison systems. For politicians and citizens alike, the notion of a strict, military-style punishment as an alternative to extended incarceration is attractive. But do they work? Because there are so many different types of boot camps (e.g., some have a military-style atmosphere whereas others do not), there is no easy answer to this question.

Doris MacKenzie and her colleagues have evaluated boot camp program efficacy in eight states: Florida, Georgia, Illinois, Louisiana, New York, Oklahoma, South Carolina, and Texas. These sites were selected because they incorporated the core elements of a boot camp program, including (a) strict rules, discipline, and a military boot camp-like atmosphere; (b) mandatory participation in military drills and physical training; and (c) separation of program participants from other prison inmates.

The evaluation was extensive and resulted in many publications (Brame and MacKenzie 1996; MacKenzie 1994; MacKenzie et al. 1995; MacKenzie and Piquero 1994; MacKenzie and Souryal 1995). Rather than focusing on one measure of program success, such as recidivism reduction, MacKenzie et al. developed five different components to their evaluation: a process evaluation of the programs based on interviews with staff and inmates, official program materials, and observation; a study of inmate attitudinal change during incarceration; a study of offender recidivism; a study of positive adjustment during community supervision; and a study of prison bed–space savings.

We will highlight the results of the impact assessments for recidivism here. To determine whether boot camps were more likely than traditional prison time to reduce recidivism after release, MacKenzie et al. utilized a quasi-experimental design. In each state, a sample of male boot camp program graduates was used as the experimental condition. Two other offender samples were used as comparison groups and usually included regular prison parolees, probationers, and boot camp dropouts. The individuals from all samples, however, met the eligibility requirements for the boot camp programs. This nonequivalent control group design is illustrated for you in Exhibit 11.7.

After being sentenced to probation or released from boot camps and prison, subjects were tracked for a follow-up period of up to 2 years of community supervision. Recidivism was measured by arrests and revocations for new crimes and/or for technical violations.

Were boot camps successful in meeting their goals? Well, in five states (Florida, Georgia, Oklahoma, South Carolina, and Texas), MacKenzie's findings suggest that boot camp graduates appeared to recidivate at about the same rate as those from the comparison groups. In Illinois, Louisiana, and New York, however, boot camp graduates had lower recidivism rates on particular recidivism measures. Graduates in Illinois and Louisiana, for example, were less likely to have their supervision status revoked as a result of a new crime revocation than were comparison samples. And although they did not differ from the comparison sample on other measures of recidivism, New York boot camp graduates were less likely to be returned to prison as a result of a technical violation.

The weakness of this quasi-experimental design lay in the fact that MacKenzie was not able to randomly assign offenders to the boot camps or the comparison treatments. Therefore, there is less confidence in the findings, primarily because there is no assurance that the offenders were equivalent before they received the treatments. To control for these differences, MacKenzie and colleagues utilized strong statistical evidence that served to increase the internal validity of their findings.

In addition, even for the modest effects found in the three states, there is still some ambiguity about how the independent variable, in this case the type of incarceration, influenced the dependent variable (recidivism).

Exhibit 11.7	Nonequivalent Control Group Design Used to Evaluate Boot Camps

Subjects	Group	Treatment/Condition	Posttest
Boot camp–eligible offenders	Experimental group →	Boot camp →	Recidivism
	Comparison →	Prison →	Recidivism
	Comparison →	Probation →	Recidivism

Source: Brame and MacKenzie 1996.

MacKenzie does, however, speculate about the reasons why the Illinois, Louisiana, and New York programs showed reduced recidivism rates compared to their respective comparison programs. In fact, MacKenzie contends that one of the reasons may have had little to do with the boot camps themselves:

> These programs stand out as the only boot camps in the study that have developed an intensive supervision phase for boot camp graduates. It is therefore very likely that differences in recidivism rates in these states were due to the type of community supervision provided to graduates, not in-prison programming. (MacKenzie and Souryal 1996:293)

In addition, these boot camps devoted a considerable amount of time per day to rehabilitative activities such as drug treatment services.

In summary, MacKenzie's (1994) results were not very favorable for boot camps. She states,

> Results clearly show that the core elements of boot camp programs—military-style discipline, hard labor, and physical training—by themselves did not reduce offender recidivism—but it is likely that some mixture of rehabilitation and intensive follow-up supervision plays an important role. (p. 65)

🗐 Case Study: Drinking and Homicide in Eastern Europe

Alcohol consumptions has been linked to violence by many researchers, not just in the United States, but in many countries. In fact the World Health Organization (WHO) estimates that nearly ¼ of homicides are attributable to alcohol worldwide (WHO, 2011). Research also reveals that the relationship between alcohol and violence is culturally mediated. That is, if the cultural ethos of getting drunk also involves violence, individuals are more likely to be violent when drunk compared to individuals whose cultural response to violence is more lethargic or peaceful. To examine the effects of alcohol consumption on rates of homicide in several Eastern European countries (Russian, Belarus, Poland, former Czechoslovakia, Hungary, and Bulgaria), Bye (2008) examined per capita alcohol consumption and homicide rate data for various time periods, generally between the 1950s through 2002. To measure alcohol consumption, Bye (2008) actually used annual sales in liters of pure alcohol per inhabitant aged 15 and older, which does not include alcohol made at home. Based on survey data, several of the countries are characterized by heavy and/or binge drinking that often leads to intoxication (e.g., Russia and Belarus), while Poland is characterized by nondaily drinking and irregular binge drinking episodes.

We won't highlight results for all countries, but instead focus on a contrast between Russia and Poland. Exhibits 11.8 and 11.9 display the alcohol sales plotted along with total, male, and female homicide rates over time for Poland and Russia respectively. For Poland, alcohol sales increased steadily until 1980 until pressures from the Solidarity movement introduced rationing and reduced state production of alcohol. Trends in Russia indicate an increasing trend in both alcohol sales and homicide rates until 1985 when policies reduced alcohol availability. After the campaign in 1988, both alcohol consumption and homicide rates began to increase again. It can also be seen that the relationship between alcohol consumption in Russia is very consistent with increases in homicide rates; as alcohol sales increase, so do homicide rates. In Poland, however, alcohol consumption remained relatively unchanged during the increase in homicide rates witnessed in the 1990s. Bye's (2008) statistical analyses confirm these descriptive displays. The effects of alcohol consumption on homicide rates was more pronounced in countries with more detrimental drinking patterns, "implying that the relative risk will depend on the patterns of drinking and of behavior associated with drinking in a particular society" (Bye 2008:24).

Exhibit 11.8	Alcohol Sales, Total, Male and Female Homicide Rates From 1959 to 2002 for Poland.

Source: Bye, Elin K. 2008. Alcohol and Homicide in Eastern Europe: A Time Series Analysis of Six Countries.

Exhibit 11.9	Alcohol Sales, Total, Male and Female Homicide Rates From 1959 to 2002 for Russia.

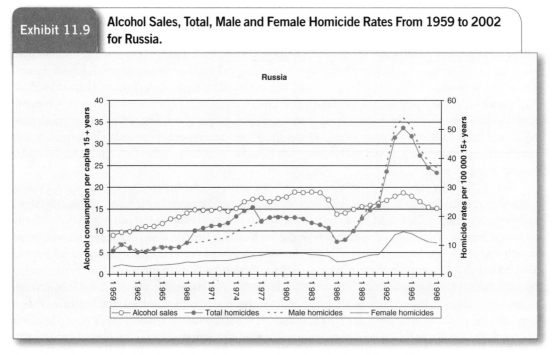

Source: Bye, Elin K. 2008. Alcohol and Homicide in Eastern Europe: A Time Series Analysis of Six Countries.

🔲 Nonexperimental Designs

Much research that is conducted to evaluate the effectiveness of programs or policies uses a nonexperimental design in which a single group is studied only once, after the treatment or program has been delivered. Unfortunately, such studies have absolutely no form of control or comparison. As such, they are "of almost no scientific value" (Campbell and Stanley 1966:6). Fortunately, their use by researchers interested in determining the efficacy of programs is decreasing dramatically. To illustrate the deficiencies of these designs in evaluation research, we provide a case study of their use—fortunately, these kinds of one-shot designs are getting harder and harder to find!

> **One-shot design** A research design that measures the dependent variable after the treatment has been delivered for only those who receive the treatment.

🔲 Case Study: Vocational Education for Serious Juvenile Offenders—A One-Shot Design

Some of the earliest programs for crime reduction have been those that provide legitimate employment or employment skills to offenders or at-risk individuals. Most of these programs target adolescents. One of the myriad programs to provide vocational education for juvenile offenders is New Pride, Inc. This program has been providing vocational services to serious young offenders (14 through 18 years of age) for almost two decades. Designed as an alternative to institutionalization in state correctional facilities, New Pride uses a holistic approach and provides a wide array of services, including diagnostic and needs assessment, intensive supervision in the community, individual and family counseling, prevocational training (e.g., basic academic and social interactional skills), vocational training and job placement, structured recreation, and cultural education. Based on results of the diagnostic and needs assessment, services are individualized to meet the specific needs of each youth and are integrated into a single treatment plan.

The planners of New Pride, understandably, have a lot of faith in their program. Unfortunately, there have been few systematic attempts to evaluate the effectiveness of this program and others like it in either increasing employment or reducing recidivism (Bushway and Reuter 1997). For example, the results of the one-shot design methodology evaluation performed by James and Granville (1984) of the New Pride program are too scientifically deficient to be of value. This methodology is displayed in Exhibit 11.10.

Basically, a one-shot design measures the dependent variable after the treatment has been delivered for only those who received the treatment. James and Granville (1984) found that over 70% of those who completed the New Pride program were successfully reintegrated into the public school system, continued part-time employment, and were not rearrested within 6 months of program completion. Unfortunately, because there was no random assignment to another comparison group—in fact, there was no comparison group whatsoever—these results tell us very little. This type of design is vulnerable

Exhibit 11.10	One-Shot Design Used to Evaluate the New Pride Program

Subjects	Treatment/Condition	Posttest
Serious young offenders (14–18 years old) →	Received New Pride program →	Recidivism and school placement

Source: James and Granville 1984.

to all the confounding effects described in Chapter 7 including selection bias, endogenous change, and history effects. Perhaps the results would have been the same for youths who had received no vocational training. The problem is we can never be sure when a one-shot design such as this is used.

Qualitative and Quantitative Methods

Evaluation research that attempts to identify the effects of a treatment, law, or program typically is quantitative. It is fair to say that when there is an interest in comparing outcomes between an experimental and a control group or in tracking change over time in a systematic manner, quantitative methods are favored.

But qualitative methods can add much to quantitative evaluation research studies, including more depth, detail, nuance, and exemplary case studies (Patton 1997). Perhaps the greatest contribution qualitative methods can make in many evaluation studies is investigating program process, finding out what is "inside the black box." Although it is possible, even recommended, to track the process of service delivery with quantitative measures like staff contact hours, frequency of complaints, and the like, the goal of finding out what is happening to program clients and how clients experience the program can often best be achieved by observing program activities and interviewing staff and clients intensively.

Another good reason for using qualitative methods in evaluation research is the importance of learning how different individuals react to the treatment. Qualitative methods can also help in understanding how social programs actually operate. Complex social programs have many different features, and it is not always clear whether it is the combination of those features or some particular features that are responsible for the program's effect, or for the absence of an effect. Lisbeth B. Schorr, director of the Harvard Project on Effective Interventions, and Daniel Yankelovich, president of Public Agenda, put it this way: "Social programs are sprawling efforts with multiple components requiring constant mid-course corrections, the involvement of committed human beings, and flexible adaptation to local circumstances" (Schorr and Yankelovich 2000:A19).

The more complex the social program, the more value that qualitative methods can add to the evaluation process. Schorr and Yankelovich (2000) point to the TenPoint Coalition, an alliance of African American ministers who helped reduce gang warfare in Boston through multiple initiatives, "ranging from neighborhood probation patrols to safe havens for recreation" (p. A19). Qualitative methods would help describe a complex, multifaceted program like this.

For the most part, the strengths and weaknesses of methodologies used in evaluation research are those of the methods we have already discussed throughout this text. As Patton (1997) contends, "There are no perfect [evaluation] studies. And there cannot be, for there is no agreement on what constitutes perfection" (p. 23). There are, however, methods that are better able to infer cause and effect. Because the basic question of most impact evaluations is "Does the program (cause) have its intended consequences (effect)?" there are basic methodological criteria we can use to judge the methods discussed in this chapter.

In their review of the crime prevention evaluation literature, Sherman et al. (1997) adopted a way to judge the "methodological rigor" of evaluation studies using a 5-point scale. The researchers gave each study examined in their review a "scientific methods score" of 1 to 5, with 5 being the strongest scientific evidence. Only studies that used random assignment to a program (experimental group) and comparison group (control groups) were assigned a score of 5. Studies that used a comparison between multiple groups with and without a program, controlling for other factors received a score of 4.

Despite the fact that a randomized experiment is the best way to determine the impact of a program, it is also important to remember that the methodology selected for an evaluation project should be relevant to the policymakers and planners who intend to use the results. Although some researchers vehemently contend that only a randomized experimental design can provide reliable information on the impacts of a program, others just as vehemently disagree.

For example, in his utilization-focused method of evaluation, Patton (1997) believes that when making evaluation methods decisions, the primary focus should be on getting the best possible data to answer primary users' questions. This cannot be done without involving them in the decision-making process to begin with. For methods decisions, the emphasis is on the appropriateness of the method to answer the practitioner's questions. Patton contends that only when these decisions are made in collaboration with the primary users will they be perceived as credible and, thus, more likely to be used.

It should also be noted that evaluation research faces obstacles not faced by general social research. We have already highlighted a few of these including the obstacle of obtaining support and cooperation from program staff and sponsors. In their review of evaluation research on crime prevention programs, Sherman et al. (1997) delineate several other obstacles. For example, one obstacle noted is the structural separation of research and program funding. In everyday life, this often means that an evaluator is brought in after a program has been implemented and asked to assess its consequences. This, of course, leads to several problems. How can the consequences be accurately assessed if the evaluator did not have the opportunity to monitor the dependent variable (outcomes) before the program was started? How can the consequences be accurately assessed if the evaluator had no chance to obtain a comparison group by randomly assigning some units (e.g., individuals or communities) to the program or treatment condition and others elsewhere? To ameliorate this problem, Sherman recommends that Congress produce financial incentives for partnerships to be created between local agencies implementing programs and researchers evaluating them.

▣ Increasing Demand for Evidence-Based Policy

As you have seen in this chapter, evaluation studies come in many forms. A single study, such as the Minneapolis Domestic Violence Experiment (first introduced in Chapter 2), can be very influential and have an enormous effect on police policies. But we have seen that replications of studies answering the same question often result in very different conclusions. Obviously learning what works should rely on more than one study. Evaluation specialists are increasingly encouraging policymakers to enact evidence-based policies, which are based on a **systematic review** of all available evidence that assesses what works and what doesn't. Petrosino and Lavenberg (2007) define systematic reviews as follows:

> In systematic reviews, researchers attempt to gather relevant evaluative studies, critically appraise them, and come to judgments about what works using explicit, transparent, state-of-the-art methods. In contrast to traditional syntheses, a systematic review will include detail about each stage of the decision process, including the question that guided the review, the criteria for studies to be included, and the methods used to search for and screen evaluation reports. It will also detail how analyses were done and how conclusions were reached. (p. 1)

> **Systematic review** Summary review about the impact of a program wherein the analyst attempts to account for differences across research designs and samples, often using statistical techniques such as a meta-analysis.

The reviews often try to quantify the successfulness of particular programs and interventions, sometimes using a technique called meta-analysis, which we describe later. Although these reviews are designed to be objective, there are still controversies surrounding any particular review, including conflict about the inclusion or exclusion of studies and what qualifies as a rigorous study design (e.g., is a true experimental design the only way to determine causality?).

Systematic reviews are increasingly sponsored by both private and government entities. One private organization that has become a leader in publicizing reviews related to criminal justice policy research is the **Campbell Collaboration**. The Campbell Collaboration is an international research network that prepares and disseminates

Campbell Collaboration Group producing systematic reviews of programs and policies in many areas including criminal justice, social work, and education.

systematic reviews of social science evidence in three fields including crime and justice, education, and social welfare. The collaboration's mission "is to promote positive social change, by contributing to better-informed decisions and better-quality public and private services around the world" (www.campbellcollaboration.org). All reports are peer reviewed and are available on the collaboration's Web site. One example from the online Campbell Library (www.campbellcollaboration .org/library.php) is a systematic review by Tolan et al. (2008) that examined the impact of mentoring interventions in decreasing delinquency and other problems. If you read the report, you will see that all decisions made by the authors are explicitly stated. For example, they were very specific in their criteria for mentoring, which had to meet four criteria: (a) an interaction between two individuals over an extended period of time; (b) inequality of experience, knowledge, or power between the mentor and mentee, with the mentor possessing the greater share; (c) the mentee is in a position to imitate and benefit from the knowledge, skill, ability, or experience of the mentor; and (d) the absence of inequality that typifies other helping relationships and is marked by professional training, certification, or predetermined status differences such as parent-child or teacher-student relationships.

When selecting studies for their review, Tolan et al. (2008) also clearly stated four criteria: (a) studies that focused on youth who were at risk for juvenile delinquency or who were currently involved in delinquent behavior; (b) studies that focused on prevention or treatment for those at-risk youth; (c) studies that measured at least one quantitative effect on at least one outcome including delinquency, substance abuse, academic achievement, or aggression; and (d) studies that were conducted in predominately English-speaking countries reported between 1980 and 2005. As you can see, systematic reviews are, well, extremely systematic! For the record, the review found that there was a modest impact of mentoring in reducing delinquency and aggression, but less of an effect was found between mentoring and drug use and academic achievement. Meta-analyses, which are often used in systematic reviews, will be discussed in the next chapter.

▣ Basic Science or Applied Research

Alfred Blumstein (2009) has argued that criminologists and other social scientists who do research on criminal justice-related issues are "constantly in a battle with ideology that argues policy positions from a strongly ideological and moralistic position rather than one based on scientific knowledge of how to be effective in policy" (p. 1). For example, you can find many examples of criminal justice policies that were implemented based on political imperatives that were not based on empirical evidence such as "three strikes" laws, many drug-related laws including the mandatory minimum sentences, sexual offender registry laws, and so on. This reality is being played out at a time when funding agencies are increasingly demanding that policy relevance be addressed in research proposals.

Evaluation research like the studies examined in this chapter and elsewhere in the text seeks to determine whether one program or policy has a more desirable impact than another. This knowledge can then be applied to policy formation and, as such, is termed applied research. In contrast, basic science is generally used for the discipline itself, for advancing general knowledge and "more precisely for generating and testing hypotheses serving to support, modify or innovate theory" (Junger-Tas 2005:147). In distinguishing between basic science and applied research, Junger-Tas further explains, "The most important distinction . . . is that the former addresses scientific questions, such as the accumulation or extension of knowledge, and aims at theoretical conclusions, while the

Basic science In contrast to applied research, the main motivation of basic science is to advance general knowledge and/or to test theoretical propositions.

latter addresses political and policy decisions, and as such is action-oriented" (p. 148). Canton and Yates (2008) identify three basic questions that applied criminology should address:

1. What is to be done about offenders?

2. What is to be done about crime?

3. What is to be done on behalf of victims of crime?

Do you think that doing applied research would be good for society as well as for social researchers? Or do you think that a focus on how to improve society might lead social researchers to distort their understanding of how society works? Regardless of your own orientation, you have lots of company in the debate. In the 19th century, sociologist Lester Frank Ward (soon to be the American Sociological Society's first president) endorsed applied research: "The real object of science is to benefit man. A science which fails to do this, however agreeable its study, is lifeless" (Ward 1897:xxvii). But in 1929, American Sociological Society President William Fielding Ogburn urged sociologists to be guided by a basic research orientation: "Sociology as a science is not interested in making the world a better place to live. . . . Science is interested directly in one thing only, to wit, discovering new knowledge" (Ogburn 1930:300–301).

While many criminological researchers view applied and basic research as complementary, tension between these two orientations has continued ever since these early disputes. For example, Joyner (2003) recently stated, "I argue that the call for social science research to be 'value-free' is untenable and that a legitimate role for the [researcher] involves using one's disciplinary perspective and research to inform program and policy development in an attempt to improve the quality of life for marginalized groups" (p. 5).

Others have articulated warnings about where the demand for policy relevance may lead. For example, even Garvin and Lee (2003), who have engaged in policy-related research of their own, have asked researchers to critically examine the dangers of this increased demand for policy relevance and how these demands might affect research decisions. The first decision that may be affected, of course, is the research question itself. Garvin and Lee state,

> If our gaze leads us to seek only policy-relevant data and findings, what might we overlook? What questions might we *not* ask? . . . We may miss some of the most interesting parts of the work, as well as subtle yet critical power relations, in our hurry to solve problems. More dangerously, we may simply pass over the more challenging research questions because they may not seem policy-relevant at a particular place or time. (p. 44)

Walters (2006) goes even further and argues that participation in government research is to endorse a biased agenda that omits topics of national and global concern in favor of regulating the poor and the powerless.

Researchers who seek funding for their work are even more constrained by the solicitation for "requests for proposals" by funding agencies such as the National Institute of Justice, the U.S. Department of Justice's main funding source for research. To obtain funding, researchers must generally fit their research questions into the research needs mandated by funding agencies. Junger-Tas (2005) echoes this danger when he states,

> We have seen successive trends in research topics, which were directly influenced by the agenda of the country's criminal justice administration. This explains the different waves of research on incapacitation and career criminals, followed by research on drugs and now, of course, on organized crime and terrorism. There is indeed a danger in allowing (funding) administrative authorities to decide exclusively on research topics, since this may seriously restrict the field of research. (p. 150)

Clearly, most of us would not be in this discipline if we did not have an inherent desire to help society in some way. In the end, we should constantly reflect on decisions we are making in research and how these decisions may be influenced by external influences. After reading this text, you undoubtedly have a good understanding of the difference between these orientations, but we can't predict whether you'll decide which one is preferable. Perhaps you'll conclude, like we do, that they both have merit.

▣ Ethics in Evaluation

Evaluation research can make a difference in people's lives while it is in progress, as well as after the results are reported. Educational and vocational training opportunities in prison, the availability of legal counsel, and treatment for substance abuse—each is a potentially important benefit, and an evaluation research project can change both the type and the availability. This direct impact on research participants and, potentially, their families heightens the attention that evaluation researchers have to give to human subjects concerns. Although the particular criteria that are at issue and the decisions that are most ethical vary with the type of evaluation research conducted and the specifics of a particular project, there are always serious ethical as well as political concerns for the evaluation researcher (Boruch 1997; Dentler 2002).

Assessing needs, determining evaluability, and examining the process of treatment delivery have few special ethical dimensions. Cost-benefit analyses in themselves also raise few ethical concerns. It is when program impact is the focus that human subjects considerations multiply. What about assigning persons randomly to receive some social program or benefit? One justification given by evaluation researchers has to do with the scarcity of these resources. If not everyone in the population who is eligible for a program can receive it, due to resource limitations, what could be a fairer way to distribute the program benefits than through a lottery? Random assignment also seems like a reasonable way to allocate potential program benefits when a new program is being tested with only some members of the target recipient population. However, when an ongoing entitlement program is being evaluated and experimental subjects would normally be eligible for program participation, it may not be ethical simply to bar some potential participants from the programs. Instead, evaluation researchers may test alternative treatments or provide some alternative benefit while the treatment is being denied.

There are many other ethical challenges in evaluation research:

- How can confidentiality be preserved when the data are owned by a government agency or are subject to discovery in a legal proceeding?
- Who decides what level of burden an evaluation project may tolerably impose upon participants?
- Is it legitimate for research decisions to be shaped by political considerations?
- Must evaluation findings be shared with stakeholders rather than only with policymakers?
- Is the effectiveness of the proposed program improvements really uncertain?
- Will a randomized experiment yield more defensible evidence than the alternatives?
- Will the results actually be used?

The Health Research Extension Act of 1985 (Public Law 99-158) mandated that the Department of Health and Human Services require all research organizations receiving federal funds to have an institutional review board (IRB) to assess all research for adherence to ethical practice guidelines. We have already reviewed the federally mandated criteria (Boruch 1997):

- Are risks minimized?
- Are risks reasonable in relation to benefits?

- Is the selection of individuals equitable? (Randomization implies this.)

- Is informed consent given?

- Are the data monitored?

- Are privacy and confidentiality ensured?

Evaluation researchers must consider whether it will be possible to meet each of these criteria long before they even design a study.

The problem of maintaining subject confidentiality is particularly thorny, because researchers, in general, are not legally protected from the requirements that they provide evidence requested in legal proceedings, particularly through the process known as "discovery." However, it is important to be aware that several federal statutes have been passed specifically to protect research data about vulnerable populations from legal disclosure requirements. For example, the Crime Control and Safe Streets Act (28 CFR Part 11) includes the following stipulation:

> Copies of [research] information [about persons receiving services under the act or the subjects of inquiries into criminal behavior] shall be immune from legal process and shall not, without the consent of the persons furnishing such information, be admitted as evidence or used for any purpose in any action, suit, or other judicial or administrative proceedings. (Boruch 1997:60)

When it appears that it will be difficult to meet the ethical standards in an evaluation project, at least from the perspective of some of the relevant stakeholders, modifications should be considered in the study design. Several steps can be taken to lessen any possibly detrimental program impact (Boruch 1997):

- Alter the group allocation ratios to minimize the number in the untreated control group.

- Use the minimum sample size required to be able to adequately test the results.

- Test just parts of new programs rather than the entire program.

- Compare treatments that vary in intensity (rather than presence or absences).

- Vary treatments between settings rather than among individuals within a setting.

Essentially, each of these approaches limits the program's impact during the experiment and so lessens any potential adverse effects on human subjects. It is also important to realize that it is costly to society and potentially harmful to participants to maintain ineffective programs. In the long run, at least, it may be more ethical to conduct an evaluation study than to let the status quo remain in place.

🖾 Conclusion

In recent years, the field of evaluation research has become an increasingly popular and active research specialty within the fields of criminology and criminal justice. Many social scientists find special appeal in evaluation research because of its utility.

The research methods applied to evaluation research are not different from those covered elsewhere in this text; they can range from qualitative intensive interviews to rigorous randomized experimental designs. In process evaluations, qualitative methodologies can be particularly advantageous. However, the best method for determining cause and effect, or for determining whether a program had its intended consequences (impacts), is the randomized experimental design. Although this may not always be possible in the field, it is the "gold standard" with which to compare methodologies used to assess the impacts of all programs and/or policies.

Key Terms

Accuracy   316
Applied research   315
Basic science   342
Black box evaluation   328
Campbell Collaboration   341
Cost-benefit analysis   326
Cost-effectiveness analysis   326
Efficiency analysis   326
Evaluability assessment   320
Evidence-based policy   315
Experimental designs   324
Feasibility   316
Feedback   318
Formative evaluation   323

Impact evaluation (or impact analysis)   323
Improvement-oriented evaluation   319
Inputs   317
Integrative approaches   330
Judgment-oriented evaluation   319
Knowledge-oriented evaluation   319
Mechanism   333
Needs assessment   320
Nonequivalent control group design   335
One-shot design   339
Outcomes   318
Outputs   318
Process evaluation (program monitoring)   321

Program process   317
Program theory   328
Propriety   316
Quasi-experimental design   335
Random assignment   332
Social science approaches   330
Stakeholder approaches (responsive evaluation)   329
Stakeholders   318
Systematic review   341
Theory-driven evaluation   328
Time series design   335
Utility   316

Highlights

- Whenever people implement a program for a specific purpose, they pay attention to the consequences of it, even if this attention is not in the form of rigorous scientific methods. Evaluation research, however, has become increasingly used to assess the impacts of programs and policies since the 1950s.

- The evaluation process can be modeled as a feedback system, with inputs entering the program, which generates outputs and then outcomes, which feed back to program stakeholders and affect program inputs.

- The evaluation process as a whole, and the feedback process in particular, can be understood only in relation to the interests and perspectives of program stakeholders.

- The process by which a program has an effect on outcomes is often treated as a "black box," but there is good reason to open the black box and investigate the process by which the program operates and produces, or fails to produce, an effect.

- A program theory may be developed before or after an investigation of program process is completed. It may be either descriptive or prescriptive.

- Evaluation research is done for a client, and its results may directly affect the services, treatments, or punishments that program users receive. Evaluation researchers differ in the extent to which they attempt to orient their evaluations to program stakeholders.

- There are five primary types of program evaluation: needs assessment, evaluability assessment, process evaluation (including formative evaluation), impact evaluation (also termed summative evaluation), and efficiency (cost-benefit) analysis.

- The evaluation of need generally aims to describe the nature and scope of the problem along with the target population in need of services.

- The evaluation of process determines the extent to which implementation has taken place, whether the program is reaching the target population, whether the program is actually operating as expected, and what resources are being expended. Qualitative methods are typically utilized in process evaluations.

- Impact evaluations determine whether the program or policy produced the desired outcomes. Quantitative methods are typically utilized in impact evaluations.

- The evaluation of efficiency relates program outcomes to program costs.

- True randomized experiments are the most appropriate method for determining cause and effect and, as such, for determining the impact of programs and policies.

- Evaluation research raises complex ethical issues because it may involve withholding desired social benefits.

- Systematic reviews synthesize the results of the best available research on a given topic using transparent procedures.

- Research seeking to contribute to basic science focuses on expanding knowledge by testing theories and providing results to other researchers. Applied research seeks to have an impact on social practice and to share results with a wide audience.

Research in the News

Predicting Criminal Propensity

Nowhere is needs assessment more needed than in predicting the risk of recidivism among applicants for parole. In the 1920s, sociologist Ernest Burgess studied previously released inmates' criminal histories and classified them on the basis of 22 variables as hobos, ne'er-do-wells, farm boys, drug addicts, gangsters, and recent immigrants. Illinois had used a classification like this for 30 years, while other states relied on "clinical judgment." Now most states use a quantitative risk assessment tool in which risk predictions are based on identified correlates of future criminality, such as age at first arrest, job and relationship history, history of drug abuse and gang activity, and behavior while incarcerated.

Source: Neyfakh, Leon. 2011. "You will Commit a Crime in the Future, True, False: Inside the Science of Predicting Violence." *Boston Sunday Globe,* February 20: K1, K4.

Exercises

1. Read one of the articles reviewed in this chapter. Fill in the answers to the article review questions (Appendix B) not covered in the chapter. Do you agree with the answers to the other questions discussed in the chapter? Could you add some points to the critique provided by the author of the text or to the lessons on research design drawn from these critiques?

2. Evaluate the ethics of one of the studies reviewed in which human subjects were used. Sherman and Berk's (1984) study of domestic violence raises some interesting ethical issues, but there are also points to consider in most of the other studies. Which ethical guidelines (see Chapter 3) seem most difficult to adhere to? Where do you think the line should be drawn between not taking any risks at all with research participants and developing valid scientific knowledge? Be sure to consider various costs and benefits of the research. Now do the same for one of the articles reviewed in this chapter.

3. Propose a randomized experimental evaluation of a social program with which you are familiar. Include in your proposal a description of the program and its intended outcomes. Discuss the strengths and weaknesses of your proposed design.

4. Identify the key stakeholders in a local social or educational program. Interview several stakeholders to determine their goals for the program and what tools they use to assess goal achievement. Compare and contrast the views of each stakeholder and try to account for any differences you find.

Developing a Research Proposal

Imagine that you are submitting a proposal to the U.S. Justice Department to evaluate the efficacy of a new treatment program for substance abusers within federal correctional institutions.

1. What would your research question be if you proposed a process evaluation component to your research?

2. For the outcome evaluation, what is your independent variable, and what would your dependent variable be? How would you operationalize both?

3. What type of research design would you propose to answer both the process evaluation and outcome evaluation components in your proposal?

STUDENT STUDY SITE

Log on to the Web-based student study site at **www.sagepub.com/bachmanprccj5e** for additional study tools including eFlashcards, Web quizzes, links to SAGE journal articles, podcasts, videos, data sets and codebooks, Web exercises, Web resources, and additional appendices.

Web Exercises

1. Go to the American Evaluation Association Web site at www .eval.org. Choose "Publications" and then "Guiding Principles for Evaluators." What are the five guiding principles discussed in this document? Provide a summary of each principle.

   a. How adequate are juvenile court records? Go to the Bureau of Justice Statistics Web site at www.ojp.usdoj.gov/bjs/ and find a report that uses juvenile data and write a brief summary.

   b. Propose a research project to evaluate the adequacy of the juvenile justice system in the collection and maintenance of juvenile law enforcement records and/or juvenile court records.

2. Describe the resources available for evaluation researchers at the following Web site: www.world bank.org/oed/.

3. Check out the latest information regarding the D.A.R.E. program at www.dare.com. What is the current approach? Can you find information on the Web about current research on D.A.R.E.?

4. Go to the Campbell Collaboration Web site (www.campbellcol laboration.org) and access the library. Find a study that evaluates a topic of interest to you. What were the selection criteria used for the review? How did the researchers operationalize the constructs they were measuring (e.g., mentoring, delinquency, recidivism)? What do they conclude?

Ethics Exercises

1. The Manhattan Bail Project randomly assigned some defendants with strong community ties to be recommended for release without bail and some not to be recommended. There was a very high (99%) rate of appearance at trial for those released without bail, but of course, the researchers did not know that this would be the case before they conducted the study. Would you consider this study design ethical? What if one of the persons in the 1% who did not come to trial murdered someone when they should have been at court? Are there any conditions when randomization should not be permitted when evaluating criminal justice programs?

2. A large body of evaluation research suggested that the D.A.R.E. program was not effective in reducing drug use in schools, but many school and police officials and parents and students insisted

on maintaining the program without change for many years. Do you think that government agencies should be allowed to defund programs that numerous evaluation research studies have shown to be ineffective? Should government agencies be *required* to justify funding for social programs on the basis of evaluation research results?

3. Some of you may have participated in an experiment as part of the requirements for an Introduction to Psychology course. Discuss some of the ethical dilemmas and challenges this poses for researchers and professors. If students did not want to participate in an experiment, should they be allowed to get credit through another activity? Do you believe that students who consent to participate in an experiment are actually voluntarily doing so?

SPSS or Excel Exercises

1. There are many factors that affect the willingness of crime victims to report their victimization to police. Female victims of violence, particularly violence perpetrated by known offenders such as intimate partners, are generally the least likely to report their victimizations to police. The data in NCVS.ASSULT.POR contain information about assault victimizations against men and women obtained from a random sample of these victimizations from the National Crime Victimization Survey during 1992–2005. The question we want to explore with these data is, "What are the factors that affect a victim's willingness to report his or her victimization to police?" Obtain a frequency distribution of the variables of interest: *REPORTED, V4241*, and *INJURED*. Describe the results.

2. Notice that there are some missing cases for these data, so the appropriate percents to examine in the frequency output are under the "valid percents" column. *V4241* indicates the relationship between the victim and the offender for each victimization as "knew before," "stranger," or "don't know." Let's recode this variable into strangers and nonstrangers. We want to call the new variable STRANGER. You can recode the categories of 1 (knew before) and 2 (stranger) into the same values they now have or into different values, but the main goal is to reclassify "don't know" responses, which are coded 3 and 8, into missing values to create a two-category variable. Also, because this variable is for victimizations that involve

only one offender, the cases that are now coded 9 will also have to be coded missing since they are cases involving multiple offenders. Check your newly created variable using the frequencies command to make sure it was recoded correctly.

3. Now let's examine the bivariate relationship between police reporting behavior (*REPORTED*) and whether the offender was known or a stranger (*STRANGER*). Ask for a cross-tabulation of the two variables. Let's keep with the practice of placing the independent variable (*RELATION*) in the columns and the dependent variable (*REPORTED*) in the rows. Make sure you ask for the appropriate percentages to be calculated, which would be based on the column totals since the independent variable will be displayed in the columns of the table. What do you conclude about the relationship between these two variables?

4. Now let's examine the bivariate relationship between police reporting behavior (*REPORTED*) and whether or not the victim sustained an injury as the result of her victimization (*INJURED*). Let's keep with the practice of placing the independent variable (*INJURED*) in the columns and the dependent variable (*REPORTED*) in the rows. Remember to ask for the appropriate percentages. What do you conclude about the null hypothesis that these two variables are independent or not related?

CHAPTER 12

Mixing and Comparing Methods

Today, over 7.2 million people are under some form of correctional supervision in the United States, including nearly 4.9 million adults under community supervision (Bonczar and Glaze 2011). Except those under sentences of death or life without the possibility of parole (LWOP), the majority of these individuals will be returning to their communities. For example, during 2009, almost 731,000 prisoners were released from our nation's prisons back into the streets (West, Sabol, and Greenman 2010). A large percent of individuals under correctional supervision have been convicted of drug law violations, primarily possession (Dorsey and Zawitz 2005), and once released, a majority of these offenders will return to prison for new offenses or for parole violations (Langan and Levin 2002). Research indicates that the drug-addicted offender appears to be particularly vulnerable to long-term patterns of relapse and reoffending. Except for intensive experiences with long term aftercare programming (Inciardi and Harrison 2000), there appears to be very few programs that significantly increase the probability of success for ex-offenders attempting to become conforming members of society, particularly for those with drug addictions. For example, a recent evaluation of a large federally funded reentry initiative to develop projects to improve the reentry prospects of offenders to the community concluded that the "Serious and Violent Offender Reentry Initiative (SVORI) has not been promising." Overall, the evaluation project indicated that there were only modest effects on recidivism for offenders exposed to enhanced reentry programming 15 months postrelease compared to those who did not receive the enhanced programming (Lattimore and Visher 2010). The high number of offenders reentering society annually coupled with the less than ideal projection for their future success gives urgency to the present study.

Sampson and Laub contended that martial attachment and job stability were key factors associated with desistance from crime (Sampson and Laub 1993; Laub and Sampson 2003). The sample studied by Sampson and Laub, however, was exclusively white and came of age in the 1950s when the American economy was expanding. Recent research has questioned the ability of their theory to explain desistance for contemporary samples of offenders (Giordano, Cernkovich, and Rudolph 2002). A recent project by one of the authors (Bachman et al. 2012) sought to increase our understanding about the process of desistance from crime and drug use among current urban, drug-involved, largely minority, and increasingly female criminal offenders. We consciously developed our project using a mixed methods design to "combine the inherent strengths of both qualitative and quantitative methodologies to maximize our understanding of the life-course trajectories of substance abuse and crime for a contemporary cohort of drug using offenders" (Bachman et al. 2012:32). This decision is not unique. As you can see in Exhibit 12.1, mixed methods research is experiencing a rebirth in the social sciences in general and in the criminological sciences in particular. Of course, using mixed methods is not new in our discipline. Members of the early Chicago School applied both quantitative and qualitative methods to their study of crime and juvenile delinquency in communities in the early 1920s. However, despite these early roots, the majority of published work in the last 50 years can be divided into the broad categories of qualitative methods compared to quantitative methods.

In earlier chapters, we have given you examples of research that has combined research methods, but in this chapter, we will explain in more detail the logic of mixed methods and different ways of combining methods. We then review the strengths and limitations of the methods we have discussed; this review will help you choose the most appropriate research design for a particular investigation and decide when a combination of methods—"mixed methods"—is most useful. Finally, we introduce the methods of meta-analysis and meta-synthesis, which allows systematic evaluation of findings from numerous published studies that have all used similar quantitative and qualitative methods.

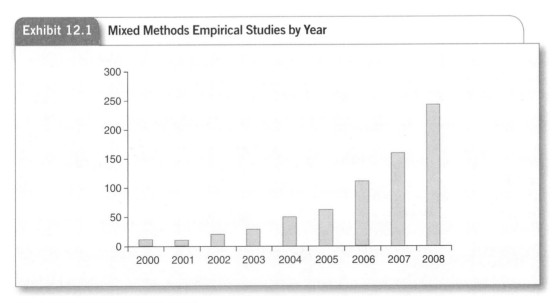

Exhibit 12.1 | **Mixed Methods Empirical Studies by Year**

Source: vankova and Kawamura (2010, p. 591).

▣ Mixed Methods

What exactly is mixed methods research? While there are many definitions of mixed methods research, the operationalization provided by the National Institute of Health's Office of Behavioral and Social Sciences Research is useful. It defines mixed methods as "focusing on research questions that call for real-life contextual understandings . . . employing rigorous quantitative research assessing the magnitude and frequency of constructs and rigorous qualitative research exploring the meaning and understanding of constructs . . . intentionally integrating or combining these methods to draw on the strengths of each" (Creswell et al. 2011:4). As you can see, the use of mixed methods should be an intentional design decision, not the addition of another aspect of research that is an afterthought or fishing expedition.

You learned in Chapter 2 that research involves both deductive processes (testing ideas against observations) and inductive processes (developing ideas from observations). You have also learned that quantitative methods are used most often in deductively oriented research and that qualitative methods are often used in inductively oriented research. A common reason for mixing both quantitative and qualitative methods in one research project is to take advantage of the unique strengths of each methodological approach when engaged in different stages of the research process (Teddlie and Tashakkori 2010).

Another reason for mixing methods is to add unique insights about the intervention process that cannot easily be obtained from the primary method used in an investigation. This function is underscored in the name often given to mixed methods research, **triangulation**. The term triangulation is actually derived from land surveying, where knowing a single landmark allows you to locate yourself only somewhere along a lone in a single direction from the landmark. However, with two landmarks, you can take bearings on both and locate yourself at their intersection. Extrapolated to research, triangulation suggests that a researcher can get a clearer picture of the social reality being studied by viewing it from two different perspectives, or two different methods.

> **Triangulation** The use of multiple methods to study one research question. Also used to mean the use of two or more different measures of the same variable.

Should Methods Be Mixed?

Increasingly in our discipline, the boundaries separating different methods of data collection often overlap. Experiments may be conducted in the field, and field research may utilize quantitative counts of phenomena or random samples of events. The bottom line is that no one method can be graded superior to the others, and each varies in its suitability to different research questions and goals. But *should* methods be mixed? That's a decision you will have to make for yourself. Methodological purists believe that only qualitative or quantitative methods provide adequate tools for investigating the social world, while methodological pragmatists believe that different methods should be used to answer the questions to which they are most suited (Onwuegbuzie and Combs 2010). Methodological pluralists believe the social world is composed of multiple realities that cannot be understood without multiple methods: a subjective reality reflected in individual experiences; an intersubjective reality reflected in social structures, languages, and social institutions; and an objective reality comprised of material things and physical processes (Johnson and Gray 2010). Qualitative methods may be best suited to investigate subjective reality, while quantitative methods may be most appropriate for investigating objective reality; an investigation of intersubjective reality may require some of both methods.

In addition to these philosophical questions, you should also consider some practical questions before you decide to mix methods in an investigation or review other investigations using mixed methods. Is a mixed methods approach consistent with your own goals and prior experiences? Are you well trained to mix methods, or will you need to include collaborators? Do your research questions allow for unanticipated results? Are your different research questions congruent, and do they convey a need for integration? Is it feasible to carry out a mixed methods design, or do you lack sufficient time or resources to carry it out? Are participants accessible to you (Plano Clark and Badiee 2010)?

Types of Mixed Methods Designs

If you do conclude that a mixed methods design fits the purpose of the study and provides the best strategy to answer your research question, then you have different options for your design. Creswell and Plano Clark (2011) identify six major mixed methods designs (see Exhibit 12.2):

1. *Convergent parallel design.* The quantitative and qualitative methods are implemented at the same time. The findings are integrated and interpreted together.

2. *Exploratory sequential design.* The qualitative method is implemented first followed by the quantitative method.

3. *Embedded design.* This occurs when the primary method is qualitative or quantitative but the researcher adds the other component to gain additional insight. For example, a quantitative design might be supplemented by a case study. These designs may be either concurrent or sequential.

4. *Transformative design.* Cresswell and Plano Clark (2011) suggest that the unique feature of a transformative design is that it uses a theoretical perspective with a social justice focus such as feminist research or participatory action research. Such research is done to improve the well-being of vulnerable populations.

5. *Multiphase design.* This design involves a series of quantitative and qualitative designs; each design and the findings inform the next phase.

> ***Convergent parallel design*** In mixed methods research, when quantitative and qualitative methods are implemented at the same time. The findings are integrated and interpreted together.
>
> ***Exploratory sequential design*** The qualitative method is implemented first followed by the quantitative method.
>
> ***Transformative design*** In mixed methods research, this design uses theoretical perspective with a social justice focus to improve the well-being of vulnerable populations.
>
> ***Embedded design*** In mixed methods research, when the primary method is qualitative or quantitative but the researcher adds the other component to gain additional insight.
>
> ***Multiphase design*** In mixed methods research, this design involves a series of quantitative and qualitative designs; each design and the findings inform the next phase.

Exhibit 12.2 | **Six Major Mixed Methods Research Designs**

(a) The convergent parallel design

Quantitative Data Collection and Analysis → Compare or relate → Interpretation

Qualitative Data Collection and Analysis → Compare or relate

(Continued)

Exhibit 12.2 (Continued)

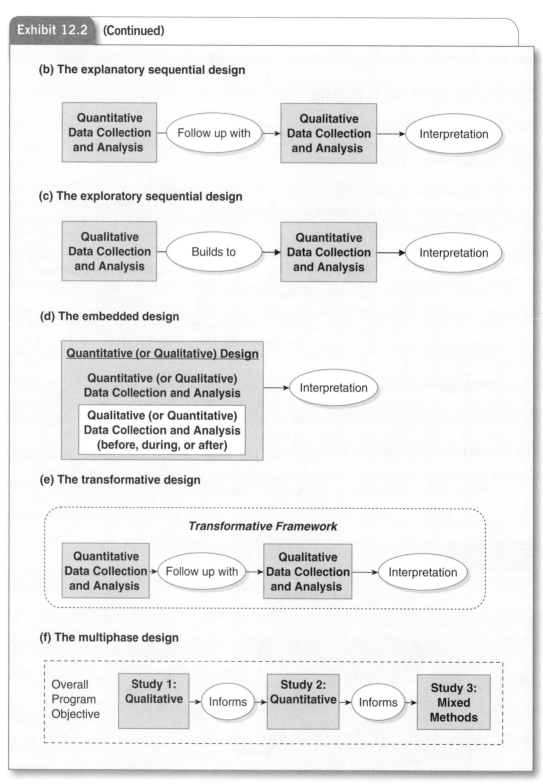

(b) The explanatory sequential design

Quantitative Data Collection and Analysis → Follow up with → Qualitative Data Collection and Analysis → Interpretation

(c) The exploratory sequential design

Qualitative Data Collection and Analysis → Builds to → Quantitative Data Collection and Analysis → Interpretation

(d) The embedded design

Quantitative (or Qualitative) Design

Quantitative (or Qualitative) Data Collection and Analysis → Interpretation

Qualitative (or Quantitative) Data Collection and Analysis (before, during, or after)

(e) The transformative design

Transformative Framework

Quantitative Data Collection and Analysis → Follow up with → Qualitative Data Collection and Analysis → Interpretation

(f) The multiphase design

Overall Program Objective — Study 1: Qualitative → Informs → Study 2: Quantitative → Informs → Study 3: Mixed Methods

Source: Creswell & Plano Clark, 2011, pp. 69–70.

Creswell (2010) has helped popularize a simple notational system for distinguishing different ways of mixing quantitative and qualitative methods. This system distinguishes the priority given to one method over the other and the sequence in which they are used in a research project. For example,

- QUAL + QUAN: equal importance of the two approaches and their concurrent use;

- QUAL à quan: sequenced use, with qualitative methods given priority;

- QUAN(qual): qualitative methods embedded within a primarily quantitative project.

Sometimes researchers will develop a study flowchart to describe the mixed methods process and sequence of events.

Rather than being planned in advance, steps to combine research designs may emerge naturally as a project is developed: An experiment conducted in the field can be supplemented with qualitative observations about delivery of the experimental treatment; some intensive open-ended questions can follow closed-ended survey questions; field research may utilize quantitative counts of phenomena or random samples of events; comparative historical studies may add survey research results to an inspection of historical documents or compilation of national statistics.

Case Study of Convergent Parallel Design: School Security and Discipline

Aaron Kupchik provides an excellent example of triangulation in practice in his book *Homeroom Security* (2010). His methodology would be classified as a *convergent parallel design* because both quantitative and qualitative methods were implemented at the same time and the findings were integrated together. The research question was primarily interested in how school security measures, particularly the presence of police officers, affect students. In four high schools, two in a Southwestern state, and two in a mid-Atlantic state, Kupchik engaged in over 100 hours of observation at each school, shadowing administrators and security guards, and surveying classrooms and common areas. He also conducted over 100 semi-structured interviews with administrators, security personnel, students, and parents. These interviews "sought to acquire an understanding of the respondents' views of the school rules and punishments, his or her experiences with school discipline, and his or her perceptions of school violence and appropriate responses to it." (Kupchik 2010:225). In addition to these two methods, student survey data were also collected at each school, and among other things, students were asked about their experiences with punishment at school and their perceptions of the fairness of these incidents. Thus, to more fully understand the reality of school discipline, Kupchik used three very different research methods, each providing him with a somewhat different angle to examine the issue, and each method complemented the other's weaknesses.

The school observations allowed Kupchik to observe the interactions in the school in real time. He observed on numerous occasions how relatively minor problems escalated into larger problems as a result of police involvement, resulting in students unnecessarily being sent to the criminal justice system rather than having their issues dealt with at the school level only. With the in-depth interviews, Kupchik was able to identify how some of the school administrators perceived the behavior of the police officers in their schools. For example, one school administrator stated,

> The biggest problem that I see is that . . . police officers are trained to deal with adults. . . . [T]hey are not trained to deal with children. . . . They deal with them terribly. In their day-to-day interactions. . . . [T]hey deal with them like criminals, they do not trust anything they say, they assume they are lying before they even open their mouths. And it's not their fault. They've been trained to do that. (Kupchik 2010:108)

Finally, the survey data allowed him to make generalizations regarding perceptions and experiences of discipline to the larger student population. For example, the survey data indicated that boys were more likely to report getting in trouble for rule violations than girls, as were African American and Latino/a students compared to whites.

Of course, these are only a sampling of the many findings from this research. The central point we want to illustrate is how the use of all three methodologies provided a more complete picture of school discipline compared to the use of a single method. The research provided both in-depth detailed descriptions of the reality of school discipline from both administrator and student perspectives. It also provided a quantitative assessment of students' experiences that could be generalized to a larger student population.

▣ Case Study of Exploratory Sequential Design: American Indian Homicide

As noted above, some mixed methods designs begin with a qualitative method to explore a phenomenon and then conduct a quantitative method for confirmatory purposes. This is referred to as an *exploratory sequential design*. This was the design used by Bachman (1992) when studying the social causes of homicide within contemporary American Indian communities. Although other researchers had noted high rates of American Indian homicide, virtually no attempts were made to explore the factors that contributed to such high rates. Are the causal mechanisms that create these high rates the same as those that were documented in the population in general? Or are the social forces that were identified as increasing both African American and white homicide rates different from those forces that contribute to American Indian homicide? Because there was virtually no research examining the social factors related to American Indian homicide, Bachman first wanted to gain some insight and understanding of the structural and cultural conditions that may contribute to lethal violence at the individual level. Accordingly, she selected the qualitative method of intensive interviewing as her first method. Bachman (1992) conducted face-to-face interviews with homicide offenders at three Midwestern state prisons. Offenders responded to a lengthy set of open-ended questions and probes concerning the circumstances surrounding their crime, their life before the crime, and their attitudes about crime in general. Thus, she started with inductive research, beginning with qualitative interview data, which were then used to develop (induce) a general explanation (a theory) to account for the data.

The theoretical model that emerged from her interview data is displayed in Exhibit 12.3. The model demonstrates the causal forces of social disorganization, economic deprivation, a culture of honor or violence, and the psychological mechanisms of culture conflict and perceived powerlessness with the intervening variable of alcohol or drug abuse. Also included in the theoretical guide is the antecedent variable to each of these concepts, internal colonialism. Although this concept was not explicitly derived from the qualitative analysis, Bachman explained, "No model explaining any phenomenon with regard to American Indians would be complete without acknowledgment of the colonization process to which our government has subjected this population" (p. 36).

Using this theoretical model, Bachman (1992) next collected state and county level data on homicide rates from the Supplementary Homicide Reports (SHR) and combined these data with social indicators of poverty and social disorganization from the U.S. Census. Thus began the deductive phase of her research to test three hypotheses:

1. The higher the level of social disorganization within a reservation community, the higher the rate of homicide.

2. The higher the level of economic deprivation within a reservation community, the higher the rate of homicide.

3. The more traditional and integrated a reservation community, the lower the rate of homicide.

Results indicated that American Indian communities with higher levels of both social disorganization and economic deprivation also had higher rates of homicide. Bachman (1992) did not find support in her data for the third hypothesis. In addition to guiding her deductive research, the qualitative interview data also provided Bachman's

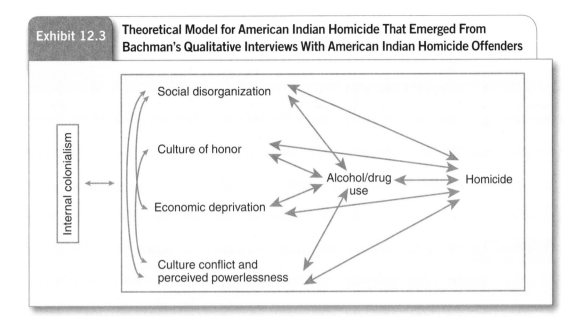

| Exhibit 12.3 | Theoretical Model for American Indian Homicide That Emerged From Bachman's Qualitative Interviews With American Indian Homicide Offenders |

research with a wealth of narratives that added meaning and depth to the statistical relationships that were found at the aggregate level. For example, many homicide offenders revealed what conditions of social disorganization and economic deprivation were like in their own lives. One offender talked about the reality of his disorganized childhood, being placed in multiple foster homes:

> I was pretty much living in foster homes since I was about two. I guess my parents weren't doing too good—you know, drinking and partying. My brother got put into a different foster home, but my sister and I got in the same one. After several moves, we all eventually got placed in the same home. We moved around quite a bit. (p. 38)

Finding support for relationships between the independent and dependent variables at two different levels— the individual level and the community level—provided validity to Bachman's (1992) conclusions that both social disorganization and economic deprivation are related to homicide in American Indian communities. Campbell and Fiske (1959) explain the validity-enhancing qualities of triangulation:

> If a hypothesis can survive the confrontation of a series of complementary methods of testing, it contains a degree of validity unattainable by one tested within the more constricted framework of a single method. . . . Findings from this latter approach must always be subject to the suspicion that they are method-bound: Will the comparison totter when exposed to an equally prudent but different testing method? (p. 82)

Case Study: Adding Qualitative Data to Official Juvenile Records

It makes sense to use official records to study the treatment of juveniles accused of illegal acts because these records document the critical decisions to arrest, to convict, or to release (Dannefer and Schutt 1982). But research based on official records can be only as good as the records themselves. In contrast to the controlled interview process in a research study, there is little guarantee that officials' acts and decisions were recorded in a careful and unbiased manner.

Research on official records can be strengthened by interviewing officials who create the records or by observing them while they record information. A participant observation study of how probation officers screened cases in two New York juvenile court intake units shows how important such information can be (Needleman 1981). As indicated in Exhibit 12.4, Needleman found that the concepts most researchers believe they are measuring with official records differ markedly from the meaning attached to these records by probation officers. Researchers assume that sending a juvenile case to court indicates a more severe disposition than retaining a case in the intake unit, but probation officers often diverted cases from court because they thought the court would be too lenient. Researchers assume that probation officers evaluate juveniles as individuals, but in these settings, probation officers often based their decisions on juveniles' current social situation (e.g., whether they were living in a stable home), without learning anything about the individual juvenile. Perhaps most troubling for research using case records, Needleman found that probation officers decided how to handle cases first and then created an official record that appeared to justify their decisions.

Exhibit 12.4 **Researchers' and Juvenile Court Workers' Discrepant Assumptions**

Researchers' Assumptions	Intake Workers' Assumptions
• Being sent to court is a harsher sanction than diversion from court.	• Being sent to court often results in more lenient and less effective treatment.
• Screening involves judgments about individual juveniles.	• Screening centers on the juvenile's social situation.
• Official records accurately capture case facts.	• Records are manipulated to achieve the desired outcome.

Source: Needleman 1981:248–56.

Comparing Research Designs

You have now seen the value of mixing methods. The central features of true experiments, quasi-experiments, surveys, participant observation, intensive interviews, etc. provide distinct perspectives even when used to study the same social processes. This should be your golden rule: *The choice of a data collection method should be guided in large part by the aspect of validity that is of most concern and the best method for answering your research question!*

As you can see in Exhibit 12.5, none of these methods is superior to the others in all respects, and each varies in its suitability to different research questions and goals. Choosing among them for a particular investigation requires consideration of the research problem, opportunities and resources, prior research, philosophical commitments, and research goals.

True experimental designs are strongest for testing nomothetic causal hypotheses and are most appropriate for studies of treatment effects, as well as research questions that are believed to involve basic social-psychological processes. Random assignment reduces the possibility of preexisting differences between treatment and comparison groups to small, specifiable, chance levels, so many of the variables that might create a spurious association are controlled. But despite this clear advantage, an experimental design requires a degree of control that cannot always be achieved in other settings. Researchers may be unable to randomly assign participants to groups or have too few

Exhibit 12.5	Comparison of Research Methods

Design	Measurement Validity	Generalizability	Type of Causal Assertions	Causal Validity
Experiments	+	–	Nomothetic	+
Surveys	+	+	Nomothetic	+/–[a]
Participant Observation and Intensive Interviewing	–/+[b]	–	Idiographic	–
Historical/Comparative[c]	–	–/+	Both	–

[a]Surveys are a weaker design for identifying causal effects than true experiments, but use of statistical controls can strengthen causal arguments.

[b]Reliability is low compared to surveys, and evaluation of measurement validity is often not possible. However, direct observations may lead to a greater understanding of the concepts being measured.

[c]All conclusions about these designs vary with the specific approach used.

participants to assign to groups, and unfortunately, most field experiments also require more access arrangements and financial resources than can often be obtained. In lieu of these difficulties, quasi- and nonexperimental designs are used, but at the cost of causal validity.

Surveys typically use standardized, quantitative measures of attitudes, behaviors, or social processes. Closed-ended questions are most common and are well suited for the reliable measurement of variables that have been studied in the past and whose meanings are well understood. Of course, surveys often include measures of many more variables than are included in an experiment, but this feature is not inherent in either design. Many surveys rely on random sampling for their selection of cases from some larger population, and this feature makes them preferable for research that seeks to develop generalizable findings. However, survey questionnaires can only measure what respondents are willing to report; they may not be adequate for studying behaviors or attitudes that are regarded as socially unacceptable. Surveys are also often used to test hypothesized causal relationships. When variables that might create spurious relationships are included in the survey, they can be controlled statistically in the analysis and thus eliminated as rival causal influences.

Qualitative methods such as participant observation and intensive interviewing presume an exploratory measurement approach in which indicators of concepts are drawn from direct observation or in-depth commentary. This approach is most appropriate when it is not clear what meaning people attach to a concept or what sense they might make of particular questions about it. Qualitative methods are also suited to the exploration of new or poorly understood social settings when it is not even clear what concepts would help to understand the situation. Further, these methods are useful in uncovering the process of a program or the implementation of an intervention. They may also be used instead of survey methods when the population of interest is not easily identifiable or seeks to remain hidden. For these reasons, qualitative methods tend to be preferred when exploratory research questions are posed or when new groups are investigated. But, of course, intensive measurement necessarily makes the study of large numbers of cases or situations difficult, resulting in the limitation of many field research efforts to small numbers of people or unique social settings. The individual field researcher may not require many financial resources, but the amount of time required for many field research projects serves as a barrier to many would-be field researchers.

A researcher should always consider whether data of another type should be collected in single-method studies and whether additional research using different methods is needed before the research question can be answered with sufficient confidence. But the potential for integrating methods and combining findings does not decrease the importance of single studies using just one method of data collection. The findings from well-designed studies in carefully researched settings are the necessary foundation for broader, more integrative methods. There is little point in combining methods that are poorly implemented or in merging studies that produced invalid results. Whatever the research question, we should consider the full range of methodological possibilities, make an informed and feasible choice, and then carefully carry out our strategy. As you saw in Chapter 2, research questions are never completely answered. Research findings regarding a particular question are added to the existing literature to inform future research, and the research circle continues.

🔲 Comparing Results Across Studies

Meta-Analysis

> **Meta-analysis** The quantitative analysis of findings from multiple studies.

Meta-analysis is a quantitative method for identifying patterns in findings across multiple studies of the same research question (Cooper and Hedges 1994). Unlike a traditional literature review, which describes previous research studies verbally, meta-analyses treat previous studies as cases whose features are measured as variables and are then analyzed statistically. It is like conducting a survey in which the respondents are previous studies. Meta-analysis shows how evidence about interventions varies across research studies. If the methods used in these studies varied, then meta-analysis can be used to describe how this variation affected study findings. If social contexts or demographic characteristics varied across the studies, then a meta-analysis can indicate how social context or demographic characteristics affected study findings. Meta-analysis often accompanies systematic reviews that summarize what we know about the effectiveness of a particular intervention. By integrating different study samples and controlling for social context and demographic characteristics, meta-analysis enhances the generalizability of the findings. As noted in the last chapter, meta-analyses are often used to provide a systematic reviews for evidence-based policies.

Meta-analysis can be used when a number of studies have attempted to answer the same research question with similar quantitative methods. It is not typically used for evaluating results from multiple studies that employed different methods or measured different dependent variables. It is also not very sensible to use meta-analysis to combine study results when the original case data from these studies are available and can actually be combined and analyzed together (Lipsey and Wilson 2001). Rather, meta-analysis is a technique to combine and statistically analyze the statistical findings in published research reports.

After a research problem is formulated about prior research, the literature must be searched systematically to identify the entire population of relevant studies. Typically, multiple bibliographic databases are used; some researchers also search for related dissertations and conference papers. Eligibility criteria must be specified carefully to determine which studies to include and which to omit as too different. Mark Lipsey and David Wilson (2001) suggest that eligibility criteria include the following:

- *Distinguishing features.* This includes the specific intervention tested and perhaps the groups compared.
- *Research respondents.* These specify the population to which generalization is sought.
- *Key variables.* These must be sufficient to allow tests of the hypotheses of concern and controls for likely additional influences.
- *Research methods.* Apples and oranges cannot be directly compared, but some trade-off must be made between including the range of studies about a research question and excluding those that are so different in their methods as not to yield comparable data.
- *Cultural and linguistic range.* If the study population is going to be limited to English language publications, or limited in some other way, this must be acknowledged and the size of the population of relevant studies in other languages should be estimated.

- *Time frame.* Social processes relevant to the research question may have changed for such reasons as historical events or new technologies, so temporal boundaries around the study population must be considered.

- *Publication type.* Will the analysis focus only on published reports in professional journals, or will it include dissertations and/or unpublished reports? (pp. 16–21)

Once the studies are identified, their findings, methods, and other features are coded (e.g., sample size, location of sample, strength of the association between the independent and dependent variables). Statistics are then calculated to identify the average effect of the independent variable on the dependent variable, as well as the effect of methodological and other features of the studies (Cooper and Hedges 1994). The **effect size** statistic is the key to capturing the association between the independent and dependent variables across multiple studies. The effect size statistic is a standardized measure of association—often the difference between the mean of the experimental group and the mean of the control group on the dependent variable, adjusted for the average variability in the two groups (Lipsey and Wilson 2001).

> **Effect size** A standardized measure of association—often the difference between the mean of the experimental group and the mean of the control group on the dependent variable, adjusted for the average variability in the two groups.

The meta-analytic approach to synthesizing findings from several studies can result in more generalizable findings than those obtained with just one study. Methodological weaknesses in the studies included in the meta-analysis are still a problem; it is only when other studies without particular methodological weaknesses are included can we estimate effects with some confidence. In addition, before we can place any confidence in the results of a meta-analysis, we must be confident that all (or almost all) relevant studies were included and that the information we need to analyze was included in all (or most) of the studies (Matt and Cook 1994).

One of the challenges of meta-analysis is that the authors of the articles to be reviewed may not always report sufficient information. For example, the study reports (whether a journal article or unpublished report) may not contain information about participant characteristics, an especially important variable if we are to consider the generalizability of the results to different population groups. Littell (2005) noted that to conduct her meta-analysis of Multisystemic Therapy, she had to contact principal investigators to obtain more information about participant characteristics, interventions, and outcomes.

Meta-Synthesis

Meta-synthesis is a related method used to analyze and integrate findings from qualitative studies (Thorne et al. 2004). This type of analysis requires not just aggregating findings from different qualitative studies, but also reinterpreting the data once in aggregate. Similar to meta-analyses, attention to eligibility criteria for selection into a meta-synthesis is extremely important.

> **Meta-synthesis** The qualitative analysis of findings from multiple qualitative studies.

🔲 Case Study of Meta-Synthesis: Female Drug Dealers

Maher and Hudson (2007) performed a meta-synthesis examining the qualitative literature on women in the illicit drug economy to identify and integrate key themes. The authors spelled out their methods meticulously describing the characteristics they used to select studies that met their criteria. They first searched many data bases (e.g., Criminal Justice Abstracts, Sociological Abstracts) for research using various key terms such as *drug market, drug economy, women dealing.* Studies were only selected if they "generated findings in relation to female participation in the drug economy," and the "primary data collection used qualitative or ethnographic research" (Maher and Hudson 2007:809). Of 36 studies located, only 15 met their criteria and provided thick descriptions of female experiences using field notes or narrative data from transcribed interviews. A sample of the selected studies included in the meta-synthesis are described in Exhibit 12.6.

| Exhibit 12.6 | Example of the Studies for Metasynthesis of Female Drug Dealers |

Author(s)	Study Location	Sample
Rosenbaum (1981)	San Francisco and New York	100 women
Adler (1985)	Southwest County close to Mexico border	65 dealers/smugglers, 6 women
Miller, E. M. (1986)	Milwaukee	64 women "hustlers"
Waldorf, Reinarman, and Murphy (1991)	San Francisco	80 sellers, 26 female
Taylor (1993)	Glasgow, Scotland	26 women
Maher (1997)	New York	211 women
Dunlap, Johnson, and Maher (1997)	New York	111 dealers, 39 women
Sterk (1999)	Atlanta, GA	149 women
Denton (2001)	Melbourne, Australia	16 women recently released from prison

Source: Adapted from Maher and Hudson. 2007. "Women in the Drug Economy: A Metasynthesis of the Qualitative Literature." *Journal of Drug Issues* 37:805–27

After reading that qualitative material from the 15 studies examined, Maher and Hudson (2007) identified six themes that captured the nature and experience of women's participation in the illicit drug economy. One of the key findings was that gender-stratified nature of women's involvement; all studies regardless of time or place found that women tended to occupy subordinate roles to men, even those women identified as successful dealers. They also concluded that most women were introduced to dealing through relationships with sex partners. They concluded, "our results suggest that while women rely on a diverse range of income sources and juggle different roles both within the drug economy and in relation to dealing and domestic responsibilities, most women in most drug markets remain confined to low level and marginal roles" (Maher and Hudson 2007:821).

Case Study of Meta-Analysis: The Effectiveness of Anti-Bullying Programs

The 2005 School Crime Supplement to the National Crime Victimization Survey reported that about 14% of teens between the ages of 12 and 18 had been bullied in the past 6 months. The effects of bullying are numerous and include perceived fear, behavior problems, negative consequences for school performance, depression, and other physical ailments. There have been many different programs designed to decrease bullying in schools, but the effectiveness of these programs remains largely unknown. To examine the effects of anti-bullying programs across studies, Ferguson et al. (2007) performed a meta-analysis of randomized experimental studies examining the efficacy of such programs.

Studies included in the Ferguson et al. (2007) meta-analysis had several selection criteria: (a) they had to be published between 1995 and 2006; (b) the outcome variables had to clearly measure some element of bullying behavior toward peers; (c) they had to involve some form of control group to test program effectiveness; (d) the intervention programs had to be school-based; and (e) only manuscripts published in peer-reviewed journals were included. Results of the meta-analysis indicated that the impact of anti-bullying programs ranged from less than 1% for low-risk children to 3.6% for high-risk children. Ferguson and his colleagues (2007) stated, "Thus, it can be said that although anti-bullying programs produce a small amount of positive change, it is likely that this change is too small to be practically significant or noticeable" (p. 408).

Meta-analyses such as this make us aware of how hazardous it is to base understanding of social processes on single studies that are limited in time, location, and measurement. Of course, we need to have our wits about us when we read reports of meta-analytic studies. It is not a good idea to assume that a meta-analysis is the definitive word on a research question just because it cumulates the results of multiple studies.

Meta-analyses and meta-syntheses make us aware of how hazardous it is to base understandings of social processes on single studies that are limited in time, location, and measurement. Although one study may not support the hypothesis that we deduced from what seemed to be a compelling theory, this is not a sufficient basis for discarding the theory itself, nor even for assuming that the hypothesis is no longer worthy of consideration in future research. You can see that a meta-analysis combining the results of many studies may identify conditions for which the hypothesis is supported and others for which it is not.

Case Study of Meta-Analysis: Do Parent Training Programs Prevent Child Abuse?

Brian Lundahl, Janelle Nimer, and Bruce Parsons (2006) were interested in the effect of parent training and parent education programs on reducing risk factors associated with child abuse. They included only studies that met six eligibility criteria including: the training was conducted with families in which there were no parent or child developmental or cognitive delays; the training was directed to preventing physical abuse, child neglect, or emotional abuse and not sexual abuse; there was actual training, and pretests and posttests were given to at least five participants. Using three keywords (*child abuse*, *child neglect*, and *parent training*) they searched three databases (ERIC, PsychInfo, and Social Work Abstracts) for any articles published between 1970 and 2004. Of 186 studies, they found 23 studies that met the eligibility criteria. They coded outcome measures including parents' emotional adjustment, child-rearing attitudes, child-rearing behaviors, and documented abuse and moderating and independent variables including participant characteristics, parent training program characteristics, and the methodological rigor of the studies.

Overall, they found that parent training had a moderate effect and was effective in changing parental beliefs and attitudes toward children, improving parental emotional well-being, altered child-rearing behaviors, and reducing documented abuse. They also found that specific program characteristics influenced these outcomes. For example programs that included home visitors had a greater impact than programs without home visitors and programs that did training in both the home and the office were more effective than programs that limited training to one site.

Conclusion

We began this chapter by asking what mixed methods research has to tell us about our social world. The mixed methods examples from this chapter demonstrate that a research design is an integrated whole. Designing research means deciding how to measure empirical phenomena, how to identify causal connections, and how to generalize findings—not as separate decisions, but in tandem, with each decision having implications for the others. The choice of a data collection method should be guided in part by the aspect of validity that is of most concern, but each aspect of validity must be considered in attempting to answer every research question. A basic question the researcher must ask is: Will a mixed methods approach give a better picture of the research target than a single-method approach? If the answer is yes, then the researcher must consider which combination of methods will offer the best mix of validity, generalizability, and rich, accurate data on the target research question.

The ability to apply diverse techniques to address different aspects of a complex research question is one mark of a sophisticated researcher. Awareness that one study's findings must be understood in the context of a larger body of research is another. And the ability to speculate on how the use of different methods might have altered a study's findings is a prerequisite for informed criticism of research.

Finally, realistic assessment of the weaknesses as well as the strengths of each method of data collection should help you to remember that humility is a virtue in research. Advancement of knowledge and clear answers to specific research questions are attainable with the tools you now have in your methodological toolbox. Perfection, however, is not a realistic goal. No matter what research method we use, our mental concepts cannot reflect exactly what we measured, our notions of causation cannot reveal a tangible causal force, and our generalizations always extend beyond the cases that were actually studied. This is not cause for disillusionment, but it should keep us from being excessively confident in our own interpretations or unreasonably resistant to change. Final answers to every research question we pose cannot be achieved; what we seek are new, ever more sophisticated questions for research.

Key Terms

Convergent parallel design   353
Effect Size   364
Embedded design   353

Exploratory sequential design   353
Meta-analysis   360
Meta-synthesis   361

Multiphase design   353
Transformative design   353
Triangulation   352

Highlights

- The use of mixed methods, sometimes referred to as triangulation, is intentionally combining two or more research methods to study a one research question.

- Mixed methods research has been increasing for the past 25 years primarily because most researchers are not convinced that research on most topics can be improved by using mixed methods.

- There are several designs available in mixed methods research including those that give equal weight to both quantitative and

qualitative methodologies and those that give differential weight to one or the other method.

- Researchers can test statistically for patterns across multiple studies with meta-analysis. This technique can be used only in areas of research in which there have been many prior studies using comparable methods.

- Meta-synthesis is the analysis tool for assessing the results of multiple studies that have relied on qualitative methods.

Research in the News

Pushing Back at Bullying

The vast majority of school districts across the nation are incorporating anti-bulling programs into their curriculums, including a program called "Names Can Really Hurt Us." In this story, the journalist

focuses exclusively on accounts from administrators and students from Greenwich, Connecticut, about how fabulous the program has worked in their schools. The program rests on a foundation of "open-mike" days in which students provide testimonies to either being bullied or being a bystander of a bullying incident who intervened. A social studies teacher stated, "I was impressed by the student panelists and the kids who got up in the open-mike segment. I was amazed. I came back and said, 'Let's get it done.'" Although the methodology was not revealed, the article did note that a "follow-up survey of the 'Names' program in San Diego in 2000 found that 60% of students said that after the session they would be less likely to call someone a name." What would you want to know about this study to determine whether the program had causal validity?

Source: Hirshey, Gerri. 2007. "Pushing Back at Bullying." *The New York Times,* January 28. Retrieved June 23, 2012 (http://www.nytimes.com/2007/01/28/nyregion/nyregionspecial2/28rbully.html?pagewanted=print).

Exercises

1. Some research projects use an "inverted pyramid" data collection strategy, with broad, quantitative measures gathered from a large population on top, narrowing to more intensive qualitative measures (focus groups, individual interviews) with a smaller subset of the population at the bottom. Design a research project that resembles such an inverted pyramid, showing what measures and what sample size and research subjects you would use at each level of the design.

2. Think of at least three areas of criminological research where you believe much research has been done—for example, understanding why some people engage in crime. Where are you likely to find such studies? What sources would you use to see if a meta-analysis had been done in these areas in the last 5 to 8 years? Choose two of these topic areas and try to find a recent meta-analysis. You may wish to start by looking on ERIC and in JSTOR. Almost all meta-analyses have the word "meta-analysis" in the article title.

Developing a Research Proposal

Now is the time to mix your methods.

1. Add a component involving a second method to your research proposal. If you already developed alternative approaches in answer to the exercises in earlier chapters, just write a justification for these additions that point out the potential benefits.

2. Consider the possible influences of social context factors on the variables pertinent to your research question. Write a rationale for including a test for contextual influences in your proposed research.

3. Describe a method for studying the contextual influences in Question 2.

STUDENT STUDY SITE

Log on to the Web-based student study site at **www.sagepub.com/bachmanprccj5e** for additional study tools including eFlashcards, Web quizzes, links to SAGE journal articles, podcasts, videos, data sets and codebooks, Web exercises, Web resources, and additional appendices.

Web Exercises

1. Find the Web site for the online *Journal of Mixed-Methods Research* (mmr.sagepub.com). On the home page, click the button "Current Issue." When the table of contents for the current issue comes up, click on the abstracts for three of the articles, and for each article, write down the two more methods that the authors used to conduct their research. Did any methods occur more than once? Were there any methods you had never heard of before?

2. Go to the home page of the *Journal of Mixed-Methods Research*. At the button for "Article Statistics," click on "Most Read." When the most-read article titles come up, read the abstracts for the top five articles. What themes or main points do you see running through these articles? Based on the top-five abstracts, write a paragraph or two describing the most important issues currently being discussed or investigated by mixed method researchers.

3. Go to the National Criminal Justice Reference Service Web site (www.ncjrs.gov) and search for the term *mixed methods*. Find at least two studies that have used a mixed methods approach. What strengths did this approach provide the study compared to using just one of the methods?

Ethics Exercises

1. You learned in this book that Sampson and Raudenbush (1999) had observers drive down neighborhood streets in Chicago and record the level of disorder they observed. What should have been the observers' response if they observed a crime in progress? What if they just suspected that a crime was going to occur? What if the crime was a drug dealer interacting with driver at a curb? What if it was a prostitute soliciting a customer? What, if any, ethical obligation does a researcher studying a neighborhood have to residents in that neighborhood? Should research results be shared at a neighborhood forum or community meeting?

2. Some research investigating the effects of alcohol have actually had research subjects drink to the point of intoxication. If you were a student member of your university's institutional review board, would you vote to approve a study like this? Why or why not? Would you ban an experiment that involves alcohol altogether, or would you set certain criteria for the experimental conditions? What would such criteria be? How about female students who may be potentially pregnant? Can you think of any other circumstances in which you would allow an experiment involving the administration of illegal drugs?

SPSS or Excel Exercises

In the data set GSS2010x, let's learn how causal hypotheses can be evaluated with nonexperimental data.

1. Specify four hypotheses in which CAPPUN is the dependent variable and the independent variable is also measured with a question in the 2010 GSS. The independent variables should have no more than a few valid values (e.g., values that are not missing).

2. Inspect the frequency distributions of each independent variable in your hypotheses along with your dependent variable. If it appears that any has little valid data or was coded with more than 10 categories, substitute another independent variable.

3. Generate cross-tabulations that show the association between CAPPUN and each of the independent variables. Make sure that you ask for the percentages to be calculated relative to where you place the independent variable. For example, if you place an independent variable on the column, you should ask for percentages to be calculated for the column variable.

4. Does support for capital punishment vary across the categories of any of the independent variables? By how much? Would you conclude that there is an association, as hypothesized, for any pairs of variables?

CHAPTER 13

Quantitative Data Analysis

"Oh no, not data analysis and statistics!" We now hit the chapter that you may have been fearing all along, the chapter on data analysis and the use of statistics. This chapter describes what you need to do after your data have been collected. You now need to analyze what you have found, interpret it, and decide how to present your data so that you can most clearly make the points you wish to make.

What you probably dread about this chapter is something that you either sense or know from a previous course: The studying of data analysis and statistics will lead you into that feared world of mathematics. We would like to state at the beginning, however, that you have relatively little to fear. The kind of mathematics required to perform the data analysis tasks in this chapter is minimal. If you can add, subtract, multiply, and divide and are willing to put some effort into carefully reading the chapter, you will do well in the statistical analysis of your data. In fact, it is our position that the analysis of your data will require more in the way of careful and logical thought than in mathematical skill. One helpful way to think of statistics is that it consists of a set of tools that you will use to examine your data to help you answer the questions that motivated your research in the first place. Right now, the toolbox that holds your statistical tools is fairly empty (or completely empty). In the course of this chapter, we will add some fundamental tools to that toolbox. We would also like to note at the beginning that the kinds of statistics you will use on criminological data are very much the same as those used by economists, psychologists, political scientists, sociologists, and other social scientists. In other words, statistical tools are statistical tools, and all that changes is the nature of the problem to which those tools are applied.

This chapter will introduce several common statistics in social research and highlight the factors that must be considered in using and interpreting statistics. Think of it as a review of fundamental social statistics, if you have already studied them, or as an introductory overview, if you have not.

Two preliminary sections lay the foundation for studying statistics. In the first, we will discuss the role of statistics in the research process, returning to themes and techniques you already know. In the second preliminary section, we will outline the process of acquiring data for statistical analysis. In the rest of the chapter, we will explain how to describe the distribution of single variables and the relationship between variables. Along the way, we will address ethical issues related to data analysis. This chapter will be successful if it encourages you to see statistics responsibly and evaluate them critically and gives you the confidence necessary to seek opportunities for extending your statistical knowledge.

It should be noted that, in this chapter, we focus primarily on the use of statistics for descriptive purposes. Those of you looking for a more advanced discussion of statistical methods used in criminal justice and criminology should seek other textbooks (e.g., Bachman and Paternoster 2008). Although many colleges and universities offer social statistics in a separate course, we don't want you to think of this chapter as something that deals with a different topic than the rest of the book. Data analysis is an integral component of research methods, and it's important that any proposal for quantitative research include a plan for the data analysis that will follow data collection.

▣ Introducing Statistics

Frequency distributions Numerical display showing the number of cases, and usually the percentage of cases (the relative frequencies), corresponding to each value or group of values of a variable.

Statistics play a key role in achieving valid research results, in terms of measurement, causal validity, and generalizability. Some statistics are useful primarily to describe the results of measuring single variables and to construct and evaluate multi-item scales. These statistics include **frequency distributions**, graphs, measures of central tendency and variation, and reliability tests. Other statistics are useful primarily in achieving causal validity, by helping us describe the association among variables and control for, or otherwise take into account, other variables.

Cross-tabulation is one technique for measuring association and controlling other variables and is introduced in this chapter. All these statistics are called **descriptive statistics** because they are used to describe the distribution of and relationship among variables.

You learned in Chapter 5 that it is possible to estimate the degree of confidence that can be placed in generalizations for a sample and for the population from which the sample was selected. The statistics used in making these estimates are called inferential statistics, and they include confidence intervals, to which you were exposed in Chapter 5. In this chapter we will refer only briefly to inferential statistics, but we will emphasize later in the chapter their importance for testing hypotheses involving sample data.

Criminological theory and the results of prior research should guide our statistical plan or analytical strategy, as they guide the choice of other research methods. In other words, we want to use the statistical strategy that will best answer our research question. There are so many particular statistics and so many ways for them to be used in data analysis that even the best statistician can become lost in a sea of numbers if she is not using prior research and theorizing to develop a coherent analysis plan. It is also important for an analyst to choose statistics that are appropriate to the level of measurement of the variables to be analyzed. As you learned in Chapter 3, numbers used to represent the values of variables may not actually signify different quantities, meaning that many statistical techniques will be inapplicable. Some statistics, for example, will only be appropriate when the variable you are examining is measured at the nominal level. Other kinds of statistics will require interval-level measurement. To use the right statistic, then, you must be very familiar with the measurement properties of your variables (and you thought that stuff would go away!).

> **Cross-tabulation (cross-tab)** A bivariate (two-variable) distribution, showing the distribution of one variable for each category of another variable.

> **Descriptive statistics** Statistics used to describe the distribution of and relationship among variables.

> **Inferential statistics** Mathematical tools for estimating how likely it is that a statistical result based on data from a random sample is representative of the population from which the sample was selected.

🖳 Case Study: The Causes of Delinquency

In this chapter, we will use research on the causes of delinquency for our examples. More specifically, our data will be a subset of a much larger study of a sample of approximately 1,200 high school students selected from the metropolitan and suburban high schools of a city in South Carolina. These students, all of whom were in the 10th grade, completed a questionnaire that asked about such things as how they spent their spare time; how they got along with their parents, teachers, and friends; their attitudes about delinquency; whether their friends committed delinquent acts; and their own involvement in delinquency. The original research study was designed to test specific hypotheses about the factors that influence delinquency. It was predicted that delinquent behavior would be affected by such things as the level of supervision provided by parents, the students' own moral beliefs about delinquency, their involvement in conventional activities such as studying and watching TV, their fear of getting caught, their friends' involvement in crime, and whether these friends provided verbal support for delinquent acts. All these hypotheses were derived from extant criminological theory, theories we have referred to throughout this book. One specific hypothesis, derived from deterrence theory, predicts that youths who believe they are likely to get caught by the police for committing delinquent acts are less likely to commit delinquency than others. This hypothesis is shown in Exhibit 13.1. The variables from this study that we will use in our chapter examples are displayed in Exhibit 13.2.

Exhibit 13.1	**Perceived Fear of Punishment and Delinquency**

Fear of getting caught by police ⟶ Delinquency

Exhibit 13.2 List of Variables for Class Examples of Causes of Delinquency

Variable	SPSS Variable Name	Description
Gender	V1	Sex of respondent.
Age	V2	Age of respondent.
TV	V21	Number of hours per week the respondent watches TV.
Study	V22	Number of hours per week the respondent spends studying.
Supervision	V63	Do parents know where respondent is when he or she is away from home?
Friends think theft wrong	V77	How wrong do respondent's best friends think it is to commit petty theft?
Friends think drinking wrong	V79	How wrong do respondent's best friends think it is to drink liquor under age?
Punishment for drinking	V109	If respondent was caught drinking liquor under age and taken to court, how much of a problem would it be?
Cost of vandalism	V119	How much would respondent's chances of having good friends be hurt if he or she was arrested for petty theft?
Parental supervision	PARSUPER	Added scale from items that ask respondent if parents know where he or she is and whom he or she is with when away from home. A high score
Friend's opinion	FROPINON	Added scale that asks respondent if his or her best friends thought that committing various delinquent acts was all right. A high score means more support
Friend's behavior	FRBEHAVE	Added scale that asks respondent how many of his or her best friends commit delinquent acts.
Certainty of punishment	CERTAIN	Added scale that measures how likely respondent thinks it is that he or she will be caught by police if he or she were to commit delinquent acts. A high
Morality	MORAL	Added scale that measures how morally wrong respondent thinks it is to commit diverse delinquent acts. A high score means strong moral inhibitions
Delinquency	DELINQ1	An additive scale that counts the number of times respondent admits to committing a number of different delinquent acts in the past year. The higher the score, the more delinquent acts committed.

▣ Preparing Data for Analysis

Our analysis of the causes of delinquency in this chapter is an example of **secondary data analysis**. As we described in Chapter 10, it is secondary because we received the data secondhand; we did not design the data-collection instrument ourselves. Using secondary data in this way has a major disadvantage; if you did not design the study yourself, it is unlikely

> **Secondary data analysis** Analysis of data collected by someone other than the researcher or the researcher's assistant.

that all the variables you think should have been included actually were included and that they were measured in the way that you prefer. In addition, the sample may not represent the population in which you are interested, and the study design may be only partially appropriate to your research question. For example, this particular study was completed before recent theoretical work in criminology on self-control. It also contains only self-reported delinquency and no measures as to whether these delinquent acts resulted in an arrest or a juvenile court appearance. Furthermore, because it is a survey of individuals, the study has no measures of the kinds of communities within which the students lived—for example, the level of crime in the community or measures of informal community control. Because the survey sample is selected only from one city in South Carolina, we cannot make generalizations to youths in other cities or in other states.

Although they come with many disadvantages, there is one important advantage of secondary data: They are readily available. It is the availability of secondary data that makes their use preferable for many purposes. A great many high-quality data sets (such as the data set on delinquency we are using) are available for reanalysis from the Inter-University Consortium for Political and Social Research (ICPSR) at the University of Michigan. Other data sets for secondary data analysis can be obtained from the government, individual researchers, and other research organizations. Most of these data sets are stored on computer disks or CD-ROMs, ready for use without any further effort. Therefore, for a great many research problems, a researcher should first check what data sets on the question already are available. An enormous savings in time and resources may be the result.

If you have conducted your own survey or experiment, your quantitative data must be prepared in a format suitable for computer entry. You learned in Chapter 8 that questionnaires and interview schedules can be precoded to facilitate data entry by representing each response with a unique number (see Exhibit 13.3). This method allows direct

Exhibit 13.3	Section of the National Violence Against Men and Women Survey on Stalking Victimizations Given to Female Respondents

SECTION H: STALKING VICTIMIZATION

H1. Now I'd like to ask you some questions about following or harassment you may have experienced on more than one occasion by strangers, friends, relatives, or even husbands and partners. Not including bill collectors, telephone solicitors, or other salespeople, has anyone, male or female, ever . . . MARK ALL THAT APPLY

    01 Followed you or spied on you?

    02 Sent you unsolicited letters or written correspondence?

    03 Made unsolicited phone calls to you?

    04 Stood outside your home, school, or workplace?

    05 Showed up at places you were even though he or she had no business being there?

    06 Left unwanted items for you to find?

(Continued)

Exhibit 13.3 **(Continued)**

07 Tried to communicate with you in other ways against your will?

08 Vandalized your property or destroyed something you loved?

09 (Volunteered) Don't Know   GO TO SECTION I

10 (Volunteered) Refused   GO TO SECTION I

11 (Volunteered) None   GO TO SECTION I

H2.   If H1 = ANY OF 1–8 (RESPONDENT HAS BEEN STALKED) GO TO H3, ELSE GO TO SECTION I.

H3.   Has anyone ever done any of these things to you on more than one occasion?

1 Yes

2 No   GO TO SECTION I

3 (Volunteered) Don't Know   GO TO SECTION I

4 (Volunteered) Refused   GO TO SECTION I

H4.   How many different people have ever done this to you on more than one occasion?

_____ Number of people [RANGE IS 1–97]

98 (Volunteered) Don't Know   GO TO SECTION I

99 (Volunteered) Refused   GO TO SECTION I

H5.   Was this person/these persons . . . MARK ALL THAT APPLY

01 Your current spouse?

02 An ex-spouse?

03 A male live-in partner?

04 A female live-in partner?

05 A relative?

06 Someone else you know?

07 A stranger?

08 (Volunteered) Don't Know

09 (Volunteered) Refused

Source: Tjaden and Thoennes 2000.

---

entry of the precoded responses into a computer file, after responses are checked to ensure that only one valid answer code has been circled (extra written answers can be assigned their own numerical codes). Most survey research organizations now use a database management program to control data entry. The program prompts the data entry clerk for each response, checks the response to ensure that it is a valid response for that variable, and then saves the response in the data file. Not all studies have used precoded data entry, however, and individual researchers must enter the data themselves. This is an arduous and time-consuming task, but not for us if we use secondary data. After all, we get the data only after they have been coded and computerized.

Of course, numbers stored in a computer file are not yet numbers that can be analyzed with statistics. After the data are entered, they must be checked carefully for errors, a process called **data cleaning**. If a data entry program has been used and programmed to flag invalid values, the cleaning process is much easier. If data are read in from a text file, a computer program must be written that defines which variables are coded in which columns, attaches meaningful labels to the codes, and distinguishes values representing missing data. The procedures for doing so vary with each specific statistical

> **Data cleaning** The process of checking data for errors after the data have been entered in a computer file.

package. We used the Windows version of the Statistical Package for the Social Sciences (SPSS) for the analysis in this chapter; you will find examples of SPSS commands required to define and analyze data on the Student Study Site for this text, www.sagepub.com/bachmanprccj5e. More detailed information on using SPSS is contained in SPSS manuals or in other "how to" books such as Wagner (2010).

Displaying Univariate Distributions

The first step in data analysis is usually to display the variation in each variable of interest in what are called *univariate frequency distributions*. For many descriptive purposes, the analysis may go no further. Frequency distributions and graphs of frequency distributions are the two most popular approaches for displaying variation; both allow the analyst to display the distribution of cases across the value categories of a variable. Graphs have the advantage over numerically displayed frequency distributions because they provide a picture that is easier to comprehend. Frequency distributions are preferable when exact numbers of cases with particular values must be reported, and when many distributions must be displayed in a compact form.

No matter which type of display is used, the primary concern of the data analyst is to accurately display the distribution's shape—that is, to show how cases are distributed across the values of the variable. Three features of the shape of a distribution are important: **central tendency**, **variability**, and **skewness** (lack of symmetry). All three of these features can be represented in a graph or in frequency distribution.

These features of a distribution's shape can be interpreted in several different ways, and they are not all appropriate for describing every variable. In fact, all three features of a distribution can be distorted if graphs, frequency distributions, or summary statistics are used inappropriately.

A variable's level of measurement is the most important determinant of the appropriateness of particular statistics. For example, we cannot talk about the skewness (lack of symmetry) of a qualitative variable (measured at the nominal level). If the values of a variable cannot be ordered from lowest to highest, if the ordering of the values is arbitrary, we cannot say whether the distribution is symmetric because we could just reorder the values to make the distribution more (or less) symmetric. Some measures of central tendency and variability are also inappropriate for qualitative variables.

The distinction between variables measured at the ordinal level and those measured at the interval or ratio level should also be considered when selecting statistics to use, but social researchers differ on just how much importance they attach to this distinction. Many social researchers think of ordinal variables as imperfectly measured interval-level variables and believe that in most circumstances statistics developed for interval-level variables also provide useful summaries for ordinal variables. Other social researchers believe that variation in ordinal variables will often be distorted by statistics that assume an interval level of measurement. We will touch on some of the details of these issues in the following sections on particular statistical techniques.

We will now examine graphs and frequency distributions that illustrate these three features of shape. Summary statistics used to measure specific aspects of central tendency and variability will be presented in a separate section. There is a summary statistic for the measurement of skewness, but it is used only rarely in published research reports and will not be presented here.

> **Central tendency** A feature of a variable's distribution, referring to the value or values around which cases tend to center.
>
> **Variability** A feature of a variable's distribution, referring to the extent to which cases are spread out through the distribution or clustered in just one location.
>
> **Skewness** A feature of a variable's distribution; refers to the extent to which cases are clustered more at one or the other end of the distribution rather than around the middle.

Graphs

It is true that a picture often is worth a thousand words. Graphs can be easy to read, and they very nicely highlight a distribution's shape. They are particularly useful for exploring data because they show the full range of variation and identify data anomalies that might be in need of further study. And good, professional-looking graphs can now be produced relatively easily with software available for personal computers. There are many types of graphs, but the most common and most useful are bar charts and histograms. Each has two axes, the vertical axis (*y*-axis) and the horizontal axis (*x*-axis), and labels to identify the variables and the values with tick marks showing where each indicated value falls along the axis. The vertical *y*-axis of a graph is usually in frequency or percent units, whereas the horizontal *x*-axis displays the values of the variable being graphed. There are different kinds of graphs you can use to descriptively display your data, depending upon the level of measurement of the variable.

> **Bar chart** A graphic for qualitative variables in which the variable's distribution is displayed with solid bars separated by spaces.
>
> **Percentage** Relative frequencies, computed by dividing the frequency of cases in a particular category by the total number of cases, and multiplying by 100.
>
> **Mode** The most frequent value in a distribution; also termed the probability average.

A **bar chart** contains solid bars separated by spaces. It is a good tool for displaying the distribution of variables measured at the nominal level and other discrete categorical variables because there is, in effect, a gap between each of the categories. In our delinquency data, one of the questions asked of respondents was if their parents knew where they were when they were away from home. We graphed the responses to this question in a bar chart, which is shown in Exhibit 13.4. In this bar chart we report both the frequency count for each value and the **percentage** of the total that each value represents. The bar chart in Exhibit 13.4 indicates that very few of the respondents (only 16, or 1.3%) reported that their parents "never" knew where they were when they were not at home. Almost one half (562, or 44.3%) of the youths reported that their parents "usually" knew where they were. What you can also see by noticing the height of the bars above "usually" and "always" is that most youths report that their parents provide very adequate supervision. You can also see that the most frequent response was "usually" and the least frequent was "never." Because the response "usually" is the most frequent value, it is called the **mode** or modal response. With ordinal data like these, the mode is the most appropriate measure of central tendency. (More about this later.)

Notice that the cases tend to cluster in the two values of "usually" and "always"; in fact, about 80% of all cases are found in those two categories. There is not much variability in this distribution, then. In Exhibit 13.5, we show another bar chart from the delinquency data. In this example, the variable is the attitude of one's friends toward drinking under age. Respondents were asked how wrong their best friends thought it was to drink liquor under age. As you can see, unlike the case in Exhibit 13.4, the frequencies are more evenly spread out across the various values (the heights of the bars don't differ as much in this bar chart), so there is more variability in this variable than for the one shown in Exhibit 13.4.

A **histogram** is like a bar chart, but it has bars that are adjacent, or right next to each other, with no gaps. This is done to indicate that data displayed in a histogram, unlike the data in a bar chart, are quantitative variables that vary along a continuum (see the discussion of levels of measurement for variables in Chapter 4). Exhibit 13.6 shows a histogram from the delinquency data set we are using. The variable being graphed is the number of hours per week the respondent reported to be studying. Notice that the cases cluster at the low end of the values. In other words, there are a lot of youths who spend between 0 and 15 hours per week studying. After that, there are only a few cases at each different value with a "spike" occurring at 25, 30, 38, and 40 hours studied. This distribution is clearly not symmetric. In a symmetric distribution there is a lump of cases or a "spike" with an equal number of cases to the left and right of that spike. In the distribution shown in Exhibit 13.6, most of the cases are at the left end of the distribution (i.e., at low values), and the distribution trails off on the right side. The ends of a histogram like this are often called the tail of a distribution. In a symmetric distribution, the left and right tails are approximately the same length. As you can

> **Histogram** A graphic for quantitative variables in which the variable's distribution is displayed with adjacent bars.

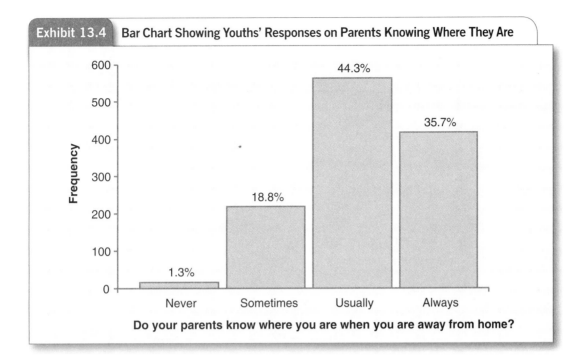

Exhibit 13.4 Bar Chart Showing Youths' Responses on Parents Knowing Where They Are

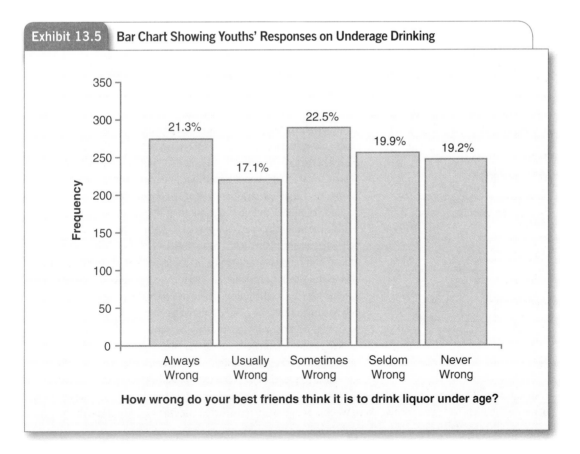

Exhibit 13.5 Bar Chart Showing Youths' Responses on Underage Drinking

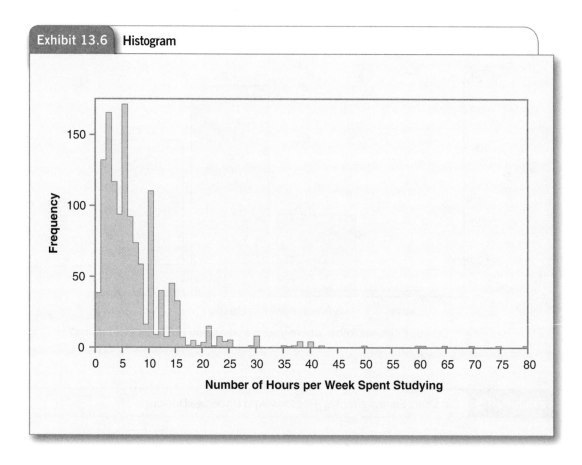

Exhibit 13.6 | Histogram

clearly see in Exhibit 13.6, however, the right tail is much longer than the left tail. When the tails of the distribution are uneven the distribution is said to be asymmetrical or skewed. A skew is either positive or negative. When the cases cluster to the left and the right tail of the distribution is longer than the left, as in Exhibit 13.6, our variable distribution is **positively skewed**. When the cases cluster to the right side and the left tail of the distribution is long, our variable distribution is **negatively skewed**.

In a **frequency polygon**, a continuous line connects the points representing the number or percentage of cases with each value. The frequency polygon is an alternative to the histogram when the distribution of a quantitative, continuous variable must be displayed; this alternative is particularly useful when the variable has a wide range of values. We used the same number of hours studying data shown in Exhibit 13.6 to make the frequency polygon in Exhibit 13.7. Notice that the frequency polygon is constructed by making a point or dot to represent the frequency of each value and then drawing a line by connecting the dots. The frequency polygon gives us the same impression of the data as the histogram. These data cluster near the low values (representing fewer hours studied), and there are only a very few respondents who report studying more than 25 hours per week. Because the right tail is long, relative to the left tail of the distribution, we have a positive skew. We could have easily constructed both the histogram and the frequency polygon with percentages rather than raw frequencies.

Positively skewed Describes a distribution in which the cases cluster to the left and the right tail of the distribution is longer than the left.

Negatively skewed A distribution in which cases cluster to the right side and the left tail of the distribution is longer than the right.

Frequency polygon A graphic for quantitative variables in which a continuous line connects data points representing the variable's distribution.

Exhibit 13.7   Frequency Polygon

If graphs are misused, they can distort, rather than display, the shape of a distribution. Compare, for example, the two graphs in Exhibit 13.8. The first graph shows that high school seniors reported relatively stable rates of lifetime use of cocaine between 1980 and 1985. The second graph, using exactly the same numbers, appeared in a 1986 *Newsweek* article on the coke plague (Orcutt and Turner 1993). To look at this graph, you would think that the rate of cocaine usage among high school seniors increased dramatically during this period. But, in fact, the difference between the two graphs is due simply to changes in how the graphs are drawn. In the "plague" graph (B), the percentage scale on the vertical axis begins at 15 rather than 0, making what was about a one-percentage-point increase look very big indeed. In addition, omission from the plague graph of the more rapid increase in reported usage between 1975 and 1980 makes it look as if the tiny increase in 1985 were a new, and thus more newsworthy, crisis.

Adherence to several guidelines (Tufte 1983) will help you spot these problems and avoid them in your own work:

- The difference between bars can be exaggerated by cutting off the bottom of the vertical axis and displaying less than the full height of the bars. Instead, begin the graph of a quantitative variable at 0 on both axes. It may at times be reasonable to violate this guideline, as when an age distribution is presented for a sample of adults, but in this case be sure to mark the break clearly on the axis.

- Bars of unequal width, including pictures instead of bars, can make particular values look as if they carry more weight than their frequency warrants. Always use bars of equal width.

- Either shortening or lengthening the vertical axis will obscure or accentuate the differences in the number of cases between values. The two axes usually should be of approximately equal length.

- Avoid chart junk that can confuse the reader and obscure the distribution's shape (a lot of verbiage, numerous marks, lines, lots of cross-hatching, etc.).

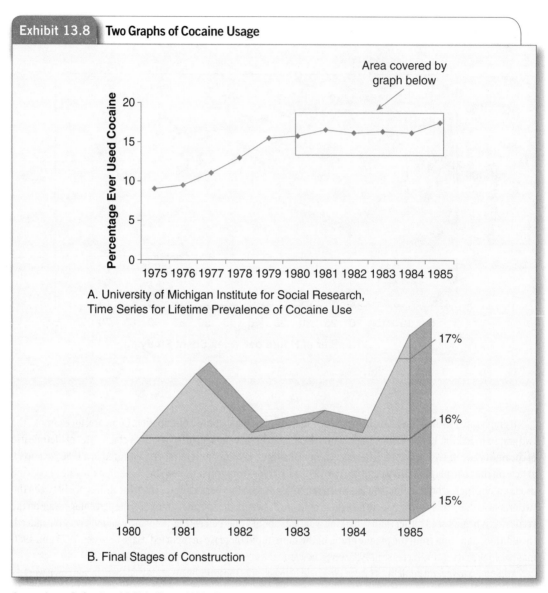

Exhibit 13.8 Two Graphs of Cocaine Usage

A. University of Michigan Institute for Social Research, Time Series for Lifetime Prevalence of Cocaine Use

B. Final Stages of Construction

Source: James D. Orcutt and J. Blake Turner, 1993. "Shocking Numbers and Graphic Accounts." *Social Problems,* Vol. 49, No. 2, pp. 190–206. © 1993 by the Society for the Study of Social Problems. Reprinted by permission.

Frequency Distributions

A frequency distribution displays the number, the percentage (the relative frequencies), or both for cases corresponding to each of a variable's values or a group of values. The components of the frequency distribution should be clearly labeled, with a title, a stub (labels for the values of the variable), a caption (identifying whether the distribution includes frequencies, percentages, or both), and perhaps the number of missing cases. If percentages are presented rather than frequencies (sometimes both are included), the total number of cases in the distribution (the Base N) should be indicated (see Exhibit 13.9). Remember that a percentage is simply a relative frequency. A percentage shows the frequency of a given value relative to the total number of cases times 100.

Base N The total number of cases in a distribution.

Exhibit 13.9	Frequency Distribution

How much of a problem would it be if you went to court for drinking liquor under age?

Value	Frequency (f)	Percentage (%)
No problem at all	14	1.1
Hardly any problem	53	4.2
A little problem	196	15.4
A big problem	421	33.1
A very big problem	588	46.2
Total	1,272	100.0

Ungrouped Data

Constructing and reading frequency distributions for variables with few values is not difficult. In Exhibit 13.9, we created the frequency distribution from the variable "Punishment for Drinking" found in the delinquency data set (see Exhibit 13.2). This variable asked the youths to respond to the following question: "How much of a problem would it be if you went to court for drinking liquor under age?" The frequency distribution in Exhibit 13.9 shows the frequency for each value and its corresponding percentage.

As another example of calculating the frequencies and percentages, suppose we had a sample of 25 youths and asked them their gender. From this group of 25 youths, 13 were male and 12 were female. The frequency of males (symbolized here by f) would be 13 and the frequency of females would be 12. The percentage of males would be 52%, calculated by f/ the total number of cases × 100 (13 / 25 × 100 = 52%). The percentage of females would be 12 / 25 × 100 = 48%.

In the frequency distribution shown in Exhibit 13.9, you can see that only a very small number (14 out of 1,272) of youths thought that they would experience "no problem" if they were caught and taken to court for drinking liquor under age. You can see that most, in fact 1,009 of these youths or 79.3% of them, thought that they would have either "a big problem" or "a very big problem" with this. If you compare Exhibit 13.9 to Exhibit 13.4, you can see that a frequency distribution (see Exhibit 13.9) can provide much of the same information as a graph about the number and percentage of cases in a variable's categories. Often, however, it is easier to see the shape of a distribution when it is graphed. When the goal of a presentation is to convey a general sense of a variable's distribution, particularly when the presentation is to an audience not trained in statistics, the advantages of a graph outweigh those of a frequency distribution.

Exhibit 13.9 is a frequency distribution of an ordinal-level variable; it has a very small number of discrete categories. In Exhibit 13.10, we provide an illustration of a frequency distribution with a continuous quantitative variable. This variable is one we have already looked at and graphed from the delinquency data, the number of hours per week the respondent spent studying. Notice that this variable, like many continuous variables in criminological research, has a large number of values. Although this is a reasonable frequency distribution to construct—you can, for example, still see that the cases tend to cluster in the low end of the distribution and are strung way out at the upper end—it is a little difficult to get a good sense of the distribution of the cases. The problem is that there are too many values to easily comprehend. It would be nice if we could simplify distributions like these that have a large number of different values. Well, we can. We can construct what is called a grouped frequency distribution.

Grouped frequency distribution A frequency distribution in which the data are organized into categories, either because there are more values than can be easily displayed or because the distribution of the variable will be clearer or more meaningful.

Grouped Data

Many frequency distributions, such as those in Exhibit 13.10, and many graphs require grouping of some values after the data are collected. There are two reasons for grouping:

1. There are more than 15–20 values to begin with, a number too large to be displayed in an easily readable table.

2. The distribution of the variable will be clearer or more meaningful if some of the values are combined.

Exhibit 13.10	Frequency Distribution With Continuous Quantitative Data: Hours Studied per Week	
Value	*Frequency (f)*	*Percentage (%)*
0	38	3.0
1	132	10.4
2	165	13.0
3	116	9.1
4	94	7.4
5	171	13.4
6	92	7.2
7	73	5.7
8	58	4.6
9	16	1.3
10	110	8.6
11	9	0.7
12	40	3.1
13	7	0.6
14	45	3.5
15	32	2.5
16	7	0.6
17	5	0.4
18	4	0.3
19	1	0.1
20	15	1.2
21	8	0.6

Value	Frequency (f)	Percentage (%)
22	1	0.1
23	1	0.1
24	4	0.3
25	5	0.4
29	1	0.1
30	8	0.6
35	1	0.1
37	1	0.1
40	4	0.3
42	1	0.1
50	1	0.1
60	1	0.1
61	1	0.1
65	1	0.1
70	1	0.1
75	1	0.1
80	1	0.1
Total	1,272	100.0

Inspection of Exhibit 13.10 should clarify these reasons. In this distribution it is very difficult to discern any shape, much less the central tendency. What we would like to now do to make the features of the data more visible is change the values into intervals of values, or a range of values. For example, rather than having five separate values of 0, 1, 2, 3, and 4 hours studied per week, we can have a range of values or an interval for the first value, such as 0–4 hours studied. Then we can get a count or frequency of the number of cases (and percentage of the total) that fall within that interval.

Once we decide to group values, or categories, we have to be sure that in doing so we do not distort the distribution. Adhering to the following guidelines for combining values in a frequency distribution will prevent many problems:

- Categories should be logically defensible and preserve the distribution's shape.

- Categories should be mutually exclusive and exhaustive, so every case is classifiable in one and only one category.

- The first interval must contain the lowest value, and the last interval must contain the highest value in the distribution.

- Each interval width, the number of values that fall within each interval, should be the same size.

- There should be between 7 and 13 intervals. This is a tough rule to follow. The key is not to have so few intervals that your data are clumped or clustered into only a few intervals (you will lose too much information about your distribution) and not to have so many intervals that the data are not much clearer than an ungrouped frequency distribution.

Let us use the data in Exhibit 13.10 on the number of hours studied by these youths to create a grouped frequency distribution. We will follow a number of explicit steps:

Step 1. Determine the number of intervals you think you want. This decision is arbitrary, but try to keep the number of intervals you have in the 7–13 range. For our example, let us say we initially decided we wanted to have 10 intervals. (Note, if you do your frequency distribution and it looks too clustered or there are too many intervals, redo your distribution with a different number of intervals.) Don't worry; there are no hard and fast rules for the correct number of intervals, and constructing a grouped frequency distribution is as much art as science. Just remember that the frequency distribution you make is supposed to convey information about the shape and central tendency of your data.

Step 2. Decide on the width of the interval (symbolized by w_i). The interval width is the number of different values that fall into your interval. For example, an interval width of 5 has five different values that fall into it, say, the values 0, 1, 2, 3, and 4 hours studied. There is a simple formula to approximate what your interval width should be given the number of intervals you decided on in the first step: Determine the range of the data, where the range is simply the highest score in the distribution minus the lowest score. In our data, with the number of hours studied, the range is 80 because the high score is 80 and the low score is 0, so range = 80 – 0 = 80. Then determine the width of the interval by dividing the range by the number of intervals you want from Step 1. We wanted 10 intervals, so our interval width would be $w_i = 80 / 10 = 8$. We should therefore have an interval width of 8. If you use this simple formula for determining your interval width and you end up with a decimal, say 8.2 or 8.6, then simply round up or down to an integer.

Step 3. Make your first interval so that the lowest value falls into it. Our lowest value is 0 (for studied 0 hours per week), so our first interval begins with the value 0. Now, if the beginning of our first interval is 0 and we want an interval width of 8, is the last value of our interval 7 (with a first interval of 0–7 hours), or is the last value of our interval 8 (with a first interval of 0–8 hours)? One easy way to make a grouped frequency distribution is to do the following: Take the beginning value of your first interval (in our case, it is 0), and add the interval width to that value (8). This new value is the first value of your next interval. What we know, then, is that the first value of our first interval is 0, and the first value of our second interval is 8 (0–?, 8–?). This must mean that the last value to be included in our first interval is one less than 8, or 7. Our first interval, therefore, includes the range of values 0–7. If you count the number of different values in this interval you will find that it includes eight different values (0, 1, 2, 3, 4, 5, 6, 7). This is our interval width of 8.

Step 4. After your first interval is determined, the next intervals are easy. They must be the same width and not overlap (mutually exclusive). You must make enough intervals to include the last value in your variable distribution. The highest value in our data is 80 hours per week, so we construct the grouped frequency distribution as follows:

0–7

8–15

16–23

24–31

32–39

40–47

48–55

56–63

64–71

72–79

80–87

Notice that in order to include the highest value in our data (80 hours) we had to make 11 intervals instead of the 10 we originally decided upon in Step 1. No problem. Remember, the number of intervals is arbitrary and this is as much art as science.

Step 5. Count the number or frequency of cases that appear in each interval and their percentage of the total. The completed grouped frequency distribution is shown in Exhibit 13.11. Notice that this grouped frequency distribution conveys the important features of the distribution of these data. Most of the data cluster at the low end of the number of hours studied. In fact, more than two thirds of these youths studied fewer than 8 hours per week. Notice also that the frequency of cases thins out at each successive interval. In other words, there is a long right tail to this distribution indicating a positive skew because fewer youths studied a high number of hours. Notice also that the distribution was created in such a way that the interval widths are all the same and each case falls into one and only one interval (i.e., the intervals are exhaustive and mutually exclusive). We would have run into trouble if we had two intervals like 0–7 and 7–14 because we would not know where to place those youths who spent 7 hours a week studying. Should we put them in the first or second interval? If the intervals are mutually exclusive, as they are here, you will not run into these problems.

| Exhibit 13.11 | Example of a Grouped Frequency Distribution From Hours Studied |

Value	Frequency (f)	Percentage (%)
0–7	881	69.26
8–15	317	24.92
16–23	42	3.30
24–31	18	1.42
32–39	2	0.16
40–47	5	0.39
48–55	1	0.08
56–63	2	0.16
64–71	2	0.16
72–79	1	0.08
80–87	1	0.08
Total	1,272	100.00

Note: Total may not equal 100.0% due to rounding error.

▣ Summarizing Univariate Distributions

Summary statistics, sometimes called descriptive statistics, focus attention on particular aspects of a distribution and facilitate comparison among distributions. For example, suppose you wanted to report the rate of violent crimes for each city in the United States with over 100,000 in population. You could report each city's violent crime rate, but it is unlikely that two cities would have the same rate, and you would have to report approximately 200 rates, one for each city. This would be a frequency distribution that many, if not most, people would find difficult to comprehend. One way to interpret your data for your audience would be to provide a summary measure that indicates what the average violent crime rate is in large U.S. cities. That is the purpose of the set of summary statistics called measures of central tendency. You would also want to provide another summary measure that shows the variability or heterogeneity in your data—in other words, a measure that shows how different the scores are from each other or from the central tendency. That is the purpose of the set of summary statistics called measures of *variation* or *dispersion*. We will discuss each type of measurement in turn.

Measures of Central Tendency

Central tendency is usually summarized with one of three statistics: the mode, the median, or the mean. For any particular application, one of these statistics may be preferable, but each has a role to play in data analysis. To choose an appropriate measure of central tendency, the analyst must consider a variable's level of measurement, the skewness of a quantitative variable's distribution, and the purpose for which the statistic is used. In addition, the analyst's personal experiences and preferences inevitably will play a role.

Mode

The mode is the most frequent value in a distribution. For example, refer to the data in Exhibit 13.11, which shows the grouped frequency distribution for the number of hours studied. The value with the greatest frequency in those data is the interval 0–7 hours; this is the mode of that distribution. Notice that the mode is the most frequently occurring value; it is not the frequency of that value. In other words, the mode in Exhibit 13.11 is 0–7 hours; the mode is not 881, which is the frequency of the modal category. To show how the mode can also be thought of as the value with the highest probability, refer to Exhibit 13.12. Suppose you had this grouped frequency distribution but knew nothing else about each of the 1,272 youths in the study. If you were to pick a case at random from the distribution of 1,272 youths and were asked how many hours the youth studied per week, what would your best guess be? Well, since 881 of the 1,272 youths fall into the first interval of 0–7 hours studied, the probability that a randomly selected youth studied from 0 to 7 hours would be .696 (881 / 1,272). This is higher than the probability of any other interval. It is the interval with the highest probability because it is the interval with the greatest frequency or mode of the distribution. When a variable distribution has one case or interval that occurs more often than the others, it is called a **unimodal distribution**.

Sometimes a distribution has more than one mode because there are two values that have the highest frequency. This distribution would be called **bimodal**. Some distributions are trimodal in that there are three distinctively high frequency values. And some distributions have no mode. Look back at the graph of the frequency distribution in Exhibit 13.5. There is no one value with a frequency much higher than another. In fact, if you calculate the probabilities of a randomly selected person falling into each of the different values, they would not be all that different. In other words,

> **Unimodal distribution** A distribution of a variable in which there is only one value that is the most frequent.

> **Bimodal distribution** A distribution that has two nonadjacent categories with about the same number of cases, and these categories have more cases than any other categories.

the outcomes are equiprobable, or there is no mode. In saying that there is no mode, though, you are communicating something very important about the data: that no case is more common than the others. Another potential problem with the mode is that it might happen to fall far from the main clustering of cases in a distribution. It would be misleading in this case, then, to say simply that the variable's central tendency was the same as the modal value.

Nevertheless, there are occasions when the mode is very appropriate. Most important, the mode is the only measure of central tendency that can be used to characterize the central tendency of variables measured at the nominal level. In Exhibit 13.12 we have the frequency distribution of the conviction offense for 1,000 offenders convicted in a criminal court. The central tendency of the distribution is property offense, because more of the 1,000 offenders were convicted of a property crime than any other crime. For the variable "type of offense convicted of," the most common value is property crime. The mode also is often referred to in descriptions of the shape of a distribution. The terms *unimodal* and *bimodal* appear frequently, as do descriptive statements such as "The typical (most probable) respondent was in her 30s." Of course, when the issue is determining the most probable value, the mode is the appropriate statistic.

Median

The **median** is the score in the middle of a rank-ordered distribution. It is, then, the score or point that divides the distribution in half (the 50th percentile). The median is inappropriate for variables measured at the nominal level because their values cannot be put in ranked order (remember, there is no "order" to nominal-level data), and so there is no meaningful middle position. To determine the median, we simply need to do the following. First, rank-order the values from lowest to highest. If there is an odd number of scores, then you can find the position of the median in the rank order of scores by using the following simple formula:

> *Median* The position average, or the point that divides a distribution in half (the 50th percentile).

$$\frac{N+1}{2},$$

where N is equal to the total number of cases. If there is an even number of scores, then you can find the position of the median in the rank order of scores by finding the midpoint of the scores in the following two positions:

$$\text{Position 1} = \frac{N}{2}$$

$$\text{Position 2} = \frac{N+2}{2}.$$

Exhibit 13.12   **Frequency Distribution of Offense Convicted for 1,000 Offenders**

Offense	Frequency (f)
Violent	125
Drug	210
Property	480
Public order	100
Other	85
Total	1,000

The midpoint of the two scores can be found by adding the scores in the two positions and dividing by 2. Please note that in both formulas you use the formula to find the position of the median; the formula does not give you the value of the median. Let us do an example.

In Exhibit 13.13, we first list a sample of nine U.S. cities and their rate of violent crime. In the bottom panel of Exhibit 13.13, we drop one of the cities (San Francisco) and have eight cities.

Let us determine the median for both lists. First, we rank-order the violent crime rates for the first list:

Rank	Crime Rate
1	1,322
2	1,461
3	1,530
4	1,589
5	1,861
6	1,887
7	1,916
8	2,059
9	3,571

Exhibit 13.13   **Rate of Violent Crime for Selected U.S. Cities**

City	Number of Violent Crimes per 100,000
Atlanta	3,571
Boston	1,916
Cleveland	1,530
Dallas	1,589
Los Angeles	2,059
New Orleans	1,887
New York	1,861
Philadelphia	1,322
San Francisco	1,461
Atlanta	3,571
Boston	1,916
Cleveland	1,530
Dallas	1,589
Los Angeles	2,059
New Orleans	1,887
New York	1,861
Philadelphia	1,322

Because we have an odd number of scores ($N = 9$), the position of the median is determined by $(9 + 1) / 2 = 10 / 2 = 5$. The median violent crime rate, then, is in the fifth position in this rank order. Starting either at the top of the scores and counting down to the fifth position or at the bottom and counting up, we find that in the fifth position is the score 1,861 violent crimes per 100,000, which is the median violent crime rate for these nine U.S. cities. Now, let us find the median in the second list. We first rank-order these eight scores:

Rank	Crime Rate
1	1,322
2	1,530
3	1,589
4	1,861
5	1,887
6	1,916
7	2,059
8	3,571

Because we now have an even number of scores (notice that the violent crime rate for San Francisco is missing from this list), we know that the median position is the midpoint in between the fourth ($8 / 2 = 4$) and fifth ($[8 + 2] / 2$) positions. The score at the fourth position is 1,861 and at the fifth is 1,887. The value of the median can now be found by adding these two scores and dividing by 2. The median rate of violent crime is equal to $(1,861 + 1,887) / 2 = 1,874$ violent crimes per 100,000 population.

The median is the score at the 50th percentile, so in a frequency distribution it is determined by identifying the value corresponding to a cumulative percentage of 50. We show you how to do this in Exhibit 13.14. These data are a repeat of the data in Exhibit 13.10 and show the number of hours studied for the youths in the delinquency data set. To find the 50th percentile, we simply added a new column to these data, labeled cumulative percentage. Cumulative percentages are found by taking the percentage of the interval percentage plus all others below it. So the first value (3.0%) would be entered as the first cumulative percentage because there are no other intervals below the first. This cumulative percentage simply means that 3% of the youths studied for 0 hours per week. Then we add the percentage in the next value (10.4%) to this to arrive at a cumulative percentage of 13.4%. This means that 13.4% of the youths studied for 1 hour per week or less. This becomes the second entry in the cumulative percentage column. We continue adding each adjacent percentage value until we reach 50%. There is a cumulative percentage of 56.3% at the value of 5 hours per week. The median number of hours studied per week, then, is 5 hours. Of the respondents, 50% studied less than 5 hours per week, and 50% studied more than 5 hours per week.

Mean

The **mean** is simply the arithmetic average of all scores in a distribution. It is computed by adding up the value of all the cases and dividing by the total number of cases, thereby taking into account the value of each case in the distribution:

Mean = Sum of value of all cases / number of cases.

The symbol for the mean is $\bar{X}$ (pronounced "X-bar"). In algebraic notation, the equation is

Mean The arithmetic, or weighted, average, computed by adding up the value of all the cases and dividing by the total number of cases.

$$\bar{X} = \frac{\sum_{1}^{N} x_i}{N},$$

Exhibit 13.14 Frequency Distribution With Continuous Quantitative Data: Hours Studied per Week

Value	Frequency (f)	Percentage (%)	Cumulative Percentage
0	38	3.0	3.0
1	132	10.4	13.4
2	165	13.0	26.4
3	116	9.1	35.5
4	94	7.4	42.9
5	141	13.4	56.3 (includes 50th percentile)
6	92	7.2	
7	73	5.7	
8	58	4.6	
9	16	1.3	
10	110	8.6	
11	9	0.7	
12	40	3.1	
13	7	0.6	
14	45	3.5	
15	32	2.5	
16	7	0.6	
17	5	0.4	
18	4	0.3	
19	1	0.1	
20	15	1.2	
21	8	0.6	
22	1	0.1	
23	1	0.1	
24	4	0.3	
25	5	0.4	
29	1	0.1	
30	8	0.6	

Value	Frequency (f)	Percentage (%)	Cumulative Percentage
35	1	0.1	
37	1	0.1	
40	4	0.3	
42	1	0.1	
50	1	0.1	
60	1	0.1	
61	1	0.1	
65	1	0.1	
70	1	0.1	
75	1	0.1	
80	1	0.1	
Total	1,272	100.0	

where x_i is a symbol for each ith score and i's go from 1 to N; N is the total number of cases. What the algebraic equation says to do is to sum all scores, starting at the first score and continuing until the last, or Nth, score; then divide this sum by the total number of cases (N).

We will calculate the mean rate of violent crime for the nine U.S. cities listed in Exhibit 12.13:

$$\bar{X} = \frac{(3,571+1,916+1,530+1,589+2,059+1.887+1,861+1,332+1,461)}{9} = 1,910.7.$$

The mean rate of violent crime for these nine U.S. cities, then, is 1,910.7 violent crimes per 100,000 population. Notice that in calculating the mean we do not have to first rank-order the scores. The mean takes every score into account, so it does not matter if we add 3,571 first, in the middle, or last.

Computing the mean requires adding up the values of the cases, so it makes sense to compute a mean only if the values of the cases can be treated as actual quantities—that is, if they reflect an interval or ratio level of measurement, or if they are ordinal and we assume that ordinal measures can be treated as interval. It would make no sense, however, to calculate the mean for the variable racial or ethnic status. Imagine a group of four people in which there were two Caucasians, one African American, and one Hispanic. To calculate the mean you would need to solve the equation (Caucasian + Caucasian + African American + Hispanic) / 4 = ? Even if you decide that Caucasian = 1, African American = 2, and Hispanic = 3 for data entry purposes, it still does not make sense to add these numbers because they do not represent real numerical quantities. In other words, just because you code Caucasian as "1" and African American as "2," that does not mean that African Americans possess twice the race or ethnicity as Caucasians. To see how numerically silly this is, note that we would just as easily have coded African Americans as "1" and Caucasians as "2." Now, with one arbitrary flip of our coding scheme Caucasians have twice the race or ethnicity as African Americans. Thus, both the median and the mean are inappropriate measures of central tendency for variables measured at the nominal level.

Median or Mean?

Both the median and the mean are used to summarize the central tendency of quantitative variables, but their suitability for a particular application must be carefully assessed.

The key issues to be considered in this assessment are the variable's level of measurement, the shape of its distribution, and the purpose of the statistical summary. Consideration of these issues will sometimes result in a decision to use both the median and the mean and will sometimes result in neither measure being seen as preferable. But in many other situations, the choice between the mean and median will be clear-cut as soon as the researcher takes the time to consider these three issues.

Level of measurement is a key concern because to calculate the mean, we must add up the values of all the cases, a procedure that assumes the variable is measured at the interval or ratio level. So even though we know that coding Agree as 2 and Disagree as 3 does not really mean that Disagree is one unit more of disagreement than Agree, the mean assumes this evaluation to be true. Calculation of the median requires only that we order the values of cases, so we do not have to make this assumption. Technically speaking, then, the mean is simply an inappropriate statistic for variables measured at the ordinal level (and you already know that it is completely meaningless for nominal variables). In practice, however, many social researchers use the mean to describe the central tendency of variables measured at the ordinal level, for the reasons outlined earlier.

The shape of a variable's distribution should also be taken into account when deciding whether to use the median or the mean. When a distribution is perfectly symmetric (i.e., when the distribution is bell shaped), the distribution of values below the median is a mirror image of the distribution of values above the median, and the mean and median will be the same. But the values of the mean and median are affected differently by skewness, or the presence of cases with extreme values on one side of the distribution but not the other side. The median takes into account only the number of cases above and below the median point, not the value of these cases, so it is not affected in any way by extreme values. The mean is based on adding the value of all the cases, so it will be pulled in the direction of exceptionally high (or low) values. When the value of the mean is larger than the median, we know that the distribution is skewed in a positive direction, with proportionately more cases with lower than higher values. When the mean is smaller than the median, the distribution is skewed in a negative direction.

This differential impact of skewness on the median and mean is illustrated in Exhibit 13.15. We show in the first list the crime rate per 1,000 residents for seven neighborhoods in a hypothetical city. The crime rates range from a low of 51.7 per 1,000 to 135.3 per 1,000. When we calculate the mean crime rate for these seven neighborhoods we find that it is 94.8 crimes per 1,000; the median is 98.7 crimes per 1,000. Notice that this is a relatively symmetrical distribution, with the values of the mean and the median very comparable to each other. With these data both the mean and the median provide an accurate description of the central tendency.

In the second list of neighborhoods, we replace the neighborhood that had the highest crime rate (i.e., King's Crossing) with West Chester, which has a substantially higher crime rate: 697.5 per 1,000. It is, then, an unusually high score. When we calculate the mean for these data, we find that it is 175.1 per 1,000; it has increased from its previous value of 94.8. The median, however, remains the same; it is still 98.7 crimes per 1,000. When an unusually high score is added to a distribution, then, the mean gets inflated relative to the median. In distributions that are positively skewed, the mean is of greater magnitude than the median. Notice also that with this unusually high crime rate added, the median is still an accurate picture of the central tendency, whereas the mean of 175.1 is no longer accurate.

In the third list of neighborhoods, we replace the neighborhood that has the lowest crime rate (i.e., Valley View) with Pleasantville, which has a substantially lower crime rate, 5.3 per 1,000. It is, then, an unusually low score. When we calculate the mean for these data, we find that it is 88.1 per 1,000; it has decreased from the value in the first list, which was 94.8. The median, however, remains the same; it is still 98.7 crimes per 1,000. When an unusually low score is added to a distribution, then, the mean gets deflated relative to the median. In distributions that are negatively skewed, the mean is less than the median. Notice also that even with this unusually low crime rate added, the median is still an accurate picture of the central tendency, whereas the mean of 88.1 is no longer as accurate.

This example illustrates one of the problems with using the mean as a measure of central tendency. If the data are skewed (either positively or negatively), then the mean will be affected by the extreme scores in the distribution and will

Exhibit 13.15	Rates of Crime in Selected Neighborhoods

Community	Crime Rate per 1,000
Valley View	51.7
Glen Commons	63.1
Springdale	75.3
Green Acres	98.7
Oceanside	113.4
Meadowbrook	125.9
King's Crossing	135.3
Valley View	51.7
Glen Commons	63.1
Springdale	75.3
Green Acres	98.7
Oceanside	113.4
Meadowbrook	125.9
West Chester	697.5
Pleasantville	5.3
Glen Commons	63.1
Springdale	75.3
Green Acres	98.7
Oceanside	113.4
Meadowbrook	125.9
King's Crossing	135.3

not give as accurate an estimate of the central tendency of the data as the median. The lesson is that one should probably report both the mean and the median. In general, the mean is the most commonly used measure of central tendency for quantitative variables, because it takes into account the value of all cases in the distribution and it is the foundation for many other more advanced statistics. However, the mean's very popularity results in its use in situations for which it is inappropriate. Keep an eye out for this problem.

Measures of Variation

You have learned that central tendency is only one aspect of the shape of a distribution. Although the measure of center is the most important aspect for many purposes, it is still just a piece of the total picture. A summary of distributions based only on their central tendency can be very incomplete, even misleading. For example, three towns might have the same mean and median crime rate but still be very different in their social character due to the shape of the crime distributions. We show three distributions of community crime rates for three different towns in Exhibit 13.16. If you calculate the mean and median crime rate for each town, you will find that the mean and median crime rate is the same for all three. In terms of its crime rate, then, each community has the same central tendency. As you can see, however, there is something very different about these towns. Town A is a very heterogeneous town; crime rates in its neighborhoods are neither very homogeneous nor clustered at either the low or high end. Rather, the crime rates in its communities are spread out from one another. Crime rates in these neighborhoods are, then, very diverse. Town B is characterized by neighborhoods with very homogeneous crime rates; there are no real high or low crime areas because each neighborhood is not far from the overall mean of 62.4 crimes per 1,000. Town C is characterized by neighborhoods with either very low crime rates or very high crime rates. Crime rates in the first four neighborhoods are much lower than the mean (62.4 crimes per 1,000), whereas those in the last four neighborhoods are much higher than the mean. Although they share identical measures of central tendency, these three towns have neighborhood crime rates that are very different.

The way to capture these differences is with statistical measures of variation. Four popular measures of variation are the range, the interquartile range, the variance, and the standard deviation (which is the most popular measure of variability). To calculate each of these measures, the variable must be at the interval or ratio level. Statistical measures of variation are used infrequently with qualitative variables, so these measures will not be presented here.

Range

The **range** is a simple measure of variation, calculated as the highest value in a distribution minus the lowest value:

> **Range** The true upper limit in a distribution minus the true lower limit (or the highest rounded value minus the lowest rounded value, plus one).

$$\text{Range} = \text{Highest value} - \text{Lowest value}.$$

It often is important to report the range of a distribution, to identify the whole range of possible values that might be encountered. However, because the range can be drastically altered by just one exceptionally high or low value (called an **outlier**), it does not do an adequate job of summarizing the extent of variability in a distribution. For our three towns in Exhibit 13.16, the range in crime rates for Town A is 89.9 (109.4 – 19.5), for Town B it is 6.9 (65.0 – 58.7), and for Town C, it is 106.4 (115.3 – 8.9).

Exhibit 13.16 **Neighborhood Crime Rates in Three Different Towns**

Town A	Town B	Town C
19.5	58.1	8.9
28.2	59.7	15.4
35.7	60.1	18.3
41.9	62.7	21.9
63.2	63.2	63.2
75.8	63.9	103.5
92.0	64.2	104.2
95.7	64.5	110.7
109.4	65.0	105.3

Interquartile Range

A version of the range statistics, the interquartile range, avoids the problem created by unusually high or low scores in a distribution. It is the difference between the scores at the first and third quartiles. Quartiles are the points in a distribution corresponding to the first 25% of the cases (the first quartile), the first 50% of the cases (the second quartile), and the first 75% of the cases (the third quartile). You already know how to determine the second quartile, corresponding to the point in the distribution covering half of the cases; it is another name for the median. The first and third quartiles are determined in the same way, but by finding the points corresponding to 25% and 75% of the cases, respectively.

Outlier An exceptionally high or low value in a distribution.

Interquartile range The range in a distribution between the end of the first quartile and the beginning of the third quartile.

Quartiles The points in a distribution corresponding to the first 25% of the cases, the first 50% of the cases, and the top 25% of the cases.

Variance

If the mean is a good measure of central tendency, then it would seem that a good measure of variability would be the distance each score is away from the mean. Unfortunately, we cannot simply take the average distance of each score from the mean. One property of the mean is that it exactly balances negative and positive distances from it, so if we were to sum the difference between each score in a distribution and the mean of that distribution, it would always sum to zero. What we can do, though, is to square the difference of each score from the mean so the distance retains its value. This is the notion behind the variance as a measure of variability.

The variance is the average square deviation of each case from the mean, so it takes into account the amount by which each case differs from the mean. The equation to calculate the variance is

Variance A statistic that measures the variability of a distribution as the average squared deviation of each score from the mean of all scores.

$$\sigma^2 = \frac{\sum_1^N \left(X - \bar{X} \right)^2}{N}.$$

In words, this formula says to take each score and subtract the mean, then square this difference, then sum all these differences, and then divide this sum by N or the total number of scores. We will calculate the variance for the crime rate data from Town A in Exhibit 13.16.

X	(X-X̄)	(X-X̄)²
19.5	(19.5~62.4) = −42.9	1,840.41
28.2	(28.2~62.4) = −34.2	1,169.64
35.7	(35.7~62.4) = −26.7	712.89
41.9	(41.9~62.4) = −20.5	420.25
63.2	(63.2~62.4) = −0.8	0.64
75.8	(75.8~62.4) = 13.4	179.56
92.0	(92.0~62.4) = 29.6	876.16
95.7	(95.7~62.4) = 33.3	1,108.89
109.4	(109.4~62.4) = 47.0	2,209.00
	Σ(x − X̄)	Σ (X − X̄)² =8.517.44

We can now determine that the variance is

$$\sigma^2 = \frac{8,517.44}{9} = 946.38 \,.$$

The variance of these data, then, is 946.38. In "squared deviation units," the variance tells us the amount of variation the distribution has around its mean. We had to square the original deviation units before summing them because $\sum(X - \overline{X}) = 0$. For most people, however, it is difficult to grasp "squared deviation units." For this reason, we typically take the square root of this value, called the standard deviation, to bring the variable back to its original units of measurement.

Standard Deviation

Standard deviation The square root of the average squared deviation of each case from the mean.

The **standard deviation** is simply the square root of the variance. It is the square root of the average squared deviation of each case from the mean:

$$\sigma = \sqrt{\frac{\sum_1^N (X - \overline{X})^2}{N}} \,.$$

To find the standard deviation, then, simply calculate the variance and take the square root. For our example, the standard deviation is

$$\sigma = \sqrt{946.38} = 30.76 \,.$$

When the standard deviation is calculated from sample data, the denominator is supposed to be $N - 1$, rather than N, an adjustment that has no discernible effect when the number of cases is reasonably large. This value tells us that, on average, the neighborhood crime rates in Town A vary 30.76 around their mean of 62.4.

The standard deviation has mathematical properties that make it the preferred measure of variability in many cases. In particular, the calculation of confidence intervals around sample statistics, which you learned about in Chapter 5, relies on an interesting property of normal curves. Areas under the normal curve correspond to particular distances from the mean, expressed in standard deviation units. If a variable is normally distributed, 68% of the cases will lie between plus and minus 1 standard deviation from the distribution's mean, and 95% of the cases will lie between 1.96 standard deviations above and below the mean. Cases that fall beyond plus or minus 1.96 standard deviations from the mean are termed outliers. Because of this property, the standard deviation tells us quite a bit about a distribution, if the distribution is normal. This same property of the standard deviation enables us to infer how confident we can be that the mean (or some other statistic) of a population sampled randomly is within a certain range of the sample mean (see Chapter 5).

Cross-Tabulating Variables

Most data analyses focus on relationships among variables to test hypotheses or just to describe or explore relationships. For each of these purposes, we must examine the association among two or more variables. Cross-tabulation (cross-tab) is one of the simplest methods for doing so. A cross-tabulation displays the distribution of one variable for each category of another variable; it can also be called a *bivariate distribution*. Cross-tabs also provide a simple tool for statistically controlling one or more variables while examining the associations among others. In this section, you will learn how cross-tabs used in this way can help test for spurious relationships and evaluate causal models. Cross-tabulations are usually used when both variables are measured at either the nominal or the ordinal level—that is, when the values of both variables are categories.

We are going to provide a series of examples of cross-tabulations from our delinquency data. In our first example, the independent variable we are interested in is the youth's gender (V1, see Exhibit 13.2), and the dependent variable is the youth's self-reported involvement in delinquent behavior (DELINQ1). To use the delinquency variable in a cross-tabulation, however, we first need to recode it into a categorical variable. We will make three approximately equal categories of self-reported delinquency: low, medium, and high. Using the SPSS recode command, we will create another variable called DELINQ2, which was made from the following recode commands:

$$(0 - 2 = 1)$$

$$(3 - 13 = 2)$$

$$(14 - 118 = 3)$$

Anyone who reported from none to two delinquent acts is now coded as 1, or low delinquency; anyone reporting from three to 13 delinquent acts is now coded as 2, or medium delinquency; and anyone reporting 14 or more delinquent acts is now coded as 3, or high delinquency. If you were to do a frequency distribution of this new variable, DELINQ2, you would see that there are three approximately equal groups.

We are interested in the relationship between gender and delinquency because a great deal of delinquency theory would predict that males are more likely to be delinquent than females. The gender of the youth is the independent variable, and the level of self-reported delinquency is the dependent variable.

Exhibit 13.17 shows the cross-tabulation of gender with DELINQ2. Some explanation of this table is in order. Notice that there are two values of gender (male and female) that comprise the two rows of the table and three values of delinquency (low, medium, and high) that comprise the three columns of the table. Cross-tabulations are usually referred to by the number of rows and columns the table has. Our cross-tabulation in Exhibit 13.17 is a 2 × 3 (pronounced "two-by-three") table because there are two rows and three columns. Notice also that there are values at the end of each row and at the end of each column. These totals are referred to as the *marginals* of the table. These **marginal distributions** provide the sum of the frequencies for each column and

> **Marginal distributions** The summary distributions in the margins of a cross-tabulation that correspond to the frequency distribution of the row variable and of the column variable.

Exhibit 13.17 Cross-Tabulation of Respondents' Gender by Delinquency

		SELF-REPORTED DELINQUENCY			
		Low	*Medium*	*High*	*Total*
GENDER	Female	275 40.4%	182 26.8%	223 32.8%	680 100%
	Male	175 29.6%	166 28.0%	251 42.4%	592 100%
	Total	450	348	474	1,272

each row of the table. For example, there are 680 females in the data and 592 males. These row marginals should sum to the total number of youths in the data set: 1,272. There are 450 youths who are low in delinquency, 348 youths who are medium in delinquency, and 474 youths who are high on the delinquency variable. These column marginals should also sum to the total number of youths in the data set: 1,272.

Now notice that there are 2 × 3 or 6 data entries in the table (let us ignore the percentages for now). These data entries are called the *cells* of the cross-tabulation and represent the joint distribution of the two variables: gender and delinquency. The table in Exhibit 13.17 has six cells for the joint distribution of two levels of gender with three levels of delinquency. In other words, notice where the value for female converges with the value of low for delinquency. You see a frequency number of 275 in this cell. This frequency is how many times there is the joint occurrence of a female and low delinquency; it shows that 275 females were also low in delinquency. Moving to the cell to the right of this, we see that there are 182 females who were medium in delinquency, and moving to the right again we see that there are 223 females who were high in delinquency. The sum of these three numbers is equal to the total number of females, 680. The row for the males shows the joint distribution of males with each level of delinquency.

What we would like to know is whether there is a relationship or an association between gender and delinquency. In other words, are males more likely to be delinquent than females? Because raw frequencies can provide a deceptive picture, we determine whether there is any relationship between our independent and dependent variables by looking at the percentages. Keep in mind that the idea in looking at relationships is that we want to know if variation on the independent variable has any effect on the dependent variable. To determine this, what we always do in cross-tabulation tables is to calculate our percentages on each value of the independent variable. For example, notice that in Exhibit 13.17, gender is our independent variable. We calculated our percentages so that for each value of gender the percentages sum to 100% at the end of each row. The percentages for both females and males, therefore, sum to 100% at the end of the row. Now we take a given category of the dependent variable and ask what percentage of each independent variable value falls into that category of the dependent variable. Another way to say this is that we calculate our percentages on the independent variable and compare them on the dependent variable. We compare the percentages for different levels of the independent variable on the same category or level of the dependent variable.

In Exhibit 13.17, for example, notice that 40.4% of the female youths were low in delinquency, but only 29.6% of the males were low. This tells us that females are more likely to be low in delinquency than males. Now let us look at the *high* category. We can see that 32.8% of the females were high in delinquency and 42.4% of the males were high. Together, this tells us that females are more likely to be low in delinquency and males are more likely to be high in delinquency. There is, then, a relationship between gender and delinquency. Also notice that the independent variable was the row variable and the dependent variable was the column variable. It does not always have to be this way; the independent variable could just as easily have been the column variable. The important general rule to remember is to always calculate your percentages on the levels of the independent variable (e.g., use marginal totals for the independent variable as denominators) and compare percentages on a level of the dependent variable.

In Exhibit 13.18, we report the same data as in Exhibit 13.17, this time switching the rows and the columns. Now, the independent variable (gender) is the column variable, so we calculate our percentage going down each of the two columns. We then compare percentages across rows. For example, we still see that 40.4% of the females were low in delinquency, whereas only 29.6% of the males were. And 42.4% of the males were high in delinquency, but only 32.8% of the females were high in delinquency.

Describing Association

A cross-tabulation table reveals four aspects of the association between two variables:

- *Existence*. Do the percentage distributions vary at all between categories of the independent variable?
- *Strength*. How much do the percentage distributions vary between categories of the independent variable?

- *Direction*. For quantitative variables, do values on the dependent variable tend to increase or decrease with an increase in value of the independent variable?

- *Pattern*. For quantitative variables, are changes in the percentage distribution of the dependent variable fairly regular (simply increasing or decreasing), or do they vary (perhaps increasing, then decreasing, or perhaps gradually increasing, then rapidly increasing)?

In Exhibit 13.17, an association exists, although we can only say that it is a modest association. The percentage difference at the low and high ends of the delinquency variables is approximately 10 percentage points.

We provide another example of a cross-tabulation in Exhibit 13.19. This is a 3 × 3 table that shows the relationship between how morally wrong a youth thinks delinquency is (the independent variable) and his or her self-reported involvement in delinquency (the dependent variable). This table reveals a very strong relationship between moral beliefs and delinquency. We can see that 5.6% of youths with weak moral beliefs are low on delinquency; this increases to 33.8% for those with medium beliefs and to 62.8% for those with strong moral beliefs. At the high end, over two

Exhibit 13.18 Cross-Tabulation of Respondents' Delinquency by Gender

		GENDER		
		Female	Male	Total
SELF-REPORTED DELINQUENCY	**Low**	275 40.4%	175 29.6%	450
	Medium	182 26.8%	166 28.0%	348
	High	223 32.8%	251 42.4%	474
	Total	680 100%	592 100%	1,272

Exhibit 13.19 Cross-Tabulation of Respondents' Morals by Delinquency

		SELF-REPORTED DELINQUENCY			
		Low	Medium	High	Total
MORALS	**Weak**	20 5.6%	79 22.3%	256 72.1%	355 100%
	Medium	170 33.8%	185 36.8%	148 29.4%	503 100%
	Strong	260 62.8%	84 20.3%	70 16.9%	414 100%
	Total	450	348	474	1,272

thirds (72.1%) of those youths with weak moral beliefs are high in delinquency, 29.4% of those with medium moral beliefs are high in delinquency, and only 16.9% of those youths with strong moral beliefs are high in delinquency. Clearly, then, having strong moral beliefs serves to effectively inhibit involvement in delinquent behavior. This is exactly what control theory would have us believe.

Exhibit 13.19 is an example of a negative relationship between an independent and a dependent variable. As the independent variable increases (i.e., as one goes from weak to strong moral beliefs), the likelihood of delinquency decreases (one becomes less likely to commit delinquency). The independent and dependent variables move in opposite directions, so this is a negative relationship. The pattern in this table is close to what is called monotonic. In a **monotonic relationship**, the value of cases consistently increases (or decreases) on one variable as the value of

> **Monotonic relationship** A pattern of association in which the value of cases on one variable increases or decreases fairly regularly across the categories of another variable.

cases increases (or decreases) on the other variable. Monotonic is often defined a bit less strictly, with the idea that as the value of cases on one variable increases (or decreases), the value of cases on the other variable tends to increase (or decrease), and at least does not change direction. This describes the relationship between moral beliefs and delinquency. Delinquency is most likely when moral beliefs are low, less likely when moral beliefs are medium, and least likely when moral beliefs are strong.

We present another cross-tabulation table for you in Exhibit 13.20. This table shows the relationship between the variable "number of hours studied" and the variable "certainty of punishment" (see Exhibit 13.2). Both variables were originally continuous variables that we recoded into three approximately equal groups for this example. We hypothesize that those youths who study more will have a greater perceived risk of punishment than those who study less, so hours studied is our independent variable and certainty is the dependent variable. Comparing levels of hours studied for those with high certainty, we see that there is not much variation. Of those who did not study very much (0–3 hours), 39.2% were high in perceived certainty. Of those who studied from 4 to 6 hours, 35.6% were high in perceived certainty, and 40.3% of those who studied more than 7 hours per week were high in perceived certainty. Much the same levels prevail at low levels of perceived certainty. Those who do not study very much are no more or less likely to perceive a low certainty of punishment than those who study a lot. Variation in the independent variable, then, is not related to variation in the dependent variable. It looks like there is no association between the number of hours a youth studies and the extent to which he or she thinks punishment for delinquent acts is certain.

You will find when you read research reports and journal articles that social scientists usually make decisions about the existence and strength of association on the basis of more statistics than just percentage differences in a cross-tabulation table. A **measure of association** is a type of descriptive statistic used to summarize the strength of

| Exhibit 13.20 | Cross-Tabulation of Respondents' Morals by Delinquency |

		CERTAINTY OF PUNISHMENT			
		Low	*Medium*	*High*	*Total*
NUMBER OF HOURS STUDIED	0–3 Hours	126 27.9%	148 32.8%	177 39.2%	451 100%
	4–6 Hours	117 32.8%	113 31.7%	127 35.6%	357 100%
	7+ Hours	129 27.8%	148 31.9%	187 40.39%	464 100%
	Total	372	409	491	1,272

an association. There are many measures of association, some of which are appropriate for variables measured at particular levels. One popular measure of association in cross-tabular analyses with variables measured at the ordinal level is gamma. As with many measures of association, the possible values of gamma vary from –1, meaning the variables are perfectly associated in a negative direction; to 0, meaning there is no association of the type that gamma measures; to +1, meaning there is a perfect positive association of the type that gamma measures.

> **Measure of association** A type of descriptive statistic that summarizes the strength of an association.
>
> **Gamma** A measure of association sometimes used in cross-tabular analyses.

Inferential statistics are used in deciding whether it is likely that an association exists in the larger population from which the sample was drawn. Even when the association between two variables is consistent with the researcher's hypothesis, it is possible that the association was just due to chance or to the vagaries of sampling on a random basis (of course, the problem is even worse if the sample is not random). It is conventional in statistics to avoid concluding that an association exists in the population from which the sample was drawn unless the probability that the association was due to chance is less than 5%. In other words, a statistician normally will not conclude that an association exists between two variables unless he or she can be at least 95% confident that the association was not due to chance. This is the same type of logic that you learned about in Chapter 5, which introduced the concept of 95% confidence limits for the mean. Estimation of the probability that an association is not due to chance will be based on one of several inferential statistics, chi-square being the one used in most cross-tabular analyses. The probability is customarily reported in a summary form such as "$p < .05$," which can be translated as "the probability that the association was due to chance is less than 5 out of 100 [5%]."

When an association passes muster in this way, when the analyst feels reasonably confident (at least 95% confident) that it was not due to chance, it is said that the association is statistically significant. Statistical significance means that an association is not likely to be due to chance, according to some criterion set by the analyst. Convention (and the desire to avoid concluding that an association exists in the population when it does not) dictates that the criterion be a probability less than 5%.

> **Chi-square** An inferential statistic used to test hypotheses about relationships between two or more variables in a cross-tabulation.

> **Statistical significance** An association that is not likely to be due to chance, judged by a criterion set by the analyst (often that the probability is less than 5 out of 100, or $p < .05$).

But statistical significance is not everything. You may remember from Chapter 5 that sampling error decreases as sample size increases. For this same reason, an association is less likely to appear on the basis of chance in a larger sample than in a smaller sample. In a table with more than 1,000 cases, such as those involving the delinquency data set, the odds of a chance association are often very low indeed. For example, with our table based on 1,272 cases, the probability that the association between gender and delinquency (see Exhibit 13.18) was due to chance was less than 1 in 1,000 ($p < .001$)! The association in that table was fairly weak, as indicated by a gamma of .20. Even weak associations can be statistically significant with such a large sample, which means that the analyst must be careful not to assume that just because a statistically significant association exists, it is therefore important. In a large sample, an association may be statistically significant but still be too weak to be substantively significant or important. All this boils down to another reason for evaluating carefully both the existence and the strength of an association.

Controlling for a Third Variable

Cross-tabulation can also be used to study the relationship between two variables while controlling for other variables. We will focus our attention on controlling for a third variable in this section, but we will say a bit about controlling for more variables at the section's end. We will examine three different uses for three-variable cross-tabulation: identifying an intervening variable, testing a relationship for spuriousness, and specifying the conditions for a relationship. Each of these uses for three-variable cross-tabs helps determine the validity of our findings, either by evaluating criteria for

> **Elaboration analysis** The process of introducing a third variable into an analysis in order to better understand—to elaborate—the bivariate (two-variable) relationship under consideration; additional control variables also can be introduced.

causality (nonspuriousness and identification of a causal mechanism) or by increasing our understanding of the conditions required for a relationship to hold, an indication of the cross-population generalizability of the findings. All three uses are aspects of elaboration analysis—the process of introducing control variables into a bivariate relationship in order to better understand—to elaborate the relationship (Rosenberg 1968). We will examine the gamma and chi-square statistics for each table in this analysis.

Intervening Variables

We have already discovered that females are less likely to be delinquent than males (see Exhibit 13.17). Finding this relationship between gender and delinquency is just the beginning of our work, however. What we would now like to know and investigate is why this relationship exists. What is it about females that makes them less likely to commit delinquent acts than males? Let us first rule out strictly biological factors and explore some possible social reasons for this gender difference in delinquency. One possibility is that because they are more closely supervised than males, females have fewer opportunities to be delinquent. In other words, females are under more strict parental supervision, and it is because they are under more strict supervision that they are less likely than males to commit delinquency. This possible relationship is shown in Exhibit 13.21. Notice that in this relationship the variable "parental supervision" intervenes between gender and delinquency. It explains why females are at lower risk for delinquency compared to males. To determine whether parental supervision intervenes in the relationship between gender and delinquency and whether it explains this relationship, we must examine the relationship between gender and delinquency while controlling for difference in parental supervision. If parental supervision intervenes in the gender-delinquency relationship, the effect of controlling for this third variable would be to eliminate, or at least substantially reduce, the original relationship between gender and delinquency.

To examine this possibility, we first recode the parental supervision variable (PARSUPER; see Exhibit 13.2) into two approximately equal levels: weak supervision and strong supervision. We then look at two subtables of the gender-delinquency relationship: once under the condition of weak parental supervision and once under the condition of strong parental supervision (see Exhibit 13.22). For ease of presentation, we will report only the cell percentages and not the frequencies. What we see is that once parental supervision is controlled, there is no real relationship between gender and delinquency. That is, if males and females have the same amount of supervision from their parents, they do not differ that much in their risk of being delinquent. For example, among females

> **Subtables** Tables describing the relationship between two variables within the discrete categories of one or more other control variables.

with weak parental supervision, 46.0% are high in delinquency, and among males with weak parental supervision 49.6% are delinquent. There is less than four percentage points' difference between males and females in their risk of being high delinquents under these conditions. Among those with strong parental supervision, 19.8% of the females were high in delinquency and 23.6% of the males were high, less than four percentage points' difference.

This percentage analysis is borne out by the chi-square tests and measures of association. Under both the weak and strong levels of parental supervision, the relationship between gender and delinquency is not significant, and gamma is only .067 when supervision is weak and .136 when supervision is strong. In neither case is the obtained

---

Exhibit 13.21 | **Example of an Intervening Variable**

| Gender | ⟶ | Parental supervision | ⟶ | Delinquency |

Exhibit 13.22	Cross-Tabulation of Respondents' Gender by Delinquency Within Levels of Parental Supervision

Weak Parental Supervision

		SELF-REPORTED DELINQUENCY			
GENDER		Low	Medium	High	Total
	Female	26.1%	27.9%	46.0%	337
	Male	23.2%	27.2%	49.6%	427
	Total				764

$\chi 2 = 1.220$ ($p > .05$), Gamma = .067

Strong Parental Supervision

		SELF-REPORTED DELINQUENCY			
GENDER		Low	Medium	High	Total
	Female	54.4%	25.7%	19.8%	343
	Male	46.1%	30.3%	23.6%	165
	Total				508

$\chi 2 = 3.193$ ($p > .05$), Gamma = .136

gamma very different from zero (indicating no relationship). Collectively, these results would lead us to the conclusion that parental supervision intervenes in the relationship between gender and delinquency. A very important reason females are less delinquent than males, therefore, is that females are under stricter supervision from their parents than are males, and strong parental supervision leads to a reduced risk of delinquency.

Extraneous Variables

Another reason for introducing a third variable into a bivariate relationship is to see whether the original relationship is spurious due to the influence of an **extraneous variable**, which is a variable that causes both the independent and dependent variables. The only reason why the independent and dependent variables are related, therefore, is that they both are the effects of a common cause (another independent variable).

> **Extraneous variable** A variable that influences both the independent and dependent variables so as to create a spurious association between them that disappears when the extraneous variable is controlled.

Exhibit 13.23 shows what a spurious relationship would look like. In this case, the relationship between x and y exists only because both are the effects of the common cause z. Controlling for z, therefore, will eliminate the x-y relationship. Ruling out possible extraneous variables will help considerably strengthen the conclusion that the relationship between the independent and dependent variables is causal, particularly if all the variables that seem to have the potential for creating a spurious relationship can be controlled.

Notice that if a variable is acting as an extraneous variable, then controlling for it will cause the original relationship between the independent and dependent variables to disappear or substantially diminish. This was also

Exhibit 13.23   Example of a Spurious Relationship

Original relationship between *x* and *y* disappears

the empirical test for an intervening variable. Therefore, the difference between intervening and extraneous variables is a logical one and not an empirical one. In both instances, controlling for the third variable will cause the original relationship to diminish or disappear. There should, therefore, be sound theoretical grounds for suspecting that a variable is acting as an intervening variable, explaining the relationship between the independent and dependent variables.

As an example of a possible extraneous relationship, we will look at the association between a youth's perception of the certainty of punishment and self-reported involvement in delinquency. Deterrence theory should lead us to predict a negative relationship between perceived certainty and delinquency. Indeed, this is exactly what we observe in our delinquency data. We will not show you the cross-tabulation table, but when we looked at the relationship between perceived certainty and delinquency we found that 53.2% of youth who were low in certainty were high in delinquency; 39.1% of those who perceived medium certainty were high in delinquency; and only 23.6% of those who perceived a high certainty of punishment were high in delinquency. Youth who believed they would get caught if they engaged in delinquency, then, were less likely to be delinquent. The gamma value for this table was –.382, indicating a moderate negative relationship between perceived certainty and delinquency, exactly what deterrence theory would lead us to expect.

Someone may reasonably argue, however, that this discovered negative relationship may not be causal but instead may be spurious. It could be suggested that what is actually behind this relationship is the extraneous variable, moral beliefs. The argument is that those with strong moral inhibitions against committing delinquent acts think that punishment for morally wrongful actions is certain *and* refrain from delinquent acts. Thus, the observed negative relationship between perceived certainty and delinquency is really due to the positive effect of moral beliefs on perceived certainty and the negative effect of moral beliefs on delinquency (see Exhibit 13.24). If moral beliefs are actually the causal factor at work, then controlling for them will eliminate or substantially reduce the original relationship between perceived certainty and delinquency.

To look at this possibility, we examined the relationship between perceived certainty and delinquency under three levels of moral beliefs (weak, medium, and strong). The cross-tabulations are shown in Exhibit 13.25. What we can see

Exhibit 13.24   A Spurious Relationship Between *x* and *y*

Moral beliefs → Perceived certainty

Moral beliefs → Delinquency

is that in each of the subtables there is a negative and significant association between the perceived certainty of punishment and delinquency. In two of the three subtables, however, the relationship is weaker than what was in the original table (there the gamma was –.382); we obtained gammas of –.271 and –.197. Under the condition of strong moral beliefs, however, the original relationship is unchanged. What we would conclude from this elaboration analysis is that the variable "moral beliefs" is not acting as a very strong extraneous variable. Although some of the relationship between perceived risk and delinquency is due to their joint relationship with moral beliefs, we cannot dismiss the possibility that the perceived certainty of punishment has a causal influence on delinquent behavior.

Specification

Specification A type of relationship involving three or more variables in which the association between the independent and dependent variables varies across the categories of one or more other control variables.

By adding a third variable to an evaluation of a bivariate relationship, the data analyst can also specify the conditions under which the bivariate relationship occurs. A **specification** occurs when the association between the independent and dependent variables varies across the categories of one or more other control variables—that is, when the original relationship is stronger under some condition or conditions of a third variable and weaker under others.

Exhibit 13.25	Cross-Tabulation of Perceived Risk by Delinquency Within Levels of Moral Beliefs

Weak Moral Beliefs

			SELF-REPORTED DELINQUENCY		
		Low	Medium	High	Total
PERCEIVED CERTAINTY	Low	3.8%	14.7%	81.4%	156
	Medium	8.6%	27.3%	64.1%	128
	High	4.2%	29.6%	66.8%	71
	Total				355

$\chi2 = 13.646$ ($p < .001$), Gamma = $-.271$

Medium Moral Beliefs

			SELF-REPORTED DELINQUENCY		
		Low	Medium	High	Total
PERCEIVED CERTAINTY	Low	22.0%	42.5%	35.4%	127
	Medium	33.9%	35.6%	30.5%	174
	High	41.1%	34.2%	24.8%	202
	Total				503

$\chi2 = 13.646$ ($p < .001$), Gamma = $-.197$

Strong Moral Beliefs

			SELF-REPORTED DELINQUENCY		
		Low	Medium	High	Total
PERCEIVED CERTAINTY	Low	42.7%	28.1%	29.2%	89
	Medium	58.9%	17.7%	23.4%	107
	High	72.9%	18.3%	8.7%	218
	Total				414

$\chi2 = 13.646$ ($p < .001$), Gamma = $-.393$

In criminology, social learning theory would predict that youths who are exposed to peers who provide verbal support for delinquency are at greater risk for their own delinquent conduct. We found support for this hypothesis in our delinquency data set. We examined this relationship by recoding into two approximately equal groups the variable FROPINON (see Exhibit 13.2). The first group had weak verbal support from peers, whereas the second group had strong verbal support. Among those youths who reported that their peers provided only weak verbal support for delinquency, 15% were highly delinquent. Among those with strong verbal support from peers, nearly 58% were highly delinquent. The gamma value for this relationship was .711, a very strong positive relationship. Clearly, then, having friends give you verbal support for delinquent acts (e.g., "It's OK to steal") puts you at risk for delinquency.

It is entirely possible, however, that this relationship exists only when friends' verbal support is backed up by their own behavior. That is, verbal support from our peers might not affect our delinquency when they do not themselves commit delinquent acts or when they commit only a very few. In this case, their actions (inaction in this case) speak louder than their words, and their verbal support does not influence us. When they also commit delinquent acts, however, the verbal support of peers carries great weight.

We looked at this possibility to examine the relationship between friends' verbal support for delinquency and a youth's own delinquency within two levels of friends' behavior (FRBEHAVE; see Exhibit 13.2). We recoded FRBEHAVE into two approximately equal groups. In the first group, fewer of one's friends are delinquent (few delinquent friends) than the other (many delinquent friends). This attempt to specify the relationship between friends' opinions and our own delinquency is shown in Exhibit 13.26. What we see is a little complex. When only a few of a youth's friends are also committing delinquent acts, their verbal support still has a significant and positive effect on self-reported delinquency. The gamma value in this subtable is .416, which is moderately strong but less than the original gamma of .771. When many of a youth's friends are delinquent, however, the positive relationship between peers' verbal support and self-reported delinquency is much stronger, with a gamma of .608. The behavior of our peers, then, only weakly specifies the relationship between peer opinion and delinquency. Clearly, then, what our peers say about delinquency matters even if they are not committing delinquent acts all the time themselves.

Our goal in introducing you to cross-tabulation has been to help you think about the association among variables and to give you a relatively easy tool for describing association. To read most statistical knowledge, in addition to the statistical techniques we have considered here and the inferential statistics we discussed previously, you should learn about the summary descriptive statistics used to indicate the strength and direction of association. Until you do so, you will

---

Exhibit 13.26 Cross-Tabulation of Friends' Verbal Support by Delinquency Within Levels of Friends' Delinquent Behavior

Few Delinquent Friends

		SELF-REPORTED DELINQUENCY			
		Low	Medium	High	Total
FRIENDS' VERBAL SUPPORT	Weak	67.3%	23.8%	8.9%	437
	Strong	44.3%	34.3%	21.4%	140
	Total				577

$\chi 2 = 27.374$ ($p > .001$), Gamma = .416

Many Delinquent Friends

		SELF-REPORTED DELINQUENCY			
		Low	Medium	High	Total
FRIENDS' VERBAL SUPPORT	Weak	30.5%	38.5%	31.0%	174
	Strong	7.5%	24.8%	67.4%	521
	Total				695

$\chi 2 = 87.508$ ($p > .001$), Gamma = .608

find it difficult to state with precision just how strong an association is. You also should learn about a different statistical approach to characterizing the association between two quantitative variables, called regression or correlation analysis. Statistics based on regression and correlation analyses are used very often in social science and have many advantages over cross-tabulation, as well as some disadvantages. You will need to take a course in social statistics, however, to become proficient in the use of statistics based on regression and correlation.

▣ Analyzing Data Ethically: How Not to Lie About Relationships

When the data analyst begins to examine relationships among variables in some real data, social science research becomes most exciting. The moment of truth, it would seem, has arrived. Either the hypotheses are supported or not. But, in fact, this is also a time to proceed with caution and to evaluate the analyses of others with even more caution. Once large data sets are entered into a computer, it becomes very easy to check out a great many relationships; when relationships are examined among three or more variables at a time, the possibilities become almost endless.

This range of possibilities presents a great hazard for data analysis. It becomes very temping to search around in the data until something interesting emerges. Rejected hypotheses are forgotten in favor of highlighting what's going on in the data. It is not wrong to examine data for unanticipated relationships; the problem is that inevitably some relationships between variables will appear just on the basis of chance association alone. If you search hard and long enough, it will be possible to come up with something that really means nothing.

A reasonable balance must be struck between deductive data analysis to test hypotheses and inductive analysis to explore patterns in a data set. Hypotheses formulated in advance of data collection must be tested as they were originally stated; any further analyses of these hypotheses that involve a more exploratory strategy must be labeled as such in research reports. Serendipitous findings do not need to be ignored, but they must be reported. Subsequent researchers can try to deductively test the ideas generated by our explorations.

We also have to be honest about the limitations of using survey data to test causal hypotheses. The usual practice for those who seek to test a causal hypothesis with nonexperimental survey data is to test for the relationship between the independent and dependent variables, controlling for other variables that might possibly create spurious relationships. This is what we did by examining the relationship between the perceived certainty of punishment and delinquency while controlling for moral beliefs (see Exhibit 13.25). But finding that a hypothesized relationship is not altered by controlling for just one variable does not establish that the relationship is causal; nor does controlling for two, three, or many more variables. There always is a possibility that some other variable that we did not think to control, or that was not even measured in the survey, has produced a spurious relationship between the independent and dependent variables in our hypothesis (Lieberson 1985). We must always think about the possibilities and be cautious in our causal conclusions.

▣ Conclusion

This chapter has demonstrated how a researcher can describe phenomena in criminal justice and criminology, identify relationships among them, explore the reasons for these relationships, and test hypotheses about them. Statistics provide a remarkably useful tool for developing our understanding of the social world, a tool that we can use to test our ideas and generate new ones.

Unfortunately, to the uninitiated, the use of statistics can seem to end debate right there; you cannot argue with the numbers. But you now know better than that. The numbers will be worthless if the methods used to generate the data are not valid; and the numbers will be misleading if they are not used appropriately, taking into account the type of data to which they are applied. And even assuming valid methods and proper use of statistics, there is one more critical step, for the numbers do not speak for themselves. Ultimately, it is how we interpret and report the numbers that determines their usefulness. It is this topic we turn to in the next chapter.

Key Terms

Bar chart   374
Base N   378
Bimodal distribution   384
Central tendency   373
Chi-square   399
Cross-tabulation (cross-tab)   369
Data cleaning   372
Descriptive statistics   368
Elaboration analysis   400
Extraneous variable   401
Frequency distributions   368
Frequency polygon   376
Gamma   399

Grouped frequency distribution   379
Histogram   374
Inferential statistics   369
Interquartile range   393
Marginal distributions   395
Mean   387
Measure of association   398
Median   385
Mode   374
Monotonic relationship   398
Negatively skewed   376
Outlier   392
Percentage   374

Positively skewed   376
Quartiles   393
Range   392
Secondary data analysis   371
Skewness   373
Specification   402
Standard deviation   394
Statistical significance   399
Subtables   400
Unimodal distribution   384
Variability   373
Variance   393

Highlights

- Data collection instruments should be precoded for direct entry, after verification, into a computer. Use of secondary data can save considerable time and resources but may limit data analysis possibilities.

- Bar charts, histograms, and frequency polygons are useful for describing the shape of distributions. Care must be taken with graphic displays to avoid distorting a distribution's apparent shape.

- Frequency distributions display variation in a form that can be easily inspected and described. Values should be grouped in frequency distributions in a way that does not alter the shape of the distribution. Following several guidelines can reduce the risk of problems.

- Summary statistics are often used to describe the central tendency and variability of distributions. The appropriateness of the mode, mean, and median varies with a variable's level of measurement, the distribution's shape, and the purpose of the summary.

- The variance and standard deviation summarize variability around the mean. The interquartile range is usually preferable to the range to indicate the interval spanned by cases, due to the effect of outliers on the range. The degree of skewness of a distribution is usually described in words rather than with a summary statistic.

- Cross-tabulations should normally be percentaged within the categories of the independent variable. A cross-tabulation can be used to determine the existence, strength, direction, and pattern of an association.

- Elaboration analysis can be used in cross-tabular analysis to test for spurious and intervening relationships and to identify the conditions under which relationships occur.

- Inferential statistics are used with sample-based data to estimate the confidence that can be placed in a statistical estimate of a population parameter. Estimates of the probability that an association between variables may have occurred on the basis of chance are also based on inferential statistics.

Research in the News

Stories vs. Statistics

An online commentary on the *New York Times* Web site by mathematician John Allen Paulos celebrated the increased communication between literature and the scientific domain. In it, Dr. Paulos contended that, because of works of literature, most of us know that notions of central tendency, like the mean and median, probably led to words like *usual*, *typical*, or *normal*. Moreover, notions of statistical variation—as in the standard deviation, variance, and so on, probably led to words like *extreme*, *unlike*, and *different*. Dr. Paulos, however, believes that when we listen to stories, we do not judge but simply want to be entertained. In contrast, when we evaluate a piece of statistical evidence, we are generally very critical so we are not fooled. Do you think there is a tension between literature and statistics?

Source: Paulos, John Allen. 2010. "Stories vs. Statistics." October 24, Opinionator, *The New York Times,* Retrieved May 30, 2010 (http://opinionator.blogs.nytimes.com/2010/10/24/stories-vs-statistics/).

Exercises

1. Create frequency distributions from lists in the Federal Bureau of Investigation (FBI) Uniform Crime Reports on characteristics of arrestees in at least 100 cases (cites). You will have to decide on a grouping scheme for the distribution scheme of variables such as race, age, and crime committed, and how to deal with outliers in the frequency distribution.

   a. Decide what summary statistics to use for each variable of interest. How well were the features of each distribution represented by the summary statistics? Describe the shape of each distribution.

   b. Propose a hypothesis involving two of these variables, and develop a cross-tabulation to evaluate the support for this hypothesis.

   c. Describe each relationship in terms of the four aspects of an association, after making percentages within each table within the categories of the independent variable. Which hypotheses appear to have been supported?

2. Become a media critic. For the next week, scan a newspaper or some magazines for statistics related to crime or criminal victimization. How many can you find using frequency distributions, graphs, and the summary statistics introduced in this chapter? Are these statistics used appropriately and interpreted correctly? Would any other statistics have been preferable or useful in addition to those presented?

3. The table below shows a frequency distribution of "trust in people" as produced by the Statistical Package for the Social Sciences (SPSS) with the General Social Survey 2006 data. As you can see, the table includes abbreviated labels for the variable and its response choices, as well as the raw frequencies and three percentage columns. The first percentage column (Percent) shows the percentage in each category; the next percentage column (Valid Percent) is based on the total number of respondents who gave valid answers (3,929 in this instance). It is the Valid Percent column that normally should be used to construct a frequency distribution for presentation. The last percentage column is Cumulative Percent, adding up the valid percents from top to bottom.

Redo the table for presentation, using the format of the frequency distributions presented in the text.

		Frequency	Percent
Valid	CAN TRUST	1279	28.4
	CANNOT TRUST	2458	54.5
	DEPENDS	192	4.3
	Total	3929	87.1

(Continued)

(Continued)

		Frequency	Percent
Missing	NAP	575	12.7
	NA	6	.1
	Total	581	12.9
Total		4510	100.0

Developing a Research Proposal

Use the General Social Survey data to add a pilot study to your proposal. A pilot study is a preliminary effort to test out the procedures and concepts that you have proposed to research.

1. Review the GSSCRJ2K variable list and identify some variables that have at least some connection to your research problem. If possible, identify one variable that might be treated as independent in your proposed research and one that might be treated as dependent.

2. Request frequencies for these variables.

3. Request a cross-tabulation of the dependent variable by the independent variable (if you were able to identify any). If necessary, recode the independent variable to three or fewer categories.

4. Write a brief description of your findings and comment on their implications for your proposed research. Did you learn any lessons from this exercise for your proposal?

STUDENT STUDY SITE

Log on to the Web-based student study site at **www.sagepub.com/bachmanprccj5e** for additional study tools including eFlashcards, Web quizzes, links to SAGE journal articles, podcasts, videos, data sets and codebooks, Web exercises, Web resources, and additional appendices.

Web Exercises

1. Search the Web for a crime-related example of statistics. The Bureau of Justice Statistics is a good place to start: www.ojp.usdoj.gov/bjs/. Using the key terms from this chapter, describe the set of statistics you have identified. What phenomena does this set of statistics describe? What relationships, if any, do the statistics identify?

2. Do a Web search for information on a criminological subject that interests you. How much of the information that you find relies on statistics as a tool for understanding the subject? How do statistics allow researchers to test their ideas about the subject and generate new ideas? Write your findings in a brief report, referring to the Web sites that you found.

Ethics Exercises

1. Review the frequency distributions and graphs in this chapter. Change one of these data displays so that you are "lying with statistics." (You might consider using the graphic technique discussed by Orcutt and Turner 1993.)

2. Consider the relationship between gender and delinquency that is presented in Exhibit 13.19.

    What third variable do you think should be controlled in the analysis to better understand the basis for this relationship? How might criminal justice policies be affected by finding out that this relationship was due to differences in teacher expectations rather than to genetic differences in violence propensity?

SPSS or Excel Exercises

1. Develop a description of homicide defendants and their sentence lengths from HOMICIDE.POR. Examine each characteristic with three statistical techniques: a graph, a frequency distribution, and a measure of central tendency.

2. Describe the distribution of each variable, noting any skewness and/or outliers.

3. Collapse the categories for defendant's age (DAGE) and sentence length (PRITIME). Examine the data distributions using a graph and frequency distribution. Does the general shape of the distributions change as a result of changing how the data are measured?

4. Look at the relationship between these two variables. Indicate which variable is the dependent variable and which variable is the independent variable.

5. Run a cross-tabulation on these data (use your newly created categorical variables). Be sure to obtain percentiles for categories of the independent variable (either row or column).

6. Propose two variables that might create a spurious relationship between defendant's age and sentence length. Explain your thinking. Propose a variable that might result in a conditional effect of age on sentence length so that the relationship between age and sentence length would vary across the categories of the other variable. Test these propositions with three variable cross-tabulations. Were any supported? How would you explain your findings?

CHAPTER 14

Reporting
Research Results

The goal of research is not just to discover something but to communicate that discovery to a larger audience—other social scientists, government officials, your teachers, the general public—perhaps several of these audiences. Whatever the study's particular outcome, if the research report enables the intended audience to comprehend the results and learn from them, the research can be judged a success. If the intended audience is not able to learn about the study's results, the research should be judged a failure no matter how expensive the research, how sophisticated its design, or how much of yourself you invested in it.

This conclusion may seem obvious, and perhaps a bit unnecessary. After all, you may think that all researchers write up their results for other people to read. But the fact is that many research projects fail to produce a research report. Sometimes the problem is that the research is poorly designed to begin with and cannot be carried out in a satisfactory manner; sometimes unanticipated difficulties derail a viable project. But too often the researcher just never gets around to writing a report. And then there are many research reports that are very incomplete or poorly written or that speak to only one of several interested audiences. The failure may not be complete, but the project's full potential is not achieved.

The stage of reporting research results is also the point at which the need for new research is identified. It is the time when, so to speak, "the rubber hits the road"—when we have to make our research make sense to others. To whom will our research be addressed? How should we present our results to them? Should we seek to influence how our research report is used?

The primary goals of this chapter are to guide you in comparing writing worthwhile reports of your own and communicating with the public about research. This chapter also gives particular attention to the writing process itself and points out how that process can differ when writing up qualitative versus quantitative research. We will conclude by considering some of the ethical issues unique to the reporting process, with special attention to the problem of plagiarism.

Research Report Goals

The research report will present research findings and interpretations in a way that reflects some combination of the researcher's goals, the research sponsor's goals, the concerns of the research subjects, and perhaps the concerns of a wider anticipated readership. Understanding the goals of these different groups will help the researcher begin to shape the final report even at the start of the research. In designing a proposal and in negotiating access to a setting for the research, commitments often must be made to produce a particular type of report, or at least cover certain issues in the final report. As the research progresses, feedback about the research from its participants, sponsoring agencies, collaborators, or other interested parties may suggest the importance of focusing on particular issues in the final report. Social researchers traditionally have tried to distance themselves from the concerns of such interested parties, paying attention only to what is needed to advance scientific knowledge. But in recent years, some social scientists have recommended bringing these interested parties into the research and reporting process itself.

Advance Scientific Knowledge

Most social science research reports are directed to other social scientists working in the area of study, so they reflect orientations and concerns that are shared within this community of interest. The traditional scientific approach encourages a research goal to advance scientific knowledge by providing reports to other scientists. This approach also treats value considerations as beyond the scope of science: "An empirical science cannot tell anyone what he should do but rather what he can do and under certain circumstances what he wishes to do" (Weber 1949:54).

The idea is that developing valid knowledge about how society is organized or how we live our lives does not tell us how society should be organized or how we should live our lives. There should, as a result, be a strict separation between the determination of empirical facts and the evaluation of these facts as satisfactory or unsatisfactory (Weber 1949). Social scientists must not ignore value considerations, which are viewed as a legitimate basis for selecting a research problem to study. After the research is over and a report has been written, many scientists also consider it acceptable to encourage government officials or private organizations to implement the findings. During a research project, however, value considerations are to be held in abeyance.

Shape Social Policy

As we highlighted in our discussion of applied research in Chapter 11, many social scientists seek to influence social policy through their writing. By now, you have been exposed to several such examples in this text, including all the evaluation research (Chapter 11). These particular studies, like much policy-oriented social science research, are similar to those that aim strictly to increase knowledge. In fact, these studies might even be considered contributions to knowledge first and to social policy debate second. What distinguishes the reports of these studies from strictly academic reports is their attention to policy implications.

Other social scientists who seek to influence social policy explicitly reject the traditional scientific, rigid distinction between facts and values (Sjoberg and Nett 1968). Bellah et al. (1985) have instead proposed a model of "social science as public philosophy," in which social scientists focus explicit attention on achieving a more just society:

> Social science makes assumptions about the nature of persons, the nature of society, and the relation between persons and society. It also, whether it admits it or not, makes assumptions about good persons and a good society and considers how far these conceptions are embodied in our actual society.

> Social science as public philosophy, by breaking through the iron curtain between the social sciences and the humanities, becomes a form of social self-understanding or self-interpretation. . . . By probing the past as well as the present, by looking at "values" as much as at "facts," such a social science is able to make connections that are not obvious and to ask difficult questions. (p. 301)

This perspective suggests more explicit concern with public policy implications when reporting research results. But it is important to remember that we all are capable of distorting our research and our interpretations of research results to correspond to our own value preferences. The temptation to see what we want to see is enormous, and research reports cannot be deemed acceptable unless they avoid this temptation.

Organize Social Action—Participatory Action Research

For the same reasons that value questions are traditionally set apart from the research process, many social scientists consider the application of research a nonscientific concern. William Foote Whyte, whose *Street Corner Society* (1943) study you encountered in Chapter 9, has criticized this belief and proposed an alternative research and reporting strategy he calls **participatory action research** (PAR). Whyte (1991:285) argues that social scientists must get "out of the academic rut" and engage in applied research to develop better understanding of social phenomena.

Participatory action research A type of research in which the researcher involves some organizational members as active participants throughout the process of studying an organization; the goal is making changes in the organization.

In PAR, the researcher involves as active participants some members of the setting studied. Both the organizational members and the researcher are assumed to want to develop valid conclusions, to bring unique insights, and to desire change, but Whyte (1991) believed that these objectives were more likely to be obtained if the researcher collaborated actively with the persons he studied. PAR can bring researchers into closer contact with participants in the research setting through groups that discuss and plan research steps and then take steps to implement research findings. Stephen Kemmis and Robin McTaggart (2005:563–68) summarize the key features of PAR research as "a spiral of self-reflecting cycles" involving

- planning a change,
- acting and observing the process and consequences of the change,

- reflecting on these processes and consequences,

- replanning, and

- acting and observing again.

In contrast with the formal reporting of results at the end of a research project, these "cycles" make research reporting an ongoing part of the research process.

🔲 Case Study: Seeking Higher Education for Inmates

While prison populations in the United States have been significantly increasing, access to college programs within prisons has been essentially eliminated. Primarily because of the "tough on crime" policies of the 1990s, by 1995, only 8 of the existing 350 college programs in prisons remained open nationwide (Torre and Fine 2005). To remedy this situation, Torre and Fine became involved in participatory action research to facilitate a college and college-bound program at the Bedford Hills Correctional Facility (BHCF), a maximum-security women's prison in New York. To conduct a study of the effects of the program, Michelle Fine was the principal investigator along with four prisoner-researchers and four researchers from the Graduate Center of the City University of New York. This "participatory research team" asked several questions: (a) Who are the women in the college program? (b) What is the impact of the college experience on inmate students and their children? (c) What is the impact of the college experience on the prison environment? (d) What is the impact of the college experience beyond college on recidivism? (e) What is the cost of such a program to taxpayers? The researchers used a triangulated methodology employing quantitative analysis of recidivism rates and costs of the program along with in-depth interviews with the participants; focus groups with inmates, faculty, children, and college presidents; and surveys of faculty who taught in the program. Although not using a randomized experimental design, Torre and Fine along with their co-investigators tracked participants in the college program after release and found that women who had not participated in the program were four times more likely to be returned to custody than women who participated.

The narratives from the interviews with college inmates also illuminated the positive benefits of the education. One inmate college student said, "Because when you take somebody that feels that they're not gonna amount to anything, and you put them in an environment, like, when you're in college it takes you away from the prison, . . . it's like you're opening your mind to a whole different experience" (Torre and Fine 2005:582). The positive impact of college on the inmates was also transferred to their children. The cost-benefit analysis of the program indicated that the savings based on decreased recidivism rates for those who attended the college far outweighed the initial cost of the program itself. In sum, with just a small grant from a private foundation, the participatory action research team brought together universities, prisoners, churches, community organizations, and prison administrators to resurrect a college at BHCF. The authors concluded, "Key elements of this program include broad-based community involvement, strong prisoner participation in design and governance, and the support of the prison administration" (p. 591). A full report of this research can be found at web.gc.cuny.edu/che/changingminds.html. As you can see, participatory action research has the potential to be life changing for all involved!

Dialogue With Research Subjects

Guba and Lincoln (1989) have carried the notion of involving research subjects and others in the design and reporting of research one step further. What they call the **constructivist paradigm** is a methodology that

> **Constructivist paradigm** Methodology based on rejection of belief in an external reality; it emphasizes the importance of exploring the way in which different stakeholders in a social setting construct their beliefs.

emphasizes the importance of exploring how different stakeholders in a social setting construct their beliefs. As we noted in Chapter 3, this approach rejects the assumption that there is a reality around us to be studied and reported on. Instead, social scientists operating in the constructivist paradigm try to develop a consensus among participants in some social process about how to understand the focus of inquiry, a program that is often evaluated. A research report will then highlight different views of the social program and explain how a consensus can be reached.

The constructivist approach provides a useful way of thinking about how to best make sense of the complexity and subjectivity of the social world. Other researchers write reports intended to influence public policy, and often their findings are ignored. Such neglect would be less common if social researchers gave more attention to the different meanings attached by participants to the same events, in the spirit of constructivist case reports. The philosophy of this approach is also similar to the utilization-based evaluation research approach advanced by Patton (1997; see Chapter 11) that involves all stakeholders in the research process.

▣ On Writing Research

The goal of research is not just to discover something but also to communicate that discovery to a larger audience: other social scientists, government officials, your teachers, the general public—perhaps several of these audiences. Whatever the study's particular outcome, if the intended audience for the research comprehends the results and learns from them, the research can be judged a success. If the intended audience does not learn about the study's results, the research should be judged a failure—no matter how expensive the research, how sophisticated its design, or how much you (or others) invested in it.

Successful research reporting requires both good writing and a proper publication outlet. We will first review guidelines for successful writing before we look at particular types of research publications.

Consider the following principles formulated by experienced writers (Booth, Colomb, and Williams 1995):

- Respect the complexity of the task and don't expect to write a polished draft in a linear fashion. Your thinking will develop as you write, causing you to reorganize and rewrite.

- Leave enough time for dead ends, restarts, revisions, and so on, and accept the fact that you will discard much of what you write.

- Write as fast as you comfortably can. Don't worry about spelling, grammar, and so on until you are polishing things up.

- Ask anyone whom you trust for reactions to what you have written.

- Write as you go along, so you have notes and report segments drafted even before you focus on writing the report.

It is important to outline a report before writing it, but neither the report's organization nor the first written draft should be considered fixed. As you write, you will get new ideas about how to organize the report. Try them out. As you review the first draft, you will see many ways to improve your writing. Focus particularly on how to shorten and clarify your statements. Make sure that each paragraph concerns only one topic. Remember the golden rule of good writing: Writing is revising!

You can ease the burden of report writing in several ways:

- Draw on the research proposal and on project notes.

- Use a word processing program on a computer to facilitate reorganizing and editing.

- Seek criticism from friends, teachers, and other research consumers before turning in the final product.

We often find it helpful to use what is called **reverse outlining**: After you have written a first complete draft, outline it on a paragraph-by-paragraph basis, ignoring the actual section headings you used. See if the paper you wrote actually fits the outline you planned. How could the organization be improved? Most important, leave yourself enough time so that you can revise, several times if possible, before turning in the final draft. Revision is essential until complete clarity is achieved.

> ***Reverse outlining*** Outlining the sections in an already written draft of a paper or report to improve its organization in the next draft.

For more suggestions about writing, see Becker (1986), Booth et al. (1995), Cuba (2002), Strunk and White (2000), and Turabian (1996). And we don't need to point out that students (and professional researchers) often leave final papers (and reports) until the last possible minute (often for understandable reasons, including other coursework and job or family responsibilities). But be forewarned: *The last-minute approach does not work for research reports.*

🔲 Research Report Types

Research projects designed to produce student papers and theses, applied research reports, and academic articles all have unique features that will influence the final research report. For example, student papers are written for a particular professor or for a thesis committee and often are undertaken with almost no financial resources and in the face of severe time constraints. Applied research reports are written for an organization or agency that usually also has funded the research and has expectations for a particular type of report. Journal articles are written for the larger academic community and will not be published until they are judged acceptable by some representatives of that community (e.g., after the article has gone through extensive peer review).

These unique features do not really match up so neatly with the specific types of research products. For example, a student paper that is based on a research project conducted in collaboration with a work organization may face some constraints for a project designed to produce an applied research report. An academic article may stem from an applied research project conducted for a government agency. An applied research report often can be followed by an academic article on the same topic. In fact, one research study may lead to all three types of research reports, as students write course papers or theses for professors who write both academic articles and applied research reports.

Student Papers and Theses

What is most distinctive about a student research paper or thesis is the audience for the final product: a professor or, for a thesis, a committee of professors. In light of this, it is important for you to seek feedback early and often about the progress of your research and about your professor's expectations for the final paper. Securing approval of a research proposal is usually the first step, but it should not be the last occasion for seeking advice prior to writing the final paper. Do not become too anxious for guidance, however. Professors require research projects in part so that their students can work through, at least somewhat independently, the many issues they confront. A great deal of insight into the research process can be gained this way. So balance your requests for advice with some independent decision making.

Most student research projects can draw on few resources beyond the student's own time and effort, so it is important that the research plan not be overly ambitious. Keep the paper deadline in mind when planning the project, and remember that almost every researcher tends to underestimate the time required to carry out a project.

Group Projects

Pooling your resources with those of several students in a group project can make it possible to collect much more data but can lead to other problems. Each student's role should be clarified at the outset and written into the research proposal as a formal commitment. Group members should try to help each other out, rather than competing to do the least work possible or to receive the most recognition. Complaints about other group members should be made to the professor when things just cannot be worked out among group members. Each group member should have a clear area of responsibility in the final report, and one may want to serve as the final editor.

The Thesis Committee

Students who are preparing a paper for a committee, usually during the senior year of a BA or at the MA or PhD level, must be prepared to integrate the multiple perspectives and comments of committee members into a plan for a coherent final report. (The thesis committee chair should be the primary guide in this process; careful selection of faculty to serve on the committee is also important.) As much as possible, committee members should have complementary areas of expertise that are each important for the research project: perhaps one methodologist, one specialist in the primary substantive area of the thesis, and one specialist in a secondary area. Theses using data collected by service agencies or other organizations often benefit if an organizational representative is on the committee.

It is very important that you work with your committee members in an ongoing manner, both individually and collectively. In fact, it is vitally important to have a group meeting with all committee members at the beginning of the project to ensure everyone on the committee supports the research plan. Doing this will avoid obstacles that arise due to miscommunication later in the research process.

Journal Articles

It is the peer review process that makes preparation of an academic journal article most unique. Similar to a grant review, the journal's editor sends submitted articles to two or three experts, peers, who are asked whether the paper should be accepted more or less as is, revised and then resubmitted, or rejected. Reviewers also provide comments, sometimes quite lengthy, to explain their decision and to guide any required revisions. The process is an anonymous one at most journals; reviewers are not told the author's name, and the author is not told the reviewers' names. Although the journal editor has the final say, editors' decisions are normally based on the reviewers' comments.

> **Peer review** A process in which a journal editor sends a submitted article to two or three experts who judge whether the paper should be accepted, revised and resubmitted, or rejected; the experts also provide comments to explain their decision and guide any revisions.

This peer review process must be anticipated in designing the final report. Peer reviewers are not pulled out of a hat. They are expert in the field or fields represented in the paper and usually have published articles themselves in that field. It is critical that the author be familiar with the research literature and be able to present the research findings as a unique contribution to that literature. In most cases, this hurdle is much harder to jump with journal articles than with student papers or applied research reports. In fact, most leading journals have a rejection rate of over 90%, so that hurdle is quite high indeed. Of course, there is also a certain luck of the draw in peer review. One set of two or three reviewers may be inclined to reject an article that another set of reviewers would accept (see the next case study). But in general, the anonymous peer review process results in higher-quality research reports because articles are revised prior to publication in response to the suggestions and criticisms of the experts.

Criminological and criminal justice research is published in a myriad of journals within several disciplines, including criminology, law, sociology, psychology, and economics. As a result, there is no one formatting style that all criminological literature abides by. If, for example, you are submitting your paper to a psychology-related journal, you must abide by the formatting style dictated by the *Publication Manual of the American Psychological Association* (2009). The easiest way to determine how to format a paper for a particular journal is to examine recent volumes of the journal and format your paper accordingly. To give you a general idea of what a journal article looks like, an article in its entirety has been reprinted in Appendix C, along with an illustration of how to read a journal article. There are also numerous articles available on the Student Study Site for this text.

Despite the slight variations in style across journals, there are typically seven standard sections within a journal article in addition to the title page (see Exhibit 14.1).

Exhibit 14.1 | **General Sections of a Journal Article**

1. *Abstract*. This should be a concise and nonevaluative summary of your research paper (no more than 120 words) that describes the research problem, the sample, the method, and the findings.

2. *Introduction*. The body of a paper should open with an introduction that presents the specific problem under study and describes the research strategy. Before writing this section, you should consider the following questions: What is the point of the study? How do the hypotheses and the research design relate to the problem? What are the theoretical implications of the study, and how does the study relate to previous work in the area? What are the theoretical propositions tested, and how were they derived? A good introduction answers these questions in a few paragraphs by summarizing the relevant argument and the data, giving the reader a sense of what was done and why.

3. *Literature Review*. Discuss the relevant literature in a way that relates each previous study cited to your research, not in an exhaustive historical review. Citation of and specific credit to relevant earlier works is part of the researchers' scientific and scholarly responsibility. It is essential for the growth of cumulative science. This section should demonstrate the logical continuity between previous research and the research at hand. At the end of this section, you are ready to conceptually define your variables and formally state your hypotheses.

4. *Method*. Describe in detail how the study was conducted. Such a description enables the reader to evaluate the appropriateness of your methods and the reliability and validity of your results. It also permits experienced investigators to replicate the study if they so desire. In this section, you can include subsections that describe the sample, the independent and dependent variables, and the analytical or statistical procedure you will use to analyze the data.

5. *Results*. Summarize the results of the statistical or qualitative analyses performed on the data. This can include tables and figures that summarize findings. If statistical analyses are performed, tests of significance should also be highlighted.

6. *Discussion*. Take the opportunity to evaluate and interpret your results, particularly with respect to your original hypotheses and previous research. Here, you are free to examine and interpret your results as well as draw inferences from them. In general, this section should answer the following questions: What have I contributed to the literature here? How has my study helped resolve the original problem? What conclusions and theoretical implications can I draw from my study? What are the limitations of my study? What are the implications for future research?

7. *References*. All citations in the manuscript must appear in the reference list, and all references must be cited in the text.

Applied Reports

Unlike journal articles, applied reports are usually commissioned by a particular government agency, corporation, or nonprofit organization. As such, the most important problem that applied researchers confront is the need to produce a final report that meets the funding organization's expectations. This is called the hired gun problem. Of course, the extent to which being a hired gun is a problem varies greatly with the research orientation of the funding organization and with the nature of the research problem posed. The ideal situation is to have few constraints on the nature of the final report, but sometimes research reports are suppressed or distorted because the researcher comes to conclusions that the funding organization does not like.

Applied reports that are written in a less highly charged environment can face another problem—even when they are favorably received by the funding organization, their conclusions are often ignored. This problem can be more a matter of the organization not really knowing how to use research findings than a matter of not wanting to use them. And this is not just a problem of the funding organization; many researchers are prepared only to present their findings, without giving any thought to how research findings can be translated into organizational policies or programs.

An Advisory Committee

An advisory committee can help the applied researcher avoid the problems of incompatible expectations for the final report and insufficient understanding of how to use the research results, without adopting the more engaged strategy of Whyte's (1991) participatory action research or Guba and Lincoln's (1989) constructivist inquiry. An advisory committee should be formed before the start of the project to represent the various organizational segments with stakes in the outcomes of the research. The researcher can use the committee as a source of intelligence about how particular findings may be received and as a sounding board for ideas about how the organization or agency can use research findings. Perhaps most important, an advisory committee can help the researcher work out many problems in research design, implementation, and data collection. Because an advisory committee is meant to comprise all stakeholders, it is inevitable that conflicts will arise between advisory group members. In our experience, however, these conflicts almost invariably can be used to strategize more effectively about the research design and the final product.

Advisory committees are particularly necessary for research investigating controversial issues. For example, after a study conducted in 1999 found that several death row inmates had been wrongly convicted of their crimes, the governor of Illinois placed a moratorium on all death sentences in the state. Other results of the study suggested that the death penalty was handed down unfairly; it found proportionally more minority and poor offenders were sentenced to death than whites and those who could afford hired legal counsel. This caused a great deal of media attention and calls for other states that practice the death penalty to institute similar moratoriums. As a consequence of this attention, other states have begun to examine their implementation of the death penalty as well. Maryland is one such state. In 2001, the state legislature in Maryland commissioned Raymond Paternoster (Paternoster et al. 2004) at the University of Maryland to conduct a study of its practice of the death penalty. The primary goal of the study was to determine whether the administration of the death penalty in the state was affected by the race of the defendant or victim.

As you can imagine, when the study was released, it was controversial. To make sure all interests were represented, Paternoster et al. (2004) set up an advisory committee before undertaking the study. The advisory committee consisted of a group of prosecutors and defense counsel who had experience in capital cases. They advised Professor Paternoster on several critical issues, including the years that the study should cover, the sources where information can be found, and the particularly important variables related to sentencing outcomes. Not only did the advisory committee provide substantive input into the research, but by having a broad spectrum of the legal community "on board," it also provided credibility to the study's findings.

Data Displays

You learned in Chapter 13 about some of the statistics that are useful in analyzing and reporting data, but there are some additional methods of presenting statistical results that can improve research reports. Combined and compressed displays are used most often in applied research reports and government documents, but they can also help communicate findings more effectively in student papers and journal articles.

> **Combined frequency display** A table that presents together the distributions for a set of conceptually similar variables having the same response categories; common headings are used for the responses.

In a **combined frequency display**, the distributions for a set of conceptually similar variables with the same response categories are presented together, with common headings for the responses. For example, you could identify the variables in the leftmost column and the value labels along the top. Exhibit 14.2 is a combined display reporting the frequency distributions in percentage form for five variables that indicate the responses of high school seniors to questions about their delinquent behavior. From this table you can infer several pieces of information besides the basic distribution of self-reported delinquency. You can determine the variation in the cohort's involvement in specific types of delinquent behavior, and you can also determine whether this behavior increased or decreased over time (1982–1994). For example, although the majority of seniors reported having an argument or a fight with their parents, only a small percentage of students (around 20% on average) reported getting into a fight where a group of their friends was against

Exhibit 14.2	Combined Frequency Display of High School Seniors Reporting Involvement in Selected Delinquent Activities in the Past 12 Months, United States (in %)

Delinquent Activity	Class of 1987 (N = 3,179)	Class of 1988 (N = 3,361)	Class of 1989 (N = 3,350)	Class of 1990 (N = 2,879)	Class of 1991 (N = 2,627)	Class of 1992 (N = 2,569)	Class of 1993 (N = 2,690)
Argued or had a fight with either of your parents?							
Not at all	8.8	9.7	9.6	9.3	10.0	9.3	12.1
Once	8.5	8.2	8.7	8.8	8.9	8.7	9.4
Twice	12.1	11.0	10.2	12.8	12.7	11.7	12.4
3 or 4 times	23.1	23.7	23.6	23.2	24.7	24.7	20.2
5 or more times	47.5	47.5	47.9	45.9	43.6	45.5	45.9
Taken part in a fight where a group of your friends was against another group?							
Not at all	80.4	80.5	79.7	81.1	79.6	78.7	77.8
Once	11.3	11.1	12.1	11.4	11.2	11.5	11.2
Twice	4.4	4.4	3.9	4.4	5.0	4.4	5.8
3 or 4 times	2.6	2.4	2.4	1.9	2.5	3.2	2.9
5 or more times	1.4	1.6	1.8	1.2	1.7	2.2	2.3
Gotten into trouble with police because of something you did?							
Not at all	75.9	77.5	76.6	75.8	77.4	77.8	90.4
Once	15.3	12.8	13.7	13.2	12.4	11.9	5.9
Twice	4.5	6.2	5.5	6.0	6.0	5.2	1.8
3 or 4 times	2.8	2.4	2.6	3.4	2.7	3.0	1.2
5 or more times	1.5	1.1	1.6	1.6	1.5	2.2	0.6

Source: Adapted from Sourcebook of Criminal Justice Statistics: 1994 (NCJ-154591). Bureau of Justice Statistics, U.S. Department of Justice, Washington, DC.

another group or getting into trouble with police (around 25% on average). You can also see that the rate of fighting behavior did not change much over the 13-year time period examined; however, the percentage of youth getting into trouble with the police actually decreased.

Compressed frequency displays can also be used to present cross-tabular data and summary statistics more efficiently, by eliminating unnecessary percentages (such as those corresponding to the second

Compressed frequency display A table that presents cross-classification data efficiently by eliminating unnecessary percentages, such as the percentage corresponding to the second value of a dichotomous variable.

value of a dichotomous variable) and by reducing the need for repetitive labels. Exhibit 14.3 presents a compressed display used to highlight the results of a survey on attitudes toward problems facing the country by several demographic characteristics. For several problem areas, respondents were asked to tell interviewers if they believed the country was "about the same today," "making progress in this area," or "losing ground" on this area. The percentages displayed are for those respondents who said that they believed the country was "losing ground" on a particular problem area.

Combined and compressed statistical displays present a large amount of data in a relatively small space. To the experienced reader of statistical reports, such displays can convey much important information. They should be used

| Exhibit 14.3 | Compressed Display of Attitudes Toward Problems Affecting the Country Today by Demographic Characteristics |

Question: "Next, as I read you some problem areas, please tell me how you think each is affecting the country today. First, do you think the problem of . . . is about the same today, is the country making progress in this area, or is the country losing ground?"

Percentage Responding "Losing Ground"

	Crime (in %)	Families Split Up (in %)	Drugs (in %)
Sex			
Male	71	73	60
Female	82	77	71
Race			
White	77	75	64
Nonwhite	77	75	79
Age			
Under 30 years	73	75	64
30 to 49 years	79	73	63
50 to 64 years	78	76	69
65 years and older	77	76	70
Education			
College graduate	71	71	64
Some college	84	79	67
High school graduate	80	77	66
Less than high school graduate	69	72	66

Source: Interview data from a nationwide sample of 1,800 adults by Princeton Survey Research Associates for the Pew Research Center for The People & The Press. Adapted from the Sourcebook of Criminal Justice Statistics: 1995 (NCJ-158900). Bureau of Justice Statistics, U.S. Department of Justice, Washington, DC.

with caution, however, because people who are not used to them may be baffled by the rows of numbers. Graphs can also provide an efficient tool for summarizing relationships among variables. Exhibit 14.4 is from the evaluation report of the Children at Risk (CAR) program performed by Harrell, Cavanagh, and Sridharan (1999). It presents the percentage of youth who used drugs at different times during the course of the evaluation for both treatment (youth who participated in the program) and control (youth who did not) groups. As you can readily see, compared to youth who did not receive the CAR program, fewer youth who participated in the CAR program used drugs at all times that were measured.

Another good example of the use of graphs to show relationships is provided by a Bureau of Justice Statistics report on homicide patterns between 1980 and 2008 (Cooper and Smith, 2011). Exhibit 14.5, taken from that report, shows how rates of intimate partner homicides have varied by gender and race over time. As you can see, homicides against African American women by their intimate partners decreased in the mid-1990s, but have been going up since then while similar homicides against white women have remained relatively stable since the 1990s, but are higher than they were in the 1980s. In contrast, intimate partner homicides against both African American and white men perpetrated by their intimate partners have declined since the 1980s, and they have remained relatively stable since 2000.

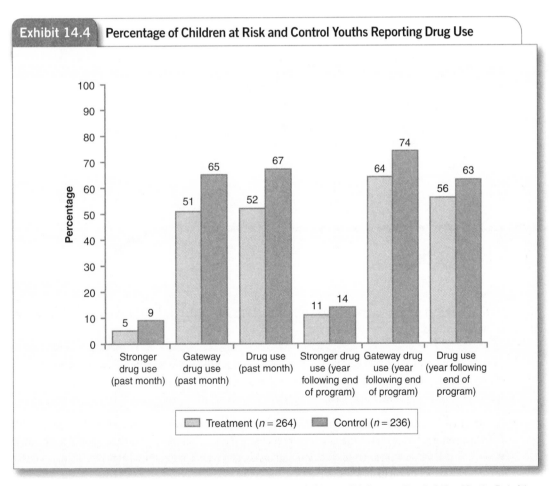

Exhibit 14.4 | **Percentage of Children at Risk and Control Youths Reporting Drug Use**

Source: A. Harrell, Cavanagh, S., and Sridharan, S. 1999. *Evaluation of the Children at Risk Program: Results 1 Year After the End of the Program* (NCJ-178914).Washington, DC: National Institute of Justice: Research in Brief.

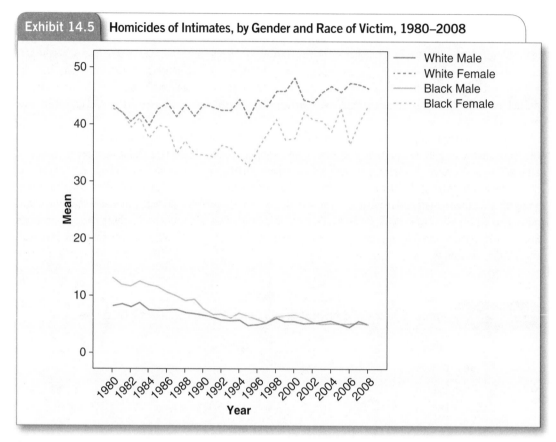

Exhibit 14.5 Homicides of Intimates, by Gender and Race of Victim, 1980–2008

Source: Cooper, Alexia and Erica Smith. 2011. Homicide Trends in the United States, 1980–2008. NCJ 236018. Bureau of Justice Statistics, U.S. Department of Justice.

🔲 Ethics and Reporting

It is at the time of reporting research results that the researcher's ethical duty to be honest becomes paramount. Here are some guidelines:

- *Provide an honest accounting of how the research was carried out and where the initial research design had to be changed.* Readers do not have to know about every change you made in your plans and each new idea you had, but they should be informed about major changes in hypotheses or research design.

- *Maintain a full record of the research project so that questions can be answered if they arise.* Many details will have to be omitted from all but the most comprehensive reports, but these omissions should not make it impossible to track down answers to specific questions about research procedures that may arise in the course of data analysis or presentation.

- *Avoid "lying with statistics" or using graphs to mislead.* (See Chapter 13.)

- *Acknowledge the sponsors of the research.* In part, this is so others can consider whether this sponsorship may have tempted you to bias your results in some way; thank staff who made major contributions.

- *Be sure that the order of authorship for coauthored reports is discussed in advance and reflects agreed-upon principles. Be sensitive to coauthors' needs and concerns.*

🔲 Communicating With the Public

Even following appropriate guidelines such as these, however, will not prevent controversy and conflict over research on sensitive issues. Does this mean that ethical researchers should avoid political controversy by sidestepping media outlets for their work? Many social scientists argue that the media offer one of the best ways to communicate the practical application of sociological knowledge and that when we avoid these opportunities, "some of the best sociological insights never reach policy makers because sociologists seldom take advantage of useful mechanisms to get their ideas out" (Wilson 1998:435).

The sociologist William Julius Wilson (1998) urges the following principles for engaging the public through the media:

1. Focus on issues of national concern, issues that are high on the public agenda.

2. Develop creative and thoughtful arguments that are clearly presented and devoid of technical language.

3. Present the big picture whereby the arguments are organized and presented so that the readers can see how the various parts are interrelated.

Ethical research reporting should not mean ineffective reporting. You need to tell a coherent story in the report and to avoid losing track of the story in a thicket of minuscule details. You do not need to report every twist and turn in the conceptualization of the research problem or the conduct of the research, but be suspicious of reports that do not seem to admit to the possibility of any room for improvement. Social science is an ongoing enterprise in which one research report makes its most valuable contribution by laying the groundwork for another, more sophisticated research project. Highlight important findings in the research report, but use the research report also to point out what are likely to be the most productive directions for future researchers.

🔲 Plagiarism

It may seem depressing to end a book on research methods with a section on plagiarism, but it would be irresponsible to avoid the topic. Of course, you may have a course syllabus detailing instructor or university policies about plagiarism and specifying the penalties for violating that policy, so we're not simply going to repeat that kind of warning. You probably realize that the practice of selling term papers is revoltingly widespread (our search of "term papers" on Google returned 5,920,000 Web sites on June 3, 2008); so we're not going to just repeat that academic dishonesty is widespread. Instead, we

> *Plagiarism* Presenting as one's own the ideas or words of another person or persons for academic evaluation without proper acknowledgment.

will use this section to review the concept of plagiarism and to show how that problem connects to the larger issue of the integrity of social research. When you understand the dimensions of the problem and the way it affects research, you should be better able to detect plagiarism in other work and avoid it in your own.

You learned in Chapter 3 that maintaining professional integrity—honesty and openness in research procedures and results—is the foundation for ethical research practice. When it comes to research publications and reports, being honest and open means avoiding plagiarism—that is, presenting as one's own the ideas or words of another person or persons for academic evaluation without proper acknowledgment (Hard, Conway, and Moran 2006).

An increasing body of research suggests that plagiarism is a growing problem on college campuses. Jason Stephens and his colleagues (2007) found in a Web-based survey of self-selected students at two universities that one quarter acknowledged having plagiarized a few sentences (24.7%) or a complete paper (.3%) in coursework within the past year (many others admitted to other forms of academic dishonesty, such as copying homework). Hard et al. (2006) conducted an anonymous survey in selected classes in one university, with almost all students participating, and found much higher plagiarism rates: 60.6% reported that they had copied "sentences, phrases, paragraphs, tables, figures or data directly or in slightly modified form from a book, article, or other academic source without using quotation marks or giving proper acknowledgment to the original author or source" (p. 1069) and 39.4% reported that they had "copied information from Internet Web sites and submitted it as [their] work" (p. 1069).

So the plagiarism problem is not just about purchasing term papers—although that is really about as bad as it gets (Broskoske 2005); plagiarism is also about what you do with the information you obtain from a literature review or an inspection of research reports. And rest assured that this is not only about student papers; it also is about the work of established scholars and social researchers who publish reports that you want to rely on for accurate information. Several noted historians have been accused of plagiarizing passages that they used in popular books; some have admitted to not checking the work of their research assistants, to not keeping track of their sources, or to being unable to retrieve the data they claimed they had analyzed. Whether the cause is cutting corners to meet deadlines or consciously fudging facts, the effect is to undermine the trustworthiness of social research.

Now that you are completing this course in research methods, it's time to think about how to do your part to reduce the prevalence of plagiarism. Of course, the first step is to maintain careful procedures for documenting the sources that you rely on for your own research and papers, but you should also think about how best to reduce temptations among others. After all, what people believe about what others do is a strong influence on their own behavior (Hard et al. 2006).

Reviewing the definition of plagiarism and how it is enforced by your discipline's professional association is an important first step. These definitions and procedures reflect a collective effort to help social scientists maintain standards throughout the discipline. Awareness is the first step (American Sociological Association [ASA] 1999). In addition, your college or university also has rules that delineate its definition of and consequences for plagiarism.

Researchers have an obligation to be familiar with their code of ethics, other applicable ethics codes, and their application to sociologists' work. Lack of awareness or misunderstanding of an ethical standard is not, in itself, a defense to a charge of unethical conduct.

ASA's (1999) Code of Ethics, which is used by the American Society of Criminology, includes an explicit prohibition of plagiarism:

14. Plagiarism

(a) In publications, presentations, teaching, practice, and service, sociologists explicitly identify, credit, and reference the author when they take data or material verbatim from another person's written work, whether it is published, unpublished, or electronically available.

(b) In their publications, presentations, teaching, practice, and service, sociologists provide acknowledgment of and reference to the use of others' work, even if the work is not quoted verbatim or paraphrased, and they do not present others' work as their own whether it is published, unpublished, or electronically available. (p. 16)

The next step toward combating the problem and temptation of plagiarism is to keep focused on the goal of social research methods: investigating the social world. If researchers are motivated by a desire to learn about social relations, to understand how people understand society, and to discover why conflicts arise and how they can be prevented, they will be as concerned with the integrity of their research methods as are those, like yourself, who read and use the results of their research. Throughout this text, you have been learning how to use research processes and practices that yield valid findings and trustworthy conclusions. Failing to report honestly and openly on the methods used or sources consulted derails progress toward that goal.

It works the same as with cheating in school. When students are motivated only by the desire to "ace" their tests and receive better grades than others, they are more likely to plagiarize and use other illicit means to achieve that goal. Students who seek first to improve their understanding of the subject matter and to engage in the process of learning are less likely to plagiarize sources or cheat on exams (Kohn 2008). They are also building the foundation for becoming successful social researchers who help others understand our world.

Conclusion

Good critical skills are essential when evaluating research reports, whether your own or those produced by others. There are always weak points in any research, even published research. It is an indication of strength, not weakness, to recognize areas where one's own research needs to be, or could have been, improved. And it is really not just a question of sharpening our knives and going for the jugular. You need to be able to weigh the strengths and weaknesses of particular research results and to evaluate a study in terms of its contribution to understanding its particular research question, not whether it gives a definitive answer for all time.

But this is not to say that anything goes. Much research lacks one or more of the three legs of validity—measurement validity, causal validity, and generalizability—and sometimes contributes more confusion than understanding about particular issues. Top journals generally maintain very high standards, partly because they have good critics in the review process and distinguished editors who make the final acceptance decisions. But some daily newspapers do a poor job of screening, and research reporting standards in many popular magazines, TV shows, and books are often abysmally poor. Keep your standards high and your view critical when reading research reports, but not so high or so critical that you turn away from studies that make tangible contributions to the literature, even if they do not provide definitive answers. And don't be so intimidated by the need to maintain high standards that you shrink from taking advantage of opportunities to conduct research yourself.

The growth of social science methods from infancy to adolescence, perhaps to young adulthood, ranks as a key intellectual accomplishment of the 20th century. Opinions about the causes and consequences of crime no longer need depend on the scattered impressions of individuals, and criminal justice policies can be shaped by systematic evidence of their effectiveness.

Of course, social research methods are no more useful than the commitment of the researchers to their proper application. Research methods, like all knowledge, can be used poorly or well, for good purposes or bad, when appropriate or not. A claim that a belief is based on social science research in itself provides no extra credibility. As you have learned throughout this book, we must first learn which methods were used, how they were applied, and whether interpretations square with the evidence. To investigate the social world, we must keep in mind the lessons of research methods.

Key Terms

Combined frequency display   418
Compressed frequency display   419
Constructivist paradigm   413

Participatory
  action research   412
Plagiarism   423

Peer review   416
Reverse outlining   415

Highlights

- Proposal writing should be a time for clarifying the research problem, reviewing the literature, and thinking ahead about the report that will be required.

- Relations with research subjects and consumers should be developed in a manner that achieves key research goals and preparation of an effective research report. The traditional scientific approach of minimizing the involvement of research subjects and consumers in research decisions has been challenged by proponents of participatory action research and adherents of the constructivist paradigm.

- Different types of reports typically pose different problems. Authors of student papers must be guided in part by the expectations of their professor. Thesis writers have to meet the requirements of different committee members but can benefit greatly from the areas of expertise represented on a typical thesis committee. Applied researchers are constrained by the expectations of the research sponsor; an advisory committee from the applied setting can help avoid problems. Journal articles must pass a peer review by other social scientists and often are much improved in the process.

- Research reports should include an introductory statement of the research problem, a literature review, a methodology section, a findings section with pertinent data displays, and a conclusions section that identifies any weaknesses in the research design and points out implications for future research and theorizing. This basic report format should be modified according to the needs of a particular audience.

- All reports should be revised several times and critiqued by others before they are presented in final form.

- Some of the data in many reports can be displayed more efficiently by using combined and compressed statistical displays.

- The central ethical concern in research reporting is to be honest. This honesty should include providing a truthful accounting of how the research was carried out, maintaining a full record about the project, using appropriate statistics and graphs, acknowledging the research sponsors, and being sensitive to the perspectives of coauthors.

- Plagiarism is a grievous violation of scholarly ethics. All direct quotes or paraphrased material from another author's work must be appropriately cited.

Research in the News

Scientist Resigns at Harvard After Accusations of Scientific Misconduct

The *New York Times* reported several stories in 2011 about the psychologist, Marc Hauser, a leading researcher in his field, for academic misconduct. Dr. Hauser resigned before the verdict of the accusations could be announced. This article notes that "scientific misconduct is generally understood to connote grave offenses like fraud or plagiarism." As such, beware. Plagiarism may not only result in an F in your class or getting kicked out of school, it may mean the end of your career.

Source: Wade, Nicholas. "Scientist Under Inquiry Resigns From Harvard." *The New York Times,* July 20: A17.

Exercises

1. Select a recent article published in a peer-reviewed criminological journal and answer the following questions: How effective is the article in conveying the design and findings of the research? Could the article's organization be improved at all? Are there bases for disagreement about the interpretation of the findings?

2. Call a local criminal justice official and arrange for an interview. Ask the official about his or her experience with applied research reports and his or her conclusions about the value of social research and the best techniques for reporting to practitioners.

3. Rate four criminological journal articles for overall quality of the research and for effectiveness of the writing and data displays. Discuss how each could have been improved.

4. How firm a foundation do social research methods provide for understanding the social world? Stage an in-class debate, with the pro and con arguments focusing on the variability of social research findings across different social contexts and the difficulty of understanding human subjectivity.

Developing a Research Proposal

Now, it is time to bring all the elements of your proposal together.

1. Organize the proposal material you wrote for previous chapters in a logical order. Based on your research question, select the most appropriate research method as your primary method (see Chapters 5–10).

2. To add a multiple component to your research design, select another research method that could add knowledge about your research question.

3. Rewrite the entire proposal, adding an introduction. Also add sections that outline a budget and state the limitations of your study.

STUDENT STUDY SITE

Log on to the Web-based student study site at **www.sagepub.com/bachmanprccj5e** for additional study tools including eFlashcards, Web quizzes, links to SAGE journal articles, podcasts, videos, data sets and codebooks, Web exercises, Web resources, and additional appendices.

Web Exercises

1. Go to the National Science Foundation's Law and Social Sciences Program Web site at www.nsf.gov/funding/pgm_summ.jsp?pims_id=5422. What are the components that this program looks for in a proposed piece of research? Write a detailed outline for a research proposal to study a subject of your choice to be submitted to the National Science Foundation for funding.

2. Using the Web, find five different examples of criminological research projects that have been completed. Briefly describe each. How does each differ in its approach to reporting the research results? To whom do you think the author(s) of each is "reporting" (i.e., who is the "audience")? How do you think the predicted audience has helped shape the author's approach to reporting the results? Be sure to note the Web sites at which you located each of your five examples.

Ethics Exercises

1. Plagiarism is not a joke. What are the regulations on plagiarism in class papers at your school? What do you think the ideal policy would be? Should this policy take into account cultural differences in teaching practices and learning styles? Do you think this ideal policy is likely to be implemented? Why or why not? Based on your experiences, do you believe that most student plagiarism is the result of misunderstanding about proper citation practices, or is it the result of dishonesty? Do you think that students who plagiarize while in school are less likely to be honest as social researchers?

2. Full disclosure of sources of research as well as of other medically related funding has become a major concern for medical journals. Should researchers publishing in criminology and criminal justice journals also be required to fully disclose all sources of funding? Should full disclosure of all previous funds received by criminal justice agencies be required in each published article? What about disclosure of any previous jobs or paid consultations with criminal justice agencies? Write a short justification of the regulations you propose.

3. Some researchers do not make their data publicly available. As such, other researchers are not able to replicate the original findings. Would you recommend legal regulations about the release of research data? What would those regulations be? Would they differ depending on the researcher's source of funding? Would you allow researchers exclusive access to their own data for some period of time after they have collected it?

SPSS or Excel Exercises

1. How do friends' opinions and support for delinquent activities influence levels of delinquency among youth? A combined frequency display of the distributions of a series of YOUTH.POR variables will help you answer this question.

   a. Obtain a frequency distribution and descriptive statistics for the index of friends' attitudes toward delinquent acts (FROPINION), the index of friends' engagement in delinquent acts (FRBEHAVE), and the delinquency index at time 11 (DELINQ1).

   b. Using the mean as the measure of center, recode the three indexes to measure low and high levels of each variable (e.g., all values below the mean represent low levels of a given variable, and all values above the mean represent high levels of the given variable).

   c. Use the percentages in these distributions to prepare a combined frequency display.

   d. Discuss what you have learned about the influence of friends' delinquent tendencies on delinquency levels among youth.

2. Repeat Exercise 1 using the parental index (PARNT2), the certainty of punishment index (CERTAIN), and the morality index (MORAL). Note: The scale for the variables of interest in this exercise is measured opposite the delinquency scale. For example, high scores on the parental index indicate high parental supervision, which in theory should correspond with low levels of delinquency. Be sure to place the percentages for DELINQ1 accordingly (make note of the placement of the percentiles for this variable or create more intuitive column labels).

3. Write a short report based on the analyses you conducted for the SPSS exercises throughout this book, including the data displays you have just prepared. Include in your report a brief introduction and literature review. In a short methods section, review the basic methods used and list the variables you have used for the analysis. In your conclusions section, include some suggestions for additional research on support for capital punishment.

Appendix A

Questions to Ask About a Research Article

1. What is the basic research question or problem? Try to state it in just one sentence. (Chapter 2)

2. Is the purpose of the study explanatory, evaluative, exploratory, or descriptive? Did the study have more than one purpose? (Chapter 1)

3. Was the theoretical framework presented? What was it? Did it seem appropriate for the research question addressed? Can you think of a different theoretical perspective that might have been used? (Chapter 2)

4. What prior literature was reviewed? Was it relevant to the research problem? To the theoretical framework? Does the literature review appear to be adequate? Are you aware of (or can you locate) any important omitted studies? (Chapter 2)

5. How well did the study live up to the guidelines for science? Do you need additional information in any areas to evaluate the study? To replicate it? (Chapter 2)

6. Did the study seem consistent with current ethical standards? Were any trade-offs made between different ethical guidelines? Was an appropriate balance struck between adherence to ethical standards and use of the most rigorous scientific practices? (Chapter 2 and in each methods chapter)

7. What were the major concepts in the research? How, and how clearly, were they defined? Were some concepts treated as unidimensional that you think might best be thought of as multidimensional? (Chapter 3)

8. Were any hypotheses stated? Were these hypotheses justified adequately in terms of the theoretical framework? In terms of prior research? (Chapter 2)

9. What were the independent and dependent variables in the hypothesis or hypotheses? Did these variables reflect the theoretical concepts as intended? What direction of association was hypothesized? Were any other variables identified as potentially important? (Chapter 2)

10. Did the instruments used—the measures of the variables—seem valid and reliable? How did the author attempt to establish this? Could any more have been done in the study to establish measurement validity? (Chapter 3)

11. What were the units of analysis? Were they appropriate for the research question? If some groups were the units of analysis, were any statements made at any point that are open to the ecological fallacy? If individuals were the units of analysis, were any statements made at any point that suggest reductionist reasoning? (Chapter 4)

12. Was the study design cross-sectional or longitudinal, or did it use both types of data? If the design was longitudinal, what type of longitudinal design was it? Could the longitudinal design have been improved in any way, as by collecting panel data rather than trend data, or by decreasing the dropout rate in a panel design? If cross-sectional data were used, could the research question have been addressed more effectively with the longitudinal data? (Chapter 5)

13. Were any causal assertions made or implied in the hypotheses or in subsequent discussion? What approach was used to demonstrate the existence of causal effects? Were all three criteria for establishing causal relationships addressed? What, if any, variables were controlled in the analysis to reduce the risk of spurious relationships? Should any other variables have been measured and controlled? How satisfied are you with the internal validity of the conclusions? (Chapters 5, 6)

14. Was a sample or the entire population of elements used in the study? What type of sample was selected? Was a probability sampling method used? Did the authors think the sample was generally representative of the population from which it was drawn? Do you? How would you evaluate the likely generalizability of the findings to other populations? (Chapter 4)

15. Was the response rate or participation rate reported? Does it appear likely that those who did not respond or participate were markedly different from those who did participate? Why or why not? Did the author(s) adequately discuss this issue? (Chapters 4, 6)

16. Was an experimental, survey, participant observation, or some other research design used? How well was this design suited to the research question posed and the specific hypotheses tested, if any? Why do you suppose the author(s) chose this particular design? How was the design modified in response to research constraints? How was it modified in order to take advantage of research opportunities? (Chapters 6–10)

17. Was an evaluation research design used? Which type was it? What was the primary purpose of the evaluation? (Chapter 11)

18. Were multiple methods used? Were findings obtained with different methods complementary? (Chapter 11)

19. Was any attention given to social context? To biological processes? If so, what did this add? If not, would it have improved the study? Explain. (Chapter 5)

20. Summarize the findings. How clearly were statistical and/or qualitative data presented and discussed? Were the results substantively important? (Chapters 9, 13)

21. Did the author(s) adequately represent the findings in the discussion and/or conclusions sections? Were conclusions well grounded in the findings? Are any other interpretations possible? (Chapter 14)

22. Compare the study to others addressing the same research question. Did the study yield additional insights? In what ways was the study design more or less adequate than the design of previous research? (Chapters 2, 10, 13)

23. What additional research questions and hypotheses are suggested by the study's results? What light did the study shed on the theoretical framework used? On social policy questions? (Chapters 2, 10, 13)

Appendix B

How to Read a Research Article

The discussions of research articles throughout the text may provide all the guidance you need to read and critique research on your own. But reading about an article in bits and pieces in order to learn about particular methodologies is not quite the same as reading an article in its entirety in order to learn what the research discovered. The goal of this appendix is to walk you through an entire research article, answering the review questions introduced in Appendix A. Of course, this is only one article, and our "walk" will take different turns from one taken by a review of other articles, but after this review, you should feel more confident when reading other research articles on your own.

For this example, we will use an article by Alarid, Burton, and Cullen (2000) on gender and crime among felony offenders (reprinted in this volume on pp. 436–455). It focuses on a topic important to explaining the similarities and differences between male and female offending patterns as well as to questions of the generalizability of central criminological theoretical perspectives. Moreover, the article is published in a reputable criminological journal, the *Journal of Research in Crime and Delinquency*, indicating the article makes an important contribution to what is known about the etiology of criminal offending across gender groups.

We have reproduced below each of the article review questions from Appendix A, followed by our answers to them. After each question, we indicate the article page or pages that we are referring to. You can also follow our review by reading through the article itself and noting our comments.

1. *What is the basic research question or problem? Try to state it in just one sentence.* (Chapter 2)

The clearest statement of the research question actually consists of two questions: "[Can] social control and differential association theories . . . help account for participation in crime among young adult male and female felons?" (p. 174 in the original article). Prior to this point, the authors focus on the research problem, describing the limitations of past research and why exploring social control and differential association theories across gender groups among felony offenders is important.

2. *Is the purpose of the study explanatory, evaluative, exploratory, or descriptive? Did the study have more than one purpose?* (Chapter 1)

This study is exploratory in nature. The literature review (pp. 171–174) makes it clear that the primary purpose of this research is exploratory since new ground is being covered based on the limitations of past research. In addition, the problem statement indicates the exploratory character of the study: It "attempts to test the generality of social control and differential association theories to a population that has been infrequently studied" (p. 173).

3. *Was the theoretical framework presented? What was it? Did it seem appropriate for the research question addressed? Can you think of a different theoretical perspective that might have been used?* (Chapter 2)

This study uses two theoretical perspectives, "social control" and "differential association." This framework is very appropriate for the research questions addressed because this study explores the applicability of these theories to adult populations and their generalizability across gender groups. Because the research question focuses specifically on the applicability and generalizability of these specific theoretical perspectives, no other theoretical framework would be applicable.

4. *What prior literature was reviewed? Was it relevant to the research problem? To the theoretical framework? Does the literature review appear to be adequate? Are you aware of (or can you locate) any important omitted studies?* (Chapter 2)

Literature is reviewed from the article's first page until the "method" section (pp. 171–174). All the literature seems relevant to the particular problem as well as the general theoretical framework. The first few paragraphs generalize the findings of several studies that measures of both theories are related to criminal involvement (pp. 171–172). The authors then discuss the limited focus of previous studies and their rationale for selecting social control and differential association as their focus for this study (pp. 172–174). We leave it to you to find out whether any important studies were omitted.

5. *How well did the study live up to the guidelines for science? Do you need additional information in any areas to evaluate the study? To replicate it?* (Chapter 2)

It would be best to return to this question after reading the whole article. The study clearly involves a test of ideas against empirical reality to the extent that reality could be measured; it was carried out systematically and disclosed, as far as we can tell. Because the authors used a sample of newly incarcerated felons, it may be difficult for others to replicate the authors' findings. Drawing from previous research, the authors make some general assumptions about what factors best measure social control and differential association (p. 177). However, in previous studies, those factors measuring social control and differential association have been applied primarily to juvenile populations (p. 172). Intuitively, the same measures or indicators may not be applicable to adult populations (e.g., parental attachment and peer attachment), but we have no empirical evidence of this. The authors also assume respondents' reports of past criminal behavior are valid (pp. 177–178). It appears these are reasonable assumptions, but they are unproved assumptions that could be challenged. This is not in itself a criticism of the research, since some assumptions must be made in any study. The authors specified the meaning of key terms, as required in scientific research. The authors did search for regularities or patterns in their data, thus living up to another guideline. A skeptical stance toward current knowledge is apparent in the literature review and in the authors' claim that "social control and differential association theory appear to have general effects" on young adult felons and across gender

groups (pp. 189–190). They encourage the development of new theories but emphasize the importance of "older" theoretical perspectives and their application to underresearched topics (p. 192). The study thus seems to exemplify adherence to basic scientific guidelines and to be very replicable.

6. *Did the study seem consistent with current ethical standards? Were any trade-offs made between different ethical guidelines? Was an appropriate balance struck between adherence to ethical standards and use of the most rigorous scientific practices?* (Chapter 2)

To the best of our knowledge, the study was consistent with current ethical standards. "All data were collected directly from the participants themselves" (p. 175). In accordance with the American Sociological Association (ASA) code of ethics, participation in the study was voluntary, and the participants gave their informed consent to participate. The reporting seems honest and open. The original survey used by the authors is not likely to have violated any ethical guidelines concerning the treatment of human subjects, although it would be necessary to inspect the survey instrument itself to evaluate this.

7. *What were the major concepts in the research? How, and how clearly, were they defined? Were some concepts treated as unidimensional that you think might best be thought of as multidimensional?* (Chapter 3)

There are two key concepts in this study, social control and differential association. These concepts are the focus of the study and are discussed at length. These concepts, however, were not defined so that a layperson would understand what these concepts mean.

8. *Were any hypotheses stated? Were these hypotheses justified adequately in terms of the theoretical framework? In terms of prior research?* (Chapter 2)

Three hypotheses are stated, although they are labeled as theoretical predictions, which are derived from previous research (p. 173). The first hypothesis is that social control will account for variation in offending across gender groups. The second hypothesis is that differential association will account for variation in offending across gender groups. Finally, the third hypothesis is that the effect of the competing theory will be spurious.

9. *What were the independent and dependent variables in the hypothesis(es)? Did these variables reflect the theoretical concepts as intended? What direction of association was hypothesized? Were any other variables identified as potentially important?* (Chapter 2)

The dependent variable for this study is past criminal activity. For purposes of analysis, past criminal behavior is divided into three subscales resulting in four dependent variables: general crime (the total of all criminal activities), violent crime, property crime, and drug crime (p. 177). There are eight independent variables included in this study. The independent variables for the first hypothesis include five social control indicators. These include marital/partner attachment (0 = not married/unattached and 1 = married/attached), attachment to parents (a three-item composite index, higher values represent stronger attachment), attachment to friends (a two-item index, higher values represent stronger attachment), involvement in conventional activities (a two-item index measuring how much free time individual has, higher values represent more free time), and moral belief in the law (measured by a two-item index with higher values representing stronger belief) (pp. 178–180).

The independent variables for the second hypothesis include three indicators of differential association. These include individual definitions toward crime (a five-item index, higher values represent greater tolerance of criminal behavior), others' definitions toward crime (a three-item index, higher values represent greater association with individuals who hold favorable definition toward violating the law), and criminal friends (continuous variable indicating the number of close friends who have broken the law) (pp. 180–182).

Can you identify the variables in the final hypothesis?

10. *Did the instruments used—the measures of the variables—seem valid and reliable? How did the author attempt to establish this? Could any more have been done in the study to establish measurement validity?* (Chapter 3)

The measurement of the dependent variable was straightforward. The authors report the scale used has been identified as a valid and reliable self-report assessment of antisocial behavior (p. 176). In addition, reliability was assessed using Cronbach's alpha method, which indicated the general scale and the subscales are a reliable measure of criminal behavior. The measurement of the independent variables was also straightforward. The authors report the scales used have been identified as valid measures of social control and differential association indicators. In addition, Cronbach's alpha reliability testing shows the measures are reliable.

11. *What were the units of analysis? Were they appropriate for the research question? If some groups were the units of analysis, were any statements made at any point that*
are open to the ecological fallacy? If individuals were the units of analysis, were any statements made at any point that suggest reductionist reasoning? (Chapter 4)

The authors sampled young adult, first-time felony offenders sentenced to a residential court-ordered boot camp program. The units of analysis are appropriate for the research question. No statements were made at any point that suggest reductionist reasoning.

12. *Was the study design cross-sectional or longitudinal, or did it use both types of data? If the design was longitudinal, what type of longitudinal design was it? Could the longitudinal design have been improved in any way, as by collecting panel data rather than trend data, or by decreasing the dropout rate in a panel design? If cross-sectional data were used, could the research question have been addressed more effectively with the longitudinal data?* (Chapter 5)

The survey was cross-sectional. The research question could have been addressed more effectively with longitudinal data that followed people from childhood into adulthood, since many of the authors' interpretations reflect their interest in how individuals' past experiences shape their propensity for criminal behavior.

13. *Were any causal assertions made or implied in the hypotheses or in subsequent discussion? What approach was used to demonstrate the existence of causal effects? Were all three criteria for establishing causal relationships addressed? What, if any, variables were controlled in the analysis to reduce the risk of spurious relationships? Should any other variables have been measured and controlled? How satisfied are you with the internal validity of the conclusions?* (Chapters 5, 6)

The explanatory hypotheses indicate that the authors were concerned with causality. However, the lack of previous research on their chosen population suggests an exploratory approach to causality. In order to reduce the risk of spuriousness in the presumed causal relationships, three control variables were included in the analysis: age, race/ethnicity, and gender (p. 188); these variables have been shown to be strongly related to criminal activity. There are other variables that might have created a spurious relationship, but at least several of the most likely contenders have been controlled. For example, some of the differences in social control and differential association measures may be due to social class—that is, individuals who were raised in more affluent families are more likely to have had greater social control in their lives and less opportunity to be involved with individuals who favor, or at least justify, criminal behavior. Income has also been shown to be negatively related to criminal activity—that is, the higher an individual's income, the less likely he or she is to engage in criminal activity.

14. *Was a sample or the entire population of elements used in the study? What type of sample was selected? Was a probability sampling method used? Did the authors think the sample was generally representative of the population from which it was drawn? Do you? How would you evaluate the likely generalizability of the findings to other populations?* (Chapter 4)

The sample was a nonrandom (nonprobability) sample of young, first-time felony offenders. A purposive sampling technique was used when sampling women; the authors "focused [their] efforts on obtaining responses from the entire [female] population . . . in the program over a 15-month period" (p. 175). The authors did not focus on sampling the entire male population; therefore, the authors obtained an availability sample of males sentenced to the program over the same time period. The authors admit the sample is not representative of "felony crimes committed by men and women in prison, [but] closely resembles first-time felony offenders in other shock incarceration programs as an alternative to jail or prison incarceration" (p. 176). Do you believe the authors can generalize their findings to similar populations? Why or why not?

15. *Was the response rate or participation rate reported? Does it appear likely that those who did not respond or participate were markedly different from those who did participate? Why or why not? Did the author(s) adequately discuss this issue?* (Chapters 4, 6)

The response rate was reported. The authors obtained responses from 122 of 124 (or 98.4%) female offenders and 1,031 (or 85.9%) of male offenders (p. 175). With the exception of female offenders, the authors did not discuss differences among those who did and did not participate with the study. Of the two female offenders who did not participate in the study, one did not speak English and the other woman escaped from the facility (p. 175). In general, it is reasonable to believe those who did not participate in the study were not markedly different from those who did participate. The large sample of males and females obtained for this study should have provided good variability.

16. *Was an experimental, survey, participant observation, or some other research design used? How well was this*

design suited to the research question posed and the specific hypotheses tested, if any? Why do you suppose the author(s) chose this particular design? How was the design modified in response to research constraints? How was it modified in order to take advantage of research opportunities? (Chapters 6–10)

Survey research was the method of choice and probably was used for this article because it provided the most cost-effective means of gathering data. Survey research seems appropriate for the research questions posed.

17. *Was an evaluation research design used? Which type was it? What was the primary purpose of the evaluation?* (Chapter 10)

This study did not use any type of evaluation research.

18. *Were multiple methods used? Were findings obtained with different methods complementary?* (Chapter 10)

This study used only survey methods.

19. *Was any attention given to social context? To biological processes? If so, what did this add? If not, would it have improved the study? Explain.* (Chapters 5, 10)

Social context is given attention in this study on an individual level. The majority of social control and differential association indicators are measures of social conditions and experiences of the respondents. However, no attention is given to the potential importance of larger social contexts, such as neighborhood or region of the country. Biological factors that may increase the propensity for criminality are not considered in this study.

20. *Summarize the findings. How clearly were statistical and/or qualitative data presented and discussed? Were the results substantively important?* (Chapters 9, 13)

Statistical data are presented clearly using descriptive statistics, examination of bivariate relationships, and multiple regression analysis (a multivariate statistical technique) that highlight the most central findings. No qualitative data are presented. The findings seem substantively important, since they identify social control and differential association theories that can be applied to adult populations across gender groups (pp. 184–188).

21. *Did the author(s) adequately represent the findings in the discussion and/or conclusion sections? Were conclusions well grounded in the findings? Are any other interpretations possible?* (Chapter 13)

The findings are well represented in the discussion and conclusion section (pp. 188–192). The authors point out in their literature review that the focus for testing social control and differential association theories data is often limited to juvenile delinquent populations and frequently fails to consider possible differences between males and females. The findings suggest these theoretical perspectives can be applied to adult criminal populations and are important in explaining variation in criminal behavior across gender groups. You might want to consider what other interpretations of the findings might be possible. Remember that other interpretations are always possible for particular findings—it is a question of the weight of the evidence, the persuasiveness of the theory used, and the consistency of the findings with other research.

22. *Compare the study to others addressing the same research question. Did the study yield additional insights? In what ways was the study design more or less adequate than the design of previous research?* (Chapters 2, 10, 13)

This study investigated the relationship between social control and differential association on a population that had not previously received much attention (young adult felony offenders). This helped the authors to gain additional insights into the influence of social control and differential association on young adults across gender groups.

23. *What additional research questions and hypotheses are suggested by the study's results? What light did the study shed on the theoretical framework used? On social policy questions?* (Chapters 2, 10, 13)

The authors suggest no additional research questions or hypotheses. However, the study does shed light on the importance of "traditional" theoretical perspectives in explaining variation in criminal behavior among adults across gender groups. The authors note the importance of new theoretical paradigms but emphasize "that the value of 'older' theoretical perspectives should be remembered and . . . applied to under-researched topics" (p. 192).

Gender and Crime Among Felony Offenders

Assessing the Generality of Social Control and Differential Association Theories

Leanne Fiftal Alarid

Velmer S. Burton, Jr.

Francis T. Cullen

lthough often tested empirically on high school samples, differential association and social control theories have only infrequently been used to explain offending by felons. Based on a sample of 1,153 newly incarcerated felons, the authors examine the ability of differential association and social control theories to explain self-reported offending across types of crime and gender groups. Overall, the analyses lend support to both perspectives and suggest that they are "general" theories of crime. It also appears, however, that differential association theory has more consistent effects, especially for men. Parental attachment is a significantly stronger predictor of female than male participation in violent crime. These results indicate that future studies of criminal behavior risk being misspecified if they do not include measures of these "traditional" theories of crime.

Since the 1969 publication of Hirschi's *Causes of Delinquency*, social control or control theory and differential association or "cultural deviance" theory have competed vigorously against one another for the status of the preeminent micro-level sociological theory of crime (see also Kornhauser 1978).

Even today, spirited exchanges occur in which the logical and empirical adequacy of the theories is debated (see Akers 1996, 1998; Costello 1997; Hirschi 1996; Matsueda 1988, 1997). These paradigms continue to guide research (see, e.g., Akers 1998; Sampson and Laub 1993) not only because of their theoretical parsimony and elegance but also because they accrue a measure of empirical support (Akers 1996; Krohn 1995).

Although noteworthy exceptions exist, most of the tests of social control and differential association theory have been conducted using self-report surveys on juveniles. Particularly instructive are empirical studies in which measures of both theories have been incorporated in the analysis. In general, this research suggests that measures of both theories are related to delinquent or adult criminal involvement, although in some studies, the strength of the differential association variables is greater (Benda 1994; Conger 1976; Kandel and Davies 1991; Macdonald 1989; Matsueda 1982; Matsueda and Heimer 1987; McGee 1992; see also Akers 1998; Burton 1991; Krohn 1995).

A key concern, however, is the generality of social control and differential association theories. These perspectives typically have been seen as having the ability to explain various forms of crime for all people (see, e.g., Akers 1998; Sutherland and Cressey 1955; Hirschi 1969; Sampson and Laub 1993). Clearly, the theoretical power of each of these perspectives hinges on their ability to achieve the status of a general theory. Accordingly, a central empirical and thus theoretical issue is whether social control and differential association theories can explain criminal behavior that extends beyond the delinquency found among community samples of youth.

There have been studies conducted on adult samples that have found support for differential association/social learning theory (Akers 1998; Akers and LaGreca 1988, 1991; Akers et al. 1989; Boeringer, Shehan, and Akers 1991; Dull 1983; Orcutt 1987; Tittle, Burke, and Jackson 1986). Research on social control theory with adult samples also suggests that adult social bonds may reduce criminal behavior (Horney, Osgood, and Marshall 1995; Lasley 1988; Sampson and Laub 1993). Even so, the empirical literature assessing whether social control and differential association theories can explain adult criminal behavior remains limited, especially when one searches for studies that include in their analyses measures of both theoretical perspectives.[1] Among the few adult studies testing social control versus differential association theory, the results show mixed support for both perspectives. Thus, two studies using community samples of adults found stronger support for differential association theory (Burton 1991; Macdonald 1989), while another study revealed that social control theory was better able to account for variation in arrests for men and women drug offenders (Covington 1985).

Even with this research, however, there are typically two limitations. First, especially with adult samples, studies often do not explore whether the effects of variables measuring traditional criminological theories vary by gender. Traditional theories have been criticized for their perceived inability to explain female criminality (Adler 1975; Daly and Chesney-Lind 1988; Leonard 1982) and for ignoring how gender-related factors—such as patriarchal power relations—differentially shape the involvement of gender groups in crime (Heidensohn 1985; Messerschmidt 1993) and victimization (Chesney-Lind and Shelden 1992). In turn, it is argued that scholars should formulate separate or different theories of crime for women (Leonard 1982; Messerschmidt 1993; Naffine and Gale 1989; Smart 1976).

Second, tests of social control and differential association theory have only infrequently been conducted on samples that include a high base rate of serious offending. As a result, we have only limited information on whether these theories explain more than relatively minor forms of criminal involvement.

As Messner and Rosenfeld (1994:47) note, this "neglect of serious offending by contemporary criminologists" means that it is necessary to employ "other ways of obtaining information from people who commit serious crimes (e.g., they can be interviewed in prison)." Although still not widespread, criminologists increasingly are undertaking tests of criminological theories that employ serious offenders interviewed in prison or in the community (see Covington 1985; Horney and Marshall 1992; Horney et al. 1995; Longshore, Turner, and Stein 1996; Sampson and Laub 1990, 1993).

Among this body of research on samples of adult offenders, however, research testing social control and differential association theories is rare; research that conducts such studies by gender is virtually nonexistent. The only known exception is Covington's (1985) study of adult heroin addicts in which an attempt is made to explain self-reported total arrests and arrests for property crimes. Covington's analysis revealed that measures of social control were better predictors of women's criminal involvement in property crime and in both men's and women's involvement in overall offending behaviors; differential association measures, however, were able to explain men's property arrests.[2]

In light of the status of the existing research, the current study attempts to test the generality of social control and differential association theories to a population that has been infrequently studied: young adult felons drawn from the inner city. Social control and differential association theories were selected because they have been found, among existing sociological theories, to have the most consistent empirical support in studies of juveniles.[3] Social control theory is also used to explain adult crime in recent important studies (Horney et al. 1995; Sampson and Laub 1993). These theories both predict that their effects will be general—that is, they will account for variation in offending and that this effect will hold for males and females.

These theories also predict that the effects of the competing theory will be spurious (Hirschi 1969). The spuriousness issue is important because most tests with adults have not included measures of both theories (e.g., Horney et al. 1995; Sampson and Laub 1993). As such, findings from previous theoretical tests could be misspecified if the effects of differential association variables account for the findings of social control variables.

Based on previous research on community samples of adults and juveniles that have used both sets of measures, we would anticipate that both variables will have effects. Like members of the community, offenders can be expected to vary in their levels of social control (Horney et al. 1995; Sampson and Laub 1993). We can also expect variation in differential associations and crime-related attitudes. Still, given the lack of previous research testing these theories with a population of offenders extensively involved in crime, the relationship of the theories to criminal involvement remains to be empirically determined.

Thus, the purpose of this article is to test the generality of social control and differential association theories with a sample of young adult felons drawn from the inner city. The study also has the advantage of including males and females.

Using a self-report survey, the study examines both overall offending and involvement in specific forms of criminal conduct. By testing the two theories against each other, the central focus will be to discern which theory—if not both theories—can explain variation in offending among young adult men and women felony offenders from an urban area. That is, are social control and differential association theories mainly explanations of juvenile delinquency, or can they help account for participation in crime among young adult male and female felons?

▣ Method

The procedures used to test differential association and social control theory with 1,153 felony women and men in a community corrections program have been organized into four categories: (1) data collection, (2) sample characteristics, (3) dependent variables, and (4) independent variables.

Data Collection

Data for this study were gathered from felons sentenced to a residential court-ordered boot camp program in Harris County, Texas, which includes the Houston metropolitan area. The boot camp program was designed for a 17- to 25-year-old male or female adult who had been convicted as a first-time felon and had been sentenced to prison. Offenders were considered for the program by judges as a "last stop before prison." The type of convicted offender (violent, property, or drug) in this program was thus was a reflection of judicial discretion.

The three-month coed program emphasized discipline, physical labor, and drills and offered GED education, life skills, and drug awareness classes. The program housed a maximum capacity of 30 women in one smaller barrack and approximately 240 men in five program barracks, with a sixth housing barrack available for incoming "new boots." Up to 48 men entered the program as a cohort, were housed in the same barracks, and graduated together three months later. Since only about 2 women entered the program every week, there were no distinct female cohorts. Rather, female "new boots" were mixed with more senior women offenders, and the barracks never filled to capacity during the data collection period. For both women and men, the residential stay in the boot camp program

was an alternative to jail or prison incarceration. The program was followed by a two-year period of intensive supervision probation in the community (Burton et al. 1993).

Data were collected on participants who entered the boot camp between June 1992 and September 1993. Since a smaller number of women were sentenced to boot camp, we focused our efforts on obtaining responses from the entire population of 124 women in the program over a 15-month time period. Out of the female population in the boot camp program, we were successful at obtaining consent from 122 (or 98.4 percent) of the women. One woman who did not participate could not understand or speak English, while another woman escaped from the facility prior to our weekly visit. Of approximately 1,200 males who entered the program during that time period, we collected questionnaire responses from 1,031 (or 85.9 percent) of the men offenders.

All data were collected directly from the participants themselves, who completed a paper-and-pencil questionnaire in the facility housing barracks within two weeks of their arrival. The male cohorts completed their surveys in a group setting with one trained researcher available to answer questions. The women participants completed their surveys individually with one trained research team member (recall that only two to three women entered the program weekly). We do not believe that the differences in the two data collection methods were significant enough to affect response reliability or validity. The benefits of obtaining a high response rate for the women outweighed any negative effects caused by conducting the men's questionnaire sessions in larger groups. A total of 1,153 usable questionnaires were completed, 10.6 percent by women respondents.

| Table c.1 | Sample Characteristics | |

Characteristic	Women (n = 122)	Men (n = 1,031)
Age (17–28 years)	20.6	19.5
Race/ethnicity (percentage)		
African American	44.3	44.4
Caucasian	45.1	31.4
Hispanic	10.7	23.8
Formal education (years)	10.5	10.3
Marital/partner attachment		
(percentage attached)	32.0	35.1
Number of children (percentage)		
None	46.7	69.8
One	30.3	21.3
Two	9.8	6.1
Three or more	13.1	2.9
Median household income (in dollars)	16,800	27,500
Current conviction (percentage)		
Drug	41.8	28.9
Person	19.7	19.5
Property	38.5	51.6

🔲 Sample Characteristics

The sample characteristics of the 1,031 men and 122 women indicated that the vast majority lived in the inner city or surrounding urban area at the time of arrest for their most recent conviction. Men and women were both between the ages of 17 and 28 years, with the average age calculated at 19.5 for men and 20.6 years for women. The African American composition of both samples was identical (44 percent). However, there were more Caucasian women (45.1 percent) than men (31.4 percent), and there were more Hispanic men than women (23.8 percent and 10.7 percent, respectively). The amount of formal education completed ranged between 6th grade and three years of higher education, with a mean of a 10th-grade education. Single/unattached women (68.0 percent) and men (64.9 percent) comprised the majority of the sample relative to married and cohabiting women and men.

The demographic differences between the men and women in the sample were number of children, median household income, and current conviction. First, about 46.7 percent of women and 69.8 percent of men had no dependent children. Of all the fathers and mothers, the women more often reported being the primary caretaker and sole financial respondent for the children. As primary caretakers, the women lived in households that generated much lower incomes than men.

The median household income for women (most with children) was $16,800, while men's reported annual household income was $27,500.

As for the most recent conviction, crimes of violence were comparably represented by gender; in the sample, 19.7 percent of women and 19.5 percent of men were violent offenders. More women (41.8 percent) than men (28.9 percent) were convicted of a drug offense. Bear in mind that the offense type of each convicted offender (violent, property, or drug) does not represent felony crimes committed by men and women in prison. Even though women are increasingly being sentenced for felony drug offenses as a result of the war on drugs (U.S. Bureau of Justice Statistics 1994; Immarigeon and Chesney-Lind 1993), our sample more closely resembles first-time felony offenders in other shock incarceration programs as an alternative to jail or prison incarceration (MacKenzie and Brame 1994).

▣ Dependent Variables

Dependent variable measures for the analysis were originally derived from Elliott and Ageton's (1980) scale of delinquent behaviors offenses found in the National Youth Survey (NYS). The NYS is currently "the most highly respected self-report assessment of antisocial behavior" (Caspi et al. 1994). We adjusted certain measures to apply to our young adult sample. Respondents were asked whether they had ever committed 35 different deviant and criminal acts (Hindelang, Hirschi, and Weis 1981). Our prevalence dimension of crime measures offense participation or the number of crime types committed. Other researchers have preferred the use of the prevalence measure of variety:

> Variety scores are useful for individual-differences research for several reasons. First, they show the extent of involvement in different types of crimes. . . . Second, they are less skewed than frequency scores. Third, they give equal weight to all delinquent acts, unlike frequency scores, which give more weight to minor crimes that are committed more frequently (e.g., underage drinking) and less weight to serious, less frequent crimes (e.g., rape). (Caspi et al. 1994:170–71)[4]

In the current study, one point was assigned if a respondent admitted involvement in a specific act; if respondents did not admit involvement, no points were assigned. The general crime scale was summed to obtain a composite score, which ranged from 0 to 35. Items in the general crime scale have been employed in previous tests of criminological theories using samples of adults (Burton et al. 1993, 1994, 1998). In addition, we distinguished type of criminal behavior by dividing the offenses into three subscales: violent, property, and drug. Table C.2 shows the means, standard deviations, and reliability for all dependent and independent variables used in the analysis.

Using Cronbach's (1951) alpha method, the 35-item general crime scale was reliable at .82 for women and .90 for men; the 15-item property crime subscale had a reliability level for women and men of .72 and .85, respectively; the 11-item drug subscale was .76 for women and .81 for men; and the 9-item violent crime subscale was reliable for females at .61 and .66 for males (see the appendix for individual offenses included in each subscale and accompanying frequencies separated by gender). Table C.2 shows that men admitted past involvement in an average of nine crimes: three drug offenses, four property crimes, and two violent crimes. Women engaged in an average of nine total crimes: four drug offenses, three property crimes, and two violent crimes. Although the property crime rate differed slightly for men and women, the types of drug offenses and violent crimes committed by both men and women were similar (see English 1993).[5]

Independent Variables

The items used in this study to measure social control and differential association variables were all drawn from previous theoretical tests (see Burton 1991; Burton et al. 1993, 1994, 1998; Fiftal 1993; Matsueda 1982).[6] Participants in our sample responded to each item by using a 6-point Likert scale that ranged from *strongly agree* (6) to *strongly disagree* (1). Some responses were recoded so that a high score on an item indicated the presence of differential association or social control. The reliability of each composite independent theory measure was checked by Cronbach's (1951) alpha method. Finally, factor analysis was performed on each composite measure to ensure that each of the individual measures

Exhibit c.2 Individual Dependent and Independent Variables by Gender

Variable	Number of Items	Women		Men		Sample
		Reliability	Mean (SD)	Reliability	Mean (SD)	F-Ratio
Dependent						
General crime	35	.82	8.57 (5.12) (range: 0–26)	.90	9.49 (6.85) (range: 0–31)	2.06
Violent crime	9	.61	1.64 (1.25) (range: 0–6)	.66	1.72 (1.70) (range: 0–9)	0.27
Property crime	15	.72	2.98 (2.60) (range: 0–11)	.85	4.19 (3.76) (range: 0–17)	11.99**
Drug crime	11	.76	3.96 (2.55) (range: 0–11)	.81	3.62 (2.72) (range: 0–11)	1.68
Independent						
Social control						
Marital/partner attachment	1	—	0.32 (0.47)	—	0.35 (0.48)	0.48
Parental ttachment	3	.75	15.25 (2.98)	.64	14.87 (3.02)	1.77
Peer attachment	2	.81	6.84 (2.91)	.73	7.68 (2.79)	9.58**
Involvement	2	.69	6.44 (2.89)	.56	6.09 (2.69)	1.82
Belief	2	.63	8.88 (2.41)	.51	8.11 (2.40)	11.23**
Differential association						
Individual definitions	5	.77	10.97 (4.95)	.62	11.98 (4.52)	5.30*
Others' definitions	3	.71	9.50 (3.79)	.66	10.11 (3.61)	3.11
Criminal friends	1	—	2.87 (1.66)	—	2.77 (1.85)	0.30

$*p < .05.$ $**p < .01.$

loaded on one factor. The mean, standard deviation, and reliability of each independent variable, separated by gender, can be found in Table C.2.

Social Control Theory

Hirschi's (1969) social control theory was originally formulated to rival differential association or "cultural deviance" theory as an explanation of why some juveniles conform and others engage in delinquency. More recent research has applied this perspective to adult criminality. Social control theory asserts that individuals with strong ties to family and friends (Covington 1985; Sampson and Laub 1990, 1993) will be protected from criminal involvement. In this study, we measure the adult social bond by marital attachment, attachment to parents, attachment to friends, involvement, and belief.[7]

Marital/partner attachment. Attachment to a significant other of the opposite sex by cohabiting or marriage is perceived as providing informal social control by protecting individuals from participation in criminal and other antisocial activities (Rand 1987; Sampson and Laub 1993). In our analysis, we use marital/partner attachment status as one of the adult social bond measures (0 = not married/unattached and 1 = married/attached).

Attachment to parents. We include three items to measure attachment to parents to determine the effect of longstanding connections to parents by gender: "Throughout my life, I have had a lot of respect for my mother and father" (LaGrange and White 1985; Rosenbaum 1987). The second item asks whether respondents have "gotten along" well with their parents throughout their lives. This measure is modified from previous tests of social control (Eve 1978; Simons et al. 1980). The third component states, "My family is the most important thing in my life." The level of reliability for the attachment to parents scale is .75 for women and .64 for men.

Attachment to friends. The bond to friends is an important part of conventional attachment. The items used in the questionnaire yielded a reliability level of .81 for women and .73 for men. Respondents were asked to respond to the following two items: "It is important for me to spend time with my friends," and "My friends are a very important part of my life" (Agnew 1985; Burton 1991; Canter 1982; Friedman and Rosenbaum 1988; Hindelang 1973; Johnson, Marcos, and Bahr 1987; Matsueda 1982; Paternoster and Triplett 1988; Rosenbaum 1987).

Involvement. Involvement in conventional activities is measured by how much free time individuals have (Agnew 1985; Burton 1991; Canter 1982; Johnson 1979; Rosenbaum 1987). The following two items (reliable at .69 for women and .56 for men) were borrowed from Burton's (1991) study: "Between work, family, and community activities, I don't have much free time," and "Before coming here, I had a lot of free time on my hands."

Belief. Finally, the conventional bond is measured by moral belief in the law, specifically in the police, as measured by the following statement: "I have a lot of respect for the police" (Hindelang 1973; Hirschi 1969). The second item, "It is all right to get around the law if you can get away with it," was also used by Hirschi (1969) in previous tests. The two items have a reliability level of .63 for women and .51 for men.

Differential Association Theory

According to Sutherland's (1947) theory of differential association, individuals develop internalized definitions that are favorable or nonfavorable toward violating the law. As individual exposure to procriminal values, patterns, and associates increases, the likelihood of criminal involvement also increases. As in previous studies, we use three differential association variables to measure the likelihood of criminal exposure: individual definitions toward the law, others' definitions toward the law, and number of criminal friends.

Individual definitions toward crime. The five-item scale measuring individual definitions toward crime examined an individual's degree of tolerance for criminal behavior, the moral validity of violating the law, and the level of agreement with committing criminal acts. Cronbach's (1951) alpha reliability for the scale for women is .77 and .62 for men. To measure disapproval toward violating the law, we asked for a response to the following item: "No matter how small the crime, breaking the law is a serious matter" (Akers et al. 1989; Jackson, Tittle, and Burke 1986; Short 1960). A second item, "It is morally wrong to break the law," also assessed anticriminal definitions (see Jackson et al. 1986; Matsueda 1989; Silberman 1976; Tittle et al. 1986). In contrast, to measure adults' willingness to violate the law, three items were included: "Sometimes you just don't have any choice but to break the law" (Krohn, Lanza-Kaduce, and Akers 1984; Short 1960), "If someone insulted me, I would be likely to hit or slap them," and "If breaking the law really doesn't hurt anyone, and you can make a quick buck doing it, then it's really not all that wrong" (Burton 1991).

Others' definitions toward crime. According to Sutherland (1947), criminal behavior is influenced primarily through exposure to other individuals holding definitions favorable toward violating the law. Relying on previous tests of differential association (Akers et al. 1979; Cressey 1953; Dull 1983; Griffen and Griffen 1978; Jaquith 1981; Johnson et al. 1987; Short 1960; Tittle et al. 1986), we included the following item: "Many of the people I associate with think it's okay to break the law if you can get away with it." The second item is designed to determine the type of people (criminal or noncriminal) with whom an individual associates. Thus, respondents were presented with the following item: "Most of the people I associate with would never break the law." In previous research, items similar to this have been related to delinquent involvement (Akers et al. 1989; Krohn et al. 1984; Jackson et al. 1986; Orcutt 1987). Finally, the third item assesses the extent to which individuals are "often in situations where people encourage [them] to do something illegal." This three-item scale has a reliability coefficient of .71 for women and .66 for men.

Criminal friends. Many empirical tests of differential association theory have relied on the number of criminal associates as evidence of interaction with criminal members within an individual's primary group (see, e.g., Akers et al. 1979; Dull 1983; Johnson et al. 1987; Warr and Stafford 1993; Winfree, Griffith, and Sellers 1989). In our study, we apply a measure of the actual number of criminal friends in our model by asking, "In the last 12 months, how many of your five closest friends have done something they could have gotten arrested for?"

Findings

We assessed the bivariate relationships between the eight independent variables and crime by zero-order correlations. Tables C.3 and C.4 show that for the sample as a whole, all three of the differential association variables (individual definitions, others' definitions, and number of criminal friends) were significantly and directly correlated with property, violent, and drug offenses.[8] Similarly, these tables reveal that the social control variables of attachment to parents, involvement in conventional activities, and belief in the law were significantly and inversely correlated with criminal behavior. On the other hand, marriage reduced involvement only in property crime, and attachment to peers was positively correlated with all types of crime.[9]

General Criminal Behavior and Gender

Following the bivariate analysis, we used ordinary least squares (OLS) regression to examine the effects of independent variables on dependent variables. The first dependent variable (general crime) was regressed on three control variables (age, race, and gender), five social control variables, and three differential association variables.[10] Race was dummy coded (White vs. non-White), while age was a continuous variable. Regression coefficients were determined with all variables entered simultaneously into the equation. Table C.5 shows the standardized and unstandardized regression coefficients for men and women when both theories were regressed against each other. Gender groups were analyzed both independently and together.

Social control. Table C.5 shows that three out of five social control variables were significantly related to the overall measure of criminal behavior for the sample. Attachment to peers was significantly and positively related to criminal behavior. Attachment to parents and involvement in conventional activities were significantly and inversely related to involvement in criminal behavior. Those who got along well with their parents and considered them an important part of their lives were less likely to engage in criminal behavior. Furthermore, respondents who were immersed in time-consuming activities (i.e., work, family, and community activities) were also less likely to commit crimes.

We conducted a difference of slopes test on the significant unstandardized regression coefficients and their corresponding standard errors to determine if any significant differences existed between men and women. When conducting a hypothesis test of two samples of this nature, we relied on the formula suggested by Paternoster et al. (1998). We found that attachment to parents ($z = -2.214$) was a significantly stronger predictor of female ($b = -.533$; $SE = .129$) as opposed to male ($b = -.208$; $SE = .070$) crime participation. On the other hand, there were no significant differences between women and men and the level of involvement as a predictor of criminal participation. The effect, then, of involvement on participation in crime is similar for men and women.

One of the strongest predictors for a woman's involvement in crime was whether she lived with a mate or was married. The significance of this relationship was not in the predicted direction of social control theory, which would hypothesize that family relationships, including marriage, insulate against criminal involvement. On the other hand, marital attachment was not significant for predicting men's criminal behavior.

One factor that was significantly related to men's participation in crime was peer attachment. Young men who were attached to their friends were more likely to engage in criminal behavior—a relationship in the direction opposite to that predicted by social control theory. Other studies have interpreted peer attachment and increased criminal involvement as indirect support for differential association theory, depending on whether the friends were delinquent (Conger 1976).[11]

Exhibit c.3 Zero-Order Correlations of Theoretical Variables and Crime Scales (men)

	General Crime	Violent Crime	Property Crime	Drug Crime	Peer Attachment	Parental Attachment	Marital/ Partner Attachment	Involvement	Individual Belief	Other Definitions	Criminal Definitions	Friends
General crime	1.00											
Violent crime	.75**	1.00										
Property crime	.91**	.60**	1.00									
Drug crime	.80**	.44**	.53**	1.00								
Peer attachment	.15**	.09**	.14**	.13**	1.00							
Parent attachment	-.23**	-.16**	-.22**	-.18**	-.05	1.00						
Marital/ partner attachment	-.05	-.01	-.10**	-.00	-.07*	.04	1.00					
Involvement	-.19**	-.12**	-.20**	-.14**	-.10**	-.01	.10**	1.00				
Belief	-.25**	-.24**	-.20**	-.18**	-.02	.21**	-.02	.18**	1.00			
Individual definitions	.27**	.29**	.24**	.18**	.04	-.22**	-.02	-.17**	-.54**	1.00		
Others' definitions	.37**	.32**	.34**	.24**	.02	-.18**	-.07*	-.28**	-.29**	.28**	1.00	
Criminal friends	.39**	.30**	.37**	.29**	.02	-.12**	-.09**	-.22**	-.27**	.27**	.42**	1.00

*$p < .05$. **$p < .01$.

Exhibit c.4 Zero-Order Correlations of Theoretical Variables and Crime Scales (women)

	General Crime	Violent Crime	Property Crime	Drug Crime	Peer Attachment	Parental Attachment	Marital/ Partner Attachment	Involvement	Individual Belief	Other Definitions	Criminal Definitions	Friends
General crime	1.00											
Violent crime	.61**	1.00										
Property crime	.86**	.41**	1.00									
Drug crime	.83**	.32**	.50**	1.00								
Peer attachment	.32**	.13	.31**	.27**	1.00							
Parent attachment	−.35**	−.24**	−.33**	−.25**	−.12	1.00						
Marital/ partner attachment	−.30**	−.09	−.29**	−.26**	−.20*	.08	1.00					
Involvement	−.26**	−.38**	−.13	−.19*	−.10	−.12	−.07	1.00				
Belief	−.22*	−.17	−.19*	−.16	−.13	.27**	.10	.09	1.00			
Individual definitions	.28**	.23*	.21*	.24**	.19*	−.20*	−.01	−.16	−.50**	1.00		
Others' definitions	.47**	.35**	.35**	.42**	.17	−.24**	−.00	−.32**	−.18*	.33**	1.00	
Criminal friends	.31**	.22**	.28**	.23**	.03	−.10	−.00	−.13	−.12	.14	.28**	1.00

* $p < .05$. ** $p < .01$.

Exhibit c.5	Effects of Social Control and Differential Association Variables on General Crime: Standardized Betas (unstandardized B coefficients) Reported					
Variable Name	Women (n = 122)		Men (n = 1,031)		Women and Men (N = 1,153)	
Social control						
Marital/partner attachment						
(0 = not attached)	.21	(2.27)**	.01	(.08)	.02	(.33)
Parental attachment	−.31	(−.53)**	−.09	(−.21)**	−.12	(−.32)**
Peer attachment	.07	(.12)	.06	(.16)*	.07	(.16)*
Involvement	−.24	(−.43)**	−.06	(−.16)*	−.07	(−.18)*
Belief	.03	(.05)	−.06	(−.17)	−.05	(−.15)
Differential association						
Individual definitions	.11	(.11)	.12	(.19)**	.12	(.17)**
Others' definitions	.18	(.31)*	.16	(.31)**	.16	(.30)**
Criminal friends	.16	(.50)*	.26	(.98)**	.26	(.94)**
Control variables						
Age	−.08	(−.15)	.03	(.08)	.01	(.04)
Gender (0 = male)	—	—	—	—	−.05	(−.93)
Race (0 = non-White)	.22	(2.23)**	.19	(2.75)**	.19	(2.64)**
R^2		.51		.29		.30

*$p < .05$. **$p < .01$.

Differential association. In Table C.5, others' definitions and criminal friends significantly predicted both male and female involvement in crime. A difference of slopes test on criminal friends indicated there were no significant differences between women and men; the effect of criminal friends on participation in crime is similar for men and women.

Individual definitions, although in the expected direction for women, were significant only for men. Furthermore, for men, differential association variables had stronger effects than social control theory variables in predicting their participation in crime. For women, there was some tendency for the social control variables to have stronger effects. The overall explanatory power for both theories in the model for women was $R^2 = .51$ and for men was .29.

Control variables. Race/ethnicity significantly predicted criminal involvement for women and men. Specifically, Anglo men and women were more likely to have been involved in crime than non-White individuals. Age was not a significant predictor of overall rates of criminal behavior. To more precisely measure the nature of gender differences and similarities for overall crime, a separate *t*-test for independent samples was conducted using unstandardized partial regression coefficients while using gender as the grouping variable. Results indicated that the mean for the men (9.88) was significantly higher than for women (8.56) for the general crime scale.

Type of Criminal Behavior and Gender

Table C.6 shows the contribution of social control and differential association theories to individually and simultaneously explain young men's and women's involvement in drug, property, and violent crimes.

Social control. A consistent and significant predictor of all three crime types for women was parental attachment.

Exhibit c.6 — Effects of Social Control and Differential Association Variables on Drug, Property, and Violent Crime: Standardized Betas (and unstandardized coefficients) Reported

Variable Name	Drug Crime			Property Crime			Violent Crime		
	Women	Men	Sample	Women	Men	Sample	Women	Men	Sample
Social control									
Marital/partner									
attachment	.16 (.89)*	.04 (.24)	.06 (.33)*	.21 (1.17)**	−.04 (−.32)	−.02 (−.18)	.08 (.21)	.02 (.07)	.02 (.08)
Parental attachment	−.18 (−.15)*	−.06 (−.05)	−.06 (−.07)*	−.29 (−.26)**	−.10 (−.12)**	−.12 (−.18)**	−.29 (−.12)**	−.06 (−.04)**	−.10 (−.07)**
Peer attachment	−.02 (−.02)	.06 (.06)	.06 (.06)*	.15 (.14)	.06 (.08)*	.07 (.09)*	.01 (.00)	.06 (.04)	.05 (.03)
Involvement	−.22 (−.20)**	−.07 (−.07)*	−.09 (−.08)**	−.10 (−.09)	−.07 (−.10)*	−.07 (−.09)*	−.34 (−.15)**	.01 (.01)	−.02 (−.01)
Belief	.01 (.01)	−.08 (−.09)*	−.07 (−.08)*	.02 (.02)	−.02 (−.03)	−.02 (−.03)	.01 (.01)	−.05 (−.04)	−.04 (−.03)
Differential association									
Individual definitions	.11 (.06)	.08 (.05)*	.09 (.05)*	.06 (.03)	.10 (.08)**	.09 (.08)**	.09 (.02)	.15 (.06)**	.14 (.05)**
Others' definitions	.15 (.18)*	.08 (.06)*	.10 (.08)**	.14 (.21)*	.16 (.16)**	.15 (.15)**	.10 (.03)	.17 (.08)**	.16 (.07)**
Criminal friends	.15 (.22)*	.23 (.34)**	.22 (.33)**	.17 (.23)*	.24 (.50)**	.24 (.48)**	.05 (.04)	.18 (.17)**	.17 (.16)**
Control variables									
Age	.14 (.14)*	.16 (.20)**	.16 (.19)**	−.18 (−.18)*	−.06 (−.11)*	−.08 (−.13)**	−.23 (−.11)**	−.03 (−.02)	−.04 (−.03)
Gender (0 = male)	—	—	.01 (.06)	—	—	−.09 (−1.04)**	—	—	−.01 (.07)
Race (0 = non-White)	.44 (2.25)**	.26 (1.51)**	.28 (1.62)**	.03 (.14)	.13 (1.07)**	.12 (.96)**	−.07 (−.17)	.02 (.08)	−.00 (−.00)
R^2	.49	.23	.25	.40	.25	.26	.36	.18	.19

$*p < .05.$ $**p < .01.$

Parental attachment was also significant in the direction predicted by social control theory for men's property and violent crime. Attachment to parents served as an effective insulator for men and women against criminal involvement, a finding consistent in delinquency studies (Burton et al. 1995). A difference of slopes test indicated that the effect of parental attachment ($z = -2.136$) was a significantly stronger predictor for women ($b = -.122$; $SE = .036$) than for men ($b = -.036$; $SE = .018$) for violent crime participation. The effect of parental attachment on property crime ($z = 1.62$) is similar for males and females since the difference was found to be not statistically significant.

Lack of involvement in conventional activities significantly predicted men's and women's participation in drug crime, as well as women's violent crime and men's property crime. Difference of slopes tests verified that lack of involvement in activities has similar effects for men's and women's involvement in drug crime and overall crime participation.

Marital attachment significantly predicted women's involvement in drug and property crimes but not in the direction predicted by social control theory. In other words, women who were married or living with a mate or boyfriend were more likely to be involved in drugs and/or property offenses. Marital attachment for men, however, did not insulate against or foster crime.

Differential association. For men, all three measures of differential association theory were significantly and positively related to all three types of crime. Thus, when criminal behavior was separated by type, differential association theory more consistently explained men's participation in drug, property, and violent criminal behaviors than did social control theory. For women, though, both differential association and social control theory were related to explaining female drug and property offenses, while social control variables were stronger predictors of women's participation in violent crime. Difference of slopes tests were conducted to detect significant effects on others' definitions and criminal friends between men and women. None of the differences was statistically significant for participation in property, drug, or overall crime. In other words, the effects of criminal friends and others' definitions on criminal participation were similar for men and women.

Control variables. Of the three control variables, age and race/ethnicity were the most consistent and strongest predictors of differences in rates of offending for men and women. As the age of male and female adults increased, involvement in drug crimes also significantly increased, while male and female property and female violent crimes significantly decreased. Anglo men and women were more likely to have been involved in drug crime than non-White men and women. Also, Anglo men were more likely than were African American and Hispanic men to have been involved in property crime.

The only type of crime that varied by gender was property offenses. Men were more likely than women to have committed crimes against property. For independent samples, *t*-tests were conducted for each of the three subscales, using unstandardized partial regression coefficients. Gender was used in each *t*-test as the grouping variable to more precisely measure the nature of gender differences and similarities for drug, property, and violent offenses. Results confirmed that the mean for the men (4.37) was significantly higher than for women (2.98) for the property crime subscale. However, for drug offenses, there was no difference between men (3.75) and women (3.94). The same held true for the violent crime subscale, in which men (1.77) were found to have a mean similar to that of women (1.64).

🔲 Discussion

If psychology is sometimes referred to as the "science of college sophomores," then criminology might earn the label of the "science of high school sophomores"; while psychologists run experiments on their students, criminologists rely, over and over again, on samples of adolescents in school. To be sure, such self-report research is important and has considerably advanced our understanding of crime causation. Nonetheless, the skewness in focusing on adolescents and on minor delinquencies means that the applicability of criminological theory to serious and adult offending for men and women has been examined too infrequently.

A strategy employed episodically to rectify this omission has been to test theories on samples of convicted offenders, who have higher base rates of serious criminality (see, e.g., Covington 1985; Horney et al. 1995; Longshore et al. 1996; Sampson and Laub 1993). Building on this research, we have attempted to assess the generality of social control and differential association theories and to explain self-report crime across gender among first-time convicted felons serving a three-month sentence in a shock probation program, as an alternative to jail or prison incarceration. Several salient results were found.

First, both social control theory and differential association theory appear to have general effects. For the sample as a whole, the support for differential association is especially strong and consistent: The three differential association variables are significantly related to the general crime scale and to the drug, property, and violent crime subscales. Note that many studies that assess differential association use only the single measure of "number of delinquent peers." In a cross-sectional study, the peer-delinquency relationship is subject to the claim of spuriousness—that it is merely a case of "birds of a feather flocking together" (see Hirschi 1969; Gottfredson and Hirschi 1990). In our analysis, however, it is noteworthy that the attitudinal measures of others' definitions and one's own individual definitions also are related to all the crime scales for the sample. Some additional support for differential association theory can be drawn from the positive relationships of peer attachment to all the crime measures for the sample. This result is contrary to Hirschi's (1969) prediction. Furthermore, to the extent that the members of the sample are likely to have delinquent friends, then such attachment might be viewed as an indicator of differential association.

The findings for the social control measures are less impressive but nonetheless offer support for the perspective. Parental attachment had a consistent negative relationship to all of the crime measures for the sample. It appears, therefore, that bonds to parents have continuing effects on serious felons into early adulthood (Sampson and Laub 1993). Furthermore, with the exception of violent crime, involvement in conventional activities was negatively and significantly associated with the crime measures. Previous research on social control theory exploring the relationship between involvement and criminality has revealed mixed findings. While some studies have reported that involvement has few effects on offending (see, e.g., Hirschi 1969), others have found that involvement in conventional activities has a significant and inverse relationship both to minor forms of deviance (Agnew 1985; Friedman and Rosenbaum 1988; Rosenbaum 1987) and to adult offending behavior (Fiftal 1993; Lasley 1988).

Second, the analyses suggest that the "traditional" criminological perspectives can account for offending across the genders. This is not to say, however, that gender-specific theories could not expand our understanding not only of female crime but also of male criminal participation (see, e.g., Chesney-Lind 1989; Hagan 1989; Messerschmidt 1993). Still, the data reveal that differential association and social control variables—albeit

with some variation—have similar effects across male and female felons. In fact, for every crime measure, the amount of explained variation is higher for the female sample than it is for the male sample. Furthermore, our results are consistent with a recent meta-analysis of predictors of criminal behavior, which reports that antisocial attitudes/associates and parental/family factors have similar effects for males and females (Andrews and Bonta 1994:68).

Some differences do emerge, however, when analyzing the effects of theoretical variables by gender. We should caution that making interpretations is difficult because the large sample size for the male offenders (1,031 men vs. 122 women) means that the analyses of the males have more power to detect statistically significant relationships. With this caveat stated, it appears that the differential association variables have consistent effects not only across crime types but also across male and female offenders. Only with individual definitions are any gender differences apparent; even here, the relationships, though not significant for women, are in the same direction.

In contrast, the effects of social control variables were stronger for the women than for the men in our sample. We found that the effects of parental attachment significantly and inversely affected males' offending, but the impact of parental attachment on females was significantly stronger for participation in violent offenses. This difference between men and women was not found for property crime, and parental attachment was not significant for male drug crime participation. The effect of a lack of parental attachment as a significant predictor of female violent crime is especially noteworthy for furthering our understanding of female offending.

Covington's (1985) analysis revealed that measures of social control theory were stronger predictors of adult women's criminal involvement. She suggests that as adolescents, females generally are exposed to more parental supervision than male adolescents. Thus, females may be more negatively influenced when familial relations are problematic or when parental supervision is reduced or nonexistent. Covington raises the additional possibility that these findings indicate differential perception of female and male adolescent offending by the juvenile justice system. While male adolescent offending may stem from a variety of causes, "many of the early female [juvenile] arrests may have been based on their detached and unsupervised status as juveniles rather than serious criminality" (Covington 1985:350).

We should note that with the exception of violent crime, being married or attached to a male partner was positively and significantly related to criminal involvement for women. For males, female partner attachment had no effects on any crime scale. The result for males is consistent with Sampson and Laub (1993), who found that marriage only had effects on their sample of former delinquents when marital quality is taken into account (see also Laub, Nagin, and Sampson 1998). Unfortunately, we do not have detailed information on the nature of the marital relationship to disentangle why marriage or attachment fosters criminality.

From a differential association perspective, it may be that the female felons in the sample are involved with men who reinforce their criminality. Research on battered women offenders found that being involved in intimate violent relationships was a main pathway to increasing the risk of offending (Richie 1996). Another possibility is that women from abusive, dysfunctional homes—those who are at a high risk for offending (see, e.g., Chesney-Lind 1989)—attempt to escape family victimization through early marriages and attachments (Miller 1986). These attachments, in turn, influenced the roles these women played in criminal behavior in relation to men (see Alarid et al. 1996). Future research should take into account the quality of the marital relationship, as well as the role that battering and intimate abuse have on subsequent involvement with the criminal justice system.

Another noteworthy finding is that for both males and females, being Caucasian was associated with higher rates of self-reported crime for every scale with the exception of violent offending. These differences could reflect racial differences in criminal justice processing: Compared to minorities, Whites had to have more involvement in self-reported crime before being arrested and incarcerated.

An added finding that may have resulted from decisions made during prosecutorial and judicial case processing was the offending patterns of men and women. While men reported having committed more overall crime than women, particularly more property offenses, women and men did not differ significantly in the type and number of drug and violent crimes. These similarities may mean that judges who sentenced young, first-time felony offenders to shock incarceration as a prison alternative were impartial to gender.

In closing, the analyses reported here lend continuing support to the traditional theories of social control and, especially, differential association/social learning. Importantly, the data support the claim that these are "general" theories, explaining variations in self-report criminality among felony offenders and across men and women. As Cole (1975) demonstrates, however, the fate of crime and deviance theories does not always or usually hinge on their empirical vitality but on whether newer "paradigms" offer fresh research opportunities. New theories, of course, should be welcomed and their explanatory power assessed. But in doing so, we would caution that the value of "older" perspectives should be remembered and, as in our research, applied to underresearched topics.

| Appendix | Prevalence of Self-Reported Criminal Behavior: "Have You Ever . . . ?" |

	Women	Men	n (%)	n (%)
Property crime subscale (15 items)				
1. Avoided paying at restaurants, the movie theater, etc.?	29	(23.8)	346	(33.7)*
2. Knowingly bought, held, sold stolen property?	50	(41)	531	(51.8)*
3. Taken someone else's vehicle without their permission?	33	(27)	379	(36.9)*
4. Taken anything ($5 or less) from your job?	11	(9)	152	(14.8)
5. Taken anything (between $5 and $50) from your job?	11	(9)	118	(11.5)
6. Taken anything (over $50) from your job?	3	(2.5)	102	(10.0)**
7. Taken anything ($5 or less) from someone (other than work)?	46	(37.7)	317	(31.0)
8. Taken anything (between $5 and $50) from someone (other than work)?	25	(20.5)	306	(30.0)*
9. Taken anything (over $50) from someone else (other than work)?	31	(25.4)	346	(33.7)
10. Damaged/destroyed property belonging to relative/family of origin?	15	(12.3)	166	(16.2)

	Women	Men	n (%)	n (%)
11. Purposely damaged/destroyed property belonging to an employer?	2	(1.6)	59	(5.7)*
12. Purposely damaged/destroyed property belonging to spouse/partner/friend (someone other than family of origin or an employer)?	22	(18.0)	327	(31.9)**
13. Broken into a building/vehicle?	25	(20.5)	423	(41.2)**
14. Stolen or attempted to steal a motor vehicle?	19	(15.6)	314	(30.6)**
15. Thrown objects at cars/property?	41	(33.6)	419	(40.9)
Drug crime subscale (11 items)				
1. Drank alcoholic beverages before age 21?	92	(75.4)	788	(76.8)
2. Drove a car while drunk?	51	(41.8)	471	(46.0)
3. Bought/provided beer/liquor for someone under 21?	51	(41.8)*	340	(33.2)
4. Had marijuana/hashish?	86	(70.5)**	572	(55.8)
5. Used hallucinogens/LSD?	26	(21.3)	226	(22.0)
6. Had amphetamines?	17	(13.9)	129	(12.6)
7. Had barbiturates?	14	(11.5)	91	(8.9)
8. Had heroin?	6	(4.9)	32	(3.1)
9. Had cocaine?	60	(49.2)**	278	(27.1)
10. Sold marijuana?	34	(27.9)	359	(35.2)
11. Sold hard drugs (cocaine, crack, heroin)?	46	(37.7)	435	(42.5)
Violent crime subscale (9 items)				
1. Been involved in a gang fight?	25	(20.5)	232	(22.6)
2. Used physical force to get money from a relative/family of origin?	4	(3.3)	48	(4.7)
3. Used physical force to get money from someone at work?	1	(0.8)	35	(3.4)
4. Used physical force to get money from someone, a family member, or someone at work?	12	(9.8)	151	(14.7)
5. Hit or threatened to hit a relative/member of family of origin?	42	(34.4)	337	(32.9)
6. Hit or threatened to hit someone at work?	5	(4.1)	144	(14.0)**
7. Hit or threatened to hit friend/partner/spouse?	80	(65.6)**	528	(51.7)
8. Had or tried to have sex with someone against their will?	1	(0.8)	31	(3.0)
9. Attacked someone with the idea of seriously hurting/killing them?	30	(24.6)	264	(25.7)

Note: Women, $n = 122$; men, $n = 1,031$.

*$p < .05$. **$p < .01$.

回 NOTES

1. There have been several adult tests of social control and differential association measures assessed against deterrence, low self-control, social learning, strain, or subcultural theory measures (see, e.g., Burton et al. 1994; Ginsberg and Greenley 1978; Makkai and Braithwaite 1991; Tittle 1980).

2. Covington's (1985) tests of social control and differential association theories differed from the variables presented in this study. For example, involvement was not included as a social control variable, and individual definitions toward crime were not included as a differential association variable.

3. Strain theory, a fundamental perspective that also offers explanations on criminal behavior, was not included in the final analysis. Although Agnew's (1985) general strain theory has received some empirical support, Merton's social strain theory has received less support in previous studies. We originally included social strain variables that tested relative deprivation and blocked opportunities for both men and women in the data set. The variables measuring blocked opportunities were not reliable (.44) and were not used in the analysis. The variables measuring relative deprivation (reliable at .74) were regressed separately with all dependent crime variables. Relative deprivation was not significant for women for any type of crime and was significant only for male property crime but not for male drug or violent offenses. When relative deprivation was regressed against social control theory and/or differential association theory, relative deprivation had no effect for any type of crime.

4. Incidence data (how many times in the past year) were collected on all criminal behaviors but were not used due to a low reliability of the incidence subscales. The 35-item general crime incidence scale was, however, reliable at .61.

5. We are not suggesting that women are becoming more violent in their criminal involvement, especially as they relate to the women's self-reported involvement of violent crime, particularly the three "hit or threatened to hit" measures in the violent crime subscale (see appendix). The similarities in self-reported crime participation by women and men in our study can be accounted for in part by English (1993:373), who found that incarcerated adult women and men prisoners had similar participation rates for assault, robbery, motor vehicle theft, fraud, and dealing drugs. Our data show, however, that women and men participate in a wide variety of criminal behaviors, from less serious to more serious, which may or may not be related to their conviction offense.

6. A potential weakness of our measures is the varying time frame of our independent and dependent variables (e.g., the time frame for "peer attachment" and "marital attachment" is current, the time frame for "criminal friends" is in the past year, while the time frame for the dependent measure of prevalence is lifetime). We are largely assuming that our measures of our independent variables are relatively stable over time. Furthermore, we believe that our analysis has merit despite these issues. Future research would benefit from longitudinal analysis to determine the stability of theoretical variables over time.

7. Commitment, an element of Hirschi's (1969) social bond, was not used in the analysis due to its low reliability.

8. Men and women were also analyzed separately using correlations between differential association variables with the dependent variables. Our analyses revealed that a significant correlation existed between all variables. For the sample as a whole, the three differential association measures are more highly correlated with each other than are the five measures of social control. This may increase the likelihood of finding greater consistency with differential association measures.

9. When bivariate correlations were analyzed separately by gender, a mixed portrayal emerged for social control variables. Attachment to parents for both men and women was significantly and inversely related to all types of crime. For men, attachment to friends, involvement, and belief were significantly related to all crime types, with the exception of marital attachment, which was significant only for property crime. For women, attachment to friends and marital attachment were related to drug and property crimes but not violent crime. On the other hand, involvement was significantly related to women's drug and violent crimes but not women's property offenses. Finally, belief was significantly related to women's property crime and violent crime but was not significantly related to women's drug crime.

10. We separately analyzed the control variables with each of the theories before regressing them together as shown in Table C.5. The results of the separate regressions show a significant relationship between age, race, and self-reported offending behavior. Age was inversely related to crime—that is, as age increased, less crime was committed. Men and women of color reported they committed significantly less crime than did Caucasian men and women. When social control theory was introduced into the equation with the three control variables, all social control variables, except for marital attachment, were significantly related to criminal offending. All social control variables were significant in the predicted direction, except for attachment to friends. When social control variables were removed and differential association variables were regressed with the three control variables, all three differential association variables were significantly and directly related to crime in the predicted direction.

11. To detect the presence of an interaction between peer attachment and criminal friends, we introduced a multiplicative term into each regression equation. A hierarchical F-test indicated that an interaction effect was not present for women, but an interaction existed for men for drug, property, and general crime scales (Jaccard, Turrisi, and Wan 1990). The difference between the R^2 values in the main effect and interactive models indicated that the interaction contributed less than 1 percent to each model (.63 percent for drug, .89 percent for general crime, and .90 percent for property offenses).

▣ References

Adler, Freda. 1975. *Sisters in Crime: The Rise of the New Female Offender.* New York: McGraw-Hill.

Agnew, Robert. 1985. "Social Control Theory and Delinquency: A Longitudinal Test." *Criminology* 23:47–61.

Akers, Ronald L. 1996. "Is Differential Association/Social Learning Cultural Deviance Theory?" *Criminology* 34:229–47.

———. 1998. *Social Learning and Social Structure: A General Theory of Crime and Deviance.* Boston: Northeastern University Press.

Akers, Ronald L., Marvin Krohn, Lonn Lanza-Kaduce, and Marcia Radosevich. 1979. "Social Learning and Deviant Behavior: A Specific Test of a General Theory." *American Sociological Review* 44:636–55.

Akers, Ronald L., and Anthony LaGreca. 1988. "Alcohol, Contact with the Legal System, and Illegal Behavior among the Elderly." In *Older Offenders,* edited by Belinda Mccarthy and Robert Langworthy. New York: Praeger.

———. 1991. "Alcohol Use among the Elderly: Social Learning, Community Context, and Life Events." In *Society, Culture, and Drinking Patterns Re-Examined,* edited by David J. Pittman and Helene Raskin White. New Brunswick, NJ: Rutgers Center of Alcohol Studies.

Akers, Ronald L., Anthony LaGreca, John Cochran, and Christine Sellers. 1989. "Social Learning Theory and Alcohol Behavior among the Elderly." *Sociological Quarterly* 30:625–38.

Alarid, Leanne Fiftal, Velmer S. Burton, James W. Marquart, Francis T. Cullen, and Steven J. Cuvelier. 1996. "Women's Roles in Serious Offenses: A Study of Adult Felons." *Justice Quarterly* 13:431–54.

Andrews, D. A., and James Bonta. 1994. *The Psychology of Criminal Conduct.* Cincinnati, OH: Anderson.

Benda, Brent B. 1994. "Testing Competing Theoretical Concepts: Adolescent Alcohol Consumption." *Deviant Behavior* 15:375–96.

Boeringer, Scot, Constance L. Shehan, and Ronald L. Akers. 1991. "Social Contexts and Social Learning in Sexual Coercion and Aggression: Assessing the Contribution of Fraternity Membership." *Family Relations* 40:558–64.

Burton, Velmer S. 1991. "Explaining Adult Criminality: Testing Strain, Differential Association, and Control Theories." Ph.D. dissertation, University of Cincinnati.

Burton, Velmer S., Francis T. Cullen, T. David Evans, Leanne Fiftal Alarid, and R. Gregory Dunaway. 1998. "Gender, Self-Control, and Crime." *Journal of Research in Crime and Delinquency* 35:123–47.

Burton, Velmer S., Francis T. Cullen, T. David Evans, and R. Gregory Dunaway. 1994. "Reconsidering Strain Theory: Operationalization, Rival Theories, and Adult Criminality." *Journal of Quantitative Criminology* 10:213–40.

Burton, Velmer S., Francis T. Cullen, T. David Evans, R. Gregory Dunaway, Sesha R. Kethineni, and Gary L. Payne. 1995. "The Impact of Parental Controls on Delinquency." *Journal of Criminal Justice* 23:111–26.

Burton, Velmer S., James W. Marquart, Steven J. Cuvelier, Robert J. Hunter, and Leanne Fiftal. 1993. "The Harris County CRIPP Program: An Outline for Evaluation, Part 1." *Texas Probation* 8:1–8.

Canter, Rachelle J. 1982. "Family Correlates of Male and Female Delinquency." *Criminology* 20:149–67.

Caspi, Avshalom, Terrie E. Moffitt, Phil A. Silva, Magda Stouthamer-Loeber, Robert F. Krueger, and Pamela S. Schmutte. 1994. "Are Some People Crime Prone? Replications of the Personality-Crime Relationship across Countries, Genders, Races, and Methods." *Criminology* 32:163–95.

Chesney-Lind, Meda. 1989. "Girls' Crime and Woman's Place: Toward a Feminist Model of Female Delinquency." *Crime and Delinquency* 35:5–29.

Chesney-Lind, Meda, and Randall G. Shelden. 1992. Girls, *Delinquency, and Juvenile Justice*. Pacific Grove, CA: Brooks/Cole.

Cole, Stephen. 1975. "The Growth of Scientific Knowledge: Theories of Deviance as a Case Study." In *The Idea of Social Structure: Papers in Honor of Robert K. Merton*, edited by Lewis A. Coser. New York: Harcourt Brace.

Conger, Rand. 1976. "Social Control and Social Learning Models of Delinquency: A Synthesis." *Criminology* 14:17–40.

Costello, Barbara. 1997. "On the Logical Adequacy of Cultural Deviance Theories." *Theoretical* Criminology 1:403–28.

Covington, Jeanette. 1985. "Gender Differences in Criminality among Heroin Users." *Journal of Research in Crime and* Delinquency 22:329–53.

Cressey, Donald. 1953. *Other* People's *Money*. Glencoe, IL: Free Press.

Cronbach, Lee J. 1951. "Coefficient Alpha and the Internal Structure of Tests." *Psychometrika* 16:297–334.

Daly, Kathleen, and Meda Chesney-Lind. 1988. "Feminism and Criminology." *Justice Quarterly* 5:497–538.

Dull, R. Thomas. 1983. "Friend's Use and Adult Drug and Drinking Behavior: A Further Test of Differential Association Theory." *Journal of Criminal Law and Criminology* 74:1608–19.

Elliott, Delbert S., and Suzanne S. Ageton. 1980. "Reconciling Race and Class Differences in Self-Reported and Official Estimates of Delinquency." *American Sociological Review* 45:95–110.

English, Kim. 1993. "Self Reported Crime Rates of Women Prisoners." *Journal of Quantitative Criminology* 9:357–82.

Eve, Raymond. 1978. "A Study of the Efficacy of Interactions of Several Theories for Explaining Rebelliousness among High School Students." *Journal of Criminal Law and Criminology* 69:115–25.

Fiftal, Leanne E. 1993. "Assessing Adult Female Criminality: Testing Differential Association and Social Control Theories." Master's thesis, Sam Houston State University.

Friedman, Jennifer, and Dennis P. Rosenbaum. 1988. "Social Control Theory: The Salience of Components of Age, Gender, and Type of Crime." *Journal of Quantitative Criminology* 4:363–81.

Ginsberg, Irving J., and James R. Greenley. 1978. "Competing Theories of Marijuana Use: A Longitudinal Study." *Journal of Health and Social Behavior* 19:22–34.

Gottfredson, Michael R., and Travis Hirschi. 1990. *A General Theory of Crime*. Stanford, CA: Stanford University Press.

Griffin, Brenda S., and Charles T. Griffin. 1978. "Marijuana Use among Students and Peers." *Drug Forum* 7:155–65.

Hagan, John. 1989. *Structural Criminology*. New Brunswick, NJ: Rutgers University Press.

Heidensohn, Frances M. 1985. *Women and Crime*. New York: Macmillan.

Hindelang, Michael J. 1973. "Causes of Delinquency: A Partial Replication and Extension." *Social Problems* 20:471–87.

Hindelang, Michael J., Travis Hirschi, and Joseph G. Weis. 1981. *Measuring Delinquency*. Beverly Hills, CA: Sage.

Hirschi, Travis. 1969. *Causes of Delinquency*. Berkeley: University of California Press.

———. 1996. "Theory without Ideas: Reply to Akers." *Criminology* 34:249–56.

Horney, Julie, and Ineke Haen Marshall. 1992. "Risk Perceptions among Serious Offenders: The Role of Crime and Punishment." *Criminology* 30:575–94.

Horney, Julie, D. Wayne Osgood, and Ineke Haen Marshall. 1995. "Criminal Careers in the Short-Term: Intra-Individual Variability in Crime and Its Relation to Local Life Circumstances." *American Sociological Review* 60:655–73.

Immarigeon, Russ, and Meda Chesney-Lind. 1993. "Women's Prisons: Overcrowded and Overused." In *It's a Crime: Women and Justice*, edited by Roslyn Muraskin and Ted Alleman. Englewood Cliffs, NJ: Regents/Prentice Hall.

Jaccard, James, Robert Turrisi, and Choi K. Wan. 1990. *Interaction Effects in Multiple Regression*. Newbury Park, CA: Sage.

Jackson, Elton F., Charles R. Tittle, and Mary Jean Burke. 1986. "Offense-Specific Models of the Differential Association Process." *Social Problems* 33:335–56.

Jaquith, Susan M. 1981. "Adolescent Marijuana and Alcohol Use: An Empirical Test of Differential Association Theory." *Criminology* 19:271–80.

Johnson, Richard. 1979. *Juvenile Delinquency and* Its *Origins: An Integrated Theoretical Approach*. New York: Cambridge University Press.

Johnson, Richard E., Anastasios C. Marcos, and Stephen J. Bahr. 1987. "The Role of Peers in the Complex Etiology of Adolescent Drug Use." *Criminology* 25:323–40.

Kandel, Denise, and Mark Davies. 1991. "Friendship Networks, Intimacy, and Illicit Drug Use in Young Adulthood: A Comparison of Two Competing Theories." *Criminology* 29:441–69.

Kornhauser, Ruth. 1978. *Social Sources of* Delinquency. Chicago: University of Chicago Press.

Krohn, Marvin. 1995. "Control and Deterrence Theories of Criminality." In *Criminology: A Contemporary Handbook*, 2nd ed., edited by Joseph F. Sheley. Belmont, CA: Wadsworth.

Krohn, Marvin, Lonn Lanza-Kaduce, and Ronald Akers. 1984. "Community Context and Theories of Deviant Behavior: An Examination of Social Learning and Social Bonding Theories." *The Sociological Quarterly* 25:353–71.

LaGrange, Randy L., and Helene Raskin White. 1985. "Age Differences in Delinquency: A Test of Theory." *Criminology* 23:19–45.

Lasley, James R. 1988. "Toward a Control Theory of White-Collar Offending." *Journal of Quantitative Criminology* 4:347–62.

Laub, John H., Daniel S. Nagin, and Robert J. Sampson. 1998. "Trajectories of Change in Criminal Offending: Good Marriages and the Desistance Process." *American Sociological Review* 63:225–38.

Leonard, Eileen B. 1982. *Women, Crime, and Society: A Critique of Theoretical Criminology.* New York: Longman.

Longshore, Douglas, Susan Turner, and Judith A. Stein. 1996. "Self-Control in a Criminal Sample: An Examination of Construct Validity." *Criminology* 34:209–28.

Macdonald, Patrick T. 1989. "Competing Theoretical Explanations of Cocaine Use: Differential Association Versus Control Theory." *Journal of Contemporary Criminal Justice* 5:73–88.

MacKenzie, Doris Layton, and Robert Brame. 1994. "Shock Incarceration and Positive Adjustment during Community Supervision: A Multi-Site Evaluation." Presented at the annual meeting of the Academy of Criminal Justice Sciences, June, Chicago.

Makkai, Toni, and John Braithwaite. 1991. "Criminological Theories and Regulatory Compliance." *Criminology* 29:191–220.

Matsueda, Ross L. 1982. "Testing Control Theory and Differential Association: A Causal Modeling Approach." *American Sociological Review* 47:489–504.

———. 1988. "The Current State of Differential Association Theory." *Crime and Delinquency* 34:277–306.

———. 1989. "The Dynamics of Moral Beliefs and Minor Deviance." *Social Forces* 68:428–57.

———. 1997. "'Cultural Deviance Theory': The Remarkable Persistence of a Flawed Term." *Theoretical Criminology* 1:429–52.

Matsueda, Ross L., and Karen Heimer. 1987. "Race, Family Structure, and Delinquency: A Test of Differential Association and Social Control Theories." *American Sociological Review* 52:826–40.

McGee, Zina T. 1992. "Social Class Differences in Parental and Peer Influence on Adolescent Drug Use." *Deviant Behavior* 13:349–72.

Merton, Robert. 1938. "Social Theory and Anomie." *American Sociological Review* 3:672–82.

Messerschmidt, James W. 1993. *Masculinities and* Crime. Lanham, MD: Rowman & Littlefield.

Messner, Steven F., and Richard Rosenfeld. 1994. *Crime and the American Dream.* Belmont, CA: Wadsworth.

Miller, Eleanor M. 1986. *Street Woman.* Philadelphia, PA: Temple University Press.

Naffine, Ngaire, and Fay Gale. 1989. "Testing the Nexus: Crime, Gender, and Unemployment." *British Journal of Criminology* 29:144–56.

Orcutt, James. 1987. "Differential Association and Marijuana Use: A Closer Look at Sutherland (with a Little Help from Becker)." *Criminology* 25:341–58.

Paternoster, Raymond, Robert Brame, Paul Mazerolle, and Alex Piquero. 1998. "Using the Correct Statistical Test for the Equality of Regression Coefficients." *Criminology* 36:859–66.

Paternoster, Raymond, and Ruth Triplett. 1988. "Disaggregating Self-Reported Delinquency and Its Implications for Theory." *Criminology* 26:591–625.

Rand, Alicia. 1987. "Transitional Life Events and Desistance from Delinquency and Crime." In *From Boy to Man: From Delinquency to Crime,* edited by Marvin Wolfgang, Terence P. Thornberry, and Robert M. Figlio. Chicago: University of Chicago Press.

Richie, Beth E. 1996. *Compelled to Crime: The* Gender *Entrapment of Battered Black Women.* New York: Routledge Kegan Paul.

Rosenbaum, James L. 1987. "Social Control, Gender and Delinquency: An Analysis of Drug, Property and Violent Offenders." *Justice Quarterly* 4:117–32.

Sampson, Robert J., and John H. Laub. 1990. "Crime and Deviance over the Life Course: The Salience of Adult Social Bonds." *American Sociological Review* 55:609–27.

———. 1993. *Crime in the Making.* Cambridge, MA: Harvard University Press.

Short, James F. 1960. "Differential Association as a Hypothesis: Problems of Empirical Testing." *Social Problems* 8:14–24.

Silberman, Matthew. 1976. "Toward a Theory of Deterrence." *American Sociological Review* 41:442–61.

Simons, Ronald L., Martin G. Miller, and Stephen M. Aigner. 1980. "Contemporary Theories of Deviance and Female Delinquency: An Empirical Test." *Journal of Research in Crime and Delinquency* 17:42–57.

Smart, Carol. 1976. *Women, Crime and Criminology: A Feminist Critique.* Boston: Routledge Kegan Paul.

Sutherland, Edwin H. 1947. *Principles of Criminology.* 4th ed. Philadelphia, PA: Lippincott.

Sutherland, Edwin H., and Donald Cressey. 1955. *Principles of Criminology.* Philadelphia, PA: Lippincott.

Tittle, Charles R. 1980. Sanctions *and Social Deviance.* New York: Praeger.

Tittle, Charles, Mary Jean Burke, and Elton Jackson. 1986. "Modeling Sutherland's Theory of Differential Association: Toward an Empirical Clarification." *Social Forces* 65:405–32.

U.S. Bureau of Justice Statistics. 1994. *Special Report, March, 1994.* Washington, DC: Government Printing Office.

Warr, Mark, and Mark Stafford. 1993. "Age, Peers, and Delinquency." *Criminology* 31:17–40.

Winfree, L. Thomas Curt, T. Griffiths, and Christine Sellers. 1989. "Social Learning Theory, Drug Use and American Indian Youths: A Cross-Cultural Test." *Justice Quarterly* 6:395–418.

Glossary

Academy of Criminal Justice Sciences (ACJS), Code of Ethics: The Code of Ethics of ACJS sets forth 1) General Principles and 2) Ethical Standards that underlie members of the Academy's professional responsibilities and conduct, along with the 3) Policies and Procedures for enforcing those principles and standards. Membership in the Academy of Criminal Justice Sciences commits individual members to adhere to the ACJS Code of Ethics in determining ethical behavior in the context of their everyday professional activities.

Accuracy: The accuracy standards are intended to ensure that an evaluation will reveal and convey technically adequate information about the features that determine worth or merit of the program being evaluated.

Alternate-forms reliability: A procedure for testing the reliability of responses to survey questions in which subjects' answers are compared after the subjects have been asked slightly different versions of the questions or when randomly selected halves of the sample have been administered slightly different versions of the questions.

Analytic comparative research: Research that seeks to understand how national systems work and the factors related to their operations.

Anchors: Key dates of important events like birthdays that help trigger recall for respondents.

Anomalous findings: Unexpected patterns in data, which stimulate new ideas or theoretical approaches.

Anonymity: Provided by research in which no identifying information is recorded that could be used to link respondents to their responses.

Applied research: Research that has an impact on policy and can be immediately utilized and applied.

Arrestee Drug Abuse Monitoring (ADAM): Uses standardized drug testing methodologies and predictive models to measure the consequences of drug abuse within and across the United States boundaries.

Association: A criterion for establishing a causal relationship between two variables: variation in one variable is related to variation in another variable as condition to determine causality.

Authenticity: When the understanding of a social process or social setting is one that reflects fairly the various perspectives of participants in that setting.

Availability sampling: Sampling in which elements are selected on the basis of convenience.

Bar chart: A graphic for qualitative variables in which the variable's distribution is displayed with solid bars separated by spaces.

Base N: The total number of cases in a distribution.

Basic science: In contrast to applied research, the main motivation of basic science is to advance general knowledge and/or to test theoretical propositions.

Before-and-after designs: A quasi-experimental design consisting of several before-and-after comparisons involving the same variables but different groups.

Belmont Report: A 1979 National Commission for the Protection of Human Subjects of Biomedical and Behavioral Research report that established three basic ethical principles for the protection of human subjects, including respect for persons, beneficence, and justice.

Beneficence: Minimizing possible harms and maximizing benefits.

Bimodal distribution: A distribution that has two nonadjacent categories with about the same number of cases, and these categories have more cases than any other categories.

Black box evaluation: This type of evaluation occurs when an evaluation of program outcomes ignores, and does not identify, the process by which the program produced the effect.

Campbell Collaboration: Group producing systematic reviews of programs and policies in many areas including criminal justice, social work, and education.

Case report: A report that helps the reader realize (in the sense of making real) not only the states of affairs that are believed by constructors [research respondents] to exist but also of the underlying motives, feelings, and rationales leading to those beliefs

Case-oriented understanding: An understanding of social processes in a group, formal organization, community, or other collectivity that reflects accurately the standpoint of participants.

Causal effect (nomothetic perspective): When variation in one phenomenon, an independent variable, leads to or results, on average, in variation in another phenomenon, the dependent variable.

Causal effect (idiographic perspective): When a series of concrete events, thoughts, or actions result in a particular event or individual outcome.

Causal effect: The finding that change in one variable leads to change in another variable, *ceteris paribus* (other things being equal).

Causal validity (internal validity): The type of validity that is achieved when a conclusion that one phenomenon leads to or results in another phenomenon—or doesn't lead to or result in another—is correct.

Census: Research in which information is obtained through the responses that all available members of an entire population give to questions.

Central tendency: A feature of a variable's distribution, referring to the value or values around which cases tend to center.

Certificate of Confidentiality: Document that protects researchers from being legally required to disclose confidential information.

Ceteris paribus: Latin term meaning "all other things being equal."

Chi-square: An inferential statistic used to test hypotheses about relationships between two or more variables in a cross-tabulation.

Closed-ended (fixed-choice) questions: Survey questions providing preformulated response choices for the respondent to circle or check.

Cluster: A naturally occurring, mixed aggregate of elements of the population.

Cognitive interview: A technique for evaluating questions in which researchers ask people test questions, then probe with follow-up questions to learn how they understood the questions and what their answers mean.

Cohort: Individuals or groups with a common starting point. Examples of a cohort include college class of 1997, people who graduated from high school in the 1980s, General Motors employees who started work between 1990 and the year 2000, and people who were born in the late 1940s or the 1950s (the baby boom generation).

Cohort study (event-based design): A type of longitudinal study in which data are collected at two or more points in time from individuals in a cohort.

Combined frequency display: A table that presents together the distributions for a set of conceptually similar variables having the same response categories; common headings are used for the responses.

Comparative research: Research comparing data from more than one time period and/or more than one nation.

Compensatory rivalry (John Henry effect): A type of contamination in experimental and quasi-experimental designs that occurs when control group members are aware that they are being denied some advantage and increase their efforts by way of compensation. This problem has also been referred to as the John Henry effect.

Complete observation: A role in participant observation in which the researcher does not participate in group activities and is publicly defined as a researcher.

Compressed frequency display: A table that presents cross-classification data efficiently by eliminating unnecessary percentages, such as the percentage corresponding to the second value of a dichotomous variable.

Computer-assisted personal interviewing (CAPI): An interview in which the interviewer carries a laptop computer programmed to display the interview questions and processes the responses that the interviewer types in, as well as checking that these responses fall within the allowed ranges.

Computer-assisted telephone interview (CATI): A telephone interview in which a questionnaire is programmed into a computer, along with relevant skip patterns that must be followed. It essentially combines the tasks of interviewing, data entry, and some data cleaning.

Computer-assisted qualitative data analysis: Uses special computer software to assist qualitative analyses through creating, applying and refining categories; tracing linkages between concepts; and making comparisons between cases and events.

Computer-assisted self-interviewing (CASI): A system within which respondents interact with a computer-administered questionnaire by using a mouse and following audio instructions delivered via headphones.

Computer Interactive Voice Response (IVR): Software that uses a touch-tone telephone to interact with people in order to acquire information from or enter data into a database.

Concept: A mental image that summarizes a set of similar observations, feelings, or ideas.

Conceptualization: The process of specifying what we mean by a term. In deductive research, conceptualization helps to translate portions of an abstract theory into testable hypotheses involving specific variables. In inductive research, conceptualization is an important part of the process used to make sense of related observations.

Confidence interval: The range defined by the confidence limits for a sample statistic.

Confidence limits: The upper and lower bounds around an estimate of a population parameter based on a sample statistic. The confidence limits show how much confidence can be placed in the estimate.

Constant: A number that has a fixed value in a given situation; a characteristic or value that does not change.

Construct validity: The type of validity that is established by showing that a measure is related to other measures as specified in a theory.

Constructivist paradigm: Methodology based on rejection of belief in an external reality; it emphasizes the importance of exploring the way in which different stakeholders in a social setting construct their beliefs.

Contamination: A source of causal invalidity that occurs when the experimental and/or the comparison group is aware of the other group and is influenced in the posttest as a result.

Content analysis: A research method for systematically analyzing and making inferences from text.

Content validity: The type of validity that establishes a measure covers the full range of the concept's meaning.

Context: A focus of causal explanation; a particular outcome is understood as part of a larger set of interrelated circumstances.

Contextual effect: Relationships between variables that vary between geographic units or other contexts.

Contingent question: Questions that are asked of only a subset of survey respondents.

Control or comparison group: The group of subjects who are either exposed to a different treatment than the experimental group or who receive no treatment at all.

Convergent parallel design: In mixed-methods research, when quantitative and qualitative methods are implemented at the same time. The findings are integrated and interpreted together.

Conversation analysis: Developed from ethnomethodology, this qualitative method focuses on the sequence and details of conversational interaction and focuses on how reality is constructed.

Cost-benefit analysis: A type of evaluation research that compares program costs to the economic value of program benefits.

Cost-effectiveness analysis: A type of evaluation research that compares program costs to actual program outcomes.

Counterfactual: The outcome that would have occurred if the subjects who were exposed to the treatment actually were not exposed but otherwise had had identical experiences to those they underwent during the experiment.

Cover letter: The letter sent with a mailed questionnaire. It explains the survey's purpose and auspices and encourages the respondent to participate.

Covert (complete) participation: A role in field research in which the researcher does not reveal his or her identity as a researcher to those who are observed. The covert participant has adopted the role of a "complete participant."

Crime mapping: Geographical mapping strategies used to visualize a number of things including location, distance, and patterns of crime and their correlates.

Criminological research question: A question about some aspect of crime or criminals, the answer to which is sought through collection and analysis of the firsthand, verifiable, empirical data.

Criterion validity: The type of validity that is established by comparing the scores obtained on the measure being validated to those obtained with a more direct or already validated measure of the same phenomenon (the criterion).

Cross-population generalizability (external validity): Exists when findings about one group, population, or setting hold true for other groups, populations, or settings.

Cross-sectional research design: A study in which data are collected at only one point in time.

Cross-tabulation (cross-tab): A bivariate (two-variable) distribution, showing the distribution of one variable for each category of another variable.

Data cleaning: The process of checking data for errors after the data have been entered in a computer file.

Debriefing: A researcher's informing subjects after an experiment about the experiment's purposes and methods and evaluating subjects' personal reactions to the experiment.

Deductive reasoning: The type of reasoning that moves from the general to the specific.

Deductive research: The type of research in which a specific expectation is deducted from a general premise and is then tested.

Dependent variable: A variable that is hypothesized to change or vary depending on the variation in another variable.

Descriptive comparative research: Research that seeks to understand the structure, nature, or scope of a nation's or nations' criminal justice systems or rates of crime.

Descriptive research: Research in which social phenomena are defined and described.

Descriptive statistics: Statistics used to describe the distribution of and relationship among variables.

Deterministic causal approach: An approach in which there is a relationship between an independent and a dependent variable; the independent variable

has an effect on the dependent variable in every case under consideration.

Dichotomy: A variable having only two values.

Differential attrition: A problem that occurs in experiments when comparison groups become different because subjects are more likely to drop out of one of the groups for various reasons.

Direction of association: A pattern in a cross-tabulation; the values of variables tend to change consistently in relation to change on the other variable. Direction of association can be either positive or negative.

Discriminant validity: An approach to construct validation; scores on the measure to be validated are compared to scores on another measure of the same variable and to scores on variables that measure different but related concepts. Discriminant validity is achieved if the measure to be validated is related most strongly to its comparison measure and less so to the measures of other concepts.

Disproportionate stratified sampling: Sampling in which elements are selected from strata in different proportions from those that appear in the population.

Distribution of benefits: An ethical issue about how much researchers can influence the benefits subjects receive as part of the treatment being studied in a field experiment.

Documentation: A list and/or copy of all contacts, interviews, and written documents that preserves a record of the project.

Double-barreled question: A single survey question that actually asks two questions but allows only one answer.

Double-blind procedure: An experimental method in which neither subjects

nor the staff delivering experimental treatments know which subjects are getting the treatment and which are receiving a placebo.

Double-negative question: A question or statement that contains two negatives, which can muddy the meaning.

Ecological fallacy: An error in reasoning in which incorrect conclusions about individual level processes are drawn from group-level data.

Ecometrics: The process of evaluating the reliability and validity of measures about organizations, neighborhoods, or other collective units.

Effect size: A standardized measure of association—often the difference between the mean of the experimental group and the mean of the control group on the dependent variable, adjusted for the average variability in the two groups.

Efficiency analysis: A type of evaluation research that compares program costs to program effects. It can be either a cost-benefit analysis or a cost-effectiveness analysis.

Elaboration analysis: The process of introducing a third variable into an analysis in order to better understand—to elaborate—the bivariate (two-variable) relationship under consideration; additional control variables also can be introduced.

Electronic survey (Web-based survey): A survey that is sent and answered by computer, either through e-mail or on the Web.

Embedded design: In mixed methods research, when the primary method is qualitative or quantitative but the researcher adds the other component to gain additional insight.

Empirical generalizations: Statements that describe patterns found in data.

Endogenous change: A source of causal invalidity that occurs when natural developments or changes in the subjects (independent of the experimental treatment itself) account for some or all of the observed change from the pretest to the posttest.

Enumeration units: Units that contain one or more elements and that are listed in a sampling frame.

Epistemology: A branch of philosophy that studies how knowledge is gained or acquired.

Ethnography: The study of a culture or cultures that some group of people shares, using participant observation over an extended period of time.

Ethnomethodology: A qualitative research method focused on the way that participants in a social setting create and sustain a sense of reality.

Evaluability assessment: A type of evaluation research conducted to determine whether it is feasible to evaluate a program's effects within the available time and resources.

Evaluation research: Research about social programs or interventions.

Event-based design (cohort study): A study in which data are collected at two or more points in time from individuals in a cohort.

Event-structure analysis: A systematic method of developing a causal diagram showing the structure of action underlying some chronology of events; the end result is an idiographic causal explanation.

Evidence-based policy: A policy that has been evaluated with a methodologically rigorous design and has been proven to be effective.

Ex post facto control group design: Nonexperimental design in which comparison groups are selected after the treatment, program, or other variation in the independent variable has occurred.

Exhaustive attributes: A variable's attributes or values in which every case can be classified as having one attribute.

Exhaustive responses: A variable's attributes or values in which every case can be classified as having one attribute.

Expectancies of the experimental staff: A source of treatment misidentification in experiments and quasi-experiments that occurs when change among experimental subjects is due to the positive expectancies of the staff who are delivering the treatment, rather than to the treatment itself; also called a *self-fulfilling prophecy.*

Experience sampling method (ESM): A technique for drawing a representative sample of everyday activities, thoughts, and experiences; participants carry a pager and are beeped at random times over several days or weeks; upon hearing the beep, participants complete a report designed by the researcher

Experimental approach: An approach in which the researcher assigns individuals to two or more groups in a way that equates the characteristics of individuals in the groups (with a certain chance of error), except for variation in the groups' exposure to the independent variable.

Experimental designs: Refers to a plan for assigning subjects to treatment conditions. A good experimental design serves three purposes: causation, which allows the experimenter to make causal inferences about the relationship between independent variables and a dependent variable; control, which allows the experimenter to rule out alternative explanations due to the confounding effects of extraneous variables (i.e., variables other than the independent variables); and variability, which reduces variability within treatment conditions, which makes it easier to detect differences in treatment outcomes.

Experimental group: In an experiment, the group of subjects that receives the treatment or experimental manipulation.

Explanatory research: Research that seeks to identify causes and/or effects of social phenomena.

Exploratory research: Research in which social phenomena are investigated without a priori expectations, in order to develop explanations of them.

Exploratory sequential design: The qualitative method is implemented first followed by the quantitative method.

External events (history effect): A source of causal invalidity that occurs when something other than the treatment influences outcome scores; also called an effect of external events.

External validity (cross-population generalizability): A type of validity that occurs when a treatment effect (or noneffect) occurs across subgroups within an experiment or other study or across different populations, times, or settings.

Extraneous variable: A variable that influences both the independent and dependent variables so as to create a spurious association between them that disappears when the extraneous variable is controlled.

Face validity: The type of validity that exists when an inspection of the items used to measure a concept suggests that they are appropriate "on their face."

Factorial survey: A survey in which randomly selected subsets of respondents are asked different questions, or are asked to respond to different vignettes, in order to determine the causal effect of the variables represented by these differences.

Falsifiable: When a theory can be tested and falsified or otherwise not supported by empirical evidence.

Feasibility: The feasibility standards are intended to ensure that an evaluation will be realistic, prudent, diplomatic, and frugal.

Federal Policy for the Protection of Human Subjects: Federal regulations established in 1991 that are based on the principles of the Belmont Report.

Feedback: Information about service delivery system outputs, outcomes, or operations that is available to any program inputs.

Fence-sitters: Survey respondents who see themselves as being neutral on an issue and choose a middle (neutral) response that is offered.

Field experiment: An experimental study conducted in a real-world setting.

Field notes: Notes that describe what has been observed, heard, or otherwise experienced in a participant observation study; these notes usually are written after the observational session data analysis.

Field research: Research in which natural social processes are studied as they happen and left relatively undisturbed.

Filter question: A survey question used to identify a subset of respondents who then are asked other questions.

Fixed-choice question: A question format in which respondents are provided with explicit responses from which to select.

Fixed-sample panel design (panel study): A type of longitudinal study in which data are collected from the same individuals—the panel—at two or more points in time. In another type of panel design, panel members who leave are replaced with new members.

Floaters: Survey respondents who provide an opinion on a topic in response to a closed-ended question that does not include a "don't know" option, but will choose "don't know" if it is available.

Focus groups: Unstructured group interviews in which the focus group leader actively encourages discussion among participants on the topics of interest.

Formative evaluation: Process evaluation that is used to shape and refine program operations.

Frequency distributions: Numerical display showing the number of cases, and usually the percentage of cases (the relative frequencies), corresponding to each value or group of values of a variable.

Frequency polygon: A graphic for quantitative variables in which a continuous line connects data points representing the variable's distribution.

Gamma: A measure of association sometimes used in cross-tabular analyses.

Generalizability: The type of validity that is achieved when a conclusion holds true for the population, group, or groups that we say it does, given the conditions that we specify.

Geographic Information System (GIS): The software tool that has made crime mapping increasingly available to researchers since the 1990s.

Grounded theory: Systematic theory developed inductively, based on observations that are summarized into conceptual categories, reevaluated in the research setting, and gradually refined and linked to other conceptual categories.

Group-administered survey: A survey that is completed by individual respondents who are assembled in a group.

Grouped frequency distribution: A frequency distribution in which the data are organized into categories, either because there are more values than can be easily displayed or because the distribution of the variable will be clearer or more meaningful.

Hawthorne effect: A type of contamination in experimental and quasi-experimental designs that occurs when members of the treatment group change in terms of the dependent variable because their participation in the study makes them feel special.

Hermeneutic circle: Represents the dialectical process in which the researcher obtains information from multiple stakeholders in a setting, refines his or her understanding of the setting, and then tests that understanding with successive respondents.

Histogram: A graphic for quantitative variables in which the variable's distribution is displayed with adjacent bars.

Historical events research: Research in which social events of only one time period in the past are studied.

History effect (external events): A source of causal invalidity that occurs when something other than the treatment influences outcome scores; also called an effect of external events.

Hypothesis: A tentative statement about empirical reality involving the relationship between two or more variables.

Idiographic causal explanation: An explanation that identifies the concrete, individual sequence of events, thoughts, or actions that resulted in a particular outcome for a particular individual or that led to a particular event; may be termed an individualist or historicist explanation.

Idiosyncratic variation: Variation in responses to questions that is caused by individuals' reactions to particular words or ideas in the question instead of by variation in the concept that the question is intended to measure.

Illogical reasoning: Prematurely jumping to conclusions and arguing on the basis of invalid assumptions.

Impact evaluation (or impact analysis): Analysis of the extent to which a treatment or other service has the intended effect.

Improvement-oriented evaluation: Evaluations that seek to improve a program rather than simply rendering a summative judgment about the program's merit or effectiveness.

Inaccurate observation: Observations based on faulty perceptions of empirical reality.

Independent variable: The variable that is hypothesized to cause, or lead to, variation in another variable.

Index: A composite measure based on summing, averaging, or otherwise combining the responses to multiple questions that are intended to measure the same variable.

Indicator: The question or other operation used to indicate the value of cases on a variable.

Inductive reasoning: The type of reasoning that moves from the specific to the general.

Inductive research: The type of research in which specific data are used to develop (induce) a general explanation.

Inferential statistics: Mathematical tools for estimating how likely it is that a statistical result based on data from a random sample is representative of the population from which the sample was selected.

In-person interview: A survey in which an interviewer questions respondents and records their answers.

Inputs: Resources, raw materials, clients, and staff that go into a program.

Institutional review board (IRB): Committee in all research organizations including universities that reviews research proposals to ensure the protection of human subjects.

Integrative approaches: An orientation to evaluation research that expects researchers to respond to concerns of people involved with stakeholders as well as to the standards and goals of the social scientific community.

Intensive interviewing: Open-ended, relatively unstructured questioning in which the interviewer seeks in-depth information on the interviewee's feelings, experiences, and/or perceptions.

Interitem reliability: An approach that calculates reliability based on the correlation among multiple items used to measure a single concept.

Internal validity (causal validity): The type of validity that is achieved when a conclusion that one phenomenon leads to or results in another phenomenon—or doesn't lead to or result in another—is correct.

Interobserver reliability: When similar measurements are obtained by different observers rating the same persons, events, or places.

Interpretive questions: Questions included in a questionnaire or interview schedule to help explain answers to other important questions.

Interpretivism (interpretivist philosophy): The belief that reality is socially constructed and that the goal of social scientists is to understand what meanings people give to that reality.

Interquartile range: The range in a distribution between the end of the first quartile and the beginning of the third quartile.

Intersubjective agreement: Agreement between scientists about the nature of reality; often upheld as a more reasonable goal for science than certainty about an objective reality.

Interval level of measurement: A measurement of a variable in which the numbers indicating a variable's values represent fixed measurement units, but have no absolute, or fixed, zero point.

Intervening variables: Variables that are influenced by an independent variable and in turn influence variation in a dependent variable, thus helping to explain the relationship between the independent and dependent variables.

Interview schedule: The survey instrument containing the questions asked by the interviewer for an in-person or phone survey.

Intraobserver reliability (intrarater reliability): Consistency of ratings by an observer of an unchanging phenomenon at two or more points in time.

John Henry effect: See *compensatory rivalry.*

Jottings: Brief notes that are jotted down quickly during the observation period that will be expanded into more extensive field notes.

Judgment-oriented evaluation: Evaluations aimed at determining the overall merit, worth, or value of something.

Justice (in research): Distributing benefits and risks of research fairly.

Knowledge-oriented evaluation: Used to influence thinking about issues in a general way.

Level of measurement: The complexity of the mathematical means that can be used to express the relationship between a variable's values. The nominal level of measurement, which is qualitative, has no mathematical interpretation; the quantitative levels of measurement (ordinal, interval, and ratio) are progressively more complex mathematically.

Life calendar: An instrument that helps respondents recall events in their past by displaying each month of a given year along with key dates noted within the calendar, such as birthdays, arrests, holidays, anniversaries, etc.

Likert-type responses: Survey responses in which respondents indicate the extent to which they agree or disagree with statements.

Longitudinal research design: A study in which data are collected that can be ordered in time; also defined as research in which data are collected at two or more points in time.

Mailed (self-administered) survey: A survey involving a mailed questionnaire to be completed by the respondent.

Marginal distributions: The summary distributions in the margins of a cross-tabulation that correspond to the frequency distribution of the row variable and of the column variable.

Matching: A procedure for equating the characteristics of individuals in different comparison groups in an experiment. Matching can be done on either an individual or an aggregate basis. For individual matching, individuals who are similar in terms of key characteristics are paired prior to assignment, and then the two members of each pair are assigned to the two groups. For aggregate matching, groups are chosen for comparisons that are similar in terms of the distribution of key characteristics.

Matrix: A form that systematically records particular features of multiple cases or instances and how they are related.

Mean: The arithmetic, or weighted, average, computed by adding up the value of all the cases and dividing by the total number of cases.

Measure of association: A type of descriptive statistic that summarizes the strength of an association.

Measurement validity: The type of validity that is achieved when a measure measures what it is presumed to measure.

Mechanism: A discernible process that creates a causal connection between two variables.

Median: The position average, or the point that divides a distribution in half (the 50th percentile).

Meta-analysis: The quantitative analysis of findings from multiple studies.

Meta-synthesis: The qualitative analysis of findings from multiple qualitative studies.

Method of agreement: A method proposed by John Stuart Mill for establishing a causal relation, in which the values of cases that agree on an outcome variable also agree on the value of the variable hypothesized to have a causal effect, whereas they differ in terms of other variables.

Mixed-mode survey: Surveys that are conducted by more than one method, allowing the strengths of one survey design to compensate for the weaknesses of another and maximizing the likelihood of securing data from different types of respondents; for example, nonrespondents in a mailed survey may be interviewed in person or over the phone.

Mode: The most frequent value in a distribution; also termed the probability average.

Monotonic relationship: A pattern of association in which the value of cases on one variable increases or decreases fairly regularly across the categories of another variable.

Multiphase design: In mixed methods research, this design involves a series of quantitative and qualitative designs; each design and the findings inform the next phase.

Multiple-group before-and-after design: A quasi-experimental design consisting of several before-and-after comparisons involving the same variables but different groups.

Multistage cluster sampling: Sampling in which elements are selected in two or more stages, with the first stage being the random selection of naturally occurring clusters and the last stage being the random selection of multi-level elements within clusters.

Mutually exclusive attributes: A variable's attributes or values are mutually exclusive if every case can have only one attribute.

Mutually exclusive responses: Response choices on a survey that do not overlap.

Narrative analysis: A form of qualitative analysis in which the analyst focuses on how respondents impose order on the flow of experience in their lives and so make sense of events and actions in which they have participated.

Needs assessment: A type of evaluation research that attempts to determine the needs of some population that might be met with a social program.

Negative relationship: The independent and dependent variables move in opposite directions; as one increases the other decreases.

Negatively skewed: A distribution in which cases cluster to the right side and the left tail of the distribution is longer than the right.

Nominal level of measurement: Variables whose values have no mathematical interpretation; they vary in kind or quality but not in amount.

Nomothetic causal explanation: A type of causal explanation involving the belief that variation in an independent variable will be followed by variation in the dependent variable, when all other things are equal.

Nonequivalent control group design: A quasi-experimental design in which there are experimental and comparison groups that are designated before the treatment occurs but are not created by random assignment.

Nonprobability sampling methods: Sampling methods in which the probability of selection of population elements is unknown.

Nonresponse: People or other entities who do not participate in a study although they are selected for the sample.

Nonspuriousness: A relationship that exists between two variables that is not due to variation in a third variable.

Normal distribution: A symmetric distribution shaped like a bell and centered around the population mean, with the number of cases tapering off in a predictable pattern on both sides of the mean.

Nuremberg War Crimes Trials: U.S. court trials that exposed horrific medical experiments conducted by Nazi doctors and others in the name of "science."

Office for Protection From Research Risks in the National Institutes of Health: The organization within the federal government that monitors all IRBs, ensuring federal standards are followed.

Omnibus survey: A survey that covers a range of topics of interest to different social scientists.

One-shot design: A research design that measures the dependent variable after the treatment has been delivered for only those who receive the treatment.

Open-ended questions: Survey questions to which the respondent replies in his or her own words, either by writing or by talking.

Operation: The procedure for actually measuring the concepts we intend to measure, identifying the value of a variable for each case.

Operationalization: The process of specifying the operations that will indicate the value of a variable for each case.

Ordinal level of measurement: A measurement of a variable in which the numbers indicating a variable's values specify only the order of the cases, permitting "greater than" and "less than" distinctions.

Outcomes: The impact of the program process on the cases processed.

Outlier: An exceptionally high or low value in a distribution.

Outputs: The services delivered or new products produced by the program process.

Overgeneralization: An error in reasoning that occurs when we conclude that what we have observed or know to be true for a subset of cases holds true for the entire set.

Participant observation: A type of field research in which a researcher develops a sustained and intensive relationship with people while they go about their normal activities.

Participatory action research: A type of research in which the researcher involves some organizational members as active participants throughout the process of studying an organization; the goal is making changes in the organization.

Peer review: A process in which a journal editor sends a submitted article to two or three experts who judge whether the paper should be accepted, revised and resubmitted, or rejected; the experts also provide comments to explain their decision and guide any revisions.

Percentage: Relative frequencies, computed by dividing the frequency of cases in a particular category by the total number of cases, and multiplying by 100.

Periodicity: A sequence of elements (in a list to be sampled) that varies in some regular, periodic pattern.

Philip Zimbardo's Stanford Prison Experiment: A 2-week experiment that simulated the prison life of both prisoners and guards that was ended in just 6 days because of what the simulation was doing to college students who participated.

Phone survey: A survey in which interviewers question respondents over the phone and then record their answers.

Phrenology: A now defunct field of study, once considered a science in the 19th century, that held that bumps and fissures of the skull determined the character and personality of a person.

Placebo effect: A source of treatment misidentification that can occur when subjects receive a treatment that they consider likely to be beneficial, and improve because of that expectation rather than because of the treatment itself.

Plagiarism: Presenting as one's own the ideas or words of another person or persons for academic evaluation without proper acknowledgment.

Population: The entire set of elements (e.g., individuals, cities, states, countries, prisons, schools) in which we are interested.

Population parameter: A statistic computed for the entire population.

Positive relationship: The independent and dependent variables move in the same direction; as one increases the other decreases.

Positively skewed: Describes a distribution in which the cases cluster to the left and the right tail of the distribution is longer than the left.

Positivism: The belief, shared by most scientists, that there is a reality that exists quite apart from our own perception of it, although our knowledge of this reality may never be complete.

Postpositivism: The belief that there is an empirical reality but that our understanding of it is limited by its complexity and by the biases and other limitations of researchers.

Posttest: Measurement of an outcome (dependent) variable after an experimental intervention or after a presumed independent variable has changed for some other reason.

Pretest: Measurement of an outcome (dependent) variable prior to an experimental intervention or change in a presumed independent variable for some other reason. The pretest is exactly the same "test" as the posttest, but it is administered at a different time.

Privacy Certificate: Document that protects researchers from being legally required to disclose confidential information.

Probability of selection: The likelihood that an element will be selected from the population for inclusion in the sample. In a census of all the elements of a population, the probability that any particular element will be selected is 1.0 because everyone will be selected. If half the elements in the population are sampled on the basis of chance (say, by tossing a coin), the probability of selection for each element is one-half, or .5. When the size of the sample as a proportion of the population decreases, so does the probability of selection.

Probability sampling method: Sampling methods that rely on a random, or chance, selection method so that the probability of selection of population elements is known.

Process analysis: A research design in which periodic measures are taken to determine whether a treatment is being delivered as planned, usually in a field experiment.

Process evaluation (program monitoring): Evaluation research that investigates the process of service delivery.

Program process: The complete treatment or service delivered by the program.

Program theory: A descriptive or prescriptive model of how a program operates and produces effects.

Progressive focusing: Process in which a qualitative analyst interacts with the data and gradually refines his or her focus.

Proportionate stratified sampling: Sampling methods in which elements are selected from strata in exact proportion to their representation in the population.

Propriety: The propriety standards are intended to ensure that an evaluation will be conducted legally, ethically, and with due regard for the welfare of those involved in the evaluation, as well as those affected by its results.

Pseudoscience: Dubious but fascinating claims that are touted as "scientifically proven" and bolstered by fervent, public testimonials of believers who have experienced firsthand or have claimed to have witnessed the phenomenon; however, such evidence is not based on the principles of the scientific method.

Psychometrics: The process of evaluating the reliability and validity of measures about individuals.

Purposive sampling: A nonprobability sampling method in which elements are selected for a purpose, usually because of their unique position. Sometimes referred to as *judgment sampling.*

Qualitative comparative analysis (QCA): A systematic type of qualitative analysis that identifies the combination of factors that had to be present across multiple cases to produce a particular outcome.

Qualitative methods: Methods such as participant observation, intensive interviewing, and focus groups that are designed to capture social life as participants experience it, rather than in categories predetermined by the researcher. These methods typically involve explanatory research questions, inductive reasoning, an orientation to social context and human subjectivity, and the meanings attached by participants to events and to their lives.

Quantitative methods: Methods such as surveys and experiments that record variation in social life in terms of categories that vary in amount. Data that are treated as quantitative are either numbers or attributes that can be ordered in terms of magnitude.

Quartile: The points in a distribution corresponding to the first 25% of the cases, the first 50% of the cases, and the top 25% of the cases.

Quasi-experimental design: A research design in which there is a comparison group that is comparable to the experimental group in critical ways, but subjects are not randomly assigned to the comparison and experimental groups.

Questionnaire: The instrument containing the questions on a self-administered survey.

Quota sampling: A nonprobability sampling method in which elements are selected to ensure that the sample represents certain characteristics in proportion to their prevalence in the population.

Random assignment: A procedure by which each experimental and control group subjects are placed in a group randomly.

Random digit dialing (RDD): The random dialing by a machine of numbers within designated phone prefixes, which creates a random sample for phone surveys.

Random number table: A table containing lists of numbers that are ordered solely on the basis of chance; it is used for drawing a random sample.

Random sampling error: Differences between the population and the sample that are due only to chance factors (random error), not to systematic sampling error. Random sampling error may or may not result in an unrepresentative sample. The magnitude of sampling error due to chance factors can be estimated statistically.

Random selection: The fundamental element of probability samples; the essential characteristic of random selection is that every element of the population has a known and independent chance of being selected into the sample.

Range: The true upper limit in a distribution minus the true lower limit (or the highest rounded value minus the lowest rounded value, plus one).

Ratio level of measurement: A measurement of a variable in which the numbers indicating a variable's values represent fixed measuring units and an absolute zero point.

Reactive effect: The changes in individual or group behavior that are due to being observed or otherwise studied.

Reductionist fallacy (reductionism): An error in reasoning that occurs when incorrect conclusions about group-level processes are based on individual-level data.

Refereed journals: Journals that selected research papers for publication based on the peer reviews of other social scientists.

Reference period: A time frame in which a survey question asks respondents to place a particular behavior (e.g., in the last 6 months).

Reflexivity: An accounting by a qualitative researcher of that describes the natural history of the development of evidence; this enables others to more adequately evaluate the findings.

Regression effect: A source of causal invalidity that occurs when subjects who are chosen for a study because of their extreme scores on the dependent variable become less extreme on the posttest due to natural cyclical or episodic change in the variable.

Reliability: A measure is reliable when it yields consistent scores or observations of a given phenomenon on different occasions. Reliability is a prerequisite for measurement validity.

Reliability measures: Special statistics that help researchers decide whether responses are consistent.

Repeated cross-sectional design (trend study): A type of longitudinal study in which data are collected at two or more points in time from different samples of the same population.

Repeated measures panel design: A quasi-experimental design consisting of several pretest and posttest observations of the same group.

Replacement sampling: A method of sampling in which sample elements are returned to the sampling frame after being selected, so they may be sampled again. Random samples may be selected with or without replacement.

Replications: Repetitions of a study using the same research methods to answer the same research question.

Representative sample: A sample that looks like the population from which it was selected in all respects that are potentially relevant to the study. The distribution of characteristics among the elements of a representative sample is the same as the distribution of those characteristics among the total population. In an unrepresentative sample, some characteristics are over-represented or underrepresented and sampling error emerges.

Research circle: A diagram of the elements of the research process, including theories, hypotheses, data collection, and data analysis.

Resistance to change: Reluctance to change ideas in light of new information, due to ego-based commitments, excessive devotion to tradition, or uncritical agreement with authorities.

Respect for persons: Treating persons as autonomous agents and protecting those with diminished autonomy.

Reverse outlining: Outlining the sections in an already written draft of a paper or report to improve its organization in the next draft.

Sample: A subset of elements from the larger population.

Sample generalizability: Exists when a conclusion based on a sample, or subset, of a larger population holds true for that population.

Sample statistic: An estimated statistic (e.g., proportion, mean) from the one sample we actually selected from a population.

Sampling distribution: A distribution of the value of a statistic from many samples.

Sampling error: Any difference between the characteristics of a sample and the characteristics of a population. The larger the sampling error, the less representative the sample.

Sampling frame: A list of the elements of a population from which a sample actually is selected.

Sampling interval: The number of cases from one sampled case to another in a systematic random sample.

Sampling units: The units actually selected in each stage of sampling.

Saturation point: The point at which subject selection is ended in intensive interviewing, when new interviews seem to yield little additional information.

Scale: A composite measure of one concept created from a series of two or more questions.

Science: A set of logical, systematic, documented methods with which to investigate nature and natural processes; the knowledge produced by these investigations.

Secondary data analysis: Analysis of data collected by someone other than the researcher or the researcher's assistant.

Selection bias: A source of internal (causal) invalidity that occurs when characteristics of experimental and comparison group subjects differ in any way that influences the outcome.

Selective observation: Observations chosen because they are in accord with preferences or beliefs of the observer.

Self-fulfilling prophecy: See *expectancies of the experimental staff*.

Serendipitous findings (anomalous findings): Unexpected patterns in data, which stimulate new ideas or theoretical approaches.

Simple random sampling: A method of sampling in which every sample element is selected only on the basis of chance, through a random process.

Skewness: A feature of a variable's distribution; refers to the extent to which cases are clustered more at one or the other end of the distribution rather than around the middle.

Skip patterns: The unique combination of questions created in a survey by filter questions and contingent questions.

Snowball sampling: A method of sampling in which sample elements are selected as they are identified by successive informants or interviewees.

Social science: The use of scientific methods to investigate individuals, societies, and social processes including questions related to criminology and criminal justice; the knowledge produced by these investigations.

Social science approaches: An orientation to evaluation research that expects researchers to emphasize the importance of researcher expertise and maintenance of autonomy from program stakeholders.

Solomon four-group design: An experimental design in which there are four groups. Two of the groups represent a classic experimental design in which there is an experimental and a control group that each receive a pretest. The final two groups represent an experimental and a control group but neither receives a pretest. This design helps to identify the interaction of testing and treatment.

Specification: A type of relationship involving three or more variables in which the association between the independent and dependent variables varies across the categories of one or more other control variables.

Split-ballot design: Unique questions or other modifications in a survey administered to randomly selected subsets of the total survey sample, so that more questions can be included in the entire survey or so that responses to different question versions can be compared.

Split-halves reliability: Reliability achieved when responses to the same questions by two randomly selected halves of a sample are about the same.

Spurious relationship: A relationship between two variables that is due to variation in a third variable.

Stakeholders: Individuals and groups who have some basis of concern with the program.

Stakeholder approaches (responsive evaluation): An orientation to evaluation research that expects researchers to be responsive primarily to the people involved with the program.

Standard deviation: The square root of the average squared deviation of each case from the mean.

Stanley Milgram's experiments on obedience to authority: Experiments by Stanley Milgram that sought to identify the conditions under which ordinary citizens would be obedient to authority figures' instructions to inflict pain on others.

Statistical control: A technique used in nonexperimental research to reduce the risk of spuriousness. One variable is held constant so the relationship between two or more other variables can be assessed without the influence of variation in the control variable.

Statistical significance: An association that is not likely to be due to chance, judged by a criterion set by the analyst (often that the probability is less than 5 out of 100, or $p < .05$).

Stratified random sampling: A method of sampling in which sample elements are selected separately from population strata that are identified in advance by the researcher.

Subject fatigue: Problems caused by panel members growing weary of repeated interviews and dropping out of a study or becoming so used to answering the standard questions in the survey that they start giving stock or thoughtless answers.

Subtables: Tables describing the relationship between two variables within the discrete categories of one or more other control variables.

Surveys: Popular and versatile research instruments using a question format. Surveys can either be self-administered or read by an interviewer.

Survey research: Research in which information is obtained from a sample of individuals through their responses to questions about themselves or others comparison of designs.

Systematic observation: A strategy that increases the reliability of observational data by using explicit rules that standardize coding practices across observers.

Systematic random sampling: A method of sampling in which sample elements are selected from a list or from sequential files, with every nth element being selected after the first element is selected randomly within the first interval.

Systematic review: Summary review about the impact of an program or program wherein the analyst attempts to account for differences across research designs and samples, often using statistical techniques such as a meta-analysis.

Systematic sampling error: Overrepresentation or underrepresentation of some population characteristics in a sample due to the method used to select the sample. A sample affected by systematic sampling error is a biased sample.

Systemic social observation (SSO): A careful method of observing phenomena.

Tacit knowledge: In field research, a credible sense of understanding of social processes that reflects the researcher's awareness of participants' actions as well as their words, and of what they fail to state, feel deeply, and take for granted.

Target population: A set of elements larger than or different from the population sampled and to which the researcher would like to generalize study findings.

Test-retest reliability: A measurement showing that measures of a phenomenon at two points in time are highly correlated, if the phenomenon has not changed, or have changed only as much as the phenomenon itself.

Theoretical construct: Parts of a theory that describe what is important to look at to understand, explain, predict, and "do something about" the subject.

Theoretical sampling: A sampling method recommended for field researchers by Glaser and Strauss (1967).

A theoretical sample is drawn in a sequential fashion, with settings or individuals selected for study as earlier observations or interviews indicate that these settings or individuals are influential.

Theory: A logically interrelated set of propositions about empirical reality. Examples of criminological theories are social learning, routine activities, labeling, general strain, and social disorganization theory.

Theory-driven evaluation: A program evaluation that is guided by a theory that specifies the process by which the program has an effect.

Thick description: A rich description that conveys a sense of what it is like from the standpoint of the participants in that setting.

Time order: A criterion for establishing a causal relation between two variables; the variation (the dependent variable) indicating its effect.

Time series design (repeated measures panel design): A quasi-experimental design consisting of many pretest and posttest observations of the same group.

Transformative design: In mixed methods research, this design uses theoretical perspective with a social justice focus to improve the well-being of vulnerable populations.

Transnational research: Explores how cultures and nations deal with crime that transcends their borders.

Transparent: An important feature of the scientific method that requires procedures, methods, and data analyses of any study to be presented clearly for the purposes of replication.

Treatment: The manipulation that exposes subjects in an experiment to a particular value of the independent variable.

Treatment misidentification: A problem that occurs in an experiment when the treatment itself is not what causes the outcome, but rather the outcome is caused by some intervening process that the researcher has not identified and is not aware of.

Trend study: See *repeated cross-sectional design*.

Triangulation: The use of multiple methods to study one research question. Also used to mean the use of two or more different measures of the same variable.

True experiment: Experiment in which subjects are assigned randomly to an experimental group that receives a treatment or other manipulation of the independent variable and a comparison group that does not receive the treatment or receives some other manipulation. Outcomes are measured in a posttest.

Unimodal distribution: A distribution of a variable in which there is only one value that is the most frequent.

Units of analysis: The level of social life on which a research question is focused, such as individuals.

Units of observation: The cases about which measures actually are obtained in a sample.

Unobtrusive measures: Measures that allow researchers to collect data about individuals or groups without their direct knowledge or participation.

Utility: The utility standards are intended to ensure that an evaluation will serve the practical information needs of intended users.

Variability: A feature of a variable's distribution, referring to the extent to which cases are spread out through the distribution or clustered in just one location.

Variable: Characteristics or properties that can vary (take on different values or attributes).

Variance: A statistic that measures the variability of a distribution as the average squared deviation of each score from the mean of all scores.

Verstehen: German term for "understanding."

Web-based survey: see *electronic survey*.

References

Abbott, Andrew. 1992. "From Causes to Events: Notes on Narrative Positivism." *Sociological Methods* 20(May):428–55.

Abbott, Andrew. 1994. "History and Sociology: The Lost Synthesis." In *Engaging the Past: The Uses of History Across the Social Sciences*, 77–112. Durham, NC: Duke University Press.

Abma, Tineke A. 2005. "Responsive Evaluation: Its Meaning and Special Contribution to Health Promotion." *Evaluation and Program Planning* 28:279–89.

Abrams, Philip. 1982. *Historical Sociology*. Ithaca, NY: Cornell University Press.

Academy of Criminal Justice Sciences (ACJS). 2000. "Code of Ethics." Retrieved September 26, 2009 (http://www.acjs.org/pubs/167_671_2922.cfm).

Adair, G., T. W. Dushenko, and R. C. L. Lindsay. 1985. "Ethical Regulations and Their Impact on Research Practice." *American Psychologist* 40:59–72.

Adler, P. A. 1985. *Wheeling and Dealing: An Ethnography of an Upper-Level Drug Dealing and Smuggling Community*. New York: Columbia University Press.

Agnew, R. 1992. "Foundations for a General Strain Theory of Crime and Delinquency." *Criminology* 30:475–99.

Agnew, R. 2006. "Storylines as a Neglected Cause of Crime." *Journal of Research in Crime and Delinquency* 43(2):119–47.

Alarid, Leanne Fiftal, Velmer S. Burton Jr., and Francis T. Cullen. 2000. "Gender and Crime Among Felony Offenders: Assessing the Generality of Social Control and Differential Association Theories." *Journal of Research in Crime and Delinquency* 37:171–99.

Alfred, Randall. 1976. "The Church of Satan." In *The New Religious Consciousness*, edited by Charles Glock and Robert Bellah, 180–202. Berkeley: University of California Press.

Altheide, David L. and John M. Johnson. 1994. "Criteria for Assessing Interpretive Validity in Qualitative Research." In *Handbook of Qualitative Research*, edited by Norman K. Denzin and Yvonna S. Lincoln, 485–99. Thousand Oaks, CA: Sage.

Altman, L. 1987. "U.S. and France End Rift on AIDS." *The New York Times*, April 1. Retrieved May 28, 2007 (http://www.nytimes.com/1987/04/01/us/us-and-france-end-rift-on-aids.html).

Altman, L. 1998. "Getting It Right on the Facts of the Death." *The New York Times*, December 22. Retrieved May 28, 2007 (http://www.nytimes.com/1998/12/22/health/the-doctor-s-world-getting-it-right-on-the-facts-of-death.html).

Alvarez, A. and R. Bachman. 2008. *Violence: The Enduring Problem*. Thousand Oaks, CA: Sage.

Amenta, E. and J. D. Poulsen. 1994. "Where to Begin: A Survey of Five Approaches to Selecting Independent Variables for Qualitative Comparative Analysis." *Sociological Methods and Research* 23(1):22–53.

American Psychiatric Association. 1994. *Diagnostic and Statistical Manual of Mental Disorders (DSM-IV)*. 4th ed. Washington, DC: Author.

American Psychological Association. 2009. *Publication Manual of the American Psychological Association*. 6th ed. Washington, DC: Author.

American Sociological Association. 1999. *Code of Ethics and Policies and Procedures of the ASA Committee on Professional Ethics*. Washington, DC: Author.

Anderson, Elijah. 1990. *Streetwise: Race, Class, and Change in an Urban Community*. Chicago: University of Chicago Press.

Anderson, Elijah. 1999. *Code of the Street: Decency, Violence, and the Moral Life of the Inner City*. New York: Norton.

Anderson, Elijah. 2003. "Jelly's Place: An Ethnographic Memoir." *Symbolic Interaction* 26:217–37.

Anderson, Tammy. 2009. *Post-Rave Dance Scenes and Cultural Change*. Philadelphia: Temple University Press.

Anglin, M. D., D. Longshore, and S. Turner. 1999. "Treatment Alternatives to Street Crime: An Evaluation of Five Programs." *Criminal Justice and Behavior* 26(2):168–95.

Archer, Dane and Rosemary Gartner. 1984. *Violence and Crime in Cross-National Perspective*. New Haven, CT: Yale University Press.

Arwood, T. and S. Panicker. 2007. "Assessing Risk in Social and Behavioral Sciences." Collaborative Institutional Training Initiative. Retrieved June 5, 2008 (https://www.citiprogram.org/membners/learners).

Asmussen, Kelly J. and John W. Creswell. 1995. "Campus Response to a Student Gunman." *Journal of Higher Education* 66(5):575–91.

Babor, Thomas F., Robert S. Stephens, and G. Alan Marlatt. 1987. "Verbal Report Methods in Clinical Research on Alcoholism: Response Bias and Its Minimization." *Journal of Studies on Alcohol* 48(5):410–24.

Bachman, Ronet. 1992. *Death and Violence on the Reservation: Homicide, Family Violence, and Suicide in American Indian Populations*. Westport, CT: Auburn House.

Bachman, Ronet. 2000. "A Comparison of Annual Incidence Rates and Contextual Characteristics of Intimate Perpetrated Violence Against Women From the National Crime Victimization Survey (NCVS) and the National Violence Against Women Survey (NVAWS)." *Violence Against Women* 6(8):839–67.

Bachman, Ronet and Raymond Paternoster. 2008. *Statistics for Criminology and Criminal Justice*. 3rd ed. New York: McGraw-Hill.

Bachman, Ronet and Linda Saltzman. 1995. "Violence Against Women: Estimates From the Redesigned National Crime Victimization Survey." *Bureau of Justice Statistics Special Report* (NCJ 154348). Washington, DC: U.S. Department of Justice.

Bachman, Ronet and Bruce Taylor. 1994. "The Measurement of Rape and Family Violence by the Redesigned National Crime Victimization Survey." *Justice Quarterly* 11:702–14.

Bachman, Ronet, Erin Kerrison, Daniel O'Connell, and Raymond Paternoster. 2012. *Roads Diverge: Long-term Patterns of Relapse, Recidivism, and Desistance for a Cohort of Drug Involved Offenders* (Final Report, Grant Number 2008-IJ-CX-0017). National Institute of Justice, U.S. Department of Justice.

Bakalar, Nicholas. 2010. "Child Abuse Investigations Didn't Reduce Risk, A Study Finds." *The New York Times*. October 12:D3.

Bandura, Albert, Dorothea Ross, and Sheila A. Ross. 1963. "Imitation of Film-Mediated Aggressive Models." *Journal of Abnormal and Social Psychology* 66:3–11.

Barnett, Jim. 2011. "Justice Department Finds Seattle Police Department Engaged in Excessive Force." CNN, December 16. Retrieved June 1, 2011 (http://www.cnn.com/2011/12/16/justice/washington-seattle-police/index.html).

Baskin, Deborah R. and Ira B. Sommers. 1998. *Casualties of Community Disorder: Women's Careers in Violent Crime*. Boulder, CO: Westview.

Baumrind, D. 1964. "Some Thoughts on Ethics of Research: After Reading Milgram's 'Behavioral Study of Obedience.'" *American Psychologist* 19(6):421–23.

Baumrind, D. 1985. "Research Using Intentional Deception: Ethical Issues Revisited." *American Psychologist* 40(2):165–74.

Bayley, David H. 1994. *Police for the Future*. Oxford, UK: Oxford University Press.

Becker, Howard S. 1958. "Problems of Inference and Proof in Participant Observation." *American Sociological Review* 23:652–60.

Becker, Howard S. 1963. *The Outsiders: Studies in the Sociology of Deviance*. New York: Free Press.

Becker, Howard S. 1986. *Writing for Social Scientists*. Chicago: University of Chicago Press.

Bellah, Robert N., Richard Madsen, William M. Sullivan, Ann Swidler, and Steven M. Tipton. 1985. *Habits of the Heart: Individualism and Commitment in American Life*. New York: Harper & Row.

Belli, Robert F., Frank P. Stafford, and Duane F. Alwin. 2009. *Calendar and Time Diary: Methods in Life Course Research*. Thousand Oaks, CA: Sage.

Belousov, Konstantin, Tom Horlick-Jones, Michael Bloor, Jakov Gilinsky, Valentin Golbert, Jakov Kostikovsky, Michael Levi, and Dmitri Pentsov. 2007. "Any Port in a Storm: Fieldwork Difficulties in Dangerous and Crisis-Ridden Settings." *Qualitative Research* 7:155–75.

Bench, Lawrence L. and Terry D. Allen. 2003. "Investigating the Stigma of Prison Classification: An Experimental Design." *The Prison Journal* 83(4):367–82.

Bennet, Lauren, Lisa Goodman, and Mary Ann Dutton. 1999. "Systematic Obstacles to the Criminal Prosecution of a Battering Partner: A Victim Perspective." *Journal of Interpersonal Violence* 14:761–72.

Bennett, R. R. 2004. "Comparative Criminology and Criminal Justice Research: The State of Our Knowledge." *Justice Quarterly* 21(1):1–21.

Berger, Peter L. and Thomas Luckmann. 1966. *The Social Construction of Reality*. New York: Doubleday & Co.

Berk, Richard A., Alice Campbell, Ruth Klap, and Bruce Western. 1992. "The Deterrent Effect of Arrest in Incidents of Domestic Violence: A Bayesian Analysis of Four Field Experiments." *American Sociological Review* 57:698–708.

Binder, Arnold and James W. Meeker. 1993. "Implications of the Failure to Replicate the Minneapolis Experimental Findings." *American Sociological Review* 58(December):886–88.

Black, M. C., K. C. Basile, M. J. Breiding, S. G. Smith, M. L. Walters, M. T. Merrick, J. Chen, and M. R. Stevens. 2011. *The National Intimate Partner and Sexual Violence Survey (NISVS): 2010 Summary Report*. Atlanta, GA: National Center for Injury Prevention and Control, Centers for Disease Control and Prevention.

Black, Donald J., ed. 1984. *Toward a General Theory of Social Control*. Orlando, FL: Academic Press.

Blackwell, Brenda Sims and Alex R. Piquero. 2005. "On the Relationships Between Gender, Power Control, Self-Control, and Crime." *Journal of Criminal Justice* 33:1–17.

Blau, Peter M. and Judith R. Blau. 1982. "The Cost of Inequality: Metropolitan Structure and Violent Crime." *American Sociological Review* 47:114–29.

Blumstein, Alfred. 2009. "What Role Should ASC Take in Policy Advocacy?" *The Criminologist* 34(3):1–3.

Boba, Rachel. 2009. *Crime Analysis With Crime Mapping*. Thousand Oaks, CA: Sage.

Bollen, Kenneth A., Barbara Entwisle, and Arthur S. Alderson. 1993. "Macrocomparative Research Methods." *Annual Review of Sociology* 19:321–51.

Bonczar, T. P. and L. E. Glaze. 2011. *Probation and Parole in the United States, 2010* (NCJ-236019). Washington, DC: Bureau of Justice Statistics, U.S. Department of Justice.

Booth, Wayne C., Gregory G. Colomb, and Joseph M. Williams. 1995. *The Craft of Research*. Chicago: University of Chicago Press.

Borg, Marian J. 1998. "Vicarious Homicide Victimization and Support for Capital Punishment: A Test of Black's Theory of Law." *Criminology* 36:537–67.

Boruch, Robert F. 1997. *Randomized Experiments for Planning and Evaluation: A Practical Guide*. Thousand Oaks, CA: Sage.

Bourgois, Philippe, Mark Lettiere, and James Quesada. 1997. "Social Misery and the Sanctions of Substance Abuse: Confronting HIV Risk Among Homeless Heroin Addicts in San Francisco." *Social Problems* 44:155–73.

Braga, Anthony A., David L. Weisburd, Elin J. Waring, Lorraine Green Mazerolle, William Spelman, and Francis Gajewski. 1999. "Problem-Oriented Policing in Violent Crime Places: A Randomized Controlled Experiment." *Criminology* 37(4):541–80.

Brame, Robert and Doris L. MacKenzie. 1996. "Shock Incarceration and Positive Adjustment During Community Supervision: A Multisite Evaluation." In *Correctional Boot Camps: A Tough Intermediate Sanction*, edited by D. L. MacKenzie and E. E. Herbert (NCJ 57639). Washington, DC: National Institute of Justice, U.S. Department of Justice.

Brennan, T. and J. Austin. 1997. *Women in Jail: Classification Issues*. Washington, DC: Department of Justice, National Institute of Corrections.

Brewer, J. and A. Hunter. 1989. *Multimethod Research: A Synthesis of Styles*. Newbury Park, CA: Sage.

Bridges, George S. and Joseph G. Weis. 1989. "Measuring Violent Behavior: Effects of Study Design on Reported Correlates of Violence." In *Violent Crime, Violent Criminals*, edited by Neil Alan Weiner and Marvin E. Wolfgang, 14–34. Newbury Park, CA: Sage.

Brody, Jane. 2008. "Curbing Binge Drinking Takes Group Effort." *The New York Times*, September 8:F7.

Broskoske, Steve. 2005. "How to Prevent Paper Recycling." *The Teaching Professor* 19:1–4.

Bureau of Justice Statistics. 2009a. "Homicide Trends in the U.S." Retrieved November 23, 2009 (http://ojp.usdoj .gov/bjs/homicide/city.htm).

Bureau of Justice Statistics. 2009b. "Prison Statistics." Retrieved June 26, 2009 (http://www.ojp.usdoj .gov/bjs/prisons .htm).

Burt, Martha R. 1996. "Homelessness: Definitions and Counts." Pp. 15–23 in *Homelessness in America*, edited by Jim Baumohl. Phoenix, AZ: Oryx.

Bushman, Brad J. 1995. "Moderating Role of Trait Aggressiveness in the Effects of Violent Media on Aggression." *Journal of Personality and Social Psychology* 69(5):950–60.

Bushman, Brad J. and Rowell L. Huesmann. 2012. "Effects of Violent Media on Aggression." In *Handbook of Children and the Media*. 2nd ed., edited by B. J. Bushman and R. L. Huesmann. Thousand Oaks, CA: Sage.

Bushway, S. and P. Reuter. 1997. "Labor Markets and Crime Risk Factors." In *Preventing Crime: What Works, What Doesn't, What's Promising*, edited by L. W. Sherman, D. Gottfredson, D. MacKenzie, J. Eck, P. Reuter, and S. Bushway. Unpublished report by the Department of Criminology and Criminal Justice, University of Maryland.

Buzawa, Eva S. and Carl G. Buzawa. 1996. *Domestic Violence: The Criminal Justice Response*. 2nd ed. Thousand Oaks, CA: Sage.

Bye, Elin K. 2008. "A Time Series Analysis of Six Countries." *Homicide Studies* 12:7–27.

Campbell, Donald T. and M. Jean Russo. 1999. *Social Experimentation*. Thousand Oaks, CA: Sage.

Campbell, Donald T. and Julian C. Stanley. 1966. *Experimental and Quasi-Experimental Designs for Research*. Chicago: Rand McNally.

Campbell, Richard T. 1992. "Longitudinal Research." In *Encyclopedia of Sociology*, edited by Edgar F. Borgatta and Marie L. Borgatta, 1146–58. New York: Macmillan.

Campbell, T. T. and D. W. Fiske. 1959. "Convergent and Discriminant Validity by the Multi-Trait, Multi-Method Matrix." *Psychological Bulletin* 56:126–39.

Campbell, Wilson. 2002. "A Statement From the Governmental Accounting Standards Board and Performance Measurement Staff." American Society for Public Administration. Retrieved July 20, 2002 (http://www.aspanet. org/cap/forum_ statement.html#top).

Canton, R. and Yates, J. 2008. "Applied Criminology." In *Applied Criminology*, edited by Brian Stout, Joe Yates, and Brian Williams, 1–16. Thousand Oaks, CA: Sage.

Cantor, David. 1984. *Comparing Bounded and Unbounded Three and Six Month Reference Periods in Rate Estimation*. Washington, DC: Bureau of Social Science Research.

Cantor, David. 1985. "Operational and Substantive Differences in Changing the NCS Reference Period." In *Proceedings of the American Statistical Association, Social Statistics Section*, 125–37. Washington, DC: American Statistical Association.

Cao, L., A. Adams, and V. J. Jensen. 1997. "A Test of the Black Subculture of Violence Thesis: A Research Note." *Criminology* 35(2):367–79.

Carrington, P. J. and J. L. Schulenberg. 2008. "Structuring Police Discretion: The Effect on Referrals to Youth Court." *Criminal Justice Policy Review* 19:349–67.

Castillo, Mariana. 2012. "Guatemalans to file appear over STD Experiments."

CNN, Friday, June 15. Retrieved June 17, 2012 (http://www.cnn.com/2012/06/15/us/guatemala-std-experiments/index.html).

Cava, A., R. Cushman, and K. Goodman. 2007. "HIPPA and Human Subjects Research." Collaborative Institutional Training Initiative. Retrieved June 5, 2008 (https://www.citiprogram.org/members/learners).

Cavender, Gray and Lisa Bond-Maupin. 2000. "Fear and Loathing on Reality Television: An Analysis of *America's Most Wanted* and *Unsolved Mysteries*." In *Criminology: Perspectives*, edited by Steven Cooper, 51–57. Bellevue, WA: Coursewise.

Chalk, Rosemary and Joel H. Garner. 2001. "Evaluating Arrest for Intimate Partner Violence: Two Decades of Research and Reform." *New Directions for Evaluation* 90:9–23.

Chen, Huey-Tsyh. 1990. *Theory-Driven Evaluations*. Thousand Oaks, CA: Sage.

Chen, Huey-Tsyh and Peter Rossi. 1987. "The Theory Driven Approach to Validity." *Evaluation and Program Planning* 10:95–103.

Cloward, Richard and Lloyd E. Ohlin. 1960. *Delinquency and Opportunity: A Theory of Delinquent Gangs*. New York: Free Press.

CNN. 2012. "Drunken Driving Declines in U.S.: Drug Use 'Troubling' Agency Says." Retrieved June 10, 2012 (http://www.cnn.com/2009/CRIME/07/13/drunken.driving/index.html).

Coffey, Amanda and Paul Atkinson. 1996. *Making Sense of Qualitative Data: Complementary Research Strategies*. Thousand Oaks, CA: Sage.

Cohen, Lawrence E. and Marcus Felson. 1979. "Social Change and Crime Rate Trends: A Routine Activity Approach." *American Sociological Review* 44: 588–608.

Colbert, D. L., R. Paternoster, and S. Bushway. 2002. "Do Attorneys Really Matter? The Empirical and Legal Case for the Right of Counsel at Bail." *Cardozo Law Review* 23(5):1719–93.

Converse, Jean M. 1984. "Attitude Measurement in Psychology and Sociology: The Early Years." In *Surveying Subjective Phenomena*, vol. 2, edited by Charles F. Turner and Elizabeth Martin, 3–40. New York: Russell Sage.

Cook, Philip J. and John H. Laub. 1998. "The Epidemic in Youth Violence." In *Youth Violence: Crime and Justice*, vol. 24, edited by Michael Tonry and Mark H. Moore. Chicago: University of Chicago Press.

Cook, Thomas D. and Donald T. Campbell. 1979. *Quasi-Experimentation: Design and Analysis Issues for Field Settings*. Chicago: Rand McNally.

Cooper, Alexia and Erica L. Smith. 2011. *Homicide Trends in the United States, 1980–2008* (NCJ 236018). Bureau of Justice Statistics, U.S. Department of Justice.

Cooper, Harris and Larry V. Hedges. 1994. "Research Synthesis as a Scientific Enterprise." In *The Handbook of Research Synthesis*, edited by Harris Cooper and Larry V. Hedges, 3–14. New York: Russell Sage.

Core Institute. 1994. "Core Alcohol and Drug Survey: Long Form." Carbondale: FIPSE Core Analysis Grantee Group, Core Institute, Student Health Programs, Southern Illinois University.

Corse, Sara J., Nancy B. Hirschinger, and David Zanis. 1995. "The Use of the Addiction Severity Index With People With Severe Mental Illness." *Psychiatric Rehabilitation Journal* 19(1):9–18.

Creswell, J. W., A. C. Klassen, V. L. Clark, and K. C. Smith. 2011. *Best Practices for Mixed Methods Research in the Health Sciences*. National Institutes of Health.

Cresswell, J. W. and V. L. Plano Clark. 2011. *Designing and Conducting Mixed Methods Research*. 2nd ed. Thousand Oaks, CA: Sage.

Cuba, L. 2002. *A Short Guide to Writing About Social Science*. 4th ed. New York: Addison-Wesley.

Czaja, Ronald and Bob Blair. 1996. *Survey Research*. Newbury Park, CA: Pine Forge.

D'Amico, Elizabeth J. and Kim Fromme. 2002. "Brief Prevention for Adolescent Risk-Taking Behavior." *Addiction* 97:563–74.

Dannefer, W. Dale and Russell K. Schutt. 1982. "Race and Juvenile Justice Processing in Court and Police Agencies." *American Journal of Sociology* 87(March):1113–32.

Davey, Monica. 2012. "Rate of Killings Rises 38 Percent in Chicago in 2012." *The New York Times*, June 25. Retrieved September 20, 2012 (http://www.nytimes.com/2012/06/26/us/rate-of-killings-rises-38-percent-in-chicago-in-12.html?emc=eta1&_r=0).

Davis, James A. and Tom W. Smith. 1992. *The NORC General Social Survey: A User's Guide*. Newbury Park, CA: Sage.

Decker, Scott H. and Barrik Van Winkle. 1996. *Life in the Gang: Family, Friends, and Violence*. Cambridge, UK: Cambridge University Press.

Denton, B. 2001. *Dealing: Women in the Drug Economy*. Sydney: University of New South Wales Press.

Dentler, Robert A. 2002. *Practicing Sociology: Selected Fields*. Westport, CT: Praeger.

Denzin, Norman K. and Yvonna S. Lincoln. 1994. "Introduction: Entering the Field of Qualitative Research." In *Handbook of Qualitative Research*, edited by Norman K. Denzin and Yvonna S. Lincoln, 1–17. Thousand Oaks, CA: Sage.

Department of Health, Education, and Welfare. 1979. "The Belmont Report." Retrieved September 26, 2009 (http://www.hhs.gov/ohrp/humansubjects/guidance/belmont.htm).

Dewan, Shaila K. 2004a. "As Murders Fall, New Tactics Are Tried Against Remainder." *The New York Times*, December 31, pp. A24–A25.

Dewan, Shaila K. 2004b. "New York's Gospel of Policing by Data Spreads Across U.S." *The New York Times*, April 26, pp. A1, C16.

Dillman, Don A. 1978. *Mail and Telephone Surveys: The Total Design Method*. New York: Wiley.

Dillman, Don A. 1982. "Mail and Other Self-Administered Questionnaires." Chapter 12 in *Handbook of Survey Research*, edited by Peter Rossi, Kames Wright, and Andy Anderson. New York: Academic Press. Reprinted on pp. 637–38 in Delbert C. Miller. 1991. *Handbook of Research Design and Social Measurement*. 5th ed. Newbury Park, CA: Sage.

Dillman, Don A. 2000. *Mail and Internet Surveys: The Tailored Design Method*. 2nd ed. New York: John Wiley.

Dillman, Don A. 2007. *Mail and Internet Surveys: The Tailored Design Method*. 2nd ed. Update with New Internet, Visual, and Mixed-Mode Guide. Hoboken, NJ: Wiley.

Dillman, Don A., James A. Christenson, Edwin H. Carpenter, and Ralph M. Brooks. 1974. "Increasing Mail Questionnaire Response: A Four-State Comparison." *American Sociological Review* 39(October):744–56.

Dorsey, T. L. and M. W. Zawitz. 2005. *Drugs and Crime Facts* (NCJ-165148). Washington, DC: Bureau of Justice Statistics, U.S. Department of Justice.

Duggan, Paul, Michael D. Shear, and Marc Fisher. 1999. "Killers Fused Violent Fantasy, Reality." *The Washington Post*, April 22, p. A1.

Duncombe, Jean and Julie Jessop. 2002. "'Doing Rapport' and the Ethics of 'Faking Friendship.'" In *Ethics in Qualitative Research*, edited by Melanie Mauthner, Maxine Birch, Julie Jessop, and Tina Miller, 107–122. Thousand Oaks, CA: Sage.

Dunford, Franklyn W., David Huizinga, and Delbert Elliott. 1990. "The Role of Arrest in Domestic Assault: The Omaha Police Experiment." *Criminology* 28:183–206.

Dunlap, E., B. D. Johnson, and L. Maher. 1997. "Female Crack Sellers in New York City: Who They Are and What They Do." *Women and Criminal Justice* 8(4):25–55.

Durkheim, Emile. [1951] 1987. *Suicide*. New York: Free Press.

Duwe, G., Donnay, W., and Tewksbury, R. 2008. "Does Residential Proximity Matter? A Geographic Analysis of Sex Offense Recidivism." *Criminal Justice and Behavior* 35:484–505.

Elliott, Delbert and Suzanne Ageton. 1980. "Reconciling Race and Class Differences in Self-Reported and Official Estimates of Delinquency." *American Sociological Review* 45:95–110.

Elliott, Delbert A., David Huizinga, and Suzanne S. Ageton. 1985. *Explaining Delinquency and Drug Use*. Newbury Park, CA: Sage.

Ellsberg, M. and Heise, L. 2005. *Researching Violence Against Women: A Practical Guide for Researchers and Activists*. Washington, DC: World Health Organization, PATH.

Emerson, Robert M., ed. 1983. *Contemporary Field Research*. Prospect Heights, IL: Waveland.

Emerson, Robert M., Rachel I. Fretz, and Linda L. Shaw. 1995. *Writing Ethnographic Fieldnotes*. Chicago: University of Chicago Press.

Erikson, Kai T. 1966. *Wayward Puritans: A Study in the Sociology of Deviance*. New York: Wiley.

Erikson, Kai T. 1967. "A Comment on Disguised Observation in Sociology." *Social Problems* 12:366–73.

Farrington, David P. 1977. "The Effects of Public Labeling." *British Journal of Criminology* 17(2):112–25.

Fenno, Richard F., Jr. 1978. *Home Style: House Members in Their Districts*. Boston: Little, Brown.

Ferguson, C. J., C. San Miguel, J. C. Kilburn, J. R. Sanchez, and P. Sanchez. 2007. "The Effectiveness of School-Based Anti-bullying Programs: A Meta-analytic Review." *Criminal Justice Review* 32(4):401–14.

Fink, Arlene. 2005. *Conducting Research Literature Reviews: From the Internet to Paper*. 2nd ed. Thousand Oaks, CA: Sage.

Fischer, Constance T. and Frederick J. Wertz. 2002. "Empirical Phenomenological Analyses of Being Criminally Victimized." In *The Qualitative Researcher's Companion*, edited by A. Michael Huberman and Matthew B. Miles, 275–304. Thousand Oaks, CA: Sage.

Fisher, Bonnie. 2009. "The Effects of Survey Question Wording on Rape Estimates: Evidence from a Quasi-experimental Design." *Violence Against Women* 15:133–47.

Fleury-Steiner, Benjamin. 2003. *Jurors' Stories of Death: How America's Death Penalty Invests in Inequality*. Ann Arbor: University of Michigan Press.

Forero, Juan. 2000. "Census Takers Top '90 Efforts in New York City, With More to Go." *The New York Times*, June 12, p. A29.

Fowler, Floyd J. 1988. *Survey Research Methods*. Rev. ed. Newbury Park, CA: Sage.

Fowler, Floyd J. 1995. *Improving Survey Questions: Design and Evaluation*. Thousand Oaks, CA: Sage.

Freedman, David A. 1991. "Statistical Models and Shoe Leather." In *Sociological Methodology*, vol. 21, edited by Peter V. Marsden, 291–313. Oxford, UK: Basil Blackwell.

Gallup, George 1986. *Public Opinion, 1985*. Wilmington, DE: Scholarly Resources Press.

Garner, Joel, Jeffrey Fagan, and Christopher Maxwell. 1995. "Published Findings From the Spousal Assault Replication Program: A Critical Review." *Journal of Quantitative Criminology* 11:3–28.

Garvin, T. and Gravois Lee, R. 2003. "Reflections on the 'Policy-Relevant Turn' in Research." *Social Justice* 30(4):FY 40–53.

Geertz, Clifford. 1973. "Thick Description: Toward an Interpretive Theory of Culture." In *The Interpretation of Cultures*, edited by Clifford Geertz, 3–30. New York: Basic Books.

"'Get Tough' Youth Programs Are Ineffective, Panel Says." 2004. *The New York Times*, October 17, p. 25.

Gill, Hannah E. 2004. "Finding a Middle Ground Between Extremes: Notes on Researching Transnational Crime and Violence." *Anthropology Matters Journal* 6:1–9.

Giordano, P .C., S. A. Cernkovich, and J. L. Rudolph. 2002. "Gender, Crime, and Desistance: Toward a Theory of

Cognitive Transformation." *American Journal of Sociology* 107(4):990–1064.

Glaser, Barney G. and Anselm L. Strauss. 1967. *The Discovery of Grounded Theory: Strategies for Qualitative Research.* London: Weidenfeld and Nicholson.

Glover, Judith. 1996. "Epistemological and Methodological Considerations in Secondary Analysis." In *Cross-National Research Methods in the Social Sciences*, edited by Linda Hantrais and Steen Mangen, 28–38. New York: Pinter.

Glueck, Sheldon and Eleanor Glueck. 1950. *Unraveling Juvenile Delinquency.* New York: Commonwealth Fund.

Goffman, Erving. 1961. *Asylums: Essays on the Social Situation of Mental Patients and Other Inmates.* Garden City, NY: Doubleday.

Goldfinger, Stephen M., Russell K. Schutt, Larry J. Seidman, Winston M. Turner, Walter E. Penk, and George S. Tolomiczenko. 1996. "Self-Report and Observer Measures of Substance Abuse Among Homeless Mentally Ill Persons in the Cross-Section and Over Time." *The Journal of Nervous and Mental Disease* 184(11):667–72.

Goleman, Daniel. 1993. "Placebo Effect Is Shown to Be Twice as Powerful as Expected." *The New York Times*, August 17, p. C3.

Goleman, Daniel. 1995. *Emotional Intelligence.* New York: Bantam.

Goode, Erica. 2011. "Sending the Police Before There's a Crime." *The New York Times*, August 16, A11.

Gordon, Raymond. 1992. *Basic Interviewing Skills.* Itasca, IL: Peacock.

Gottfredson, D. C. and T. Hirschi. 1990. *A General Theory of Crime.* Palo Alto, CA: Stanford University Press.

Gray, Kevin M. 2011. "Problem behaviors of students pursuing policing careers." *Policing* 34(3):541–52.

Griffin, Larry. 1993. "Narrative, Event-Structure Analysis, and Causal Interpretation in Historical Sociology." *American Journal of Sociology* 98:1094–1133.

Grinnell, Frederick. 1992. *The Scientific Attitude.* 2nd ed. New York: Guilford.

Grossman, David C., Jolly J. Neckerman, Thomas D. Koepsell, Ping-Yu Liu, Kenneth N. Asher, Kathy Beland, Darin Frey, and Frederick P. Rivara. 1997. "Effectiveness of a Violence Prevention Curriculum Among Children in Elementary School: A Randomized Controlled Trial." *The Journal of the American Medical Association* 277(20):1605–12.

Groves, Robert M. 1989. *Survey Errors and Survey Costs.* New York: Wiley.

Groves, Robert M. and D. L. Cork. (2008). *Surveying Victims: Options for Conducting the National Crime Victimization Survey.* Washington, DC: National Research Council.

Groves, Robert M. and Mick P. Couper. 1998. *Nonresponse in Household Interview Surveys.* New York: Wiley.

Groves, Robert M. and Robert L. Kahn. 1979. *Surveys by Telephone: A National Comparison With Personal Interviews.* New York: Academic Press. Adapted in Delbert C. Miller. 1991. *Handbook of Research Design and Social Measurement.* 5th ed. Newbury Park, CA: Sage.

Gruenewald, Paul J., Andrew J. Treno, Gail Taff, and Michael Klitzner. 1997. *Measuring Community Indicators: A Systems Approach to Drug and Alcohol Problems.* Thousand Oaks, CA: Sage.

Guba, Egon G. and Yvonna S. Lincoln. 1989. *Fourth Generation Evaluation.* Newbury Park, CA: Sage.

Guba, Egon G. and Yvonna S. Lincoln. 1994. "Competing Paradigms in Qualitative Research." In *Handbook of Qualitative Research*, edited by Norman K. Denzin and Yvonna S. Lincoln, 105–17. Thousand Oaks, CA: Sage.

Gubrium, Jaber F. and James A. Holstein. 1997. *The New Language of Qualitative Method.* New York: Oxford University Press.

Gubrium, Jaber F. and James A. Holstein. 2000. "Analyzing Interpretive Practice." In *The Handbook of Qualitative Research.* 2nd ed., edited by Norman Denzin and Yvonna S. Lincoln, 487–508. Thousand Oaks, CA: Sage.

Guerino, Paul, Paige M. Harrison, and William J. Sabol, 2011. *Prisoners in 2010* (NCJ 236096). Bureau of Justice Statistics, U.S. Department of Justice.

Groves, Robert M. and Daniel L. Cork. 2008. *Surveying Victims: Options for Conducting the National Crime Victimization Survey.* National Research Council. Washington, DC: National Academies Press.

Hagan, J., A. R. Gillis, and J. Simpson. 1985. "The Class Structure of Gender and Delinquency: Toward a Power-Control Theory." *American Journal of Sociology* 90:1151–76.

Hagan, John. 1994. *Crime and Disrepute.* Thousand Oaks, CA: Pine Forge.

Hage, Jerald and Barbara Foley Meeker. 1988. *Social Causality.* Boston: Unwin Hyman.

Hagedorn, John. 1988. *People and Folks.* Chicago: Lake View.

Hakimzadeh, Shirin and D'Vera Cohn. 2007. *English Usage Among Hispanics in the United States.* Washington, DC: Pew Hispanic Center. Retrieved May 24, 2008 (http://pewhispanic.org/files/reports/82.pdf).

Haney, C., C. Banks, and Philip G. Zimbardo. 1973. "International Dynamics in a Simulated Prison." *International Journal of Criminology and Penology* 1:69–97.

Hantrais, Linda and Steen Mangen. 1996. "Method of Management of Cross-National Social Research." In *Cross-National Research Methods in the Social Sciences*, edited by Linda Hantrais and Steen Mangen, 1–12. New York: Pinter.

Hard, Stephen F., James M. Conway, and Antonia C. Moran. 2006. "Faculty and College Student Beliefs About the Frequency of Student Academic Misconduct." *The Journal of Higher Education* 77:1058–80.

Harrell, Adele, S. Cavanagh, and S. Sridharan. 1999. *Evaluation of the Children at Risk Program: Results 1 Year After the End of the Program* (NCJ 178914). Washington, DC: National Institute of Justice, U.S. Department of Justice.

Harris, Anthony R., Stephen H. Thomas, Gene A. Fisher, and David J. Hirsch. 2002. "Murder and Medicine: The Lethality of

Criminal Assault 1960–1999." *Homicide Studies* 6:128–66.

Hart, Chris. 1998. *Doing a Literature Review: Releasing the Social Science Research Imagination*. London: Sage.

Heckathorn, Douglas D. 1997. "Respondent-Driven Sampling: A New Approach to the Study of Hidden Populations." *Social Problems* 44:174–99.

Hirschel, J. David, Ira W. Hutchison, III, and Charles W. Dean. 1992. "The Failure of Arrest to Deter Spouse Abuse." *Journal of Research in Crime and Delinquency* 9(2):7–33.

Hirshey, Gerri. 2007. "Pushing Back at Bullying." *The New York Times*, January 28. Retrieved 23, 2012 (http://www.nytimes.com/2007/01/28/nyregion/nyregionspecial2/28rbully.html?pagewanted=print).

Horney, Julie, D. Wayne Osgood, and Ineke Haen Marshall. 1995. "Criminal Careers in the Short-Term: Intra-Individual Variability in Crime and Its Relation to Local Life Circumstances." *American Sociological Review* 60:655–73.

Howell, J. C. 2003. *Preventing and Reducing Juvenile Delinquency: A Comprehensive Framework*. Thousand Oaks, CA: Sage.

Hoyle, Carolyn and Andrew Sanders. 2000. "Police Response to Domestic Violence: From Victim Choice to Victim Empowerment." *British Journal of Criminology* 40:14–26.

Huberman, A. Michael and Matthew B. Miles. 1994. "Data Management and Analysis Methods." In *Handbook of Qualitative Research*, edited by Norman K. Denzin and Yvonna S. Lincoln, 428–44. Thousand Oaks, CA: Sage.

Humphrey, Nicholas. 1992. *A History of the Mind: Evolution and the Birth of Consciousness*. New York: Simon & Schuster.

Humphreys, Laud. 1970. *Tearoom Trade: Impersonal Sex in Public Places*. Chicago: Aldine.

Hunt, Morton. 1985. *Profiles of Social Research: The Scientific Study of Human Interactions*. New York: Russell Sage.

Huston, Patricia and C. David Naylor. 1996. "Health Services Research: Reporting on Studies Using Secondary Data Sources." *Canadian Medical Association Journal* 155:1697–1702.

Inciardi, J. A. and L. D. Harrison, eds. 2000. *Harm reduction*. Thousand Oaks, CA: Sage.

Irwin, John. 1970. *The Felon*. Englewood Cliffs, NJ: Prentice Hall.

Jalbert, Sarah K., William Rhodes, Christopher Flygare, and Michael Kane. 2010. "Testing Probation Outcomes in an Evidence-Based Practice Setting: Reduced Caseload Size and Intensive Supervision Effectiveness." *Journal of Offender Rehabilitation* 49(4):233–53.

James, Thomas S. and Jeanne M. Granville. 1984. "Practical Issues in Vocational Education for Serious Juvenile Offenders." In *Violent Juvenile Offenders: An Anthology*, edited by R. Mathias, P. DeMuro, and R. Allison. San Francisco, CA: National Council on Crime and Delinquency.

Jervis, Robert. 1996. "Counterfactuals, Causation, and Complexity." In *Counterfactual Thought Experiments in World Politics: Logical, Methodological, and Psychological Perspectives*, edited by Philip E. Tetlock and Aaron Belkin, 309–16. Princeton, NJ: Princeton University Press.

Johnson, Burke and Robert Gray. 2010. "A History of Philosophical and Theoretical Issues for Mixed Methods Research." In *Sage Handbook of Mixed Methods in Social and Behavioral Research*. 2nd ed., edited by Abbas Tashakkori and Charles Teddlie, 69–94. Thousand Oaks, CA: Sage.

Johnston, Lloyd D., Jerald G. Bachman, and Patrick M. O'Malley. 1994. *Sourcebook of Criminal Justice Statistics: 1994* (NCJ 154591). Washington, DC: Bureau of Justice Statistics, U.S. Department of Justice.

Joint Committee on Standards for Education Evaluation. 1994. *The Program Evaluation Standards*. Thousand Oaks, CA: Sage.

Joyner, L. M. 2003. "Applied Research in the Pursuit of Justice: Creating Change in the Community and the Academy." *Social Justice* 30(4):5–20.

Junger-Tas, J. 2005. "The Scientific Integrity of Applied Research." *European Journal on Criminal Policy and Research* 11:143–58.

Kandakai, Tina L., James H. Price, Susan K. Telljohann, and Carter A. Wilson. 1999. "Mothers' Perceptions of Factors Influencing Violence in Schools." *Journal of School Health* 69(5):189–205.

Kaplan, Fred. 2002. "NY Continues to See Plunge in Number of Felonies." *The Boston Globe*, April 15, p. A3.

Kaplan, Thomas. 2012. "Cuomo Seeks Cut in Frisk Arrests." *The New York Times*, June 4:A1.

Kaufman, Sharon R. 1986. *The Ageless Self: Sources of Meaning in Late Life*. Madison: University of Wisconsin Press.

Kemmis, S. and R. McTaggart. 2005. "Participatory Action Research: Communicative Action and the Public Sphere." In *The Sage Handbook of Qualitative Research*. 3rd ed., edited by Norman K. Denzin and Yvonna S. Lincoln, 559–603. Thousand Oaks, CA: Sage.

Kincaid, Harold. 1996. *Philosophical Foundations of the Social Sciences: Analyzing Controversies in Social Research*. Cambridge, UK: Cambridge University Press.

King, Gary, Robert O. Keohane, and Sidney Verba. 1994. *Scientific Inference in Qualitative Research*. Princeton, NJ: Princeton University Press.

Kobelarcik, E. L., C. A. Alexander, R. P. Singh, and G. M. Shapiro. 1983. "Alternative Reference Periods for the National Crime Survey." In *Proceedings of the American Statistical Association: Section on Survey Methods*. Washington, DC: American Statistical Association.

Koegel, Paul. 1987. *Ethnographic Perspectives on Homeless and Homeless Mentally Ill Women*. Washington, DC: Alcohol, Drug Abuse, and Mental Health Administration; Public Health Service; U.S. Department of Health and Human Services.

Kohn, Melvin L. 1987. "Cross-National Research as an Analytic Strategy." *American Sociological Review* 52:713–31.

Kohn, Alfie. 2008. "Who's Cheating Whom?" *The Education Digest* 73:4–11.

Korn, J. H. 1997. *Illusions of Reality: A History of Deception in Social Psychology.* Albany: State University of New York Press.

Kraemer, Helena Chmura and Sue Thiemann. 1987. *How Many Subjects? Statistical Power Analysis in Research.* Newbury Park, CA: Sage.

Krueger, Richard A. 1988. *Focus Groups: A Practical Guide for Applied Research.* Newbury Park, CA: Sage.

Kupchik, Aaron. 2010. *Homeroom Security: School Discipline in an Age of Fear.* New York: New York University Press.

Kvale, Steinar. 1996. *Interviews: An Introduction to Qualitative Research Interviewing.* Thousand Oaks, CA: Sage.

Kvale, Steinar. 2002. "The Social Construction of Validity." In *The Qualitative Inquiry Reader,* edited by Norman K. Denzin and Yvonna S. Lincoln, 229–325. Thousand Oaks, CA: Sage.

Labaw, Patricia J. 1980. *Advanced Questionnaire Design.* Cambridge, MA: ABT Books.

Langan, P. A. and D. J. Levin. 2002. *Recidivism of prisoners released in 1994.* NCJ 193427. Washington, DC: Bureau of Justice Statistics, U.S. Department of Justice.

Latour, Francie. 2002. "Marching Orders: After 10 Years, State Closes Prison Boot Camp." *The Boston Sunday Globe,* June 16, pp. B1, B7.

Lattimore, P. K. and C. A. Visher. 2010. *The multi-site evaluation of SVORI: Summary and Synthesis* (NCJ 230421). Washington, DC: Bureau of Justice Statistics, U.S. Department of Justice.

Laub, J. H. and R. J. Sammpson. 2003. *Shared Beginnings, Divergent Lives: Delinquent Boys to Age 70.* Cambridge, MA: Harvard University Press.

Lavin, Danielle and Douglas W. Maynard. 2001. "Standardization vs. Rapport: Respondent Laughter and Interviewer Reaction During Telephone Surveys." *American Sociological Review* 66:453–79.

Lavrakas, Paul J. 1987. *Telephone Survey Methods: Sampling, Selection, and Supervision.* Newbury Park, CA: Sage.

Lazarsfeld, Paul F. and Anthony R. Oberschall. 1965. "Max Weber and Empirical Research." *American Sociological Review* (April):185–99.

Lempert, Richard. 1989. "Humility Is a Virtue: On the Publicization of Policy-Relevant Research." *Law and Society Review* 23:146–61.

Lempert, Richard and Joseph Sanders. 1986. *An Invitation to Law and Social Science: Desert, Disputes, and Distribution.* New York: Longman.

Levine, James P. 1976. "The Potential for Crime Overreporting in Criminal Victimization Surveys." *Criminology* 14:307–30.

Levy, Paul S. and Stanley Lemeshow. 1999. *Sampling of Populations: Methods and Applications.* 3rd. ed. New York: Wiley.

Lewin, Tamar. 2001. "Income Education Is Found to Lower Risk of New Arrest." *The New York Times,* November 16, p. A18.

Lichtblau, Eric. 2000. "Crime Dip Levels Off; Assault, Rape Up." *The New York Times,* December 19, p. A2.

Lieberson, Stanley. 1985. *Making It Count: The Improvement of Social Research and Theory.* Berkeley: University of California Press.

Lieberson, Stanley. 1991. "Small *N*'s and Big Conclusions: An Examination of the Reasoning in Comparative Studies Based on a Small Number of Cases." *Social Forces* 70:307–20.

Linsky, Arnold, Ronet Bachman, and Murray Straus. 1995. *Stress Culture and Aggression in the United States.* New Haven, CT: Yale University Press.

Lipsey, Mark W. and David B. Wilson. 2001. *Practice Meta-Analysis.* Thousand Oaks, CA: Sage.

Liptak, Adam. 2004. "Long Term in Drug Case Fuels Debate on Sentencing." *The New York Times,* September 12, p. 16.

Listwan, S. J., J. L. Sundt, A. M. Holsinger, and E. H. Katessam. 2003. "The Effect of Drug Court Programming on Recidivism: The Cincinnati Experience." *Crime and Delinquency* 49:389–411.

Littell, Julia H. 2005. "Lessons From a Systematic Review of Effects of Multisystemic Therapy." *Children and Youth Services Review* 27:445–63.

Litwin, Mark S. 1995. *How to Measure Survey Reliability and Validity.* Thousand Oaks, CA: Sage.

Lo, C. C., Y. S. Kim, and C. Cheng. 2008. "Offense Specialization of Arrestees: An Event History Analysis." *Crime and Delinquency* 54:341–65.

Locke, Lawrence F., Stephen J. Silverman, and Waneen Wyrick Spirduso. 1998. *Reading and Understanding Research.* Thousand Oaks, CA: Sage.

Lofland, John and Lyn H. Lofland. 1984. *Analyzing Social Settings: A Guide to Qualitative Observation and Analysis.* 2nd ed. Belmont, CA: Wadsworth.

Loftus, Louise. 2011. "Data on Rape in E.U. Difficult to Compare." *The New York Times,* October, 24. Retrieved June 12, 2012 (http://www.nytimes.com/2011/10/25/world/europe/data-on-rape-in-eu-difficult-to-compare.html).

Lovibond, S. H., X. Mithiran, and W. G. Adams. 1979. "The Effects of Three Experimental Prison Environments on the Behaviour of Non-Convict Volunteer Subjects." *Australian Psychologist* 14:273–87.

Lundahl, Brad W., Janelle Nimer, and Bruce Parsons. 2006. "Preventing Child Abuse: A Meta-Analysis of Parent Training Programs." *Research in Social Work Practice* 16:151–62.

Lynch, James P. 1996. "Clarifying Divergent Estimates of Rape From Two National Surveys." *Public Opinion Quarterly* 60:410–30.

Lynch, Michael and David Bogen. 1997. "Sociology's Asociological 'Core': An Examination of Textbook Sociology in Light of the Sociology of Scientific Knowledge." *American Sociological Review* 62:481–93.

MacDonald, J. M., A. R. Piquero, R. F. Valois, and K. J. Zullig. 2005. "The Relationship Between Life Satisfaction, Risk-Taking Behaviors, and Youth Violence. " *Journal of Interpersonal Violence* 20:1495–1518.

MacKenzie, Doris L. 1994. "Results of a Multisite Study of Boot Camp Prisons." *Federal Probation* 58(2):60–66.

MacKenzie, Doris L., Robert Brame, David McDowall, and C. Souryal. 1995. "Boot Camp, Prisons and Recidivism in Eight States." *Criminology* 33(3):401–30.

MacKenzie, Doris L. and Alex Piquero. 1994. "The Impact of Shock Incarceration Programs on Prison Crowding." *Crime and Delinquency* 40(2):222–49.

MacKenzie, Doris L. and C. Souryal. 1995. "Inmate Attitude Change During Incarceration: A Comparison of Boot Camp With Traditional Prison." *Justice Quarterly* 12(2):125–50.

MacKenzie, Doris L. and C. Souryal. 1996. "Multisite Study of Correctional Boot Camps." In *Correctional Boot Camps: A Tough Intermediate Sanction*, edited by D. L. MacKenzie and E. E. Herbert (NCJ 157639). Washington, DC: National Institute of Justice, U.S. Department of Justice.

Maher, Lisa and Susan L. Hudson. 2007. "Women in the Drug Economy: A Metasynthesis of the Qualitative Literature." *Journal of Drug Issues* 37:805–26.

Mangione, Thomas W. 1995. *Mail Surveys: Improving the Quality*. Thousand Oaks, CA: Sage.

Marini, Margaret Mooney and Burton Singer. 1988. "Causality in the Social Sciences." In *Sociological Methodology*, vol. 18, edited by Clifford C. Clogg, 347–409. Washington, DC: American Sociological Association.

Marshall, G. D. and P. G. Zimbardo. 1979. "Affective Consequences of Inadequately Explained Physiological Arousal." *Journal of Personality and Social Psychology* 37:970–88.

Martin, Lawrence L. and Peter M. Kettner. 1996. *Measuring the Performance of Human Service Programs*. Thousand Oaks, CA: Sage.

Matt, Georg E. and Thomas D. Cook. 1994. "Threats to the Validity of Research Syntheses." In *The Handbook of Research Synthesis*, edited by Harris M. Cooper and Larry V. Hedges, 503–20. New York: Russell Sage.

Maxwell, Joseph A. 1996. *Qualitative Research Design: An Interactive Approach*. Thousand Oaks, CA: Sage.

McLellan, A. Thomas, Lester Luborsky, John Cacciola, Jeffrey Griffith, Frederick Evans, Harriet L. Barr, and Charles P. O'Brien. 1985. "New Data From the Addiction Severity Index: Reliability and Validity in Three Centers." *The Journal of Nervous and Mental Disease* 173(7):412–23.

Menand, Louis. 2001. *The Metaphysical Club: A Story of Ideas in America*. New York: Farrar, Straus, and Giroux.

Merton, Robert K. 1938. "Social Structure and Anomie." *American Sociological Review* 3:672–82.

Merton, Robert K., Marjorie Fiske, and Patricia L. Kendall. 1956. *The Focused Interview*. Glencoe, IL: Free Press.

Messner, Steven F. and Richard Rosenfeld. 1994. *Crime and the American Dream*. Belmont, CA: Wadsworth.

Miethe, Terance D., Wendy C. Regoeczi, and Kriss A. Drass. 2004. *Rethinking Homicide: Exploring the Structure and Process Underlying Deadly Situations*. Cambridge, UK: Cambridge University Press.

Milgram, S. 1963. "Behavioral Study of Obedience." *The Journal of Abnormal and Social Psychology* 67(4):371–78.

Milgram, Stanley. 1964. "Issues in the Study of Obedience: A Reply to Baumrind." *American Psychologist* 19:848–52.

Milgram, Stanley. 1965. "Some Conditions of Obedience and Disobedience to Authority." *Human Relations* 18:57–75.

Milgram, Stanley. 1974. *Obedience to Authority: An Experimental View*. New York: Harper & Row.

Milgram, Stanley. 1992. *The Individual in a Social World: Essays and Experiments*. 2nd ed. New York: McGraw-Hill.

Mill, John Stuart. 1872. *A System of Logic: Ratiocinative and Inductive*. 8th ed., vol. 2. London: Longmans, Green, Reader, & Dyer.

Miller, Arthur G. 1986. *The Obedience Experiments: A Case Study of Controversy in Social Science*. New York: Praeger.

Miller, Delbert C. 1991. *Handbook of Research Design and Social Measurement*. 5th ed. Newbury Park, CA: Sage.

Miller, E. 1986. *Street Woman*. Philadelphia: Temple University Press.

Miller, H. G., J. N. Gribble, L. C. Mazade, and C. F. Turner. 1998. "Abortion and Breast Cancer: Facto or Artifact?" In *Science of Self Report*, edited by A. Stone. Mahwah, NJ: Lawrence Erlbaum.

Miller, Jody. 2000. *One of the Guys: Girls, Gangs, and Gender*. New York: Oxford University Press.

Miller, J. 2003. "An Arresting Experiment: Domestic Violence Victim Experiences and Perceptions." *Journal of Interpersonal Violence* 18:695–716.

Miller, J. 2008. *Getting Played: African American Girls, Urban Inequality, and Gendered Violence*. New York, NY: New York University Press.

Miller, Susan. 1999. *Gender and Community Policing: Walking the Talk*. Boston: Northeastern University Press.

Miller, Susan L. and C. Burack. 1993. "A Critique of Gottfredson and Hirschi's General Theory of Crime: Selective (in) Attention to Gender and Power Positions." *Women and Criminal Justice* 4:115–34.

Miller, William L. and Benjamin F. Crabtree. 1999a. "Clinical Research: A Multimethod Typology and Qualitative Roadmap." In *Doing Qualitative Research*. 2nd ed., edited by Benjamin F. Crabtree and William L. Miller, 3–30. Thousand Oaks, CA: Sage.

Miller, William L. and Benjamin F. Crabtree. 1999b. "The Dance of Interpretation." In *Doing Qualitative Research*, edited by Benjamin F. Crabtree and William L. Miller, 127–43. Thousand Oaks, CA: Sage.

Mills, C. Wright. 1959. *The Sociological Imagination*. New York: Oxford University Press.

Mohr, Lawrence B. 1992. *Impact Analysis for Program Evaluation*. Newbury Park, CA: Sage.

Monkkonen, Eric H. 1994. "Introduction." In *Engaging the Past: The Uses of History Across the Social Sciences*, 1–8. Durham, NC: Duke University Press.

Mooney, Christopher Z. and Mei Hsien Lee. 1995. "Legislating Morality in the American States: The Case of Abortion Regulation Reform." *American Journal of Political Science* 39:599–627.

Moore, Joan W. 1978. *Homeboys: Gangs, Drugs, and Prison in the Barrios of Los Angeles*. Philadelphia: Temple University Press.

Moore, Joan W. 1991. *Going Down to the Barrio: Homeboys and Homegirls in Change*. Philadelphia: Temple University Press.

Morrill, Calvin, Christine Yalda, Madeleine Adelman, Michael Musheno, and Cindy Bejarano. 2000. "Telling Tales in School: Youth Culture and Conflict Narratives." *Law & Society Review* 34:521–65.

Mosher, Clayton J., Terance D. Miethe, and Dretha M. Phillips. 2002. *The Mismeasure of Crime*. Thousand Oaks, CA: Sage.

Mueser, Kim T., Paul R. Yarnold, Douglas F. Levinson, Hardeep Singhy, Alan S. Bellack, Kimmy Kee, Randall L. Morrison, and Kashinath G. Yadalam. 1990. "Prevalence of Substance Abuse in Schizophrenia: Demographic and Clinical Correlates." *Schizophrenia Bulletin* 16(1):31–56.

National Institute on Alcohol Abuse and Alcoholism (NIAAA). 1994. "Alcohol-Related Impairment." *Alcohol Alert* 25(July):1–5.

National Institute on Alcohol Abuse and Alcoholism (NIAAA). 1997. "Alcohol Metabolism." *Alcohol Alert* 35(January):1–4.

National Opinion Research Center. 1992. *The NORC General Social Survey: Questions and Answers*. Mimeographed. Chicago: National Data Program for the Social Sciences.

National Victim Center and the Crime Victims Research and Treatment Center. 1992. *Rape in America: A Report to the Nation*. Arlington, VA: National Victim Center and the Crime Victims Research and Treatment Center.

Needleman, Carolyn. 1981. "Discrepant Assumptions in Empirical Research: The Case of Juvenile Court Screening." *Social Problems* 28(February): 247–262.

Nester, Paul. G. and Russell K. Schutt. 2012. *Research Methods in Psychology: Investigating Human Behavior*. Thousand Oaks, CA: Sage.

Neuendorf, Kimberly A. 2002. *The Content Analysis Guidebook*. Thousand Oaks, CA: Sage.

Neyfakh, Leon. 2011. "You will Commit a Crime in the Future, True, False: Inside the Science of Predicting Violence." *Boston Sunday Globe,* February 20: K1, K4.

Oberschall, Anthony. 1972. "The Institutionalization of American Sociology." In *The Establishment of Empirical Sociology: Studies in Continuity, Discontinuity, and Institutionalization*, edited by Anthony Oberschall, 187–251. New York: Harper & Row.

Ogburn, William F. 1930. "The Folkways of a Scientific Sociology." *Scientific Monthly* 30:300–306.

Olzak, Susan, Suzanne Shanahan, and Elizabeth H. McEneaney. 1996. "Poverty, Segregation, and Race Riots: 1960 to 1993." *American Sociological Review* 61:590–613.

Onwuegbuzie, Anthony J. and Julie P. Combs. 2010. "Emergent Data Analysis Techniques in Mixed Methods Research: A Synthesis." In *Sage Handbook of Mixed Methods in Social and Behavioral Research,* 2nd ed, edited by Abbas Tashakkori and Charles Teddlie, 397–430., Thousand Oaks, CA: Sage.

Orcutt, James D. and J. Blake Turner. 1993. "Shocking Numbers and Graphic Accounts: Quantified Images of Drug Problems in the Print Media." *Social Problems* 49(May):190–206.

Orshansky, Mollie. 1977. "Memorandum for Daniel P. Moynihan. Subject: History of the Poverty Line." In *The Measure of Poverty. Technical Paper I: Documentation of Background Information and Rationale for Current Poverty Matrix*, edited by Mollie Orshansky, 232–37. Washington, DC: U.S. Department of Health, Education, and Welfare.

Padilla, Felix M. 1992. *The Gang as an American Enterprise*. New Brunswick, NJ: Rutgers University Press.

Pager, D. 2007. *Marked: Race, Crime and Finding Work in an Era of Mass Incarceration*. Chicago: University of Chicago Press.

Papineau, David. 1978. *For Science in the Social Sciences*. London: Macmillan.

Parks, Kathleen A., Ann M. Pardi, and Clara M. Bradizza. 2006. "Collecting Data on Alcohol Use and Alcohol-Related Victimization: A Comparison of Telephone and Web-Based Survey Methods." *Journal of Studies on Alcohol* 67:318–23.

Parlett, Malcolm and David Hamilton. 1976. "Evaluation as Illumination: A New Approach to the Study of Innovative Programs". In *Evaluation Studies Review Annual,* vol. 1, edited by, G. Glass, 140–57. Thousand Oaks, CA: Sage.

Pate, Anthony M. and Edwin E. Hamilton. 1992. "Formal and Informal Deterrents to Domestic Violence: The Dade County Spouse Assault Experiment." *American Sociological Review* 57:691–97.

Paternoster, Raymond. 1991. *Capital Punishment in America*. New York: Lexington.

Paternoster, Raymond, Robert Brame, Ronet Bachman, and Lawrence W. Sherman. 1997. "Do Fair Procedures Matter? The Effect of Procedural Justice on Spouse Assault." *Law & Society Review* 31(1):163–204.

Paternoster, Raymond, Robert Brame, Sarah Bacon, and Andrew Ditchfield. 2004. "Justice by Geography and Race: The Administration of the Death Penalty in Maryland 1978–1999." *Margins* 4(1):1–97.

Patton, Michael Quinn. 1997. *Utilization Focused Evaluation: The New Century Text*. 3rd ed. Thousand Oaks, CA: Sage.

Patton, Michael Quinn. 2002. *Qualitative Research and Evaluation Methods*. 3rd ed. Thousand Oaks, CA: Sage.

Paulos, John Allen. 2010. "Stories vs. Statistics." October 24, Opionionator. *The New York Times,* Retrieved May 30, 2010 (http://opinionator.blogs.nytimes.com/2010/10/24/stories-vs-statistics/).

Pepinsky, Harold E. 1980. "A Sociologist on Police Patrol." In *Fieldwork Experience: Qualitative Approaches to Social Research*, edited by William B. Shaffir, Robert A. Stebbins, and Allan Turowetz, 223–34. New York: St. Martin's.

Peterson, R. A. 2000. *Constructing Effective Questionnaires*. Thousand Oaks, CA: Sage.

Petrosino, A. and J. Lavenberg. 2007. "Systematic Reviews and Meta-Analyses: Best Evidence on 'What Works' for Criminal Justice Decision Makers." *Western Criminology Review* 8(1):1–15.

Pew Hispanic Center. 2008. Statistical Portrait of the Foreign-Born Population in the United States, 2006. Statistical tables from 2000 Census and 2006 American Community Survey, Retrieved May 24, 2008 (http://pewhispanic.org/factsheets/factsheet/php?FactsheetID=36).

Phoenix, Ann. 2003. "Neoliberalism and Masculinity: Racialization and the Contradictions of Schooling for 11- to 14-Year-Olds." *Youth & Society* 36:227–46.

Piliavin, J. A. and I. R. Piliavin. 1972. "Effect of Blood on Reactions to a Victim." *Journal of Personality and Social Psychology* 23:353–61.

Plano Clark, Vicki L. and Manijeh Badiee. 2010. "Research Questions in Mixed Methods Research." In *Sage Handbook of Mixed Methods in Social and Behavioral Research*. 2nd ed., edited by Abbas Tashakkori and Charles Teddlie, 275–304. Thousand Oaks, CA: Sage.

Posavac, E. J. and R. G. Carey. 1997. *Program Evaluation: Methods and Case Studies*. Upper Saddle River, NJ: Prentice Hall.

Powell, Kenneth E., Lois Muir-McClain, and Lakshmi Halasyamani. 1995. "A Review of Selected School-Based Conflict Resolution and Peer Mediation Projects." *Journal of School Health* 65(10):426–32.

Presley, Cheryl A., Philip W. Meilman, and Rob Lyerla. 1994. "Development of the Core Alcohol and Drug Survey: Initial Findings and Future Directions." *Journal of American College Health* 42:248–55.

Price, Richard H., Michelle Van Ryn, and Amiram D. Vinokur. 1992. "Impact of a Preventive Job Search Intervention on the Likelihood of Depression Among the Unemployed." *Journal of Health and Social Behavior* 33:158–67.

Pruitt, Matthew V. 2008. "Deviant Research: Deception, Male Internet Escorts, and Response Rates." *Deviant Behavior* 29(1):70–82.

Punch, Maurice. 1994. "Politics and Ethics in Qualitative Research." In *Handbook of Qualitative Research*, edited by Norman K. Denzin and Yvonna S. Lincoln, 83–97. Thousand Oaks, CA: Sage.

Putnam, Israel. 1977. "Poverty Thresholds: Their History and Future Development." In *The Measure of Poverty. Technical Paper I: Documentation of Background Information and Rationale for Current Poverty Matrix*, edited by Mollie Orshansky, 272–83. Washington, DC: U.S. Department of Health, Education, and Welfare.

Pyrczak, Fred. 2005. *Evaluating Research in Academic Journals: A Practical Guide to Realistic Evaluation*. 3rd ed. Glendale, CA: Pyrczak.

Ragin, Charles C. 1987. *The Comparative Method: Moving Beyond Qualitative and Quantitative Strategies*. Berkeley: University of California Press.

Ragin, Charles C. 1994. *Constructing Social Research*. Thousand Oaks, CA: Pine Forge.

Rashbaum, William K. 2002. "Reasons for Crime Drop in New York Elude Many." *The New York Times*, November 29, p. A28.

Raudenbush, Stephen W. and Robert J. Sampson. 1999. "Ecometrics: Toward a Science of Assessing Ecological Settings, With Application to the Systematic Social Observation of Neighborhoods." *Sociological Methodology* 29:1–41.

Regoli, R. M. and J. D. Hewitt. 1994. "Delinquency in Society: A Child-Centered Approach." New York: McGraw-Hill.

Reicher, Stephen and S. Alexander Haslam. 2006. "Rethinking the Psychology of Tyranny: The BBC Prison Study." *British Journal of Social Psychology* 45:1–40.

Reiss, Albert J., Jr. 1971. *The Police and the Public*. New Haven, CT: Yale University Press.

Reiss, Albert J. and Jeffrey A. Roth. 1993. *Understanding and Preventing Violence*. Washington, DC: National Academy Press.

Reynolds, Paul Davidson. 1979. *Ethical Dilemmas and Social Science Research*. San Francisco: Jossey-Bass.

Richards, Thomas J. and Lyn Richards. 1994. "Using Computers in Qualitative Research." In *Handbook of Qualitative Research*, edited by Norman K. Denzin and Yvonna S. Lincoln, 445–62. Thousand Oaks, CA: Sage.

Richardson, Laurel. 1995. "Narrative and Sociology." In *Representation in Ethnography*, edited by John Van Maanen, 198–221. Thousand Oaks, CA: Sage.

Riedel, Marc. 2000. *Research Strategies for Secondary Data: A Perspective for Criminology and Criminal Justice*. Thousand Oaks, CA: Sage.

Riessman, Catherine Kohler. 2002. "Narrative Analysis." In *The Qualitative Researcher's Companion*, edited by

A. Michael Huberman and Matthew B. Miles, 217-70. Thousand Oaks, CA: Sage.

Riessman, Catherin Kohler. 2008. *Narrative Methods for the Human Sciences*. Thousand Oaks, CA: Sage.

Ringwalt, Christopher L., Jody M. Greene, Susan T. Ennett, Ronaldo Iachan, Richard R. Clayton, and Carl G. Leukefeld. 1994. *Past and Future Directions of the D.A.R.E. Program: An Evaluation Review*. Research Triangle, NC: Research Triangle Institute.

Rise, Eric W. 1995. *The Martinsville Seven: Race, Rape, and Capital Punishment*. Charlottesville: University Press of Virginia.

Rives, Norfleet W., Jr., and William J. Serow. 1988. *Introduction to Applied Demography: Data Sources and Estimation Techniques*. Sage University Paper Series on Quantitative Applications in the Social Sciences, Series No. 07–039. Newbury Park, CA: Sage.

Roan, Shari. 2007. "Put to the Test." *The Los Angeles Times,* May 21:A15.

Rodríguez, Havidán, Joseph Trainor, and Enrico L. Quarantelli. 2006. "Rising to the Challenges of a Catastrophe: The Emergent and Prosocial Behavior Following Hurricane Katrina." *The Annals of the American Academy of Political and Social Science* 604:82–101.

Rosen, Lawrence. 1995. "The Creation of the Uniform Crime Report: The Role of Social Science." *Social Science History* 19:215–38.

Rosenbaum, David E. 2000. "Seeking Answers, Census Is Raising Privacy Questions." *The New York Times*, April 1, pp. A1, A9.

Rosenbaum, M. 1981. *Women on Heroin*. New Brunswick: Rutgers University Press.

Rosenberg, Morris. 1968. *The Logic of Survey Analysis*. New York: Basic Books.

Rosenfeld, Richard, Timothy M. Bray, and Arlen Egley. 1999. "Facilitating Violence: A Comparison of Gang-Motivated, Gang-Affiliated, and Nongang Youth Homicides." *Journal of Quantitative Criminology* 15(4):496–516.

Rossi, Peter H. 1989. *Down and Out in America: The Origins of Homelessness*. Chicago: University of Chicago Press.

Rossi, Peter H. and Howard E. Freeman. 1989. *Evaluation: A Systematic Approach*. 4th ed. Newbury Park, CA: Sage.

Rubin, Herbert J. and Irene S. Rubin. 1995. *Qualitative Interviewing: The Art of Hearing Data*. Thousand Oaks, CA: Sage.

Rueschemeyer, Dietrich, Evelyne Huber Stephens, and John D. Stephens. 1992. *Capitalist Development and Democracy*. Chicago: University of Chicago Press.

Ruggles, Patricia. 1990. *Drawing the Line: Alternative Poverty Measures and Their Implications for Public Policy*. Washington, DC: The Urban Institute Press.

Sacks, Stanley, Karen McKendrick, George DeLeon, Michael T. French, and Kathryn E. McCollister. 2002. "Benefit-Cost Analysis of a Modified Therapeutic Community for Mentally Ill Chemical Abusers." *Evaluation and Program Planning* 25:137–48.

Sampson, Robert J. 1987. "Urban Black Violence: The Effect of Male Joblessness and Family Disruption." *American Journal of Sociology* 93 (September):348–82.

Sampson, Robert J. and John H. Laub. 1993. *Crime in the Making: Pathways and Turning Points Through Life*. Boston: Harvard University Press.

Sampson, Robert J. and John H. Laub. 1993. "Structural Variations in Juvenile Court Processing: Inequality, the Underclass, and Social Control." *Law and Society Review* 27(2):285–311.

Sampson, Robert J. and Janet L. Lauritsen. 1994. "Violent Victimization and Offending: Individual-, Situational-, and Community-Level Risk Factors." In *Understanding and Preventing Violence*, vol. 3, *Social Influences*, edited by Albert J. Reiss, Jr., and Jeffrey A. Roth, 1–114. Washington, DC: National Academy Press.

Sampson, Robert J. and Stephen W. Raudenbush. 1999. "Systematic Social Observation of Public Spaces: A New Look at Disorder in Urban Neighborhoods." *American Journal of Sociology* 105:603–51.

Sampson, Robert J., Stephen W. Raudenbush, and Felton Earls. 1997. "Neighborhoods and Violent Crime: A Multilevel Study of Collective Efficacy." *Science* 277:918–24.

Sanchez-Jankowski, Martin. 1991. *Islands in the Street*. Berkeley: University of California Press.

Saretsky, H. 1972. "The OEO P. C. Experiment and the John Henry Effect." *Phi Delta Kappan* 53:579–81.

Savage, J., R. R. Bennett, and M. Danner. 2008. "Economic Assistance and Crime: A Cross-National Investigation." *European Journal of Criminology* 5:217–38.

Savelsberg, Joachim L., Ryan King, and Lara Cleveland. 2002. "Politicized Scholarship? Science on Crime and the State." *Social Problems* 49:327–48.

Savin, H. B. 1973. "Professors and Psychological Researchers: Conflicting Values in Conflicting Roles." *Cognition* 2:147–49.

Schorr, Lisbeth B. and Daniel Yankelovich. 2000. "In Search of a Gold Standard for Social Programs." *The Boston Globe*, February 18, p. A19.

Schuman, Howard and Stanley Presser. 1981. *Questions and Answers in Attitude Surveys: Experiments on Question Form, Wording, and Context*. New York: Academic Press.

Schutt, Russell K., Suzanne Gunston, and John O'Brien. 1992. "The Impact of AIDS Prevention Efforts on AIDS Knowledge and Behavior Among Sheltered Homeless Adults." *Sociological Practice Review* 3(1):1–7.

Schwandt, Thomas A. 1994. "Constructivist, Interpretivist Approaches to Human Inquiry." In *Handbook of Qualitative Research*, edited by Norman K. Denzin and Yvonna S. Lincoln, 118–37. Thousand Oaks, CA: Sage.

Scriven, Michael. 1972. "The Methodology of Evaluation." In *Evaluating Action Programs: Readings in Social Action and Education*, edited by Carol H. Weiss, 123–36. Boston: Allyn & Bacon.

Scull, Andrew T. 1988. "Deviance and Social Control." In *Handbook of Sociology*, edited by Neil J. Smelser, 667–93. Newbury Park, CA: Sage.

Sechrest, Lee and Souraya Sidani. 1995. "Quantitative and Qualitative Methods: Is There an Alternative?" *Evaluation and Program Planning* 18:77–87.

Seidman, Larry J. 1997. "Neuropsychological Testing." In *Psychiatry*, vol. 1, edited by Allan Tasman, Jerald Kay, and Jeffrey Lieberman, 498–508. Philadelphia: W. B. Saunders.

Selm, Martine Van and Nicholas W. Jankowski. 2006. "Conducting Online Surveys." *Quality & Quantity* 40:435–56.

Seltzer, Richard A. 1996. *Mistakes That Social Scientists Make: Error and Redemption in the Research Process.* New York: St. Martin's.

Seron, C., J. Pereira, and J. Kovath, 2006. "How Citizens Assess Just Punishment for Police Misconduct." *Criminology* 44(4):925–60.

Shadish, William R., Thomas D. Cook, and Laura C. Leviton, eds. 1991. *Foundations of Program Evaluation: Theories of Practice.* Thousand Oaks, CA: Sage.

Shaw, Clifford R. and Henry D. McKay. 1942. *Juvenile Delinquency and Urban Areas.* Chicago: University of Chicago Press.

Shepherd, Jane, David Hill, Joel Bristor, and Pat Montalvan. 1996. "Converting an Ongoing Health Study to CAPI: Findings From the National Health and Nutrition Study." In *Health Survey Research Methods Conference Proceedings*, edited by Richard B. Warnecke, 159–64. Hyattsville, MD: U.S. Department of Health and Human Services.

Sherman, Lawrence W. 1992. *Policing Domestic Violence: Experiments and Dilemmas.* New York: Free Press.

Sherman, Lawrence W. 1993. "Implications of a Failure to Read the Literature." *American Sociological Review* 58:888–89.

Sherman, Lawrence W. 1997. "Thinking About Crime Prevention." In *Preventing Crime: What Works, What Doesn't, What's Promising*, edited by L. W. Sherman, D. Gottfredson, D. MacKenzie, J. Eck, P. Reuter, and S. Bushway. Unpublished report by the Department of Criminology and Criminal Justice, University of Maryland.

Sherman, Lawrence W. and Richard A. Berk. 1984. "The Specific Deterrent Effects of Arrest for Domestic Assault." *American Sociological Review* 49:261–72.

Sherman, Lawrence W., P. Gartin, and M. Buerger. 1989. "Hot Spots of Predatory Crime: Routine Activities and the Criminology of Place." *Criminology* 27:27–56.

Sherman, Lawrence W., D. Gottfredson, Doris MacKenzie, J. Eck, P. Reuter, and S. Bushway. 1997. *Preventing Crime: What Works, What Doesn't, What's Promising.* Unpublished Report by the Department of Criminology and Criminal Justice, University of Maryland.

Sherman, Lawrence W., Douglas A. Smith, Janell D. Schmidt, and Dennis P. Rogan. 1992. "Crime, Punishment, and Stake in Conformity: Legal and Informal Control of Domestic Violence." *American Sociological Review* 57:680–90.

Short, James F., Jr. and Ivan Nye. 1957–58. "Reported Behavior as a Criterion of Deviant Behavior." *Social Problems* 5:207–13.

Sieber, J. E. 1992. *Planning Ethically Responsible Research: A Guide for Students and International Review Boards.* Thousand Oaks, CA: Sage.

Sjoberg, Gideon, ed. 1967. *Ethics, Politics, and Social Research.* Cambridge, MA: Schenkman.

Sjoberg, Gideon and Roger Nett. 1968. *A Methodology for Social Research.* New York: Harper & Row.

Skinner, Harvey A. and Wen-Jenn Sheu. 1982. "Reliability of Alcohol Use Indices: The Lifetime Drinking History and the MAST." *Journal of Studies on Alcohol* 43(11):1157–70.

Skocpol, Theda. 1984. "Emerging Agendas and Recurrent Strategies in Historical Sociology." In *Vision and Method in Historical Sociology*, edited by Theda Skocpol, 356–91. New York: Cambridge University Press.

Smith, J. 1991. "A Methodology for Twenty-First Century Sociology." *Social Forces* 70:1–17.

Smyth, Jolene D., Don A. Dillman, Leah Melanie Christian, and Michael J. Stern. 2004. "How Visual Grouping Influences Answers to Internet Surveys." Extended version of paper presented at the Annual Meeting of the American Association for Public Opinion Research, Phoenix, AZ, May 13. Retrieved July 5, 2005 (http:// survey .sesrc.wsu.edu/dillman/papers.htm).

Snow, David L., Jacob Kraemer Tebes, and Michael W. Arthur. 1992. "Panel Attrition and External Validity in Adolescent Substance Use Research." *Journal of Consulting and Clinical Psychology* 60:804–7.

Sobell, Linda C., Mark B. Sobell, Diane M. Riley, Reinhard Schuller, D. Sigfrido Pavan, Anthony Cancilla, Felix Klajner, and Gloria I. Leo. 1988. "The Reliability of Alcohol Abusers' Self-Reports of Drinking and Life Events That Occurred in the Distant Past." *Journal of Studies on Alcohol* 49(2):225–32.

Sosin, Michael R., Paul Colson, and Susan Grossman. 1988. *Homelessness in Chicago: Poverty and Pathology, Social Institutions and Social Change.* Chicago: Chicago Community Trust.

St. Jean, Peter K. B. 2007. *Pockets of Crime: Broken Windows, Collective Efficacy, and the Criminal Point of View.* Chicago: University of Chicago Press.

Stake, Robert E. 1995. *The Art of Case Study Research.* Thousand Oaks, CA: Sage.

Stephens, Jason M., Michael F. Young, and Thomas Calabrese. 2007. "Does Moral Judgment Go Offline When Students are Online? A Comparative Analysis of Undergraduates' Beliefs and Behaviors Related to Conventional and Digital Cheating." *Ethics & Behavior* 17:233–54.

Sterk, C. E. 1999. *Fast Lives: Women Who Use Crack Cocaine*. Philadelphia: Temple University Press.

Stewart, David W. 1984. *Secondary Research: Information Sources and Methods*. Beverly Hills, CA: Sage.

Stickle, W. P., N. M. Connell, D. M. Wilson, and D. Gottfredson. 2008. "An Experimental Evaluation of Teen Courts." *Journal of Experimental Criminology* 4:137–63.

Straus, Murray. 1979. "Measuring Intrafamily Conflict and Violence: The Conflict Tactics (CT) Scales." *Journal of Marriage and the Family* 41:75–88.

Strunk, William, Jr., and E. B. White. 2000. *The Elements of Style*. 4th ed. New York: Macmillan.

Sudman, Seymour. 1976. *Applied Sampling*. New York: Academic Press.

Surrette, R. 1998. *Media, Crime, and Justice: Images and Realities*. Belmont, CA: West/Wadsworth.

Tannenbaum, F. 1938. *Crime and the Community*. New York: Columbia University Press.

Taylor, A. 1993. *Women Drug Users: An Ethnography of a Female Injecting Community*. Oxford: Clarendon Press.

Teddlie, Charles and Abbas Tashakkori. 2010. "Overview of Contemporary Issues in Mixed Methods Research." In *Sage Handbook of Mixed Methods in Social and Behavioral Research*. 2nd ed., edited by Abbas Tashakkori and Charles Teddlie, 1–41. Thousand Oaks, CA: Sage.

Thacher, David. 2011. "The Distribution of Police Protection." *Journal of Quantitative Criminology* 27(3):275–298.

The Washington Post. January 16, 2011. "Topic A: Gun Control's Prospects After Tucson." Retrieved June 10, 2012 (http://www.washingtonpost.com/wp-dyn/content/article/2011/01/14/AR2011011406881.html).

Thornberry, T. P, M. Krohn, A. Lizotte, and S. Bushway. 2008. "The Rochester Youth Development Survey." Hindelang Criminal Justice Research Center, University of Albany. Retrieved June 23, 2009 (http://www.albany.edu/hindelang/youth_study.html).

Thorne, Noreen C., Edward E. Hunter, Lorraine Murray, Lisa Ninci, Elaine M.Rolfs, and Leonie Pallikkathayil. 2008. "The Experience of Living With Chronic Mental Illness: A Photovoice Study." *Perspectives in Psychiatric Care* 44:14–24.

Thrasher, Frederic. 1927. *The Gang: A Study of 1,313 Gangs in Chicago*. Chicago: University of Chicago Press.

Tjaden, Patricia and Nancy Thoennes. 1998. "Violence and Threats of Violence Against Women and Men in the United States, 1994–1996." Inter-University Consortium for Political and Social Research (ICPSR) Study No. 2566. Retrieved July 15, 2009 (http://www.icpsr.umich.edu/icpsrweb/ICPSR/studies/2566/detail?archive=ICPSR&q=national+violence+against+womens+survey#methodology).

Tjaden, Patricia and Nancy Thoennes. 2000. "Extent, Nature, and Consequences of Intimate Partner Violence." In *Findings From the National Violence Against Women Survey* (NCJ 181867). Washington, DC: National Institute of Justice, U.S. Department of Justice.

Toby, Jackson. 1957. "Social Disorganization and Stake in Conformity: Complementary Factors in the Predatory Behavior of Hoodlums." *Journal of Criminal Law, Criminology and Police Science* 48:12–17.

Tolan, P., D. Henry, M. Schoeny, and A. Bass. 2008. "Mentoring Interventions to Affect Juvenile Delinquency and Associated Problems." *Campbell Systematic Reviews* 2008(16). Retrieved November 15, 2009 (http://www.campbellcollaboration.org/library.php).

Tonry, Michael and Mark H. Moore. 1998. *Youth Violence: Crime and Justice*. Vol. 24. Chicago: University of Chicago Press.

Torre, M. E. and M. Fine. (2005). "Bar None: Extending Affirmative Action to Higher Education in Prison." *Journal of Social Issues* 61(3):569–94.

Tourangeau, R. and T. W. Smith. 1996. "Asking Sensitive Questions: The Impact of Data Collection Mode, Question Format, and Question Context." *Public Opinion Quarterly* 60:275–301.

Tourangeau, Roger. 2004. "Survey Research and Societal Change." *Annual Review of Psychology* 55:775–801.

Tufte, Edward R. 1983. *The Visual Display of Quantitative Information*. Cheshire, CT: Graphics.

Turabian, Kate L. 1996. *A Manual for Writers of Term Papers, Theses, and Dissertations*. Rev. 6th ed. Chicago: University of Chicago Press.

Turner, C. F., L. Ku, S. M. Rogers, L. D. Lindberg, J. H. Pleck, and F. L. Sonenstein. 1998. "Adolescent Sexual Behavior, Drug Use, and Violence: Increased Reporting With Computer Survey Technology." *Science* 280:867–73.

Turner, Charles F. and Elizabeth Martin, eds. 1984. *Surveying Subjective Phenomena*. Vols. I and II. New York: Russell Sage.

Turner, Stephen P. 1980. *Sociological Explanation as Translation*. Cambridge, UK: Cambridge University Press.

Tyler, Tom. 1990. *Why People Obey the Law*. New Haven, CT: Yale University Press.

U.S. Bureau of the Census. 1999. *United States Census 2000, Updated Summary: Census 2000 Operational Plan*. Washington, DC: U.S. Department of Commerce, Bureau of the Census.

U.S. Bureau of the Census. 2000. "Census Bureau Directory Says 92 Percent of U.S. Households Accounted for: Thanks President and Vice President for Message to Census Workers." In *United States Department of Commerce News*. Retrieved May 31, 2000 (http://www.census.gov/Press-Release/www/2000/cb00cn41.html).

U.S. Department of Health and Human Services. 2002. "Health Information Privacy: The Privacy Rule." Retrieved September 26, 2009 (http://www.hhs.gov/ocr/privacy/hipaa/administrative/privacyrule/index.html).

Vaillant, George E. 1995. *The Natural History of Alcoholism Revisited*. Cambridge, MA: Harvard University Press.

Van Maanen, John. 1982. "Fieldwork on the Beat." In *Varieties of Qualitative Research*, edited by John Van Maanen, James M. Dabbs, Jr., and Robert R. Faulkner, 103–51. Beverly Hills, CA: Sage.

Van Maanen, John. 1995. "An End to Innocence: The Ethnography of Ethnography." In *Representation in Ethnography*, edited by John Van Maanen, 1–35. Thousand Oaks, CA: Sage.

Van Maanen, John. 2002. "The Fact of Fiction in Organizational Ethnography." In *The Qualitative Researcher's Companion*, edited by A. Michael Huberman and Matthew B. Miles, 101–17. Thousand Oaks, CA: Sage.

Venkatesh, Sudhir Alladi. 1997. "The Social Organization of Street Gang Activity in an Urban Ghetto." *American Journal of Sociology* 103:82–102.

Venkatesh, Sudhir Alladi. 2000. *American Project: The Rise and Fall of a Modern Ghetto*. Cambridge, MA: Harvard University Press.

Vidich, Arthur J. and Stanford M. Lyman. 1994. "Qualitative Methods: Their History in Sociology and Anthropology." In *Handbook of Qualitative Research*, edited by Norman K. Denzin and Yvonna S. Lincoln, 23–59. Thousand Oaks, CA: Sage.

Vigil, James Diego. 1988. *Barrio Gangs*. Austin: University of Texas Press.

Wade, Nicholas. "Scientist Under Inquiry Resigns From Harvard." *The New York Times*, July 20: A17.

Wagner, William E., III. 2010. *Using SPSS for Social Statistics and Research Methods*. Thousand Oaks, CA: Sage.

Waldorf, D., C. Reinarman, and S. Murphy. 1991. *Cocaine Changes: The Experience of Using and Quitting*. Philadelphia: Temple University Press.

Wallace, Walter L. 1971. *The Logic of Science in Sociology*. Chicago: Aldine.

Wallace, Walter L. 1983. *Principles of Scientific Sociology*. New York: Aldine.

Wallerstein, J. S. and C. J. Wyle. 1947. "Our Law-Abiding Law Breakers." *Probation* 25:107–12.

Walter, Shoshana. 2012. "Shootings Soar in Oakland: Children Often Victims." *The New York Times*, January 8: A29A

Walters, Pamela Barnhouse, David R. James, and Holly J. McCammon. 1997. "Citizenship and Public Schools: Accounting for Racial Inequality in Education for the Pre- and Post-Disfranchisement South." *American Sociological Review* 62:34–52.

Walters, R. 2006. "Boycott, Resistance, and the Role of the Deviant Voice." *Criminal Justice Matters* 62:6–7.

Ward, Lester Frank. 1897. *Dynamic Sociology*. 2nd ed. New York: D. Appleton.

Watson, Charles G., Curt Tilleskjor, E. A. Hoodecheck-Schow, John Pucel, and Lyle Jacobs. 1984. "Do Alcoholics Give Valid Self-Reports?" *Journal of Studies on Alcohol* 45(4):344–48.

Watson, Roy E. L. 1986. "The Effectiveness of Increased Police Enforcement as a General Deterrent." *Law and Society Review* 20(2):293–99.

Weatherby, Norman L., Richard Needle, Helen Cesari, Robert Booth, Clyde B. McCoy, John K. Waters, Mark Williams, and Dale D. Chitwood. 1994. "Validity of Self-Reported Drug Use Among Injection Drug Users and Crack Cocaine Users Recruited Through Street Outreach." *Evaluation and Program Planning* 17(4):347–55.

Webb, Eugene, Donald T. Campbell, Richard D. Schwartz, and Lee Sechrest. [1966] 2000. *Unobtrusive Measures: Nonreactive Research in the Social Sciences*. Chicago: Rand McNally.

Weber, Max. 1949. *The Methodology of the Social Sciences*. Translated and edited by Edward A. Shils and Henry Finch. New York: Free Press.

Weber, Robert Philip. 1985. *Basic Content Analysis*. Beverly Hills, CA: Sage.

Weber, Robert Philip. 1990. *Basic Content Analysis*. 2nd ed. Newbury Park, CA: Sage.

Wechsler, Henry, Andrea Davenport, George Dowdall, Barbara Moeykens, and Sonia Castillo. 1994. "Health and Behavioral Consequences of Binge Drinking in College: A National Survey of Students at 140 Campuses." *JAMA:*

The Journal of the American Medical Association 272(21):1672–77.

Weisburd, David, L. Maher, and Lawrence Sherman. 1992. "Contrasting Crime General and Crime Specific Theory: The Case of Hot Spots of Crime." *Advances in Criminological Theory* 4:45–69.

Weisburd, David, Stanton Wheeler, Elin Waring, and Nancy Bode. 1991. *Crimes of the Middle Class: White-Collar Offenders in the Federal Courts*. New Haven, CT: Yale University Press.

Weiss, Carol H. 1993. "Where Politics and Evaluation Research Meet." *Evaluation Practice* 14:93–106.

West, H. C., W. J. Sabol, and S. J. Greenman. 2010. *Prisoners in 2009* (No. NCJ 231675). Washington, DC: Bureau of Justice Statistics.

Whyte, William Foote. 1943. *Street Corner Society: The Social Structure of an Italian Slum*. Chicago: University of Chicago Press.

Whyte, William Foote. 1955. *Street Corner Society*. Chicago: University of Chicago Press.

Whyte, William Foote. 1991. *Social Theory for Social Action: How Individuals and Organizations Learn to Change*. Newbury Park, CA: Sage.

Williams, B. N. and M. Stahl. 2008. "An Analysis of Police Traffic Stops and Searchers in Kentucky: A Mixed-Methods Approach Offering Heuristic and Practical Implications." *Policy Science* 41:221–43.

Williams, Christine and E. Joel Heikes. 1993. "The Importance of Researcher's Gender in the In-depth Interview: Evidence From Two Case Studies of Male Nurses." *Gender and Society* 7:280–91.

Wilson, William Julius. 1987. *The Truly Disadvantaged: The Inner City, the Underclass, and Public Policy*. Chicago: University of Chicago Press.

Wilson, William Julius. 1998. "Engaging Publics in Sociological Dialogue Through the Media." *Contemporary Sociology* 27:435–38.

Wines, Michael. 2006. "To Fill Notebooks, and Then a Few Bellies." *The New York Times*, August 27, Week in Review.

Wolcott, Harry F. 1995. *The Art of Field-work*. Walnut Creek, CA: AltaMira.

Wolff, N., C. L. Blitz, J. Shi, R. Bachman, and J. Siegel. 2006. "Sexual Violence Inside Prisons: Rates of Victimization." *Journal of Urban Health* 83(5):835–51.

World Health Organization. 2011. *Global Status Report on Alcohol and Health*. Geneva, Switzerland: World Health Organization.

Wright, Richard and Scott Decker. 1994. *Burglars on the Job: Streetlife and Residential Break-ins*. Boston: Northeastern University Press.

Zaret, David. 1996. "Petitions and the 'Invention' of Public Opinion in the English Revolution." *American Journal of Sociology* 101:1497–1555.

Zimbardo, Philip G. 1971. *Prison Life Study: General Information*. Retrieved July 3, 2009 (http://www .prisonexperiment .org).

Zimbardo, Philip G. 1973. "On the Ethics of Intervention in Human Psychological Research: With Special Reference to the Stanford Prison Experiment." *Cognition* 2:243–56.

Zimbardo, Philip G. 2004. "A Situationist Perspective on the Psychology of Evil: Understanding How Good People Are Transformed Into Perpetrators." In *The Social Psychology of Good and Evil: Understanding Our Capacity for Kindness and Cruelty*, edited by Arthur G. Miller, 21–50. New York: Guilford.

Zimbardo, Philip G. 2007. *The Lucifer Effect: Understanding How Good People Turn Evil*. New York: Random House.

Zimbardo, Philip G. 2009. "Revisiting the Stanford Prison Experiment: A Lesson in the Power of Situation." Retrieved July 2, 2009 (http://www.lucifer effect.com).

Zimbardo, Philip G., W. Curtis Banks, Craig Haney, and David Jaffe. 1973. "The Mind Is a Formidable Jailer: A Pirandellian Prison." *The New York Times Magazine*, April 8, p. 38.

Index

About the Authors

Ronet Bachman, PhD, is a professor in the Department of Sociology and Criminal Justice at the University of Delaware. She is coauthor of *Statistical Methods for Criminology and Criminal Justice* and coeditor of *Explaining Criminals and Crime: Essays in Contemporary Criminal Theory*. In addition, she is the author of *Death and Violence on the Reservation*, coauthor of *Stress, Culture, and Aggression*, coauthor of *Murder American Style*, and coauthor of *Violence: The Enduring Problem*, along with numerous articles and papers that examine the epidemiology and etiology of violence, with particular emphasis on women, the elderly, and minority populations. She is currently the coprincipal investigator on a National Institute of Justice–funded grant to study the long-term desistance trajectories of drug-involved offenders who were originally released from prison in 1990.

Russell K. Schutt, PhD, is a professor and the chair of sociology at the University of Massachusetts, Boston, and a lecturer on sociology in the Department of Psychiatry at the Harvard Medical School (Massachusetts Mental Health Center). He completed his BA, MA, and PhD (1977) degrees at the University of Illinois at Chicago and was a postdoctoral fellow in the Sociology of Social Control Training Program at Yale University (1977–1979). In addition to *Investigating the Social World: The Process and Practice of Research*, now in its seventh edition, *Making Sense of the Social World*, now in its fourth edition (with Dan Chambliss), and coauthored versions for the fields of psychology, social work, and education), he is the author most recently of *Homelessness, Housing, and Mental Illness* (Harvard University Press), as well as of *Organization in a Changing Environment*, coeditor of *The Organizational Response to Social Problems*, and coauthor of *Responding to the Homeless: Policy and Practice*. He has authored and coauthored numerous journal articles, book chapters, and research reports on criminal justice, homelessness, service preferences and satisfaction, mental health, organizations, and teaching research methods. His research has been funded by the Massachusetts Department of Public Health, the National Cancer Institute, the National Institute of Mental Health, the Fetzer Institute (a study of a violence reduction program), and local sources.

⑤SAGE researchmethods

The essential online tool for researchers from the world's leading methods publisher

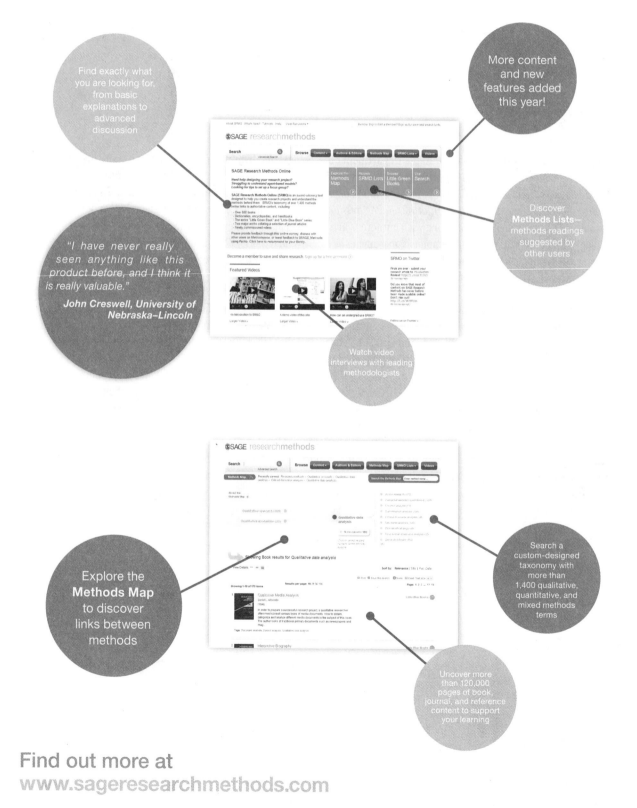

Find exactly what you are looking for, from basic explanations to advanced discussion

More content and new features added this year!

"I have never really seen anything like this product before, and I think it is really valuable."

John Creswell, University of Nebraska–Lincoln

Discover **Methods Lists**— methods readings suggested by other users

Watch video interviews with leading methodologists

Explore the **Methods Map** to discover links between methods

Search a custom-designed taxonomy with more than 1,400 qualitative, quantitative, and mixed methods terms

Uncover more than 120,000 pages of book, journal, and reference content to support your learning

Find out more at
www.sageresearchmethods.com